ENLIGHTENING THE BRITISH

Knowledge, discovery and the museum in the eighteenth century

ENLIGHTENING THE BRITISH
Knowledge, discovery and the museum in the eighteenth century

edited by

R.G.W. Anderson, M.L. Caygill, A.G. MacGregor and
L. Syson

THE BRITISH MUSEUM PRESS

First published in 2003 by The British Museum Press
A division of The British Museum Company Ltd
46 Bloomsbury Street, London WC1B 3QQ

A catalogue record for this book is available from the British Library

ISBN 0-7141-5010-X

Printed in England by Cambridge University Press

Acknowledgements

The contents of this volume represent essentially the texts delivered at the British Museum's 250th Anniversary conference, titled 'Enlightening the British: Knowledge, discovery and the museum in the eighteenth century', which took place at the Museum on 4–6 April 2002. The conference, which attracted some 250 delegates, was supported by the Friends of the British Museum and the British Academy.

Acknowledgement must also be made to Sir David Attenborough, Dr Jim Bennett, Dr Iain Gordon Brown, Professor Michael Hunter, Luke Syson and Sir Keith Thomas who acted as chairmen of sessions at the conference. Like the audience, they contributed many useful observations to the discussions, which in turn influenced the texts as reproduced here.

The text was amended at various stages during the editing process. The editors are grateful to Suzanne Anderson and Christine Lawrence for help with retyping and to Glennis Hoggarth and Christine Lawrence for their part in organizing the Conference. Thanks are also due to the Editor at British Museum Press, Laura Brockbank, to BMP's Managing Editor Teresa Francis for her support for the publication, and to the copy-editor Johanna Stephenson.

Contents

List of illustrations

Notes on the Contributors

Robert Anderson was Director of the British Museum from 1992 to 2002. He has published widely in the history of science and in museum history. Recently he has been at the Institute for Advanced Study, Princeton, and Churchill College, Cambridge, conducting research on the interaction of the working classes with collections in the nineteenth century.

Ken Arnold has worked in a variety of museums on both sides of the Atlantic. He joined the Wellcome Trust in 1992 on completing his PhD on the history of museums. He now runs an exhibitions department involved in a variety of arts projects that explore the culture of medicine—its art, science and history. He regularly writes and lectures on museums and on contemporary relations between the arts and sciences.

Malcolm Baker is Head of the Medieval and Renaissance Galleries Project at the Victoria and Albert Museum, London, and Professor of Art History at the University of Southern California, Los Angeles, where he directs the USC-Getty Program in the History of Collecting and Display. His latest book is *Figured in Marble: The making and viewing of eighteenth-century sculpture* (2000).

David Bindman is Professor of the History of Art at University College London. He has written on William Blake and William Hogarth, and was author of *The Shadow of the Guillotine: Britain and the French Revolution* (1989). His most recent book is *Ape to Apollo: Aesthetics and the idea of race, c.1700–1800* (2002).

Marjorie Caygill joined the British Museum in 1973 and has published a number of books and articles on its history and collections. These include *The Story of the British Museum* (1981), *Treasures of the British Museum* (1985), *The British Museum A–Z Companion* (1999) and *The British Museum: 250 Years* (2003). She has co-edited (with John Cherry) *Augustus Wollaston Franks: Nineteenth-century collecting and the British Museum* (1997).

Neil Chambers is Research Curator and Executive Director of the Banks Research Project, which is currently located at The Natural History Museum, London. He is preparing for publication, in a series of volumes, *The Scientific Letters of Sir Joseph Banks (1743–1820)*.

Celina Fox holds a senior fellowship from the Paul Mellon Centre for Studies in British Art to write a book on art and industry in eighteenth-century Europe. Having been Keeper of Paintings, Prints and Drawings at the Museum of London, she organized the exhibition *London: World City 1800–40* at the Villa Hügel, Essen in 1992.

T.G.H. James served on the curatorial staff of the British Museum from 1951 to 1988, and was Keeper of Egyptian Antiquities from 1974 until his retirement. He has worked in the field in Egypt, and published scholarly works on the monuments, inscriptions, papyri and history of ancient Egypt, and more recently on the history of the early years of Egyptology.

Lisa Jardine is Director of the AHRB Centre for Editing Lives and Letters and Professor of Renaissance Studies at Queen Mary University of London. Her most recent books are *On a Grander Scale: The outstanding career of Sir Christopher Wren* (2002) and a biography of Robert Hooke, *The Curious Life of Robert Hooke: The man who measured London* (2003).

Ian Jenkins joined the curatorial staff of the British Museum in 1978. His books include *Archaeologists and Aesthetes* (1992) and *The Parthenon Frieze* (1994). He has recently been appointed Keeper of the new Department of Presentation, with responsibility for the intellectual and visual coherence of the Museum's galleries and special exhibitions. Prior to this he was Senior Curator in the Department of Greek and Roman Antiquities.

Bengt Jonsell is Professor Bergianus emeritus at the Royal Swedish Academy of Sciences. He was born in 1936, and graduated with a DPhil from Uppsala University in 1968, specializing in taxonomic botany. He was appointed Professor and Director of the Bergius Botanic Garden in Stockholm in 1983, and retired in 2001. Besides papers about Nordic and tropical botany, he has written about Linnaeus and his disciples and was from 1985 to 1998 President of the Swedish Linnaean Society.

Joseph M. Levine is Distinguished Professor of History at Syracuse University. He is the author of *Dr Woodward's Shield: History, science and satire in Augustan England* (1977) and *The Battle of the Books: History and literature in the Augustan Age* (1991), as well as other books and many articles on the intellectual history of modern Britain. He is currently completing a book on The Rise and Decline of English Neoclassicism.

Arthur MacGregor is a Senior Assistant Keeper at the Ashmolean Museum, Oxford, and a former Director of the Society of Antiquaries. He has published widely on the history of museums and has edited several volumes on the subject, including *Tradescant's Rarities* (1983), *The Late King's Goods* (1989) and *Sir Hans Sloane* (1994), and co-edited *The Origins of Museums* (1985). He is joint general editor of *The Paper Museum of Cassiano dal Pozzo* and joint editor of the *Journal of the History of Collections*.

John Mack is Keeper of Ethnography at the British Museum, where he specializes in African visual and material culture. He is the author or editor of thirteen books, the most recent of which, *Museum of the Mind: Art and memory in world cultures* (2003), accompanied one of the Museum's 250th anniversary exhibitions.

David McKitterick is Librarian and Fellow of Trinity College, Cambridge, and author of the standard history of Cambridge University Library in the eighteenth and nineteenth centuries. The third (and final) volume of his history of Cambridge University Press is to be published in 2004. He is a general editor of the *Cambridge History of the Book in Britain*.

Debora J. Meijers is Associate Professor of Art History at the University of Amsterdam. She has worked on several topics relating to the history of collecting. Her publications include *Kunst als Natur: Die Habsburger Gemäldegalerie um 1780* (1995). Currently she is supervising, together with Renée Kistemaker and Natalja Kopaneva, the Russian-Dutch research project *The 'Paper Museum' of the Academy of Sciences in Saint Petersburg (c.1725–1760)*.

Partha Mitter is Research Professor in Art History at the University of Sussex. He has been Fellow of Clare Hall, Cambridge, Mellon Fellow at the Institute for Advanced Study, Princeton, Reader of the British Academy and Radhakrishnan Lecturer at Oxford. He is the author of *Much Maligned Monsters: History of European reactions to Indian art* (1977), *Art and Nationalism in Colonial India 1850–1922* (1994) and *Indian Art* (2001).

Hugh Pagan is Managing Director of Hugh Pagan Limited, antiquarian booksellers specializing in architecture and its allied arts. He is a Fellow of the Society of Antiquaries of London, a past President (and current Vice-President) of the British Numismatic Society, and a member of the British Academy Committee for the Sylloge of Coins of the British Isles.

Sam Smiles is Professor of Art History at the University of Plymouth. He has published widely on British eighteenth- and nineteenth-century art and has a special interest in art and antiquarianism. His books include *The Image of Antiquity: Ancient Britain and the Romantic imagination* (1994) and *Eye Witness: Artists and visual documentation in Britain, 1770–1830* (2000).

Sir Keith Thomas is a fellow of All Souls College, Oxford, and a Trustee of the British Museum. He was previously President of Corpus Christi College, Oxford, and is a past President of the British Academy. He is the author of *Religion and the Decline of Magic: Studies in popular beliefs in sixteenth- and seventeenth-century England* (1978), *Man and the natural world: Changing attitudes in England 1500–1900* (1983) and other works on the social and cultural history of early modern England.

Hugh Torrens trained as a stratigrapher at Oxford, Leicester and Palermo before settling at Keele University, where he taught for thirty years. His interests soon evolved to include not only the history of the earth but also those who had studied it. He retired in 2000.

Giles Waterfield is a Senior Research Fellow at the Institute of Historical Research, acting senior lecturer at the Courtauld Institute of Art and Director of the Attingham Summer School and Royal Collection Studies. He is a Trustee of the Heritage Lottery Fund. His interest in the history of museums and galleries in Britain led to the publication of *Palaces of Art* (1993) and *Art for the People* (1995), and to his curatorship of the exhibition *Art Treasures of England* (Royal Academy of Arts, London, 1999). He has published two novels.

Richard Yeo is an Australian Professorial Fellow in the Faculty of Arts, Griffith University, Brisbane. He has written on the history of eighteenth- and nineteenth-century science, and his books include *Defining Science: William Whewell, natural knowledge and public debate in early Victorian Britain* (1993), *Encyclopaedic Visions: Scientific dictionaries and Enlightenment culture* (2001) and *Science in the Public Sphere: Natural knowledge in British culture, 1800–1860* (2001).

Introduction
Robert Anderson

It is almost too trite to say that the British Museum was a product of its age, born into that period of remarkable intellectual flowering, the European Enlightenment. At the very least, some further explanation is needed. If a large and comprehensive state museum was a natural (though by no means inevitable) outcome of the Enlightenment in Great Britain, why was it not a natural outcome for the other nations of Europe, or indeed, for even one of the other nations of Europe? And why did it emerge in the particular form that it did?

The conference held at the British Museum in April 2002, 'Enlightening the British', was not intended to treat the foundation and early history of the Museum, but rather to consider the cultural environment from which it emerged and into which it was born.[1] All twenty-two papers read at that meeting are published here, together with the summing-up. The diversity of their coverage reflects the preoccupations of the Augustan age and what followed: the classical world and neoclassicism, libraries, publishing, physical science, natural history, exploration, ethnography, antiquarianism and the world of cabinets and proto-museums. Of course, the range of topics could not be comprehensive, but the intended outcome is that it should provide a context to be considered in relation to histories of the British Museum and, indeed, to other institutions founded at about the same time.

Various claims have been made for the British Museum's mid-eighteenth-century foundation, such as that it was the world's first public museum. Clearly it was not, but there are problems of definition which need to be addressed, such as what constitutes a museum, and what exactly is a 'public museum'. The fact is that there were accessible museums long before 15 January 1759, the day on which the British Museum first opened its doors to the public. This question was considered in part at the tercentenary conference of the Ashmolean Museum in 1983, which offered an opportunity to consider collections and museums of the sixteenth to early eighteenth centuries.[2]

It is clear that there was not, in the middle of the eighteenth century, a sudden transition from private cabinet of curiosities to public museum, from the personal to the communal, from the astonishing to the rational. A good number of cabinets were more or less accessible, to some parts of the public at least, and certain natural history collections were ordered 'scientifically' to provide understanding of relationships between specimens. On the other hand, the British Museum, though in theory open to all, was quite difficult for much of the public to penetrate, and it was, at least initially, to display its fair share of monstrosities (though it is difficult to be certain just how the early displays were organized). The Museum may have been the earliest of its kind, but its accompanying national library came relatively late on to the European scene; it had been long awaited by scholars in Britain.

The Royal Society of London, founded in 1660, the year of restitution of the monarchy and the year of birth of Sir Hans Sloane, started its collection almost immediately. By 1681 an impressive catalogue of its holdings was published.[3] It consisted, overwhelmingly, of natural history specimens (including *materia medica*), but coins, scientific instruments and ethnographic items were also included. The collection underwent various vicissitudes and Robert Hooke's purpose-built Repository was abandoned in a move to new premises. Dissemination of the Society's contributions to knowledge was promoted by publication of the *Philosophical Transactions* from 1665. The Society of Antiquaries of London, whose activities encouraged the collecting of antiquities and topographical description, started meeting from 1707 and though there were earlier monographs (for example, works delineating the English coinage), its periodical *Archaeologia* appeared from 1770. Links were created between the British Museum, and the Royal Society and the Society of Antiquaries, through ex-officio trusteeships of their Presidents to the Museum's Board.

Founded for the purpose of applying knowledge to practical problems of the day, the Society for the Encouragement of Arts, Manufactures and Commerce (with its motto '*Utile et Dulce*') was instigated in 1754, began collecting mechanical models in 1760 and started publishing its *Transactions* in 1783. Concerning itself with science, production and design, the Society provided a natural locus for entrepreneurs such as Josiah Wedgwood, who presented one of his six 'First Day's Vases' to the British Museum in 1769. In accepting this, it is clear that the early Museum was interested both in contemporary material and in industrial production. In the provinces, societies on a smaller scale developed at about the same time, and some of them formed collections of antiquities and natural specimens which were thoroughly discussed at meetings. That created by the Gentlemen's Society of Spalding, Lincolnshire, established particularly early in 1710, is an unexpected survival to the present day. It is clear that networks between these organizations themselves and with some of the leading scholars of the day, were set up, all this leading to the conclusion that the provinces were much less provincial than might have been imagined. Significant private collections were to be found outside London but several of these were disturbingly ephemeral and peripatetic.

Perhaps the collection in Great Britain which was to prove to be the most significant of its age, in the long term, was that formed by father and son who shared the same name of John Tradescant. From the early years of the seventeenth century, the elder Tradescant collected botanical and other specimens in the Low Countries, France and Russia. Later he obtained material from America, and set up his museum at Lambeth, to the south of London. Visitors were admitted, for a fee, and in 1656 a catalogue was published.[4] After the death of the younger

Tradescant the collection was acquired by the herald, astrologer and alchemist Elias Ashmole, who presented it to the University of Oxford. The University provided a purpose-built edifice which opened in 1683. The building encompassed an exhibition gallery, lecture room and laboratory, exhibiting even at this early date the functions that museums were later to develop: display, education and research. Though within a university, it had a public aspect and visitors were admitted on payment of a charge. The Ashmolean Museum thus has a claim to be the first public museum.

In the year the Ashmolean opened, Hans Sloane graduated in medicine at the University of Orange in France. Sloane was an Ulsterman by birth, a botanist by inclination, a physician by profession and a collector by obsession.[5] He never undertook the Grand Tour and did not experience the great collections of classical antiquities which were already being assembled. His early passion was for natural history; acting as the Duke of Albemarle's private doctor, Sloane went to Jamaica where he amassed plant and animal specimens. On his return to London he set up in private practice, became physician to the Queen and accrued wealth in a variety of ways. His collecting mania was funded by his success in medicine (and his marriage), and he was able to develop it efficiently by purchasing the entire collections of others, though on many occasions material was also presented to him. Sloane's main focus was on flora and fauna, native and exotic, though he collected in many diverse fields, including numismatics, antiquities, books and manuscripts. He acquired a fine collection of Dürer drawings and watercolours, but his primary interest may well have been focused on their natural history subject-matter rather than their aesthetic qualities; other collectors, such as fellow physician Richard Mead, might be considered to be greater connoisseurs. Sloane became an establishment figure, being elected both President of the Royal College of Physicians in 1717 and, succeeding Sir Isaac Newton on his death in 1727, President of the Royal Society of London. In truth, though, Sloane was not an outstandingly inventive scientist or physician of his day, as can be judged by consulting his slight output of publications. His contribution to intellectual life was in the creation of a huge collection, which he made freely available to fellow spirits of his time. Even the great Swedish taxonomist Linnaeus was lured to Chelsea in 1736, having heard of the reputation of Sloane's material, though he was uncomplimentary about the state in which he found it when he arrived. Towards the end of Sloane's life, the organization of his collection could no longer be said to follow the precepts of the day. The praise offered by the usually curmudgeonly Zacharias Conrad von Uffenbach in 1710 (the corals, he said, were 'especially charming . . . not only of unusual size and quality') would not count after 1735, the date of publication of Linnaeus's *Systema Naturae*. Visual appeal and rarity seem to have been the guiding principles for at least some part of Sloane's collection, though in truth little is known about its detailed arrangement. Nevertheless, what can be deduced from the organization of other parts of the collection, for example the ethnographic material, indicates an underlying Enlightenment rationale.

Sloane lived to an old age, and towards the end became concerned about what would happen to his lifetime's accretions. By means of a subtly worded will, trustees were required to offer the collection first to the King and then to

Parliament. Acceptance by the latter meant that not only the first state-owned museum would come into being but a national library in combination with it, comprising Sloane's collection along with the Cotton library, since 1700 state property and rich in manuscripts, the Harleian library, accumulated by the Earls of Oxford and also containing a fine collection of manuscript material, and the old Royal Library. The Act of Parliament specified the name 'British Museum', though the reason for this choice was not suggested at the time and has never been determined with any certainty. The Museum Trustees met for the first time on 11 December 1753, Montagu House (the British Museum's first home, a seventeenth-century mansion which used to stand on the site of the present building) was purchased on 5 April 1755, and the first Principal Librarian (equivalent to the post of Director) received his appointment on 21 May 1756. A further two and a half years would have to elapse before the new establishment would be ready to receive its first visitors.

The Enlightenment in England can be characterized by a spread of the spirit of curiosity amongst newly developing classes of society, release from attitudinal constraints of the past, and a creative desire for knowledge which was satisfied in a variety of ways: by experimentation, by exploration, by books and by forms of public spectacle. All of these would be encapsulated in the British Museum when it emerged mid-century. The investigations soberly pursued by the fellowship of the Royal Society were transmitted to the public through the phenomenon of the public lecturer in science who, on payment of a fee, would perform dramatic experiments before the very eyes of spectators with a battery of demonstration apparatus. But the worlds were not entirely apart: Francis Hauksbee the Elder could, at the same time, be instrument maker, expositor of natural philosophy to his subscribers, and curator of experiments to the Royal Society, to which body, significantly, he was elected a Fellow. The spirit of science was increasingly felt. The public's yearning to experience it at first hand led to the formation of a community of itinerant lecturers, whose instrumental needs were supplied by a burgeoning group of innovative artisans. That Tobias Smollett's Matthew Bramble, with or without irony, proposed 'for the honour of the nation', that courses of mathematics and experimental philosophy should be taught in the newly established British Museum, should be no cause for surprise.

Literacy in England grew throughout the eighteenth century. By the time the British Museum was established, 60 per cent of men and 40 per cent of women could read, these levels being higher still in London. Ownership of books in households increased significantly[6] and for the well-to-do, reading matter became available in coffee shops and from circulating libraries. The 1662 Licensing Act, which provided government with controls for censuring publications, lapsed in 1695. From that time onward, book production expanded, though taxation provided another means of constraint on publication. It was not only books which were produced in larger numbers: periodicals and newspapers saw a significant rise. Most of the books published were concerned with religion, politics, literature, history and geography. Relatively few dealt with the subjects of philosophy, science, technology, or were in a foreign language (Latin, Greek and French were by far the most common of this minority group). A genre which did flourish was the encyclopaedia[7] – a vehicle for organizing knowledge – and, indeed, it was a Fellow (later Secretary) of the Royal Society, John Harris, who in 1704 produced the first volume of *Lexicon technicum; or, An universal English dictionary of the arts and sciences*. His connections allowed him to call on specialist advice and, unlike earlier attempts by others, his efforts were seen as authoritative. Five editions were published by 1736. By this date, Ephraim Chambers' great *Cyclopaedia: or, An Universal Dictionary of Arts and Sciences*, incorporating Newtonian philosophy, was already available and later it was to act as a stimulus for the even mightier editorial project of Denis Diderot and Jean Le Rond D'Alembert, the *Encyclopédie, ou Dictionnaire raisonné des sciences, des arts et métiers*, published between 1751 and 1757 in thirty-five volumes. In turn, this led to the project developed by Andrew Bell, Colin Macfarquhar and William Smellie, *Encyclopaedia: or, a dictionary of arts and sciences, compiled upon a new plan,* issued between 1769 and 1771. The 'new plan' was that the three-volume work incorporated thirty long entries of many pages each, so that the product was a combination of short dictionary-length entries, interspersed with monographs written by noted academic figures. Though its arrangement has evolved in a convoluted way over its long history, it remains with us as *Encyclopaedia Britannica*. Pierre Bayle's great dictionary was first published in Paris in 1697 (in whose praise de Saint Evremond versified: 'Qu'on admire le grand savoir, L'erudition infinie, Où l'on ne voit pas, ni génie, Je ne saurois le concevoir: Mais je trouve BAYLE admirable . . .'). The 1702 edition was translated into English in 1710, and there was an influential second edition, *The Dictionary Historical and Critical of Peter Bayle*, in 1734, which energized the production of *Biographia Britannica . . . Collected from the Best Authorities . . . and Digested in the Manner of Mr Bayle's . . . Dictionary*, of 1747.

Other great projects of scholarly organization in the eighteenth century involved the compilation of dictionaries.[8] In Britain, the century opened with the publication of John Kersey's *A New English Dictionary* of 1702, the first English dictionary to cover common as well as exotic words. Kersey then revised and expanded Edward Philips's *The New World of English Words*, incorporating scientific terms from Harris's *Lexicon Technicum*. The major achievement of the century was Samuel Johnson's 1755 *A Dictionary of the English Language*, which was based on historical usage and which included illustrative quotations. Johnson accepted that he could scarcely stabilize the language as the *Dictionnaire de l'Académie Françoise* of 1694 was intended to do, but Johnson's work was considered at the very least an adequate response to the great French project.

In various senses, the establishment of the British Museum can be considered the means by which the natural and artificial worlds could be organized, even taxonomized, by bringing them together under one roof. Thus the Museum acted as though it were an encyclopaedia, or a dictionary based on historical principles, with sequences of rooms, their layout, and the juxtaposition of objects within them providing a means of understanding relationships within the three-dimensional world of objects and specimens. The need to elucidate the structure of nature and of artefacts was becoming increasingly important as objects that had never previously been experienced came flooding through London as a result of

increased exploration, trade and commerce. It seemed that no part of the world was too remote for Britain's merchant and naval fleets. Imported textiles from India strongly affected fashionable taste in clothes, and export ceramics from China and Japan were commissioned by every family of wealth. These were to be intermixed with classical antiquities being brought back from Mediterranean countries by those indulging in the Grand Tour. Sloane's collection reflected these activities, though it has to be said that they did not represent his priority areas for collecting: his acquisitions were more likely to be natural history specimens from the Americas. Some thought that the whole of the natural world could be represented in Sloane's cabinet. An anonymous 'poem occasion'd by the viewing of Dr. Sloans musaeum London Dec: 1712' includes the stanza:

> No more the Traveller from pole to pole
> Shall search the seas or round the globe shall rowll
> Safe from the dangers of the deep may be
> And visit nature while he visits thee.[9]

Sloane's collection became the basis of what shortly became the most comprehensive public museum of the Enlightenment. A major part of the answer to the question 'Why did it happen in Britain?' is that collections owned by commoners of the size and significance of Sloane's simply did not exist elsewhere. An additional factor was that there was nobody to inherit, let alone curate, the collection after Sloane's death, and so he made the most elaborate arrangements to pass it on to a public body. But this does not explain its existence in the first place. First, there was Sloane's obsessional behaviour, which verged on addiction. Second, the collection was created over a very long lifetime: Sloane started collecting as a young man in the final decades of the seventeenth century and continued with little abatement until his death in 1753 at the age of ninety-two. Third, conditions in Britain were especially conducive to the possibility of creating a large collection of international character. There was a high level of intellectual inquiry, fuelled to a large extent by Newton's revolutionary science and its aftermath. This was aided by the nation being relatively stable – at least compared with Continental Europe. England had experienced her political revolution well before Sloane's collecting activity began and, apart from skirmishes with Jacobites, no war-like activities took place on British soil throughout the eighteenth century. The country could be judged a republic with the monarch as titular head of state. For these reasons, the Enlightenment in England and Scotland was distinctive from those varieties in other European nations and antipathy between the State and intellectuals did not exist as it did in, say, France. Academicians in Europe were sometimes in the direct employ of the ruler. Hierarchies in Britain, though clearly existing, were somewhat looser than elsewhere and knowledge could flow more naturally. Fourth, the success of Britain's trade, for example through the East India Company (leading to 'the British Discovery of Hinduism'), by the activities of the American colonists, and by military action, was to bring all manner of exotic material to Britain. (These acquisitions were frequently of significance: soon after the Museum's foundation, objects collected on voyages by Sir Joseph Banks were to add a more rigorous scientific dimension to curating, while an Egyptian stele which found its way to the British Museum directly resulted in the understanding of hieroglyphic script.) And lastly, although this issue is not yet settled, the Protestant ethic, including particularly its Nonconformist components, did offer a less constricting and controlling environment than Catholicism.

As it happens, the creation of the British Museum was touch-and-go until the transformation of the Bill into the British Museum Act which received the Royal Assent on 7 June 1753. If the British nation had not agreed to Sloane's conditions, the collection might have been offered to the academies of St Petersburg, Paris, Berlin or Madrid; or it could have been sold. The Exchequer was wary, and as a result, the setting-up costs of the Museum did not come from the State, but from the proceeds of a public lottery (though approved by Parliament). Those people who bought lottery tickets to provide for the arrangements made by Sloane's trustees and for the purchase of Montagu House were not, when it came to it, thinking that their gambled money was going to result in the establishment of a great new public institution of objects saved for the nation: they were hoping for cash prizes. It was a damn'd close-run thing.

Notes and references

1   A new history of the British Museum was published for the 250th Anniversary of its foundation: David M. Wilson, *The British Museum: A history* (London, 2002); this includes a valuable bibliography, pp.394–406. For the Museum's history, other general works which should be consulted are Edward Miller, *That Noble Cabinet: A history of the British Museum* (London, 1973); W.T. Stearn, *The Natural History Museum: A history of the British Museum (Natural History) 1753–1980* (London, 1981); P.R. Harris, *A History of the British Museum Library 1753–1973* (London, 1998). A good short summary is Marjorie Caygill, *The Story of the British Museum* (London, 2002).

2   Oliver Impey and Arthur MacGregor, *The Origins of Museums: The cabinet of curiosities in sixteenth- and seventeenth-century Europe* (Oxford, 1985). This book contains the published proceedings of the Ashmolean Museum's 300th Anniversary Conference.

3   Nehemiah Grew, *Musæum Regalis Societatis* (London, 1681).

4   J. Tradescant, *Musæum Tradescantianum: or, a Collection of Rarities, preserved at South-Lambeth neer London* (London, 1656).

5   See A. MacGregor (ed.), *Sir Hans Sloane: Collector, scientist, antiquary; founding father of the British Museum* (London, 1994).

6   Lorna Weatherill, 'The meaning of consumer behaviour in late seventeenth- and early-eighteenth century England', in John Brewer and Roy Porter (eds), *Consumption and the World of Goods* (London, 1993), pp.206–227.

7   Robert Collinson, *Encyclopaedias: Their history throughout the ages* (London, 1963), pp.99–137.

8   Sidney I. Landau, *Dictionaries: The art and craft of lexicography* (Cambridge, 2001), pp.43–66.

9   Kate Whitaker, 'The culture of curiosity', in N. Jardine, J.A. Secord and E.C. Spary (eds), *Cultures of Natural History* (Cambridge, 1996), pp.88,89.

Chapter 1

Anticipating the Enlightenment

Museums and galleries in Britain before the British Museum

Giles Waterfield

Whether or not the early British Museum was a giant, it was certainly surrounded by pygmies. Since the early seventeenth century, museums had existed in London and in large provincial cities, as well as in private hands, but by the 1750s they were largely in a poor state. Although many of these collections were private, those with institutional associations offer the most interesting points of comparison with the fledgling institution in Montagu House. This chapter touches on the nature of some of these early museums, and aims to sketch the intellectual background which inspired them and which produced an attempt, however limited, to communicate with some sort of a public. Visual records of these early museums and their displays are very limited and our impressions have to be based primarily on the comments of visitors and on the (relatively numerous) printed catalogues.

In one important respect these early institutional museums did not at all resemble those we know today. Fine art, as we would now call it, did not yet enjoy the privileged position it was to achieve in the nineteenth century. The assumption prevailed that works of art deserved a place in a museum collection primarily for iconographic purposes or as examples of skilful craftsmanship rather than as objects in their own right. Thus, even in the Tradescant collection, as augmented by Elias Ashmole and given to the University of Oxford to form the museum that was to bear his name, the picture collection was effectively restricted to portraits of the founders, of English and foreign men of learning, and of recent kings of England – in other words to historical and loyalist associations. The taxonomical system adopted in the early Tradescant catalogue allowed no special place for works of art. The handful of paintings which were not portraits, such as the early *Landscape* by Nathaniel Bacon (probably the first pure landscape painting to be produced by a British artist), were listed in the 1656 catalogue in what now seems the somewhat inglorious category of 'Mechanick artificiall Works in Carvings, Turnings, Sowings and Paintings'.[1]

Such an attitude to paintings tended to be restricted to the 'public' sphere, since the creation of private (and generally princely) galleries devoted to paintings and sculpture was a long-established custom in Italy and elsewhere. On the Continent, these galleries became gradually more accessible to the public from the mid-eighteenth century onwards, and a similar practice developed in Britain. The attitude to what we would now characterize as works of art which was evident at the seventeenth-century Ashmolean applied also at the British Museum, even though Sloane's collection contained numerous

objects which we would define in those terms. It was perhaps the survival of this attitude, at least within the British Museum, that persuaded some commentators (including trustees) to suppose in the 1820s, when the foundation of a new National Gallery was being discussed, that the new institution would be subsumed in the existing museum.[2]

The early museums in Britain shared a number of characteristics. They were set up – with one notable exception – either by private individuals or by learned societies. While sometimes open to the general public and generally to the noble and scholarly classes, such regular access was not a significant feature of their life, unless enforced by financial pressures. It would be inappropriate to categorize these institutions in modern terms: they were not museums specifically of archaeology or natural history; rather they aspired to a comprehensive coverage of the productions of art and nature. In many cases it is apparent from contemporary descriptions that the collections were assembled with a moral purpose, to show forth the glory of God. This aspect applied particularly to the natural history studies pursued by such eminent collectors and writers – the two activities were often closely associated – as in the case of the distinguished botanist John Ray. These collections merged seamlessly with the libraries which almost invariably formed part of the holdings of museums. While these institutions tended to open in a bustle of learned activity, by the time of the creation of the British Museum this early excitement had generally subsided into a state of indolent torpor. In so far as their collections were intended to assist in the deciphering of the universe through scientific investigation rather than ecclesiastical dogma, they were symbols of Enlightenment thinking. Not only were the collections used as tools of research supporting the learned discussions, lectures and experiments conducted on the same premises, but their codification in manuscript or printed catalogues was regarded as a crucial element of the institution's work. The taxonomical principles on which these catalogues were based were diverse and necessarily experimental, but in their various forms they did give the collections some intellectual coherence. It is a field that would sustain further investigation.

So what were these museums? It may prove illuminating to examine three such collections, different in institutional character but comparable in contents and history: the Royal Society, the Gentlemen's Society of Spalding, and the Ashmolean Museum. The Royal Society, whose founders had already met together informally for some years, was set up with a Royal Charter at Gresham College in 1660. Its premises included a room intended for meetings, which also held portraits of leading figures in the Society – a very characteristic practice in an official interior of this type. Such tributes to the founders were also typical of early museums. It also boasted a 'Repository', on which work began at an early stage of the Society's life, intended both to house instruments used for regular scientific experiments and to bring together objects which would combine to create a microcosm. As Michael Hunter has observed, 'Aspirations for the collections seem to have been linked to hopes that it might be possible to construct a universal taxonomy which would accurately mirror the order of nature.'[3] In the achievement of this goal certain museums on the Continent (notably the famous anatomical collection at the University of Leiden) provided models. Although by the 1680s the Society's research activities had diminished, in 1681 Nehemiah Grew published a comprehensive catalogue, *Musæum Regalis Societatis*. This volume aimed to present 'A Prospect of the whole WORK of the Musaeum'.[4] It was divided into four major parts. Part 1, 'Of Animals', had seven sections: Human Rarities, Quadrupeds, Serpents, Birds, Fishes, Shells, Insects. The following parts were devoted respectively to Plants, Minerals, and 'Artificial Matters'. This final section was particularly ambitious, covering 'things relating to chemistry', 'things relating to mathematicks; and some Mechanicks'. 'Mechanicks' included ingenious inventions such as a 'Box-Hive' for bees contrived by Christopher Wren and designed to keep bees warmer with various beneficial results, and a hammock from the Indies described with an accompanying exegesis. This section of the display, which also included scientific instruments, reflects an interest in assembling objects which potentially had a strong practical application. This idea of bringing together ingenious inventions with a functional character was regarded by early members of the Society, all of them supporters of the New Philosophy, as one of their most important purposes. As Thomas Sprat, its first historian and a strong champion of Bacon, wrote in his *History of the Royal Society of London*, published in 1677 and frequently reprinted: 'Is it not evident, in these last hundred years . . . that almost a new Nature has been revealed to us . . . more noble secrets in optics, medicine, anatomy, astronomy, discovered, than in all those credulous and doting ages, from Aristotle to us?'[5] This belief in the practical application of museum collections was to be a shared characteristic of these early institutions, even though it did not always fit happily with more intellectual intentions.

Characteristically, the fine arts hardly had a place at the Royal Society. Sculpture was represented by a few objects notable primarily for their ingenuity of execution (such as 'Andromeda carved on a mother of pearl shell')[6] and some coins and other Roman antiquities excavated in London. We may suppose that the display within the museum was organized, at least theoretically, on the principles enunciated in the catalogue. There emerges from the early descriptions one problem which recurs in these early museums. On the one hand those who conceived them aimed to present the universe in miniature. On the other hand, collections were largely dependent on gifts rather than purchases, even though in some cases these were carefully chosen: for the Royal Society's museum, the secretary, Henry Oldenburgh, solicited the presentation of certain particularly desirable objects from other

learned bodies throughout Europe. This dependence on donations meant that repositories tended to include numbers of curiosities and freaks of nature of various sorts, survivals of an older fascination with exotica which generally offered only individual significance. At the Royal Society, for example, Grew lists a 'BONE said to be taken out of a MAREMAIDS HEAD',[7] though in some of his accounts of exotic objects he displays a degree of cheerful scepticism as though as he is as much interested in the myths around the supposed rarity as in the object itself.

While no views of the Museum survive, its character a generation later may be gauged from the description given by Zacharias Conrad von Uffenbach, an ill-tempered and anglophobic German who visited Britain in 1710. Uffenbach's vigorous description of the decline of the Repository should perhaps be viewed with a certain scepticism, but it does give an impression of the condition of contemporary institutions. He remarks that:

> . . . it is the sight of the Museum that is most astounding. It consists of what appear to be two long narrow chambers, where lie the finest instruments and other articles . . . not only in no sort of order or tidiness but covered with dust, filth and coal-smoke, and many of them broken and utterly ruined. If one inquires after anything, the operator who show strangers round . . . will usually say: 'A Rogue had it stolen away,' or he will show you pieces of it, saying: 'It is corrupted or broken'; and such is the care they take of things!

The conclusion reached by Uffenbach appears to have applied to all too many learned institutions by the early eighteenth century:

> But that is the way with all public societies. For a short time they flourish, while the founder and original members are there to set the standard; then come all kinds of setbacks . . . their final state is one of indifference and sloth.[8]

During the first half of the eighteenth century, scientific collections such as those held by the Royal Society and the Ashmolean tended to remain in an inert condition and, as Uffenbach suggested, to languish in the absence of any concentrated curatorial attention. The idea that the general public might be admitted to such museums and offered instruction on their contents was not general in Britain, even though the concept of learned societies – whether official or private – continued to flourish. In the early days of the British Museum, the new institution, while theoretically open to all, in practice erected an elaborate system which had the effect of making visits to the collection both difficult and unrewarding.

Michael Hunter has discussed the diffusion of the Royal Society's ideals throughout England in the second half of the seventeenth century.[9] From the late 1660s comparable societies were established not only in such large centres as Oxford, Norwich and York but in smaller towns, a phenomenon which continued through the eighteenth and into the nineteenth century. An interesting outbreak of learned bodies in and around Lincolnshire in the early eighteenth century, for example, in Stamford and Peterborough, as well as in Doncaster to the north, a succession of societies was established, each a modest version of the Royal Society. Usually the most prominent members were local schoolmasters, clergymen, tradesmen and merchants; some had gentry members and possibly the patronage of a local nobleman, though in some cases there were strong links with other societies and with prominent scholars in London. They followed the Royal Society in holding regular meetings at which papers were presented and objects of interest discussed, and often also in forming collections.[10]

Of these early institutions, the ancestors of the literary and philosophical institutes of the late eighteenth and early nineteenth centuries, one remarkable example survives. The Gentlemen's Society of Spalding began to form around 1710 under the influence of the Lincolnshire antiquary Maurice Johnson. Though he spent most of his life in Spalding, Johnson was very well-connected and was a prime mover in the re-establishment of the Society of Antiquaries of London in 1717. The Spalding Society was in regular correspondence with the Antiquaries, and included among its members such celebrated persons as Hans Sloane, Isaac Newton, Alexander Pope and J.M. Rysbrack.

The interests of the Gentlemen's Society were comprehensive. 'We deal', remarked Maurice Johnson to a fellow member in 1746, 'in all arts and sciences, and exclude nothing from our conversation but politics, which would throw us all into confusion and disorder.'[11] Its aim was 'to excite a spirit of enquiry'.[12] In fact, one of the prevailing interests of the Society was the study of antiquities and natural history, with a strong local bias. From its earliest days the Society assembled a collection which is close to being unique for a private society of this nature in having maintained a continuous life to the present. Within this collection, the library naturally formed a crucial element. The museum's character is suggested by the *Rules and Orders* of 1725: while the books were to be kept in the church or grammar school, the remainder, 'with all MSS, charts, maps, plans, drawings, prints, coins, casts, carvings, and other curiosities in nature or art, purchased by or bestowed on this Society . . . [are] to be kept in the classes in its museum under the rules and direction of this Society.'[13] One must suppose that this museum, organized by category like a three-dimensional catalogue, functioned primarily as a private repository. There is no record of public admission, and the objects were presumably kept in wooden cabinets, perhaps of the type typically used by Dr Woodward for the display of his highly important collection of fossils and natural history specimens, now surviving in the Sedgwick Museum in Cambridge.[14]

At Spalding, one of the most important elements in the museum's life was antiquarian study. Antiquarianism was a field that had revived steadily during the sixteenth century as scholars became increasingly interested in the early history of Britain and the problem of the Ancient Briton. The idea that one could rely on the myth-based accounts of such writers as the twelfth-century monk Geoffrey of Monmouth was replaced, under the influence of men like William Camden, by a desire to study original sources at first hand and if possible to establish the role of Britain as 'a member of the fellowship of nations who drew their strength from roots struck deep in the Roman Empire.'[15] In this tradition, works such as John Aubrey's *Monumenta Britannica* aimed to apply to material associated with pre-Roman and Roman remains 'the same classificatory method and presentation as his colleagues in the Royal Society were using in the natural sciences.'[16] For the museums examined here, antiquarian study was a crucial element of their work. Thus, by 1660 the rudimentary Royal Society included antiquarian study within its interests. At the Ashmolean, both

of the earliest keepers were leading antiquaries. Robert Plot, who was the *custos* of the Ashmolean from its foundation until his retirement in 1690, published two major works: *The Natural History of Oxford-shire*, in 1677, and the similar volume for Staffordshire issued in 1686. These works were based partly on his own collection, which ultimately he donated to the museum. They were pioneering attempts to undertake a systematic study of the counties' ancient and recent history and archaeology, together with their geographical characteristics. It was an interest shared by his successor, Edward Lhwyd, who was to become a highly important scholar. It was no coincidence that Lhwyd (who worked in a junior capacity at the museum almost from its foundation) was not only a pioneer in the study of Celtic philology, but a biologist, geologist, and antiquary. In terms of collections and their display, the objects assembled in the pursuit of these antiquarian studies tended to be selected for their value as documents (based on local historical and geographical considerations) as much as for their interest as curiosities. Public display was not a prime consideration: museums functioned, rather, as depositories of informative specimens for a learned or at least semi-learned audience.

Very much more public in its aspirations than the Gentlemen's Society of Spalding (though not necessarily more ambitious intellectually) were the collections of the Tradescants, father and son, and of Elias Ashmole, which in 1683 jointly formed the founding collections of the Ashmolean Museum. The Tradescants' collection had resulted from the travels of the elder John Tradescant, his botanical researches and his accumulation of curiosities of art and nature from donors with contacts around the world. Privately owned though it was when kept in the Ark, the Tradescants' house in Lambeth, from the 1630s onwards they allowed easy access to the house and the botanical garden which formed an important element of the whole. In terms of its accessibility to the general public it has been described as 'probably the first museum of its kind in Britain'.[17] The collection was published as the *Musæum Tradescantianum* in 1656. Its reputation is apparent from the decision of Charles II in 1661 to quash an order from the Master of the Revels against the display at the Ark, without authority, of what the Master described as 'severall strainge creatures': as the king put it, 'Our express pleasure is that the Said Tredeskyn bee suffered, freely and quietly to proceed, as formerly, in entertaining & receiving all persons, whose curiosity shall invite them to the delight of seeing his rare & ingenious Collections of Art and nature.'[18]

From a relatively early date it was intended that the collection should become a public institution. In his will (which was successfully challenged by Ashmole after an acrimonious lawsuit), Tradescant the Younger had stipulated that the collection should be bequeathed to Oxford or Cambridge University. Ashmole was particularly interested in the future use of the collection as a school for the study of the natural sciences. As an active scholar who had attended the University at Oxford during the Civil War, he would have considered (not altogether wisely, as it turned out) that that university would be a particularly suitable beneficiary for a collection for which he envisaged a continuing life as an academic resource, rather than as a collection of random curios. Later seventeenth-century Oxford, where the talents of Christopher Wren, Robert Boyle and numerous others centred round John Wilkins, Warden of

Wadham College, had stimulated, from the 1650s onwards, a vigorous climate of Baconian enquiry, certainly appeared the ideal home for an innovative museum as centre for scientific research. The University and the individual colleges already possessed a number of collections, notably at the Bodleian Library, which could be viewed at least by a limited public, but these were scarcely used other than to amuse visitors. The Ashmolean was revolutionary in a British context as a centre of academic activity within a university. In spite of the hostility of many traditional members of the University still allied to the older philosophy, a new building was erected, in fact at much greater expense than the University could afford. The early character of the Museum is conveyed by the physician and natural historian Thomas Molyneaux, writing in 1683. Molyneaux found that Dr Plot, the first Keeper, was

> ... very civil and obliging, and shewed me all the new building on the west side of the theatre, built of square freestone, containing ... the Museum Ashmoleanum; Schola Historiae Naturalis, et Officina chymica. It consists only of these three rooms, one a-top of the other, and a large staircase. The Museum Ashmoleanum is the highest; the walls of which are all hung round with John Tradescant's rarities, and several others of Mr. Ashmol's own gathering, his picture hangs up at one end of the room, with a curious carved frame about it, of Mr Gibbins his work ... Under this rome is the Schola Hist. Nat, very spacious and high, curiously wainscoted, at the end a very pretty white marble chimney-piece stained up and down with red ... In this place Dr Plott reads lectures to all that go thro' a course of chymistry with him, and to those only ... Under this is the Officina chymica, the greatest part of which is under ground, and therefore it is very cold, even in the summer time ... it is very well contrived with great variety of furnaces, and those very convenient for all the operations in chymistry ... [19]

While following the tradition of the Royal Society in postulating a close relationship between the Repository and the academic programme of the institution, the Ashmolean was innovatory as a museum in attempting to provide an organized course of study in the context of a university. As it turned out the experiment achieved only limited success but ultimately it was to have many followers.

From the beginning the Museum was open to visitors; indeed financially it was wholly dependent on admission fees. This made a strong impact on its character. Uffenbach describes the museum in 1710, hardly thirty years after its foundation. He was shocked. On viewing the museum, he remarked:

> On our first entrance we wondered not a little that there should be such talk made over this museum outside this island, and more particularly of course within it ... The specimens ... might also be much better arranged and preserved ... But it is surprising that things can be preserved even as well as they are, since the people impetuously handle everything in the usual English fashion and ... even the women are allowed up here for sixpence; they run here and there, grabbing at everything and taking no rebuff from the Sub-Custos. [20]

Although the Museum was not in notably good order at the time of Uffenbach's visit, these deficiencies may have been due to the Keeper at the time rather than to any fundamental lack of interest, within the University, in its objectives. In spite of various difficulties, the Ashmolean continued to house scientific experiments and to receive important gifts (notably the Alfred Jewel, in 1718), to the arrangement of which much attention was given. A number of the men involved in the Museum in these years were also connected with Sir Hans Sloane or with the young British Museum, so that the Ashmolean can be seen, in spite of the vicissitudes it sometimes suffered, as creating a continuous link between the burst of scientific activity of the late seventeenth century and the establishment of the first national museum in the world in 1753. [21]

The inclusion of historical specimens in a museum was no novelty. In the same period there also existed a set of displays – which effectively were museums – that contravened all the ideas outlined above, displays that relied on prejudice and the distortion of history for political ends, through the use of unresearched and inaccurate information, presented in a wholly unhistorical way. These manifestations were also, it has to be said, extremely successful in terms of public presentation, and remained in various forms open until the late nineteenth century. They relied on (and developed) the royal collections, which in the sixteenth and seventeenth centuries (as nowadays) were intimately, but indefinably, linked to state ownership. When Paul Hentzner, a German lawyer, made an extensive tour of England in 1597, he was able without apparent difficulty to view the curiosities at Whitehall Palace, Windsor Castle and Hampton Court. Most significantly, he saw the Tower of London, already a regular place of resort for visitors. In addition to the old-established royal menagerie, he was greatly impressed by two aspects of royal magnificence. In the royal wardrobe they 'were shown ... a hundred pieces of arras belonging to the Crown, made of gold, silver, and silk ... saddles ... an immense quantity of Bed-furniture, such as canopes, and the like ... some Royal Dresses, so extremely magnificent, as to raise any one's admiration at the sums they must have cost.'[22] The Armoury was equally remarkable, with its 'spears from which you may shoot ... rich Halberds ... lances ... and the body armour of Henry VIII ... Cross-bows, Bows & Arrows ...'. Warming to his theme, Hentzner asks excitedly, '... but who can relate all that is to be seen here? Eight or nine men, employed by the year, are scarce sufficient to keep all the Arms bright.'[23] This collection was essentially a display of royal wealth and military power rather than a museum in the sense considered above. It maintained, very loosely, the tradition of the medieval cathedral treasury.

After the Restoration – clearly a highly sensitive moment for the monarchy – the displays at the Tower were extended into three departments, which were regularly open to visitors for a fee. The 'Line of Kings', already in place a year or so after 1660, was expanded in 1688. In this visually impressive display, many of the monarchs from William the Conqueror to the seventeenth century, but with some tactful omissions, were shown mounted on horseback in striking if wildly anachronistic armours. (William I, for example, held a musket.)[24] Also in the Tower, the Spanish Armoury demonstrated the horrors of foreign invasion and particularly the evils associated with a great Roman Catholic power through an eye-watering display of weapons and instruments of torture which were supposedly trophies of the Spanish Armada (though in fact almost all of them had been in the Armoury for many years before 1588). These displays, supplemented by the artistically arranged weaponry shown in the Grand Storehouse, represented the first attempts at what one might, if somewhat anachronistically, describe as a national museum. They reflect the growing interest in national history and national pride, themes which sometimes appeared in other, less overtly bellicose museum displays. The displays at the Tower remained on view throughout the eighteenth century, untouched by any ideas of the brotherhood of man.

One important aspect of the Oxford collections, as touched upon earlier, looked forward to one of the most important aspects of the British Museum: the display of classical sculpture. Immediately next to the museum were exhibited the marbles acquired from second decade of the seventeenth century onwards by Thomas Howard, 2nd Earl of Arundel. The marbles had originally been displayed in a consciously didactic scheme at Arundel House on the Strand, where Peacham described them:

> Arundel House is the chief English scene of ancient inscriptions, which Master John Selden, the best and learnedst antiquary in this kingdom, hath collected together under the title of Marmora Arundelliana. You shall find all the walls of the house inlaid with them and speaking Greek and Latin to you. The garden especially will afford you the pleasure of a world of learned lectures in this kind.[25]

The idea of incorporating marbles, and particularly inscriptions, into the walls of buildings, derived ultimately from classical precedents and more recently from the practice, current at least as early as the mid-sixteenth century in Rome, of attaching recently excavated antiquities to the walls of great palaces. There they testified to the ancient connections and erudition of the owners, and contributed in the ideal of the re-creation of ancient Rome. The idea was followed in England. Robert Cotton, the antiquary whose library formed one of the founding collections of the British Museum, showed antiquities on the walls of his country house at Conington in Huntingdon-shire, at the beginning of the seventeenth century, and the same principle was followed in other private museums such as the Senhouse collection of classical antiquities at Netherhall in Cumberland.

As David Howarth has pointed out, the display of sculpture was discussed by Francis Junius, Arundel's librarian, in his *De Pictura Veterum* of 1637: he stressed the morally improving effect of sculpture displays, and suggested that the physical presence of statues – and presumably inscriptions – could inspire glorious deeds in the beholder.[26] A similar approach was followed at Oxford when part of the Marbles, particularly the inscriptions, were given to the University through the good offices of John Evelyn in 1667. Though they were not integrated into the collections of the Ashmolean Museum, physically they were closely linked, since following Roman and British precedent they were displayed in the open air on the walls enclosing the adjacent Sheldonian Theatre.

The development, during the first half of the eighteenth century, of the scientific collections associated with learned and private societies and with museums has already been suggested: they tended to subside into indolent desuetude. Private collections, whether antiquarian or tending increasingly towards classical antiquity, continued to flourish, sometimes under the patronage of such notable figures as the physician Richard Mead. Mead was not only a collector of books and notable works of art: the catalogue of his possessions lists coins and medals, antiquities and 'antique pictures', as well as fossils and natural history specimens.[27] His house in Great Ormond Street in London – regarded at the time as the finest collection in the country – functioned as an unofficial academy, described by his biographer as 'Temple of Nature, and a Repository of Time'.[28] It was open freely to 'Ingenious men',[29] a place where the naturalist, the mathematician, the antiquary, the scholar and the painter could meet. A further link between these private collections and the intellectual climate surrounding the British Museum is the fact that Mead's biographer, and fervent admirer, was Matthew Maty, who was to become the second Principal Librarian of the British Museum.

Mead's establishment was a striking example of the peculiarly British tendency for private individuals to create private institutes of learning in the absence of active patronage by the state. Perhaps the most interesting development in the history of collecting in Britain in this period lay in the gradually changing story of art galleries, a story strongly influenced, as David Solkin has discussed,[30] by the expanding bourgeois market of Hanoverian London. In contrast to the position of early scientific museums, the pressure on public provision for the fine arts was largely commercial, as evidenced by the success of Vauxhall Gardens as a showplace for work by young British artists. A strong nationalistic interest in the potential achievement of the British School was a further important factor, an interest in which a number of leading artists such as William Hogarth played a leading role. The State continued, as it had in the seventeenth century other than through the personal patronage of the monarch, to play a nugatory role, at least until the foundation of the British Museum, when it assumed a crucial, but imperfectly realized, new importance.

A French observer who knew London intimately summed up the situation in the middle of the eighteenth century (just after the foundation of the British Museum): '. . . the arts are not made an object of the public attention in England; for there is no foundation or institution in their favour, neither by the government in general, nor in particular by the crown.'[31] Contemporary accounts of London in mid-century do, however, list numerous private art collections. In the absence of public galleries, these collections were in one way or another in the public domain since they were often published, if not necessarily easily accessible physically: thus R. and J. Dodsley's *London and its Environs Described* of 1761 summarizes the works of art belonging to Sampson Gideon, John Barnard, the Duke of Northumberland and other notable owners, and in some cases indicates how these collections might be seen. The growing interest in the contribution to be made in the public sphere by the fine arts was celebrated by the foundation in 1739 of the Foundling Hospital in London. This remarkable institution in Bloomsbury, established by Captain Thomas Coram for the benefit of children who would previously have been left to die by their penniless mothers, followed the example of charitable foundations in Venice and Florence (such as the fifteenth-century Ospedale degli Innocenti in Florence, an institution which must have inspired Coram and his associates in general concept as well as in detail), in supporting the care of the needy by providing public displays of art and music of the highest quality. At the Foundling Hospital, the leading young British artists of the day were given the opportunity to exhibit their skills in the Court Room, in which scenes of Biblical philanthropy and depictions of the London hospitals adorned the walls. The Foundling Hospital became a place of popular resort, where a new bourgeois public was able to parade in a setting sanctified both by the practice of good works and by the finest works of the emergent British school.

When the new trustees of the British Museum confronted the problem of how to establish and run their new institution, the array of public institutions in Britain in the middle of the eighteenth century was not notably impressive. It included scientific museums of some antiquity on the one hand; and on the other, an emerging type of private art collection from which, generally, the new museum was unwilling to learn. It was perhaps this shortage of convincing precedent – a shortage which applied equally in Continental Europe – that made the early years of the new national museum so experimental and, in some respects, so unsatisfactory.

Notes and references

1 Arthur MacGregor, *Tradescant's Rarities: Essays on the founding of the Ashmolean Museum, 1683* (Oxford, 1983), p.298.
2 For the most recent discussion of this issue see David Wilson, *The British Museum: A history* (London, 2002), pp.78–9.
3 Michael Hunter, 'The cabinet institutionalized', in Oliver Impey and Arthur MacGregor (eds), *The Origins of Museums: The cabinet of curiosities in sixteenth- and seventeenth-century Europe* (Oxford, 1985), p.164.
4 Nehemiah Grew, *Musæum Regalis Societatis* (London, 1681), title page.
5 Thomas Sprat, *History of the Royal Society of London* (London, 1671), p.xviii.
6 Grew, op. cit. (note 4), p.371.
7 Grew, op. cit. (note 4), p.81.
8 W.H. Quarrell and Margaret Mare (trans. and eds), *London in 1710 from the Travels of Zacharias Conrad von Uffenbach* (London, 1934), p.98.
9 Michael Hunter, *Science and Society in Restoration England* (Cambridge, 1981), *passim*.
10 Hunter, op. cit. (note 9), pp.81ff.
11 John Nichols (publisher and ed.), 'An account of the Gentlemen's Society at Spalding', in *Antiquities in Lincolnshire (1790) being the third volume of the Bibliotheca Topographica Britannica* (London, 1746–1826), p.iv. The Lincolnshire volume also contains the Statutes and Minute Books of the Society.
12 Nichols, op. cit. (note 11), p.xvii.
13 Nichols, op. cit. (note 11), p.vi.
14 David Price, 'John Woodward and a surviving British geological collection from the early eighteenth century', *Journal of the History of Collections* 1 (1989), pp.79–95, figs 2–3.
15 Stuart Piggott, *Ruins in a Landscape* (Edinburgh, 1976), p.12.
16 Piggott, op. cit. (note 15), p.15.
17 MacGregor, op. cit. (note 1), p.23.
18 Quoted in Macgregor, op. cit. (note 1), p.23.
19 Thomas Molyneux, quoted in MacGregor, op. cit. (note 1), p.59.
20 Z.C. von Uffenbach, *Oxford in 1710, from the Travels of Zacharias Conrad von Uffenbach*, trans. and ed. by W.H. and W.J.C. Quarrell (Oxford, 1928), p.31.
21 See A. MacGregor and A.J. Turner, 'The Ashmolean Museum', in *The History of the University of Oxford*, vol.v, *The Eighteenth Century*, ed. L.S. Sutherland and L.G. Mitchell (Oxford, 1986), pp.639–58.
22 Paul Hentzner, *A Journey into England in the Year MDMXCVIII* (Edinburgh, 1881), p.37.
23 Hentzner, op. cit. (note 22), p.38.
24 See, *inter alia*, anon., *Curiosities in the Tower of London* (London, 1741); Alan Borg, 'Two studies in the history of the Tower Armouries for the Society of Antiquaries', *Archaeologia* 105 (1975), pp. 317–29.
25 Thomas Peacham, *The Compleat Gentleman,* 2nd edn (London, 1634), quoted in David Howarth, *Lord Arundel and his Circle* (New Haven and London, 1985), p.120.
26 Quoted in Howarth, op. cit. (note 25), p.79.
27 *Museum Meadianum sive Catalogus Nummorum Veteris Aevi cum aliis quibusdam Artis recentoris et naturae Operibus quae vir clarissimus Richardus Mead M.D.* (London, 1755), *passim*.
28 [Matthew Maty], *Authentic Memoirs of the Life of Richard Mead, M.D.* (London, 1755), p.51.
29 Maty, op. cit. (note 29), pp.53–7.
30 David Solkin, *Painting for Money* (New Haven and London, 1993), *passim*.
31 André Rouquet, *The Present State of the Arts in England* (London, 1755), p.14.

Chapter 2

Sir Hans Sloane and the European Proto-Museum

Debora J. Meijers

Taking as its starting point the will of Sir Hans Sloane, the following contribution attempts to reconstruct a view of contemporary European museum culture from Sloane's own perspective and to assess how his declared ambition, that his collection should live on as a public museum after his death, fits into the European museum landscape of the 1730s and 1740s. The principal concern here will be with one particular kind of institution whose character was consolidated in the course of the eighteenth century – financed by public funds, equipped to promote the arts and sciences within national boundaries, conceived with a 'systematic' arrangement, and open to the public. This essay will argue that Sloane's will continued a practice that had its origins as early as the seventeenth century, and that the individual founders of such collections, at first unconsciously but from around 1700 more deliberately, contributed materially to the genesis of the museum in this specific sense. Viewed from this perspective, the contention that in drawing up his will Sloane could not have envisaged an institution of that kind proves unsustainable and we are forced to challenge the long held view that in institutional terms he was 'embarking on largely uncharted waters'.[1]

Our starting point must be to pose the following question: what did Sloane have in mind when, in 1739, he decided to offer his collection for a reasonable price first of all to George II, or, if the king were to turn down the offer, successively to three British scientific institutions – the Royal Society, the University of Oxford, and the College of Physicians in Edinburgh – and to four foreign Royal Academies of Science – Paris, St Petersburg, Berlin and Madrid?[2] In order to construct a frame of reference we must examine conventional European practice before that date. The conclusion to which we are led is that from an organizational point of view, the form of governance by a body of trustees as envisaged by Sloane existed nowhere else but in Britain (most notably with the Board of Visitors of the Ashmolean Museum and the trustees of the legacy of Sir John Cotton), but that in his ambitions to preserve the collection, to render it accessible to the public and make it an object of utility to the nation, he had no shortage of precedents to follow.

Concentration of existing collections

During a period of almost three-quarters of a century in which Sloane reaped the benefits of international travel, wide reading and correspondence with countless scholars at home and abroad, he had ample opportunity to observe the behaviour of other collectors, from the private sphere on the one hand and at a monarchical or institutional level on the other. From European cultural centres such as Florence, Vienna, Dresden and St Petersburg, he could have learned of a process of concentration in royal courts or in academies of science that by the middle of the eighteenth century had led to the crystallization of a number of 'proto-museums': in other words, a confluence of existing private collections towards monarchs or academies, who organized them systematically in increasingly monumental architectural complexes with the intention of promoting national interest in the arts and sciences and of serving the public good. It is easy to see how Sloane himself could have envisaged the foundation of an institution of this kind, but what was unusual in his case was the fact that he made it clear before his death that he personally wanted to create such an institution.

There is no shortage of examples of such monarchical or academic proto-museums built up in the manner described. Every scholar in Europe knew of Ole Worm, for example, especially following the publication of his *Museum Wormianum*,[3] which appeared a year after his death in 1654, and they probably knew also that his collection had been incorporated in its entirety into the *Kunstkammer* of the Danish king. To what extent Worm himself had planned that purchase, however, is debatable.[4] The rare examples of a deliberate legacy to a particular community took place within a specific state form, in republics such as Venice, Switzerland and the Netherlands,[5] or exceptionally in Britain with examples like the collections of Ashmole and Cotton.

While Sloane's brand of civic morality within a monarchical setting was relatively new, there were numerous examples of collectors who attempted to capitalize on their collections by selling them to a particular head of state. Despite this fundamental difference, however, these private transactions may have had more of an influence on Sloane's action than we might suppose. For instance, there was the Amsterdam apothecary Albert Seba, one of Sloane's correspondents, who sold his entire cabinet to Tsar Peter the Great in 1716 (fig. 1).[6] There was clearly no question of a legacy in this case: the apothecary was still full of life, and since he had been providing the Tsar with medicines for years, the sale of his cabinet seems rather to belong within this context. After the transaction had been concluded, he immediately set about forming a new collection, which ultimately was to exceed the first one in size.[7] But although Seba himself displayed no explicit signs of civic virtue, the sale did have the effect of ensuring that his collection remained intact, for it came to serve as the basis (along with the collection of the Amsterdam physician Frederik Ruysch) for the so-called *Kunstkamera* in St Petersburg – an institution that satisfied most of the characteristics of the 'proto-museum' mentioned earlier, as we shall see.

Perhaps inspired by the successes of Seba and Ruysch, the Dutch linen merchant Levinus Vincent wrote to Sloane that he would prefer to sell his cabinet to 'un grand prince curieux' than to entertain the idea that it would be auctioned after his death. He also wrote in the same vein to the French court and to Cosimo III de' Medici, but to no avail, for today we know of his collection only from the splendid plates of the *Wonder-Tooneel der Nature (Theatre des merveilles de la nature)* that he published in 1706–15.[8] Vincent's decision to approach the Grand Duke of Tuscany is less surprising than might at first appear, for in the years following a visit to the Netherlands, Cosimo had on several occasions shown signs of interest in the activities of the scientists and collectors there. By means of all sorts of purchases, including in 1682 the acquisition of six chests of shells from the famous researcher of the island of Ambon, Georg Everhard Rumph, he sought to maintain the system of patronage of his ancestors and to continue to expand the collections in the Uffizi.[9]

It must not be forgotten, however, that the process of concentration had already begun within the circles of private collectors themselves: the apothecary and collector James Petiver had made purchases for Sloane in the Netherlands in 1711 at the auction of the 'Indian cabinet' of the Leiden professor Paul Hermann, and his own expanded collection subsequently passed into Sloane's hands, a process repeated with several other collectors.[10] What other fate could be considered for Sloane's own mega-collection than acquisition by a monarch or a learned society, or indeed the founding of an independent museum? Sloane opted for a combination of the first and the third possibilities, and that in itself was new – an innovation born of necessity, indeed, for unlike most rulers on the Continent the British monarch had no designated cabinet of art and *naturalia* to which additions could be made.

Sloane, therefore, is likely to have been familiar with examples of this kind of confluence of existing private cabinets into a few larger – usually princely – collections. They formed part of a long-term process that began in the seventeenth century. It is important that the genesis of the public museum should be understood in this way, rather than being regarded as a process instigated at a particular moment by a specific individual (such as Sloane) or by a specific political event (such as the French Revolution), to mention two widely held ideas. By acknowledging this fact we can obtain a more realistic picture of the process by which the public museum gradually assumed its character, a process that is connected with the concentration of wealth, power and knowledge in several European centres, and a concentration not only in terms of objects but also of expertise.

Specialist keepers and new arrangements

As an example of such a process we may note that, in addition to Seba's collection, Peter the Great also bought almost the entire œuvre of Maria Sibylla Merian in Amsterdam in a single purchase, on the very day on which she breathed her last in February 1717. But along with her numerous books and drawings he also contracted the eldest of Merian's two gifted daughters, Dorothea Maria, to work as a plant and insect specialist and as an artist in St Petersburg.

We see this phenomenon – the recruitment of experts along with the collection – on a frequent basis. In several cases it was accompanied by an adaptation of the existing cabinets or even the construction of a new type of building, comprising a series of interconnected rooms in which the disciplines could be distinguished without actually being separated. In the Viennese court the Emperor Franz Stephan took an important step in this direction when he bought a collection of minerals and fossils from Jean Baillou in 1748, had them transferred from Florence (where Baillou had been director of the gallery of the last Medici duke, Gian Gastone) and appointed him as keeper of the imperial cabinet of natural history in Vienna. In 1765, immediately after the death of Franz Stephan, the project was completed with the addition of a museum wing to the Hofbibliothek, which provided a series of cabinets distinguished by discipline.[11] The Empress Maria Theresia commissioned a monumental painting in honour of her dead spouse, showing him in the presence of his four cabinet directors (fig. 2). They are represented in the mineral room, which offers a view into the other rooms, with their collections arranged by discipline.

It was not only in Vienna that this process of concentration was accompanied by an interest in more specialized management and in the arrangement and presentation of the collections in new series of rooms. In most of the larger courtly collections the various categories of objects gradually acquired their own keepers. Nevertheless, this form of division of labour should not be confused with our notion of specialization: the keepers with their respective departments remained above all connected with one another through the encyclopaedic principle of 'unity in diversity', a notion that crops up repeatedly in this context.

We can recognize this principle in the well-known formulation of the British Museum Act of 1753, that 'all Arts and Sciences have a Connexion with each other'.[12] This credo, closely associated with the concept on which Diderot and D'Alembert's *Encyclopédie* was based, was first expounded in volume 1 of that work in 1751. But here too we should recognize that it was a principle that was already firmly established in the academic and museum culture that can be traced back to Francis Bacon, to whom Diderot and D'Alembert explicitly refer. Sloane was equally imbued with this way of thinking in terms of 'unity in diversity' long before the *Encyclopédie* appeared, if we may judge from the words of Gottfried Bayer, a member of the Academy in St Petersburg, uttered in 1733: according to Bayer, Sloane was a man 'whose excellent mind has compassed so many parts of learning' as to enable him 'to have an insight into the connection all sorts of knowledge have with each other'.[13] The characterization is one equally fitting for Sloane in his capacity as an indefatigable cataloguer, for his interest in arrangement and presentation applied not only to three-dimensional exposition but also to presentation of his collection in the form of inventories. Although Sloane's catalogues were never printed, his activities in this area were broadly in line with contemporary practice in several private collections as well as in courtly proto-museums. A good example is formed, once again, by the museum of the Academy of Sciences in St Petersburg, where everything was meticulously registered in an orderly fashion and even recorded in drawings. The Russians followed the example of the Dutch collectors in this respect, particularly that of Seba with his *Thesauri* (fig. 3).[14]

For the benefit of the public

There are further parallels between Sloane's orientation and developments in the rest of Europe. Besides his contribution to the process of concentration, his encyclopaedic frame of mind and his propensity for orderly cataloguing, Sloane's emphasis on the usefulness that his collection would have to the nation and his desire for its (relative) accessibility to the public were also current topics of the period when he drew up his will – both amongst private collectors and (although this is less widely recognized) in the context of princely cabinets. For example, some courtly collections of minerals and stones were allied with research not only for the mining industry but also for the development of porcelain production. And as far as a concern for accessibility is concerned, like their private counterparts royal collections needed a degree of accessibility in order to perform their representative function, since representation can operate only if a sufficient number of people are familiar with the monarch's possessions.

A striking example is formed by the 'Palais des Sciences' in Dresden, organized in accordance with the instructions of Augustus the Strong. In 1728 Augustus formulated a decree in which all of the components of the proto-museum were present in principle: 'to the glory of our court, for the promotion of the sciences and arts, and for the benefit of the public, I order that our books and curiosities be displayed in the best arrangement in a suitable place and that a special building be constructed for that purpose'.[15] The fact that he eventually chose an existing building (the recently constructed Zwinger complex) is of less direct consequence in this context.

In summary, it may be reiterated that the characteristics of the proto-museum are not exclusively derived from the initiatives of private individuals, but can also be observed in court culture of the early eighteenth century, where they served an important function.

Institutional collections

In considering Sloane's perspective and in examining the kind of setting for a museum that might have recommended itself to him, from Britain or from elsewhere in Europe, we must focus especially on the institutional collections – that is, those of the universities and the academies of science. After all, Sloane did include a number of such institutions in his will: London, Oxford, Edinburgh, Paris, St Petersburg, Berlin and Madrid. But was this course of action so different in principle from choosing to benefit a princely museum? Closer investigation shows that by 1739 there was little to choose between offering a collection to a monarch or to an Academy, at least in an absolutist state such as France or Russia. The Academicians in Paris and St Petersburg were in the immediate employ of the monarch, in the midst of his collections. The situation of the Royal Society in London and that of the British universities was different because they had a relatively autonomous status, a feature that carried with it the consequence that they had less money at their disposal.[16]

Leaving a collection to the Royal Society carried no guarantee that it would be preserved properly: this was why Sloane abandoned that particular alternative in 1749, together with those offered by the universities of Oxford and Edinburgh.[17] But he had also changed the order of preference of the remaining academies so that St Petersburg had risen to first place. This meant that if Sloane's native country were to refuse his offer, the Russian Academy would be next in line.[18]

Russian connections

The St Petersburg Academy of Sciences was allied to a very up-to-date museum which corresponded as closely as any of the other examples mentioned so far to the characteristics that were to emerge in the second quarter of the eighteenth century. This museum, known as the *Kunstkamera*, was charged with the promotion of the arts and sciences within the Russian Empire; it was open to the public for that reason, and it was systematically arranged (at least by the norms of the day). One particularly noteworthy feature was that, from 1728 onwards, it was housed in an independent building specially constructed for the purpose, adjacent to the seat of the Academy (figs 4–6) – that is to say, it had no physical connection with any of the palaces of the Tsar.[19]

As we have seen, the nucleus of the collection had been built up from purchases made by Peter the Great during his travels in Europe, especially those made in the Netherlands from Seba, Ruysch and others in 1716–17. Through his correspondence with Seba, Sloane must already have been aware of the existence of this museum, and indeed in 1721 he had received a visit from its keeper, Johann Daniel Schumacher. Under the instructions of the Tsar himself, Schumacher was then undertaking a tour of his own with the dual aims of attracting European scholars to professorships at the projected Academy and of making purchases for the collection. At this period the construction of the new museum on the banks of the Neva was already under way.

In 1730 Sloane received another visitor from St Petersburg, the historian and ethnographer Gerhard Friedrich Müller: on this occasion Müller's task was to invite Sloane to accept an honorary fellowship of the Academy.[20] It is inconceivable that these emissaries, sent to interest Sloane in this cultural centre on the periphery of Europe, could have failed to provide him with full accounts of the academic facilities being assembled and hence it is highly likely that Sloane was closely familiar with the character of the museum in St Petersburg. When Müller and Sloane met, the interior of the building was still being fitted out (fig. 6).

But there was yet another way in which Sloane had knowledge of the Academy and the *Kunstkamera* in St Petersburg, through years of correspondence with his former assistant, the botanist Johann Amman, who in 1733 had been bold enough to accept the challenge of a professorship in that distant centre. Amman, in charge of the botanical garden of the Academy, sent seeds of Russian plants to Sloane, for which he received in return specimens from Carolina and Virginia. It was the era of the second Kamchatka expedition to the most north-easterly corner of the Russian Empire, a venture that considerably enriched the botanical, zoological and ethnographic collections of the *Kunstkamera*. A Kalmuck cheese that Sloane received from Amman was probably one of those spoils, as well as the 'Alphabet of the Callmuck language' and 'a very curious reddish sand from ye Lake Baikal' that were sent to him from St Petersburg.[21]

Following his visit to Sloane, Gerhard Friedrich Müller had become a prominent member of this expedition, led by Vitus Bering, one of whose principal missions was to discover whether the American continent was linked to Asia. The progress made by Russian 'museum culture' by around 1735 can be seen from Müller's account of a journey up the River Irtysh from Tobolsk: 'We found ourselves in a paradise of flowers mostly growing on plants as yet unknown, in a zoological garden where the rare animals of Asia had been gathered together for us, in a museum of antique heathen tombs holding rare treasures – in a word, in a place which no one had set out to investigate ever before'.[22] Here we can recognize the traditional concept of Nature as 'God's *Kunstkammer*' presented in a more secular light. But despite the lack of explicitly religious overtones, the accounts brought to Sloane must have struck a deep chord, for when he drew up his will on 9 October 1739 the Academy of St Petersburg was included as the sixth in a series of eight potential beneficiaries.

Besides the contacts with various researchers at St Petersburg as outlined above (and especially with Amman), there was also a certain pro-Russian climate predominating in Britain at the time that may have contributed to Sloane's decision. In the same year in which Sloane drew up his will, the historian Thomas Birch published a biography of Peter the Great that triggered a 'veritable explosion of British Petromania', as Anthony Cross has phrased it.[23] Sloane knew the writer well, so it is not far-fetched to suspect that Birch (to whom we are indebted for many biographical details of Sloane's own life)[24] could have acted as an additional stimulus. Peter the Great, who had been responsible for founding both a museum and an academy, had introduced western European science to Russia within the space of a few years, and had opened up for investigation the routes to east and south Asia, was undoubtedly a figure who appealed to Sloane.

In a codicil of 10 July 1749 Sloane extensively overhauled the list of beneficiaries, excluding the British scientific institutions and giving St Petersburg priority over Paris.[25] Christine Thomas has already suggested a relation here with the visit in 1748 of yet another delegate from Russia, Johann Caspar Taubert. Taubert came to investigate how the elderly Sloane intended to dispose of his collection and what it might actually contain.[26] During the past few years, however, thanks to research by Natalja Kopaneva and Jozien Driessen, much more has been discovered about the St Petersburg *Kunstkamera*, from which it may be suggested that Sloane's advanced age was not the only motive for Taubert's trip to London. Some months earlier a fierce fire had broken out in the *Kunstkamera*, reducing part of the collection to ashes. A number of steps were then taken to make good the resulting gaps,[27] and it now looks as though the visit to Sloane was the first of these. Was it the disaster in the *Kunstkamera* that prompted him to change his will? The concatenation of circumstances is tempting, but firm proof is lacking for this interpretation. For the moment we can do no more than reiterate the thesis presented here, that Sloane was perfectly well acquainted with developments in the European museum context in the period of the 1730s and 1740s and that in drawing up his will for the disposal of his collection he might

easily have been expected to picture its incorporation into a relatively advanced form of institution like those existing in Florence, Vienna, Dresden, and especially in St Petersburg. The one aspect of the resulting settlement to which this does not apply is the combination he envisaged between royal (or rather parliamentary) funding and a relatively autonomous form of management under a board of trustees, for this is a form of management by which museums of the Anglo-Saxon world are distinguished from those of the rest of the world, even to this day.

Notes and references

1 M. Caygill, 'Sloane's will and the establishment of the British Museum', in A. MacGregor (ed.), *Sir Hans Sloane: Collector, scientist, antiquary; founding father of the British Museum* (London, 1994), p.46.

2 Caygill, op. cit. (note 1), p.45. In the course of the years all these Academies had elected Sloane as a foreign member: Paris in 1709, Berlin in 1712, St Petersburg in 1734 and Madrid in 1735, followed by Göttingen in 1752. In the case of the Royal Society of London, he was elected a Fellow in 1684, Secretary 1694–1713 and President 1727–41. See A. MacGregor, 'The life, character and career of Sir Hans Sloane', in MacGregor, op. cit. (note 1), pp.21, 41.

3 In the Netherlands, for example, the *Museum Wormianum* has been traced in seventeen out of twenty-four libraries belonging to collectors between 1679 and 1729. See J. van der Waals, 'Met boek en plaat. Het boekenen atlassenbezit van verzamelaars', in E. Bergvelt and R. Kistemaker (eds), *De wereld binnen handbereik. Nederlandse kunst- en rariteitenverzamelingen, 1585–1735*, exh. cat., Amsterdams Historisch Museum (Zwolle, 1993), p.206. Sloane often referred to it: see J. Thackeray, 'Mineral and fossil collections', and J.C.H. King, 'Ethnographic collections', both in MacGregor, op. cit. (note 1), pp.123, 242 n.82.

4 Schepelern indicates only that Frederik III bought the collection after Worm's death. See H.D. Schepelern, 'Natural philosophers and princely collectors: Worm, Paludanus and the Gottorp and Copenhagen collections', in O. Impey and A. MacGregor (eds), *The Origins of Museums. The cabinet of curiosities in sixteenth- and seventeenth-century Europe* (Oxford, 1985; paperback edn London, 2001), pp.170–1.

5 For example Michiel Hinloopen left his extensive print collection to the city of Amsterdam in 1708, where it became part of the public *Kunstkammer* in the Town Hall. See J. van der Waals, *De prentschat van Michiel Hinloopen 1619–1708* (Amsterdam, 1988), pp.9–10. In 1661, to mention another example, the city and university of Basle bought the collection of Basilius Amerbach. See H.C. Ackermann, 'The Basle cabinets of art and curiosities in the sixteenth and seventeenth centuries', in Impey and MacGregor, op. cit. (note 4), p.84. In the Republic of Venice, Cardinal Domenico Grimani left his collection of sculptures and paintings to the city as early as 1523, where it developed into the 'Statuario pubblico' a few decades later. See G. Olmi, 'Italiaanse verzamelingen van de late middeleeuwen tot de zeventiende eeuw', in E. Bergvelt, D.J. Meijers and M. Rijnders (eds), *Van rariteitenkabinet tot kunstmuseum* (Heerlen/Houten, 1993), p.99. See also K. Pomian, 'Sammlungen – eine historische Typologie', in A. Grote (ed.), *Microcosmos in Macrocosmo. Die Welt in der Stube. Zur Geschichte des Sammelns 1450 bis 1800* (Opladen, 1994), p.118.

6 The contacts between Sloane and Seba date back to at least 1723, that is, well before the apothecary became a Fellow of the Royal Society (1728). See K. van Berkel, 'Citaten uit het boek der natuur. Zeventiende-eeuwse Nederlandse naturaliënkabinetten en de ontwikkeling van de natuurwetenschap', in Bergvelt and Kistemaker, op. cit. (note 3), p.187.

7 Seba died in 1736 in the age of seventy-one. The public sale of his second cabinet, starting on 14 April 1752, attracted as buyers, among others, Arnout Vosmaer, the future keeper of the cabinet of Stadholder Willem V, and the Russian Academy of Sciences in St Petersburg. See J. Driessen, 'Waarom er in 1752 in Amsterdam op de veiling van de nieuwe collectie van Albert Seba is gekocht voor de Kunstkamera van de Akademie van Wetenschappen in Sint-Petersburg', lecture in memory of Ninel Kaljazina, January 2001. See also F.J.J.M. Pieters, 'Het schatrijke naturaliënkabinet van

Stadhouder Willem V onder directoraat van topverzamelaar Arnout Vosmaer', in B. Sliggers (ed.), *Het verdwenen museum. Natuurhistorische verzamelingen 1750–1850*, exh. cat., Teylers Museum (Haarlem/Blaricum, 2002), p.22.

8 R. van Gelder, 'De wereld binnen handbereik. Nederlandse kunst- en rariteitenverzamelingen, 1585–1735', and id., 'Liefhebbers en geleerde luiden. Nederlandse kabinetten en hun bezoekers', in Bergvelt and Kistemaker, op. cit. (note 3), pp.37, 280.

9 Another example is Cosimo's invitation to Jan Swammerdam the Younger to enter his service. However, Swammerdam not only refused the post but also turned down the Duke's offer to buy his unique cabinet of anatomical preparations and insects for 12,000 guilders. Some years later, however, in 1679, Swammerdam composed a catalogue with the hope now of selling the collection to Cosimo, or else to the Royal Society, but in vain: the cabinet was subsequently auctioned and dispersed. See van Gelder, op. cit. (note 8), p.37 and van Berkel, op. cit. (note 6), p.179.

10 For Hermann and for other acquisitions by Sloane like the collections of William Courten (or Charleton) (1702) and Engelbert Kaempfer (1723 and 1725) see Bergvelt and Kistemaker, op. cit. (note 3): cat., pp.41–2, 44; MacGregor, op. cit. (note 2), p.23.

11 D. J. Meijers, *Kunst als Natur. Die Habsburger Gemäldegalerie um 1780* (Vienna/Milan, 1995), pp.105, 123 nn.5, 6.

12 Caygill, op. cit. (note 1), p.50.

13 C.G. Thomas, 'Sir Hans Sloane and the Russian Academy of Sciences', *British Library Journal* 14 (1988), p.25 quotes Sloane MS 4026. English trans., Royal Society, B.3.36.

14 Albertus Seba, *Naauwkeurige beschrijving van het schatrijke kabinet der voornaamste seldzaamheden der natuur van Albertus Seba. Locupletissimi rerum naturalium thesauri accurata descriptio et iconibus artificiosissimis expressio per universam physices historiam*, 4 vols (Amsterdam 1734, 1735, 1759, 1765). The publication also appeared in a French-Latin edition. See for the drawings of the objects of the *Kunstkamera*, R. Kistemaker, N. Kopaneva, D.J. Meijers and G. Vilinbachov, *The 'Painted Museum' of the Academy of Sciences in Saint Petersburg, c.1725–1760*, (forthcoming; St Petersburg, 2003).

15 G. Heres, *Dresdener Kunstsammlungen im 18. Jahrhundert* (Leipzig, 1991), p.69 quotes E. Hempel, *Der Dresdener Zwinger* (Leipzig, 1964), p.126.

16 See, for example, R. Hahn, *The Anatomy of a Scientific Institution: The Paris Academy of Sciences, 1666–1803* (Berkeley, Los Angeles and London, 1971), p.18. In contrast to the French Academicians, the members of the Royal Society were not paid by the king and the Society maintained its own collection.

17 See Impey and MacGregor, op. cit. (note 4), p. 210, concerning the diminished scientific status of these institutions around the middle of the eighteenth century. On the shortcomings of the Repository of the Royal Society, see M. Hunter, 'The cabinet institutionalized: the Royal Society's "Repository" and its background', in id., p.225. Eventually the opposite of what Sloane originally intended happened: in 1779 the Society presented its collection to the British Museum.

18 Thomas, op. cit. (note 13), p.33; MacGregor, op. cit. (note 2), p.41.

19 Until 1718 the *Kunstkamera* had been incorporated in Peter the Great's Summer Palace. The large number of acquisitions made during his European travels, however, led to the decision to erect a new building. During construction of the new *Kunstkamera* the collections were on show in the house of an expelled nobleman. When in the meantime the Academy of Sciences was founded

(1724/25) the museum became a part of that institution. See O. Neverov, 'De collecties van de Kunstkamera van Peter de Grote', in R. Kistemaker, N. Kopaneva and A. Overbeek (eds), *Peter de Grote en Holland. Culturele en wetenschappelijke betrekkingen tussen Rusland en Nederland ten tijde van tsaar Peter de Grote* (Bussum, 1996), pp.18–19.

20 A further question remains as to whether Müller's visit was related to the restoration of Russian–British relations in 1730. In that year Prince Antiokh Kantemir was appointed as ambassador in London. See A. Cross, *Peter the Great through British Eyes: Perceptions and representations of the Tsar since 1698* (Cambridge, 2000), p.61. Beside the acquisition of honorable and real members (professors) for the Academy, Müller's mission included the engagement of engravers and making contact with British booksellers who might be interested in selling the publications of the Russian Academy. See Thomas, op. cit. (note 13), p.23. On this occasion Muller himself was elected a Fellow of the Royal Society, under Sloane's presidency. Three years later, Muller would leave for north-eastern Asia as a participant in the second Kamchatka expedition of Vitus Bering (1733–43). See W. Hintzsche and Th. Nickol (eds), *Die Grosse Nordische Expedition. Georg Wilhelm Steller (1709–1746), ein Lutheraner erforscht Sibirien und Alaska* (Gotha, 1996). Sloane also knew the work of the botanist Johann Georg Gmelin through his *Flora Sibirica* of 1747–9, which was sent to him by the Russian Academy.

21 King, op. cit. (note 3), p.233. Furthermore, Sloane owned a Tartar weapon, 'a muscovite knife', 'muscovite womans shoes', 'the habit of the inhabitants of Kamchatchki of furs & needlework from Mr. Captn. Jenkins from Petersburg. Coat Britches, shoes & stockings' (ibid., pp.236–7). Thomas, op. cit. (note 13), p.35 lists the books received by Sloane from the Russian Academy, among others: J. Amman, *Stirpium rariorum* (St Petersburg, 1735); J. Chr. Buxbaum, *Plantarum minus cognitarum centuria I (–V)* (St Petersburg, 1728–40); L. Euler, *Mechanica* (St Petersburg, 1736); J. G. Gmelin, *Flora Sibirica*, vols I–II (St Petersburg, 1747–9).

22 Thomas, op. cit. (note 13), pp.28–9.

23 Cross, op. cit. (note 20), pp.66–7. It was one of the biographies written by Birch for a British edition of Pierre Bayle's *Dictionaire historique et critique* (1st edn Rotterdam, 1697; 4th edn 1730): J.P. Bernard, T. Birch, J. Lochman, *A General Dictionary, Historical and Critical in which a New and Accurate Translation of that of the Celebrated Mr. Bayle, with the Corrections and Observations printed in the late Edition at Paris, is included; and interspersed with several thousand Lives never before published*, 10 vols (London, 1732–41). Peter I is in vol.VIII (1739), pp.333–45.

24 Birch compiled notes for a biography of Sloane, seemingly based on personal interviews: see MacGregor, op. cit. (note 2), pp.11, 36 n.3. In 1752 he was elected secretary of the Royal Society, so that *ex officio* he became a trustee of Sloane's will. Caygill, op. cit. (note 1), pp.53, 64.

25 In 1749 the sequence was that, after the King or the Parliament, came the Academies of Science of St Petersburg, Paris, Berlin or Madrid. See Caygill, op. cit. (note 1), p.46.

26 Thomas, op. cit. (note 13), p.33.

27 Four years after his visit to Sloane, Taubert ordered the acquisition of new zoological material at the sale of Seba's second cabinet in Amsterdam. In addition, in 1753–6 a delegation was sent to China with orders to buy substitutes for the destroyed Chinese objects. See Driessen, op. cit. (note 7), p.7.

Figure 1
Albert Seba (1731), engraving
by Jacob Houbraken after a painting
by Jan Maurits Quinkhard.
Amsterdams Historisch Museum.

Figure 2
Franz Messmer and Jacob Kohl,
*Emperor Franz Stephan with his four
cabinet directors* (c.1775), oil on
canvas, 304 x 284cm (119³/₄ x
111⁷/₈in). Far left: Jean Baillou;
the others are Gerhard van Swieten
(library), Valentin Duval (coins and
medals) and Jean Marcy (instruments).
Vienna, Naturhistorisches Museum.

Figure 3
Albert Seba, *Thesaurus* (1734), vol.I,
tab.XXXVIII. Amsterdams Historisch
Museum.

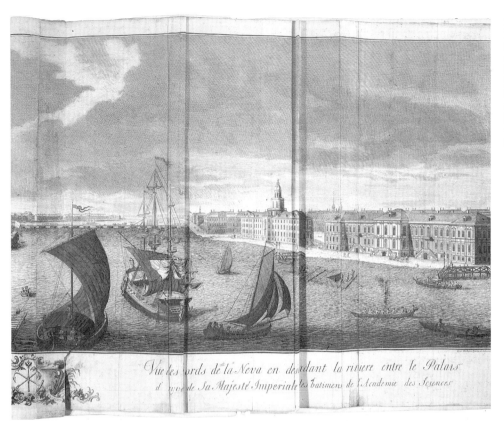

Figure 4
I. Sokolov and M. Machaev,
Plan de la capitale de St. Petersbourgh avec ses avenues les plus illustres (St Petersburg, 1753). Bank of the Neva with the new building of the *Kunstkamera*, recognizable by its observatory (architect George Johann Mattarnovi). To the right is the Academy of Sciences, located in an existing building.

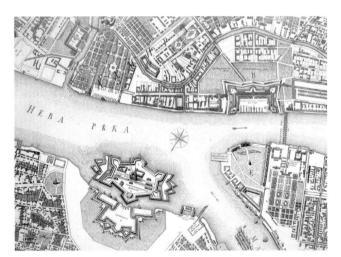

Figure 5
I. Sokolov and M. Machaev,
Plan de la capitale de St. Petersbourgh avec ses avenues les plus illustres (St Petersburg, 1753). Ground plan of the city showing the *Kunstkamera* and the Academy of Sciences (in section E). Across the river are the Winter Palace and the Admiralty (top) and the Peter and Paul Fortress (left).

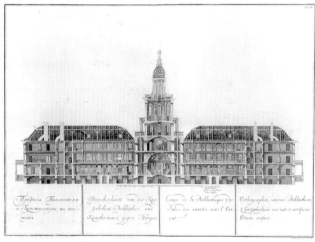

Figure 6
Palaty Sankt-Peterboergskoj Imperatorskoj Akademii Nauk, Biblioteki i Kunstkamery, kotorych predstavleny plany, fasady i profili (St Petersburg, 1741). Cross-section of the *Kunstkamera* and Library. The buildings were specially designed for this collection, in the form of two wings connected by a tower with an anatomical theatre and an observatory. The right wing served as the library, while the left wing housed the *Kunstkamera* proper. Here too the objects were arranged by type: anatomy and zoology on the first and second floors, artefacts on the gallery of the second floor.

Chapter 3

From Private Collection to Public Museum

The Sloane collection at Chelsea and the British Museum in Montagu House

Marjorie L. Caygill

In assessing eighteenth-century collections, it is not only the objects which are of interest, but also the manner in which those objects were presented and juxtaposed. Unfortunately, among the features held in common by the eighteenth-century British Museum and the collection privately displayed by its founder Sir Hans Sloane (1660–1753) is the fact that no visual record of the displays in either is known to exist. This chapter will attempt to reconstruct from the written word the appearance of both presentations and the impression they made on visitors.

Sloane maintained an extensive catalogue which gives an indication of his scientific approach to his collection. But, in addition to his intellectual pursuits, he also aimed to 'promote the good of man' and to 'manifest the glory of God', to awe visitors with the sight of nature. Sloane is also said to have set great store by diversity. His curator, James Empson (d.1765), wrote:

> The late Sir Hans always protested against such a Notion . . . [that is, of displaying only one object in its class or division] . . . [for he held] that when Things distinguish themselves from one another, either by their Colour, or Shape, or Impressions and Marks on them, Transparency or Opacity, Softness or Hardness, different Mixtures either in them or adhering to them, Places of Nativity, to which a good many other Characteristicks could be added, that all these so differently distinguish'd Productions cannot be called the same, or be represented by one Sample, but that they are different Specimens, though going under one general Name.[1]

He was generous with access. His curator – or, for favoured visitors, Sloane himself – would preside over a tour. Two lengthy, oft quoted, descriptions of the collection were left by visitors in 1748,[2] one by Per Kalm, the other an account of a visit by the Prince and Princess of Wales. Both are impressionistic but if read against a brief inventory made by Empson after Sloane's death in 1753,[3] they enable us to some extent to recreate Sloane's sequence of rooms and their contents.

Sloane's house (fig. 7) formed 'a square of above 100 feet each side'.[4] There must have been other rooms in which the household lived – perhaps including those described by Kalm as being hung with pictures – but it is a reasonable assumption that Empson lists all those occupied by the collection.

On the first floor, says Empson, Rooms 1–7 contained the library. This suite is easy to identify in the other accounts. Kalm describes 'eight . . . rooms, all the walls of which were filled from floor to ceiling with books'. The royal visit proceeded through 'several rooms filled with books, among these many hundred volumes of dry'd plants' and 'a room full of choice and

valuable manuscripts'. From Kalm we learn that Sloane's apparatus for reading multiple books stood near the herbarium.

Empson's Room 8 was the Gallery, with thirty-three cabinets, four shelves of books and 'many Things placed in the Spaces between the Cabinets and upon them'. Above these, continued all round, were four shelves of books, two of folios, one of quartos and one of octavos. This was the showpiece. It is described in the royal account as 110 ft in length, housing

> . . . the most beautiful corals, crystals and figured stones, the most brilliant butterflies and other insects, shells painted with as great variety as the precious stones; and feathers of birds vying with gems [and] the remains of the Antediluvian world.

This seems to be Kalm's 110 ft-long 'little narrow room where most of Sir Hans Sloane's treasures are'. Kalm gives us some idea of the furnishings, writing that

> Along the sides the bottom-most cabinets contain all sorts of natural curiosities with other exhibits lying on them or hanging from the wall; but about six feet up from the floor and above the exhibits, the walls are covered with books . . .

The insects were

> . . . mounted in large drawers. Each species or individual was laid in a rectangular box, the bottom of which was wooden . . . some had both the cover and the bottom of the box made of a crystal-clear glass, while some had only a transparent glass lid.

There was a cupboard with little drawers full of all kinds of seeds. Kalm describes birds' eggs and nests, stuffed fish, birds and reptiles and a Lapp drum.

Room 9 was allocated to 'Books of Drawings, etc.' which Kalm noted were 'of different kinds of natural objects'. Room 10 was the Bedchamber with three cabinets. Next to it were rooms 11, with three cabinets of medals, and 12, housing two cabinets. This seems to be where Sloane kept his most valuable objects, which were taken out and displayed to the royal visitors in three rooms towards the front of the house. Kalm mentions elsewhere eight drawers of precious stones, noting that the 1,300 most expensive stones lay in little round holes hollowed out in the drawers of a distinctive cabinet with a top like a pitched roof, constructed so that each drawer locked the one beneath it and the bottom-most drawer locked all the others.

Rooms 13 to 18 were on the ground floor. Rooms 13 and 14 comprised the Halls, decorated, according to Empson, with 'Horns of different Animals', and with Indian and other weapons. These were not mentioned by Kalm, but the royal account refers to passing 'the horns of divers creatures' and 'weapons of different countries'. In Room 15 were the 'skeletons, etc' corresponding to Kalm's description of 'an Egyptian mummy, all sorts of anatomical objects, human skeletons, etc'. Room 16 was allocated to antiquities. Kalm mentions 'all sorts of Roman and other antiquities . . . such as clay pitchers and bowls', while the royal visit records 'curious and venerable antiquities of Egypt, Greece, Hetruria, Rome, Britain and even America'.

In Room 17 were collected together 'things in Spirits of Wine, etc'. Kalm refers to 'a collection of fishes, birds, insects, lacertae, snakes, different kinds of small animals, various examples of human beings and animals, all kept in spirit' and is relieved to discover that here is the cobra of which Linnaeus had asked him to note the number of scales and abdominal plates. Somewhat aggrieved, he records: '. . . while the others went around and looked at everything, I had to spend my time trying to count them up, which was very difficult, since the snake was in a flask which was sealed at the top.' The royal account mentions 'the great saloon lined on every side with bottles filled with spirits, containing various animals'.

In the final ground-floor room, number 18, were 'stuff'd Skins of Animals, with Indian and other Habits, etc'. This matches Kalm's room with clothes of native people, a stuffed camel, a striped donkey . . . West Indian boats made of bark'.

Kalm, alone, briefly refers to Sloane's collection of paintings, hung throughout the house, being particularly taken by a 'picture which consisted entirely of naked women who twisted themselves in various postures' to spell out Sloane's name. His visit concluded with the sight of the head of a whale housed in an outbuilding.

The focus appears, therefore, to have been the Gallery – an *omnium gatherum* – which was meant to delight the eye and produce a sense of wonder. Elsewhere there seems to have been a certain basic logic in the arrangement of the collection by category: books, manuscripts and the herbarium; precious stones, coins, medals and other objects of high value where Sloane could keep an eye on them; horns and weapons on the walls; skeletons; antiquities; things in spirits; all separate, although stuffed animals and human clothing seem today to be odd neighbours.

Sloane made meticulous arrangements to secure the future of his collection after his death and in his will lie the origins of the British Museum.[5] He bequeathed the collection to the nation in return for £20,000 to his two daughters and appointed influential trustees to implement his wishes. His appeal to national patriotism was reinforced by the threat that should the British nation refuse the bequest it was to be offered in turn to a series of continental academies.

Parliament took the bait and with the passing of the British Museum Act on 7 June 1753 the old Sloane museum was no more. A new type of public institution emerged – national museum and national library – combining antiquarian and scientific interests. Thanks to Parliament three libraries (Cotton,[6] Harley[7] and Edwards[8]) had been added to the Sloane bequest. In 1757 King George II donated a fourth – the Old Royal Library of the Sovereigns of England.[9] The Museum's future was assured by the appointment of a new Board of Trustees, with perpetual succession. Although individuals might have an influence on its development, the new Museum now had a different, corporate, ethos which contrasted with Sloane's private domain. Adaptations and arrangements were made by

Committee, or at least with Committee approval. Access for visitors and the behaviour of the salaried staff were to be prescribed by printed Statutes and Rules. Initial funding was provided by a public lottery which was used to pay Sloane's two heirs, purchase the Harleian collection and a repository. The remainder was invested to cover running costs.

The Act was in many ways an enlightened document. Section 1, page 333, for example, proclaimed:

> Whereas all Arts and Sciences have a Connexion with each other, and Discoveries in Natural Philosophy and other Branches of speculative Knowledge, for the Advancement and Improvement whereof the said Museum or Collection was intended, do and may in many Instances give Help and success to the most useful Experiments and Inventions.

The question of utility is one to which the Trustees continually returned. In the first years they showed enormous energy, meeting first on 11 December 1753. The Board was led by three Principal Trustees: the Archbishop of Canterbury, the Lord Chancellor and the Speaker of the House of Commons. Although the composition of the Board looks elitist, in fact a significant number of the most active Trustees were members of the professional classes. These included such individuals as John Ward (c.1679–1758), Professor of Rhetoric at Gresham College, the Revd Thomas Birch (1705–66), Secretary of the Royal Society, and William Watson (1715–87), son of a city tradesman, and the only professional scientist.

The Trustees of the British Museum had responsibility for around 88,000 books and volumes of manuscripts, 24,000 coins and medals, 43,000 natural history specimens and perhaps 5,000 antiquities and modern curiosities. The Board also had two ambiguous directives from Parliament[10] to the effect that '. . . the said Museum or collection . . . be preserved and maintained, not only for the Inspection and Entertainment of the learned and the curious, but for the general use and benefit of the Public', and also that 'a free Access to the said general Repository, and to the Collections therein contained, shall be given to all studious and curious persons'.

After some debate,[11] the Trustees prudently concluded that 'studious and curious' did not include the lower orders, but rather 'the learned and those of polite behaviour and superiour degree'. If not viewed from a nineteenth-century or later egalitarian point of view, this seems to be a reasonable decision. Sloane's collection, much of it easily portable, was alone worth some £8 million at today's prices. When established, the Museum's new repository (figs 8, 9) was on the edge of London, near the setting of Hogarth's *Gin Lane*, with extensive gardens, poorly protected to the north. In 1756 staff were appointed. The security staff consisted of two incompetent watchmen, backed by a porter (frequently drunk), an overworked and disgruntled messenger and a manservant. For immediate assistance in a major emergency there were seven curators (some elderly), the Keeper of the Reading Room and four maids.

The ascendancy of the library collections in the new institution is indicated by the titles of the curators: a Principal Librarian, three Under Librarians, and three Assistant Librarians. The Principal Librarian, the inventor Dr Gowin Knight (1713–72), and two Under Librarians, Dr Matthew Maty (1718–76) and Dr Charles Morton (1716–99), were medically trained; the exception was James Empson, whose mother was

Sloane's housekeeper, and who had to some extent been inherited along with the Sloane collection. Two of their three Assistants[12] were clergymen, and included a numismatist and a botanist.

The Sloane collection at Chelsea was much as its founder had left it. Sloane had at one time indicated a preference for his collection to remain there but this was not legally binding. The Trustees decided after an inspection that, since many objects were lying 'loose' and would have to be protected against the public by wire and glass, it could not be shown in its present home. Having dismissed the possibility of a purpose-built museum at Westminster on grounds of cost and time, they acquired in 1754–5 a seventeenth-century mansion, Montagu House, in Bloomsbury,[13] and proceeded to adapt it to its new purpose.

James Empson, Sloane's erstwhile curator, now head of the Department of Natural and Artificial Productions, alone among his colleagues had experience of arranging a collection and pointed out that a new approach was required. He wrote in August 1756:[14]

How much soever a private Person may be at Liberty arbitrarily to dispose & place his Curiosities; we are sensible, that the British Museum, being a public Institution subject to the Visits of the Judicious & Intelligent, as well as Curious, Notice will be taken, whether or no the Collection has been arranged in a methodical Manner.

Scientific classification was one thing but Empson pointed out that it was also necessary

... in disposing of each Subdivision, to take particular Care, that those Matters may be brought nearest the Sight, as are most pleasing to the Eye and of most Consideration; placing the Rest, in Proportion as they are less so, higher & higher on the Shelves above them and those that are still inferiour in the Drawers under each Subdivision ...

After what appears on occasion to have been hectic activity, the Museum opened on Monday, 15 January 1759. Perhaps the best way to gain an impression of how the collections were arranged is to join a group who have applied for free tickets, who have returned weeks later to collect them, and who now present themselves at the gate on Great Russell Street, presided over by the Porter in a 'Gown ... of a plain drab colour with a yellow tuft' carrying a staff, 'black, tipt with silver on the top'. The eager visitors would then be conducted by the messenger through a colonnade and across what was then termed the 'great court'. The Museum's archives give some indication of what they would see and there are also two detailed sources – a guide-book (fig. 10) written by Edmund Powlett and published by R. and J. Dodsley (1761 and 1762)[15] and an unpublished playlet written in 1767.[16]

Those Montagu House interiors which were not covered by seventeenth-century fresco paintings or recently repainted the colour of stone were papered with green flock wallpaper.[17] As visitors entered the 'First State Story' (the ground floor on the south side of the House) they were confronted, in the elegantly painted hall, by their first sight of the Museum's collections (fig. 11): a somewhat mixed arrangement of objects, presumably intended to attract their attention and also (because of their weight) to relieve pressure on the floors in the upper storey. Here were Sir Hans Sloane's seven blocks of basalt from the Giant's Causeway in Ireland, a milestone from the Appian Way,

fragments of Roman granite columns, pebbles, Roman terms, pieces of serpentine and lava, and the genealogical tree of a noble Venetian Family. There was the skeleton said to be of the 'unicorn fish', the head of an Indian water buffalo and stones inscribed in Latin, Greek and other languages.

On turning left towards the grand staircase (fig. 12), through one of two stone arches, visitors would be awed by one of the finest seventeenth-century interiors in London, meticulously restored for the Trustees by Arthur Pond. On the ceiling, in a painting by Charles de la Fosse (1636–1716) was the legend of Phaeton begging to drive the chariot of the sun-god; to the side were Roman military scenes and a Bacchic revel. There were landscape and architectural decorations throughout, painted by Jacques Rousseau (1631–91) and Jean-Baptiste Monnoyer (1634–99). By the first window, next to the iron gate, a partitioned box had been erected for the Messenger, forced out of his office by the deluge of books.

At the top of the stairs was the bust of Sir Hans Sloane by Michael Rysbrack and beyond, on the 'Second State Story' (fig. 13), was the vestibule (which can be faintly glimpsed in a mid-nineteenth-century watercolour).[18] In the 1760s this room, lined with cabinets, was being used for recent acquisitions: an Egyptian mummy in a glass case in a corner on the north side, its coffin opposite and other Egyptian antiquities given by the Lethieullier family in 1756 to, as they put it, 'the Public Museum at Montagu House'. The Museum was interactive, for the coffin could be turned 'at pleasure'. In the playlet the guide declares:

Do you observe that small spring handle there? It is the easiest thing in the world, believe me, to turn round a dead – ay, or a living Mummy, if you can but find out, and touch and twirl the proper Spring.[19]

The ceiling here depicted 'The Fall of Phaeton'. Also on display were several large corals, a cabinet containing a wasp's nest, and a number of items bottled in spirits, among them a vulture's head from Surinam given by the Keeper of Printed Books, snakes, birds, spiders, lizards, a brainstone and a stuffed flamingo. At this stage the Museum had virtually no funds for making purchases and was dependent on private donations, some of them very odd and more suited to a cabinet of curiosities. It was not until later in the century that Parliament began to make special grants for acquisitions and to provide regular funding.

Turning left, the visitors entered the grand saloon where they would wait on Virginia walnut chairs for the full company to assemble. The oak floors here and elsewhere were laid out in a geometrical pattern, the fireplaces were of marble and heating was provided by iron stoves. Here were further paintings by la Fosse, centred on 'A Council of the Gods' in which Minerva was said to be modelled on Nell Gwynn. On a table was a wax model of the Belvedere statue of Laocoön. The visitors had a splendid view through the windows of the distant hills of Hampstead and Highgate and of the Museum's botanical gardens, where there were 600 species of plants.[20]

According to a number of accounts, at this point several gentry may have experienced an unwelcome phenomenon for, in spite of the Trustees' rules, respectable working people did manage to gain admittance. When, for example, an attempt was made in 1759 to require the Principal Librarian to fill in for absent members of staff he protested that it would not be proper for him to be 'shewing the Collection and attending on the company, though they shou'd be the meanest mechanicks or servants out of livery'.[21] Carl Philip Moritz in 1782 wrote: 'The visitors were of all classes and both sexes, including some of the lowest class; for, since the Museum is the property of the nation, everyone must be allowed the right of entry.'[22] And in 1784 when the Trustees considered charging for admission they concluded that this would be a waste of time since, on inspecting the list of admissions '. . . they consisted chiefly of Mechanics and Persons of the lower Classes, few of whom would probably have been at any expence to satisfy mere Curiosity'.[23]

How they got in is not known. On at least one occasion the Porter was accused of selling tickets, possibly from 'no-shows'. Although the list of visitors applying for tickets was submitted to the Principal Librarian for vetting, as Gowin Knight perceptively remarked at the outset, he saw only the list, while the Porter took the names. There is no record of any named person being refused admittance but there is a glimpse of a breakdown in the Trustees' intended arrangements with the order in 1759 that '. . . when it plainly appears, that the Persons who bring Tickets are not the Persons to whom they were granted, they be refused admittance'.[24]

From its first opening, guided tours of the entire museum were offered daily, although not at weekends or on public holidays. Two groups of five visitors were admitted each hour (broadly 9–12 noon or 4–8 p.m. in summer), to spend an hour in each of three Departments – Manuscripts and Medals, Natural and Artificial Productions, and Printed Books.[25] But the Trustees misjudged the public taste and in 1761 they accepted a revised scheme,[26] put forward by the Keeper of Printed Books. This acknowledged the public's preference for natural history and suggested, not without a certain degree of self-interest on the Keeper's part, that 'The two hours wasted by [visitors] amongst Books or Manuscripts, which few care for, and most are disgusted with, will be for the greatest part employed in seeing things, which are the chief, if not the only, object of their curiosity.' Visitors were now admitted in groups of fifteen which allowed for around 10,000 tickets to be available each year – not an immense number, but not as few as is sometimes suggested. Promptly at 9, 11 and 1 (Mondays and Thursdays in the summer only at 4 and 6 p.m.) a Librarian would appear in the Saloon to collect the tickets. The tour lasted two hours and the party could decide where they would spend the most time. A minority might linger behind if something caught their interest. It should be noted that the eighteenth-century Museum's reputation today for the speed with which visitors were forced through the rooms, appears to rely largely on two bad-tempered reports from the eighteenth century and one from the nineteenth century.[27] The criticism may therefore not be entirely merited. Other visitors were more complimentary, although many were overawed by the size of the collections and the impossibility of seeing everything.[28]

The company would embark on the tour,[29] escorted by one of the six curators, moving through the door on the right to where the main collection of manuscripts was housed in a suite of four rooms distinguished by the names of the major donors.[30] Here were the Bibliotheca Regia, Cottoniana and Harleiana.

The Museum's oil paintings, largely of 'learned Britons', were spread throughout Montagu House.[31] Resplendent above the marble chimneypiece in the first room was King George II, painted for the Trustees by Shackleton. The manuscripts were stored in newly constructed cabinets, without breaks or pediments, painted the colour of mahogany and protected by wooden-framed doors wired in an octagonal pattern. These doors were designed to be of equal widths, with a plain bead between them and were arranged so that they opened over circular library staircases. There were also low portable deal steps.

The Museum's libraries bore traces of their private origins in their contrasting methods of arrangement. The Cottonian collection, of around 861 volumes, had been stored in fourteen presses surmounted by bronze busts (all now lost) of the twelve Roman emperors listed by Suetonius, together with Cleopatra and Faustina. The contents of each cabinet acquired the names of the presiding rulers. No system of division by subject could be discerned. The old arrangement was retained at the British Museum (and is reflected today in the entries used in the British Library catalogue). Charters, deeds and loose papers were stored in drawers under the windows. On request, the conducting librarian might unlock a cabinet and display one item at a time. The popularity of Magna Carta, however, led to its being shown in a glass case with an accompanying transcript. The Trustees had attempted to keep the foundation collections separate but were increasingly having to double up collections as additions arrived. Thus also housed here were around 2,000 manuscripts from the Old Royal Library, including the Codex Alexandrinus. These retained their old numeration by press and shelf.

The Harleian collection occupied the next three rooms. It consisted of some 7,660 volumes of manuscripts, properly arranged in sequence according to Humphrey Wanley's catalogue and placed in classed order, so far as was consistent with the size of the volumes. In the first room, in a glass-topped cabinet, was also a display of English coins from William Rufus to contemporary issues, and in the third where the 14,236 original rolls, charters, deeds and other legal documents were kept, was a display of French medals which 'may, by turning a Button, be viewed both in Front and Reverse'.[32]

The main coin and medal collection, part of the Department of Manuscripts, was housed in the next room, in considerable disarray and therefore not included in the tour. The Sloane items had been 'so loosely packed up, as to be shook out of their places' during their transfer from Chelsea and the curators were attempting to sort them with the aid of newly purchased reference books and scales. The Museum's coins and medals came largely from Sloane, but the Cotton collection also included 549 specimens. The Trustees decided that Sloane's coin cabinets were unfit to be used and had thirty new ones made. These were of mahogany, a foot square, with brass fittings and numbered on an ivory plate inlaid on the front. In the next room, facing out on to the great court, were the Sloane manuscripts and a table-case containing a small display of pontifical medals.

In the room just before the vestibule the visitors entered the Department of Natural and Artificial Productions to see first the Museum's relatively meagre collection of antiquities, again largely from Sloane but with some items from Cotton or recently given by Thomas Hollis (1720–74). The 1761 guidebook noted 'We may here see the Progress of Art in the different Ages of the World, exemplified in a Variety of Utensils that each Nation in each century has produced.'[33] Some items were displayed in wall cabinets, others in table-cases. Objects such as framed fragments of Roman paintings, shields from India, and hats, were hung on the walls. Costumes were stored in deal drawers, painted mahogany. Empson recommended that the inside of the repositories not concealed by books be painted whitish, or some light colour.

Here the visitors would first encounter the Museum's rudimentary labelling system. The 1761 guide-book refers to 'the inscriptions on the several repositories' and there is a note in the Trustees' papers that inscriptions in the Department of Natural and Artificial Productions should be printed in gold.[34] Some specimens had catalogue numbers painted on them and in some instances – for example an Indian spoon from the Sloane collection, supposedly made from the breastbone of a penguin – the object had its description written on it and was marked 'Anno 1702'. In this room, therefore, were cabinets bearing the labels *Antiquitates* '*Aegyptiacae*', '*Hetruscae*' (four cabinets), '*Romanae*' (six cabinets) and '*Variae*'. The '*Variae*' included Peruvian and Mexican ceramics, a Japanese temple model, hubble-bubbles and a nest of baskets made of bark. In repositories near the windows were modern curiosities, among them North American pipes, drums from China, America and Lapland, brushes of roots and feathers, and the mathematical instruments.

The party would return through the vestibule and the saloon to reach, on the north side of Montagu House, the natural curiosities. Here the display was intended to be rather more scientifically ordered than at Chelsea. There was some selection since the Trustees had also agreed that the presentation should consist of such objects 'as were judged most deserving of the publick view'. The display was not static for they had decided that 'when any Specimens . . . shall be presented, which shall tend to render Sir Hans Sloane's Collection of Natural and Artificial Productions more compleat, the Officers of that department do insert them in their proper place in that Collection'.[35]

A report by the Principal Librarian,[36] who supervised Empson, set out a plan for dealing with Sloane's collection according to the then current theory of the 'Chain of Being':

> The Greatest and most valuable part of this Collection consists of things relating to Natural History . . . and will merit a particular Regard in the general distribution.
>
> All the Articles that come under this head may be properly classed in the three general divisions of Fossils, Vegetables, and Animals. Of these the Fossils are the most simple; and therefore may properly be disposed in the first Rank; next to them the Vegetables; and lastly the Animal Substances. By this Arrangement the Spectator will be gradually conducted from the simplest to the most compound and most perfect of Nature's Productions.

Knight added:

> . . . since there is found in Nature a gradual and almost insensible transition from one kind of Natural Production to Another, I would endeavour both in the general and particular Arrangement to exemplifie those gradual transitions as much as possible.

He also had to take into account public sensibilities and therefore recommended that

> . . . the Monsters and Anatomical preparations, will be best joined with the Skeletons, and other parts of Anatomy in the Base Story: More especially as all these are not proper Objects for all persons, particularly Women with Child.

The collections were arranged in wall cabinets 11 ft (3m 35cm) high, 18 ft (5m 49cm) long and about 14 in (36cm) deep, fitted above with shelves and glass doors and with seven drawers in the lower part. The cabinets were made of deal faced with mahogany, surmounted by a carved pediment and with 'a Festoon on the face of the Pilasters and a Rose in the centre of the Freeze over the Truss'. The wall-cases being insufficient to house all the objects, there were also table-cases and in some rooms – 'shew tables of Mahogany with glass doors at the top placed close to the windows and, by means of casters under the legs, occasionally removed' – where objects could be seen in a good light.

The first room was allocated to the Sloane minerals and fossils. At this time the term 'fossil' could be used for all items dug out of the ground but Sloane had been aware, as were the writers of the playlet and the guide, that the fossil bones, shells and leaves were the remains of once-living animals and plants. As in the antiquities section, the cases were labelled in Latin beginning with *Silices* and *Achates*. In a cabinet by the window were copies of notable precious stones including Pitt's 'Brilliant'.[37] Items which we would regard as *objets d'art* were shown here: crystals made into vases, cups, boxes, beads, crystal balls, carved coral, and jewellery. As well as the minerals, there were two large tables of fossils including ammonites and echinites and in a cabinet between the windows was a further collection of fossils given by Gustavus Brander in 1757.

In the next room the 'recent shells', in a display reminiscent of a princely cabinet, attracted the eye of visitors. But here too were more fossils of shells and plants, human and animal 'incrustations', 'stalactites', a human skull and sword found in the Tiber, bezoars and human gallstones, mammoth bones, alchemist's knives and more objects made of, or decorated with, semi-precious stones.

The company next moved into the room displaying plants and insects. With the cabinets of sponges and others of corals located here, was a gift of corals from Mr Ellis, 'who thinks them animals'. Nests of insects and birds progressed to eggs, starfish, crabs and three large tables of sea-shells. A particular favourite was the now discredited 'vegetable lamb of Tartary' (fig. 14).[38] There were also more worked objects – rings, set with cameos, intaglios and seal impressions.

In the next room, on shelves around the walls, in deal cabinets painted mahogany, with doors screened with brass wire, were plant specimens, quadrupeds and snakes preserved in spirits. The bottles were identifiable to the curators by numbers engraved on them. In some bottles lurked parasitic worms from the human body and also prominent was the one-eyed 'Cyclops' pig. Above the cabinets were animal horns. There were dried fish and animals, parts of birds and parts of fish, stuffed skins and even the skeleton of a very young whale and 'a great table' of insects. This was indeed a display reminiscent of Horace Walpole's facetious reference to Sloane's collection as comprising 'sharks with one ear and spiders as big

as geese'.[39] More appealing to the eye was a glass case with a
bird of paradise and humming birds.

In the final room were gathered a varied selection of
so-called 'modern curiosities' in cabinets and glass cases. These
included glass vessels, North American feather headdresses,
necklaces and wampum, European, Chinese and Japanese
carvings, Chinese porcelain, a horn said to have grown out of a
woman's head,[40] a portrait of Mary Davis (also famed for her
horns) and below it two fine Chelsea vases presented in 1763.[41]

The visitors were now led down the back stairs, decorated
by a painting of dead game, where hung a North American
canoe and a Greenland kayak. At the bottom of the stairs, in the
'little gilt room' between his private apartment and the library,
furnished with a 'proper shew table', the Principal Librarian
displayed his inventions[42] – improved sea compasses and
several magnets.

The entire ground floor ('First State Story') was occupied by
the Department of Printed Books. The rooms were lined by
presses painted in mahogany colour. Some doors (but not all)
appear to have been fitted with a protective trellis of brass wire.
In each room was a deal table covered with green cloth. Shelves
for books had been constructed above the marble fireplaces.
Inscriptions on the bookcases were painted in white letters on a
black ground. The books were now public property and, from
1757, they and the manuscripts were marked with the British
Museum stamp.

The 9,000 printed books of the Old Royal Library of the
Sovereigns of England beginning with Edward IV were located
in the first two library rooms. Here their original arrangement
had been continued with the collection divided by the reign in
which the books were acquired. One advantage, said the
curators, was to retain

> The curiosity of observing the different methods of binding, in
> different ages, and the pleasing sight which arises from the uni-
> formity of elegant coverings in any considerable sett of books . . .
> Books, that in themselves deserve no great attention, or would be
> lost if joined to their own class, stand a chance of acquiring some
> degree of importance, when it will be seen to whom they once
> belonged.[43]

The Bibliotheca Sloaniana occupied the next six rooms,
facing on to the garden. The Trustees had considered that the
Sloane library was ' . . . disposed in a Very Irregular Manner,
with little regard either to the Subjects or even Size of them
[the books]'.[44] The Sloane books and the 3,800 elegantly bound
volumes of the adjacent Major Edwards's Library, were
therefore now placed in what the Librarians termed 'a classical
arrangement':

> According to that method, books are first divided under some
> general heads, and afterwards subdivided into particular classes,
> properly connected with one another. The size and language of the
> books are circumstances here intirely subordinated to subjects and
> to dates, and each book is supposed to have its place, from which it
> could not without impropriety be removed.[45]

In the second room of this suite were Sloane's drawings and the
Hortus Siccus. In the middle room 'a table covered with green
cloth with shelves underneath' was provided for books
containing large maps and surveys.

The visitors then passed the Trustees' Committee Room
with its festoon curtains of green moreen and entered Major

Edwards's Library which occupied the first room to the south
overlooking the courtyard. The final room was set aside for new
acquisitions and used for deposits from the Stationers'
Company accruing to the Royal Library and gifts to George II.

The Trustees considered that ' . . . the Liberty of Studying in
the Museum is the part of this Institution from which the
Publick is like to reap the greatest Benefit'.[46] Therefore, in the
corner room of the basement on the north front, though not
seen by the general visitor, was the Reading Room, a large
vaulted apartment, uncarpeted and damp and with only two
windows. This was furnished with twenty chairs, a wainscot
table covered with green baize, and reading stands. Readers
had to be known personally, or by recommendation, to Trustees
or staff. Books, manuscripts, and objects from elsewhere in the
collections could be consulted here. Josiah Wedgwood and
Thomas Bentley looked at 'Roman and Etruscan earthenware' in
1769; Matthew Boulton made drawings of antique vases in 1770.

In 1759 the Trustees stated that priority must be given to
' . . . preparing catalogues for publication; which last the
Committee think so necessary a work, that till it is performed,
the several collections can be but imperfectly usefull to the
publick'.[47] But it was not until the nineteenth century that
catalogues began to be published in any numbers. Apart from
the meagre salaries, which meant that staff had to hold down
additional jobs in order to survive, the Department of
Manuscripts and Medals early on raised the difficulty of
balancing the needs of the studious and the curious:

> The . . . Department . . . is filled with Company from nine o'clock in
> the morning, to one in the afternoon. During which Time, your two
> Officers of the said Department, are to furnish Matters of
> Entertainment, and to answer all the Questions of 40 different
> Persons, from the Mechanic up to the first Scholar and Person of
> Quality in the Kingdom; who come all whetted with the Edge of
> Curiosity; and of whom, there are hardly any two that apprehend
> alike, or do not require the same thing to be represented to them in
> different Lights; or who would not be extremely offended, at any
> imaginary Incivility.
> The Fact is, that at the End of the four Hours' continued
> Attention and, if we may so call it, Debate; Your officers of this
> Department are fit for nothing, but to sleep or to take the necessary
> Alternative of Motion and the free Air.[48]

It is instructive to view the Museum and its collections
through the eyes of the writers of the 1761 guide-book and the
1767 playlet. In the latter, characters talk of Pope's essays,
mixing eighteenth-century rationality with credulity, and
entertainment with instruction, as did the collections
themselves at this time. A thinly disguised Assistant Librarian,
Dr Gifford, enters and the visitors' attention is ponderously
drawn to a framed display of corallines:

> You may recollect I presume the opinion of the philosophers, that
> the Scale or Chain of Being is composed of a variety of Degrees or
> Links? . . . They convey the idea of inanimate petrified matter, Yet
> are indisputedly allowed to be Animal. Here, then, you may
> suppose more lifeless inert Matter to connect with Animation and
> to ascend to the next Degree of Being. [49]

Yet at the next moment the ladies are speechless at the brilliant
colour of the butterflies, shrieking in mock fright at the
crocodile from the Jumna or gazing in amazement at the
Cyclops pig and the horned woman. Powlett writes assertively
that the turquoise is the bone of an animal fallen into a copper
mine, but he abruptly dismisses the Scythian lamb as myth.

So far as the experience of wonderment was concerned, the public Museum was thus not so far removed from the old Sloane museum. But paradoxically, although the arrangement of the natural curiosities at first sight appears to be more muddled than Sloane's, it was a rational attempt to illustrate various concepts in an eighteenth-century fashion.

The British Museum was to be increasingly neglected over the next half century. Though the Trustees placed high priority on catalogues, very few appeared. The collections rotted, displays became increasingly cramped as more objects arrived, 'duplicates' were sold and the printed books combined into one library, thereby losing their identity. Towards the end of the century the first of the great influx of antiquities began to arrive, together with more enlightened management. In 1810 guided tours ceased and the general public 'of decent appearance' were free to wander as they wished throughout Montagu House, although the library collections were now closed to them.

The Museum began with an optimism it was to regain at a later period. While it is difficult to see it in its infancy as the epitome of eighteenth-century Enlightenment thought, the seeds had been sown. In 1761 Powlett wrote approvingly:

> Nothing can conduce more to preserve the Learning which this latter Age abounds with, than having Repositories in every Nation to contain its Antiquities, such as is the Museum of *Britain*.[50]

Notes and references

References to manuscripts in the Central Archives at the British Museum are shown thus: CE 1/- General Meetings; CE 3/- Standing Committee Minutes; CE 4/- Original Papers. All citations use the relevant folio number.

1 James Empson 'Proposal of a Plan . . .', BM CE 4/1, 39–45 (27 August 1756).
2 In Arthur MacGregor (ed.), *Sir Hans Sloane: Collector, scientist, antiquary; founding father of the British Museum* (London, 1994), pp.31–5. Per (or Pehr) Kalm (1716–79) was a Swedish Professor of Natural History and Economy at the University of Åbo in Finland who travelled in Russia, England and America. The text of Kalm's account is adapted from 'Pehr Kalm, Journey in England on his way to North America', translated from Dr Martti Kerkonnen's transcript of the original manuscript by Professor Mead. A copy of the complete transcript is held in the library of the Linnean Society, London, with the description on pp.336–42. The account by Cromwell Mortimer of the visit of Frederick Louis, Prince of Wales (1707–51) was first published in the *Gentleman's Magazine* 18 (1748), pp.301–2.
3 BM CE 3/1 5–6 (22 January 1754).
4 The exterior of Sloane's house is depicted by Thomas Faulkner, *An Historical and Topographical Description of Chelsea and its Environs* in an engraving by J. Barlow from an old drawing (Chelsea, 1810 edn), frontispiece, and (1829 edn) vol.I, p.311. See Penelope Hunting, *From Manor House to Museum: A history of Chelsea manor house* (London, in association with the Cadogan Estate, 1995). The house was at one time owned by Henry VIII. It was doubled in size by the Marquis of Hamilton who bought it in 1638 and the newer western section became the episcopal palace of the Bishops of Winchester. In 1712 Sir Hans Sloane purchased the eastern part of the building from Lord Cheyne. He moved in permanently on retiring from Bloomsbury in 1742. The house was bequeathed to his two daughters, the younger of whom had married the 2nd Baron Cadogan who was responsible for the demolition of the house.
5 For a discussion of Sloane's will see Marjorie Caygill, 'Sloane's will and the establishment of the British Museum', in MacGregor, op. cit. (note 2), pp.45–68.
6 The Cotton collection was begun by Sir Robert Bruce Cotton (1571–1631) and continued by his descendants. Sir John Cotton (1621–1702) made arrangements for its donation to the Nation and this was accomplished in 1700 by his grandson, also Sir John Cotton (1679–1731). There were originally 958 volumes of manuscripts of which 861 survived a fire in 1731 at Ashburnham House, where the collection was then stored. The library's strength lay in: manuscripts, coins and charters from the Anglo-Saxon period; monastic and other ecclesiastical records; books of the Bible and lives of saints; genealogies and heraldic material; histories, annals and chronicles, mainly of the British Isles; and state papers and maps, chiefly relating to English domestic and foreign affairs, especially in the sixteenth century. Amongst its treasures were the Lindisfarne Gospels, Beowulf, a copy of the Anglo-Saxon Chronicle and two of the four surviving copies of Magna Carta.
7 The Harleian collection was put together by Robert Harley, 1st Earl of Oxford (1661–1724) and his son Edward, the 2nd Earl (1689–1741). The manuscript collection, purchased by the British Museum for £10,000, was particularly rich in English history and biblical material. The library which was said to comprise some 50,000 printed books, over 250,000 pamphlets and 41,000 prints had been dispersed by auction in 1743.
8 With the Cotton collection was a library bequeathed to the trustees of the Cotton library by Major Arthur Edwards (d.1743) 'chiefly relating to antiquities, medals, history, geography, arts, sciences and all the branches of polite literature'. Edwards also bequeathed the sum of £7,000, subject to a life interest by Elizabeth Milles. This money came to the British Museum in 1769.
9 The 'Old Royal Library' is so called to distinguish it from George III's 'King's Library' which was donated to the Museum in 1823. The Old Royal Library was founded by Edward IV and had been lodged with the Cotton collection since 1708.
10 British Museum Act, 26 George II. c.22, Section I, p.333 and Section IX, p.341.
11 Some indications of the Trustees' thinking can be found in the papers of two members of the Board: John Ward (c.1679–1758), British Library, Additional MS 6179 and Thomas Birch (1705–66), British Library, Additional MS 4449.
12 The first Assistants were: William Webb (who did not take up his post), Henry Rimius (died 1756 shortly after his appointment), William Hudson (c.1730–93), the botanist Revd Samuel Harper (c.1733–1803) and Revd Andrew Gifford (1700–84), botanist and numismatist.
13 Montagu House, designed by Robert Hooke (see Chapter 6 below), was completed c.1676 for Ralph, Duke of Montagu (c.1638–1709). It was damaged by a fire in 1686. There is some uncertainty as to the extent of the damage which, so far as the structure was concerned, was probably not as great as once thought. Excavations on the site by the Museum in 1999 found no trace of fire. The rebuilding was said to have been carried out by a French architect referred to as 'Puget' who has so far not been conclusively identified.
14 Op. cit. (note 1), fol.40.
15 [Edmund Powlett], *The General Contents of the British Museum with Remarks. Serving as a Directory In viewing that Noble Cabinet* (London, 1761; rev. edn 1762), printed by R. and J. Dodsley. Although this guide is sometimes attributed to 'R. and J. Dodsley', a British Library copy of the 1761 edition is annotated 'E. Powlett'. In the British Library Catalogue there is an annotation against a second copy of the 1761 guide (press mark c.142.cc.19) which states that inserted in it, among other things, was '. . . a MS. copy of the agreement between the author and James Dodsley, the publisher'. It would appear that this is the source of the attribution of authorship to Powlett by a now unknown but knowledgeable cataloguer. (Information from Janet Koss.)
16 Revd Weeden Butler Snr, 'Pleasing Recollection or A Walk through the British Museum', British Library, Additional MS 27,276.
17 References to the furnishings and decoration of Montagu House are taken largely from the Minutes of the Trustees' Standing Committee and General Meeting and the Surveyors' and Workmen's Estimates in the Central Archives. Sir Frederic Madden, 'A collection of views, cuttings from newspapers and magazines, etc., illustrating the history of the Museum', 4 vols, 1755–1870, British Library, press mark c.55.i.1, contains a number of descriptions of Montagu House including (General History, fol. 34) a detailed account of the decoration surviving in 1814.
18 George Scharf, snr (1788–1860), *Staircase of the Old British Museum, Montagu House*, 1845, British Museum, Department of Prints and Drawings.

19 Op. cit. (note 16), fols 11–12. It seems probable that it was the coffin rather than the mummy which revolved. The first Egyptian coffin to enter the British Museum was that now bearing the registration number EA.6695. The top of the coffin shows signs of some 'device' having been attached to it. There is a large hole running down through the centre, presumably to hold a substantial rod, and surrounding this at least fifteen smaller holes – perhaps to attach the turning machinery. The foot end does not have the large central hole but there are some small holes drilled into the base. (Information from Dr John Taylor, Department of Ancient Egypt and Sudan, British Museum.) In the Surveyors and Workmens' Estimates, vol. II (1778–), fol. 13, British Museum, Central Archives, there is an entry, December 1783 'to refix the Machinery for turning one of the Mummies . . .'. Anne Haslund Hansen of the Danish National Museum has noted the remains of a seventeenth-century display of a mummy in that collection – three hinges and a hasp for closing the coffin, the mummy inside being held up with leather straps and a metal plate under the feet.

20 The Minutes of the General Meeting (BM CE 1/1, 102 [3 June 1756]) record that 'The Garden is now in great forwardness, and may be considered as a Valuable part of the British Museum, being well stock'd with Exotic Plants'. The Trustees, in a minute of the Standing Committee (BM CE 3/1 204–5 [4 March 1757]), ordered 'that no plants or flowers be gathered but by leave of the Committee, for medical purposes, or as specimens for such studious and curious persons as may be desirous of increasing their botanical knowledge'.

21 BM CE 4/1 86 (4 April 1759).

22 Carl Philip Moritz, *Journeys of a German in England in 1782: A walking tour of England* (London, 1965), p.59.

23 BM CE 1/4 858 (31 January 1784).

24 BM CE 3/2 516 (24 February 1759).

25 The Trustees at first thought that the Act of Parliament required them to keep the Sloane collection separate. The initial tripartite division of the collections therefore consisted of (1) the Sloane library, (2) Sloane's natural and artificial curiosities, (3) the Cottonian and Harleian manuscripts and Major Edwards's library. This somewhat impractical arrangement was abandoned in 1758.

26 BM CE 1/2 263–6 (21 June 1759); CE 1/2 349–50 (28 February 1761); CE 3/3 671–3 (13 March 1761).

27 William Hutton, *A Journey from Birmingham to London* (Birmingham, 1785), pp.186–97; Moritz, op. cit. (note 22), pp.59–60; and Louis Simond, *Journal of a Tour and Residence in Great Britain, during the years 1810 and 1811, by a French traveller* (Edinburgh, 1817), pp.106–9. For a detailed account of admission regulations see M. Caygill, 'Persons of Decent Appearance', *British Museum Magazine*, 46, Summer 2003, pp.44–8.

28 For example Maria Sophie von La Roche, in *Sophie in London, 1786: Being the Diary of Sophie v. la Roche*, trans., with an introductory essay, by Clare Williams (London, 1933), pp.103–11, 156–8.

29 The description is of the Museum in the early 1760s. With the rapid growth of the collections there were many rearrangements. For example, space had to be found for Sir William Hamilton's classical collection purchased in 1772. In 1778 the South Sea room was opened to house the Cook material. Antiquities were transferred from the old house to the new Townley Gallery in 1808. However, the route of the guided tour within Montagu House appears to have remained the same until 1810 when visitors were allowed to wander unescorted through the rooms of natural and artificial curiosities.

30 The minutes of the Trustees' General Meeting (BM CE 1/1 233 [2 December 1758]) record that 'Inscriptions have been put up in the several rooms of the Museum, distinguishing the contents thereof, and the persons to whom they have formerly belonged, or by whom they have been given'.

31 Butler, op. cit. (note 16), fol.14.

32 Powlett, op. cit. (note 15), p.35. In September 1775 the Trustees directed that the Sloane manuscripts in the south-east upper corner should be moved to the room occupied by the Harleian charters and that the latter should be transferred to a garret. The space released by the departure of the Sloane manuscripts was to be used for 'a large benefaction from the admiralty and officers employed in the several expeditions to the South Seas' and henceforth was referred to as the 'South Sea Room'. This room appears to have opened in 1778 – the Trustees' Minutes record that the joinery work had not been completed in April 1777 but that the walls were papered in March 1778.

33 Powlett, op. cit. (note 15), p.18.

34 BM CE 3/2 468 (28 September 1758).

35 BM CE 3/2 401 (23 December 1757); CE 1/1 211 (18 March 1758).

36 Gowin Knight, 'A Plan for the general distribution of Sr Hans Sloane's Collection', BM CE 4/1 51–2 (n.d.).

37 Some of the objects on display in Montagu House are illustrated in John and Andrew van Rymsdyk, *Museum Britannicum: being an exhibition of a great variety of antiquities and natural curiosities, belonging to that noble and magnificent cabinet, the British Museum* (London, 1778), the first illustrated guide to the Museum. Page 70 shows a copy of 'Governor Pitt's diamond, purchased by the late Duke of Orleans, for Louis XVth . . . weighing 136 carats'.

38 The 'vegetable lamb of Tartary' was a mythical creature supposed to be the product of a bush on which grew living lambs. Sir Hans Sloane's specimen was shown to the Royal Society in 1698 and identified as the scale-covered rhizome and leaf bases of an arborescent fern from China. See Mark Jones (ed.), *Fake? The art of deception*, exh. cat., British Museum (London, 1990), no.71, p.85.

39 Walpole to Horace Mann, 14 February 1753, quoted in *The Letters of Horace Walpole*, ed. Mrs Paget Toynbee (Oxford, 1903), vol.III, pp.142–3. Walpole was one of the trustees of Sir Hans Sloane's will.

40 Van Rymsdyk, op. cit. (note 37), pp.58–9 illustrates 'One of the Horns of Mrs French, a Woman from Tenterden, a market Town of Kent, who had a Horny substance growing out of the back part of her Head' and notes that the horn on display did not belong to the subject of the portrait, Mary Davis of Great Saughall, near Cheshire. The portrait of Mary Davis, from the collection of Dr Mead, is still in the British Museum although not on display.

41 British Museum registration numbers P&E 1763, 4–15, 1 and 2. Known as the 'Cleopatra' vases from the painted panels showing the death of Cleopatra. They were given anonymously through James Empson.

42 BM CE 1/1 233–4, 238 (2 December 1758); CE 3/2 487 (8 December 1758). See Chapter 7 below.

43 'Report by Dr Maty and the Revd Mr Harper about their scheme for arranging the Royal Library of Printed Books', BM CE 4/1 68–9 (11 November 1757).

44 BM CE 1/1 69 (13 December 1755).

45 BM CE 4/1 203 ff. (15 February 1765).

46 BM CE 1/2 325 (19 June 1760).

47 BM CE 1/2 267 (21 June 1759).

48 BM CE 4/1 91–113 (n.d. 1759).

49 Butler, op. cit. (note 16), fol.20.

50 Powlett, op. cit. (note 15), p.vii.

Figure 7
The Tudor north façade of Sir Hans Sloane's manor house at Chelsea (left) with Winchester House on the right. Engraved by J. Barlow from an old drawing and published in Thomas Faulkner, *An Historical and Topographical Description of Chelsea* (London, 1810 and 1829).

Figure 8
Montagu House, south front and courtyard, *c*. 1714. Engraving by Sutton Nicholls. London, British Museum, Central Archives CE115/1/10.

Figure 9
Montagu House, north front and gardens, *c*. 1714. Engraving by James Simon. London, British Museum, Central Archives CE115/1/11.

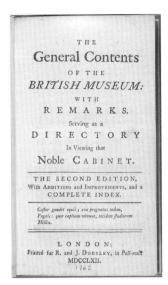

Figure 10
Frontispiece and title page of the second edition of Edmund Powlett, *The General Contents of the British Museum...* (London, 1762). The second edition describes the more usual route of the visitors' tour through the building; the author's tour in the first edition (1761) had been altered so as not to disturb a meeting of the Board of Trustees. London, British Museum, Central Library.

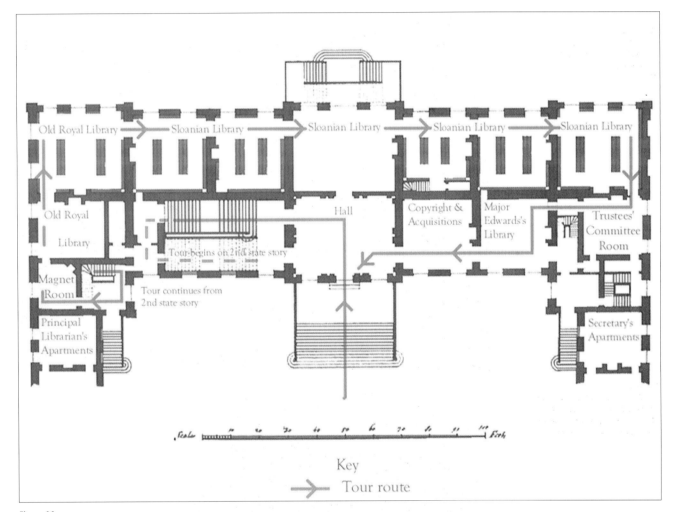

Figure 11
Montagu House, 'First State Story' showing the route of the public tour through the Department of Printed Books. Plan adapted by Tony Spence (Department of Prehistory and Early Europe, British Museum) from a plan of Montagu House by the Trustees' Surveyor, Henry Keene, *c.* 1755. London, British Museum, Central Archives.

Figure 12
The great staircase of Montagu House. Watercolour by George Scharf Snr, *c*.1845. The glimpse of the vestibule through the open door is the only known representation of the interior of the Museum's exhibition galleries in Montagu House. London, British Museum, Department of Prints and Drawings (1862-6-14-619).

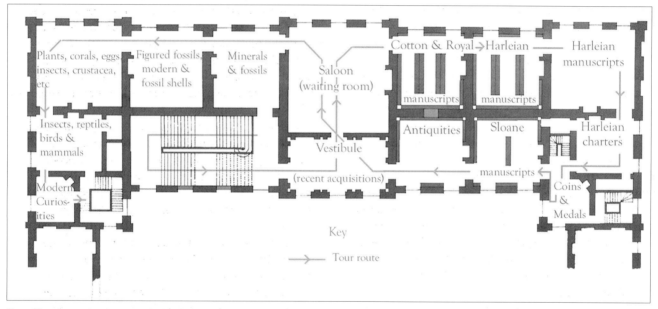

Figure 13
Montagu House, 'Second State Story' showing the route of the public tour through the Departments of Manuscripts and Natural and Artificial Productions. Plan adapted by Tony Spence (Department of Prehistory and Early Europe, British Museum) from a plan of Montagu House by the Trustees' Surveyor, Henry Keene, *c*.1755. London, British Museum, Central Archives.

Figure 14
'The vegetable lamb of Tartary'. Plate XV in J. and A. van Rymsdyk, *Museum Britannicum* (London, 1778). London, British Museum, Central Library.

Chapter 4
Encyclopaedic Collectors
Ephraim Chambers and Sir Hans Sloane
Richard Yeo

At the moment of the 250th anniversary in 2003 of the foundation of the British Museum, it should also be remembered that 2001 was the 250th anniversary of the French *Encyclopédie*, edited by Denis Diderot and Jean Le Rond D'Alembert from 1751. These two Enlightenment achievements – museum and encyclopædia – subsequently became important symbols, respectively, of British and French national culture. Nothing further will be said about the French work, but the English encyclopaedia, the *Cyclopaedia* of Ephraim Chambers (?1680–1740), on which the French work was modelled, is of relevance. Published in 1728 by a humble citizen of the Republic of Letters, this two-folio-volume dictionary of the arts and sciences did not attain the immediate notoriety, nor the later prestige, enjoyed by the *Encyclopédie*. However, it was recognized throughout eighteenth-century Europe as a significant attempt to carry the encyclopaedic tradition, from the Middle Ages and the Renaissance, into the Enlightenment, incorporating the new scientific knowledge associated with the achievement of Isaac Newton and his contemporaries. It can be usefully analysed as a way of reflecting on what might be called the encyclopaedic, or polymathic, aspirations discernible in eighteenth-century culture and illustrated in both the compilation of encyclopaedias and the collecting of objects – natural, ancient and otherwise curious.

The frontispiece to Chambers's work offers allusions to several forms of knowledge (fig. 15). Probably based on Raphael's *The School of Athens*, this image brings the participants out of the *accademia* into the *piazza* (the foreground) where learning and discovery are featured as requiring Baconian observation and experiment. Here are seen the kinds of objects that comprised collections of the period: terrestrial and celestial globes, scientific instruments of various kinds, coins and medals, heraldic shields, and one or two animal specimens. Additionally, there are books in a library, although this is very much in the background; the word 'Theologia' on the section in the left corner might conjure up, with Francis Bacon in mind, pejorative images of scholasticism. The frontispiece contrasts the active energy of measuring, observing, and experimenting with the old, and possibly useless, knowledge contained in the books stored in at least one section of the library. By comparison, Raphael's depiction of central figures such as Plato, Aristotle and Euclid has them holding the books that embody their teachings.[1] The irony, however, is that this is a frontispiece to a book – a very large one, called a *Cyclopaedia*. So in spite of any intended jibe at bookish culture in the image – an insinuation reinforced by some remarks in the Preface – Chambers had to confront the

reality that Bacon himself acknowledged: knowledge, however acquired, had to be recorded in print in order to be available for comparison and cross-checking by those living in different places and in future times. The progress of knowledge depended on reliable storage, retrieval, and communication.

It may be appropriate to reflect for a moment on the changing relations between the various practices and spaces associated with cultural collections. It needs to be recognized that the meanings now denoted by certain key terms may not match earlier usage. In the seventeenth century the word 'museum' (or 'musaeum'), used in English, did not necessarily refer to a collection of specimens and artefacts but to a scholar's study or library, nicely illustrated in a woodcut in *Orbis Sensualium Pictus* (London, 1659; 3rd edn 1672) by the Czech educational reformer Jan Comenius, in which the Latin 'Museum' is given as 'Study' (fig. 16). The Royal Society's collection was called a 'repository',[2] and well into the eighteenth century the Principal Librarian, as defined in the British Museum Act, was in charge of the entire collection.[3]

What analogies and distinctions did eighteenth-century observers draw between libraries, museums, and encyclopaedias? It is probably safe to say that all three were recognized as posing issues of selection, classification and appropriate form of display. But whereas museums and libraries were usually paired, both physically and conceptually, the encyclopaedia was a somewhat different category. For example, during the seventeenth century the concept of encyclopaedia usually referred not to a single material work (or several volumes) but to the round of subjects an educated person should pursue. This Renaissance legacy was apparent in the *Glossographia* published by Thomas Blount (1618–79) in 1656, which defined the 'encyclopedy' as 'that learning which comprehends all Liberal Sciences; an Art that comprehends all others, the perfection of all knowledge.'[4] Given this category, various collections, such as those residing in a cabinet of curiosities or a museum, a garden or a library could be seen as contributing to this encyclopaedic ideal of a well-rounded education. The range of metaphors at the time indicates this: for example, Paula Findlen has shown how the seventeenth-century Jesuit polymath Athanasius Kircher (1602–80) referred to his *Wunderkammer* situated in the College of Rome as his 'enciclopedia concreta'.[5] Similarly, when Robert Hooke voiced his wish for as 'full and complete a collection of all varieties of Natural Bodies' as possible, he described this ideal museum as a 'dictionary' that would allow one 'to read the book of nature'.[6]

Having placed his dictionary in the encyclopaedic tradition, Chambers had to say how the ideal of well rounded learning could be realized given the recent advances in the arts and sciences. The title page advertised that the work offered a 'course of antient and modern learning'; but in his long Preface Chambers acknowledged that the 'modern *Cyclopaedia*' must be more extensive than the ancient one, due to the rapid growth of knowledge since the Renaissance and the Scientific Revolution (fig. 17). Here was a major problem: the traditional (and still active) ideal of encyclopaedic learning was one of polymathy, such that the educated individual possessed an overview of the major sciences and the relations between them. As the Preface reminded its readers: 'Those who have the least acquaintance with the antient method of study, know how severe they were on this head: a man was not allowed to be an orator, historian, poet, grammarian, or even architect, or musician, much less a philosopher, without the whole circle of sciences.'[7]

Since the Renaissance there had been rival claimants for inclusion in the encyclopaedic circle of studies. Reference need only be made to the controversies between the Ancients and the Moderns, and the sometimes overlapping dispute between the defenders of traditional learning (historical and theological), such as Meric Casaubon, and the advocates of the new scientific philosophy, such as Joseph Glanville and Thomas Sprat, to see that if all priorities were included, the ideal would be impractical.[8] Chambers's point was that the encyclopaedic ideal could no longer be realized unless knowledge was efficiently summarized and collated; there were too many books, journals and transactions to read, and there was much repetition. In particular, knowledge of the arts and sciences had to be distilled and recorded in one book giving a comprehensive synopsis. The *Cyclopaedia* was such a book, and for this reason it was, in his modest estimate, 'the Best Book in Universe'.[9]

Chambers's diagnosis of the modern intellectual condition involved a survey of the state of knowledge. Although the work was alphabetically arranged, he provided a map of the sciences. This 'View of Knowledge' shows forty-seven major subjects of the arts and sciences, numbered simply according to their position on the diagram, from Meteorology to Poetry (fig. 18). In prefacing his dictionary with this map, Chambers was deferring to the traditional practice of displaying the scheme of classification by which earlier (non alphabetical) encyclopaedias were organized. His primary motive, however, was not classification but rather 'a reduction of the vast bulk of universal knowledge into a lesser compass'.[10] Unlike most collectors, Chambers did not simply want to add items; his aim was to condense knowledge of the arts and sciences in a manageable form. Wherever possible, he wanted to integrate new material into existing terms and categories so that the *Cyclopaedia* was efficient rather than unwieldy. Here the diagram came into play again: the notes attached to each subject show the cognate terms belonging to it. However, in the text of the work these terms are thrown into alphabetical order. The purpose of the diagram, and its accompanying forty-seven footnotes listing terms under each subject, is to allow for the coherence of major subjects to be reconstituted by using cross-references among the terms.[11] The diagram also reinforces Chambers's claim that the work had been collated by proper method, the terms being first collected under an appropriate 'Head', as in a private commonplace book, before

being distributed alphabetically.[12] In raising this question of the storage and retrieval of information his work signals some issues pertinent to all collections. This point will be revisited.

What, then, was Chambers's attitude to private collections, such as that of Sir Hans Sloane (1660–1753), the physician and natural historian whose private cabinet and library formed the basis of the British Museum, established by an Act of Parliament in 1753? There appears to be no reference to Sloane in the *Cyclopaedia*, but the practices associated with him are mentioned, some directly, others more obliquely. To take the first category: Chambers strongly castigates bibliophilia as a great sin; many libraries, he said, were merely opportunities for acquisition and display. Here he would have agreed with the German traveller and collector Zacharias Conrad von Uffenbach, who visited London in 1710. Apart from lamenting the poor state of most of the libraries he saw, von Uffenbach reported a conversation with a German resident familiar with the London book trade: this person (Herr Karger) said that

> . . . there were several connoisseurs who collected with so little wit that he had seen with his own eyes how a noble lord, taking a piece of string from his pocket, had measured off a row of books (most of the books in the shops being tied together in bundles) and bargained for them by the yard or ell, without glancing at their contents.[13]

Of course, Sloane was more serious about his books and lent them to people such as his friend, the philosopher, John Locke. However, in one letter mentioning that he had some 'pamphletts relating to travells, husbandry, trade and physick', Sloane added that he had sent those small books

> . . . so that you may pick out any thing you fancy and distribute the rest for making plum pyes, I confess to look over such tracts because most of them are used to such like purpose that deserve sometimes better usage for wch reason I have turn'd over many thousands within this 10 years and have bound up many volumes.[14]

Sloane's library of at least 40,000 printed volumes and some 3,000 manuscripts was not described in a printed catalogue, and hence was not easily usable, even by his friends.[15] For this reason, Sloane fell within Chambers's target-zone. Chambers insisted that books had to be used, and by this he meant mining them for essential concepts and new information. This, as indicated above, was one of the primary aims of the *Cyclopaedia*, justifying his bold claim that it would 'answer all the Purposes of a Library except Parade and Encumbrance' and would be more useful 'than any . . . [of] the Books extant.'[16]

Chambers was less specific in his opinion regarding other kinds of collection. He has no special entry on cabinets of curiosities, although these are listed as one of several kinds of 'cabinet'. However, there is an entry for 'Virtuoso', described as 'an Italian Term', lately introduced into English and denoting 'a Man of Curiosity and Learning' or 'one who loves and promotes the Arts and Sciences.' But, the entry adds, in Italy it mainly refers to those 'who apply themselves to the polite Arts of Painting, Sculpture, Turning, Mathematicks . . . ', whereas 'Among us, the Term seems affected to those who apply themselves to some curious and quaint, rather than immediately useful Art or Study: as Antiquaries, Collectors, of Rarities of any kind, Microscopical Observers etc.' Nevertheless, if this entry is unflattering towards some English virtuosi (the pejorative term in vogue was 'macaroni'), Chambers is more positive about some recent museums. After giving the classical origins of the word he states that 'The Musaeum of Oxford, call'd the Ashmolean Musaeum is a noble Pile erected at the Expence of the University, for the promoting and a carrying on several Parts of curious and useful Learning.'[17] Here the positive feature seems to be the fact that the Ashmolean is a place of learning and not merely one of display. In this sense, Chambers's comments match those later made in the *Encyclopédie*, where collections motivated by the mere curiosity of dilettanti are indicted whereas natural history collections aimed at a true understanding of nature are praised. If Chambers had been more interested in natural history he might well have admired Sloane's attempt, welcomed by John Ray and other botanists, to collate systematically the various descriptions of plants so as to avoid repetition and hence reduce the number of named species.[18]

It is worth exploring some links between Chambers and Sloane. Sloane had been a Secretary of the Royal Society of London from 1693 until 1712, for many years maintaining the *Philosophical Transactions*; he assumed the Presidency on 29 March 1727, succeeding Newton, who had died on 10 March 1727. Whereas Sloane moved in fashionable and well connected London social and intellectual circles, Chambers seems to have been a recluse, at least after leaving the employment of John Senex, the successful London globe maker and bookseller. Chambers moved to Gray's Inn and devoted himself entirely, from about 1726 until his death in 1740, to the publication of two editions of his *Cyclopaedia*. This kept him in touch with leading London booksellers such as Thomas Longman but not, as far as the evidence can confirm, with members of the scientific community. However, he was of course in touch with their books, fastidiously paraphrasing, epitomizing, abridging and common-placing their contents for integration in his dictionary. The Royal Society, with Sloane in the President's chair, acknowledged the value of this work when it approved his nomination to FRS in October 1729 as 'Author of the Universal Dictionary of Arts and Sciences'.[19]

Despite the obvious differences between the activities of Chambers and Sloane, both gained reputations for grand collections: respectively, the first major encyclopaedia of the eighteenth century, and one of the largest private collections comprising books, manuscripts, coins and medals, natural history and anthropological specimens and other curious objects. Upon visiting Sloane's collection in 1691, John Evelyn described it as 'copious', and this was even before it had been enlarged by absorbing those of other individuals, such as William Courten, Leonard Plukenet, and James Petiver, between 1702 and 1718.[20] Sloane was a collector of collections. Certain issues are raised by both cases: first, that Sloane's and Chambers's collections came to be regarded as public property; second, that they were conceived as worthy of royal notice and presented as national achievements; and finally, that both raised questions about how large collections that overwhelmed the capacities of a single mind, or memory, could be put to good public use.

Private and public collections

To take the first theme: in different ways, both private collections became public. In Sloane's case this is obvious: his personal cabinet and library were to form the foundation of a national museum – the first owned by the public by virtue of an Act of Parliament. Thus although Sloane's collection rivalled in magnitude those assembled by princes in the courts of Europe, it belonged to the world of gentlemen virtuosi or cognoscenti and came to be promoted as a public institution. In spite of the practical limits on visitors (a constant sore point into the nineteenth century), this was itself a significant development.[21] Even some thirty years later, in Germany, Johann Goethe (himself a collector) was complaining about professors at Weimar and Jena who refused to surrender the keys to their private collections for more open use by the university.[22]

In Chambers's case, this transition from private to public sphere (albeit more subtle) was also noted by contemporaries. He explained and advertised his encyclopaedia as deriving from his private reading and note-taking, in the tradition of the commonplace book recommended by humanist educators. Indeed, when Evelyn called the collection 'copious', he was using one of the standard descriptions of a well stocked commonplace book. Chambers offered this private summary of various books, journals and transactions to the public as a useful and ordered synopsis of the state of knowledge. Indeed, his defence against plagiarism – since the work was a compilation from the works of numerous authors – was that his encyclopaedia performed a public service in producing an accessible archive of knowledge available not only to scholars and philosophers but to all readers. Moreover, Chambers made a special point about compilations of scientific and technical knowledge, saying that knowledge of such utility became public property once published. The entry on 'Plagiary' reinforced this, asserting that the charge of 'author theft' could not be levelled against 'Dictionary-Writers' because:

> ... they don't pretend to set up on their own bottom, nor to treat you [the reader] at their own Cost. Their Works are supposed, in great Measure, Assemblages of other Peoples; and what they take from others they do it avowedly, and in the open Sun. In effect, their Quality gives them a Title to every thing that may be for their purpose, wherever they find it; and if they rob, they don't do it in any otherwise, than as the Bee does, for the publick Service. Their Occupation is not pillaging, but collecting Contributions.[23]

Joining in the debates stimulated by the copyright Statute of 1710, he declared:

> Tis vain to pretend any thing of property in things of this nature. To offer our thoughts to the public, and yet to pretend a right reserved therein to one's self, if it be not absurd, yet it is sordid. The words we speak, nay, the breath we emit, is not more vague and common than our thoughts, when divulged in print.[24]

Of course, objects in collections such as Sloane's, unlike ideas expressed in words carried in the air, could indeed be owned as private property. But Chambers appealed to the notion of a public domain in which knowledge of the arts and sciences became common property. This notion was a powerful one in the copyright debates; it was used by those who argued that once an author had recouped a fair return, books should be freely available for reprinting. (This position was finally upheld by the House of Lords in 1774.) Such a constant refrain, from 1710, might have formed part of the climate in which Sloane's private collection became a public asset.

Collections fit for a king

The second point of comparison is that both collections were deemed worthy of dedication to a monarch. Chambers offered his *Cyclopaedia* to George II on the occasion of the King's coronation on 11 October 1727. Of course, the dedication of books, and other objects, to members of royalty was hardly new; Sloane had dedicated the first volume of his *Voyage to the Islands Madera, Barbadoes … Jamaica, with the natural history of the last* (London, 1707) to Queen Anne. (The second volume, entitled *Natural History of Jamaica*, appeared in 1725, dedicated to George I.) But there is something more salient here. Major collections of natural history and other objects played on analogies between intellectual and political territory. From the Reformation, collections such as Sloane's were often construed as part of a virtuous attempt to reconstruct the Garden of Eden, as evidence of humanity's self-reforming efforts on Earth.[25] Once envisaged as a microcosm of the world, they could easily be seen as a symbol of political territory, of the kingdom, or indeed of an Empire such as Britain's, with possessions in far-flung places. When the Prince of Wales visited Sloane's house on 7 June 1748 the *Gentleman's Magazine* covered the story, describing the highlights of the collection and its array of objects and plants from all over the world. The Prince was reported to have expressed his pleasure in seeing 'so magnificent a collection in *England*, esteeming it an ornament to the nation'. [26]

In his dedication to the King, Chambers sought to include encyclopaedic summaries of the arts and sciences in a metaphor of intellectual territory. Indeed there were precedents, since Pliny the Elder had done so in dedicating his encyclopaedic text, the *Natural History*, to the Emperor Vespasian. Chambers referred to the *Cyclopaedia* as a 'Survey of the Republick of Learning, as it stands in Your Majesty's most auspicious Reign'. This made knowledge of the arts and sciences akin to a possession, albeit not one so tangible as a collection of minerals, plants, and animals. Chambers exploited an idea favoured by Renaissance princes: knowledge and cultivation of the arts and sciences were instruments by which political domination could be secured; and, in addition, their state of cultivation was a marker of the happiness of the people and the perfection of the realm. Addressing George II, Chambers explained that: 'Tis they [the arts and sciences], in fine, that make the Difference between your Majesty's Subjects, and the Savages of Canada, or the Cape of Good Hope.' The special function of the *Cyclopaedia* was to map the condition of knowledge at the start of the King's reign, charting the boundary between the known and unknown 'Parts of the Intelligible World'. With royal encouragement, this boundary might be extended into 'the other Hemisphere': as Chambers wrote, 'Methinks I see Trophies erecting to Your Majesty in the yet undiscover'd Regions of Science; and Your Majesty's name inscribed to inventions at present held impossible.'[27]

Dedications of this kind belonged to the Renaissance practice of courtly and aristocratic patronage; but during the eighteenth century, scientific and other cultural achievements were attached to emerging political categories – the public, and the nation. Unlike the *Encyclopaedia Britannica* (from 1768), Chambers did not use a national referent in his title: his work, like the *Encyclopédie*, reflected the cosmopolitan values of the Republic of Letters. However, the *Cyclopaedia* soon came to be seen as 'the pride of the English booksellers' and its influence on the French editors was underscored. Indeed, when it came to the crunch, Chambers's own sympathies were clear. One report says that when in France recovering from an illness, Chambers was asked to publish a new edition of his work there and dedicate it to Louis XV. The English encyclopaedist is said to have refused, viewing this suggestion as an invitation to retract 'the compliments he had paid to his lawful sovereign'.[28] By the 1780s, in Abraham Rees's editions of the *Cyclopaedia*, the new dedication assumed a more national tone, making the 'genius of Britain' an actor in its own right. Rees explained that although he had recorded 'every kind of information, which may do justice to the merit of those, of *every country*, who have distinguished themselves in the cause of Science,' he had been especially careful to include 'those inventions and improvements, which do honour to *his own country*, and to the distinguished munificence of his Sovereign'. Thus 'Britishness', noted by Linda Colley and others as a mark of cultural rhetoric after the Union of 1707, was not absent from encyclopaedias.[29] Nevertheless, the publishers of these works continued to stress that their content, especially knowledge of the arts and sciences, was not parochial, but sanctioned by the European world of learning. The tensions between cosmopolitanism and nationalism increased, however, after the French Revolution, when there was, in effect, a forcible nationalization of cultural assets. This contrasted, as observers were keen to note, with George IV's donation of the Royal Library to the nation.

Individual collectors

In spite of the rhetoric about the domain of knowledge as the possession of the King, by the time Chambers was compiling his dictionary it was conceded that individuals were unlikely to possess the knowledge required to master even their own collections. We can link this perception with concerns voiced even earlier by Gottfried Wilhelm Leibniz, Pierre Bayle and others about the ever-growing flood of books – some, of course, containing nothing of merit, but others announcing new information that demanded to be integrated with existing knowledge. What was at stake here can be seen by returning to the Prince of Wales's visit to Sloane's house.

The *Gentleman's Magazine*'s comment on the national prestige attached to such a collection has already been noted. There was also a significant remark about the way in which the Prince was able to take so much of it into his royal gaze, commenting knowingly, and drawing on his own education and reading:

> The Prince on this occasion shew'd his great reading and most happy memory; for in such a multiplicity, such a variety of the productions of nature and art; upon any thing being shewn to him he had not seen before, he was ready in recollecting where he had read it; and upon viewing the ancient and modern *medals*, he made so many judicious remarks, that he appeared a perfect master of *history* and *chronology*. [30]

This can be contrasted with Rees's dedication of his edition of the *Cyclopaedia* to George III in January 1786. Here Rees entertained the fiction that the King himself comprehended the full range of the arts and sciences and might actually correct or challenge the work's coverage. As Rees put it: 'Your Majesty's known judgement in many of the subjects, which the Dictionary comprehends, might justly alarm his [Rees's] diffidence.'[31]

In both cases, it can be argued that the royal persons are regarded not only as members of the Republic of Letters, but as exemplars of an ideal that expected educated individuals to grasp something of the circle of knowledge represented either in a museum or in an encyclopaedia. Sloane's museum and the *Cyclopaedia* were imagined as prompts to the memory, opportunities to bring previous observation or reading to bear on an object from a collection, or an entry in a dictionary. Yet, within the same breath, there is a tacit admission that this ideal was no longer feasible. It is revealing that when seeking to measure the scale of Sloane's collection, the report estimated how many volumes would be required to describe its contents: 'Fifty folio volumes would scarce contain a detail of this immense museum, consisting of above 200,000 articles.'[32] This seems to be an expression of dismay: namely, that a catalogue of this collection would be terrifying, in contrast, say, to Nehemiah Grew's already sizeable, but eminently useful, catalogue of the Royal Society's museum published in 1681 as *Musæum Regalis Societatis*. In the words of one appreciative contemporary, this catalogue made it easy 'to find likenesse and unlikenesse of things upon a suddaine'.[33]

There is evidence that Sloane's collection, both books and specimens, was used by some leading figures. Eminent borrowers of books included Locke, Samuel Pepys, Edmond Halley, Pierre Bayle, and John Ray. (In fact, Ray damaged a book; but at least he was reading it at the time, unlike George Frederic Handel who, while visiting for tea, rendered Sloane speechless by resting a buttered muffin on a valuable book). Handel is supposed to have later remarked:

To be sure, it was a careless trick, but it did no monstrous mischief; yet it put the poor old bookworm terribly out of sorts. I offered my best apologies, but the old miser would not have done with it. If it had been a biscuit, it would not have mattered . . . but muffin and butter . . . Ah mine Gott, that is the rub! It is the butter.[34]

In completing his *Historia generalis planaturum* (1687), Ray used Sloane's information on European plants, acknowledging this in his preface. In 1736 the young Swedish botanist Carl Linnaeus visited Sloane's herbarium, later expressing gratitude at being able to view this 'incomparable Museum', but also remarking to a friend that it was 'in complete disorder'.[35] The pertinent question was whether Sloane's collection was too large to be of use to an individual, and yet, in the absence of a proper printed catalogue, not accessible to others. The antiquary Thomas Hearne said as much in letter to Sloane in January 1721/2:

I am very sensible of your great Treasure and if I should come to London (where I never was yet), I would endeavour to make myself acquainted with it, especially as there is so much in it about Antiquity. I wish Catalogues of such noble Libraries and Museums as yours were published, 'twould be of great service to Learning, especially if the owners were, like yourself, of a truly publick Spirit.[36]

During the Enlightenment, there was a demand that private collections should serve a public and collaborative effort. On this score, Chambers was forward-looking: although posited on the ideal of individual encyclopaedic learning, he argued that the *Cyclopaedia* would assist the scientific community. Indeed, one kind of reader imagined in the Preface is the specialist or man of science who could consult the work to check on concepts and discoveries in areas outside his particular subject. Chambers was aware that poor communication could mean

that investigators separated by geographical or social boundaries would be unaware of what had already been discovered. The *Cyclopaedia* was a public archive that allowed the scientific community to check what had been done, thus avoiding unnecessary repetition of inquiry. By mapping the '*terra cognita*', it supplied a sound platform for future progress; acting as a record of achievements against which purported discoveries could be assessed, it might also settle priority disputes. So, playing on the concerns about patent protection for inventions, Chambers suggested that his dictionary would serve 'Inventors' by being 'a Kind of Register to secure their Property, and prevent all After-Claims of second and third Inventors.'[37] However, to be at all effective in this respect, such a dictionary required agreement on the language used in scientific and technical communication. There were already lexicons of anatomy, medicine, chemistry and other sciences, and in fact these often exposed the lack of consensus on terminology, even within the one discipline. Chambers pointed to this 'confusion of Babel' in his Preface, and as a devotee of John Locke and his analysis of language, urged the importance of clear definitions of terms. He complained about the lack of effort by established academies, such as that in France, which should have done more to protect the vocabulary in which science and learning were conducted. In the absence of such a work from an institution, he offered his own *Cyclopaedia*. In sum, his work stressed the importance of organization, standardization, and accessibility – issues relevant to all collections.

It is pertinent to conclude with a remark from William Thackeray. In 1850 he wrote from Paris to Antonio Panizzi, Principal Librarian of the British Museum, about his frustration in using the Bibliothèque Nationale:

The catalogue you consult *is the librarian* of whom however learned one cannot ask too many questions . . . instead of a catalogue at my orders, I must trust to the good memory and complaisance (both of which are very great) of the librarian.[38]

This remark captures the way in which individual memory still played a part in access to collections, even when these were based in public institutions. Over a hundred years earlier, Chambers's work provides us with one example of how this and similar matters were being confronted. His encyclopaedia of the arts and sciences rested on an uneasy combination of ideas: although it was a collection compiled and selected on the judgement of one individual, it offered itself as an archive and checkpoint for a more specialized community of investigators and readers. In this sense, it epitomized some of the tensions between the polymathic interests of individuals and the new institutions built on their collections during the eighteenth century.

Notes and references

1 E. Chambers, *Cyclopaedia* (London, 1728), vol.1, frontispiece. See also M. Hall (ed.), *Raphael's* School of Athens (Cambridge, 1997). Notwithstanding the relevance of Raphael's image, the more immediate stimulus for the engraver (J. Sturt) of this frontispiece was the work of the French painter, Sébastian Leclerc (1637–1714), especially his *L'Académie des Sciences et des Beaux-Arts*. I thank Olga Baird of the Wolverhampton Art Gallery for her advice. See also K. Scott, *The Rococo Interior: Decoration and social spaces in early eighteenth-century Paris* (New Haven, 1995), pp.66–76.

2 M. Hunter, *Science and the Shape of Orthodoxy: Intellectual change in late seventeenth-century Britain* (New York, 1995), pp.48–9. See the definition in Chambers, op. cit. (note 1), s.v. 'Musaeum' (vol.1):

'Hence the word *Musaeum* has pass'd into a general Denomination, and is now apply'd to any Place set apart as a Repository of Things that have some immediate Relation to the Arts or the *Muses*, whence the word first took its rise. See Repository.' See also P. Findlen, 'The Museum: Its Classical Etymology and Renaissance Genealogy', *Journal of the History of Collections* 1 (1989), pp.59–78.

3   E. Miller, *That Noble Cabinet: A history of the British Museum* (London, 1973), p.58; also M. Caygill, *The Story of the British Museum* (London, 1981).

4   T. Blount, *Glossographia* (London, 1656), 'Encyclopedy' and 'To the Reader'. Blount was a Roman Catholic and a Loyalist.

5   P. Findlen, *Possessing Nature: Museums, collecting, and scientific culture in early modern Italy* (Berkeley, 1994).

6   Cited in G.R. de Beer, *Sir Hans Sloane and the British Museum* (London, 1953), p.108. In the same vein the recently founded Ashmolean Museum was described as 'a new Library which may containe the most conspicuous parts of the Great Book of Nature, and rival the Bodleian's Collection of Mss. and printed volumes' (quoted in A.G. MacGregor and A.J. Turner, 'The Ashmolean Museum', in *The History of the University of Oxford,* vol.v: *The Eighteenth Century*, ed. L.S. Sutherland and L.G. Mitchell [Oxford, 1986], p.643).

7   E. Chambers, *Cyclopaedia*, 2nd edn (London, 1738), vol.i, p.xxiv. The Preface was reprinted in all editions.

8   M. Hunter, *Science and Society in Restoration England* (London, 1981), pp.154–6.

9   For the details of this claim see R. Yeo, *Encyclopaedic Visions: Scientific dictionaries and Enlightenment culture* (Cambridge, 2001), ch.5.

10   Chambers, op. cit. (note 7), vol.i, p.xxiv.

11   Chambers, op. cit. (note 1), vol.i, p.ii for the diagram; the notes continue to p.vi.

12   For this argument see R. Yeo, 'Ephraim Chambers's Cyclopaedia (1728) and the tradition of Commonplaces', *Journal of the History of Ideas* 57 (1996), pp.157–75.

13   Z.C. von Uffenbach, *London in 1710 from the Travels of Zacharias Conrad von Uffenbach*, trans. and ed. by W.H. Quarrell and M. Mare (London, 1934), pp.158–9.

14   Cited in de Beer, op. cit. (note 6), p.114.

15   See E. St John Brooks, *Sir Hans Sloane: The great collector and his circle* (London, 1953), pp.179–80. See 'The Names and Numbers of the several Things contain'd in the Musaeum', in *The Will of Sir Hans Sloane, Bart. Deceased* (London, 1753), pp.33–6 for an inventory, including the estimate of 'about 50,000 Volumes' in the library, amongst them '3516 Volumes of Manuscripts'. Sloane did draw up several private catalogues, for example, 'A catalogue of my Books taken in Febry. 1684/5 in London', British Library, Sloane MS 3995; for a full list of these catalogues, including those of objects, specimens etc., A. MacGregor (ed.), *Sir Hans Sloane: Collector, scientist, antiquary; founding father of the British Museum* (London, 1994), pp.291–4. See also J.S. Finch, 'Sir Hans Sloane's printed books', *The Library* 22 (1942), pp.67–72.

16   See Chambers, op. cit. (note 1), vol.i, p.ii.

17   Chambers, op. cit. (note 1), entries for 'Cabinet' (vol.i); 'Musaeum' and 'Virtuoso' (vol.ii). See Hunter, op. cit. (note 8), p. 75 on different groups within the scientific community. See von Uffenbach, op. cit. (note 13), pp.176–7, 185–7 for a negative view of John Woodward, the Professor of Physic at Gresham College, compared with his positive view of Sloane.

18   K. Pomian, *Collectors and Curiosities: Paris and Venice, 1500–1800*, trans. E. Wiles-Portier (London, 1990), pp.136–8. For Ray's positive

review of Sloane's catalogue of the plants of Jamaica, see *Philosophical Transactions* no. 221 (1696).

19   See Yeo, op. cit. (note 9), p.40.

20   A. MacGregor, 'The life, character and career of Sir Hans Sloane', in MacGregor op. cit. (note 15), pp.11–44, at p.22.

21   See Miller, op. cit. (note 3), p.92; P. Fara, 'The appliance of science: the Georgian British Museum', *History Today* (August 1997), pp.39–45, at pp.40, 44.

22   E.P. Hahm, 'Unpacking Goethe's collections: The public and the private in natural history collecting', *British Journal for the History of Science* 34 (2001), pp.275–300, at p.294.

23   Chambers, op. cit. (note 1), vol.ii, 'Plagiary'.

24   Chambers, op. cit. (note 7), vol.i, p.xxiv. See Yeo, op. cit. (note 9), ch.8 for the relevant eighteenth-century copyright debates.

25   See K. Whitaker, 'The culture of curiosity', in N. Jardine, J.A. Secord and E.C. Spary (eds), *Cultures of Natural History* (Cambridge, 1996), pp.75–90, at p.88 for an anonymous reflection (of 1712) on this theme: 'A poem occasion'd by the viewing of Dr. Sloane's Musaeum', held in the British Library, Sloane MS 1968, fols 192–3.

26   'An Account of the Prince and Princess of Wales visiting Sir Hans Sloane', *Gentleman's Magazine* 18 (1748), pp.301–2, at p.302. This account was written by Sloane's former amanuensis, Dr Cromwell Mortimer, Secretary of the Royal Society, who also conducted the visit. See British Library, Egerton MS 834, fols 252–5; see also St John Brooks, op. cit. (note 15), p.198.

27   Chambers, op. cit. (note 1), vol.i, 'To the King' [dedication]. This was reprinted in all editions.

28   Quoted in Yeo, op. cit. (note 9), p.231 n.18.

29   A. Rees (ed.), *Cyclopaedia*, 4 vols (London, 1778–88), vol.i, dedication; L. Colley, *Britons: Forging the nation 1710–1837* (New Haven, 1992).

30   *Gentleman's Magazine*, op.cit. (note 26), p.302.

31   Rees, op. cit. (note 29), dedication, vol.i. There were several different issues of this edition; although dated 1786, the dedication appears in the first volume of all editions.

32   *Gentleman's Magazine*, op. cit. (note 26), p.302. Sloane appreciated the need for cataloguing his natural history specimens: when he purchased James Petiver's collections he spent considerable time putting them in better order.

33   Sir John Hoskyns, cited in Hunter, op. cit. (note 8), p.67; also von Uffenbach, op. cit. (note 13), p.121 on the value of printed catalogues such as Grew's.

34   St John Brooks, op. cit. (note 15), p.123 for Ray's accident. See de Beer, op. cit. (note 6), p.124 for the Handel story.

35   See de Beer, op. cit. (note 6), pp.115, 123–4, and J.E. Dandy, *The Sloane Herbarium* (London, 1958), p.11 for the critical remark from Linnaeus's letter to Olaus Celsius.

36   Quoted in de Beer, op. cit. (note 6), p.115. Hearne also recognized the advantage of amalgamating private collections, suggesting at the time of Ralph Thoresby's death in 1725 that his collection of manuscripts 'be joined with Sir Hans Sloane's . . .'. See St John Brooks, op. cit. (note 15), p.189. On the problem of detaching the individual collector from the collection, see L. Jardine, *Ingenious Pursuits: Building the scientific revolution* (London, 1999), pp.271–2.

37   Quoted in Yeo, op. cit. (note 9), p.219 n.78. Thomas Birch made similar points about the value of Sloane's collection. See his 'Memoirs relating to the Life of Sir Hans Sloane', British Library, Additional MS 4241, fols 27–8.

38   Quoted in F. Lerner, *The Story of Libraries* (New York, 1998), p.117; author's emphasis.

Figure 15
Frontispiece of Ephraim Chambers,
Cyclopaedia, 2nd edn (London, 1738).
This frontispiece appears in all
editions. National Library of Australia.

Figure 16
Woodcut (no.XCVII) from Jan
Comenius, *Orbis Sensualium Pictus*,
3rd edn (London, 1672). National
Library of Australia.

CYCLOPÆDIA:
OR, AN
UNIVERSAL DICTIONARY
OF
ARTS AND SCIENCES;
CONTAINING
AN EXPLICATION OF THE TERMS, AND AN ACCOUNT OF THE THINGS SIGNIFIED THEREBY,
IN THE
SEVERAL ARTS, BOTH LIBERAL AND MECHANICAL;
AND THE
SEVERAL SCIENCES, HUMAN AND DIVINE:
The Figures, Kinds, Properties, Productions, Preparations, and Ufes of Things
NATURAL AND ARTIFICIAL:
The Rife, Progrefs, and State of Things
ECCLESIASTICAL, CIVIL, MILITARY, AND COMMERCIAL:
With the feveral Syftems, Sects, Opinions, &c. among
PHILOSOPHERS, DIVINES, MATHEMATICIANS, | PHYSICIANS, ANTIQUARIES, CRITICS, &c.
The whole intended as a Courfe of antient and modern Learning.
Extracted from the beft Authors, Dictionaries, Journals, Memoirs, Tranfactions, Ephemerides, &c. in feveral Languages.
By E. CHAMBERS, F. R. S.
Floriferis ut apes in faltibus omnia libant,
Omnia nos ——— LUCRET.
THE SECOND EDITION, CORRECTED AND AMENDED; WITH SOME ADDITIONS.
IN TWO VOLUMES.
VOL. I.
LONDON:
Printed for D. MIDWINTER, A. BETTESWORTH and C. HITCH, J. SENEX, R. GOSLING, W. INNYS and R. MANBY, J. and J. PEMBERTON, R. ROBINSON, C. RIVINGTON, A. WARD, J. and P. KNAPTON, E. SYMON, D. BROWN, T. LONGMAN, H. LINTOTT, and the Executors of J. DARBY and F. CLAY.
M.DCC.XXXVIII.

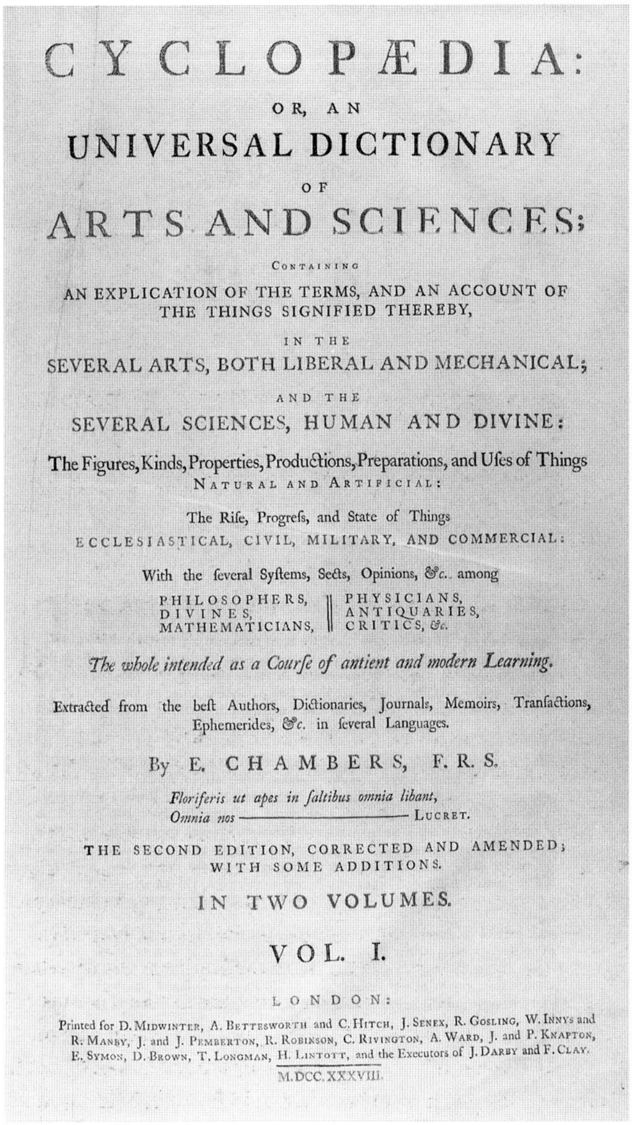

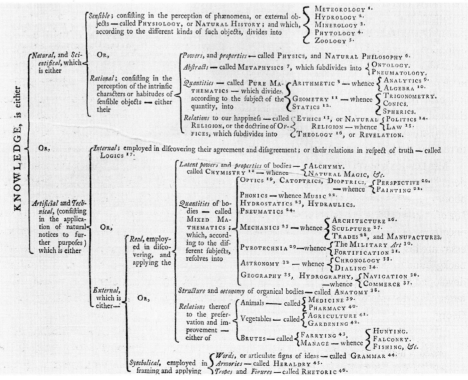

Figure 17
Title page, Ephraim Chambers, *Cyclopaedia* 2nd edn (London, 1738). National Library of Australia.

Figure 18
The 'View of Knowledge', or diagram of the arts and sciences, given in the preface of Ephraim Chambers, *Cyclopaedia*, 2nd edn (London, 1738), vol.I, p.iii. This diagram appears in all editions. National Library of Australia.

Chapter 5

Wantonness and Use

Ambitions for research libraries in early eighteenth-century England

David McKitterick

The first edition of Charlotte Lennox's novel *The female Quixote* was published in March 1752. Its heroine had grown up with access to a library 'in which, unfortunately for her, were great Store of Romances, and, what was still more unfortunate, not in the original *French*, but very bad Translations':

> Supposing Romances were real Pictures of Life, from them she drew all her Notions and Expectations. By them she was taught to believe, that Love was the ruling Principle of the World; that every other Passion was subordinate to this; and that it caused all the Happiness and Miseries of Life.[1]

As might be guessed from the novel's title, her diet of seventeenth-century romances is pivotal to the story. Quite apart from the timing of its publication, just a few months before the death of Sir Hans Sloane, this passage might usefully be introduced as a reminder that the purposes of the founders of the British Museum were broad and that libraries were not just for the scholarly. Increasingly in the eighteenth century, as the British publishing trade gained in confidence and a consumer market developed with cash and leisure to spare for books, libraries were also for entertainment, for both sexes.[2] In the mid-century there was usually no danger of confusion between different kinds of libraries. Nevertheless, the development of what quickly became the national library at the same period that witnessed a surge in popularity for the new circulating libraries is a salutary reminder of how older assumptions of use not only coloured the Museum's initial planning, but also, eventually, were to be vociferously defended. Current difficulties over the funding of publicly accessible libraries of all kinds derive from these issues. They arise partly from the fact that the boundaries are today no longer so readily definable; and, because they are not easily defined, or because different authorities – political, administrative, educational, social or geographical – wish to redraw them, they are matters for dispute.

Mrs Lennox's novel came into the world fortified by a dedication written by Samuel Johnson. He had known her for about four years, had admired her first novel, the now forgotten *Life of Harriot Stuart* (1750), and was doing what he could to encourage her literary career. The words of the title of this essay are his, and it is worth reflecting on them as a background to the purposes of the British Museum as they developed in its first years. They are drawn from his celebrated letter of advice in 1768 to Frederick Barnard, Librarian to King George III:

> Things of which the mere rarity makes the value, and which are prized at high rate by wantonness rather than by use, are always passing from poorer to richer countries . . . An eagerness for scarce books and early Editions which prevailed among the English about half a century ago, filled our shops with all the Splendour and Nicety of Literature, and when the Harleian Catalogue was published many of the books were bought for the Library of the King of France.[3]

Johnson was concerned with the distinctions between bibliophile (wanton) and scholarly values – the two not necessarily being incompatible. He was concerned with the ways and opportunities of the market. Like most of those who thought about serious collecting, he had half an eye on the French royal library (even if he was misinformed on the particular point here).[4] Above all, he was concerned with the reasons for collecting books.

The immediate subject of his discussion was early printed books, but the same considerations could be applied to books of all kinds. Johnson's knowledge of early printing was extensive and peculiar. A quarter of a century earlier he had helped to catalogue the early printed books in the Harleian library when they were put up for sale by the London bookseller Thomas Osborne.[5] He was well able to distinguish books acquired for their magnificence from their more workaday fellows. Of books frequently printed a royal library should possess, in his opinion, 'at least the most curious Edition, the most splendid, and the most useful'.[6] In stating this, he was speaking of the library of George III, but the values were equally applicable fifteen years earlier, in 1753.

The founding of the British Museum was a development conceived in London and based on collections in London. But discussion surrounding it was framed in European terms. Oxford and Cambridge were a part of this world, while other libraries, of Edinburgh and Dublin, of the major provincial English towns, of the cathedrals, of subscription libraries, parishes, schools and local societies, form a backdrop representing not so much an alternative as a complementary view. They were, however, of less importance to the immediate world in which the British Museum was born.[7] Though much of the rhetoric addressed national interest, most of those contributing their views either had direct experience of libraries overseas or were aware of them through the media of conversation, correspondence or print. For the scholarly as well as the political world, the view was European. Whether in the Europeanization of culture by means of translation, in the scholarly Republic of Letters, or in the management of public finance for political ends, culture and power walked hand in hand.[8]

The word 'library', like '*bibliotheca*', or '*bibliothèque*', has always carried many different connotations. The vocabulary of what was, in effect, a group of linked concepts requires some unravelling. This is not because there are necessarily clear distinctions to be drawn according to different social, educational or economic circumstances, but because the multiplication of meanings and cross-references in these usages implied a hierarchy of significances and purposes. The size and purpose of libraries, the degree to which they were to be comprehensive or selective, the distinction between collecting for ostentation or display and the more obvious virtues of knowledge – these had all been topics of discussion for centuries. With the increasing flood of new publications in the late sixteenth century, and more especially in the seventeenth century, the notion of 'library' was continually reformulated, and referred as often to bibliographical guidance or to processes of selection (theoretical or practical) as to collections of books. To strive for comprehensiveness, or to be selective, involved decisions that were regarded as moral or even religious issues.[9] Seneca was quoted with approval: '*Distrahit animum librorum multitudo. Itaque cum legere non possis quantum habueris, satis est habere quantum legas.*'[10] The library that emulated such selectivity was not merely practical, but was based on moral principles.

Some of the various usages that had become established by the mid-eighteenth century may be conveniently demonstrated, in the simplest manner, from the ways in which the word 'library' was applied in the titles of publications that appeared in the few years surrounding the foundation of the British Museum. They offer a verbal as well as conceptual context in which the 'library' that formed so fundamental a part of that new institution in both public and private parlance was to be understood. The Museum, and the Library, were on scales hitherto unattempted in Britain. With no direct comparisons, their meaning was for most people only to be understood by a process of linguistic exclusion.

Libraries were places of authority, in which ancient manuscripts could be found and modern manuscripts could be placed for reference. The long-celebrated *Testament of the Twelve Patriarchs*, originally published in English in 1576 and republished many times subsequently, was based on 'an auncient Greeke copye, written in parchment . . . kept in the Universitie Librarye of Cambridge'. The phrasing of the first edition was still in use in the 1750s.[11] In 1748 there appeared in London a small book, *The best and easiest Method of preserving uninterrupted Health to extreme Old Age,* which based its claims to authority not only on 'the suffrages of the most celebrated practitioners among the antients and moderns', but also on its being taken 'from a manuscript found in the library of an eminent physician lately deceased'. Using a similar device as *captatio lectoris,* the *Account of the Princes of Wales, from the first institution till Prince Henry, eldest son to King James I,* written by Richard Connak (or Connock) in 1609, was 'Publish'd out of a Manuscript in Trinity-College Library' and printed at London in 1751.[12] Another popular book was *The memoirs of Sign. Gaudentio di Lucca: taken from his confession and examination before the Fathers of the Inquisition at Bologna in Italy.* This was no translation, but was in fact written in English by Simon Berington (d. 1755). First published in 1737, by 1752 it was in its fifth edition. The claim on the title-page that it was 'Copied from the original manuscript kept in St. Mark's Library at Venice' was wholly fictitious, and intended solely to lend a spurious air of veracity.

Other kinds of library made lesser claims in a moral sense, but sometimes large ones nonetheless. Batty Langley's *Builders compleat Chest-book, or library of arts and sciences, absolutely necessary to be understood by builders and workmen in general . . . ,* first published in 1738 and with dozens of copper-plates to aid his instructions, found an audience of artisans across the country. Four editions had appeared by 1766, as it established itself as a standard if rather pedestrian authority.[13] Another book for professionals was *The Gentleman, Tradesman, and Traveller's pocket Library* (1753). The publisher was John Newbery,[14] one of the first to specialize in publishing for children and who found in the terms 'library' and 'museum' the kind of vocabulary he required to suggest the need for only a short attention span. So, for children as for adults, the word 'library' could denote little more than an anthology, such as *The Family Library: or, instructor in useful knowledge,* of which a fourth edition was published in 1752. There were plenty of books with such titles. Oliver Goldsmith and Christopher Smart were working in this tradition when they assembled their *Lilliputian Magazine: or the young gentleman & lady's golden library,* published by Newbery in 1751–2.[15] Its purpose was very similar to yet another Newbery publication, the *Museum for young Gentlemen and Ladies: or, a private tutor for little masters and misses,* first published probably in 1751.[16]

The words '*Bibliotheca*', '*Bibliothèque*' or '*Library*', much used as periodical titles from the late seventeenth century onwards, sometimes indicated their purpose as review journals, at other times denoted their selective natures, and often meant both. At the beginning of the eighteenth century, the *Bibliotheca annua* had listed new books published in England. Among the most widely familiar reviewing journals for the scholarly world were the *Bibliothèque universelle et historique,* originally published in 1686–93, and the *Bibliothèque choisie* (1703–13): both were subsequently republished several times. By the 1740s, series had appeared of a *Bibliothèque Angloise* and a *Bibliothèque Britannique,* as well as *Belgique, Française, Germanique* and *Italique.* Many of these lasted only a few years, and the *Bibliothèque des Cafés* (1739) seems to have lasted just one month. Others found a solid market throughout Europe, notably the *Bibliothèque Raisonnée des Ouvrages des Savans de l'Europe,* founded in 1728 and not closed until 1753.[17]

Such publishers' libraries had their parallels in the long-familiar association of *Bibliotheca* with bibliography and (hence) with the organization of knowledge.[18] The tradition stretched back at least to Gessner in the 1540s.[19] Ever since at least the sixteenth century, the words 'library' and 'bibliotheca' could thus denote a book, or books, or lists of books. The same words had come to serve to denote businesses. They were familiar as referring to a place of resort, especially in the comparatively recent fashion for commercial circulating libraries, whether, to select examples from imprints in the early 1750s (and there were many more like them), that of Meyer in St Martin's Lane (London),[20] or that of Robert Williamson in Liverpool.[21] These libraries, increasingly popular especially from the 1750s onwards, assumed some of the business of the old and familiar coffee-houses. By concentrating on lending out books, with a modicum of publishing on the side, they were characteristic of the increasing specialization that marks the mid-eighteenth-century consumer trade. Though very far from dominated by either sex, they seem to have catered more comfortably to a female audience, and so complemented contemporary changes in supply and demand for printed books and magazines.[22]

More well-established, there were the libraries of institutions – educational, religious or public. In these, together (to some extent) with the Royal Library, lay the most obvious comparisons with (and justifications of) the new British Museum library. Until 1753, the Bodleian Library was the closest that England had to a national library.[23] Otherwise the country offered little by way of example, despite such recent library buildings as those at Christ Church and All Souls or the Radcliffe Camera at Oxford,[24] or – a generation earlier – Trinity College at Cambridge.[25] For those having some knowledge or experience of the European continent, there above all was the Vatican library, 'the finest in the universe', collected according to contemporary tradition mainly by Sixtus V, and enriched by the spoils of the Palatine library from Heidelberg.[26] The room built in the 1580s by Domenico Fontana and decorated by Cesare Nebbia and others was part of the tourist itinerary, depicted also in engravings for those either unable to see it for themselves or wishing to have some memento. Though by no means all were openly accessible, the other libraries of Italy were well enough known by repute – at Venice, Milan, Florence, Bologna, Padua and elsewhere. The great libraries at Vienna, Wolfenbüttel and Munich dominated the German-speaking world, even if Ratisbon (Regensburg) could boast a copy of the Gospels written in letters of gold,[27] or, as Le Gallois had pointed out in 1680, the books of the Elector Friedrich Wilhelm of Brandenburg were better bound than those at Wolfenbüttel.[28] In Portugal, Dom João V employed a network of agents and ambassadors to create in the Paço da Ribeira a library European in its range and embracing both the arts and the sciences: the library seems to have been so arranged that books and scientific instruments could be used alongside each other. The very substantial print collection was obtained partly in London, and attached to the library there was a museum of natural philosophy of which the geological collections enjoyed especial fame.[29]

With the exception of the Vatican, all these tended to be eclipsed by the libraries of Paris. The Royal Library, the libraries of Mazarin, the Sorbonne and the Collège de Navarre, and the religious foundations of St Germain-des-Prés, Ste Geneviève and the Collège de Clermont were but some of the most obvious in a city that fully deserved the soubriquet accorded it by Le Gallois, 'the Athens of our age'.[30] For the French scholarly world, the most readily accessible libraries in the late seventeenth century were the Mazarine and some of the religious houses. Though available in theory, the Royal Library became more easily usable only from 1692 onwards; even then its opening hours were severely limited, and remained so for most of the eighteenth century. The Mazarine, open two days a week, was by the 1750s heavily used, and was much appreciated.[31]

Knowledge of these libraries formed the background to the debate that developed in England during the last decades of the seventeenth century and the first few years of the eighteenth on the urgent need for a library worthy of a country whose overseas interests were growing.[32] The international frame of political, social and scholarly reference was subjected to repeated reaffirmation: by the experience of royalists in exile during the mid-seventeenth century, the accession of William III

in 1688, the military campaigns of the Duke of Marlborough, and the fashionable enthusiasm for travel as education. In the learned world, the successful re-launch of university printing at Oxford by John Fell and his associates in the 1670s, and the same at Cambridge encouraged by Richard Bentley in the 1690s, were signs of new confidence – scholarly as well as financial.[33] Questions of British identity came to the fore in the first years of the eighteenth century, but the debate on libraries and national status as well as necessity was by then well in place. It was viewed partly as one of pride, but it was one with political, economic and scholarly incentives. In practical terms, the questions converged on a succession of proposals for the acquisition of various major private libraries that came on the market in the late seventeenth and early eighteenth centuries.

In 1697 Bentley drew attention to the state of the Royal Library: its numismatic collections lost, its manuscripts without covers, its books sent in under the Licensing Acts still in quires for want of binding, and no books having been bought from overseas for sixty years. He proposed not only a new building, but also that Parliament should settle an annual revenue, which was to be spent under the control of a board of curators. To raise this, Bentley suggested that there should be an increase in the tax on imported paper, a measure that would encourage domestic production. He envisaged a library of 200,000 volumes, accessible to the public. He even allowed himself also to imagine how the interior might appear:

> . . . cased on the inside with Marbles of ancient Inscriptions, Basso Relievo's, &c. either found in our own Kingdom, or easily and cheaply to be had from the *African* Coast, and *Asia* the Less. Those few Antiquities procured from the *Greek* Islands by the Lord *Arundel*, and since published both at home and abroad, are an evidence what great advancement of Learning, and honour to the Nation may be acquired by this means.[34]

He further pointed out that both de Thou's library in France,[35] and Marquard Gude's in Germany, were available for purchase. In the event, the first was mostly absorbed into the library of the Marquis de Ménars, and then sold again in 1706 to the Duc de Rohan; the Gude library was sold at Hamburg in 1706. The library of Isaac Vossius, who died at Windsor in 1689, was sold to the University of Leiden in 1690, after Bentley had hoped that it might be obtained for the Bodleian Library and Evelyn had hoped for some Maecenas to give it to adorn Wren's new library at Trinity College, Cambridge.[36] Its loss to England was still lamented by Roger Gale and Samuel Johnson in the 1740s:[37]

> The sale of *Vossius's* Collection into a Foreign Country is, to this Day, regretted by Men of Letters; and if this Effort for the Prevention of another Loss of the same Kind should be disadvantageous to him, no Man will hereafter willingly risque his Fortune in the Cause of Learning.[38]

In 1738 Roger Gale had given his own manuscripts, estimated at about 500 volumes, to Trinity College, his *alma mater*, intending thereby that they should not be dispersed or even lost.[39] Bentley had appealed to national sentiment, but no-one was more alert than he to the needs of foreign scholars as well. The two aims were not incompatible, as he spoke of advancing the glory of England 'by erecting a free Library of all sorts of Books, where every Foreigner will have such convenience of studying'.

> 'Tis our Publick Interest and Profit, to have the Gentry of Foreign nations acquainted with *England*, and have part of their Education here. And more Money will be annually imported and spent here by such Students from abroad, than the Whole Charge and revenue of the Library will amount to.

Just how great such economic benefits might have been can only be a matter for speculation. That British scholarship was a part of Europe's, and vice versa, was not a matter for dispute; and the wisdom of encouraging overseas visitors to learn more about Britain was simply an extension of the same agenda to different kinds of people. Where some of his contemporaries saw comparisons between English and foreign libraries as questions of competition, Bentley saw them, more profoundly and with a longer view, as a means of integration.

In the century between about 1660 and 1760, the scholarly focus of library provision changed from private to public, and with it changed the focus of responsibility. In England the context was defined roughly by the library clauses in the Licensing Act of 1662, and by the founding of the British Museum in 1753 (and its opening to the public in 1759). Broadly similar issues can be identified overseas.[40] In Sweden, legislation was enacted in 1661 directing that one copy of every new publication should be given to the Royal Library.[41] In Germany, the Kurfürstliche Bibliothek zu Cölln an der Spree, opened in the same year, became the foundation for the present Deutsche Staatsbibliothek; the university library at Göttingen dates from 1734.[42] In Denmark, the founding of the Royal Library in Copenhagen in the early 1660s by Frederick III was based on the acquisition of three private collections; provisions for legal deposit were introduced in 1697.[43] In Naples the Brancacci library was founded thanks to Cardinal Brancacci in 1675; in Rome the Biblioteca Casanatense was opened to the public in 1701;[44] and in Florence in 1714 the scholarly and chaotic Antonio Magliabechi left his books to the people of his city: the library was eventually opened in 1747.[45] The university library at Bologna dated its foundation from 1712, and at Turin the university library was amalgamated with the library of the Dukes of Savoy in the 1720s.[46] In Madrid the Biblioteca Nacional was opened in 1712.[47]

These new foundations, most of them coming within a single generation, differed widely in their details, but much of their apparent impetus came from widespread and frequently expressed anxieties at the increasing numbers of books being published.[48] Often, they were also responses to new forms of scientific enquiry in the widest sense. Libraries were seen as a means of controlling and re-ordering knowledge, as well as of collecting books. Though there was often provision for legal deposit, this was not always pursued with much energy. At Vienna, where the Emperor Ferdinand II had sought to ensure that four copies of every book from German publishers were deposited in the Hofbibliothek, the acquisition of a succession of private libraries (including the Fugger library and that of Tycho Brahe in the mid-seventeenth century, and that of Prince Eugene of Savoy in 1738) were of much greater significance. In France, legal deposit had been established by François I in 1537, but the book and print trades required constant reminders of

their obligations;[49] and in England, despite the agitations of Richard Bentley as Royal Librarian, the legislation was followed only very casually for the Royal Library, Oxford and Cambridge alike.[50] The real issues, however, were not about keeping pace with the flood of new books, but about transitions from private to public responsibility of all kinds – for historic manuscripts and documents, early and modern printed books and access to modern research.

As for London, there was no such library to be seen. For the public, that of Lambeth Palace stood on the other side of the river,[51] and Archbishop Thomas Tenison's more recently founded library (1684) at St Martin-in-the-Fields offered only a modicum of provision.[52] Neither was well-endowed, and at Lambeth the fortunes of the library inevitably depended heavily on the interests of the current Archbishop of Canterbury. For the City clergy there were Sion College[53] and the library of St Paul's Cathedral.[54] The library founded under the terms of the will of Daniel Williams, and opened to the public in 1729, had quickly developed into one especially for dissenters, but it had no money for purchases.[55] In 1707 there had been talk of amalgamating the Royal Library with the Cottonian and that of the Royal Society. Among other benefits, this would have brought before a wider public the wide-ranging library of the Earl of Arundel (d.1646), with more recent work; but nothing happened.[56]

The long-felt need for a public library in London that might be compared with those in Paris was not lost on the Harleys. As their library grew, so Edward Harley in particular seems to have contemplated its future as an independent endowment.[57] However, the financial retrenchment of the last months of his life meant that this idea had to be abandoned. Instead, as the learned world contemplated the dispersal of his collections, Roger Gale hoped that the manuscripts might be obtained for the Bodleian Library.[58] A little later the historian Thomas Carte put forward an audacious suggestion that the twelve great City livery companies should collaborate in erecting a library at the top of the new Mansion House currently in course of construction under the guidance of George Dance.[59] The Harleian manuscripts would serve as the foundation collection for such a collection. As a Jacobite exile working on the history of England, Carte had benefited greatly from the libraries of Paris; but in 1747 he was still complaining of London's lack of an adequate public library (by which he meant one that would meet his need for historical research):

> There is not a day in the week, but there is some well-furnished library open at *Paris*, for the inquisitive world to repair thither and peruse the authors they have occasion to consult: and for the most opulent city upon earth, the metropolis of a great and learned nation, to labour under a defect of this kind, looks as if learning, the friend and the support of liberty, met here with little encouragement from the publick, however it may be cultivated by private persons, in despight of all difficulties.[60]

Carte's proposal of 1743 was a limited one, depending on an endowment of no more than £4,000. His arguments were based (appropriately enough for the City) on commerce, and on freedom. A library was a political as well as learned tool. This was no new argument; though he did not do so, he might have reminded his readers of Cotton's purposes early in the previous century.[61] Singling out 'Trade, History, and Antiquity', he noted that

> Learning of this kind is of all others the most discouraged by a corrupt Administration, who would fain engross all the materials thereof to themselves, and care to see it in no hands but those of their own creatures, who would prostitute it to their purposes.[62]

The City was uniquely qualified. 'No Body of men have ever distinguished themselves more eminently in the cause of Liberty than the City has always done: the Nation looks upon her as one of the chief bulwarks of her liberties.' Such a library would '. . . remain to all future ages an irrefragable evidence of those rights and liberties which our ancestors enjoyed, and, conveying down inviolate to our times, have entailed upon us the obligation of transmitting them safe to posterity'.

At best, parts of Carte's arguments were special pleading, based on one interpretation of the Civil War and a view where, for the moment, the different political structures of France and Britain were concealed. Just as for others of his generation engaged in different activities, comparisons with France had to be discreetly selective.

To some extent, the preoccupations of those who, in the wake of Sloane's will, promoted the new Museum can be discovered in the ways that the British Museum Act was framed.[63] First, and most obviously, though the first element to be mentioned was the multifarious collection of Sloane, it was overwhelmingly about books: 'An Act for the Purchase of the *Museum*, or Collection of Sir *Hans Sloane*, and of the Harleian Collection of manuscripts; and for providing One General Repository for the better Reception and more convenient Use of the said Collections; and of the *Cottonian Library*, and of the Additions thereto.' Adopting the phrasing of the codicil, it went on to define Sloane's 'museum': 'consisting of all his Library of Books, Drawings, Manuscripts, Prints, Medals, and Coins, ancient and modern Antiquities, Seals, Cameos, and Intaglios, Precious Stones, Agates, Jaspers, Vessels of Agate and Jasper, Chrystals, Mathematical Instruments, Drawings, and Pictures, and all other Things in the said Collection or Museum.'

The wording of the Act reveals also the distinctions between the Sloane and Cotton[64] collections, as they were perceived by the draftsmen. In particular, the Cotton library included 'the most useful Manuscripts, written Books, Papers, Parchments, Records, and other Memorials . . . for the Knowledge and Preservation of our Constitution both in Church and State'. The Harleian manuscripts[65] were treated more summarily, perhaps (we might guess) less through ignorance or lack of appreciation than because the draftsmen saw no need to rehearse a more general collection that had been the subject of gossip for several years.

Those whose money is sought for acquisitions tend to be alert to unnecessary duplication. In this there was some necessarily careful wording so as to emphasise the complementary nature of the foundation collections, particularly Sloane's in natural philosophy and Cotton's in national history and historical identity. By contrast, the issue of access could be dealt with straightforwardly. In the 1690s the subject had lain at the centre of the row involving Richard Bentley as Royal Librarian. Both Sloane and Harley had been generous in permitting scholars to use their libraries. In this they were but

the latest representatives of a long-standing tradition, one that the Act now sought to extend to 'free access . . . to all studious and curious Persons'. Legally, if not in practice, access to the records of (amongst other matters) Church and State was to be more nearly (albeit by no means completely) democratic, not based on the autocracies of scholarship or private introductions. Though slipped into the Act quietly enough, it was one of the most innovative of all the provisions for a new kind of library.

But then the whole had to be brought together, and here the Act was explicit concerning 'the Principal Librarian to whom the Care and Custody of the said General Repository shall be chiefly committed'. This was the title that remained in use until the end of the nineteenth century.[66] In 1753, the Museum was to be in the charge of an official with the title of Librarian. In many respects, the Act was imaginative and forward-looking. It took a unique opportunity to unite the three most important private collections in the country. It arranged for the whole to be funded by a lottery, on which its extremely specific directions make clear that this was not a matter of everyday trust or familiarity. It took a cautiously populist approach, in that the new creation was 'not only for the inspection and entertainment of the learned and curious, but for the general use and benefit of the publick'. Nonetheless, in its management, and therefore in its scope, the fundamental concept was rooted in tradition.

In some respects the tradition of library as museum has become almost as familiar to modern historians as it was to the eighteenth century in practice.[67] George Vertue's engraved frontispiece to the auction catalogue of the Harleian pictures, prints and sculpture (fig.19) celebrated much more than books, and included portrait paintings, busts of classical figures, classical sculpture, urns and other remains, a numismatic collection, seals and prints – of Hollar in particular.[68] In the public re-ordering of knowledge epitomized in, for example, the removal of the geological and natural history collections to South Kensington in the 1880s[69] and extraction of the books and manuscripts to form part of the new British Library in 1973, this view of coherence in memory, inspiration and creation was later to be deliberately set aside. Knowledge was not merely to be socially defined and organized; it was to be defined and organized according to principles of divergence. The tradition exemplified in the Sloane collections was lost in the dispersal of the British Museum, but it is still to be seen, to a degree, in Paris in the Bibliothèque Nationale,[70] and (to a lesser extent, very much simplified) in the more recent formation of the Pierpont Morgan Library in New York, where books, manuscripts, paintings and other works of art are combined in a single collection. In Germany, the Stiftung Preussischer Kulturbesitz draws many of its principles from this same theme of unifying different forms of creation.[71] To the educated of the seventeenth and eighteenth centuries (as well as long before and for some time afterwards), libraries were repositories of knowledge in forms not just of books and manuscripts. Antiquities and other natural or man-made objects all contributed to a single purpose. Coins, medals, prints, drawings, paintings, sculpture and even furniture were but different forms of knowledge. So, too, were the natural history collections of Sloane.[72] By means of scientific instruments, the natural world could be investigated. Globes were obvious needs. Portrait busts and paintings were not only inspirations from past generations, a

David McKitterick

purpose given modern credence and authority by ancient practice.[73] They were also means of modern identity, whether in private family likenesses or in the choices that marked one library from another as much as did the choice of books on the shelves. Natural history collections, including geological, botanical and zoological specimens, provided knowledge of a kind that could not necessarily be drawn from books. Engravings and printed or manuscript accounts offered one range of explanations and meanings; the desiccated or fragmentary specimens offered another. The two were complementary. Even the more *outré* examples in the older cabinets of curiosities, such as unicorns' horns, maintained this relationship between the two- and the three-dimensional, the recorded and the observable. As Claude du Molinet succinctly phrased it in probably the best known of all catalogues of its kind, such collections were intended '*servir aux belles lettres*'.[74]

Understandably, the three foundation collections of the British Museum have attracted much attention. Slightly less has been paid to the gift by George II in 1757 of the so-called Old Royal Library, reaching back at least to the reign of Edward IV.[75] Ever since the fire at Ashburnham House that had so damaged the Cotton manuscripts, it had been housed with that collection in the old dormitory of Westminster School. Bentley's hopes for a better future had come to nothing, and little money had been spent since. Had Queen Mary lived, the tale might have been different, for she was generally thought to have had a stronger interest in such matters than did her husband.[76] The addition of the Royal Library to the new museum was in some measure simply a tidying-up, as it followed its companion Cotton manuscripts to Montagu House. As David Casley had remarked to Lord Hardwicke in 1742, the Cotton and the Royal Libraries made 'a better figure & one more useful together than separate'.[77] But it had a much greater resonance and significance than simply as a complement to a collection of manuscripts. It was fundamental to the subsequent development of the Museum not just in its incomparable collections of manuscripts and printed books (we may note the absence, in this instance, of other artefacts or natural curiosities), but also because of the legal advantage it enjoyed, founded on the terms of the Licensing Act of 1662. In common with the University Library at Cambridge and the Bodleian Library at Oxford, it was entitled to one copy of each book published in Britain. The much older concept of legal deposit had formed a cornerstone of the French royal library since 1537, but the similarities between the English and the French royal libraries were otherwise limited.[78]

As Royal Librarian during the 1690s, the young Richard Bentley had made considerable efforts to improve the position of the library, with respect both to its legal claims and its national position if not status. He argued, unsuccessfully, for better premises, and he looked forward to the day when funds needed for war could be freed for the promotion of the Library. He could, however, do little about access. In Paris, Louvois was providing a special room in which to seat readers using the royal library. In London, Bentley was accused (not altogether justly) of discouraging readers, but it is true that he considered the state of the library to be so bad that he preferred makeshift arrangements in his own lodgings for those wishing to consult its greatest treasure, the Codex Alexandrinus.[79]

When compared with the French Royal Library, the differences were apparent not just in scale, but also in national status and focus, and in use. Under the energetic management of Jean-Paul Bignon, *Bibliothécaire du Roi* from 1719 to 1741, its organization was put on a modern footing, and new premises were found for it in the Hôtel de Nevers, originally erected by Mazarin in the rue de Richelieu.[80] The manuscripts of Baluze had been acquired in 1719,[81] the de Mesmes collection came in 1731,[82] the early manuscripts from Limoges in 1730,[83] and the Colbert manuscripts in 1732, after four years' negotiation.[84] In all these transactions, some of them involving large sums of money, there was a willingness to invest that was wholly lacking in England. It was not just a question of scale, of England's exchequer compared with that of France; it was also a question of energy and political and public confidence. The French Royal Library did not belong to the nation in the sense that was to be established with the trustees of the British Museum; but it did stand as a centre of national identity. For anyone seeking to make comparisons, it was both the most obvious and the most relevant. The tendency for collections of national importance to gravitate from private into national responsibility, already evident in the late seventeenth century, was becoming a matter of public policy.

The public emphasis of the foundation collections of the British Museum was on manuscripts, in value as well as in content. Cotton's printed books, perhaps dispersed much earlier, were not mentioned;[85] those of the Harleian library had gone, together with a fine collection of prints, to the London bookseller Thomas Osborne, who (as we have seen) offered them in a series of catalogues in 1743–5. For printed books, as distinct from manuscripts, the Museum possessed those of Sloane, amounting to perhaps 45,000 volumes, of which perhaps as much as one-third were medical.[86] The Old Royal Library not only brought a further, and magnificent collection of manuscripts; it also brought a collection of about 9,000 printed books that complemented those of Sloane at many turns.[87] Though the most recent volumes were unbound, as they had been delivered from the book trade under the terms of legal deposit, their presence gave to the new library at least the semblance of balance that even Sloane's broad interests could not encompass. The result was very far from comprehensive, in either its subject-matter or its level of scholarship and attainment; but it provided a basis for the future.

All these issues lay behind the creation of a national library. In the absence of such a library, the onus had been on private collectors to assemble what may be called the historical record. Cotton's purpose had been political, and the British Museum Act of 1753 made clear that this was remembered as its chief justification. Its location in Westminster was in itself a powerful physical statement of a political point. When in 1733 plans were put forward by William Kent for rebuilding the Houses of Parliament, it was initially envisaged that the Cotton library would be housed in the galleries of the great basilica that was to serve as meeting ground between the Lords and Commons. In later stages of the plans this was dropped, but the topography of politics had identified the continuing national importance of a collection that had originally been assembled to meet the needs and challenges of the reign of James I.[88]

Under the terms of his original will, Sloane's collections were to be offered at the price of £20,000 first to the King, for him to purchase and present to the country.[89] There was some precedent for this, in that in 1715 George I had been persuaded by Lord Townshend, Secretary of State, to buy the library of John Moore, Bishop of Ely, and present it to the University of Cambridge. The circumstances were, however, different. Moore had left no provision for his books, and there were several parties interested in their purchase after his death; and the gift to Cambridge was heavily influenced by political need. All this was public knowledge, and Sloane had known Moore as a collector.[90] Three decades later, such a proceeding no longer seemed feasible. Instead, in a codicil Sloane provided for trustees who would apply either to the King or to Parliament for the requisite sum. Three possibilities that he had originally envisaged, of sale either to the Royal Society or to the University of Oxford or to the College of Physicians at Edinburgh, were now set aside. Instead, his next preferences were for the academies at St Petersburg, Paris, Berlin or Madrid. Sloane was connected with them all, but the nature of his challenge was unmistakable. It was to Britain: not, therefore, to an institution, but to the country. By implicitly acknowledging the difficulties that would face any of the institutions he had mentioned originally, Sloane redefined national responsibility. Just as opportunities to purchase other libraries, either domestic or from overseas, had been lost, so now there was an explicit threat of export if money was not forthcoming. Sloane's will was cast in the context of an international debate that was not only about money, but also about national resolve and self-determination.

Amidst mid-eighteenth-century questions of national identity, there were more personal issues. In conclusion, it may be suggested that one particular link may have coloured the course of thought in the events of the 1750s. Lord Hardwicke, Lord Chancellor and one of the three *ex officio* principal trustees of the British Museum, had been High Steward[91] of the University of Cambridge since 1749, having served before that as University Counsel since 1724. His son Philip Yorke (later the 2nd Earl) was one of the trustees of Sloane's will. The family connections with the University were strong, and apart from a brief interruption by William Pitt successive Earls were High Stewards from 1749 until 1834.[92] The connections were further strengthened by the proximity to Cambridge of Hardwicke's estate at Wimpole, which he had bought from Edward Lord Harley in 1739 and where James Gibbs had been employed to design a room to house many of the Harleian manuscripts and printed books.[93] These and other links between Government and Cambridge brought concomitant hopes of promotion in the minds of many people in the University.[94] More important to the future of the British Museum, they also meant that events in Cambridge were well-known in Whitehall.

On the accession of George II in 1727, the University presented a volume of printed verses by its members to the new King.[95] Such volumes, elaborately bound up, were customary for royal occasions, and their presentation at court was a matter of some moment to the University as a whole. Contributions, by its resident members, were mostly in Latin or Greek, and occasionally in Hebrew or Arabic. A few were, sometimes, in English. As usual, the contributors in 1727 included heads of houses, regius professors, fellows of colleges and a few undergraduates. The whole compilation was as much a matter of honour and politics as a spontaneous outpouring of patriotism.

The volume was intended as both a memorial to George I and a celebration of his son. Most of the contributors not unnaturally focused on the future. Nevertheless, for the University as a whole, by far the most important act of the late King had been his donation in 1715 of the entire library of John Moore. Thanks to an epigram, this was long recalled as an act inspired primarily by political need, to secure the loyalty of a body containing many people who were at best uncomfortable with the Hanoverian succession.[96] More importantly, it brought to Cambridge a library celebrated on the Continent, as well as in Britain, as one unparalleled in Moore's generation, for its manuscripts and for its early printed books. Moore, Bishop successively of Norwich and of Ely, had been in the circle that included Bentley, Locke and others who had argued for a stronger royal library as a national institution. On his death, Wanley had hoped that it might be acquired by Lord Harley.[97] Amongst his own books were the then earliest known manuscript of Bede (published by the University Press in 1722) and the finest collection of works printed by Caxton then in existence (which became the basis of a study published in 1735[98]). Its arrival not merely trebled the size of the old University Library; the privileges of copyright deposit, confirmed in the Copyright Act of Queen Anne in 1710, were now joined to an earlier collection of international importance. By his gift, George I had created a library of a status that could justifiably be defined as national.

It was this newly born library that the *Bibliothecarius* of the day, Samuel Hadderton, now celebrated at length in the verses published in the volume of 1727. Other books, acquired since 1715, extended the geographical frame of reference beyond Europe. Hadderton had more than just books to celebrate, for in 1727 he also had hopes that royal interest would be taken in the proposed new library buildings. Nothing came of the buildings. More importantly, perhaps, Moore's library was known formally, in Cambridge as in the wider world of scholarship, as the Royal Library, thus to distinguish it from the old, pre-existing, collections.

George II was reminded of all this on his coronation. However little the new King may have noted them at the time, or recalled them afterwards, they stood in print as a reminder also to those who advised him in the 1750s. The public and scholarly beneficence, and the European (not merely British) dimensions were examples that might be followed. Both bibliographically and politically, the adding of the Old Royal Library to the new British Museum was more than a convenience, a tidying-up of space left only partially occupied following the departure of the Cotton manuscripts from Westminster. If a precedent or an encouragement was to be sought for the gift by the King of the Library to the Nation, it was to be found not among the other London collections of the 1740s, but in his father's example at Cambridge.

However, there was a further and greater difference, not between 1715 and the 1750s, but between England and France. England created a national library, and in doing so not merely found a new answer to an old question, but also wrought a revolution in the way that research libraries were to be conceived, funded and organized. Until 1789, France retained the Royal Library as her principal library of record. In France, the great collections documented by Delisle were drawn towards a library that remained essentially socially exclusive, whatever the provisions for readers. The idea that a monarch might give a major collection to another library or institution, whether in Paris or in the provinces, did not arise. By contrast, the drift in England was away from the monarch. George I gave Moore's books to Cambridge, and George II gave the old Royal Library to the Nation. The privileges of legal deposit passed from the Royal Library to the new national one. Such actions had been initiated by discussions conducted in terms of bibliophily, scholarship and politics, using language that remained remarkably consistent between the 1660s and the 1750s. To a great extent, Johnson was simply developing these themes in the 1760s. Even Bentley, for all his astuteness and eagerness to press the case for the royal library with whatever arguments he could muster (in 1700 he owed his appointment as Master of Trinity College, Cambridge, to royal patronage), did not press a political point. But in the Enlightenment wording of the British Museum Act is a hint that in the 1750s political and constitutional implications were not forgotten: 'not only for the inspection and entertainment of the learned and curious, but for the general use and benefit of the publick'.

Notes and references

1   Charlotte Lennox, *The Female Quixote*, ed. Margaret Dalziel (Oxford, 1970), chap.i.
2   Various aspects of this are surveyed in John Brewer and Roy Porter (eds), *Consumption and the World of Goods* (London, 1993) and Anne Bermingham and John Brewer (eds), *The Consumption of Culture, 1600–1800: Image, object, text* (London, 1995); see also Lorna Weatherill, *Consumer Behaviour and Material Culture in Britain, 1660–1760*, 2nd edn (London, 1996) and, for a summary with further reading, James Raven, 'Du qui au comment; à la recherche d'une histoire de la lecture en Angleterre', in Roger Chartier (ed.), *Histoires de la lecture; un bilan de recherches* (Paris, 1995), pp.141–63. The majority of the most dramatic extensions to the publishing and popular library markets occurred in the second half of the century.
3   Johnson to Barnard, 28 May 1768: Samuel Johnson, *Letters*, ed. Bruce Redford, 5 vols (Princeton, 1992–4), vol.i, p.308.
4   Simone Balayé, *La Bibliothèque nationale des origines à 1800* (Geneva, 1988), offers no evidence of large-scale purchases from the Harleian books for the French Royal Library. But the Danish statesman Count Otto Thott (1703–85) was a heavy buyer, his purchases including about 150 incunabula: see Victor Madsen, *Katalog over det Kongelige Bibliotheks inkunabler*, 2 vols (Copenhagen, 1931–8).
5   Johnson's account of the Harleian library was first published in *Proposals for printing by subscription the first two volumes of Bibliotheca Harleiana* (London, 1742); it was also printed in the *Gentleman's Magazine* 12 (1742), pp.636–9, and again in the first volume of Thomas Osborne's *Catalogus Bibliothecae Harleianae* (London, 1743–5), pp.1–8. See also D. McKitterick, 'Thomas Osborne, Samuel Johnson and the learned of foreign nations; a forgotten catalogue', *Book Collector* 41 (1992), pp.55–68. For Osborne and Johnson see Thomas Kaminski, *The Early Career of Samuel Johnson* (Oxford, 1987), pp.174–84.
6   Johnson, op. cit. (note 3), vol.i, p 309: Redford notes Johnson's meaning of 'curious': 'elegant; neat; laboured; finished'.
7   In Dublin, apart from Trinity College, Archbishop Marsh's library was founded by *An act for settling and preserving a publick library for ever in the house . . . built by His Grace Narcissus, now Lord Arch Bishop of Armagh* (1707). In Edinburgh, the privileges of copyright deposit were enjoyed from 1710 onwards by the Faculty of Advocates (library opened 1689) and the University Library. See also, more generally, Thomas Kelly, *Early Public Libraries: A history of public libraries in Great Britain before 1850* (London, 1966). For cathedral libraries see the references gathered in E. Anne Read, *A Checklist of Books, Catalogues and Periodical Articles relating to the Cathedral Libraries of England* (Oxford Bibliographical Society, 1970); for Anglican parish libraries see Michael Perkin, *A Directory of the Parochial Libraries of the Church of England and the Church in Wales* (Bibliographical Society, 2003). Discussion of these and other libraries will be included in the *Cambridge History of Libraries in Britain* (3 vols, Cambridge, forthcoming).
8   Though he has little specifically to say on museums and libraries in the first half of the century, many other aspects of this connection are explored in T.C.W. Blanning, *The Culture of Power and the Power of Culture: Old Regime Europe, 1660–1789* (Oxford, 2002). For translation, see for example Bernhard Fabian, *The English Book in Eighteenth-Century Germany* (London, 1992).
9   Robert Damien, *Bibliothèque et état; naissance d'une raison politique dans la France du xviiᵉ siècle* (Paris, 1995). Gabriel Naudé's *Advis pour dresser une bibliothèque* (Paris, 1627, rev. 1644) has been published in facsimile with an introduction by Claude Jolly (Paris, 1990); John Evelyn's English translation was first published in 1661, but seems not to have found a long-term following: there was no further edition until 1903. See also Jean Viardot, 'Naissance de la bibliophilie; les cabinets de livres rares', in Claude Jolly (ed.), *Histoire des bibliothèques françaises. Les bibliothèques sous l'Ancien Régime, 1530–1789* (Paris, 1988), pp.269–89.
10 Seneca, *Epistolae*, ii. See also P. Le Gallois, *Traitté des plus belles bibliothèques de l'Europe* (Paris, 1680), p.3: 'A multitude of books is a distraction; therefore, since you cannot read everything that you may possess, possess only as many as you can manage.'
11 The manuscript is Cambridge University Library, MS Ff.1.24, given by Matthew Parker in 1574: J.C.T. Oates, *Cambridge University Library: A history; from the beginnings to the Copyright Act of Queen Anne* (Cambridge, 1986), pp.106–7, with further references.
12 Trinity College, Cambridge, MS R.5.25. This manuscript was originally prepared for Prince Henry himself.
13 Eileen Harris and Nicholas Savage, *British Architectural Books and Writers, 1556–1785* (Cambridge, 1990), pp.268–9, 273–4.
14 S. Roscoe, *John Newbery and his Successors, 1740–1814* (Wormley, 1973).
15 Ibid., cat. J219.
16 Ibid., cat. J253. About twenty editions had appeared by the end of the century.
17 Jean Sgard, *Dictionnaire des journaux*, 2 vols (Paris, 1991), with further references.
18 Theodore Besterman, *The Beginnings of Systematic Bibliography* (Oxford, 1935); Luigi Balsamo, *La bibliografia; storia di una tradizione* (Florence, 1984), trans. as *Bibliography: History of a tradition* (Berkeley, 1990). Some of these topics are explored further in Roger Chartier, *L'ordre des livres* (Aix-en-Provence, 1992), trans. as *The Order of Books* (Cambridge, 1994), chap. 3, 'Libraries without walls'.
19 Gessner's *Bibliotheca universalis* was published at Zurich in 1545, and his *Pandectarum sive partitionum universalium . . . libri xxi* in 1548. See also (in a very large literature) Hans Fischer, 'Conrad Gessner (1516–1565) as bibliographer and encyclopedist', *The Library*, 5th ser. 21 (1966), pp.269–81; Alfredo Serrai, *Conrad Gesner*, ed. Maria Cochetti (Rome, 1990); Helmut Zedelmaier, *Bibliotheca universalis und Bibliotheca selecta; das Problem der Ordnung des gelehrten Wissens in der frühen Neuzeit* (Cologne, 1992).
20 *The Spring-Garden Journal*, nos 1–4 ('Printed: and sold at Mr. Meyer's Library in May's-Buildings, St Martin's-Lane; where letters to the authoress are taken in', 1752). The author was Bonnell Thornton, one of whose targets was Henry Fielding: see Martin C. and Ruth R. Battestin, *Henry Fielding: A life* (1989), p.423. Meyer had opened his library, in an alleyway off the east side of St Martin's Lane, in 1751: Mier's (or Meyer's) coffee house had stood in King Street, Bloomsbury (the modern Southampton Row), c.1720–40: see Bryant Lillywhite, *London Coffee Houses* (London, 1963), p.366. For contemporary circulating libraries see Archibald Clarke, 'The reputed first circulating subscription library in London', *The Library* 2nd ser.1 (1900), pp.274–89; Hilda M. Hamlyn, 'Eighteenth-century circulating libraries in England', *The Library*, 5th ser. 1 (1947), pp.197–222; Paul Kaufman, 'The community library: a chapter in actions of the English social history', *Transactions of the American Philosophical Society*, new ser. 57 (1967), pp.1–65; Paul Kaufman, 'Coffee houses as reading centres', in his *Libraries and their Users: Collected papers in library history* (London, 1969), pp.115–27.
21 Zachary Langton, *An essay concerning the human rational soul. In three parts. Shewing i. The origin, ii. The nature, iii. The excellency of this soul, upon natural as well as revealed principles* (Liverpool: printed for R. Williamson at his circulating library, 1755).

22 The increase in the market specifically for women's reading was marked partly by the founding of magazines such as *The Lady's Magazine* (1733), *Queen Anne's Weekly Journal, or the Ladies Magazine* (1735), *The Female Spectator* (1744: by Eliza Haywood, and much reprinted), *The Lady's Weekly Magazine* (1747), *The Ladies Magazine* (1749), *The New Universal Magazine, or Gentleman and Lady's Companion* (1751) and *The Lady's Magazine* (1759).

23 Ian Philip, *The Bodleian Library in the Seventeenth and Eighteenth Centuries* (Oxford, 1983).

24 James Gibbs, *Bibliotheca Radcliviana* (London, 1747); S.G. Gillam, *The Building Accounts of the Radcliffe Camera* (Oxford Historical Society, new ser 13, 1948); *Bibliotheca Radcliviana, 1749–1949: Catalogue of an exhibition . . .* (Oxford, 1949); Sir Edmund Craster, *The History of All Souls College Library*, E.F. Jacob (ed.) (London, 1971); Dean Cook and John Mason (eds), *The Building Accounts of Christ Church Library, 1716–1779* (Oxford, 1988).

25 David McKitterick (ed.), *The Making of the Wren Library, Trinity College, Cambridge* (Cambridge, 1995).

26 Gregorio Leti, *The Life of Pope Sixtus the Fifth*, trans. Philip Farneworth (London, 1754), p.378. Leti's work was originally published in 1669.

27 This ninth-century manuscript was made for Charles the Bald; now Munich, Bayerische Staatsbibliothek, MS Clm 14000.

28 Le Gallois, *Traitté des plus belles bibliothèques de l'Europe* (Paris, 1680), pp.113–14. For another view, compiled without knowledge of Le Gallois, see Johannes Lomeier, *De bibliothecis*, 2nd edn (Utrecht, 1680): the most pertinent chapter has been conveniently translated and edited by John Warwick Montgomery as *A Seventeenth-Century View of European Libraries: Lomeier's De bibliothecis, chapter x* (Berkeley, 1962).

29 Angela Delaforce, *Art and Patronage in Eighteenth-Century Portugal* (Cambridge, 2002).

30 Le Gallois, op. cit. (note 10), p.122. These and other libraries are treated in Jolly, op. cit. (note 9).

31 Pierre Gasnault, 'De la bibliothèque de Mazarin à la bibliothèque Mazarine', in Jolly, op. cit. (note 9), pp.135–45, at p.143.

32 For this aspect of the Republic of Letters see Françoise Waquet, 'Qu'est-ce que la République des Lettres? Essai de sémantique historique', *Bibliothèque de l'Ecole des Chartes* 147 (1989), pp.473–502; Anne Goldgar, *Impolite Learning: Conduct and community in the Republic of Letters, 1680–1750* (New Haven, 1995).

33 Stanley Morison and Harry Carter, *John Fell, the University Press and the 'Fell' Types* (Oxford, 1967); David McKitterick, *A History of Cambridge University Press*, vol. II: *Scholarship and commerce, 1698–1872* (Cambridge, 1998).

34 Richard Bentley, *A Proposal for building a Royal Library, and establishing it by Act of Parliament* (London, 1697), reprinted in A.T. Bartholomew, *Richard Bentley, D.D.; A bibliography* (Cambridge, 1908), pp.93–6. For the Arundel marbles at Oxford see Z.C. von Uffenbach, *Merkwürdige Reisen durch Niedersachsen, Holland und Engelland* (Ulm, 1753–4), vol.III, pp.121–6. See also D.E. Haynes, *The Arundel Marbles* (Oxford, 1975) and David Howarth, *Lord Arundel and his Circle* (New Haven, 1985). Bentley had partly in mind Humphrey Prideaux, *Marmora Oxoniensia, ex Arundellianis, Seldenianis, aliisque conflata* (Oxford, 1676): see also Harry Carter, *A History of the Oxford University Press*, vol.I: *To the year 1780* (Oxford, 1975), pp.83–6.

35 Antoine Coron, 'Ut prosint aliis; Jacques-Auguste de Thou et sa bibliothèque', in Jolly, op. cit. (note 9), pp.101–25.

36 Philip, op. cit. (note 23), p.61; John Evelyn to Samuel Pepys, 12 August 1689: John Evelyn, *Diary and Correspondence*, ed. H.B. Wheatley, 4 vols (London, 1906), vol.III, p.450. The sale to Leiden is briefly recounted in K.A. de Meyer, *Codices Vossiani latini*, vol.I (Leiden, 1973), pp.ix–xii. The catalogue of Vossius's manuscripts printed in Edward Bernard, *Catalogus librorum manuscriptorum Angliae et Hiberniae in unum collecti* (Oxford, 1697–8), vol.II, pp.62–9, was made in the 1680s. In 1710 Thomas Hearne made a note of the library, and of hopes that Oxford would take an interest. Some authorities since have assumed that the collection was still for sale at that date: see, for example, W. D. Macray, *Annals of the Bodleian Library, Oxford*, 2nd edn (Oxford, 1890), p.179.

37 Gale to Stukeley, 11 December 1741: William Stukeley, *Family Memoirs*, 3 vols, vol.I (Durham, 1882–7), p.327. See also F. F. Blok, *Contributions to the History of Isaac Vossius's Library* (Amsterdam, 1974); Elfriede Hulshoff Pol, 'The library', in Th.H. Lunsingh Scheurleer and G.H. Posthumus Meyjes (eds), *Leiden University in the Seventeenth Century: An exchange of learning* (Leiden, 1975), pp. 394–459.

38 Samuel Johnson, *Proposals for printing by subscription the . . . Bibliotheca Harleiana* (London, 1742). See also note 3 above.

39 M.R. James, *The Western Manuscripts in the Library of Trinity College, Cambridge*, 4 vols (Cambridge, 1900–4), vol.III, p.vi. Gale's original letter is MS O.11.29, fol.1.

40 Summary accounts of national libraries and major university libraries are conveniently provided in David H. Stam (ed.), *International Dictionary of Library Histories*, 2 vols (Chicago, 2001).

41 Arundell Esdaile, *National Libraries of the World: Their history, administration and public services*, rev. F.J. Hill (1957), p.225. The status and nature of the collections in the Royal Library (much of which had been destroyed by fire in 1697) and Uppsala University Library were topics of concern in the mid-eighteenth century, and gave rise to two histories: see Magnus Olai Celsius, *Bibliothecae Regiae Stockholmensis historia* (Stockholm, 1751; rev. edn 1771) and Olof Celsius, *Bibliothecae Upsaliensis historia* (Uppsala, 1745).

42 Bernhard Fabian, 'An eighteenth-century research collection: English books at Göttingen University Library', *The Library*, 6th ser. 1 (1979), pp.209–24; see also his 'Göttingen als Forschungsbibliothek im achtzehnten Jahrhundert; Plädoyer für eine neue Bibliotheksgeschichte', in Paul Raabe (ed.), *Öffentliche und private Bibliotheken im 17. und 18. Jahrhundert* (Wolfenbüttel, 1977), pp.209–39.

43 Lauritz Nielsen, *Danske privatbibliotheker gennem tiderne* (Copenhagen, 1946) vol.I (no more published).

44 Carlo Pietrangeli, *La Biblioteca Casanatense* (Florence, 1993).

45 Maria Mannelli Goggioli, *La Biblioteca Magliabechiana. Libri, uomini, idee per la prima biblioteca pubblica a Firenze* (Florence, 2000).

46 Esdaile, op. cit. (note 41), p.183.

47 Ibid., p.191.

48 Some of this background is explored in Bruno Neveu, *Erudition et religion aux xviie et xviiie siècles* (Paris, 1994), pp.25–92.

49 Robert Estivals, *Le dépôt légal sous l'ancien régime de 1537 à 1791* (Paris, 1961).

50 R.C. Barrington Partridge, *The History of the Legal Deposit of Books throughout the British Empire* (London, 1938); Philip, op. cit. (note 23), pp.77–80; David McKitterick, *Cambridge University Library: A history. The eighteenth and nineteenth centuries* (Cambridge, 1986), pp.28–31, 35–44.

51 A.C. Ducarel, *The History and Antiquities of the Archiepiscopal Palace of Lambeth* (London, 1785), pp.47–76; M. R. James, 'The history of Lambeth Palace Library', *Transactions of the Cambridge Bibliographical Society* 3 (1959), pp.1–31; Geoffrey Bill, 'Lambeth Palace Library', *The Library*, 5th ser. 21 (1966), pp.192–206.

52 This library was dispersed at a series of auction sales on 3 June and 1 July 1861 and 23 January 1862. See also the evidence of Edward Edwards and the Revd Philip Hale to the Ewart Committee on Public Libraries, *Report from the Select Committee on Public Libraries* (London, 1849), paras 186–93 and 868–959.

53 William Reading, *Bibliothecae Cleri Londinensis in Collegio Sionensi catalogus* (London, 1724); E. H. Pearce, *Sion College and Library* (Cambridge, 1913). Some of the most valuable books were sold at Sotheby's on 13 June 1977; the library has since been divided between King's College, London, and Lambeth Palace, and some books have been sold.

54 This included a number of books given by Henry Compton (d. 1713) in 1692. The printed catalogue, W. Sparrow Simpson, *St Paul's Cathedral Library: A catalogue* (London, 1893), is very selective.

55 *A short account of the charity & library established under the will of the late Rev. Daniel Williams, D.D.* (London, 1917); the first catalogue had been published in 1727: *Bibliothecae quam vir doctus & admodum Reverendus, Daniel Williams . . . bono publico legavit, catalogus* (London, 1727).

56 Edward Edwards, *Lives of the Founders of the British Museum* (London, 1870), p.296. For the early Royal Society library, see *Bibliotheca Norfolciana* (London, 1681), and R.F. Sharp, *Catalogue of a Collection of Early Printed Books in the Library of the Royal Society* (1910). Many of the Arundel printed books were sold in the nineteenth century, and at Sotheby's, 4 May 1925. For the manuscripts, acquired by the British Museum in 1831, see Arundell Esdaile, *The British Museum Library: A short history and survey* (London, 1946), pp.65–6, 254–6.

57 George Vertue, *Notebooks,* 6 vols (Walpole Society 1930–55), vol.vi, pp.63–4.

58 Roger Gale to William Stukeley, 11 December 1741: Stukeley, op. cit. (note 37), p.327.

59 John Nichols, *Literary Anecdotes of the Eighteenth Century,* 8 vols (London, 1817–58), vol.ii, pp.509–12, quoting Thomas Carte's 'Proposal for erecting a library in the Mansion-House of the City of London', a paper communicated to Richard Rawlinson in 1743.

60 Thomas Carte, *General History of England,* 4 vols (London, 1747–55), vol.i, p.vi.

61 Kevin Sharpe, 'Introduction; rewriting Sir Robert Cotton', in C.J. Wright (ed.), *Sir Robert Cotton as Collector: Essays on an early Stuart courtier and his legacy* (London, 1997), pp.1–39.

62 Thomas Carte, 'Proposal', quoted in Nichols, op. cit. (note 59), p.511.

63 26 George II.c. 22.

64 Thomas Smith, *Catalogue of the Manuscripts in the Cottonian Library (1696) . . . reprinted from Sir Robert Harley's copy, annotated by Humfrey Wanley, together with documents relating to the fire of 1731,* ed. Colin G.C. Tite (Cambridge, 1984); Colin G.C. Tite, *The Manuscript Library of Sir Robert Cotton* (London, 1994); Wright, op. cit. (note 61).

65 The first summary of the Harleian manuscripts to be published after 1753 was the Preface to the *Catalogue of the Harleian Collection of Manuscripts* by Humfrey Wanley, Thomas Astle and others, published by order of the Trustees of the British Museum, 2 vols (London, 1759–63); the introduction and index, published separately as *A Preface and Index to the Harleian Collection of Manuscripts* (London, 1763), were intended to be bound up with the catalogue. See also C.E. and Ruth C. Wright (eds), *The Diary of Humfrey Wanley,* 2 vols (Bibliographical Society, 1966); C.E. Wright, *Fontes Harleiani* (London, 1972); Humfrey Wanley, *Letters,* ed. P.L. Heyworth (Oxford, 1989).

66 P.R. Harris, *A History of the British Museum Library, 1753–1973* (London, 1998), p.751. The first 'Director and Principal Librarian', to employ the term customarily employed until 1973, was Edward Maunde Thompson, who was appointed 'Principal Librarian' in 1888 and took up the new title in 1898.

67 For one well-documented survey see Franz Georg Kaltwasser, *Die Bibliothek als Museum; von der Renaissance bis heute, dargestellt am Beispiel der Bayerischen Staatsbibliothek* (Wiesbaden, 1999). A group of essays in the *Bodleian Library Record* 17 (2001), pp.180–267, has recently focused on the theme 'Beyond the book: Cultures of collecting in Oxford libraries and beyond'.

68 This part of the collection was sold by Mr Cock on 8 March 1741/2 and the five following days. Among the lots offered were several from the Arundel collection. The coins were auctioned separately.

69 Edward Miller, *That Noble Cabinet: A history of the British Museum* (London, 1973), pp.243–4.

70 Simone Balayé, *La Bibliothèque Nationale des origines à 1800* (Geneva, 1988); Thierry Sarmant, *Le Cabinet des Médailles de la Bibliothèque Nationale, 1661–1848* (Paris, 1994); Marie-Hélène Tesnière and Prosser Gifford (eds), *Creating French Culture: Treasures from the Bibliothèque Nationale de France* (New Haven, 1995).

71 The Stiftung currently consists of seventeen museums, the Geheimes Staatsarchiv and the Staatsbibliothek zu Berlin. See Klaus-Dieter Lehmann (ed.), *Cultural Treasures of the World in the collections of the Prussian Cultural Heritage Foundation* (Berlin, 2001).

72 Arthur MacGregor (ed.), *Sir Hans Sloane: Collector, scientist, antiquary; founding father of the British Museum* (London, 1994).

73 Justus Lipsius, *De bibliothecis syntagma* (Antwerp, 1602), cap. ix.

74 Claude du Molinet, *Le cabinet de la Bibliothèque Sainte-Geneviève* (Paris, 1692), preface. See also Françoise Zehnacker and Nicolas Petit, *Le cabinet de curiosités de la Bibliothèque Sainte-Geneviève des origines à nos jours* (Paris, 1989). The museum aspects of such collections have tended to attract more attention than the closely linked issues of libraries: see, for example, Oliver Impey and Arthur MacGregor (eds), *The Origins of Museums* (Oxford, 1985); Krzysztof Pomian, *Collectors and Curiosities: Paris and Venice, 1500–1800* (Cambridge, 1990); Paula Findlen, *Possessing Nature: Museums, collecting, and scientific culture in early modern Italy* (Berkeley, 1994). For the *Kunstkammer* in Wolfenbüttel see Jill Bepler and others, *Barocke-Sammellust; die Bibliothek und Kunstkammer des Herzogs Ferdinand Albrecht zu Braunschweig-Lüneburg (1636–1687)*

(Wolfenbüttel, 1988), including an inventory of 1687 (pp. 125–8). For a mid-eighteenth-century example of a cabinet of art and curiosities see Rudolf-Alexander Schütte, 'The *Kunst- und Naturalienkammer* of Duke Anton Ulrich of Brunswick-Lüneburg at Schloss Salzdahlum', *Journal of the History of Collections* 9 (1997), pp.79–115.

75 George F. Warner and Julius P. Gilson, *Catalogue of Western Manuscripts in the Old Royal and King's Collections,* 4 vols (London, 1921), vol.i, introduction: *The Old Royal Library* (London, 1957); Miller, op. cit. (note 69), pp.54–7; T.A. Birrell, *English Monarchs and their Books: From Henry VII to Charles II* (London, 1987). The Royal Library had been removed from St James's Palace in 1708. The manuscript author catalogue of the Old Royal Library, dating mainly from 1761 but including entries down to about 1770, is now c.120.h.6*, microfilm Mic A 10504: see T. A. Birrell, *The Library of John Morris: The reconstruction of a seventeenth-century collection* (London, 1976), p.xix. In 1769 the Museum began to dispose of duplicates: a marked copy of the first sale catalogue, indicating which books came from the Old Royal, Sloane, Edwards or Birch collections, is now British Library 821.i.28 (ibid, p.xx). Professor Birrell is currently preparing an account of the printed books in the Old Royal Library

76 J.H. Monk, *The Life of Richard Bentley,* 2nd edn, 2 vols (London, 1833), vol.i, p.73.

77 David Casley to Lord Hardwicke, 23 September 1742: British Library, Additional MS 36,269, fol.1.

78 The effect of joining the Sloane, Old Royal and legal deposit books together is to be seen in the weaknesses as well as the strengths of the collection described in *Librorum impressorum qui in Museo Britannico adservantur catalogus,* 2 vols (London, 1787): this catalogue was the work of P.H. Maty, Samuel Harper and Samuel Ayscough.

79 Richard Bentley, *A Dissertation upon the Epistles of Phalaris. With an answer to the objections of the Honourable Charles Boyle, Esquire* (London, 1699), p.lxv.

80 By the time of Louis XIV's death in 1715, the French Royal Library contained over 60,000 volumes. Bignon raised money, extending the collecting interests of the library, and pestered everyone for its support. Under legal deposit legislation, the library was entitled to two copies of every new book; Bignon used the second copies for exchange or for sale. By 1730 there were about 80,000 printed books alone. N.T. Le Prince, *Essai historique sur la Bibliothèque du Roi* (Paris, 1856), p.74. For the Library at this time see Simone Balayé, 'La Bibliothèque du Roi, première bibliothèque du monde, 1664–1789', in Jolly op. cit. (note 9), pp.209–33.

81 L. Delisle, *Le cabinet des manuscrits de la Bibliothèque Impériale,* 4 vols (Paris, 1868–81) vol.i, pp.364–7.

82 Ibid., pp.397–407.

83 Ibid., pp.387–97.

84 Ibid., pp. 439–547; Denise Bloch, 'La bibliothèque de Colbert', in Jolly, op. cit. (note 9), pp.157–75.

85 Colin G.C. Tite, 'A catalogue of Sir Robert Cotton's printed books?', in Wright, op. cit. (note 61), pp.183–9; see also *British Library Journal* 17 (1991), pp.1–11.

86 M.A.E. Nickson, 'Books and manuscripts', in MacGregor, op. cit. (note 72), pp.263–77, at p. 268. Sloane's own catalogues of his printed books survive in British Library, MSS Sloane 3972 A–D and 3995 and in an interleaved copy of G.A. Mercklin's *Lindenius renovatus* (Nuremberg, 1686), British Library 878. n.8: see 'Sir Hans Sloane's catalogues', in MacGregor, op. cit. (note 72), pp.291–5. The bequest of Arthur Edwards, including about 2,000 printed books, did not arrive until after 1769.

87 Esdaile, op. cit. (note 56), p.180. The 1787 catalogue does not distinguish the provenances of the books, nor does it provide the shelf-marks that could provide the clues. For related points, see Ian Willison, 'The development of the British national library to 1837 in its European context: An essay in retrospect', in K. A. Manley (ed.) *Careering along with Books: Studies in the history of British public libraries and librarianship* (*Library History* 12 [1996]), pp.31–48. The generous help of Ian Willison at several points in this essay is gratefully acknowledged.

88 H. M. Colvin (ed.), *The History of the King's Works*, vol.v: *1660–1782* (London, 1976), pp.419–21 and pls 58–9.

89 *The Will of Sir Hans Sloane, Bart. deceased* (London, 1753). The codicils relating to his collections were printed several times separately. See also Marjorie Caygill, 'Sloane's will and the

establishment of the British Museum', in MacGregor, op. cit. (note 72), pp.45–68.

90 Mike Fitton and Pamela Gilbert, 'Insect collections', in MacGregor, op. cit. (note 72) pp.112–22, at pp.117–18.

91 This was a legal position: see J.R. Tanner (ed.), *The Historical Register of the University of Cambridge* (Cambridge, 1917), pp.64–5.

92 Between 1737 and 1749 the office had been held by the Duke of Newcastle. Ever since 1689, the Chancellor of the University had been the Duke of Somerset. On his death in 1748 he was succeeded by Newcastle. In 1754 Newcastle, Secretary of State since 1748, succeeded Henry Pelham as First Lord of the Treasury. Hardwicke became Lord Chancellor in 1737, and remained in that position until 1756.

93 Royal Commission on Historical Monuments, *An Inventory of the Historical Monuments in the County of Cambridge*, vol.I: *West Cambridgeshire* (HMSO, 1968), pp.215–16; David Souden *et al.*, *Wimpole Hall, Cambridgeshire* (London, 1991).

94 D. A. Winstanley, *The University of Cambridge in the eighteenth Century* (Cambridge, 1922) is based largely on the Newcastle and Hardwicke papers in the British Library.

95 *Academiae Cantabrigiensis Luctus in obitum Serenissimi Georgii I. et Gaudia ob potentissimi Georgii II* (Cambridge, 1727).

96 For the formation and contents of Moore's library, and its reception at Cambridge, see McKitterick, op. cit. (note 50), pp.47–224.

97 McKitterick, op. cit. (note 50), pp.143–6.

98 Conyers Middleton, *Dissertation concerning the Origin of Printing in England* (Cambridge, 1735).

99 Hadderton wrote more lines than any other contributor, his verses on various aspects of the Library, with explanatory footnotes on Cambridge topography and other subjects, spreading over more than eight folio pages.

Figure 19
George Vertue, frontispiece to Cock's
auction catalogue of the Harleian
collection of pictures, prints and
sculpture, 8 March 1741/2.

Chapter 6

Paper Monuments and Learned Societies

Hooke's Royal Society Repository

Lisa Jardine

This chapter concerns the story of how, at the very beginning of the eighteenth century, the Royal Society came finally to have its own purpose-built 'Repository' – possibly the very last building designed and supervised by Sir Christopher Wren, a building long demolished, and a project almost entirely forgotten.[1]

The Royal Society had begun to accumulate materials for a Repository from its beginnings in the early 1660s. The largest single donation, in these early years, was made in the autumn of 1663 by Dr John Wilkins (founding figure of the Society, whose protégés both Robert Hooke and Wren had been in the 1650s). At about the same time, Hooke, the Society's 'Curator of Experiments' was named as 'Keeper' – a post he continued to occupy effectively until the late 1670s, when Nehemiah Grew was appointed.[2] In early 1666 it was widely known that Hooke was in the process of soliciting benefactions towards the Repository.[3] In 1673 (the year of the return of the Society to Gresham College after its displacement to Arundel House following the Great Fire), Hooke (a chronic insomniac) was up and hyperactively about before daylight during the last days of November, sawing out beams and trusses and demolishing partitions in the basement of the College so as to create additional library (and possibly laboratory) space, thereby extending the Repository premises beyond the large gallery allocated to it upstairs.[4] When the Society eventually moved from Crane Court to Somerset House in 1779, however, the Repository and its contents were dispensed with – judged no longer appropriate to a scientific institution (and too costly to maintain). The collections went to the British Museum in 1781,[5] where few traces of them seem to survive.[6]

Hooke died on 3 March 1703. Although he had stepped down from his official responsibilities at the Royal Society in the late 1690s, after several bouts of ill health, he had carried on with his scientific social life and his intellectual activities – including his passionate discussions of scientific problems with friends like Wren – until at least 1699.[7] His funeral was an appropriately grand occasion, and a fitting finale for one of the founding figures of London Restoration science. As his biographer and the friend of his later years, Richard Waller, wrote: 'His Corps was decently and handsomely interr'd in the Church of St. Hellen in London, all the Members of the Royal Society then in Town attending his Body to the Grave, paying the Respect due to his extraordinary Merit'.[8]

Why, then, was no institutional memorial to Robert Hooke established? The answer appears to be that as far as his colleagues and friends – including his lifelong friend Sir

Christopher Wren – were concerned, a lasting monument to Hooke had indeed been created, in the form of the purpose-built premises for the Royal Society which had been Wilkins's and Hooke's shared dream since the 1660s, and into which the Society moved its books, its collection of rarities, its instruments and its experimental activities, in the summer of 1712. This was a building which under other circumstances might have been called the 'Hookean Museum'.

In the last year of Hooke's life, during the summer of 1702, shortly after the accession of Queen Anne, the Royal Society had begun to make plans to expand its Gresham College premises.[9] A proposal by the Society's landlords, the Gresham College authorities themselves, for total rebuilding of the college premises, presented a golden opportunity to redesign the facilities there used by the Society to make them more suitable for their meetings. Alterations would allow for the creation of a repository (or exhibition and storage space) to house their collection of rarities and instruments, and laboratory space for their experimental activities. At the Society's invitation, Sir Christopher Wren (in his seventieth year) submitted a 'Proposal for Building a House for the R. Society' to the President, John, Lord Somers:

> It is proposed as absolutely necessary for the continuing the Royal Society at Gresham College, that they should have a place to be Seated in the said Ground, that the Coaches of the Members (some of which are of very great Quality) may have easy access, and that the Building consist of these necessary parts.
>
> 1. A Cellar under Ground so high above it, as to have good lights for the Use of an Elaboratory and House-keeper.
> 2. The Story above may have a fair Room and a large Closet.
> 3. A Place for a Repository over them.
> 4. A Place for the Library over the Repository.
> 5. A Place Covered with Lead, for observing the Heavens.
> 6. A good Stair Case from bottom to Top.
> 7. A reasonable Area behind it, to give light to the Back Rooms.
>
> All which may be comprized in a Space of Ground Forty Foot in Front and Sixty Foot Deep.[10]

Almost immediately, however, plans for expansion as part of the rebuilding of Gresham College were abruptly halted, once the precariousness of the Society's tenure there was recognized: it transpired that if the Gresham authorities could get rid of the Society they would cheerfully do so. The Society's continued occupancy of the Gresham premises was entirely contingent on Hooke's residency there: it was Hooke's position as a Gresham Professor which entitled him to residential accommodation in the buildings, and they with him. As the sitting tenant, Hooke had in fact taken court action the previous year (encouraged by the Society) to prevent the Gresham trustees from evicting him in order to begin demolitions and a rebuilding programme for which they were at that time seeking Parliamentary permission.

On 24 March, three weeks after Hooke's death, the trustees of Gresham College notified the Royal Society that they were to remove themselves and their belongings from the College, and return the keys to Hooke's lodgings forthwith. It would undoubtedly have amused Hooke, could he have known, that his death immediately presented the new President, Sir Isaac Newton (who had refused to have anything to do with the Society as long as Hooke was active within it), with a serious problem of where to house the Society.

A hastily-assembled committee succeeded in negotiating a stay of execution of the Society's eviction from Gresham College until new premises could be found. As usual with the Royal Society then, things moved impossibly slowly. A year later, in February 1704, the Council voted to place the matter of finding them new accommodation firmly in Wren's hands (he had a reputation as a man who got things done):

> They also desired Sir Christopher Wren that he would please to take the trouble of viewing the design and project and consider what accommodation the Society wanted and to resolve by Changing or purchasing Ground fit for their affairs to add to what the Committees offer for their accommodation.

It was not until 1710, however, that a property that met with the committee's approval became available.[11] On 8 September Newton informed the Council that there was an opportunity to purchase 'the late Dr. Browns House in Crane Court in Fleet Street being now to be sold being in the middle of the Town out of Noise'.[12] Evidently it was Wren and his son, Christopher Wren junior, who decided that the premises were suitable. On 13 September 1710 Newton wrote to Sir Hans Sloane, the Society's Secretary:

> [I] am glad Sr Christopher & Mr Wren like the house [&] hope they like the price also. I have inclosed a Note [to] Mr Hunt to call a Council on Saturday next at [twe]lve a clock, & beg the favour that you would send [it] to him by the Porter who brings you this.[13]

On 2 November Wren, his son and Richard Waller (the Society's Curator) were authorized to negotiate with the house's tenant to purchase any fittings which might suit the Society.[14] The committee reported back on 30 November:

> Mr. Brigstock was Ordered to have thirty Guineas for the Wainscot and other things he leaves in the House at Crane Court according to the Report of Sir Christopher Wren, Mr. Wren and Mr. Waller.

Wren senior appears to have been closely involved in the renovations needed to make the new accommodation habitable, in spite of the fact that he was by now seventy-eight years old (as with a number of other projects in these years, his son Christopher, appointed alongside him for the purpose, often deputized for him).[15]

In March 1711 it was agreed that in addition to refurbishment of the existing house, the Society would build a 'New Repository' at Crane Court. Sir Christopher Wren was asked to draw up architectural plans for it. He did better, and produced a model. On 28 March Wren junior wrote to the Secretary:

> By my father's direction a Modell is made of the room for ye Repository of ye Royal-Society in crane Court, wch. may give ye Gentlemen a better idea, then the designe on paper: It will be very light, very commodious, and the cheapest building that can be contrived: I have sent the Joyner with it to you, that you may take yr opportunity to show it to ye Councill.[16]

Once again, however, the project ground to a halt. As on every previous occasion when attempts at providing purpose-built accommodation were made, the Royal Society was unable to come up with the ready money needed actually to get the building on site. Contracts had to be negotiated with masons and carpenters, and these could only be commenced once cash, and regular settlement of bills, could be guaranteed. There had already been problems covering the purchase of Crane Court and seeing to its repairs. When estimates were produced for Wren's design, the costs came out at a figure of almost exactly twice the £200 the Society had budgeted for their new Repository.

This time, however, two active members of the Society stepped in and saved the day. Richard Waller came up immediately with £300 to get the project moving, followed by a further £100 during the period of construction.[17] Henry Hunt made available the astonishing sum of £900 (as two separate donations), thereby underwriting the entire building.[18] Two more unlikely benefactors could hardly be imagined. Waller was a man of modest means; Hunt, was simply the Society's artisan Operator, in charge of the existing, run-down Repository.[19]

The new Repository was finished within a year, and on 8 April 1712 a committee was appointed 'to take care of the due placing of the Curiosities in the New Repository built by Mr. Waller'. The very last building actively designed by Wren became the first real, properly appointed home for the Royal Society, and in particular, the first museum building designed expressly to house the Society's by now extensive collection of rarities, scientific instruments and books.

Who really paid for the Repository? Everyone involved was closely associated with Robert Hooke. The committee convened to handle the Crane Court accommodation problems which followed Hooke's death consisted of his oldest and dearest friend, Sir Christopher Wren, Wren's son (Clerk of the Royal Works, and by now substituting for his father's regular attendance at meetings of all kinds), and Richard Waller, Hooke's closest friend and confidante at the time of his death. Waller was the person who, in the absence of near relatives, took charge of Hooke's post-mortem affairs, and who edited the 1705 edition of his *Posthumous Works*, which includes a Life of Hooke.[20]

The other crucial player in the successful completion of the building was Henry Hunt, Hooke's protégé, who had begun his career as boy servant to Hooke, and risen to take over Hooke's more menial duties at the Royal Society. He was thus a mere employee of the Royal Society (their clerk and demonstrator), who had spent his entire adult life in Hooke's service, and who, as the diary entries for the period after 1688 show, attended Hooke almost daily (and sometimes several times a day) in the later years of his life, as companion and amanuensis.[21] On the basis of their involvement in the events that followed, it can be claimed with some confidence that the Crane Court Repository was in fact the final scientific and architectural collaboration between Wren and Hooke – designed by Wren and funded by Hooke.

Waller recorded that Hooke had told him he wanted his money to go, at his death, to the Royal Society, so that new quarters, meeting rooms, laboratories, and a library might be constructed:

> I indeed, as well as others, have heard him declare sometimes that he had a great Project in his Head as to the disposal of the most part of his Estate for the advancement of Natural Knowledge, and to promote the Ends and Designs for which the Royal Society was instituted: To build an handsome Fabrick for the Societies use, with a Library, Repositary, Laboratory, and other Conveniences for making Experiments, and to found and endow a perpetual 'Physico-Mechanick Lecture' of the Nature of what himself read.[22]

According to the probate inventory, Hooke left just short of £10,000 in cash, locked in an iron chest in his Gresham College lodgings; he also left two properties on the Isle of Wight.[23] He died intestate, but a draft will – unsigned – has recently come to light, drafted five days before his death and now lodged alongside the probate inventory in the Public Record Office. This draft indicates plainly that Hooke intended to divide his considerable personal wealth (in cash) between four friends, and that they had instructions on how to dispense certain sums:

> This is the Last Will & Testament of me Robert Hooke M.D. Professor of Geometry & Experimental Pholosophy [sic] in Gresham College London & Survayor of the City of London &c. Made the [blot] twenty fifth day of – February 1702/3 for the notification of the Persons to whome I do bequeath all the several parts of such goods real & Personal as it shall please God to bless me withall at the time of my decease, with the Quallifications & quantities of them. First I doe bequeath & give to my – good friends A, B, C, & D. my whole Estate Real & Personal together with all debts owing to me yet unpaid, upon trust – and Confidence that they shall & will dispose & pay unto the said persons nominated in a s[ch]edule an[n]exed to this present will signed & sealed by me the several sum[m]s therein particularised And also discharge the Charges or Expences of my funeral which I would not have to exceed the vallue of forty pounds, And the Remainder to be equally distributed between the foresaid A. B. C & D. In testimony whereof I have here unto Subscribed my name & affixed my Seale, & declared the same to be my Act & deed to the Persons following [rest of sheet blank].[24]

Waller and Wren (with Wren's son as his father's right-hand man) were the team responsible for the arrangements immediately following Hooke's death, which led to the provision of a purpose-built repository and library at Crane Court. Wren personally designed the building (waiving his fee), which contemporary guide-books describe as 'in a little paved Court' behind the main house at 'Two Crane Court in Fleetstreet'. The description continues: 'The Repository of Curiosities is a Theatrical Building, resembling that of Leyden in Holland'.[25] Hooke would have been delighted with the Dutch influence, and the allusion to the theatre he personally designed for the Royal College of Physicians, as the architect who rebuilt their premises after the Great Fire.

A cousin of Hooke's, supposedly daughter of Hooke's father's brother, inherited the major part of his fortune, as his only living heir (though in fact the story does not end there).[26] Some of the money, however, found its way to Hooke's close friend Waller, allocated to cover the costs of sorting out of his affairs, disposing of his substantial library, and editing and publishing his *Posthumous Works*. It seems reasonable to assume that Hunt too received some kind of cash gift, as the person who had taken care of Hooke in his later years and throughout his final illness, providing him with a measure of company and affection; Hunt may even have received some kind of recompense directly from Hooke during his last days.

The Royal Society Repository project was Hooke's known last wish, vehemently expressed as such to close friends. The significant sums in ready money which Waller and Hunt produced to save Wren's Repository project from being shelved, as all previous Society building projects had been, was surely Hooke's (Waller was not a wealthy man, and Hunt a mere employee). But since Sir Isaac Newton, the President of the Royal Society, could – notoriously – not bear the mention of Hooke's name, the benefaction necessarily remained anonymous. Newton had recently dealt savagely with another long-term adversary, John Flamsteed, expelling him from the Royal Society. It is unlikely that an appeal for posthumous clemency for Hooke would have fared any better.

It was in the course of the move of the Society's rarities from Gresham College to the new Repository at Crane Court that the Royal Society portrait of Hooke, seen by a German visitor to the Society the previous year, was lost, and his scientific instruments also disappeared. Was the portrait perhaps quietly removed into the custody of someone who believed that Hooke's style of science, and his legacy of scientific instruments, would be so neglected under Newton's presidency as to endanger the painting's survival? Henry Hunt was in charge of the removals to Crane Court; in late June 1711 the Council ordered Hunt to remove the Society's 'curiosities' from Gresham College and transfer them to Crane Court 'with what convenient speed he could'.[27]

That mislaid portrait may stand here – symbolically – for the kind of 'forgetting' in the history of museums, which should be recalled. Wren's Crane Court Repository – the Hookean Museum – no longer survives; the Royal Society collections of curiosities are lost, or dispersed unrecognized among other specimens at the British Museum and the Natural History Museum; nor do we have any portrait or drawing of Hooke to which we can attach the kind of continuity of memory on which our written history depends.

Behind every distinguished, and apparently systematic, museum collection stands the personal obsession of an individual – the more or less haphazardly accumulated remnants of private interest and idiosyncratic pursuit. The Royal Society's first 'museum' – its first purpose-built Repository, long since demolished – was such a one. While it stood it might have been called (by analogy with its Oxford equivalent) the Hookean Museum, had it not been for an antagonism between its benefactor and the President of the Royal Society, which outlasted the passing of the former.

There is a final, particular poignancy to this erasure of the Crane Court 'museum' and Hooke's name from the recorded history of the British Museum. It was Hooke who designed and built Montagu House for Ralph Montagu in the 1670s.[28] This, of course, was the building which first housed the British Museum. Hooke's name is not prominent in the architectural history of the British Museum, on the grounds that his Montagu House 'burned to the ground' in 1686. In fact, the current view is that the fire at Montagu House gutted the interior, but left the structure intact.[29] Thus a further opportunity to associate the name of the Royal Society's greatest enthusiast for the collecting side of the Society's activities, and enthusiast for proper museum facilities for displaying the collections, was once again lost. Such are the peculiar vagaries of the history of museums.

Lisa Jardine

Acknowledgements
I would like to express my gratitude to Dr Jim Bennett and Professor Michael Hunter, whose important work on the Royal Society Repositories has been crucial as the starting point for this piece of work.

Notes and references

1 This account of the history of the Royal Society's Repository is based on M. Hunter, 'The cabinet institutionalized: The Royal Society's "Repository" and its background', in M. Hunter, *Science and the Shape of Orthodoxy: Intellectual change in late seventeenth-century Britain* (Cambridge, 1995), pp.135–47. See also O. Impey and A. MacGregor (eds), *The Origins of Museums: The cabinet of curiosities in sixteenth- and seventeenth-century Europe* (Oxford, 1985).

2 Hunter, op. cit. (note 1), p.140.

3 Ibid., p.145; M. Hunter, A. Clericuzo, and L. M. Principe, *The Correspondence of Robert Boyle* (London, 2001), vol.III, p.46 (Oldenburg to Boyle, 27 January 1666): 'Those of the Society, that are now in London, doe endeavour to gett a good Collection of Naturall and Artificiall Curiosities for the Societies repository; and they hope, to make shortly an acquest of a very good stock of that kind, which will looke as something towards a foundation, and will invite generous men to increase it from time to time.'; vol.III, p.49 (Hooke to Boyle, 3 February 1666): 'I am now making a collection of natural rarities, and hope, within a short time, to get as good as any have been yet made in the world, through the bounty of some of the noble-minded persons of the Royal Society. I hope we shall have again a meeting, within this week or fortnight at farthest . . . and then I hope we shall prosecute experiments and observations much more vigorously; in order to which also I design, God willing, very speedily to make me an operatory, which I design to furnish with instruments and engines of all kinds, for making examinations of the nature of bodies, optical, chemical, mechanical, &c. and therein to proceed by sych a method, as may, I hope, save me much labour, charge, and study; and in this design there will be some two or three others, that will join with me, who, I hope, are of the same mind with me.'

4 Hunter, op. cit. (note 1), p.145; H. W. Robinson and W. Adams (eds), *The Diary of Robert Hooke MA MD FRS 1672–1680* (London, 1968), p.11: '[November 1672] (24) Lord Brounkers, told him of Lord Chesters Legacy. order to, take his man. Walkd with Mr. Godfry, Mr Fitch brought a horse. writ a lecture about the new phenomena of light. Nell's cozen at Coffins. at Garways. was not well and slept very little, rose next morning (25) at 6. Sawd wood.' '[29] Slept very little but (30) at 4 in the morning rose and sawd downe the trusses celler.' p.12: '[December] [6] Garways. supd early. Slept from 12 to 3 only. (7) Rose at 6, threw down middle post and beam in celler.' '(10) Wrought in the celler and threw down post and ranged timbers. Was pretty well all day. Mr. Lodowick here, Mr. Janeway here. Eat broth and slept well. (11) at home all day, Mr Colwall here in the evening, Mr. Blackburne laid here first last night. Noe news from Arundell house. Putt staples to little back door and ranged timber in celler, had a griping and voided slimy blood. Eat chicken broth. Began to learn Dutch with Mr. Blackburne. Mary here. (12) Slept well in my gown. Sawd wood, took down joyst. Kept in, rangd and catalogued Library.' [14] Lost Diamant in cleerd celler. Set up 8^TOS and smaller books, set up 3 shelves.' p.13: '(19) Fitted glasse toole in the morning, mended Repository door. DH.'

5 See Robert Anderson's references (p.59) (taken from the British Museum trustees' minutes) for the dates of offering, acquisition and final delivery of the contents of the Royal Society Respository to Montagu House.

6 Hunter, op. cit. (note 1), p.146. For the unreliability of the claim that collections are 'lost' once acquired by museums see Hugh Torrens in this volume, and also his 'Etheldred Bennett of Wiltshire, England, the first lady geologist – her fossil collection in the Academy of Natural Sciences of Philadelphia, and the rediscovery of "lost" specimens of Jurassic Trigoniidae (Mollusca: Bivalvia) with their soft anatomy preserved', *Proceedings of the Academy of Natural Sciences of Philadelphia* (2000), pp.59–123. See also Torrens in this volume (p.84) for the reidentification of two fossil specimens known to have been in the Royal Society Repository, in the British Museum (now the Natural History Museum) collections.

7 See the volume of Hooke papers in the archives of the Royal Society, RS Classified Papers vol.xx, which contain 'in progress' works, including work for the Society, down to May 1699 – latterly reading and producing synopses of new scientific books in increasingly tiny, obsessive writing.

8 R. Waller, *The Posthumous Works of Robert Hooke* (London, 1705), p.xxvi.

9 The account which follows builds on J.A. Bennett, 'Wren's last building?', *Notes and Records of the Royal Society* 27 (1972–3), pp.107–18.

10 Royal Society Register Book RBC.9.143. The letter is undated, but is copied between letters dated May 1702 and September 1702. The whole volume is strictly chronological.

11 It may have been that political quarrels within the Society forced a move on the Society in that year. See R. Westfall, *Never at Rest: A biography of Isaac Newton* (Cambridge, 1980), pp.671–9.

12 The Dr Browne in question was none other than the Edward Browne (son of Sir Thomas Browne) who had accompanied Wren on his sightseeing trip to the region outside Paris in 1665.

13 H.W. Turnbull, J.F. Scott, A.R. Hall and L. Tilling (eds), *The Correspondence of Isaac Newton* (Cambridge, 1959–77), vol.v, p.61, letter 802, Newton to Sloane, 13 September 1710.

14 'Sir Christopher Wren, Mr. Wren and Mr. Waller were Appointed a Committee to see what Mr. Brigstock leaves in the House that may be usefull to the Society and of what Value they may be.'

15 See, for example, the letter from Wren junior to Sloane (Secretary of the Royal Society): 'I have given directions to [par]ticular Workmen, Persons I know well & trust, to take an Exact Survey of all the necessary repairs of ye House; when [they] have made their Report; and my Father [has] examin'd their several Rates, I will [place] the whole before you, and ye Workmen [m]ay begin when you shall think proper' (Bennett, op. cit. [note 9], p.110). All the workmen employed on the Crane Court building came from Wren's office.

16 Bennett, op. cit. (note 9), p.111.

17 Waller contributed a total sum of £400, of which £300 was apparently treated as an interest-free loan which the Society agreed to repay to him (£300 was the sum eventually agreed as the acceptable cost of the Repository). At his death, £250 was outstanding, and his widow (as happened more than once with 'benefactions' to the Society), sued for return of the money, on the grounds that it had been a loan, not an outright gift, eventually receiving from Newton 'two hundred and fifty pounds and fifty three pounds in full Interest' (Bennett, op. cit. [note 9], p. 113).

18 Hunt advanced £464 for the project in its early stages; four months later he lent a further £450, making a total of over £900: 'To pay for the [Crane Court] house, the society put £550 down and took a mortgage for £900 at 6 percent. Before they could move in, extensive repairs had to be made, at a further expense of £310. Having taken the plunge, they decided to go all the way and authorized £200 more to build a repository . . . By the middle of January, before the bills for either the repairs or the repository arrived, the society retired the mortgage . . . partly by borrowing £464 from their clerk, Henry Hunt. By June, further gifts reduced the debt to £200. For the repairs and the repository, the society borrowed an additional £450 from Hunt and stood £650 in his debt when he died in June 1713' (Westfall, op. cit. [note 11], pp.676–7). £900 was an enormous sum for any individual to provide – Newton's own contributions, for instance, totalled well under £200. In 1663, when Archbishop Sheldon put up £1,000 to launch the building of the Sheldonian Theatre, this was regarded as an astonishing sum for one individual to produce, however personally wealthy.

19 'Henry Hunt (d. 1713) served Hooke as a boy assistant and was trained by him. Soon after the death of Richard Shortgrave, the Society's first operator, Hunt was appointed to succeed him (2 November 1676); he also carried on the making of meteorological instruments that Shortgrave had commenced for Fellows and others. On 14 January 1679/80 his salary was raised from £10 to £40 p.a. (the same as Hooke's) in return for his devoting all his time to the Society's affairs. In 1696 he was appointed Keeper of the Library and Repository. By the time of his death the Society owed him £650 advanced by him for the purchase and fitting out of Crane Court.' (note in Turnbull *et al.*, op. cit. [note 13], vol.v, p.62).

20 At the end of the manuscript of Hooke's *Diary*, now in the Guildhall Library, there is a note in Waller's hand saying that Waller could prove, were it a proper time, that Hooke was the first to invent or

hint of those things about which great heroes of renown had contested the priority. Waller also left us the most affectionate portrait of Hooke, which includes the observation: 'He was in the beginning of his being made known to the Learned, very communicative of his Philosophical Discoveries and Inventions, till some Accidents made him to a Crime close and reserv'd. He laid the cause upon some Persons, challenging his Discoveries for their own, taking occasion from his Hints to perfect what he had not; which made him say he would suggest nothing until he had time to perfect it himself, which has been the Reason that many things are lost, which he affirm'd he knew' (Guildhall Library, MS 1757).

21 R.T. Gunther, *Early Science in Oxford* (Oxford, 1920–67), vol.X, *passim*.

22 Richard Waller, 'The life of Dr. Robert Hooke', reprinted in Gunther, op. cit. (note 21), vol.VI, pp.1–68, esp. 59–66.

23 See H. Nakajima, 'Robert Hooke's family and his youth: some new evidence from the will of the Rev. John Hooke', *Notes and Records of the Royal Society* 48 (1994), pp.11–16; L. Jardine, *On a Grander Scale: The outstanding career of Sir Christopher Wren* (London, 2002).

24 Title on back of sheet reads: "Testam[en]tum Rob[er]ti Hook M D defuncti.' Public Record Office (hereafter PRO) Prob 20/1315. My gratitude to Rachel Jardine, who first spotted the unsigned will at the Public Record Office.

25 The Leiden (anatomical) theatre had animal skeletons mounted around its circumference: see W. Schupbach, 'Some cabinets of curiosities in European academic institutions', in Impey and MacGregor, op. cit. (note 1), pp.170–2, fig.63.

26 In 1707 another cousin of Hooke's, Thomas Giles, twin brother of Robert Giles, who had been Hooke's tenant on the Isle of Wight, and whose son Tom had lodged with Hooke in London, claimed the Hooke inheritance. Since he was a resident of the Isle of Wight colony in Virginia, he had not heard of Hooke's death until several years after it took place. He pursued a long-running case in the Court of Chancery to regain Hooke's wealth and property, but the outcome is not known. See PRO, Chancery Records, C9/187/46 (1706/7): Thomas Giles c. Joseph Dillon. See C9 194/40 and C24/1278 Part II no.20 and 1289 Part I no.38 2p/ Complaint of Thomas Giles, 12 Feb. 1706/7. Explains his relationship with Robert Hooke, who died in 1702 and whose estate Giles is claiming. Believes it should be shared between himself and Anne Hollis and Elizabeth Stephens, but the latter and her daughter Elizabeth Dillon, wife of Joseph Dillon took advantage of Giles' absence abroad (in Virginia) and possessed themselves of his part of the estate. Claims there should be a fairer settlement. 4p/ Answer of Joseph Dillon, 6 Nov. 1707, Details of the relationship between Robert Hooke and Elizabeth Stephens, both now deceased. Believes the estate was settled fairly. Encloses: Details of the account of the estate of Robert Hooke. PRO, C9/194/40 (1706/7–1707/8): Thomas Giles c. Lewis Stephens, Joseph Dillon et. al. See 187/46 and C24 1278 Part II no. 20. 4p/ Bill of complaint of Thomas Giles, 12 Feb. 1706/7 From Virginia. Gives details of his inheritance of land, etc. in the Isle of Wight. Did not claim his inheritance sooner because he has only just heard of certain deaths. Alleges Stephens and Dillon conspired to rob him of his due. 1p/ Piece in Latin on the case. 4p/ Answers of Joseph Dillon and Mary, his wife, no date. Details of the relationship in the family regarding the inheritance after the death of Robert Hooke in 1702. Stephens's wife was a cousin of Hooke. Dillon was employed to take an account of the estate. Encloses an inventory of the estate. 4p/ Answers of Lewis Stephens, 19 Feb. 1707/8, Details of the estate and relationships of the beneficiaries. Encloses an account of the estate. Court of Chancery Records. Town Depositions, PRO, C24–C243 p.9 no.38 Thomas Gyles c. Stephens et al. See 1278 Part II no.20. Witnesses for Gyles: 4p/ John Crouch, 19 July 1708, Case concerns an estate on the Isle of Wight of Robert Hook, deceased. Thomas Gyles lived in Virginia and in 1705 Cecily his brother Robert's widow, asked the witness to write a letter to Thomas. 4p/ Daniel Sullivan, 27 July 1708, Went to Virginia in Sept 1706 to deliver letters to Thomas Gyles concerning the estate of Dr Robert Hook. Thomas gave him a letter to take back to England. Also showed Sullivan his papers signed by John Knell and gave him a letter to deliver to Knell in England. 1p/ Daniel alias Joseph Mitchell, 27 July 1708, Last time he saw Giles was in Virginia in March last. Identifies his handwriting. Gave him two letters to deliver in England.

27 Bennett, op. cit. (note 9), p.113. If Hunt did quietly remove the portrait as a reminder of his old mentor and friend (and because

Newton's animus towards Hooke meant it would never be asked after), it is still possible that it will one day reappear.

28 See M.I. Batten, 'The architecture of Dr. Robert Hooke F.R.S.', *Walpole Society* 25 (1936–7), pp.93–6: Evelyn in his Diary has a good deal to say about Montagu House. The first entry is in May 1676, 'went to see Mr. Montagu's new palace near Bloomsberry built by Mr. Hooke, of our Society, after the French manner', but according to Hooke's Diary this would be before the roof was finished. In November 1679 Evelyn goes there again and writes, 'it was most nobly furnished, and a fine, but too much exposed garden'. He makes his final visit in October 1683 and has left a description: 'to see Montagu House, a palace lately built by Lord Montagu … It is a stately and ample palace. Signor Verrio's fresco paintings, especially the funeral pile of Dido, on the staircase, the labours of Hercules, fight with the Centaurs, his effeminacy with Dejanira, and Apotheosis or reception among the Gods, on the walls and roof of the great room above, – I think exceeds anything he has yet done, both for design, colouring, and exuberance of invention, comparable to the greatest of the old masters, or what they so celebrate at Rome. In the rest of the chamber are some excellent paintings of Holbein, and other masters. The garden is large, and in good air, but the fronts of the house not answerable to the inside. The court at entry, and wings for offices seem too near the street, and that so very narrow and meanly built, that the corridor is not in proportion to the rest, to hide the court from being overlooked by neighbours; all which might have been prevented, had they placed the house further into the ground, of which there is enough to spare. But on the whole it is a fine palace, built after the French pavilion-way, by Mr Hooke, the Curator of the Royal Society.' See also the relevant entries from Hooke's Diary, compiled by Batten: '[2 September 1674] With Mr. Montacue to Southampton Fields. September 12th, At home all day about Mr. Montacue plat. September 13th Completed Designe. October 12th. At Mr. Montacues with Mr Fitch and agreed upon setting out ground etc, At the Ground and drank with Mullett and Fitch. December 13th, Drew upright of Wings for Montacue. December 15th, With Mr. Montacue, Mr. Sidley, Fitch, Davys here. Saw module approved. Orderd all haste to be made. [5 March 1675] Finisht estimate for Mr Montacue. March 17th. Mr. Fitch here, Before he went to Mr. Montacue. Davys men brought in Module. Directed carpenter about the Ceeling of the stairs and partition and shoring plate of dining room May 22nd in Bloomsberry with Mr. Montacue Mr. Russell, Leak, etc, Measurd out Ground to a square June 29th. Set out Mr Montacues front. July 6th Set out foundations. July 24th Fell out with Mr. Fits about the stock bricks in the front of the house. September 1st. Saw the chimneys set out. November 13th. Mr. Montacue agreed with Davys. Italian painter Plaisterer and hanging maker. [28 April 1676] to Mr. Montacues. The west half of his Roof up. Resolved on the height of the wings, the rooms to be only 14 foot in the cleer. May 2nd. With Mr. Fitch at Bloomsberry Directed the placing the chimneys in the garrets. May 10th. Mr. Povey to board the upper part of the Roof. May 24th, At Mr. Montacues. Saw his new bought picture some good. Much discourse with him about high roof. To Bloomsberry. Discoursd Hayward he demanded £30 for higher roof, stair, stairhead, chimneys etc. June 29th. Scarborough here about mending chimney it was crackd and setled June 30th. Scarborough here, Newland asked £4 for new fitting chimneys. Orderd Scarborough to have them proceeded with. July 1st. With Mr. Montacue about covering chimneys … To Bloomsberry. At the top of the new flat. Directed covering and trussing chimneys. He orderd Copper guilt balls and iron work for pavilion chimneys. I directed moulding at the bottom of the chimneys. July 3rd. Directed the top of chimneys at Thomsons. July 4th. With Waters about chimney pieces. July 8th. To Thomsons and Bloomsberry. Irons for chimney done. July 24th At Mr Montacues. Discoursd about Portico and cupelos. August 17th. Spoke with Mr. Montacue … about altering the chimneys on the pavilions. September 12th, At Mr. Montacues. He allowed to leave out turret of wings. September 21st To Mr. Montacues. With him to Bloomsberry. Pleasd chimneys. Cupelos over gateways 1, etc. Discoursd with Thomson about gateway and Stepps. [13 June 1677] Set out garden. August 28th. At Bloomsberry orderd Norris £40 on chimney pieces. November 24th. Waited on Mr. Montacue and Sidley then read over Fitches demand of overwork. November 28th. With Scarborough to Mr. Montacue with him to his house and into his Garden. Deliverd Fitches papers to Mr. Scowen.

December 5th. Discoursed with Mr. Montacue, He seemd well satisfyd in all things . . . Desird me to send him the agreements, Designes and Estimates. December 6th. Mr Montacues account ended, wherein he is made Debtor to Mr. Fitch £800. [5 January 1678] Directed Thomson about stairs with corbells etc. February 4th. With Norris bespake chimney pieces and agreed for £60. March 8th. at Bloomsberry directed passages, stairs, struck stove, wainscoting, staircase. [21 January 1679] With Hayward to Montacue house. Ballisters on top **2** of house and raile on court stairs, February 28th. at Mr. Montacues with Hammond about widening stairs. [2 February 1680] to Mr Montacue. Looke with Scowan sash windows blown down. July 7th. At Mr. Montacues, spake to him for money he promised me. Speedily viewed the cracks. None but that in the turret at the east of the Cloyster.'

29 Excavations in the forecourt of the British Museum located the foundations of the wings of Montagu House and a small area of the main front. There was no evidence of fire or rebuilding, suggesting that the damage was to the staterooms, and seems only to have destroyed the floors and roof, but probably left the walls upstanding. (Information from Anthony Spence, Department of Prehistory and Europe, British Museum.)

Chapter 7

The Status of Instruments in Eighteenth-Century Cabinets

Robert Anderson

The British Museum, an innovative institution from various points of view, might have developed down several paths. A glimpse of at least one set of possibilities is provided by Tobias Smollett's *The Expedition of Humphry Clinker,* published in London in 1771. The form of Smollett's text is that of a series of letters from travellers to a range of correspondents. One traveller, Matthew Bramble, an irascible Welsh squire, writes to his confidant, friend and physician, Dr Lewis, on 2 June in the following terms:

> Yes, Doctor, I have seen the British Museum; which is a noble collection, and even stupendous, if we consider it was made by a private man, a physician, who was obliged to make his own fortune at the same time: but great as the collection is, it would appear more striking if it was arranged in one spacious saloon, instead of being divided into different apartments, which it does not entirely fill – I could wish the series of medals was connected, and the whole of the animal, vegetable, and mineral kingdoms completed, by adding to each, at the public expence, those articles that are wanting. It would likewise be a great improvement, with respect to the library, if the deficiencies were made up, by purchasing all the books of character that are not to be found already in the collection. They might be classed in centuries, according to the dates of their publication, and catalogues printed of them and the manuscripts, for the information of those that want to consult, or compile from such authorities. I could also wish, for the honour of the nation, that there was a complete apparatus for a course of mathematics, mechanics, and experimental philosophy; and a good salary settled upon an able professor, who should give regular lectures on these subjects.[1]

This critique of the young British Museum – it had been open to the public for only twelve years when *Humphry Clinker* was published – reveals some interesting attitudes towards what might be expected of a museum. There is criticism of the building, perhaps because Montagu House was not purpose-built like the earlier Ashmolean Museum of 1683 but was adapted from a domestic dwelling, however grand. The references to the animal, vegetable and mineral kingdoms recall the institutional purposes rehearsed by Elias Ashmole when the Ashmolean Museum statutes were drawn up in 1686: 'Because the knowledge of Nature is very necessarie to humaine life, health and the conveniences thereof, & because that knowledge cannot be soe well & usefully attain'd, except the history of Nature be knowne & considered . . . I have amass'd together a great variety of naturall Concretes & Bodies, & bestowed them on the University of Oxford.'[2] Finally, Smollett's wish for a teaching function for the British Museum was also to be found in the Ashmolean, where two floors were given over to

instruction. The first keeper, Robert Plot, taught chemistry and the 'history of Nature', while John Whiteside, keeper from 1714 to 1729 established courses of experimental philosophy in the Museum.

With the benefit of hindsight, a science teaching agenda for the British Museum might seem a strange aspiration. But was it so strange at the time? The Museum had been launched with a distinct lack of direction, defined only by Sir Hans Sloane's rather loosely ordered collections and by the holdings of the Cotton and Harley libraries. The Act of Parliament of 1753 and the early pronouncements of the Trustees are equally unhelpful on matters of purpose. Learning about science and mechanics had become popular in mid-eighteenth-century London, a socially desirable pastime. The interests of Trustees, in many cases, would certainly have included the gaining of scientific knowledge, while the 1753 Act contains the following assertion.

> And whereas all Arts and Sciences have a Connexion with each other, and Discoveries in Natural Philosophy and other Branches of speculative Knowledge, for the Advancement and Improvement whereof the said Museum or Collection was intended, do and may in many Instances, give Help and Success to the most useful Experiments and Inventions: Therefore, to the end that the said Museum or Collection may be preserved and maintained, not only for the Inspection and Entertainment of the learned and curious, but for the general Use and Benefit of the Public.

Perhaps Smollett's proposal was not so outlandish. To examine these possibilities further, the place of the physical sciences in museums in the eighteenth century needs to be considered. In particular, the ways in which scientific instruments were meant to be regarded by those who encountered them should be examined. Had he found them there, Smollett's Matthew Bramble clearly would have wished instruments in the British Museum to play a strongly utilitarian role. In fact there were scientific instruments in the Museum from the day it first opened to the public on 15 January 1759, but they were not for teaching mechanics or experimental philosophy; rather they found their place alongside other kinds of antiquities and curiosities. But that is not quite the full story: the Museum's public presentation of the experimental work of the first Principal Librarian, Gowin Knight, needs assessment, which throws the status of the instrumental antiquities into sharper focus.

This dichotomy between the useful and the antiquarian is present in earlier, private, cabinets of curiosity, although lines can be blurred. How, for example, was the abacus, most probably acquired by John Tradescant the Elder on his visit with Sir Dudley Digges to Archangel in 1617, regarded when it formed part of the foundation collection of the Ashmolean? Tradescant the Younger's catalogue of 1656 describes it as 'Beads strung upon stiffe wyres, and set in four-square frames wherewith the Indians cast account'; the 1685 Ashmolean manuscript catalogue calls it 'Abacus Japonicus', a label pasted on it is inscribed 'Numerical table of the Chinese', and it is now known to be a Russian form of abacus, the *schety*.[3] The confusion concerning its origin and type are strong indications that it was collected for its curiosity value and not understood as a functional calculating device. On the other hand, the huge collection of tools amassed by the Elector Augustus of Saxony listed in an inventory of 1587 was clearly for his own use, as testified by some of the surviving products of his handiwork.[4] The question remains whether other kinds of scientific object such as geodetic and gunnery instruments were used in the field, were kept indoors as demonstration items, or simply functioned as symbols of intellectual prowess, to be viewed by admirers in a museum sense.

There is a *genre* of painting which shows scientific instruments set out on tables or shelves alongside classical antiquities and collections of pictures. What is the status of these? Were they ever, in fact, displayed in this fashion? Or again, were they symbolic of the understanding of their owner or even, for astronomical items or globes, the power of the ruler over the heavens and the earth? (A persuasive explanation of the five early eighteenth-century massive masonry observatories of Maharajah Jai Singh at Jaipur and at other north Indian cities is that they symbolized his absolute control over the cosmos.[5])

Some paintings include representations of instruments in cabinets of curiosities, which give clues to attitudes adopted towards them. In a Flemish composition of about 1620, titled *Cognoscenti in a Room hung with Pictures* in the National Gallery in London, a group of scientific instruments is shown on a table on the bottom left-hand side (fig.20).[6] Four of the eleven cognoscenti seem to be engaged in discussion about them; paintings, sculptures, prints and works of art are depicted here as well as the instruments, seemingly reflecting aspects of contemporary learning and connoisseurship. The instruments are contemporary with the date of the painting, and thus are not of antiquarian interest; moreover, they appear to have no particular pedagogic function, but imply learning and status. The use of instruments as symbols of learning in paintings continued well into the eighteenth century, and evidence is offered by a few other paintings. One by Wenzel Wehrlin, now in Wimpole Hall in Cambridgeshire,[7] shows a curious scene of a gentleman *en deshabille*, with books, prints and *objets de vertue* strewn around: a mid eighteenth-century vacuum experiment is also included, as is a globe and other scientific material. This untidy scholar is represented as a man of broad cultural taste, the top of his harpsichord acting as his display table. A (perhaps slightly earlier) portrait incorporating scientific instruments as intellectual props includes a prominent orrery of perhaps 1745, of a type constructed by Benjamin Cole and known as a Grand Orrery. This is an expensive and rare device; the instruments are tidily arranged on shelves behind the sitter. Artist and sitter are unknown; the painting is in the Science Museum, London.[8]

A new genre of scientific instruments was developed from the early years of the eighteenth century, examples of which were used for teaching and entertainment. The activity has been associated with what has been referred to in the last few years as 'science as public culture', and it is closely related to the public demonstration of Newtonian natural philosophy.[9] A number of these instruments were developed at the behest of the Royal Society, which was founded in 1660 (incidentally, the year of Sloane's birth). These entered what became known as the Society's 'Repository', used in the same sense as the word 'Museum'. The first item to enter was an air pump presented by Robert Boyle in May 1661, while in the following year natural history specimens were added, including the skin of a bird of paradise and a piece of elephant hide.[10] In October 1663 the Society's 'Curator of Experiments', Robert Hooke, was also appointed to 'have the keeping of the repository' – in other words, to be the museum curator. The collection of natural rarities expanded through the early 1660s (except for the plague year of 1665), but in 1666 the Secretary wrote to Boyle to say that the physical sciences were to be catered for, mentioning as objectives 'the Collecting a Repository, the setting up a Chymicall Laboratory, a Mechanicall operatory, an Astronomicall Observatory and an Optick Chamber'. These facilities were very clearly intended for use, and there was no antiquarian component of their disposition at this stage.

In 1681 Nehemiah Grew published his *Musaeum Regalis Societatis, or a Catalogue and Description of the Natural & Artificial Rarities Belonging to the Royal Society and preserved at Gresham College.* This is a very sophisticated work, the rationale of which Grew describes in his Preface. The collection described is largely of the natural world (this occupies 350 of the 386 pages) but Part IV lists 'Artificial Matters', and includes chemical specimens, instruments of natural philosophy, 'Things relating to the Mathematicks and some Mechanicks' (a category which includes certain ethnographic items), and coins. There is some slight antiquarian feel to certain entries, with provenances relating to earlier work of Fellows of the Society (most notably Newton's in relation to the reflecting telescope which was kept in the Repository).

By 1710, the collection was in disarray: the (admittedly morose) German traveller, Zacharias Conrad von Uffenbach, found that: 'Hardly a thing is to be recognized, so wretched do they all look . . . the finest instruments and other articles [are] not only in no sort of order or tidiness but covered with dust, filth and coal-smoke, and many of them broken and utterly ruined.' The state of the collection fluctuated through the first half of the eighteenth century and, after temporary improvement, by 1752 it was again in 'a ruinous forlorn condition'. Then in 1779 it was offered to the British Museum and accepted, though neither party seems to have been in much of a hurry: the minutes of the Trustees for 24 February 1781 record: 'The President of the Royal Society acquainted the Board that the Museum of the Royal Society, which had been formerly presented to the British Museum, was ready to be delivered on being sent for.'[11] On 2 March Daniel Solander was told to arrange for the removal of the Natural Curiosities'[12] and on 15 June he was able to report that the collection was stored in the basement of Montagu House.[13] Does that mean that only the natural history specimens were transferred and not those distressed 'finest instruments' seen by von Uffenbach? The evidence is uncertain, since another Museum manuscript refers to the transfer of 'A large Collection of natural and artificial curiosities'. The situation is complicated further because it is known that a few instruments, including the revered copy of Newton's reflecting telescope, were transferred from Crane Court to the Society's headquarters at Somerset House. It therefore seems likely that by the date under consideration some scientific instruments had already gained antiquarian status. Unfortunately there are no British Museum records which might clear up the uncertainty about which instruments, if any, were transferred. No material that might have originated in the Royal Society's Repository can be identified in the present collections.[14]

Not all instruments developed for demonstration purposes were destined for such exalted surroundings as the Royal Society. From early in the eighteenth century, a significant number of entrepreneurial lecturers in natural philosophy made a living from providing courses for the public. The first such lecturer to be identified is James Hodgson, whose advertisements, which appear from January 1705, made a particular point of boasting of the instruments to be used to demonstrate scientific principles. Those subscribing would encounter items such as 'Engines for Rarafying and Condensing Air, with all their Appurtenances . . . Microscopes of the best Contrivance, telescopes of a convenient length . . . Utensils proper for Hydrostatical experiments . . .', and so on.[15] Many (if not most) of the lecturers were peripatetic and incomes were maximized in the manner of circuses, by doing the rounds of the most lucrative towns and cities. The image of Henry Moyes might be considered (fig.21): born in 1750, he was in no way exceptional as an itinerant lecturer, apart from the fact that he was blind from birth. A Scotsman, he demonstrated science first around his native land before moving to more lucrative constituencies in England, basing himself in Manchester. In 1785 he went to America to teach, returning to Scotland five years later. He then lectured throughout Ireland. He is shown discoursing with an air pump by his side;[16] some lecturers accumulated waggon-loads of instruments which they hauled round the country with them.

Specialist instrument makers established themselves, largely in London, to benefit from the demands arising from this new form of educational entertainment. It is important to distinguish the activities of these itinerants from those who were pursuing new forms of knowledge – what might be called research – even though a good number of the lecturers in the early period were elected Fellows of the Royal Society (as was, for example, Hodgson). Instrument makers might also become Fellows: perhaps the most significant at this time was Francis Hauksbee senior, a constructor of air pumps and other sophisticated equipment, who was appointed to the position of Curator of Experiments at the Royal Society. Succeeding him in this position, after Hauksbee's death in 1713, was the Huguenot J.T. Desaguliers, who demonstrated experiments to King George I, published significant texts and travelled extensively in Britain and on the Continent. Teachers of natural philosophy could be men of some status: Desaguliers was later influential at the court of King George II and Queen Caroline, and he arranged courses for Frederick, Prince of Wales, establishing a collection of mathematical and astronomical instruments in the upper room of the Prince's house at Kew. After Frederick's

death in 1751, his son George became Prince of Wales and the 3rd Earl of Bute, who incidentally possessed a fine collection of scientific instruments of his own, saw to Prince George's education by engaging another lecturer in natural philosophy, Stephen Demainbray, to offer tuition. After George became King in 1760, an observatory was built at Richmond (which became known as the Kew Observatory). A large and comprehensive collection was amassed there, partly by means of the King commissioning the finest instruments available and partly by incorporating Demainbray's own equipment.[17] The King continued his interest in the early years of his reign and the collection became the best of its kind in Great Britain. Much of it survives and some is displayed today in the Science Museum, London.[18]

While there is no visual record of how the instruments were displayed in the Kew Observatory, they are likely to have been housed in glazed cabinets. Little was added after the 1770s, but the material remained in the building largely intact until it was transferred to King's College London, opening as the King George III Museum in 1843. Over this seventy-year period, the status of these instruments changed from that of working demonstration pieces to become a collection of antiquities. But even before this evolution, the collection must have had something of the feel of a museum; by analogy with the display of natural history specimens, the instruments probably appeared to form a taxonomy of the physical sciences. In this case, the *genera* could be considered as the traditional division of physics into mechanics, dynamics, heat, light, sound, magnetism and electricity.

Something is known about the display of other eighteenth-century collections of physical apparatus. An extensive cabinet of scientific specimens and artefacts was developed by the Frenchman Joseph Bonnier, Baron de la Mosson in the 1730s in his townhouse, the Hôtel du Lude, in Paris.[19] The collection was dispersed after Bonnier's death in 1744 and the house itself was demolished in 1861 when the rue Saint-Dominique was widened and incorporated in the Boulevard Saint-Germain. Bonnier commissioned a set of drawings of the collection in its cases from the architect Jean-Baptiste Courtonne, and eight of the nine survive. These confirm the idea that mechanics and physics could be arranged in taxonomic groups and displayed in a manner analogous to natural history. The divisions were categorized as anatomy, chemistry, pharmacy, drugs, turning (which was a princely activity indulged in by a number of early collectors), natural history and finally mechanics and physics. The display cabinets in ornate rococo style were individually designed for each division, with vertical sections divided by carved palm trees. Above four doorways leading into the gallery were paintings by Jacques de Lajoüe, signed and dated 1734, part representational of Bonnier's collection and part fantasy. One of these is now in the Beit Collection, Russborough, Ireland.[20]

Though we might mourn the destruction of such an exotic presentation of science, one eighteenth-century collection does survive intact within the building and in the cabinets that were constructed for it. This is the collection in the oval room created for Teylers Stichting in Haarlem in Holland where it remains as part of Teylers Museum. Pieter Teyler, a merchant, left his estate in 1756 to a foundation set up to purchase a home for a collection of natural history.[21] In 1779 Martinus van Marum was appointed director and was set the task of creating a scientific establishment. The architect Leendaert Viervant was engaged and, when the building itself was nearly completed, he enquired as to how he should set about the construction of display and storage cases. This concentrated minds wonderfully, and van Marum proposed an ambitious plan: apparatus should be collected specifically for research and discovery; the emphasis should be on large-scale, accurate equipment, the cost of which would be beyond the reach of private individuals; and models of useful machines and demonstration apparatus should also be included. The aim was to create a resource which could be used to provide public courses in experimental natural philosophy. The creation of the collection is an heroic story, in which van Marum eventually succeeded. The centrepiece, in the middle of the oval room, was to be the vast, free-standing disc electrical machine made by John Cuthbertson. The collection is set out in the cabinets in a way that reflects the systematic teaching of natural philosophy and the overall effect is significantly more austere than the housing provided for Bonnier's collection. Nonetheless, ornamental plaster panels for the domed roof, which reflect the contents of the cases below, were provided by J.O. Husly.

It is of interest that the collections discussed so far all had their genesis between 1730 and 1750, though collecting continued well after this period. Sir Hans Sloane's interest in physical instruments also dates from around this time. His inventory entitled 'Mathematicall instruments' was compiled in 1725 and he continued this general area of collecting activity until, it must be assumed, close to the date of his death in 1753.[22] But in many ways Sloane's motivations seems to have been fundamentally different from the impetus of those who have been examined here. Sloane's own scientific background is worth bearing in mind.[23] He had, after all, qualified in medicine and had practised as a physician, having studied at the Apothecaries' Hall in London, the Physic Garden at Chelsea, and the Jardin des Plantes and the Hôpital de la Charité in Paris. Even before his time in Jamaica, Sloane cultivated the friendship of John Ray and Robert Boyle. He was elected a Fellow of the Royal Society in 1685 at the age of twenty-five, and eleven years later he published his *Catalogus Plantarum*, on the flora of Jamaica, which he dedicated to the Royal Society and the College of Physicians. Sloane was not a major scientific figure of his age but he was certainly central to the scientific establishment. He was elected President of the College of Physicians in 1715 and served as President of the Royal Society for seventeen years, succeeding Sir Isaac Newton in 1727. Obviously Sloane's medical and natural history background is pertinent to his collecting activity in the natural world, but it also needs to be borne in mind when considering the entries for these items, few of which survive today, in his manuscript catalogues that can be categorized under the heading of what would now be called 'physical science'. For example, there are twelve entries for microscopes or sets of microscopes, and the question arises as to whether these were acquired because they were needed for scientific investigation or because they were seen as historically significant relics.

Sloane compiled thirty-one catalogues in manuscript, covering the whole spectrum of his collection. Some of these volumes survey a number of different categories of material. The scientific instruments appear in two separate catalogues,

listed in one under the category 'Mathematicall instruments', and in another in the 'Miscellanies' section.[24] The former is a coherent list of fifty-six items (numbered up to 57, but number 56 omitted). In the latter, judgment has to be exercised as to what constitutes an instrument, since the range of material defined as a 'Miscellany' is very broad, including much that would today come within the purview of oriental antiquities or of ethnography. Sixty-eight of the Miscellanies might be defined as scientific instruments, of which one is an entry added to Sloane's register four years after his death. This is the only item in either catalogue which is accompanied by a date of acquisition.

The obvious question to ask is why any given instrument appears within the 'Mathematicall' classification on the one hand or under 'Miscellanies' on the other. One possible explanation is that the nature of items under the former is akin to that of antiquities, while the latter would included items that might have been used in the course of Sloane's own scientific work. The three astrolabes are 'Mathematicall', including the remarkable late thirteenth-century example known as the 'Sloane Astrolabe'. This is an instrument that will repay much further study: nothing is know of its provenance, save that Sloane paid £2 11s. 6d. for it.[25] A second, highly refined astrolabe is that made in AH 1124 (AD 1712) for the last Safavid ruler, Shah Husain (reigned from 1694 to 1722, when he was ousted by an Afghan army). Presumably it came on to the market after Husain was overthrown, which would have meant that Sloane was acquiring a recently imported, nearly contemporary instrument, a possibility that introduces a further confusing aspect on his collecting policy; doubtless he was impressed by the highly refined craftsmanship.[26] Another 'non-useful' item is 'A copy of the Antique *orbis coelestis*, made from the original marble in the Farnese palace at Rome at the desire of the late Martin Folkes Esqr and purchased at his Sale.' Other items, which are only briefly described, include sectors, compasses, long telescope tubes, and a series of objects which previously had been the property of Sloane's patron, the Duke of Albemarle. Also to be found, perhaps recently made, was 'A way wiser to be fastened to the britches & knee to measure the distance any person walks'. However, some items of a similar kind appear in both lists: these include microscopes, such as the 'set of microscopes made by Mr Musschenbroek of Holland sent me from the Prince of Orange by Mr Desmarels & brought by Mr Bentinck when sent to complement. K. James on his coming to the crown', found amongst the Micellanies, and 'A small prospective glasse made by Mr Campani'. A few items on both lists indicate makers, for example Butterfield's dials, Marshall's and Wilson's microscopes, and Hauksbee the elder's hydrostatic balance. Amongst the non-European instruments in the Miscellanies are several Chinese and Japanese steelyards, Chinese compasses (presumably of the geomantic type) and a Chinese abacus 'of brasse'.

A number of objects have particularly interesting personal associations and relate to work being discussed at the time within the Royal Society, such as a specimen of lead glass made by Robert Boyle and glass containing colloidal gold made by Robert Hooke. There is also 'A thermometer of a new invention of Mr Reaumur' and 'A mercurial thermometer made by Mr Rowley opposite to St Martin's Church in imitation of Mr Reaumur'. Concerning the survival of these, very little remains.

The three astrolabes are still in the British Museum collection, as are the two sets of telescope tubes. There is no clear evidence about other instruments which might have been transferred from Sloane's home in Chelsea to Montagu House (though see below). The provenance of certain items currently at Bloomsbury which might possibly have been listed amongst the Miscellanies (for example the Chinese compasses) is too uncertain for an association to be made. The status of the instruments would be clearer if it were known how Sloane displayed his collection, or stored it: those few visitors who did record their impressions made extensive reference to the natural history specimens, but little else.

There is some slight indication that some of the instruments were on display in the early days of the public museum. A detailed guidebook of 1761 ascribed to Edmund Powlett (the earliest: the Museum had opened to the public only two years previously) with the title, *The General Contents of the British Museum: With Remarks, serving as a Directory in Viewing that Noble Cabinet*, mentions, 'In the other Respository near the Windows are a great Number and Variety of ancient mathematical instruments, by which the learned Observer may be enabled to judge how much that particular branch of Science is improved'.[27] Gowin Knight evidently treated early scientific instruments as though they were antiquities. But these were not the only instruments which the public could view when they came to the British Museum, and the other display throws the antique objects into sharp focus.

Knight was born the son of an impoverished clergyman. He took a medical degree at Oxford and later was to become a Fellow of the Royal Society.[28] Naturally ingenious, he experimented in magnetism, and this was to form the basis of his financial and social success. Magnets were in demand for navigational instruments, but up to the eighteenth century these had to be created from naturally occurring magnetic materials. Efforts were made by various investigators to produce magnets artificially, and in this Knight excelled. In 1756, with the support of various Fellows of the Royal Society, Knight landed the Principal Librarianship of the British Museum, thus becoming the first Director. He was required to live in the Museum itself (a tradition that has continued until very recently) and he insisted that his machine for creating permanent magnets should be installed in the Museum. It was housed in a small room at the south-west corner of the ground floor ('First State Story') of Montagu House, located strategically at the bottom of a staircase. It was to become part of the standard tour which visitors were required to take. Powlett's 1761 *Guide* describes it as follows: 'The first room we enter, contains some Sea Compasses, improved by Dr. Knight, such as are now used in the Royal Navy; and several Magnets and Apparatuses, serving to show the magnetical powers in philosophical Uses'.[29]

Unexpectedly, therefore, the early British Museum contained components of both traditional science museum and modern science centre. The question arises over whether the Museum ever considered acquiring the 'complete apparatus' that Smollett wished for, and providing the course of 'mathematics, mechanics and experimental philosophy'. There is no evidence that this was ever discussed by the Trustees, though in the list of Miscellanies there is an intriguing acquisition for 2 September 1757, out of character with everything else: this is 'An intire Electrical apparatus. Presented by Mr William Watson' (Watson was a Trustee). Like other scientific instruments acquired at the time, it does not survive. Does it perhaps indicate that Knight had intentions that were not fulfilled? There is a final piece of intriguing evidence. On 6 June 1761, a rare astronomical event took place, the Transit of Venus, when the planet Venus passed across the face of the Sun. It seems that on the day (and it should be remembered that at the time there were seven members of the Royal Society's council who were trustees of the British Museum), a party of eight assembled on the roof of Montagu House (including, just possibly, the sought-after itinerant lecturer in astronomy and Fellow of the Royal Society, James Ferguson) to observe the phenomenon.[30] Was there the possibility at this point that the British Museum might have become the public face of the Royal Society, what with the Museum's early emphasis on the natural world, the collection having been transferred to Bloomsbury and the Principal Librarian being an FRS himself? And if this line had been pursued, might the British Museum have developed into a proto-Royal Institution or even, perhaps, a Science Museum?

Notes and references

1 Tobias Smollett, *Humphry Clinker*, ed. James L. Thorson (London, 1983), p.96.
2 R. F. Ovenell, *The Ashmolean Museum 1683–1894* (Oxford, 1986), p.49.
3 Arthur MacGregor (ed.) *Tradescant's Rarities* (Oxford, 1983), p.253.
4 Joachim Menzhausen, 'Elector Augustus's *Kunstkammer*: An analysis of the inventory of 1587', in Oliver Impey and Arthur MacGregor (eds), *The Origins of Museums* (Oxford, 1985), pp.69–75.
5 Andreas Volwahsen, *Cosmic Architecture in India* (Munich, 2001), pp.8, 102–4.
6 Christopher Baker and Tom Henry, *The National Gallery Complete Illustrated Catalogue* (London, 1995), p.224, no.287.
7 BM, 30/2 (15 June 1781).
8 Inv. no. 1978-467. Some consider the sitter to be George Parker, 2nd Earl of Macclesfield.
9 Larry Stewart, *The Rise of Public Science: Rhetoric, technology and natural philosophy in Newtonian Britain* (Cambridge, 1992).
10 Michael Hunter, *Establishing the New Science: The experience of the early Royal Society* (Woodbridge, 1989), pp.123–56. A.D.C. Simpson, 'Newton's telescope and the cataloguing of the Royal Society's Repository', *Notes and Records of The Royal Society of London* 38 (1983–4), pp.187–214.
11 BM CE 1/4 fol. 828 (24 February 1781).
12 BM CE 3/7 fol. 752 (2 March 1781).
13 BM CE 3/7 fol. 1766 (15 June 1781).
14 Simpson, op. cit. (note 10), p.202, believes that none of the instruments were transferred to the British Museum.
15 Alan Q. Morton and Jane A. Wess, *Private and Public Science: The King George III Collection* (Oxford, 1993), pp.41–3.
16 John Kay, *A Series of Original Portraits* (Edinburgh, 1877), pp.177–9.
17 Ibid., pp.12–17.
18 The Science Museum has kindly agreed to the loan of a number of items for display in the King's Library in the British Museum when it reopens in 2003. This room, created by the architect Robert Smirke between 1823 and 1827 simply to house the library of King George III, no longer contains his books, which are now with the British Library at St Pancras.
19 C. R. Hill, 'The cabinet of Bonnier de la Mosson', *Annals of Science* 43 (1986), pp.147–74.
20 Marianne Roland Michel, *Lajoue et l'Art Rocaille* (Neuilly-sur-Seine, 1984), pp.184–7, 415 and figs 33–43.
21 G. L'E. Turner and T. H. Levere, *Van Marum's Scientific Instruments in Teyler's Museum* in E. Lefebvre and J.G. de Bruijn, *Martinus van Marum, Life and Work*, vol.I: iv (Leiden, 1973).
22 Peter Murray Jones, 'A preliminary check-list of Sir Hans Sloane's catalogues', *British Library Journal* 13 (1987), pp.38–51.

23 Arthur MacGregor, 'The life, character and career of Sir Hans Sloane', in Arthur MacGregor (ed.), *Sir Hans Sloane: Collector, scientist, antiquary; founding father of the British Museum* (London, 1994), pp.11–44.

24 Both of these manuscript catalogues are deposited in the Department of Ethnography, the British Museum.

25 Sloane describes it as 'A brasse astrolabe made at London for the latitude of Rome, London &c. wh. A perpetual almanact upon it'. A published catalogue which includes entries for two of the three surviving Sloane (occidental) instruments is F.A.B. Ward, *A Catalogue of European Scientific Instruments in the Department of Medieval and Later Antiquities of the British Museum* (London, 1981).

The Sloane astrolabe is no.324 in Ward's catalogue and one of the two sets of telescope tubes is 446; the other is omitted.

26 The astrolabe is signed as made by Abd-al-Ali, son of Muhammed Rafi al Juzil and is engraved by his brother Muhammed Bakir. The third Sloane astrolabe is an unsigned Maghrib instrument, probably of the eighteenth century.

27 Edmund Powlett, *The General Contents of the British Museum*, published by R. and J. Dodsley (London, 1761), p.31.

28 Patricia Fara, *Sympathetic Attractions* (Princeton, 1996), pp.36–46.

29 Powlett, op. cit. (note 27) p.98.

30 John Millburn, *Wheelwright of the Heavens* (London, 1988), pp.130–2.

Figure 20
*Cognoscenti in a Room hung with
Pictures* (detail), Flemish, *c*. 1620.
National Gallery, London (NG 1287).

Figure 21
Henry Moyes, itinerant lecturer in
chemistry and natural philosophy.
Drawn and engraved by John Kay,
dated 1796.

Chapter 8
'Utile et Dulce'
Applying knowledge at the Society for the Encouragement of Arts, Manufactures and Commerce
Celina Fox

We are become members of the Society for the Encouragement of the Arts, and have assisted at some of their deliberations, which were conducted with equal spirit and sagacity. My uncle is extremely fond of the institution, which will certainly be productive of great advantages to the public, if, from its democratical form, it does not degenerate into cabal and corruption.

Thus Melford, nephew of old Squire Bramble, regales his friend and constant correspondent, Sir Watkin Phillips, with an account of their London adventures in Smollett's *Humphry Clinker* (1771). The motto, 'Utile et Dulce', of the Society for the Encouragement of Arts, Manufactures and Commerce, founded in 1754, the year after the British Museum, could have various shades of meaning; to its members 'dulce' most obviously meant enjoyment of club life. As with so many of the voluntary societies started in Georgian Britain, the opportunity it presented for getting together, combining debate with conviviality, was symptomatic of an increasingly mobile and urban society in which new forms of communication and assembly lessened the risk of isolation and atrophy.[1]

At the same time, by its very title, the Society of Arts was intended to be 'utile', concerned with applied knowledge and active improvement. While other voluntary bodies busied themselves with intellectual and educational pursuits, politics and religion, moral and philanthropic concerns, it offered cash premiums for more or less anything that would encourage the substitution of British for imported foreign – especially French – goods. By 1760 it had sharpened its focus to concentrate on six key areas: Agriculture, Mechanics, Manufactures, Chemistry, Trade and the Colonies and the Polite Arts, each run by a committee which referred its decisions back for ratification by the Society as a whole.[2]

There is another level on which we can consider 'dulce' and 'utile' in relation to the Society of Arts and that is the way in which it combined, both socially and functionally, the polite and the mechanical. That such a coalition of interests was still something of a novelty is suggested by the ingenuous tone in which an anonymous clergymen wrote to a member of the Society in 1763: 'I agree with you that Philosophical Enquiries are very amusing, but should not we endeavour sometimes to benefit the World by our researches as well as entertain ourselves?'[3] Nevertheless, 'as well as' are key words: the Society's social make-up and practical outreach demonstrate that it was part of the world of knowledge, not isolated in some peculiar and lesser realm of its own.

Socially, the Society provided an outlet for an elite band of natural and mechanical philosophers as well as for respectable artisans. Of the ten founding members of the Society of Arts, four were fellows of the Royal Society including two, Henry Baker and the Revd Stephen Hales, who were also trustees of Sir Hans Sloane's will.[4] Baker, elected FSA in 1740 and FRS the following year, was the son-in-law of Daniel Defoe and something of a polymath. A naturalist and poet, he also published *The Microscope Made Easy* in 1743 and was awarded the Copley medal for his microscopical discoveries on saline particles. Hales, FRS from 1718 and Vice-President of the Society, was also a natural historian, Copley medallist and inventor, as well as being an active curate at Teddington, Chaplain to the Princess Dowager of Wales and her son, later King George III, and a trustee of the Colony of Georgia. The Society's first President was Lord Folkestone who was succeeded on his death in 1761, until 1793, by his brother-in-law, Lord Romney.[5]

Within ten years of its foundation, the Society had 2,136 members, paying a minimum of two guineas' annual subscription. Nearly two-thirds were genteel (styling themselves Esquire or above) and the remainder tradesmen, manufacturers and craftsmen.[6] Although, or because, this was a period when the British government was largely reactive in promoting economic growth and employment, by 1760 its members included the First Lord of the Treasury, the Duke of Newcastle, Secretary of State William Pitt the Elder, future Prime Minister the Earl of Bute, and nearly all the senior ministers in the Board of Trade. As a tenth of members had titles, Baker could congratulate himself on the 'rank and dignity' of the membership and committees were invariably chaired by gentlemen who had the time to devote to the Society's affairs.

At Baker's suggestion, special provision was also made for gentlemen inventors who applied for premiums. Medals or 'honorary premiums' were struck as tokens of esteem for 'the scholar, philosopher and gentleman of estate' as alternatives to the financial incentives that Baker believed best encouraged 'the mechanic, manufacturer and planter'.[7] But as financial need did not necessarily follow class divides, some genteel premium winners like the Revd Humphrey Gainsborough, one of the artist's inventive elder brothers, received cash while some leading London craftsmen like Christopher Pinchbeck welcomed honorary medals. The £60 premium which Gainsborough won in 1761 for his invention of a tide mill was equal to his annual stipend as pastor to the Independent Chapel at Henley-on-Thames.

'Dulce' and 'utile' were also combined on a functional level, never more so than in the field designated 'Polite Arts'. A particular emphasis was placed at first on 'mixt arts' that straddled the divide. Baker was keen to promote the commercial application of drawing by offering premiums to young male and female apprentices. Since drawing, he contended, 'enlivens the conception, corrects the judgement, and supplies the fancy with a thousand varieties', Baker believed that such premiums would improve standards of design across a wide range of manufactured goods, reducing the country's dependence on French imports.[8] Similarly, the wealthy Russia merchant and gifted amateur Robert Dingley, member of the Society of Dilettanti and Fellow of the Royal Society FRS (1748), succeeded in introducing premiums for modelling on the grounds that it was both of commercial benefit to the nation and a useful and ornamental art that could be applied to a vast range of trades, from coach building to the manufacture of papier-mâché snuffboxes.[9]

But while Baker and Dingley stressed the useful application of drawing and modelling to mechanical arts, an equally strong lobby in the Society campaigned on behalf of the exclusively polite arts and for a time, in the late 1750s and early 1760s, prior to the foundation of the Royal Academy of Arts in 1768, the Society served as an embryonic academy. This apparent diversion from the commercial concerns of the Society was essentially a pragmatic response to circumstance. By creating a class in 1757 of 'honorary drawings', rewarded by medals for the sons and daughters of the nobility who practised this 'noble and ingenious art' as a polite recreation, the interest of upper-class parents could be retained in the Society's affairs. Furthermore, it was claimed that for those who were their inferior in rank and merit, they might provide an example from whom later, 'as judges and protectors of the arts', patronage might be sought.[10]

Professional artists had campaigned for several decades to establish an academy for training artists and exhibiting art, believing they should enjoy thereby the distinctions and privileges accorded to the French Académie Royale des Beaux-Arts. The Society of Arts briefly filled the gap, supplying step-by-step inducements for training youth as well as providing exhibiting facilities for mature artists. Premiums were introduced for drawing after plaster casts of the *Dancing Fawn, Farnese Hercules, Dying Gladiator*, etc., in the Duke of Richmond's gallery at his Whitehall residence, after the live model at the St Martin's Lane Academy, for landscape and for English historical subjects in painting, engraving and medal design, as well as for sculptured figures and bas-reliefs in a variety of materials. Moreover, in 1760 the Society staged a combined exhibition with professional painters, including such high art luminaries as Joshua Reynolds and Richard Wilson, which constituted the first such event to be held in London.[11] In 1765, it was even proposed that a Rome scholarship be awarded by the Society to an under-twenty-one-year-old who promised to develop a 'Genius for Historical Painting'.[12]

Not surprisingly, there were tensions in attempting to fulfil both polite and useful expectations in tandem. William Hogarth left the Society in 1757, probably on the grounds that its comprehension of art was becoming too polite. A swathe of other artists, led by Reynolds, resigned in the 1760s because the Society was not sufficiently exclusive, a move that was to lead eventually, if tortuously, to the foundation of the Royal Academy of Arts. Some of the natural historians resigned because there was too much drawing; other members

complained because there was too much agriculture. But broadly speaking, the Society succeeded in mixing 'dulce' and 'utile', the polite and mechanical.

One of the 'mixt arts' promoted by the Society through premiums was gem-engraving in intaglio and cameo, which it deemed a 'very antient, useful and curious art', both diffusing classical standards of taste and encouraging the mechanical skills employed in the jewellery trade.[13] In 1747 Robert Dingley had published a paper in *Philosophical Transactions* on the mineralogical aspects of the subject.[14] Thomas Brand MP first proposed the premium in 1758, supported by Thomas Hollis and Matthew Duane. Hollis was a gentleman of letters, FRS and Fellow of the Society of Antiquaries FSA (1757), with a reputation for republicanism.[15] Duane was a wealthy Catholic lawyer from Newcastle with an interest in improving methods of coal mining.[16] He was also both FSA (1757) and FRS (1763), and had formed one of the best medal collections of the day. In 1766 he was elected a trustee of the British Museum and compiled a list of the duplicate coins in Sloane's collection.[17] In 1763, he took over the chairmanship of the Committee of Polite Arts from Hollis, a duty he performed for twenty years.

The Committee of Chemistry proposed premiums for methods of purifying onyxes and cornelians, for establishing a factory for leaf metal and bronze and for assorted methods of dyeing and tanning, as well as for making oils and varnishes. The Committee of Manufactures supported premiums for different branches of the textile and fashion industries, as well as for different kinds of paper making. Although these awards were usually made in cash, such useful inventions and improvements had 'polite' applications, or at least benefits for a polite clientele, supplying decorative and imitative finishes in home-produced materials for a vastly enlarged range of luxury goods.

If the Society's activities in the field of Polite Arts, Chemistry and Manufactures were contiguous with those of the wider world of knowledge, so too were they in the realms of Agriculture, Trade and the Colonies. The Society's interest in new plant specimens followed the tradition of botanical collecting as manifest in Sir Hans Sloane's herbarium. Its desire to support useful plant translocation paralleled the activities of the Royal Society under Sir Joseph Banks, himself a member of the Society from 1761 to 1764 and again in 1791.[18]

The eminent agricultural innovator Arthur Young became an active member of the Society, having been awarded gold medals for his method of rearing and fattening hogs in 1769 and for an account of the culture of cole seed (rape) in 1770. He served as chairman of the Committee of Agriculture between 1773 and 1776. The premiums offered for afforestation – the planting of acorns, alder, ash, chestnut, elm, fir, larch, poplar and so on – nearly all went to landowners who of course received gold and silver medals: the Duke of Bedford in 1758, the Earl of Plymouth in 1762, the Earl of Donegal in 1779, the Bishop of Llandaf in 1789. The utility of establishing plantations was generally recognized, given the widespread fear of shortages in the timber supply to the Navy and the increasing pace of enclosure.[19] Premiums for growing different types of grass were largely made in cash, while premiums for improved or new varieties of root vegetable were more evenly balanced between medals and money premiums. The Society encouraged the growth of crops already known, for example, turnips, carrots and parsnips, and was directly responsible for introducing the swede and mangel-wurzel.

Between 1754 and 1766 the Committee of Trade and Colonies discussed premiums for encouraging botanical gardens in the tropics, particularly the West Indies, awarding a gold medal in 1773 to Dr George Young for establishing one on the island of St Vincent. Cash premiums were awarded to planters of mulberry trees in Georgia and Carolina in 1756 and for producing silk filature there from 1759 onwards. In 1777 the Society offered a premium for the successful transfer of the Tahitian breadfruit to Britain, two years after an early Society member, John Ellis, had published a treatise on the plant. Following the failure of his notorious voyage in HMS *Bounty* in 1787, Captain William Bligh eventually succeeded in 1793 in delivering breadfruit plants from Tahiti to St Helena, St Vincent, Jamaica and finally to Kew. He was duly awarded the Society's gold medal.[20]

The Society also attracted a network of eminent foreign correspondents, virtually indistinguishable from those in touch with the Royal Society. Not unnaturally, there were particularly warm contacts with the French Académie Royale des Sciences whose long gestated project, the *Descriptions des Arts et Métiers*, was finally coming to fruition. They continued throughout the Seven Years War, the Society's Secretary Dr Peter Templeman, late Keeper of the Reading Room at the British Museum, becoming a corresponding member of the Académie in 1762 and exchanging information on matters such as winter vegetables and the planting of woods. In June 1764 the celebrated botanist and agronomist Henri-Louis Duhamel du Monceau, who was chief editor of the *Descriptions*, presented the Society with his treatise on trees and an account of the draper's art.[21] In return, the Society sent him seeds of a particular kind of fir he had requested and welcomed Duhamel's nephews whom he sent as envoys.

German economic and patriotic societies concerned with agriculture and industry were established on the model of the Society of Arts, usually on the orders of the ruler. These included the Academy of Useful Sciences founded in 1754 under the protection of the Elector of Mainz and the comparable Society founded in Karlsruhe in 1765 by the Margrave of Baden-Durlach, whose Grand Tour in the 1740s had included England and who was elected a member of the Society of Arts in 1767.[22] Empress Catherine II of Russia was induced to found the Free Economic Society of St Petersburg on the basis of a favourable memorandum about the Society received in 1765.[23] In 1766 Count de Schulenburgh left at the Society

> ... some Specimens of scarce and valuable Grass Seeds, Corn, Plants & Fossils &c. which he has collected from all Parts of Germany, Russia &c. &c. and which he desired the Society to accept. His Excellency had also a very large Collection of Manuscripts, Drawings and Models of Machines used in Mines, Agriculture, Manufactures &c Models or Copies of which His Excellency generously offers the Society. He has also lent (for the perusal of the Society) Four Folio Books illustrate with Copper Plates entitled Descriptions des Arts et Métiers, published at Paris.[24]

The relationship of the Society to museums, and in particular to cabinets of mechanical models and machines, also contributed to the project of Enlightening the British. Applications for the Society's premiums in Mechanics and Manufactures were often accompanied by drawings and models

and in 1760 it was decided that all models of machines which gained premiums would in future be the property of the Society. Similar collections existed all over Europe. In order to explain the mathematical principles of mechanics and the functioning of machinery, lecturers in natural philosophy had long used simple machines representing the lever, windlass, pulley, wedge and screw. Even as early as the sixteenth century there had been an interest in accurately constructed models of actual machines in which mechanics were applied, an interest that grew with the propagation of Baconian notions of scientific utility.

By the early eighteenth century both the Royal Society and Académie Royale des Sciences had built up collections of both types of model as fitting subjects for learned discourse.[25] Furthermore, individual savants were happy to combine both philosophical and practical models in their private mechanical cabinets. The collection formed in the 1730s by the rich amateur Joseph Bonnier de la Mosson is one of the best known, for its arrangement in the Hôtel du Lude in Paris was meticulously recorded in a series of drawings made by Jean Courtonne in 1739–40.[26] Less familiar, being unrecorded visually, are the collections of a similar scope formed by British grandee amateurs and sometimes even put to practical purposes. For example, Archibald Campbell, 1st Earl of Ilay and 3rd Duke of Argyll, amassed an impressive array of scientific instruments, machines, toys and models at his home, The Whim, Peebleshire. Models of the latest improvements in agricultural machinery were sent from London and Glasgow to be made up on the spot by local wrights and carpenters.[27]

Nevertheless, the greatest drive to build up such collections developed in the context of collective endeavour, notably at the universities. In Holland, Willem Jacob 's Gravesande, Professor of Mathematics and Astronomy at the University of Leiden, added several scale-models of mills etc., constructed at his own expense, to his exceptional collection of scientific instruments. They were purchased on his death in 1742 for the university cabinet of physics (founded in 1675 – the first to be formed at a European university).[28] In Sweden, a new Chair of National Economy ('oeconomica publica') was established by the government at the University of Uppsala in 1738, also the first of its kind in Europe. The first post-holder, Anders Berch, proceeded to found a 'theatrum-oeconomico-mechanicum' in 1754, comprising models relating to agriculture and manufacture, tools and samples of raw materials, arranged according to a quasi-Linnaean method of classification. For example, thirty examples of Swedish ploughs were divided into four family types.[29]

Naturally, each country had particular areas of technical concern: the Dutch specialized in models of wind- and water-mills, the Swedes in heating stoves and mining machinery. Some models were of almost universal interest, notably anything to do with shipping or artillery. But while such collections were frequently regarded as specialist or even secret, only to be viewed by a restricted audience, by mid-century as a corollary to the popularity of public lectures on natural philosophy, a more general audience for mechanical models was countenanced on the grounds of public utility. Some of the models used by travelling lecturers for practical demonstrations even became part of museum collections, such as those accumulated by Stephen Demainbray. When he was appointed superintendent of King George III's new observatory at Richmond in 1769, Demainbray models were added to the royal cabinet of fine scientific instruments, which was eventually handed over first to King's College London and then deposited later in the Science Museum.[30]

In Stockholm in 1756, collections of all kinds of mechanical contrivances culled from the Boards of Mines and Commerce, the War Office, Fortifications Corps, Academy of Sciences and Ironmasters' Association were brought together to form the Royal Chamber of Models. Housed on the top floor of the Old Royal Palace on Riddarholmen, the collection was open to the public and its intention was clearly pedagogic. By being arranged according to the problems they were designed to solve, the models, it was believed, would help train apprentices in the different mechanical principles, as well as in the assembly of machines.[31]

A similar motivation underlay the opening up of a ground-floor model room specifically intended for the display of ingenious machines and models at the Society of Arts' splendid new building on John Adam Street, completed to Adam's design in 1774. By the time a descriptive catalogue had been prepared in 1783, they numbered 165, made up of sixty-three models relating to agriculture, twenty relating to manufactures and eighty-two not reducible to any particular class but including mills, cranes, pumps, carriages and so forth.[32]

The British Museum was not wholly immune from these developments. Among the qualifications and duties drawn up for the first Principal Librarian was that of meeting and corresponding with 'learned and Ingenious men':

At such meetings might be Introduced any Curious Invention of Art where the Inventors may be sure of a Candid and proper Examination and afterwards with the Assistance of the Trustees as the Patron of the Museum be encouraged according to their deserts and Inventions properly made known for the Use and benefit of the publick.[33]

However, the British Museum does not appear to have risen to the challenge of promoting new invention. Smollett's crotchety provincial, Matthew Bramble, might still in 1771 be wishing of the Museum 'for the honour of the nation, that there was a complete apparatus for a course of mathematics, mechanics, and experimental philosophy; and a very good salary settled upon an able professor, who should give regular lectures on these subjects.' But by this period, mechanics had taken a more frivolous turn. Indeed, mechanical museums were all the rage in London. In the early 1770s the hottest and priciest ticket in town was for James Cox's museum of sumptuously bejewelled automata in Spring Gardens: peacocks, swans, oriental temples, and so on.[34] Despite appealing principally to Londoners' love of luxury and spectacle, it also laid claim – at least for marketing purposes – to utility. In her novel *Evelina* (1778), Fanny Burney made fun of the museum guide who was asked by the brusque Captain Mirvan what was the use of it all:

'Why, Sir, as to that, Sir', said our conductor, 'the ingenuity of the mechanism, – the beauty of the workmanship, – the – undoubtedly, Sir, any person of taste may easily discern the utility of such extraordinary performances.'
'Why then, Sir' answered the Captain, 'your person of taste must be either a coxcomb, or a Frenchman; though for the matter of that, 'tis the same thing.'

The hero Lord Orville probably best summarized Fanny Burney's own opinion:

The mechanism . . . is wonderfully ingenious: I am sorry it is turned to no better account; but its purport is so frivolous, so very remote from all aim at instruction or utility, that the sight of so fine a shew, leaves only a regret on the mind, that so much work, and so much ingenuity, should not be better bestowed.

In fact, some of the innovations which Cox's one-time assistant, John Joseph Merlin, included in his Mechanical Museum, opened in the 1780s in Prince Street, Hanover Square, were useful or at the very least ingenious gadgets, including a chair for gout sufferers, a valetudinarian bedstead, a form of roller-skates and assorted mechanical musical instruments.[35]

As we have seen, in this period 'dulce' was scarcely ever wholly divorced from 'utile'. Indeed, in a pre-vocationally driven age many would have agreed with Samuel Johnson that

It may sometimes happen, that the greatest efforts of ingenuity have been exerted in trifles; yet the same principles and expedients may be applied to more valuable purposes, and the movements which put into action machines of no use but to raise the wonder of ignorance, may be employed to drain fens, or manufacture metals, to assist the architect or preserve the sailor.[36]

Jacques de Vaucanson, creator of the famous automaton flute player, tambourine and flageolet player and the digesting duck that had astonished Europe in the 1740s, went on to design an automated silk-weaving machine that in turn inspired Jean Jacquard.[37] In 1782 he bequeathed his collection of models and machines to Louis XVI and the following year the Cabinet des Machines du Roi was established in the Hôtel de Mortagne (where Vaucanson had installed his collection), open to inventors and artisans. In Britain similar connections were made, an automaton chess player being claimed as the inspiration behind Edmund Cartwright's invention of the power loom.[38]

But compared with other collections, the significance of such mechanical models and machines was transient and their future insecure, superseded by new wonders and inventions, with the result that they were preserved, if at all, almost by accident.[39] The minutes of the Society in the later decades of the eighteenth century are littered with resolutions concerning repairs to its models, even for the grandest, such as the model made by Thomas Gregory of the Coalbrookdale Bridge that Abraham Darby III presented to the Society in 1787. Older models were sold, given away or destroyed. Once the Society began to use its model room to stage temporary exhibitions, the bulk of the model collection went first in 1850 to University College London (the trustees of the College having undertaken to repair and preserve them), then to the Patent Office Museum at South Kensington, where they languished in an unsightly shed alongside the rest of the museum, and finally in 1882 to the South Kensington Museum, becoming part of an independent Science Museum in 1909.[40]

It is fitting that the home of applied knowledge in arts and sciences in the twentieth and twenty-first centuries was inspired in part by the Society of Arts, whose first public exhibition of industrial art organized in March 1847 in the Society's model room, followed by others in 1848 and 1849, was to lead to the Great Exhibition of 1851 and thence, of course, to the foundation of the South Kensington complex. But by then the fine arts were firmly seated on a high academic horse and the sciences had become so specialized as to be increasingly removed from the public sphere.

The consequences of the art-science split along Exhibition Road are evident today, despite the best efforts of Prince Albert[41] to keep them united. But the debates of the nineteenth century and later should not be read back into the eighteenth century, when utility was not narrowly conceived and pleasure not divorced from it, when the useful and ornamental could easily co-exist. Furthermore, it will have been made clear that in the eighteenth century the applied fields promoted by Society of Arts were an important part of the spectrum of knowledge, not wholly divorced from the high culture represented by the British Museum. The application of knowledge could be both 'dulce' and 'utile', of relevance, concern and enlightenment to both the polite and mechanical classes.

Notes and references

1   P. Clark, *British Clubs and Societies 1500–1800* (Oxford, 2000).

2   The most recent general histories of the Society are D. Hudson and K.W. Luckhurst, *The Royal Society of Arts 1754–1954* (London, 1954) and J.L. Abbott and D.G.C. Allan (eds), *The Virtuoso Tribe of Arts and Sciences: Studies in the eighteenth-century work and membership of the London Society of Arts* (Athens, Georgia and London, 1992).

3   Royal Society of Arts (henceforth RSA) Guard-book, 4:63. The writer went on to propose the substitution of English elm for mahogany imported from the West Indies, provided he could discover a method of staining it to produce a 'true mahogany colour'.

4   M. Caygill, 'Sloane's will and the establishment of the British Museum', in A. MacGregor (ed.), *Sir Hans Sloane: Collector, scientist, antiquary; founding father of the British Museum* (London, 1994), pp.57–9. Also, D.G.C. Allan and R.E. Schofield, *Stephen Hales: Scientist and philanthropist* (London, 1980).

5   It is perhaps significant that Sir Jacob de Bouveries (afterwards Bouverie), created Viscount Folkestone in 1747, came from a family of Turkey merchants, descended from Flemish silk-weavers who had settled in Canterbury in 1568. He was the purchaser of the Holbein portrait of Erasmus from the Mead collection. For Romney see D.G.C. Allan, 'Robert Marsham, 2nd Baron Romney (d.1793) and the Society', *RSA Journal* 143 (1995), pp.67–9.

6   The most detailed analysis of the early membership of the Society is D.G.C. Allan, 'The Society for the Encouragement of Arts, Manufactures and Commerce. Organization, membership and objectives in the first three decades (1755–84)', University of London PhD thesis (1979).

7   RSA Guard-book, 1:103.

8   [H. Baker], 'Advantages arising from the Society for encouraging Arts', *Gentleman's Magazine* 26 (1756), p.62. The original manuscript is in RSA Guard-book, 1: 83, dated 28 January 1756.

9   RSA Guard-book, 8:85, dated 6 March 1757. See also J. Appleby, 'Mills, models and Magdalens: the Dingley brothers and the Society of Arts', *RSA Journal* 140 (1992), pp.267–73.

10 R. Dossie, *Memoirs of Agriculture and other oeconomical Arts*, vol.III (London, 1782), pp.xxi–xxii.

11 B. Allen, 'The Society of Arts and the first exhibition of contemporary art in 1760', RSA 139 (1991), pp. 265–9.

12 The proposal was agreed by the Committee of Polite Arts on 20 May 1765 but when it came before the Society on 2 April 1766, objections were raised, the decision was postponed and nothing further came of it.

13 G. Seidmann, ' "A very ancient, useful and curious art": The Society and the revival of gem-engraving in eighteenth-century England', in Abbott and Allan, op. cit. (note 2), pp.120–31.

14 'Some observations upon gems or precious stones; more particularly such as the ancients used to engrave upon', *Philosophical Transactions* 44, pt 2 (1747), pp502–6.

15 J.L. Abbott, 'Thomas Hollis and the Society 1756–1774', *RSA Journal* 119 (1971), pp.711–15, 803–7, 874–8. Also, W.H. Bond, *Thomas Hollis of Lincoln's Inn: A Whig and his books* (Cambridge, 1990). The boards of Hollis's 'democratical' books were stamped with daggers and caps of liberty.

16 D.G.C. Allan, 'Matthew Duane F.R.S., F.S.A. (1707–85): Gold Medallist and active member of the Society', *RSA Journal* 144 (October 1996), pp.35–7.

17 M.M. Archibald, 'Coins and medals', in MacGregor, op.cit. (note 4), pp.150, 152, 165 nn.14, 18.

18 D.G.C. Allan, 'Joseph Banks and the Society: another "curious case of membership"?' *RSA Journal* 141 (1993), pp.811–13.

19 For the significance of forestry for the landed elite see S. Daniels, 'The political iconography of woodland in late eighteenth-century England', in D. Cosgrove and S. Daniels (eds), *The Iconography of Landscape* (Cambridge, 1988), pp.51–72. T. Williamson, *Polite Landscapes: Gardens & society in eighteenth-century England* (Stroud, 1995), pp.124–30.

20 A. David, 'Bligh's successful breadfruit voyage', *RSA Journal* 141 (1993), pp.821–4.

21 Presumably, respectively, either *Traité des arbres et des arbustes qui se cultivent en France en plein terre* (Paris, 1755), or *De l'exploitation des bois* (Paris, 1764) and *Art de la draperie* (Paris, 1765), published as part of the *Descriptions*.

22 H-J. Braun, 'Some notes on the Germanic associations of the Society in the eighteenth century', in Abbott and Allan, op. cit. (note 2), pp.237–52.

23 J.A. Prescott, 'The Russian Free (Imperial) Economic Society, 1765–1917', *RSA Journal* 114 (1965), pp.33–7, 116 (1967), pp.68–70. Also, A.G. Cross, 'Early contacts of the Society with Russia', in Abbott and Allan, op. cit. (note 2) pp.265–75.

24 RSA Minutes, vol.11, 11 June 1766. It has not been possible to trace who this particular Count Schulenburg was, but presumably he was a member of the illustrious Prussian family rather than a descendant of George I's infamous mistress.

25 Sébastien Leclerc's engraving of the physical laboratory of the Académie in the Louvre shows a wealth of models of practical hoisting equipment, windlasses, pulleys and screws combined with artillery and architectural models, relief plans of fortifications, optical and musical instruments, as well as casts after antique and *écorché* figures. See M. Préaud, *Bibliothèque nationale. Département des Estampes. Inventaire du fonds français. Graveurs du xviie siècle*, tome VIII (Paris, 1980), pp.334–6, no.1309. On the growth of the collection see R. Hahn, *The Anatomy of a Scientific Institution: The Paris Academy of Sciences, 1666–1803* (Berkeley, Los Angeles and London, 1971), p.123.

26 The fullest description of the Hôtel during Bonnier's period of residence is given in B. Pons *et al.*, *Le Faubourg Saint-Germain. La rue Saint-Dominique. Hôtels et amateurs* (Paris, 1984), pp.151–4, 157–63. See also C.R. Hill, 'The cabinet of Bonnier de la Mosson', *Annals of Science* 43 (1986), pp.147–74. The shelves of the *cabinet mécanique* are lined with wheels, pulleys, pumps, windlasses and cranes, optical and other scientific instruments, as well as models of buildings and fortifications. An illuminating commentary on the overdoors decorated by Jacques de Lajoüe with fanciful scenes relating the contents of the shelves to a broader philosophical agenda is given in K. Scott, *The Rococo Interior* (New Haven and London, 1995), pp.167–71.

27 R.L. Emerson, 'The scientific interest of Archibald Campbell, 1st Earl of Ilay, and Duke of Argyll (1682–1761)', *Annals of Science* 59 (2002), pp.21–56. Much of his collection was acquired by his nephew, Lord Bute, and dispersed by sale after his death in 1793.

28 P. de Clerq, *The Leiden Cabinet of Physics* (Leiden, 1997), particularly pp.151–71. Many pieces survive and are displayed at the Boerhaave Museum, Leiden. Also L. Roberts, 'Going Dutch: situating science in the Dutch Enlightenment', in W. Clark, J. Golinski and S. Schaffer (eds), *The Sciences in Enlightened Europe* (Chicago and London, 1999), pp.366–9.

29 M. Jensen (ed.), *Wunderkammer des Abendlandes. Museum und Sammlung im Spiegel der Zeit* (Bonn, 1994), pp.58–9.

30 A.Q. Morton and J.A. Wess, *Public and Private Science: The King George III Collection* (Oxford, 1993). It is not clear whether the contents of the Observatory were open to the public in the eighteenth century but they were certainly described in *A Compendious Gazetteer; or, Pocket companion to the Royal Palaces, towns, villages, villas, and remarkable places within sixteen miles of Windsor* (Windsor, 3rd edn, 1794). Reference contributed by John Harris.

31 S. Lindqvist, *Technology on Trial: The introduction of steam power technology into Sweden, 1715–36* (Uppsala, 1984), pp.25–33.

32 *RSA Transactions* I (1783), pp.309–22.

33 British Library Additional MS 4449, fols 8–9, quoted in David M. Wilson, *The British Museum: A history* (London, 2002), pp.27–8.

34 R. Altick, *The Shows of London* (Cambridge, Mass. and London, 1978), pp.69–72. The finest collection of mechanical trivia which survives today is to be found in the Forbidden City, Beijing, which abounds in London- and Paris-made devices presented to successive Emperors of China in the eighteenth century.

35 M. Wright, 'The Ingenious Mechanick', in A. French (ed.), *John Joseph Merlin, The Ingenious Mechanick* (London, 1985), pp.47–59.

36 *The Rambler* 83, 1 January 1751.

37 A. Doyon and L. Liaigre, *Jacques Vaucanson, mécanicien de Génie* (Paris, 1966). M. Cardy, 'Technology as play: the case of Vaucanson', *Studies on Voltaire and the Eighteenth Century* 241 (1986), pp.109–23.

38 E. Baines, *The History of the Cotton Manufacture in Great Britain* (London, 1835), pp.229–30. See also D. Brewster, *Letters on Natural Magic, addressed to Sir Walter Scott, Bart.* (London, 1832), pp.285–6, who believed – as Johnson had anticipated – the passion for mechanical exhibitions worked by wheels and pinions, which characterized the eighteenth century, had reappeared in the stupendous mechanism of spinning-machines and steam-engines: 'Those mechanical wonders which in one century enriched only the conjuror who used them, contributed in another to augment the wealth of the nation; and those automatic toys which once amused the vulgar, are now employed in extending the power and promoting the civilization of our species.'

39 Defying this trend, one of the best preserved and most extensive collections was formed at Teylers Museum in Haarlem by Martinus van Marum in the 1790s, by commissions from leading instrument makers and from the sales of collections formed by amateurs earlier in the century. The model collections of the Conservatoire des Arts et Métiers (founded 1794) were based not only on Vaucanson's bequest but also on the collections of the Académie des Sciences, aristocratic assets confiscated during the Revolution and further bequests.

40 Only two eighteenth-century models from the Society of Arts remain in the Science Museum's collection: a model of a handloom (1857–104) and the Coalbrookdale Bridge model (1882–1929).

41 Prince Albert became President of the Society of Arts in 1843 and was instrumental in the success of the Great Exhibition of 1851. For the realization of his ideal of a didactic museum combining art and science in the service of industry as a monument to the Exhibition and encompassing, like the Exhibition, raw materials, machinery, manufactures and art, see A. Burton, *Vision & Accident: The story of the Victoria & Albert Museum* (London, 1999), pp.42–7. Significantly, in George Gilbert Scott's design for the Albert Memorial (completed in 1875) the four groups of sculpture closest to the Prince represent Agriculture, Manufactures, Commerce and Engineering, raised above the podium frieze of poets, musicians, painters, architects and sculptors.

Chapter 9

Wedgwood and his Artists
David Bindman

In the chapter of *The Stones of Venice* that was separately printed as *The Nature of Gothic*, John Ruskin locates the origin of the social divisions of his time, as did many others, somewhere between the seventeenth century and the intellectual and industrial revolutions of the eighteenth and early nineteenth centuries. His explanation of the change of mentality from the medieval to the modern anticipates Michel Foucault's account of the way the classical age (broadly the Enlightenment) subjected the body to new forms of discipline, so that it becomes 'manipulated, shaped, trained . . . [until it] obeys, responds, becomes skilful and increases its forces'.[1] This new body for Foucault is represented most fully by La Mettrie's *L'homme-machine*; it rests on a principle of 'docility', by which the body is subjected, used, transformed, and improved for the benefit of the ruling powers. Ruskin, in comparable terms, saw the modern working man as dehumanized by the imposition on him of the pursuit of mindless perfection:[2]

> you can teach a man to draw a straight line, and to cut one . . . and to copy and carve any number of given lines or forms, with admirable speed and perfect precision . . . but if you ask him to think about any of those forms . . . he stops; his execution becomes hesitating . . . he makes a mistake in the first touch he gives his work as a thinking being. But you have made a man of him for all that. He was only a machine before, an animated tool.

The working man is thus liberated from 'this degradation of the operative into a machine, which, more than any other evil of the times, is leading the mass of the nations everywhere into vain, incoherent, destructive struggling for a freedom of which they cannot explain the nature to themselves'.

Ruskin's opposition of man and machine has a particular resonance for those who have read Josiah Wedgwood's letter to his partner Thomas Bentley of 7 October 1769, in which he expresses his hope that in his factory at Etruria, he might 'make such *Machines* of the *Men* as cannot Err'.[3] For Wedgwood, the problem of the mass production of pottery was as Ruskin stated it, but he *wanted* his own men at least to be like machines. When one person works alone on a complex task like making a teapot, a task which involves different processes (throwing the pot, attaching hand and spout, applying decoration and so on), he is likely to produce a result which can be judged both individual and imperfect, like the wares produced by Wedgwood's predecessors and more old-fashioned competitors in Staffordshire. With such a method of production, consistent quality and price could not be guaranteed, for the manufacturer was in varying degrees subject to the will and needs of his workers, who may have valued the independence of 'traditional' methods, or not have wanted to work on certain days, or whatever. Such a method of work was, as industrialization progressed, believed to create an

undisciplined and even unruly workforce, and the labourers working in and around the potteries were in Josiah Wedgwood's time, we are assured by his Victorian hagiographer Eliza Meteyard, notorious for their drunkenness and fornication. She informs us disapprovingly, 'Almost every Pottery village had its special wake; and the celebration of this was a saturnalia of the grossest kind.'[4] John Wesley noted that, as he preached in Wedgwood's town of Burslem, 'Deep attention sat on every face, though as yet accompanied by deep ignorance'. Some labourers laughed at him throughout the lecture and threw mud at him, but they were as nothing to the men of Walsall whom Wesley described as 'fierce Ephesian beasts'; they hurled stones at him the whole time, and threw him down the steps.[5] According to Meteyard again, Wedgwood, who was 'in feeling and habit something very different from the coarse journeyman', was able in his factory to impose virtue upon vice, and civilization upon barbarity, by means of his own abstinence from the vices of his fellows and by his paternalistic labour practices.[6] The machinelike regularity of his wares was for her, and perhaps also for Wedgwood himself, a form of social benevolence, emblematic of the imposition of a Christian order upon heathenism, and of social hierarchy upon disorder; to her contemporary Ruskin, it stood, on the contrary, for the elimination of human engagement and self-expression, which was for him the only proof against the real Ephesian beasts of the nineteenth century, the manufacturers who imposed mechanistic practices upon their workers.

In reality, Wedgwood did not suddenly bring order to the Staffordshire potteries, nor was he the first to use machines to bring clean lines and regularity to pottery.[7] The desire to make machines of men was only an aspiration, and his letters are full of complaints about the un-machinelike behaviour of his workers. Nor did Ruskin have Wedgwood specifically in mind in his attack on division of labour and the consequences of the mechanical production of consumer goods; indeed in one of his few references to the potter, in *The Two Paths* of 1859, he holds him up to manufacturers for approval as someone who made his wares 'educational instruments [rather than] mere drugs on the market'.[8] In any case it was only really in the 1960s, with the work of Neil McKendrick on the Wedgwood papers, that it became possible to see the precise nature of Wedgwood's production and sales methods. For McKendrick, the distinctive feature of Wedgwood's methods was not in fact the division of labour, or the mechanization of the workforce, or even technical innovation, but aggressive marketing: creating an air of exclusivity and fashionability around works that were relatively cheap to produce in large numbers.[9] Wedgwood's pottery was always more expensive than that of his rivals, who could often match his quality. He had, therefore, to add value to it in other ways; hence for McKendrick the most significant remark made by Wedgwood to Bentley was the claim that 'Fashion is infinitely superior to merit', to which he added, 'If you have a favourite child you wish the public to fondle and take notice of, you have only to make choice of proper sponcers.'[10] In other words, if you can make a product fashionable among high society or achieve a name for stylishness, then those who are not themselves fashionable will wish to emulate their social betters. This meant that Wedgwood kept his public prices high, and then endlessly pursued the Royal Family, aristocracy and notable connoisseurs like Sir William Hamilton, soliciting their advice, offering them exclusive opportunities for purchase, free gifts and bargains, the flattery of naming pottery after them, doing menial and loss-making commissions for them, all for the sake of being able to exploit the social cachet of their approval. As Wedgwood famously explained to Bentley in August 1772:

> The Great People have had these Vases in their Palaces long enough for them to be seen and admired by the Middling Class of People, which class we know are vastly, I had almost said, infinitely superior in number to the Great, and though a great price was, I believe, at first necessary to make the vases esteemed Ornament for Palaces, that reason no longer exists. Their character is established, and the middling People would probably b[u]y quantitys of them at a reduced price.[11]

It is in this context that we should understand Wedgwood's presentation to the British Museum in 1786 of the great Pegasus Vase (fig.22), which he described as 'the finest & most perfect I have ever made'.[12] The source for the relief design made by Flaxman was, as is well known, a Greek vase in Sir William Hamilton's collection illustrated in D'Hancarville's famous catalogue, and Wedgwood took the opportunity to present Hamilton with a separate plaque of the same motif.[13] No doubt he often quoted Hamilton's polite reply to him: 'I never saw a bas relief executed in the true simple antique style half so well as he [Flaxman] did the Apotheosis of Homer from one of my vases.'[14] On display in Montagu House, the vase with its relief design would have been a reminder to the well-born, wealthy and respectable, who were the intended visitors to the museum in the late eighteenth century, that Wedgwood wares were not mere pottery, but represented true taste in the spirit of antiquity, and it was a reminder that Moderns could aspire to the achievements of the Ancients. Wedgwood was particularly assiduous in pursuing those associated with the British Museum, like Sir Joseph and Lady Banks and Daniel Solander, of whom he issued portrait medallions (fig.23),[15] for they could not only validate a taste for Wedgwood's pottery, they were also associated with the glamour of Captain Cook's voyages to the South Seas. The Museum in Montagu House was thus itself a 'palace' in the sense of Wedgwood's letter to Bentley quoted above, for it allowed respectable members of the middling classes to witness a display of intellect and taste by their social superiors.

It was well understood by Wedgwood that he could not maintain the establishment at Etruria only by sales to the Great Folk; indeed, it is likely that many of his more exclusive items either lost money or barely covered their costs. High volume sales had to be maintained in all circumstances. This necessitated an equally high level of opportunism, the production of ever more varied offerings to the affluent public,

and the consequent insatiable need for new designs.[16] The artists Wedgwood employed were inextricably caught up in the contradictions that flowed from the need both for mass production and for exclusivity. Artists were of use to him in providing designs or bas reliefs to be translated or cast into moulds in every size to fit any setting, but they could also help to make Wedgwood wares more fashionable in London society. Three years after the founding of the Royal Academy, he wrote to Bentley in 1771: 'I wrote to you in my last concerning Busts, I suppose those at the Academy are less hackneyed and better in general than the plaister shops can furnish us with.'[17] But he adds characteristically, 'besides it will sound better to say this is from the Academy, taken from an original in the Gallery of so and so, than to say we had it from Flaxman [senior]'.

It is often said that Wedgwood's relationship to his artists was a paternal one, but if they made up a family together, they were a somewhat dysfunctional one. As far as the everyday production of moulds was concerned Wedgwood had the artist he needed all along: his most prolific modeller, the appropriately named William Hackwood, who worked for the firm for sixty-three years from 1769 to 1832.[18] He was a remarkable craftsman though he had had no formal training, working entirely and almost always anonymously at Etruria. In 1776 Wedgwood expressed the wish that he had 'half a dozen more Hackwoods', and a biddable and unambitious designer like Hackwood was certainly essential for the bulk of his production. The new breed of painters, often puffed up by the ideals of the recently founded Royal Academy and wary of commerce, were by contrast more problematic. There was little he could get out of its President Joshua Reynolds except permission to reproduce his portraits in medallions, and advice on potentially employable sculptors like Henry Webber, whose debts made him willing to sign on for the long-term as head of the ornamental workshop at Etruria.[19]

Wedgwood did, however, apply his ever-fertile mind to, among others, Joseph Wright of Derby, a semi-detached member of the Academy, who had the advantage of living in a town not far from Etruria, commissioning from him a number of paintings. From the start Wedgwood sought to use at least one of Wright's paintings, The Corinthian Maid (New Haven, Yale Center for British Art) to advertise his pots (fig.24). As he wrote to Bentley on 5 May 1778:[20]

> I should like to have a piece of this Gentlemans art, but think Debutade's daughter would be a more apropos subject for me than the Alchymist though one principal reason for my having this subject would be a sin against the Costume. I mean the introduction of our Vases into the piece for how could such fine things be supposed to exist in the earliest infancy of the Potters Art. You know what I want, & when you see Mr Wright again I wish you would consult with him upon the subject.

What is unexpected here is not the pictorial impropriety of Wedgwood's demand, to put modern commercial pots into a painting of the origin of pottery in the ancient world, but his awareness of it, and his well-placed confidence that the artist would acquiesce, for he notes also that Wright was short of commissions at the time. In brief, Wright was both obsequious and canny in his dealings with Wedgwood, but sought literally to push the pots as far as he could into the background of the picture, encouraged, it appears, by Erasmus Darwin who was against having pots in the picture in the first place. As Wright wrote to Wedgwood, 'It seems to me the elegant simplicity of the subject shoud be disturbed as little as possible by other objects; an opening into another room, wth some elegant vases upon a shelf, others on the ground, much kept down, woud mark her fathers profession & enrich the picture without disturbing the effect, but I think I would not introduce a furnace.'[21]

Though no-one could have been more biddable than Joseph Wright, Wedgwood found sculptors easier to handle than painters, not only because of his need for designs in relief, but because they were usually more habituated to the mundane demands of ornamental commissions. John Flaxman must have seemed an ideal prospect because he was already known to Wedgwood through his father, John Flaxman Snr, who had long been a supplier of designs.[22] The younger Flaxman appeared to bridge the worlds of Etruria and fashionable London through his early success as a sculptor at the Royal Academy, though he just failed to win a scholarship to Rome. In the Nottingham Castle Museum there is a garniture of three silver vases hallmarked 1774, the central one of which is incised: 'Josiah Wedgwood from this esteemed friend to John Flaxman. Well my lad I told you that your designs were meant for the eyes of Royalty. Think of that. July 6th 1776', which was Flaxman's twenty-first birthday.[23] This inscription would give a touching picture of Wedgwood's paternal attitude towards the young artist, and his unaffected pride in the talents of those who worked for him, were it not almost certainly spurious: it is very likely to have been added in the late nineteenth century, following Meteyard's and Samuel Smiles's uncritical accounts of Wedgwood.[24]

In reality, the relationship between Wedgwood and Flaxman was characterized by some misunderstanding on both sides, and little evident warmth. Even before he had met the sculptor, Wedgwood had heard him described as a coxcomb. In a letter to Bentley of August 1771 he writes of a Mr Freeman, 'a man of taste', who 'is a great admirer of young Flaxman and has advised his Father to send him to Rome, which he has promised to do. Mr Freeman says he knows young Flaxman is a Coxcomb, but does not think him a bit the worse for it, or the less likely to be a great Artist.'[25] Wedgwood noted in a letter also to Bentley of 14 January 1775, at the time he first employed him: 'I am glad … that Flaxman is so valuable an artist. It is but a few years since he was a most supreme Coxcomb, but a little more experience may have cured him of that foible.'[26] A coxcomb was, according to Johnson's dictionary, a fop or a conceited person, and there is indeed a hint of conceit in Flaxman's numerous youthful self-portraits, but then Flaxman had been exhibiting at the Royal Academy since the age of fifteen. This is most obvious in the terracotta relief in the Victoria and Albert Museum (fig.25), probably exhibited in the Royal Academy in 1779, which has an undeniably pretentious Latin inscription 'Alumnus ex academia regale. Anno aetatis xxiv A.D.MDCCLXXVIII hanc sui ipsius effigiam fecit ionnes Flaxman iunior artifex statuarium et coelator.'[27]

What was coxcombery to Wedgwood could be seen as an assertion of artistic professionalism, independence and ambition in the light of Joshua Reynolds's exhortations to the students of the Royal Academy to take the high road of art and to study the great works of antiquity and the Renaissance. Flaxman's reason for working for Wedgwood, for a twelve-year period between 1775 and 1787 when he finally went to Rome, is quite evident. As he had failed to win the Royal Academy's premium for sculpture he was faced with having to pay his own way to Rome if he wished to follow the accepted path to glory as a monumental sculptor. He had already gained some quite important commissions for monuments, and he made it quite clear to Wedgwood that they took priority over the ornamental work for Etruria. He wrote in 1785, 'I am concerned I could not send this bas relief sooner, upon which I have been chiefly obliged to work at Night and now and then have taken a day from some large Monuments I have in hand which are in great haste'.[28] This tells Wedgwood plainly that the work for him had to be fitted in around more important commissions, and it would have been all the more pointed because monuments were almost always delayed, often by years.

There are signs that Wedgwood took some pride in employing someone of Flaxman's reputation as an artist, but he also obliged him to do menial work beneath the dignity of an ambitious professional sculptor. A surviving account of the work done by Flaxman for Wedgwood in the years 1783–7 shows an extraordinary range of work, from important relief designs for *Hercules in the Garden of the Hesperides* to portraits, but also for a lampstand, odd drawings of emblems, and 'Grinding the edges of 6 snuff boxes for the Spanish ambassador'.[29] It is not surprising that, when Flaxman did finally go to Rome in 1787, he was unresponsive to Wedgwood's hopes that he would continue to provide designs for Etruria. Wedgwood complained, like an aggrieved parent, that Flaxman never replied to letters, and when the latter did respond in January 1790 it was with a lofty reply that 'one considerable work which I have finished and another I am engaged in have engrossed my time and thoughts',[30] in fact the grand commission for the full-size marble group of *The Fury of Athemas* (Ickworth House) from the Earl of Bristol.

Flaxman might well have felt uncomfortable with the Wedgwood factory's adaptation of his designs to a range of often trivial decorative purposes, but he does not seem to have been upset by the principle of transformation itself. Relief designs like *The Apotheosis of Homer* were known to William Hamilton and others to have been crafted by Flaxman[31] (though Wedgwood appears to have seen them primarily as antique designs), but they were based on a whole series of transformations. *The Apotheosis of Homer*, as has been noted, goes back to a painted design on a Greek vase that belonged to Sir William Hamilton, which was rendered in outline in d'Hancarville's edition of Hamilton's collection[32] and was then converted by Flaxman into a low relief that could be stuck on the side of a vase. A further process of transformation began once Flaxman had made the wax model and handed it over to Wedgwood, never to be further involved. The wax could be cast any number of times in plaster and then in harder biscuit, often figure by figure. This relief could be reduced and extended in any direction, figures could be added and taken away or shifted in relation to each other, all without any reference to the artist. The *Apotheosis of Homer* could go on a vase, but it could also be the central tablet of a chimneypiece, or a wall plaque, often with slight alterations as they went along. In the case of *Mercury uniting Britain and France* of 1787 all the stages of the process have survived, from the drawing through the biscuit mould, to the final work.[33]

Though Flaxman in his letters to Wedgwood makes a clear distinction between his monuments and his commercial work, in practice the former appears to have been strongly affected by the latter's methods of production. Indeed, it could be argued that Flaxman's whole practice as an artist was based on the transformation of his designs and the distancing of the final product from the hand of the artist. In mature years it was well known that he left all the carving of the marble on his monuments to assistants, of whom he had an exceptional number. The simplicity of his monuments and their lack of baroque protuberances also made replication easier. Though the monuments can be touching and graceful in their expression of grief, in the marble monuments we see time and again the same figure reused in slightly different settings, or with the iconography altered.[34]

One can see the distancing of the artist's hand even more clearly in the line engravings illustrating the works of Dante, Homer and Aeschylus, that made him celebrated all over Europe. The original drawings are exquisitely sensitive and tremulous in their line, but they were converted for publication into dry and relatively inexpressive printed outlines by Tommaso Piroli and others. But Flaxman did not repudiate the outlines: he saw them as themselves adaptable for different purposes in the form of reliefs. He wrote to his friend William Hayley in 1793, shortly after publication: 'My intention is to shew how any story may be represented in a series of compositions on principles of the Antients, of which as soon as I return to England I intend to give specimens in Sculpture of different kinds, in groups of basrelieves [*sic*], suited to all the purposes of Sacred and Civil Architecture.'[35] And so they were, in monumental form on the Royal Opera House and the façade of Ickworth, but also on more humble items throughout the Victorian period.

This essay began by highlighting Ruskin's fierce rejection of the machine aesthetic, and his abhorrence of the very precision that might well be represented by Wedgwood's pottery. There is no doubt that Wedgwood did all he could to suborn the artists he employed into producing products that were generically 'Wedgwood', but it is interesting that the resistance to what is arguably the first modern industrialization of art by manufacturers came not from romantic artists but from those who proclaimed the academic ideals of the grand manner. It was Reynolds's children who were the first to encounter the new breed of manufacturer well before the end of the eighteenth century. It is also clear, from the example of both Joseph Wright of Derby and John Flaxman (and it was even more true of George Stubbs), that artists nonetheless showed an unexpected resourcefulness in getting their own way. Wright was able to push Wedgwood's pots into the shadows of his painting, and Flaxman was able to get himself to Rome at Wedgwood's expense.

Notes and references

1 Michel Foucault, *Discipline and Punish: the Birth of the Prison* (New York, 1979), p.136.
2 E.T. Cook and A. Wedderburn, *The Works of John Ruskin* (London, 1903–12), vol.x, 'The Stones of Venice', vol.II, pp.191–2.
3 Ann Finer and George Savage, *The Selected Letters of Josiah Wedgwood* (London, 1965), pp.82–3.
4 Eliza Meteyard, *The Life of Josiah Wedgwood* (London, 1865), vol.I, p.106.
5 Ibid., pp.265–6.
6 Ibid., p.260.
7 Aileen Dawson, *British Museum: Masterpieces of Wedgwood* (London, 1995), pp.12–16.
8 Cook and Wedderburn, op. cit. (note 2), vol.xvi, pp.344–5.
9 Neil McKendrick, 'Josiah Wedgwood and the commercialisation of the Potteries', in Neil McKendrick, John Brewer and J.H. Plumb (eds), *The Birth of a Consumer Society* (London, 1983), p.103.
10 19 June 1779, ibid., p.108.
11 23 August 1772, ibid., p.131.
12 Dawson, op. cit. (note 7), p.106.
13 Ibid., fig.82 on p.108.
14 Ibid., p.107.
15 Ibid., figs 59, 64.
16 McKendrick, op. cit. (note 9), p.107 and *passim*.
17 Dawson, op. cit. (note 7), p.38.
18 Gaye Blake Roberts, 'A selection of works by Flaxman's contemporaries working for Wedgwood', in D. Bindman (ed.), *John Flaxman* (London, 1979), p.67, fig.56.
19 Rupert Gunnis, *Dictionary of British Sculptors, 1600–1851* (London, rev. edn, n.d.), p.417.
20 Benedict Nicolson, *Joseph Wright of Derby* (London, 1968), vol.I, no.224.
21 Ibid., vol.I, p.141.
22 Gunnis, op. cit. (note 19), pp.146–7.
23 Pamela J. Wood (ed.), *Mr. Wedgwood*, exh. cat., Nottingham Castle Museum (Nottingham, 1975), p.83, no. 475, illus. p.53.
24 Samuel Smiles, *Josiah Wedgwood, FRS* (London, 1894), pp.195–227.
25 Finer and Savage, op. cit. (note 3), p.114.
26 Ibid., p.172.
27 David Bindman, 'Flaxman's early drawings, 1768–87', in Bindman, op. cit. (note 18), p.39, fig.4a. The last word should perhaps be 'caelator', or worker in bas-relief.
28 Ibid., p.26.
29 Ibid., p.57, fig. 34a.
30 Bruce Tattersall, 'Flaxman and Wedgwood', in Bindman, op. cit. (note 18), p.48.
31 Dawson, op.cit. (note 7), p.107.
32 Ibid., p.108.
33 Ibid., pp.64–5, no.52 a–e.
34 Ibid., pp.45, 109, nos 15, 124–5.
35 Ibid., p.86.

Figure 22
Josiah Wedgwood, the Pegasus Vase,
presented by Wedgwood 1786
(showing *The Apotheosis of Homer*,
designed by John Flaxman), ht 46cm
(18in). London, British Museum,
Department of Prehistory and Europe
(P&E 1786,5-27,1).

Figure 23
Josiah Wedgwood,
Sir Joseph Banks (*c.* 1775), blue
jasperware, ht 27.5cm (10⁴/₅in).
London, British Museum, Department
of Prehistory and Europe
(P&E 1887, 3-7, I.60).

Figure 24
Joseph Wright of Derby,
The Corinthian Maid (1782–4),
oil on canvas, 106.3 x 130.8cm
(41⁷/₈ x 51¹/₂ in). New Haven,
Yale Center for British Art.

Figure 25
John Flaxman, *Self Portrait*, 1778–9,
terracotta relief. London, Victoria
and Albert Museum.

Chapter 10

Skulls, Mummies and Unicorns' Horns

Medicinal chemistry in early English museums

Ken Arnold

One could, with near certainty, predict finding a few highly prized and profoundly potent objects in almost any seventeenth-century English museum or collection. One was the unicorn's horn. It was, for example, listed as item 239 in Thomas Hearne's catalogue of the museum at the Oxford University's Anatomy School. Up in Yorkshire, Ralph Thoresby had a thin slice of a sea-unicorn's horn in his cabinet – the gift of a Mrs Dorcas Dyneley. In rather loftier circumstances, a specimen valued at no less than £600 was kept in the Tower of London. The high price paid for this treasure was not just an index of its curiosity and rarity: it also reflected a significant medical value. 'The *Monoceroes* his horn', explained Jean de Renou in his 1657 *Medical Dispensatory*, 'doth admirably defend the heart from poysons.'[1]

Another choice rarity cum remedy was the mummy. Hearne's catalogue duly listed 'A Blackmoore mummied', the inventory of Tradescant's curiosities included reference to 'Divers members of Mummy', and the Royal Society's Repository contained 'AN AEGYPTIAN MUMMY given by the Illustrious Prince *Henry* Duke of *Norfolk*'. According to the famous French physician Nicholas LeFevre, mummified flesh was 'one of the noblest Remedies'. Such high medical esteem again resulted in significant financial value: an apothecary's price list of 1685 quoted mummified flesh at 5s. 4d. per pound.[2]

A third and similarly common medical object found in these museums was the human skull. The Royal Society had two, which as their collection's cataloguer Nehemiah Grew noted, could be used to prepare 'several medicines'. Consult Lefevre's text on the subject and much detail is found about how to 'make the Spirit, Oyl, and Volatile Salt of Mans Bones and skull', preferably a man 'extinguished by violent death'. Again costly, the price for 'A dead man's skull . . . according to size [was] 8s. to 11s. each'.[3]

Unicorns' horns, mummified flesh and human skulls were three particularly colourful and powerful examples of the almost ubiquitous habit of keeping *materia medica* in seventeenth-century museums. To understand the reasons for their inclusion it is important first to identify two major economic changes happening in the contemporary medical marketplace. One came in the form of a vast influx of unfamiliar herbal drugs recently brought from newly discovered lands overseas. The other was a greatly increased use of chemical remedies prepared from minerals. Cumulatively, as one contemporary commentator had it, they represented nothing less than 'a large catalogue of new medicines unknown either to Galen, Hipocrates [sic] or

Paracelsus'.[4] The combined influence of the new exotic plants and Paracelsian chemical remedies not only added particular specimens to museums, but also influenced how many other objects kept there were scrutinized, highlighting their potential medicinal significance. It is worth emphasizing just how broad the category of medicinally significant materials was at this time. Apothecaries and druggists stocked not only simple 'cures' but also a range of what have since been reclassified as spices and foods. Coriander, cinnamon and nutmeg; currants and raisins; coffee, tea and cocoa; candied oranges and jams were all part of their trade-specimens, any of which were as likely to appear in museums as in apothecaries' shops. The category of *materia medica* then was extremely broad. 'All things in general, which the whole Masse of the Earth doth expose to sight and view . . . doth either serve man for Medicament or Aliment', declared Jean de Renou. In other words, the entire natural contents of a museum – a 'Magazine of the Globes Treasures a Store-house of Natures Arcana' as he had it – had some medicinal potential.[5]

Not just crammed with medicinal objects (*materia medica*), museums were also frequently run by *persona medica*. On 10 April 1633 Thomas Johnson, 'citizen and apothecarye', turned his shop window into an exhibition space by hanging there some of the first bananas to be seen in England. Almost sixty years later John Conyers, a Fleet Street apothecary, proposed, though never quite managed to open to the public, a full-scale museum. Edward Barnard, a surgeon this time, was able to gather about him a 'curious *museum*', which was sold at auction on his death in 1737.[6] A particularly large collection, later acquired by Hans Sloane, one of the wealthiest and best-known physicians of his day, was that of the apothecary James Petiver. Amongst Sloane's other acquaintances were John Woodward and Richard Mead, both doctors who used their spare time and financial wherewithal to form cabinets of curiosities, while the Tradescant collection had no fewer than five medical patrons. Clearly, early modern medical men found something attractive in the world of museums.[7]

The motivations behind their eagerness to accumulate and work with collections of curiosities were mixed. In part they were didactic, with many of the medically inspired collections being used as teaching aids, particularly for courses devoted to *materia medica*. Cabinets of medical curiosities also provided natural foci for research, supplying not only the location in which to pursue research and the material upon which to make trials, but also a place in which to store them for further reference. For a profession that was to some extent reinventing the tools of its trade and very much expanding the range of its wares, museums supported the need to study and assay a whole set of possible new medicines. Just as crucially, museums could be worn as badges of learning and curiosity, serving as emblems of professional self-fashioning. Museums provided these medical men with practical spaces in which to advance their trade and to enrich its didactic traditions, but also just as crucially semi-public platforms on which to be seen doing so.

Institutional no less than individual commitments marked this overlap between the worlds of medicine and museums, with many emergent scientific and medical organizations hatching plans for repositories. Thus in 1654 the College of Physicians opened its Harveian Museum, built and supplied from funds provided by England's most famous doctor, William Harvey. Though information about the set-up is scant, it is nonetheless clear that the museum/library formed something of an intellectual focus for a variety of the College's interests: 'Solomon's House in reality', Walter Charleton dubbed it, in a gesture to Francis Bacon's famous scheme for a multi-disciplinary research centre. At the Society of Apothecaries, with both a laboratory shop and physic garden already in place, it became natural for a number of its members, most notably Zachariah Allen, to propose 'that a repository for drugs and materia medica should be established in the hall'.[8] It was not, however, until 1753 that a permanent exhibition of drugs and medicaments was finally mounted in the Society's library.[9]

The Royal Society was another institution that saw significant medical input funnelled into its repository, with many of those involved in its founding having medical backgrounds. Almost a century later, in the 1730s, when critical reviews of the repository led to the introduction of an entirely new system of classification, it was again a doctor, Cromwell Mortimer, who fashioned the revised scheme.[10] The connections between museums and medicine found institutional embodiment in Oxford too. Here the Anatomy School, which from 1624 housed the University's anatomy lectures, gradually took on the character of a museum, which, for part of the seventeenth century, seems to have provided specimens used in medical instruction. First recorded in 1630/1, the collection was added to throughout the century. Nathaniel Highmore left his tables of muscles to the school when he died in 1684, while in 1674/5, as Thomas Hearne's early eighteenth-century catalogue reports, 'A young whale found in the river Severn below Gloucester' was, remarkably enough, brought all the way to Oxford and placed in the School's museum.

Well before the move to establish museums, physic gardens and chemical laboratories had already become common elements in the fabric of life for many seventeenth-century medical professionals, particularly in the context of universities.[11] Museums in fact seemed rather neatly to fit between the two, drawing on the rare plants of the former and the more unusual specimens of the latter. Thus all three met the growing demand for designated sites in which to handle new herbs and chemical remedies. From a practical point of view, new herbs needed to be planted, nurtured, and cultivated, and new minerals fabricated and kept. They had also to be dealt with in more abstract terms – what was needed was a cordoned-off sector of the real world where distractions could be excluded and where chemicals and plants could be experimented upon and ordered. In this respect, museums provided something akin to the 'desk-space' needed to pursue this new intellectual project. And finally, museums, just as much as gardens and laboratories, also furnished their owners and users architecturally with a sign of permanence and moreover a symbol of professional security. For in the crowded competitive medical market place of seventeenth-century England, where struggles for market share could end in the spilling of blood, gardens, laboratories, and museums came also to be used as political tools in the battles between apothecaries and physicians, druggists and spicers, distillers, grocers and mercers, not to mention all manner of other 'wise' and 'gifted' people.[12]

Stuffed full of materia medica, set up and cared for by medical men, and studied within the context of medical institutions, seventeenth-century museums provided fertile ground in which to develop a distinctive investigative methodology, one which, following the contemporary nomenclature, could be referred to as medicinal chemistry.[13] The focus of concern for this museum-based scientific sub-discipline was the quest to uncover the 'virtues' (as they were termed) of precious, medicinally efficacious substances. Of significant and extensive concern at the time (and possibly still lurking in some received wisdom about an odd museum object kept today) this was not destined to be a long-lived line of inquiry. By the end of the seventeenth century, this research was already being seriously undermined by chronic doubts about the soundness of the (mystical) premises upon which it rested. Even at that time, the earlier assumptions about the magical essences of these powerful substances were treated with increasing scepticism and were gradually replaced by a more prosaic understanding of their (at least in some cases) undeniable efficacy. Having surveyed what type of museum-based research 'medicinal chemistry' amounted to, this chapter will conclude with an examination of the more utilitarian attitude to museum objects that emerged in the eighteenth century, and that have to some extent held sway ever since.

Evidence for the nature of 'medicinal chemistry' starts with the conditions in which samples were kept. Here again, Jean de Renou's practical chemical treatise provides a useful guide. Simples derived from plants were, if dry, to be kept in dry places; others that might perish should be made up into 'spirits' and 'waters' and then kept damp and cool. The remains of human bodies on the other hand were to be preserved by the application of pitch, bitumen and other embalming agents. When scrutinized closely, these same practical details can be found in many early museological texts, for example in Nehemiah Grew's catalogue of the Royal Society's Repository. Thus in a section on serpents, Grew described how a snake or 'Great Slow Worm . . . The chief use of which is for the Medicine called Theriaca Andromachi', was 'preserved in spirit of wine', while, in the section on minerals, he considered at some length the technique for 'washing the skins or Beasts or Fowls [with alum] on both sides', which was, he claimed, 'a good way to keep them from the Moth, and growing dank in moist weather and so to preserve them for ever'. And again, this time in the section on birds, he recorded how a 'young Linet which being first embowel'd, hath been preserved sound and entire, in rectified spirit of Wine for the space of 17 years, Given by the

Honourable Mr. Boyl. who, so far as I know, was the first that made trial of preserving animals in this way.'[14]

Robert Boyle in fact related the findings of his experiments on the subject in his *Some Considerations touching the vsefvlnesse of Experimental Natural Philosophy* (1663). In it he described 'the use of Spirit of Wine for the preservation of Bodies from putrefaction', advocating in addition the use of 'boiled down Venice Turpentine as a resin for preserving insects', giving further detailed accounts of various other 'wayes of Artificial Drying and preserving' plants, insects and 'more bulky Bodies'.[15] The preservation of specimens was indeed a core issue for many museum scientists. In 1662, one year before Boyle first published *his* findings on preservation, a certain Mr Croone had already exhibited two dog embryos kept in alcohol at the Royal Society. By the end of the century such methods had become widely known, and were commonly practised by any number of collectors. William Charleton, for example, kept entire notebooks of 'Receipts for preserving and improving collections of Natural histories', in which he described, amongst others, methods for conserving eggs with saffron, 'preserving insects with wax and turpentine, taking impressions of plants on paper, and varnishing shells'. This was also the fare of James Petiver's '*Brief* Directions for the *Easie Making* and *Preserving* collections *of all* natural Curiosities'.[16]

This search for the best method of preserving organic objects constituted an emblematic part of 'medicinal chemistry' – characteristically combining elements of cookery and metaphysics. The same bridging of earth and heaven wove its way through numerous attempts to construct a new medicine based on chemical principles – ideas already foundational in Paracelsian and Helmontian mystical thought, and further developed by that jack-of-all-intellectual-trades Francis Bacon. Long before mid-seventeenth-century technical societies turned it into a ubiquitous scientific doctrine, medicinal chemists employed an experimental methodology to determine the most effective parts of *materia medica*. One of the defining characteristics of their research style was an eagerness to employ not just sight, but all the senses. Writing at the end of the seventeenth century, Robert Hooke presented an exhaustive list of observations on which to base the analysis of a material or object: a list which, as it unfolds, begins to conjure up the unmistakable image of someone handling, even pummelling, a specimen in order to understand it:

> Shiningness, or not ... Transparency or Opacity ... Sonorousness or Dulness. Smell or Taste ... Dryness, or Moisture. Fluidity, or Consistence. Density, or Rarity. Gravity, or Levity. Coarsness, or Fineness. Fastness, or Looseness. Stiffness, or Pliableness. Roughness, or Brittleness. Claminess, or Slipperiness.[17]

For Nehemiah Grew, taste was particularly important, many items he catalogued at the Royal Society's museum being duly tested in his mouth: the gum called 'Sagu', for example, which 'Chewed ... tasteth somewhat clammy', while 'a parcel of Salt taken from *Tenariffe* [in] 1674' had, he observed, 'the perfect Tast[e] of a Lixial Salt'. Robert Plot, first Keeper of the Ashmolean Museum, on the other hand, was just as convinced by smells: a piece of Marble, he reported, 'when rub'd or scraped yielded a strong ungrateful smel'. Eyes, ears, nose, tongue and the skin were all employed in investigating the material world. A typical inquiry was made by the Royal Society on 12 June

1679 into 'a parcel of hart horn', softened and kept in a glass. To determine its nature, it was 'smelt, tasted and felt, [and] seemed by all those senses to be old chedder or Parmesan cheese'.[18]

The full range of the senses were then crucial to 'medicinal chemists'; but so too was active experimentation. Their chemical investigation of the world's fabric relied on a tactile understanding of just how to prepare a spirit of wine or a pitch for embalming, or of how to candy fruit and crush bones – and, abstracted from this, the physical and operational sense that any craftsperson gains of his or her materials. Robert Hooke's essay on 'The present Defficiency of Natural Philosophy' argued therefore not only for careful 'ocular Inspection' and 'sensible examinations', but also 'manual handling ... of the very things themselves'.[19] This expectation of a close physical scrutiny of specimens could be found in almost any museum: it was certainly in evidence in Robert Hubert's catalogue of his own collection, a whole section of which was set aside for 'things of Strange Operations'.[20] And again, it was behind Martin Lister's suggestion, made in January 1683, that the Royal Society should house its collections in presses with drawers, so that, he declared, the objects 'might be readily had at any time for inspection, and other uses, that may happen'.[21] The arrival of 'a piece of heavy wood from Jamaica' at the Oxford Philosophical Society in September 1684 similarly prompted 'some Experiments [to] be tried on it very suddenly'.[22] And geologist John Woodward was adamant that 'all such *Tests* and *Methods of Scrutiny*' naturally led to the 'discover[y of] the Nature of such Parts in these Bodies, as do not immediately fall under the senses'.[23] No better record can be found of the varied 'sensible examinations' and 'manual handlings' to which *materia medica* kept in museums were treated than Grew's catalogue of the Royal Society's repository. In examining a 'Great Stone taken out of a *Dogs* Bladder', for example, he noted 'that nitrous spirits dropped here upon scarce produce any ebullitions, although dropped on the reddish Stones, bred in a mans bladder, it produceth a great one'. 'A Slag, remaining in the bottom or the *Tin Floate* sent by Mr. *Colepress*' was tested with equal vigour. The quantity of iron that it contained had only been 'accidentally perciev'd' when its owner had applied a magnet to it. When Grew came to test it, the attractive effect had diminished, but a more complicated test still produced positive results: when small sparks were made of the slag, they were found to 'leap up to the magnet'.[24]

One especially common 'trial' was the application of water. Hubert's collection, for example, contained: a stone that 'crack[ed] into small pieces' when placed in 'a glasse of water', another that looked grey out of, and clear in, water, and 'A peece of *Wood* being scrapt in a glasse of water, it makes the water appear of two colours'.[25] In a similar vein, Grew found samples of 'Terra Japonica' to 'dissolve in water', and another of gum to 'exactly represent *Frog-Sperm*' when 'Boil'd in water'. Other tests involved the investigation of electrical effects.[26] On 23 November 1683 'several of ye stones belonging to Mr. Ashmoles Museum, were examined, as to their Electricity'. Others were used to investigate magnetic properties. A letter to Plot that accompanied Lister's donation of his curiosities to the Ashmolean described the not unusual test of 'calcinating' ores and then seeing if they 'would acknowledge the Loadstone'.[27] And John Woodward's examination of his fossils involved 'try[ing] each by *Fire*, and a *Chymical Analysis*, in order to discover whether they would emit an *Halitus* or *Vapour*, or a *Smoke* or a *Flame*: whether they would yield an *Oyl*, or a *Salt* . . .'.[28]

Meanwhile, at the Royal Society a rather different experiment involved Charles Howard and John Evelyn planting some seeds sent by a German physician for the Repository, in order to see 'whether they would grow in this climate'.[29] Indeed as one of the chief institutional promoters of the experimental philosophy, it is not too surprising to find extensive evidence of experimentation upon museum specimens kept in the Royal Society's repository, particularly in Grew's work. Thus mineral specimens, to take one example, were frequently tested with 'nitrous spirits', while others were tested for magnetism. Throughout his catalogue, and particularly in the section devoted to 'things relating to chemistry', Grew made frequent references to how things were picked up, looked at, measured, tasted, burnt, as well as having their strength tested, acid dropped on them and magnets applied to them.[30]

Another museum researcher imbued with this experimental cum tactile approach to medicinal chemistry was Elias Ashmole. As an inveterate, almost obsessional collector, his efforts at establishing an institutional museum in Oxford – from which, of course, he later gained considerable eponymous glory – were distinctly in character. The story of how he converted the Tradescant collection into the Ashmolean Museum has repeatedly been well told. What has rarely been stressed, however, is the strong medical character he imposed on the museum. Though much of it was burned in a fire that destroyed his rooms in Middle Temple in 1679, the collection that he amassed independently of Tradescant's Ark included zoological specimens, precious stones, metals, minerals, 'metallica' (i.e. quicksilver, antimony, bismuth, zinc, etc.), aromatic substances and *materia medica* of all kinds. Yet in order further to fill out the ranks of medicinally relevant objects in his new museum at Oxford, Ashmole also advocated the relocation to the Ashmolean of all the rarities previously kept 'in the Phisick & Anatomy Schoole. except such as are necessary for the Anatomy Lecture'. The 'Statutes, Orders & Rules' that Ashmole drew up to regulate the use of his new museum brought out these medical concerns even more clearly. His museum, said Ashmole, was set up to allow the requisite 'inspection of Particulars, especially those as are extraordinary in their Fabrick, or useful in Medicine, or applyed to Manufacture or Trade' that would advance 'the knowledge of Nature . . . [so] very necessarie to humaine life, health, & the conveniences thereof'. As if to ensure these ends, particularly the enhancement of human health, Ashmole also specified that the 'Kings Professor in Physick' – the only member of the group identified by intellectual discipline – be included in the team of visitors charged annually to inspect the museum.

These keen medical concerns – conceivably enlivened by both his and his successive wives' bouts of ill health – also surfaced in Ashmole's studies of botany, chemistry and astrology. From the time of his first 'simpling' excursion on 6 June 1648, Ashmole began a life-long enquiry into the medical uses of trees and plants, and especially their planetary 'signatures', which both determined their medical use and suggested propitious times for gathering specimens of them. In chemistry, his interests were particularly directed to experiments aimed at harnessing alchemical and astrological

secrets. Though frustrated in his attempts, Ashmole hoped to reinforce the connection of these chemical interests to his museum by setting up a chemistry professorship attached to it. In the end he did not achieve his goal, but the Ashmolean's first curator, Robert Plot, nonetheless did give regular lectures on chemistry. The type of chemistry that concerned Ashmole, and that would no doubt have been pursued by the Ashmolean professor had such a chair been established, was that based on museum and laboratory investigations and which would have been fully supported by the theoretical principles set out in the introduction to Ashmole's *Fasciculus Chemicus*. This was a theory that explained not only the effect of 'ordinary medicines', but also the 'true medicine': the elixir of life.[31]

Ashmole's chemistry was of the same character as that worked up by Charles II's professor of chemistry, Nicholas LeFevre, one best captured in his 1670 textbook on the subject: *A Compleat Body of Chemistry*. The subtitle of LeFevre's work provides a fair summary of his chief interests: '[it] contained whatsoever is necessary for the attaining to the Curious Knowledge of this Art [chemistry]; comprehending in the General the whole Practice thereof: and teaching the most exact Preparation of *Animals*, *Vegetables*, and *Minerals*, so as to preserve their Essential Vertues.'

LeFevre's chemistry had a firm theoretical basis. For 'Whosoever meddles with chymical remedies without the previous grounds of Theory, can deserve no other name then of Empyrick'. His theory, very much supported with the help of Hermetical philosophy, was at the same time thoroughly bonded to the basic practical methods employed in medicinal trades, albeit systematized in a *practical or operative science*. The methods and investigative practices he described would have been quite familiar to any apothecary or druggist, as well as to many of those who worked in museums: namely such techniques as the preparation of 'Spirit, Oyl, and Volatile Salt of Mans Bones and skull', the 'manner of preparing Remedies out of Harts-horn', and the relative merits of different types of mummies – the best being 'Human Bodies, dried up in the hot sands of *Lybia*' described by Grew.[32]

While much divided the thinking of the three men – Grew, Ashmole and LeFevre – a good number of similarities in their approach to medicinal chemistry nonetheless simultaneously united them. Three are of particular significance: first, all of them experimented with a remarkable number of the same object types, with, that is, the *materia medica* that was to be found in almost any late-seventeenth-century museum; second, they all shared a considerable amount of the same experimental methodology, derived in large measure from common medical practices, particularly those of the apothecary; and third, in making similar inquiries into the same specimen types, all three eagerly attempted to discover what made the medicines behave as they did, that is, to uncover the nature of what were called their 'virtues'. LeFevre signalled the importance of this quest within his work elsewhere in the rambling descriptive subtitle of his *Compleat Body of Chemistry*: the understanding of 'Essential Vertues', it declared, was critical to the 'Curious Knowledge of this Art'. Ashmole made almost the same point thus: '[a] search into those hidden vertues which God has been pleased to bestow upon created things (though closely lockt up by the generall Curse) whereby we may . . . naturally apply Agents to Patients'.[33]

Grew in his work on plants similarly described how working up from observations to the analysis of 'Orders and Degrees of their Affinities', and finally on to an understanding of 'the Causes and Ends of the Varieties', his final aim was 'more probably to conjecture at their Natures and Vertues'. The fundamental idea to which all three pointed was that each object under investigation had within it a hidden distilled essence that made it what it was: a 'virtue'. The goal of medicinal chemistry was to discover, describe and understand those virtues that had a significant medical effect.[34]

This quest for an understanding of the hidden natures or virtues of medically significant objects was what united all those who practised medicinal chemistry within museums. Quite what these virtues were, and what relationships existed between them, however, was somewhat more a matter of dispute than consensus – a dispute which had ancient roots. During the Renaissance, mystical and neo-Platonic thinkers, particularly Paracelsus, sought to reinstate the significance of the unique essences of individual things themselves, and this in order to overturn the Aristotelian idea of the higher reality of 'abstract types'. Resting on the idea that specific correspond-ences existed between micro- and macrocosm – between, that is, human bodies and the world and heavens at large – Jean de Renou, for example, held that medicines could 'by a specificall property have respect to certain peculiar parts'. Haematite (bloodstone) was thus used as a cure for diseases of the blood and, 'Man's skull [employed as] a Specific Medicine in the cure of Falling-Sickness, and indeed of most Diseases of the Head'.[35]

For many these notions of sympathetic action turned on the concept of an object's 'signature'. Writing in 1654 Nicholas Culpeper, compiler of an exhaustive materia medica, declared that 'Sympathy and Antipathy [were] the two Hinges upon which the Whole Body of Physick turns'. The grandest version of this doctrine determined that each object was marked by a planetary signature inscribed at its creation, which signalled the nature of its inherent qualities. Much scholarly time has been spent attempting to understand this view of the world. Four points will be touched on here in an attempt to illuminate what is an exceptionally murky passage of intellectual history. First, as Michel Foucault forcefully insisted, this magical system of thought is simply not commensurate with much that came after.[36] We have to attempt to divest ourselves of the power of our own understanding of the world in order meaningfully to grapple with this earlier way of making sense of – but also, crucially, way of living in – the world. Second, the widespread interest in sympathetic and antipathetic actions was just one example of an almost ubiquitous interest in that which was hidden or secret. Ashmole, for example, described his fascination with all 'occult, specifick, incomprehensible, and inexplicable qualities [that lay] . . . dormant and obscured in Nature'.[37] Third, for much of this period when magical and mystical thought was questioned, it tended to be far more in terms of its moral and religious rectitude than its rational soundness. It was Ashmole again who bluntly stated that: 'If thy thoughts are devout, honest, and pure, perhaps God may at one time or other, lay open to thy Understanding, somewhat that will truly and faithfully lead thee to the knowledge of this Mystery.'[38] And fourth, much of the early modern interest in the occult had at its core fundamentally utilitarian concerns, which

gave it in modern parlance as much the character of technology as faith. This aspect of medicinal chemistry needs to be stressed, namely that is was as much humble pharmacy as magical mystery.

This way of understanding the power of these substances – one which our own patterns of thought give us but a shadowy glimpse of – was then a moral, technological quest to uncover secrets which lay hidden within the material substance of the world. That much acknowledged, criticism of this world-view and specifically of its mystical explanations of medicinally-effective objects had already started to gather momentum during the seventeenth century. The natural philosopher Robert Boyle, for example, seriously questioned whether there really were 'specifick vertues'. While Boyle himself confessed he was 'very inclinable to the Affirmative' (denying the properties of these substances was simply to fly in the face of indubitable evidence), he was nonetheless far from inclined to adopt any mystical explanations of their effects, holding instead that they were 'reconcileable to the principles of Corpuscular . . . Philosophy'.[39] Robert Hooke, one time curator of the Royal Society's Repository, was even more robust in his reductionist pronouncements: all investigations of 'virtues' would, he affirmed, in the end reduce them 'to Regularity, Certainty, Number, Weight and Measure'. He continues '[The] affects of Bodies, which have been commonly attributed to Qualities, and these confess'd to be Occult, are perform'd by the small Machines of Nature, which are not to be discern'd without these helps [microscopes].'[40]

Similar philosophical motivations led Richard Mead, who turned his house in Great Ormond Street into a museum, to publish his 1702 Mechanical Account of Poisons, while Sir Kenelm Digby (whose involvement in museums led him to become a benefactor of Tradescant's Ark) went so far as to propose a mechanical explanation for the powder which 'doth naturally, and without any Magick, cure wounds without . . . seeing of the Patient' – the so-called powder of sympathy.[41] Here, mechanical explanations were even being offered for effects which to subsequent generations have themselves seemed, to put it mildly, highly unlikely. For Grew, a similarly sceptical approach to the magical effects of powerful substances was arrived at only after extended enquiries. Writing to John Ray on 29 October 1686, a certain Mr Johnson described having 'once imagine[d] a Possibility of knowing the Medicinal Virtue of Plants by their Signatures, but', he goes on, 'when I found that Dr. Grew had hit upon the same Notion, and laid his Enquiries much deeper than mine, viewing the internal as well as external Parts of Plants, and yet could conclude nothing, I quite desisted from further Search.'[42] Coupled with a growing aversion to what he described as any 'medling with Mystick, Mythologick, or Hieroglyphic matters', these investigations led Grew to develop a fierce suspicion about the fashion in which 'the Virtues of most Plants, are with much uncertainty, and too promiscuously ascribed to them'.[43]

Though differing in detail about how to apply metaphysical principles, the likes of Boyle, Hooke, Mead, Digby and Grew all mounted investigations in order 'rationally' to absorb and reinterpret the 'virtuous effects' of the material world. These growing doubts about the usefulness of earlier magical and mystical assumptions were accumulated gradually. Though magic was, by the end of the seventeenth century, being eased out of the lives of natural philosophers, its influence on their intellectual framework (its 'conceptual infrastructure' as Charles Webster described it) lasted a good deal longer. Magical overtones in everyday habits and practices lasted even longer. Significantly, though earlier versions of the College of Physicians' pharmacopoeia reveal a gradual dethronement of one remedy after another as being mystical and therefore bogus, it was not until the middle of the eighteenth century that an explicit general declaration was made: all 'antidotes superstitiously and dotingly derived from oracles, dreams and astrological fancies' were, henceforth, to be expunged.[44] By then, the ridicule in which such remedies were commonly held had become the currency of popular entertainment: thus a scene in Edward Ward's popular satirical account of late-seventeenth-century London, *The London Spy Compleat*, depicted a pill peddler surrounded by a 'Brainless Multitude' enraptured by a 'paquet of Universal Hodg. Podg'. He also described a visit to 'Wise Acres Hall' – a thinly disguised Gresham College, where the Royal Society's Repository could be found – in which Ward and his companion were shown 'that Wonderful curiosity the *Unicorns* Horn: made, [suggested Ward] by an Ingenious Turner, of the Tusks of an *Elephant*'. The horn was, he continued, 'of an excellent Virtue; and, by report of those that know nothing of the matter, will express Poison beyond the *Mountebanks Orvieton*'.[45]

The profound though complicated changes in opinion concerning both the effectiveness of virtuous objects and the causes of their effects resulted less in a slackening of interest in medicinal objects within museums than in the style of their investigation. In his eighteenth-century medical text, a certain Monsieur Pomet acknowledged some decline of virtuosic interest: there were, he conceded, 'few persons whose leisure and fortune . . . [gave] 'em an opportunity of applying all their Time to . . . the knowledge of Druggs'. Five examples of physicians who had successfully applied themselves did nonetheless come to Pomet's mind: Mr Petiver and Drs Morison, Grew, Sloane and Woodward. What is particularly striking about this list is that four of them worked energetically with museum collections, while Robert Morison (the fifth) spent his time in a related environment: the botanical garden. In dedicating his text to Sloane, Pomet was in no doubt as to how the great doctor had arrived at his universal skills 'in all the most curious and useful Secrets of Nature'. It came about from his 'Diligence and furnishing [his] *Museum*'.[46]

The beginning of the eighteenth century saw the emergence of a number of specialist collections devoted entirely to medical material, for the most part modest cabinets used more for instructional than research purposes. In Cambridge, for example, John Francis Vigani, Professor of Chemistry from 1704, had an oak cabinet of some twenty-six drawers provided by Queen's College, from which he taught his classes on *materia medica*. Another similar collection was gathered at St John's College by Dr William Heberden who, in the middle of the eighteenth century, gave a *Course of Lectures on the Materia Medica* in thirty-one parts, while in 1730, a professor of the University, Richard Bentley, published his *Course of Lectures upon Materia Medica . . . read in the Physics School at Cambridge upon the Collections of Dr. Attinbrooke and Signor Vigani*. A careful examination of both sets of lectures reveals in the first instance that the interest in *materia medica* continued to be

focused on their 'virtues', but second that notions of what those virtues might actually *be* had shifted profoundly. The handbills printed to advertise Heberden's lectures declared that: 'a Specimen of each Particular will be shewn, and every Thing is intended to be mentioned that is useful or curious regarding its Natural History . . . Preparations, Virtues, Dose and the cautions necessary to be observed in its use'. A specimen's 'virtue' had by now become no more and no less than its observable medicinal effect.

More evidence of this altogether pragmatic and utilitarian approach to virtues was also to be found in the work of one of the medical practitioners championed by Pomet: James Petiver. In addition to acting as demonstrator of plants at the Chelsea botanical garden from 1708 until 1718, Petiver also set himself up as an apothecary. As a natural extension to his stocks of medicines Petiver further gathered about him a vast collection of other natural history specimens, accumulated for his own private study. The transition from apothecary's store to museum thus occurred almost imperceptibly somewhere along his numerous shelves of *materia medica*. These collections formed a fundamental source for Petiver's numerous printed contributions to the knowledge of the natural world – letters in the *Philosophical Transactions*; a journal, *The Monthly Miscellany, or Memoirs for the Curious*; and a whole string of catalogues. In each of these publications, his format was similarly straightforward, consisting quite simply, as he himself declared, of 'Names, Descriptions and Vertues'. Each one also bears unmistakable evidence of Petiver's work as an apothecary: 'The largest figure' in table xxxvii of his catalogue, *Gazophylacci Naturae & Artis*, vol.1, for example, showed 'the *true* Turmerick of the *Shopps*'; table xxxx, fig.14 'Shews you the *Fruit* of the true *Oriental Anacardium*, so rarely met with in the Druggists shops', and table xlvi, fig.7 exhibited the familiar unicorn's horn, this one from Nevis. His record of the Indian plant 'Naiureevee *Malab*' in an earlier issue of the same journal read, as well it might, like an apothecary's advertisement: 'The *Decoction* takes away *Swettings*, abates the sharpness of *Urine*, and eases the *Stone*, mixt with the Oyl *Seryelin* it stops pissing of Blood. The *Root* purges; being bruised and boyl'd in *Butter*, it cures *Dysentery* . . . etc.'

Petiver's interest in *materia medica*, just as that of Vigani, Bentley, Heberden and Attenbrook, was almost entirely based on pragmatic matters. All of these men's thoughts concerning a specimen's 'virtue' were quite strictly confined by the notion of medicinal effect, with scarcely any attempt being made to go beyond that. In his 'Discourse made to the Royal Society' on 10 May 1699, Petiver did explore the more abstract matter of 'some Attempts to prove, That Herbs of the same Class, or Make, generally have the like Virtue, and Tendency to work the same Effects'. But even here, it became clear that he was still primarily motivated by a quest for underlying patterns in the observable effects, which might then be rendered as rules of thumb.[47]

With the likes of Petiver, heady musings about mystical phenomena, or indeed speculation about whence these effects might be derived, came to be reduced instead to the professional search for codes of practice. Gone was the aura of magic emanating from a cabinet's specimen skull, mummy or unicorn's horn. In its stead, as John Pointer's 1740 'Explanatory Catalogue' to his own museum put it, was a collection simply to be 'esteem'd as Things of great Use & Peculiar Advantage'.[48]

Ken Arnold

Notes and references

1 For Hearne's catalogue see R.W.T. Gunther, *Early Science in Oxford*, vol.III (Oxford, 1925), p.439; Jean de Renou, *A Medical Dispensatory* 'Englished' by Richard Tomlinson (London, 1657), p.16; David Murray, *Museums: Their History and their Use*, vol.1 (Glasgow, 1904), p.45; Humphrey Humphreys, 'The horn of the unicorn', *Antiquity* 26 (1953), pp.15–19.

2 For Hearne see Gunther, op. cit. (note 1), p.439; *Musæum Tradescantianum*, reprinted in Prudence Leith-Ross, *The John Tradescants* (Bristol, 1984), p.243; Nehemiah Grew, *Musaeum Regalis Societatis* (London, 1681), p.1; Nicholas LeFevre, *A Complete Body of Chemistry* (London, 1670), p.135. *Materia medica* values come from 'Rules and prices currant of Druggs and other commodities belonging to Physick', reproduced in Charles J. Thompson, *Alchemy, Source of Chemistry and Medicine* (New York, 1974), p.210; Karl H. Dannefeldt, 'Egyptian mumia', *The Sixteenth Century Journal* 16 (1985), pp.161–80. For an extensive discussion of early-modern processes of mummification see Harold J. Cook, 'Time's bodies: crafting the preparation and preservation of Naturalia', in *Merchants and Marvels*, ed. Paula Findlen and Pamela Smith (London, 2001), pp.91–105.

3 Grew, op. cit. (note 2), p.2; LeFevre, op. cit. (note 2), p.135; Charles J. Thompson, op. cit. (note 2), p.210.

4 Letter from J. Walduck to Petiver, n.d. (1710s), British Library, Sloane MS 2302, fol.8.

5 Renou, op. cit. (note 1), pp.477, 490.

6 Juanita Burnby, *A Study of the English Apothecary from 1660 to 1760* (London, 1983), pp.22–7; C.J. Thompson, *The Mystery and Art of the Apothecary* (Detroit, 1971), pp.93–9; G.E. Trease, *Pharmacy in History* (London, 1964), pp.122–9.

7 R.F. Ovenell, *The Ashmolean Museum 1683–1894* (Oxford, 1986), pp.32–8; Michael Hunter, 'Early problems in professionalizing scientific research: Nehemiah Grew (1641–1712)', *Notes and Records of the Royal Society* 36 (1981–2), pp.189–209.

8 *A History of the Worshipful Society of Apothecaries of London*, ed. Charles Cameron, revised by E.A. Underwood, notes by Cecil Wall (London, 1963), p.173.

9 Michael Hunter, 'Between cabinet of curiosities and research collection: the history of the Royal Society's repository', in his *Establishing the New Science: The experience of the Royal Society* (Woodbridge, 1989).

10 Burnby, op. cit. (note 6), p.81; Walter Charleton, *The Immortality of the Human Soul* (London, 1657), pp.34, 41–2.

11 See Hilde de Ridder-Symoens, 'Management and resources', in *A History of the University in Europe*, gen. ed. Walter Rüegg, vol.II: *Universities in early modern Europe (1500–1800)*, ed. Hilde de Ridder-Symoens (Cambridge, 1996), pp.155–209, esp. p.192.

12 For struggles in the medical market place see Harold J. Cook, *The Decline of the Old Medical Regime in Stuart London* (Ithaca, 1986), p.22 and *passim*; Christopher Hill, 'The medical profession and its radical critics', in *Change and Continuity in Seventeenth Century England* (London, 1974), p.158; Edward Kremers, *History of Pharmacy* (Philadelphia, 3rd edn 1963), pp.90–7; C. J. Thompson, *The Mystery and Art of the Apothecary* (Detroit, 1971), p.274; and Leslie Matthews, *The History of Pharmacy in Britain* (London, 1962).

13 Nicholas LeFevre, for example, spoke of 'Iatrochymy or Medicinal Chemistry' in his *Complete Body of Chemistry*, op. cit. (note 2), pp.7–8.

14 Renou, op. cit. (note 1), p.491; Grew op. cit. (note 2), pp.48–9, 58, 343.

15 R. Boyle, *Some Considerations touching the Vsefvlnesse of Experimental Natural Philosophy* (London, 1663), pp.22–5. See too Boyle's essay, 'A way of preserving birds taken out of the egges', *Philosophical Transactions* vol. 1 no. 12 (1666), p.200, for further detail of his method for observing embryonic growth by preserving each successive stage in 'spirit of wine'. Another Society member, Robert Hooke, perfected 'a way of incloseing an Insect such as a fly worme or the like in Amber artificially which could hardly be distinguished from a naturall production of that kind' (Royal Society Archives, 'Journal Book' vol.VI [original], p.137, dated 28 November 1678).

16 For William Charleton's 'Receipts', see British Library, Sloane MS 3962, fols 186–9, 192, and *passim*; Sloane MS 3997, fols 3–8, and *passim*. James Petiver's 'Brief Directions' were republished in *Jacobi Petiveri Opera* (London, 1767). See for general comments on preservation techniques F.J. Cole, *A History of Comparative Anatomy* (New York, 1975), pp.275, 443–5.

17 *The Posthumous Works of Robert Hooke* (1st edn, London, 1705; 2nd facsimile edn, ed. Richard Waller, London, 1971), p.36.

18 Notes on 'sagu' and salt in Grew, op. cit. (note 2), pp.339, 385; Robert Plot, *The Natural History of Oxford-shire* (London, 1677), p.94; Thomas Birch, *The History of the Royal Society* (London, 1756), vol.III, p.489. For a similar use of all the senses when phosphorous was being investigated, see Jan V. Golinski, 'A noble spectacle: research on phosphorus and the public culture of science in the early Royal Society', *Isis* 80 (1989), pp.25–7.

19 Waller, op. cit. (note 17), p.338.

20 Robert Hubert, *A Catalogue of Many Natural Rarities . . .* (London, 1664), pt II, chap.v.

21 Birch, op. cit. (note 18), vol. IV, p.250.

22 Report of Oxford Philosophical Society in Gunther, op. cit. (note 1), vol.IV, p.92.

23 J. Woodward, 'Letter to Isaac Newton', in *Fossils of all Kinds, Digested into a Method . . .* (London, 1728), p.4.

24 Grew, op. cit. (note 2), pp.13, 328, 351–3, 385.

25 Hubert, op. cit. (note 20), pp.56–7.

26 Grew, op. cit. (note 2), p.385.

27 Gunther, op. cit. (note 1), vol. IV, p.31.

28 Woodward, op. cit. (note 23), p.4.

29 Birch, op. cit. (note 18), vol.II, pp.373–4.

30 Grew, op. cit. (note 2), p.385.

31 Elias Ashmole, *Fasciculus Chemicus: Or, Chymical Collections Expressing the Engress, Progress, and Egress, of the Secret Hermetic Science, out of the Choices and most Famous Authors*, presented under the name James Hasolle (London, 1650).

32 LeFevre, op. cit. (note 2), pp.125–35.

33 Elias Ashmole, *Theatrum Chemicum Britannicum* (London, 1652), pp.443–6, and Allen Debus's introduction pp.xxxv–xxxvi. See too C.H. Josten, *Elias Ashmole 1617–1692 . . .* (Oxford, 1966), pp.58–9.

34 N. Grew, 'An idea of a philosophical history of plants', *The Anatomy of Plants . . .* (n.p., 1682), p.5.

35 LeFevre, op. cit. (note 2), pp.125–35.

36 Michel Foucault, *The Order of Things* (New York, 1973), pp.26–40.

37 Ashmole, op. cit. (note 31), pp.9–10.

38 Ashmole, op. cit. (note 33), p.443. On magic as an extension of technology see Bert Hansen, 'The complementarity of science and magic before the scientific revolution', *American Scientist* 74 (1986), pp.130–5.

39 Robert Boyle, *Of the Reconcileableness of Specifick Medicines to the Corpuscular Philosophy* (London, 1685), pp.6–9, Preface.

40 Robert Hooke, *Micrographia: or some Physiological Descriptions of Minute Bodies made by Magnifying Glasses . . .* (London, 1665), Preface. See too Catherine Wilson, 'Visual surface and visual symbol: the microscope and the occult in early modern science', *Journal of the History of Ideas* 49 (1988), pp.88–9.

41 Kenelm Digby, *A late Discourse . . . Touching the Cure of Wounds by the Powder of Smpathy* [sic] (London, 1660), p.3.

42 *Philosophical Letters Between the Late Learned Mr. Ray and Several of his Ingenious Correspondents . . .* published by N. Derham (London, 1718), p.204.

43 Grew, op. cit. (note 2), Preface; Grew, op. cit. (note 34), p.2.

44 C. Webster, 'English medical reformers of the Puritan revolution: a background to the Society of Chymical Physicians', *Ambix* 14 (1967), p.40; C.J.S. Thompson, *The Mystery and Art of the Apothecary* (Detroit, 1971), p.143.

45 Edward Ward, *The London Spy Compleat* (London, 1703), pp.58, 126.

46 *A Complete History of Druggs . . . by Monsieur Pomet* (London, 1737), Preface and 'Translator's Dedication'.

47 *Philosophical Transactions* 20, no.244 (1698), p.314.

48 'The Order of a Course of Lectures . . .', handbill kept by St John's College, Cambridge.

Chapter 11

Natural History in Eighteenth-Century Museums in Britain
Hugh S. Torrens

Museums have always been of central importance to the student of nature, that subject consisting largely of the study of diversity. For such diversity to be investigated at leisure, nature must first be collected and then stored and preserved. The Museum has thus been pivotal to the history of natural history. Despite this, a check of the old British Museum library catalogue reveals only one earlier (200th) anniversary exhibition – that for the British Museum Library, held in 1953.[1] Celebrations of the equally long history of the British Museum itself seem to be entirely lacking. Now, the 250th anniversary celebration may begin with the fact that museology itself, a word first used, according to the *Oxford English Dictionary*, in 1885, is slowly becoming a field of genuine interest, fostered in Britain by the 300th anniversary of the Ashmolean Museum in 1983 and the establishment of the *Journal of the History of Collections* which grew from that occasion. The earlier growth, from 1974, of specialist museum curatorial groups, with their journals *Geological Curator* and *The Biology Curator*, has also been of significance in encouraging the history of museums, at least in Great Britain.

A century earlier, in 1888, Thomas Greenwood (1851–1908) had bemoaned the fact that his book on *Museums and Art Galleries* 'treats a subject almost without a literature'.[2] Similarly when the fine three-volume *Museums: Their History and their Use* by David Murray (1842–1928) appeared in 1904 (reprinted 2000), it was the 'first serious inquiry into the origin and growth of the museum since the work of eighteenth-century museographers'. Murray's achievement was also made despite his 'difficulty [in] getting information regarding [published and MSS] museum catalogues [which] will scarcely be credited'.[3] Museology clearly did not then exist as a subject to which attention might be drawn.

Furthermore, museology is a complex subject. It might be thought surprising that Silvio Bedini's stimulating survey of 'The evolution of science museums' was published in the journal *Technology and Culture*.[4] But museums were, and are, full of both natural and artificial (man-made) curiosities and this division is a reminder that the second category concerns technology: 'the art of making things'. By analogy with the museum, this concerns something 'made', as opposed to 'known'. So, once museums become 'unmade' or lost, dispersed or destroyed, as the great majority of British museums from the eighteenth century have been, trying to discover what was in them is similar to the often insoluble problems of trying to discover how old technology worked. This is especially so when examples do not survive. Worse, this history of things technical,

or 'done', is a subject in which the British have never taken much interest. This is demonstrated all too clearly by the recent comparison of the numbers of university chairs in the history of technology in Britain, Germany, France, Sweden and the USA.[5]

Two British museums in the early eighteenth century

If we survey museum creators in Britain during the first half of the eighteenth century, two names are pre-eminent, Dr John Woodward (?1667–1728) and Sir Hans Sloane (1660–1753), if only because their collections are well documented and have to a considerable extent survived. From these, it can immediately be seen that any idea that the museum in Britain developed during the eighteenth century, from a 'cabinet of curiosities' into a place where all was carefully classified is unfounded. Woodward's collecting, however constrained it was to the products of the mineral (or geological) kingdom, was wonderfully classified and organized. A posthumous and voluminous catalogue was issued in 1728–9, as has been explained by David Price.[6]

Of John Woodward, Roy Porter correctly wrote in 1974 that there was no reliable evidence about his family.[7] However, Woodward has since been shown to have been the son of William Woodward, yeoman of Draycot in the parish of Wilne, Derbyshire,[8] and his wife Mary. William Woodward's will suggests that he was already a man of some substance, but his premature death in November 1682 orphaned his son and only daughter Ann whilst they were still minors. That John had been attending Repton School from 1680 suggests that Joseph Levine's belief that John's true date of birth was 1667 or 1668 is well founded.[9]

After Woodward collected his first specimens – 'the first stone I ever took notice of, or gather'd, a gritty pebble of a very light brown colour, in a great gravel-pit among the new buildings by Dover street, St James, London in 1688' – and his first fossil shell – (of a yet-to-be-conceived brachiopod) in a Cotswolds vineyard on 13 January 1690[10] – he became a singularly devoted collector and classifier of all such 'fossil' objects. He collected these because he saw 'that high value, and that use in so many very important parts of human life and affairs that they merit. [They] justly challenge our utmost study and attention ... [because] a great share of our wealth and happiness ... depend very much upon them'.[11] An unpublished study of this collection by David Price describes the rationale behind Woodward's collecting methods and explores the extraordinary range of localities – both British and foreign – from which Woodward's collections had come.[12] More recently

Clayton Ray has commented from an American perspective on Woodward's 'incomparable collection': of the 655 catalogued entries for foreign true fossils, 74 are North American and make up a minimum 127 of a total 1,210 specimens, or more than 10% of both total catalogued numbers and specimens.[13]

Another fascinating historical use of the Woodward collection is in the papyrophobic world of early attempts to find minerals. Several eighteenth-century trials were made to find what would later emerge to be unattainable – coal from the locality of Shaftesbury in Dorset. One of the few pieces of 'documentation' for such an unwritten activity is represented by specimens from an early attempt made there, which survive in Woodward's collection.[14]

Sir Hans Sloane and his collection (and his will which helped establish the British Museum) need little discussion since they are well documented, most recently in the volume edited by Arthur MacGregor.[15] The Sloane collection was much less comprehensively catalogued – at least in contemporary print – than Woodward's. The extraordinary aspect of both collections, however, is the great geographical spread of the material contained in them.

A third museum collection in Britain

A third, equally impressive, collection which never came into public ownership, was that gathered by Margaret Cavendish Harley (1715–85), 3rd Duchess of Portland.[16] This was based at her country house at Bulstrode in Buckinghamshire and in her Whitehall, London, home (from where it was later sold). She had married the 2nd Duke in July 1734 and, having acquired the collecting 'bug' from her coin- and medal-collecting father, had started to gather natural history specimens by November that same year.[17] Unlike most such collections, these were well curated, the enormous shell and insect components by Daniel Solander (1736–82) and the plants by her librarian and chaplain, the Revd John Lightfoot (1735–88). On her death the collection had to be sold to meet her creditors' demands and the process took forty mornings, from 24 April to 3 July 1786. Lightfoot's introduction to the impressive sale catalogue reported that it had been 'her Grace's intention to have had every unknown species in the three kingdoms of Nature described and published to the world'.[18] These plans were sadly thwarted, first by Solander's death in 1782, and then by her own in 1785. Horace Walpole reported that of thirty-eight of these days' sales 'there are but eight that exhibit anything but shells, ores, fossils, birds' eggs and natural history',[19] good evidence of, at least, the Duchess's active interest in natural history.

A museum in the English provinces

Between the transfer of the first two of the above collections into public ownership, in 1729 and 1753 respectively, another museological movement had started: that of the British provincial museum. Among the first of these was that founded by 'Dr' Richard Greene (1716–93) in Lichfield, Staffordshire in the 1740s. Greene was born and baptized at Walsall, Staffordshire.[20] Later his family moved to Bewdley, in Worcestershire, whence he was apprenticed to a Shrewsbury apothecary (or pharmacist) between September 1732 and September 1739,[21] before settling in practice at Lichfield. Perhaps the historic nature of both these last towns helped inspire his collecting instincts, which became manifest in his

activities from 1740. Additional inspiration may have been provided by the example of Elias Ashmole (1617–92), who had been born at Lichfield and who remains one of the city's most illustrious sons. In May 1750 Green was elected an Honorary Member of the Peterborough Gentlemen's Society, showing that his reputation had already spread beyond his native county.[22]

Greene's collecting was properly curious, embracing both history and natural history. His collection was thus miscellaneous, and was noteworthy for being open to the public free of charge every day except Saturday. In 1773 he issued the first printed *Catalogue* of his museum. In the third edition, in 1786, he stated the museum had been 'collected in the space of 46 years', that is since 1740, so confirming that it must have been started as soon as Greene had arrived in Lichfield (fig.26).[23]

Greene's museum became one of Lichfield's principal attractions. Sir Joseph Banks visited it in 1767, although he was unimpressed with nearly all the natural history materials.[24] Lichfield-born Samuel Johnson (1709–84) visited it in 1774 and 1776 when he noted that it was 'truely, a wonderful collection, both of antiquities and natural curiosities, and ingenious works of art. He had all the articles accurately arranged, with their names upon labels, printed at his own little press'.[25] Greene's was the first printing press in Lichfield.

Perhaps the most interesting aspect of this museum's history today is its palpable connection with the mysterious, badly recorded but important Lunar Society based in the Midlands. Of the fourteen individuals whose membership is accepted by the main authorities on this Society,[26] at least half were contributors to the museum. These include Matthew Boulton, Erasmus Darwin, Thomas Day, James Keir, Josiah Wedgwood, John Whitehurst and William Withering. None of the abundant books and papers on the Lunar Society seems to make any mention of a connection between Greene and the Society. So far only the Wedgwood connection has been explored,[27] while William Schupbach has investigated other potential museological connections between objects in Greene's museum and Joseph Wright (1734–97), the Derby artist who so wonderfully depicted contemporary science and technology in the Midlands.[28]

It has been erroneously suggested that 'a number of the very learned and cultured people – Dr Johnson is an outstanding example – never, so far as we know, crossed the threshold of a museum of any kind'.[29] Johnson was in fact a close friend of Greene's and had even, in 1773, lent Greene archaeological material to display in his museum,[30] while the museum later enjoyed a number of Johnsonian donations including the inkwell used in the production of the famous *Dictionary*, in testimony to the close association between the museum keeper and the author.[31]

The Leverian Museum

Greene was a friend of Sir Ashton Lever (1729–88) who began another museum, initially in the provinces, until he was forced to move it to London in an attempt to recoup the losses he had incurred in building it up. Greene and Lever later exchanged a considerable amount of material for each other's collections. The second and third editions of Greene's *Catalogue* were in part dedicated to Lever, 'his principal contributor', in 1782 and 1786. Lever's life and museum-building activities have been described by W.J. Smith[32] and new light has been shed on its (especially later) contents by Jonathan King.[33]

Lever's first interests connected with the natural world seem to have centred on horse racing, but he also kept an aviary; then in 1760 his interests in natural history deepened and he began to collect sea-shells,[34] which were to form the nucleus of the enormous accumulation that became known as the Leverian Museum. Lever built up his collections at his home, Alkrington Hall, near Oldham in Lancashire, and first put some of them on public display in Manchester in 1766. This encouraged his neighbours and acquaintances to present further material and by 1770 he had issued his own 'Instructions to Collectors', which listed all the 'productions of Nature or Art or any Thing Curious from its Antiquity' that he wished to acquire. In 1771 he opened the collection to the public at Alkrington but within two years, becoming 'tired out with the insolence of the common People whom I have hitherto indulged with the sight of my museum', he announced that he had 'now come to the resolution of refusing admittance to the lower Classes'. These he cunningly took to be all those who arrived on foot, a regulation defeated by one spirited visitor, who mounted a conveniently close cow to gain entry. An enthusiastic visitor from Halifax in Yorkshire described the natural history material in some detail in 1773.[35] In that same year Lever was elected a Fellow of the Royal Society and made the acquaintance of Gilbert White (1720–93), who, however, dropped Lever from his circle of acquaintances when his general background knowledge proved inadequate to White's purposes.

The costs to Lever of acquiring and maintaining his collections were considerable and between 1772 and 1780 he was forced by financial necessity to dispose of all of his property in Manchester. In 1774 he decided that the only future for his collection lay in London, 'in order that it might be of public utility' and where there were more affluent inhabitants whom he could charge for visiting it. There he chose the best possible central situation, Leicester House in Leicester Square, where he planned 'to pursue Natural History and carry the exhibition of it to such a height as no one can imagine and to make it the most wonderful sight in the world'.

Here, in February 1775, the famous Leverian Museum opened, at the high admission price of half a guinea a head. But this stratagem failed to solve Lever's financial problems, for in 1780 he was forced to appeal for patronage to support his collecting activities. This having proved of no avail, in 1784 he was granted an Act of Parliament enabling the museum to be disposed of by lottery, whereby he hoped to recoup the enormous expense he had incurred in gathering it together. By this time it comprised the rarest productions of the animal, vegetable and mineral kingdoms with works of art and artefacts of various native peoples in North and South America, Tahiti, Australia and other places, brought back by a variety of travellers and explorers, including Captain James Cook. Lottery tickets at one guinea each went on sale from October 1784, but only 8,000 (of the 36,000 on offer) were sold. On 23 March 1786 the draw was held and the dispersal of another fascinating museum began.

A land agent, James Parkinson (1730–1813),[36] only later realized that he held the winning ticket, his (by then deceased) wife having purchased it unknown to him. Parkinson generously allowed Lever to continue to exhibit his collections

in London until September 1786. Ironically, the publicity regarding the poor sales of Lever's tickets had been immense and, helped by that, only now did the Leverian Museum become a truly popular attraction.

Parkinson at first attempted to dispose of the entire Museum as a single entity: the Empress of Russia and the Queen of Portugal were named as potential purchasers. When no buyer came forward, however, he bravely decided to form a company to build a new venue in which to reopen a rejuvenated museum to the public, to which end in December 1786 he appealed for new materials to augment the already vast collections. The naturalist Dr George Shaw (1751–1813), who was to join the staff of the British Museum in 1791, read lectures on Natural History, to popularize the Museum in May 1787. Parkinson finally closed the Leicester Square museum in September 1787, and three months later opened his new, purpose-built museum, the Rotunda, which occupied nearly a thousand square yards on the Surrey side of the Thames near Blackfriars Bridge. It had been designed by Parkinson himself and by James Burton (alias Haliburton), who was its builder. The entrance fee was 2s.6d., which some now thought too low for a building which had seventeen different apartments. Its Grand Saloon was illustrated in the never-completed *Companion* which Parkinson started publishing in 1790.

Although this new site proved to be 'most injudicious, since it was completely out of the mighty stream of human beings which never ceases to flow through the centre of the metropolis',[37] it was, as Robert Jameson's 1793 diary demonstrates, a wonderful oasis for London's naturalists and dealers, where they could study nature through the specimens which were being continually added and where they could meet each other.[38] Also, as noted by the American visitor (a notable creator of museums himself), Charles Willson Peale (1741–1827), 'the trouble to obtain a sight of the British Museum renders it of less value to the public than a private collection belonging to Mr Parkerson [sic] called the Leverian Museum'. Peale applauded this 'superb collection [as] highly useful, instructive and amusing and which may be seen at any hour for half a dollar'.[39]

Parkinson's activities in acquiring much new material (whether natural history, mineralogy or newly available ethnography) and in promoting its display were impressive – for an outsider thrown so unexpectedly into the world of museums. There is no doubt that throughout the Museum's collections real efforts were made to describe and classify material, especially in mineralogy, where Parkinson was helped by his eldest son, John. The *Companion*, when dealing with minerals, specifically lamented that the backward state of 'this most useful study should in England be so very far behind other European nations'.[40] In the end, though, running the museum proved too much for the Parkinsons and the entire accumulation was again disposed of in a memorable auction in 1806.

A slow revolution

While this museum building had been going on in England, a quiet and slow revolution had been happening.[41] This was the revolution throughout natural history, but in particular in botany, wrought by Carl von Linné or Carolus Linnaeus (1707–78) with his introduction of the binomial system for naming plants and animals (See Chapter 12).[42] Suffice it to say that British encouragement to Linnaeus was significant even before the publication of his first *Systema Naturae* of 1735. After Linnaeus's month-long visit to England in 1736[43] these contacts increased and proved a great help in establishing his reputation.[44] Contacts were augmented further when Linnaeus's pupil Daniel Solander was appointed Sir Joseph Banks's secretary and librarian in 1772 and Keeper of the British Museum's Department of Natural and Artificial Productions in 1773. But not all were immediately persuaded: Thomas Pennant in 1767 recorded his low opinion of Linnaeus's work in zoology[45] and Pieter Camper (1722–89) in the Netherlands remained equally unimpressed.[46]

Perhaps the best indication of Linnaeus's achievement, as seen through provincial English eyes, could only come later. In 1833 the Worcestershire Natural History Society was founded, with the hope that other similarly county-wide societies would follow across the country. It held its anniversary meetings on what members supposed – unfortunately wrongly – to be Linnaeus's birthday, 25 May.[47] At its second anniversary meeting in 1835, when the foundation stone for its fine new Museum was laid before an audience of 600, its members were told how:

> ...they had wisely chosen to link their society in an especial manner to the objects pursued by the immortal Linnaeus; for this purpose they had connected it with his enchanting name... [since] but for him [they] would be without a classification which would enable them to pursue the study... Let the members of the Society then make the name of Linnaeus a rallying point.[48]

One of the best demonstrations of Linnaeus's influence in Britain is the incidence of naturalists naming their sons after him. Examples are the entomologist William Henry Linnaeus Walcott (1790–1869), son of the naturalist John Walcott (1755–1832),[49] a member of the first (1779–87) Bath Philosophical Society (hereafter BPS), and William Charles Linnaeus Martin (1798–1864), writer on natural history and superintendent of the museum of the Zoological Society, son of naturalist William Martin (1767–1810).[50]

British natural history: a *Risorgimento*

This phenomenon was a product of a new burst of activity that led to the foundation of many societies in the last quarter of the eighteenth century.[51] These were by no means as closely linked to industrialization and to industrial locations as previous authors have claimed. The 1780 rules of the BPS record that 'law, physic, divinity and politics be never made the Subjects of Debate' at their weekly winter meetings, that papers were to be read and a journal carefully kept in which these debates were recorded, and that the Society would use its funds to purchase books and scientific instruments. But no mention was made of any museum or Society collection being considered as a suitable activity:[52] that particular manifestation of enlightenment still had to reach many of the provincial societies in Britain.

Nevertheless, many members collected and made observations in natural history, including the astronomer William Herschel (1738–1822) in the field of zoology,[53] the philanthropist Matthew Martin (1748–1838), who published on entomology,[54] and John Walcott (1755–1832), who had interests across the whole range of natural history, producing books on zoology, botany and fossils (fig.27).[55] Unfortunately no clue has come down to us as to whether there ever were any BPS

collections and whether these survived. All attempts to locate the personal collections of Walcott seem to end in 1976 in a former stables in Christchurch, Dorset.[56]

In the same year as the first BPS was formed, and just after Joseph Banks had begun his presidency of the Royal Society, the Society's Council offered its collections to the Trustees of the British Museum. In 1781 this offer was accepted and the collections were removed there in order to facilitate the Society's acceptance of new accommodation offered by the Government.[57] It would be useful if the surviving elements of this important Royal Society donation could be subjected to the same historical analysis that the Sloane collection has received.[58] Among the fossils are some fine specimens from this source, including R1330, the early Darwinian plesiosaur-to-be presented to the Royal Society in 1718[59] and R1087a, the Whitby crocodile found in 1758.[60] The development of the natural history collections of the British Museum, and their curation, such as it was, in the later eighteenth century have been described by A.E. Gunther[61] and W.T. Stearn.[62]

It was soon after this Royal Society donation that two French visitors recorded their reactions to the British Museum's natural history collections as a whole. The naturalist and traveller Bartélemy Faujas de St Fond (1741–1819) came in 1784. He complained, after some fascinating political comments, that:

> ...the British Museum contains many valuable collections in natural history; but with the exception of some fishes in a small apartment, which are begun to be classed, nothing is in order, every thing is out of its place; and this assemblage is rather an immense magazine, in which things seem to have been thrown together at random, than a scientific collection, intended to instruct and honour a great nation. It may be presumed, that as long as so repulsive a confusion is suffered to continue, no artist will ever be induced to go there, to acquire those branches of information which relate to the materials he uses, and the sources whence they are derived.[63]

In 1785 the La Rochefoucauld brothers came and their impression was more favourable. They noted that:

> ...until the period of the present reign [1760] London had no... repository related to the arts and sciences such as that of the *Cabinet Royal* in Paris. They bought [Old Montagu] house to... house a great and beautiful collection of natural history [Sloane's] destined to grow daily... The cabinet of natural history... is furnished almost like ours [in Paris]. They have given the greatest attention to completing the collection of national products, and consequently all have an immediately useful function. Also, the section on the minerals of the three kingdoms is not only rich in specimens of all kinds, arranged in impressive order, but the most complete you could imagine.[64]

It would be hard to reconcile two such widely differing assessments without taking into account the differing qualifications of the commentators.

The Society for Promoting Natural History (SPNH) and the Linnean Society of London

Edmund Rack (1735–87), the Quaker co-founder and first secretary of the BPS, was a keen natural historian; he read several papers[65] – or sent them to be read – before the SPNH (which on one occasion he ambiguously called 'The Fossil Society in London'). This had been founded in that city on 13 October 1782.[66] This body also seems to have been too concerned with reading and discussing papers to pay any attention to building a museum, although it met regularly until 1794 or 1795 and soldiered on, if in name only, for another twenty-seven years until its few assets were made over to its more successful rival, the Linnean Society. James Edward Smith, soon to be 'the present possessor of the Linnean cabinet', had joined the SPNH in February 1784. (Another person elected in that year, later to be credited with priming the establishment of a remarkable complex of museums, was Louis Macie, who is considered below.)

Frustrated by the increasing ineffectiveness of the SPNH, several members broke away to found the Linnean Society in February 1788. This speedily outgrew its semi-parent and, thanks to Smith's purchase of all Linnaeus's collections in October 1784, had a museum function as its central focus. In his pioneering article on natural history in the eighteenth century, David Allen (who otherwise hardly mentions museums) makes the crucial point that in any collective activity at this time, 'any jointly owned possession, such as a journal or a museum, helped cement it together'; he concluded that the success of the Linnean Society was because it 'could draw most of its strength from the enviable possession of those [Linnaean] riches'.[67]

If this were so, perhaps the fact that Smith so soon sold the Linnaean minerals (in which he clearly had little interest) at auction in 1796[68] simply represented an attempt to distance both the Linnean Society and himself further from the rival SPNH. Perhaps in Smith's eyes the SPNH had paid too much attention to past natural worlds and not enough to those of the present. When another Bath correspondent of the SPNH, the artist John Hamlyn, disposed of his collections in 1783, claiming to be 'going Abroad', they were sold at auction in Bath,[69] and show him to have been a further largely geological collector.

Smith had earlier founded yet another natural history society, for Edinburgh University students, in 1782.[70] Here Professor John Walker (1731–1803) seems to have solved any dilemma about what to do with specimens offered to that society by putting his University Museum at the society's disposal, both for holding its meetings and as a repository for its specimens.[71] In this case a cuckoo soon crept into that society's nest and temporarily took it over: the newly exciting study of chemistry.

Laissez-faire and partial patronage

The most characteristic feature of late eighteenth-century collection-forming and museum-building in Britain, despite the sterling example set by the creation of the British Museum, seems to have been what the British, having had their attention drawn to the problem by the more state-concerned French, would later call a laissez-faire attitude.[72]

One aspect of laissez-faire was the frequent auctioning-off of natural history collections in Britain during this period, as has already been noted. This must indicate one of several possibilities: that there was little interest in seeking more permanent homes for such material, that only the money raised mattered, or that suitable repositories did not yet exist. The extraordinary extent of this auctioning-off is best revealed by a register of natural history sales that was published in 1976.[73] Paula Findlen has rightly remarked on this phenomenon: '1,600 natural history auctions occurred in Great Britain alone in the eighteenth century'[74] – and those are only the auctions of which records have survived.

Commercial dealing in natural history specimens and materials was another feature of the British scene. William Swainson recorded that George Humphrey or Humphreys (1739–1826) was 'for many years, the chief commercial naturalist in this country; and from his father, who was in the same profession, he inherited immense collections both in conchology and mineralogy'.[75] Michael Cooper has recently shed welcome new light on the extent of this dealership and its manifold connections with other commercial dealers in natural history.[76] Their 'Museum Humfredianum' of 1779, so often referred to, proved merely to be the auction sale catalogue of all the Humphreys's material, brought together since about 1745 by the father and sold only because he had just gone bankrupt.[77]

Two particularly fine examples of laissez-faire museums at this time were opened in England. The first belonged to William Bullock (c.1773–1849),[78] later an auctioneer of importance. It was established first in Sheffield in about 1795; Bullock then moved it to Liverpool in 1800, to Manchester in 1805, to Hull in 1808, and to Bath in 1809 before settling it in London the year after that – only for it to be dispersed at auction in its entirety in 1819 (fig.28).[79]

The second of these museums was that created by one of the strangest of museum keepers, Robert Ferryman (1752–1837).[80] Ferryman had taken an early interest in natural history and had started to collect animals by 1769. In the 1780s he met Edward Jenner (1749–1823), the vaccinator and pioneer natural historian, who wrote to Joseph Banks in December 1787 describing how Ferryman had 'for many years been collecting British Birds and Quadrupeds ... his preparations are animated beyond description ... the eyes which he makes himself from coloured glass and enamel are exact models from nature. The whole is freed from that gaudiness which attends Sir Ashton Lever's.'[81] In 1788 Ferryman wrote to Banks about the book he hoped to write on his collections. Banks was lukewarm about its viability, but Ferryman, undaunted, issued a Prospectus from Nettleton, Gloucestershire in March 1788. In 1789, attempting to gain more subscribers, he started touring his museum of stuffed animals with a 1s. admission charge, to Bristol, Bath (both had printed catalogues) and Gloucester. In the summer of 1795 he exhibited and catalogued what was by now his extensive 'British Zoological Museum' in a temporary building in London, hoping it 'should meet with that encouragement' which would allow it to be opened again in future years. Sadly it did not (fig.29).[82]

After Ferryman had been quickly ordained a priest at Gloucester, Jenner arranged for Ferryman's museum-building to receive more secure patronage by his being given, in October 1796, by George Wyndham, 3rd Earl of Egremont (1751–1837), the rectorship of Iping and Chithurst in Sussex. This living was intended to further Ferryman's work on the Earl's new private museum at nearby Petworth, with which Ferryman's own collection was probably incorporated.[83] But within a few years Ferryman had landed in such deep financial water that he had to face his creditors and others complaining about him in both the Consistory Court and the Court of Arches. Forced to flee his creditors, he did so by becoming a missionary for the Society for the Propagation of the Gospel, in far-away Canada. There, at least, he could, and did, continue his zoological collecting.[84]

A rather more impressive – and secure – example of provincial museum building is provided by the Newcastle

Literary and Philosophical Society founded in 1793. Its *Laws* published in 1794 record 'the opportunities which its [Newcastle's] extensive commerce affords for collecting the rare productions of nature or art' and the several donations which had already been made to the Society.[85] Charles Hatchett (1766–1847), who gave his mineral collections to the British Museum in 1799, went on a collecting tour in 1796. He then recorded that the chief part of these Newcastle collections concentrated on geology,[86] understandably, in view of the coal and other mineral resources of the area.

But there were other fascinating items in these collections. When John Hunter (1737–1821), Governor of New South Wales, sent specimens of the duck-billed platypus to Britain from Australia in 1798, some went to the Newcastle Society, of which Hunter was an Honorary Member. These were used in one of the first descriptions of this most remarkable animal, which was also published in Newcastle.[87] By the time the Northumberland, Durham and Newcastle Natural History Society was founded in 1829 the prior activities of the Literary and Philosophical Society had been vital in promoting both natural history and museum-building in the region, the latter through the fine Hancock Museum.[88]

These Australian and other colonial connections were soon to provide a new and vital input to the world of British natural history as remarkable treasures from abroad came to be uncovered. Again commercial dealers were vital to this dissemination, none more so than John Mawe (1766–1829), mineralogist, conchologist, traveller and London natural history dealer.[89] In 1804 he issued special instructions to 'Gentlemen visiting the South Seas . . . with a view to encouraging the collecting of natural history' (fig.30).[90]

Two museum builders from Britain with truly international aspirations

Two significant naturalists of the last decades of the eighteenth century provide final food for thought concerning potential museum-builders of that era. One is the remarkable Robert Townson (1762–1827), who is now starting to receive the attention his work deserves.[91] In 1806 he set off for Australia in an attempt to become one of the first serious scientists to settle there. He failed because of the political situation he faced on arrival, getting involved in the 'Rum Rebellion' to depose Governor William Bligh (1754–1817). This was the second major mutiny against Bligh and Townson was directly implicated.

Townson's earlier career in Europe had been equally, if differently, blighted by his failure to attract patronage. Patronage is one of the key features of eighteenth-century British history, as Allen has rightly pointed out.[92] It continued to play an important role into the later part of the century, the period dominated in Britain by the 'industrial revolution'.[93] Sir John Sinclair (1754–1835), a man much used to awarding patronage (but who had later to be bailed out by 'subscribers' when he himself got into financial difficulties), wrote an account of why people wanted to enter Parliament. The ability to dispense patronage, he said, was crucial in this desire, as:

> . . . to be enabled to provide for friends; to succour the indigent; to patronise merit; – these are the noble objects which stimulate every young man of superior abilities to exert his utmost talents in the

British Senate, with the hope of recommending himself to the notice of his fellow men, and of rising perhaps, at some period of his life, to the rank of a minister.[94]

Townson's consistent inability to secure such patronage caused the failure of all three attempts he made to go as naturalist or mineral surveyor to Canada, India and Sierra Leone in the last decade of the century. Yet considering all that he was able to achieve travelling alone in the then Hungarian Empire in a few, revolutionary, months in 1793, he deserved better. But, as he himself recorded, 'all is brought about by influence, very little without – however reasonable the proposal'.[95] Katherine Plymley (1758–1829), the diarist who recorded this comment, came from a Shropshire land-owning family based near Townson's English home. She helpfully recorded the extent of his naturalist bent in 1795:

> . . . his appearance, when equipt for [a walk through North Wales] was curious. His pockets contain'd a little linen, a sledge hammer to break rocks in search of fossils, a tin case to preserve the insects he should catch in & and an instrument for catching butterflies & at his back was slung a large portfolio strapped between two boards to press plants in, & a gun in his hand [for hunting animals].[96]

This was a man who still thought of the whole of nature as his single quarry.

Townson duly made large collections, but in his insufficiently patronized world of the late eighteenth century he could leave these only in the private, and obviously dangerous, care of the Plymley family, at Longnor Hall, Shropshire, near his point of departure in 1806. After the foundation of the Shropshire and North Wales natural History Society in Shrewsbury in 1835 the Plymleys, in 1837, did at least later donate a few of his insect specimens to it. Sadly, nothing has since been uncovered to suggest that any of his remarkable collections has survived subsequent vicissitudes in Salopian museums.

The other Englishman (despite his being born in France) who clearly gave a lot of thought to the disposal of both his considerable wealth and natural history collections – mainly in mineralogy – was the above mentioned Louis Macie, better known today as James Smithson (1764–1829), the posthumous benefactor of the Smithsonian Institution in America.[97] He was illegitimate, as was Townson, and clearly Smithson's decision to leave his wealth and collections to a country he had never visited might be connected with that simple fact. But Smithson too had travelled widely, if only in Europe, dying in Genoa in 1829.

It is interesting to ponder why Smithson's money was intended to found a foreign institution and not support a British one. The romantic, and unexplained, nature of this bequest has generated far too much speculative history: his evident, if badly recorded, problems with the Royal Society from 1818 explain why he did not leave his fortune to that organization. Louis Agassiz (1807–73) even recorded in 1855 that 'Smithson had already made his will and left his fortune to the Royal Society of London, when certain scientific papers were offered to that body for publication . . . They were refused; upon which he changed his will and made his bequest to the United States.' Note that Agassiz did not say these were Smithson's papers.[98] In the case of France, Smithson – otherwise a most enthusiastic republican – had while in Paris in 1793 witnessed the greatest excesses of the French Revolution. An even more obvious explanation of why Germany may have been excluded is because he became a prisoner-of-war in that country in 1808–9.

So the existence of the Smithsonian, like the great benefactor's wealth, clearly rested first on the infertility of his half-brother and then on the political situations in Europe in the last part of the eighteenth and first part of the nineteenth centuries as perceived by Smithson. But uncovering all the twists and turns behind his bequest is very complex and must involve archival ferretings all over Europe and America.

Another less welcome aspect of the world of international natural history in museums now also starts to be revealed. David Murray's history and bibliography has a note on 'Spoliation of European Museums by Napoleon Bonaparte'[99] to show that the Elgin marbles are not the only problem materials in this much debated arena. The saga of the Meuse monster, later named the *Mosasaurus* in 1822, is a particularly striking example from the world of natural history.[100]

Some conclusions

The British State did at least realize that there was a real need to give its own patronage to the world of museums on one further occasion after the foundation of the British Museum and before the end of the eighteenth century. In October 1793, the surgeon and anatomist John Hunter (1728–93) died, and in his will directed that the Government be petitioned to purchase 'all my said collection of Natural History . . . in one lot at such a price as may be considered reasonable between both parties'.[101] By 1799 it had been agreed that this collection, largely of anatomical preparations, should be purchased by Parliament and given to the Royal College of Surgeons.[102] State patronage was again vital in the survival of that fine collection. (Sadly it was largely destroyed by bombing in 1941.) Hunter's collection proved of great importance to the advancement of natural history in the nineteenth century, through the way it promoted the study of comparative anatomy.

The advances made in the ninteenth century, in both the appreciation of natural history collecting and securing specimens in museums, were to prove truly remarkable. As Thomas B. Lloyd Baker (1807–86), first president of the earliest properly constituted English Naturalists' Field Club (based in the Cotswolds) noted in 1851:

> . . . some half a century ago *collectors* and *museums* were almost universally laughed at; and, I fear, in most cases justly. A museum of that day . . . appears usually to have been a collection of heterogenous objects, whose only interest consisted in their rarity, and the only pleasure contemplated by the possessor, was, the being able to say that he had got such and such things which others had not. In these days happily a better taste is shewn; and Collectors now bring together objects, not for the mere sake of the possession but with a view to the assistance which may be obtained from them in the study of nature.[103]

Acknowledgements

Thanks are due to Robert Anderson, Janet Browne, Gina Douglas, Jonathan King, Simon Knell, Alison McCann, Arthur MacGregor, Stephen Pober, Valerie Price, William Schupbach, Earle Spamer, the late John Thackray, the late Peter Whitehead and Ellis Yochelson. They have all either contributed directly to this paper or to my understanding of museology. David Allen, Gina Douglas and Arthur MacGregor also read and most helpfully commented on a first draft. Final thanks are due to Anthony Payne, whose intuitive labours on never-finished music, have duly inspired the completion of this contribution.

Notes and references

1   *British Museum General Catalogue of Printed Books* 141 (London, 1964), p.545.
2   T. Greenwood, *Museums and Art Galleries* (London, 1888), p.v.
3   D. Murray, *Museums: Their History and their Use* (Glasgow, 1904, reprinted Staten Island, 2000), Introduction, p.i and Preface, p.viii.
4   S. Bedini, 'The evolution of science museums', *Technology and Culture* 6 (1965), pp.1–29.
5   G. Hollister-Short (ed.), 'Symposium – The current state of the history of technology in Britain', *History of Technology* 22 (2000), pp.173–264 (see Introduction and p.224).
6   D. Price, 'John Woodward and a surviving British geological collection from the early eighteenth century', *Journal of the History of Collections* 1 (1989), pp.79–95. We should record that David Price (1946–91), posthumously awarded the Brighton Medal for services to geology in museums, was a victim of academic indifference to museology, in case we should imagine its recent revival has been too successful (*Cambridge Evening News*, 31 January 1992, p.3, and 10 March 1992, p.3).
7   R. Porter, 'John Woodward: "A droll sort of philosopher"', *Geological Magazine* 116 (1979), pp.335–43.
8   Lichfield Record Office, P/C/11 1683, will of William Woodward.
9   J.M. Levine, *Dr. Woodward's Shield* (Berkeley and London, 1977), pp.18, 303.
10 J. Woodward, *An attempt towards a natural History of the Fossils of England* (London, 1728–9), pt 1, p.45 and pt 2, p.46.
11 J. Woodward, *Fossils of all kinds digested into a Method* (London, 1728), pp.iii–iv.
12 D. Price, 'John Woodward and the pursuit of knowledge of the Earth in the late seventeenth and early eighteenth centuries', unpublished paper read to the Eyles Symposium, Society for the History of Natural History (Bristol, September 1988 – copy in the author's possession). On the use of this collection as a geographical source see M. Kazmer, 'Carpathian minerals in the . . . Woodward-ian Collection', *Journal of the History of Collections* 10 (1998), pp.159–68.
13 C.E. Ray and D.J. Bohaska (eds), 'Geology and paleontology of the Lee Creek Mine, North Carolina, part III', *Smithsonian Contributions to Paleobiology* 90 (2001), pp.1–365 (esp. p.12).
14 H.S. Torrens, *The Practice of British Geology 1750–1850* (Aldershot, 2002), pp.111–235.
15 A. MacGregor (ed.), *Sir Hans Sloane: Collector, scientist, antiquary; founding father of the British Museum* (London, 1994). Chapters 3 to 8 cover natural history (Humana, Vertebrates, Invertebrates, Insects, Minerals and Fossils, Botany).
16 S. Festing, 'Rare flowers and fantastic breeds: the 2nd Duchess of Portland and her circle', *Country Life*, 12 June 1986, pp.1684–6 and 19 June 1986, pp.1772–4.
17 A. Hall (ed.), *The Autobiography and Correspondence of Mary Granville, Mrs Delany* (London, 1861), vol.1, p.514.
18 Anon., 'Particular account of the sale of the Portland Museum', *Gentleman's Magazine* 56:1 (1786), pp.526–7.
19 W.S. Lewis and J.W. Reed Jnr (eds), *Horace Walpole's Correspondence with the Walpole family*, Yale edn, vol.36 (New Haven, 1973), pp.236–7.
20 A.L. Reade, *Johnsonian Gleanings*, pt 8 (London, 1937), pp.122–58.
21 Shropshire Archives Centre, Shrewsbury, MSS 6001/4263, p.43.
22 C. Dack, 'The Peterborough Gentlemen's Society', *Journal of the British Archaeological Association* (June 1899), p.19 of offprint.
23 R. Greene, *A descriptive Catalogue of the rarities in Mr G's Museum at Lichfield* ([Lichfield], 1773) and ibid. (Lichfield, 1782 and Lichfield, 1786). The first and last editions are in the British Library, the 1782 edition is in the William Salt Library, Stafford.

24 Banks's Journal, Cambridge University Library.

25 L.F. Powell (ed.), Boswell's *Life of Johnson* (Oxford, 1934), vol.II, pp.465–6.

26 E. Robinson, 'The Lunar Society: its membership and organisation', *Transactions of the Newcomen Society* 35 (1964), pp.153–77; R.E. Schofield, *The Lunar Society of Birmingham* (Oxford, 1964).

27 H.S. Torrens, 'Lichfield Museums (pre 1850)', *Newsletter of the Geological Curators Group* 1 (1974), pp.5–10, and 'Postscript', 1 (1974), pp.38–9; L. Fletcher, 'Josiah Wedgwood and Greene's Museum', *Proceedings of the Wedgwood Society* 9 (1975), pp.31–5.

28 W. Schupbach, 'A select iconography of animal experiment', pp.340–60 in N. Rupke (ed.), *Vivisection in Historical Perspective* (London, 1987), pp.347, 358, pl.I.

29 K. Hudson, *A Social History of Museums: What the visitors thought* (London, 1975), p.27.

30 B. Redford (ed.), *The Letters of Samuel Johnson* (Oxford, 1992), vol.II, p.II.

31 After Greene's death in 1793, his museum had a singularly complex history of dispersal, involving William Bullock (c.1773–1849), Walter Honywood Yate (1779–?), and Greene's grandson Richard Wright (1777–1821). It much deserves further study.

32 W.J. Smith, 'The life and activities of Sir Ashton Lever of Alkrington', *Transactions of the Lancashire and Cheshire Antiquarian Society* 72 (1965), pp.61–92.

33 J.C.H. King, 'New evidence for the contents of the Leverian Museum', *Journal of the History of Collections* 8 (1996), pp.167–86.

34 S.P. Dance, *Shell Collecting: An illustrated history* (London, 1966), pp.109–10.

35 See Smith, op. cit. (note 32), pp.69–70 (ex *Gentleman's Magazine*).

36 See *New Dictionary of National Biography* (hereafter *NDNB*) (forthcoming).

37 W. Swainson, *The Cabinet Cyclopaedia – Natural History: Taxidermy, bibliography and biography* (London, 1840), p.246.

38 J.M. Sweet, 'Robert Jameson in London', *Annals of Science* 19 (1963), pp.81–116.

39 C.W. Peale, *Discourse introductory to a course of Lectures on the Science of Nature* (Philadelphia, 1800), p.20.

40 Parkinson's *A Companion to the Museum (late Sir Ashton Lever's) 1790* and the *Sale Catalogue of the entire Collection 1806* have been reprinted (London, 1979). The quotation here comes from *A Companion to the Museum* (London, 1790), pt 2, 'Minerals', p.55.

41 D.E. Allen, 'Natural history in Britain in the eighteenth century', *Archives of Natural History* 20 (1993), pp.333–47.

42 D.M. Knight, *Ordering the World* (London, 1981).

43 W. Blunt, *The Complete Naturalist: A life of Linnaeus* (London, 1971), see pt II, chap.4.

44 G. Douglas, entry for Carl von Linné, *NDNB* (forthcoming).

45 W.R. Dawson, *The Banks Letters: A calendar of the manuscript correspondence of Sir Joseph Banks* (London, 1958), p.661.

46 A.T. Gage, *A History of the Linnean Society of London* (London, 1938), pp.II–12, and see Dawson, op. cit. (note 45), p.200.

47 Anon., 'Worcestershire Natural History Society', *Magazine of Natural History* 8 (1835), pp.403–9. The Worcestershire Society believed Linnaeus's birthday (actually on 23 May because of calendrical changes) to be on 25 May. The Linnean Society was equally but differently misinformed, and still takes 24 May as its 'anniversary day': see Gage, op. cit. (note 46), pp.16, 104.

48 *Proceedings of the Second Anniversary Festival of the Worcestershire Natural History Society* (Worcester, 1835), pt 2, pp.26–7.

49 See *NDNB* (forthcoming).

50 Ibid.

51 H.S. Torrens, 'The four Bath Philosophical Societies 1779–1959', in R. Rolls and Jean and J.R. Guy (eds), *A Pox on the Provinces* (Bath, 1990), pp.180–8.

52 A.J. Turner (ed.), *Science and Music in 18th Century Bath* (Bath, 1977), pp.88–9.

53 S. Schaffer, 'Herschel in Bedlam: Natural history and stellar astronomy', *British Journal for the History of Science* 13 (1980), pp.211–39, esp. pp.213–14.

54 A.A. Lisney, *A Bibliography of British Lepidoptera (1608–1799)* (London, 1960), pp.222–3.

55 See *NDNB* (forthcoming).

56 H.S. Torrens, 'Two horror stories of the eighteenth century, 2: a distinctly sad ending', *Newsletter of the Geological Curators Group* 1 (6) (1976), pp.191–3.

57 H. Lyons, *The Royal Society 1660–1904* (Cambridge, 1944), pp.210–11.

58 See MacGregor, op. cit. (note 15).

59 D.G. King-Hele, *Erasmus Darwin* (London, 1999), pp.2–3.

60 R. Lydekker, *Catalogue of the Fossil Reptilia and Amphibia in the British Museum (Natural History)* (London, 1888–9), pt 1, p.III and pt 2, p.259.

61 A.E. Gunther, *The Founders of Science at the British Museum 1753–1900* (Halesworth, 1980).

62 W.T. Stearn, *The Natural History Museum at South Kensington* (London, 1981).

63 B. Faujas de St Fond, *A Journey through England . . . in 1784,* ed. A. Geikie (Glasgow, 1907), vol.I, pp.85–90.

64 N. Scarfe (ed.) *Innocent Espionage: The Larochefoucauld brothers' tour of England in 1785* (Woodbridge, 1995), pp.213–15. Unfortunately this editor has wrongly taken their later comments on the 'Chevalier xxxxxx' collections (pp.215–16) to refer to the British Museum and its William Hamilton collection of antiquities, only some of which were already safely in that museum, whereas these comments clearly refer instead to the Leverian Museum, for the disposal of which – by lottery – an Act of Parliament had just been granted.

65 See Gage, op. cit. (note 46), p.5.

66 Homo Sum, *Gentleman's Magazine* 55 (1785), pp.854–6; A member of the Linnean Society, *Gentleman's Magazine* 98 (1828), pp.415–16; M.H., *Gentleman's Magazine* 98 (1828), pp.582–3.

67 See Allen, op. cit. (note 41), pp.335, 344.

68 See Gage, op. cit. (note 46), p.18.

69 See Torrens, op. cit. (note 14), pp.III–233.

70 D.E. Allen, 'James Edward Smith and the Natural History Society of Edinburgh', *Journal of the Society for the Bibliography of Natural History* 8 (1978), pp.483–93.

71 C.W.J. Withers, '"Both useful and ornamental": John Walker's keepership of Edinburgh University's Natural History Museum 1779–1803', *Journal of the History of Collections* 5 (1993), pp.65–77.

72 This term is credited in the *Oxford English Dictionary,* 2nd edn, to the Marquis of Normanby writing in 1825.

73 J.M. Chalmers-Hunt, *Natural History Auctions 1700–1972: A register of sales in the British Isles* (London, 1976).

74 P. Findlen, *Possessing Nature* (Berkeley and London, 1994), p.399.

75 See Swainson, op. cit. (note 37), pp.219–21.

76 M. Cooper, 'Keeping it in the family: the Humphreys, Forsters and Heulands', *Matrix* 9 (2001), pp.3–31.

77 For the bankruptcy of George Humphrey of St Martin's Lane [London], dealer, see *Gentleman's Magazine* 48 (August 1778), p.392; see also C.D. Sherborn, 'Note on the *Museum Humfredianum, 1779', Annals and Magazine of Natural History* (7) 16 (1905), pp.262–4.

78 E.A. Alexander, 'William Bullock: little-remembered museologist and showman', *Curator* 28 (1985), pp.117–47.

79 *Sale Catalogue of the Bullock Museum 1819,* facsimile (London, 1979).

80 See *NDNB* (forthcoming).

81 Jenner to Banks, 28 December 1787, Fitzwilliam Museum, Cambridge.

82 Ferryman's museological activities deserve to be better known. He is not mentioned in Peter Whitehead's useful survey, 'Museums in the history of zoology', *Museums Journal* 70 (1970), pp.50–6, and 70 (1971), pp.155–60.

83 A. McCann, 'A private laboratory at Petworth House, Sussex in the late eighteenth century', *Annals of Science* 49 (1983), pp.635–55, esp. p.638.

84 R.C. Murphy, 'Robert ferryman: forgotten naturalist', *Proceedings of the American Philosophical Society* 103 (1959), pp.774–7.

85 *Laws of the Literary and Philosophical Society of Newcastle upon Tyne* ([Newcastle], 1794).

86 A. Raistrick (ed.), *The Hatchett Diary* (Truro, 1967), p.79.

87 J.W. Gruber, 'Does the platypus lay eggs? The history of an event in science', *Archives of Natural History* 18 (1991), pp.51–123, esp. pp.54–5.

88 T.R. Goddard, *History of the Natural History Society of Northumberland, Durham and Newcastle upon Tyne* (Newcastle, 1929).

89 See *NDNB* (forthcoming).

90 Copy in Mitchell library, New South Wales, Australia.

91 P. Rozsa (ed.), *Robert Townson's Travels in Hungary* (Debrecen, 1999).

92 See Allen, op. cit. (note 41), p.338.

93 M.W. McCahill, 'Peers, patronage, and the Industrial Revolution, 1760–1800', *Journal of British Studies* 16 (1976), pp.84–109.

94 J. Sinclair, *The Correspondence of the Right Honourable Sir John Sinclair,* 2 vols (London, 1831), vol.I, pp. 69–70.

95 Katherine Plymley diaries, vol.73, January 1807 (Shropshire Archives Centre, Shrewsbury).

96 Katherine Plymley diaries, vol.40, 5 December 1795 (Shropshire Archives Centre, Shrewsbury).

97 See *NDNB* (forthcoming).

98 L. Agassiz, letter, *Science* 49 (1919), p.301.

99 See Murray, op. cit. (note 3), vol.II, pp.49–50.

100 G. Laurent, *Paléontologie et Evolution en France 1800–1860* (Paris, 1987), p.155.

101 *Journals of the House of Commons* 51 (1796), pp.512–17.

102 Z. Cope, *The Royal College of Surgeons of England – A History* (London, 1959), pp.22–7.

103 T.B. Lloyd Baker, 'Address to the Cotteswold Naturalists' Club', *Proceedings of the Cotteswold Naturalists' Club* 1 (1853), Appendix p.5.

Figure 26
'View of Mr Greene's Museum at Lichfield', published in the *Gentleman's Magazine* (1788). The central clock survives in the Bath City Museum and Art Gallery.

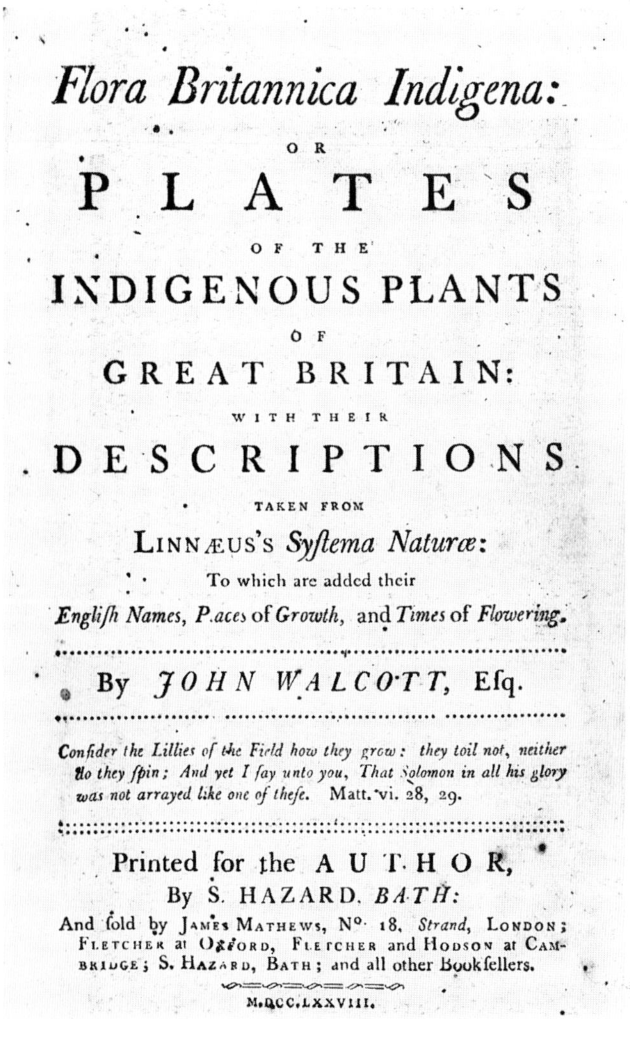

View of M.ʳ Greene's Museum at Lichfield.

Figure 27
One of two variant title pages of John Walcott's never-completed book on botany, issued just after Linnaeus's death, in fourteen monthly parts from the summer of 1778 at the 'suicidally low' price of 1s. a part.

Flora Britannica Indigena:

OR

PLATES

OF THE

INDIGENOUS PLANTS

OF

GREAT BRITAIN:

WITH THEIR

DESCRIPTIONS

TAKEN FROM

LINNÆUS'S *Syftema Naturæ:*

To which are added their

Englifh Names, P.aces of Growth, and *Times of Flowering.*

By *JOHN WALCOTT,* Efq.

Confider the Lillies of the Field how they grow: they toil not, neither do they fpin: And yet I fay unto you, That Solomon in all his glory was not arrayed like one of thefe. Matt. vi. 28, 29.

Printed for the AUTHOR,
By S. HAZARD, *BATH:*
And fold by JAMES MATHEWS, Nº 18, *Strand,* LONDON;
FLETCHER at OXford, FLETCHER and HODSON at CAM-
BRIDGE; S. HAZARD, BATH; and all other Bookfellers.

M.DCC.LXXVIII.

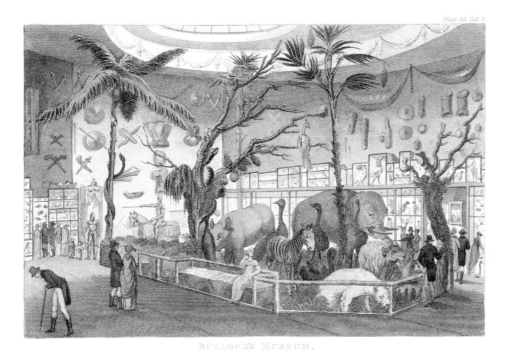

Figure 28
The final resting place of William Bullock's Museum at 22 Piccadilly, London, published in 1810 (the original, from Ackermann's *Repository of Arts*, is in colour).

Figure 29
Title page of the *Catalogue* of Robert Ferryman's 'British Zoological Museum', opened in London in the summer of 1795. London, British Library.

A

CATALOGUE

OF

BRITISH

QUADRUPEDS AND BIRDS,

CONTAINED IN THE

BRITISH

ZOOLOGICAL MUSEUM,

OXFORD STREET.

What call'st thou Solitude? Is not the Earth
With various living creatures, and the Air,
Replenish'd, and all these at thy command,
To come and play before thee? Know'st thou not
Their language and their ways? They also know,
And reason not contemptibly. With these
Find pastime, and bear rule; thy realm is large.
So spake the universal Lord.

MILTON'S PARADISE LOST.

LONDON:
PRINTED BY JOHN RIDER, No. 36, LITTLE-BRITAIN.

1795.

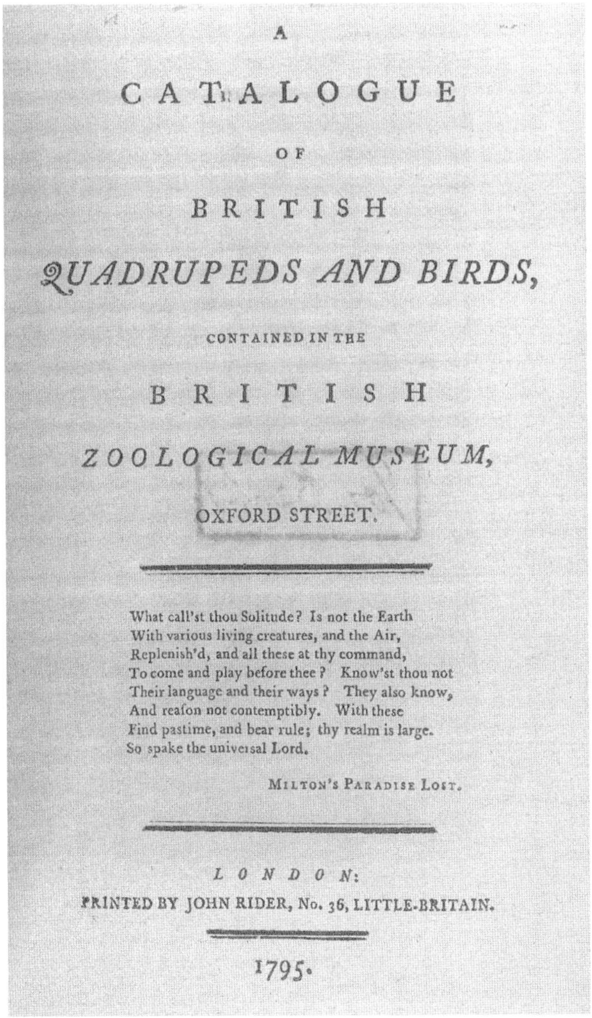

Figure 30
Title page of John Mawe's pamphlet of 1804, 'encouraging the collecting of natural history by Gentlemen who visit the South Seas and all foreign countries' (original in the Mitchell Library, Sydney, New South Wales).

163

A SHORT

TREATISE,

ADDRESSED TO

Gentlemen visiting the South Seas,

AND ALL

FOREIGN COUNTRIES;

MORE PARTICULARLY TO

Commanders, &c. of Ships,

AND

GENTLEMEN RESIDING ON SHORE,

With a View to encourage the collecting of

NATURAL HISTORY.

By JOHN MAWE,
Author of the MINERALOGY of DERBYSHIRE, &c.
No. 5, Tavistock Street, Covent Garden, London,
Where Collectors will find the largest Variety of
NATURAL HISTORY in EUROPE.

YOUNG, Printer, Brydges Street, Covent Garden.

1804.

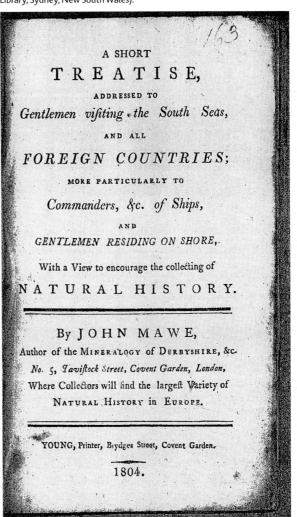

Chapter 12

Linnaeus, Solander and the Birth of a Global Plant Taxonomy
Bengt Jonsell

Fewer than 10,000 species of flowering plants and ferns were known to Linnaeus; today, more than 250,000 have been described. In his fundamental *Species plantarum* of 1753, which came to be regarded as the starting point for botanical nomenclature,[1] Linnaeus aimed to include plants from the whole world, although the great majority of those he described were, of course, European. Among the 250,000 species known today, fewer than 20,000 are from Europe, the focus having shifted definitively. By the end of the eighteenth century the number of known plant species had already tripled, the bulk of the additions being extra-European in origin. The following is a survey of the ways in which knowledge expanded and the effects, both theoretical and practical, that this had upon plant classification, that is to say, on the taxonomy of the time. The process can be followed in other parts of the world – in France and the Netherlands, for example – but it is particularly fruitful to observe it from a London perspective. Carl Linnaeus (1707–78) and Daniel Solander (1733–82) are the figures named in the title of this paper, but two more are of equal importance. One is Robert Brown (1773–1858), whose career expands into the following century, when all his main works were accomplished; the other is Sir Joseph Banks (1744–1820), instrumental in the activities of both Solander and Brown, and even mentioned as the best disciple Linnaeus never had – a reference to his aborted visit to Uppsala which was to have taken place in about 1772. Irrespective of where one chooses to study the first steps towards a global plant taxonomy, however, Linnaeus must form the starting point.

Linnaeus, his method and apostles

Following the collapse of Sweden's role as a major political power in 1718, the country rose surprisingly quickly to become one of the great scientific nations during the mid-eighteenth century, a position which it gradually lost again towards the end of the century. Among the many brilliant Swedish scientists of the era, none had a greater reputation in his own day than Linnaeus (fig.31), and none has enjoyed such long-lasting fame. The causes are manifold, but here will be discussed the two most important – Linnaeus's method of classification of plants and his many disciples who spread this methodology throughout the learned world.

The basis of Linnaeus's method for the classification of plants is the sexual system. Its strength lies in its simplicity, based as it is on the number and arrangement of the sexual organs of the plants – firstly the stamens, which define the classes, and secondly the pistils, which define the subordinate orders. In contrast to pre-Linnaean systems it operates with discrete characters: as a rule, each plant can unequivocally be placed into its appropriate class and order. The classes are illustrated in the famous plate by Georg Ehret first reproduced in the *Systema naturae*[2] of 1735. Newly discovered species can easily be located within the system. When plants increasingly came to be added from exotic parts of the globe – not least by Linnaeus's disciples – even these totally unknown forms had their numbers of stamens and arrangements of pistils which allowed them to be fitted within the system. That facility accounted for a large part of its success. Also important was the fact that Linnaeus adhered to it consistently in all his taxonomic works from the 1730s to the 1770s, effectively launching it himself as a self-conscious young man in the Netherlands in 1735–8, with visits to Britain in 1736 and France in the following year. In Britain and the Netherlands, Linnaeus's method ultimately prevailed and works arranged according to the sexual system appeared within a few years. In France, and also in Germany, on the other hand, he met with influential adversaries, the most formidable amongst whom was the Comte de Buffon in Paris. Another was Bernard de Jussieu, who introduced a 'natural' system in the Trianon garden.[3] (He was the uncle of Antoine de Jussieu who will be referred to later.) Of course the sexual system is artifical, purely practical: no one was more conscious of that than Linnaeus himself. He realized that it did not reflect a true 'affinity' among the species, which Linnaeus and other sharp eyes and minds of the time understood to exist, although they explained it in other terms than we would use today. The ambition not fulfilled by Linnaeus but published in fragments[4] was to make a faithful representation of Nature's own plan[5] – which was ultimately God's plan.

The overseas travellers among Linnaeus's disciples – his apostles, as he liked to call them – form a unique phenomenon in the history of sciences (fig.32).[6] It may be said that their efforts comprised a scientific programme for the botanical exploration of the entire globe, meeting with a range of results from full success to total catastrophe. Beginning in 1746, this impetus was maintained until 1779, when Carl Peter Thunberg, one of the latest and most successful of all, returned to Sweden with the foundations of the floras of both Japan and South Africa in his luggage. How this enterprise inspired Banks to send out botanists from Britain is a matter which will be returned to. The official driving force, which also gave rise to the necessary funding, was the hope in Sweden of making useful plant acquisitions that would make costly imports superfluous, but as these aspirations dwindled the purpose became more purely scientific. Altogether, the disciples contributed in an unequalled manner to the bringing of order out of the chaos of the world outside Europe, and they had the virtue of describing everything they found with the same kind of European eyes.[7] Travelling was as a rule performed on commercial ships, and with Sweden now politically relegated to the minor league, imperialistic ambitions could scarcely be suspected on their part. A few disciples, however, entered the foreign service, among them Forsskål who represented Denmark in Arabia, Thunberg who travelled to Japan as a Dutch physician, and indeed Solander who sailed with Cook and Banks to the South Seas. It is well known that Cook sailed with secret orders of a political nature. It has also been observed that the Swedish desire for ordering the natural history of the world flows from the highly developed bureaucracy of registration that infiltrated Swedish society in the eighteenth century.[8] The outcome of those various travels has been interpreted in very different lights, however, with Koerner recently considering them largely to be a failure.[9] This may be true from the shorter perspective of economic and commercial gains, but the extensive pioneering collections left for coming generations laid solid foundations for the study of botany.

Daniel Solander

Of special interest here is the apostle Daniel Solander (fig.33), although he owes this status thanks only to Banks, for he failed to supply Linnaeus with any plant material whatever from the unbelievably rich and sensational collections which he and Banks were to amass. Like so many of the Linnaean disciples – not to mention Linnaeus himself – Solander was the son of a provincial vicar, in his case from the north of Sweden. Like so many of them, he arrived at Uppsala University intending to study law or divinity but was seduced by the innovative – almost magnetic – teaching of Linnaeus.[10] Solander became one of the most intimate pupils of Linnaeus: 'I have kept him like a son in my house', Linnaeus wrote in his later days, giving expression to his disappointment when he received no share of the Banksian–Solander plants. In fact Solander came close to becoming both the son-in-law of and the successor to Linnaeus, and the failure of both prospects may have been contributory factors in Solander's permanent transfer to Britain. His achievements can be seen as a token of success for Linnaeus in Britain, where he helped secure acceptance of the Linnaean method. He was sent to London by Linnaeus at the instigation of Peter Collinson and John Ellis, two merchants and amateurs in natural history. The former was a personal friend of Linnaeus from 1736; he very much wanted to attract to England a person skilled in teaching Linnaean ideas, while Linnaeus saw a period spent in Britain as a necessary preparation for any successor to his chair in Uppsala.

Solander arrived in London in the summer of 1760, spending his time at first on various country estates in order to improve his English, apparently following arrangements made by Ellis. He also made a number of tours in southern England in the winter and summer of 1761 and assisted Ellis in preparing zoological items so that they could be engraved. At this time, in one letter after another, Linnaeus did his best to persuade Solander to accept a position as professor in St Petersburg; Linnaeus seems to have seen this post as an advantageous

stepping stone for Solander towards his own chair in Uppsala. Linnaeus became alarmed when he learned how quickly Solander became established in England: 'Now I am so well accustomed to the English way of life, that I am not the least bit annoyed', Solander wrote to his master only six months after his arrival. Linnaeus's old friends Ellis and Collinson were extremely anxious to keep Solander in England, and expressed concern about his being lured to St Petersburg. Collinson, in a letter to Linnaeus, pleaded their case: 'For the love and esteem I have for the Doctor, I cannot forbear expressing my concern for many reasons. First from the uncertain situation in the public affairs in that kingdom; for it is impossible that learning can flourish in tumults and riots. Who knows, in a revolution which may soon happen, how far the person of a stranger may be safe'. Later in this quite lengthy letter, he offers an alternative solution: 'No doubt but you, my dear friend, know persons less eminent, but in every way qualified in botanical science to teach Russian bears'.[11]

After some lobbying from Collinson, Ellis and others, Solander was appointed to the British Museum in February 1763. His task was to catalogue the natural history collections – there were 40,000 natural specimens in the collections bequeathed by Sir Hans Sloane, among which were the pressed plants contained in 335 volumes. He started, however, with the animals and then with plants from southern Africa. This work must have given him a much wider experience and knowledge, and also brought confirmation that the Linnaean system (to the extent that it had been developed) was a workable tool by which to arrange the specimens. In fact Solander adhered meticulously to the Linnaean method, both in his practical taxonomy and in the format of his plant descriptions. This much is clear from the accounts of floras from regions in the South Seas, which he elaborated after his circumnavigation with Cook and Banks on the *Endeavour*. That most remarkable voyage now needs to be considered.[12]

Solander and Banks

In 1764 Solander made the acquaintance of Joseph Banks, a meeting that was to prove so beneficial for the development of natural history. Banks's inclination towards botany is said to have begun one summer night at Eton; having met Solander he had obtained his perfect tutor, and at Montagu House their productive friendship developed. This led to the famous occasion when Solander offered to go with Banks to the South Seas on the *Endeavour* expedition, the primary scientific purpose of which was to study from Tahiti the transit of Venus in 1769. Banks's prompt reply to Solander is said to have been 'Someone like you would give me untold pleasures and rewards', and the arrangement was settled. The planned voyage was reported to Linnaeus, not by Solander whose communications with his old teacher were now, and were to continue to be, sporadic, but by Ellis: 'No people ever went to sea better fitted out for the purpose of Natural History, nor more elegantly . . . all this thing is owing to you and your writings'. Linnaeus nourished great expectations, not least after Solander wrote in his only letter to Linnaeus from the journey that 'we [i.e. Banks and himself] will together make the voyage to Sweden to ask professor Linnaeus to order our recruits', an expression taken from Linnaeus himself and hinting at the new plants which had been discovered. Much was indeed discovered, but not a single specimen came before the eyes of Linnaeus. After the return of the *Endeavour* in 1771, Ellis stirred up the expectations of Linnaeus by telling him that the ship came back laden with the greatest treasures of natural history ever brought into any country at one time by two people.

That was by no means an exaggeration. Judged on the basis of quantity, quality and novelty, the results have perhaps remained unsurpassed ever since. Draft manuscripts with descriptions of the species found were prepared throughout the journey, from Madeira to Saint Helena, culminating in a peak on the east coast of Australia, from Botany Bay just south of present-day Sydney, where they landed at the end of April 1770, to the Endeavour River close to the Cooktown of today, where the necessity of making cumbersome repairs to the vessel gave ample opportunity for botanizing. After their return, Solander became a well-known character on the London scene (fig.34). Sociable by nature, he was well received and also well rewarded – with an Oxford doctorate (along with Banks) and a Fellowship of the Royal Society. He was completely at home in his new life as an Englishman and made no contact with Linnaeus. Ellis received intimations of Linnaeus's disappointment:

> If I were not bound here by 64 years of age and a worn out body, I would this very day set out for London to see this great hero in botany. Moses was not permitted to enter Palestine, but only to view it from a distance: so I conceive only an idea in my mind of the acquisitions and treasures of those who have visited every part of the globe.

Ultimately Linnaeus resigned himself to an 'ungrateful Solander', who sent not one single herb or insect from all those he collected in '*Insulis australibus novis*'.

Collections from the South

The reasons why Linnaeus was excluded from taking part in the analysis of these treasures are not now totally clear, but his age and increasing illness undoubtedly played a role, implying that Uppsala was by now marginalized as a scientific centre for natural history in comparison with London. There, the Linnaean method was faithfully applied when the material came to be examined; Solander made use of it in taxonomy and terminology with a mastery that has never been surpassed (fig. 35). Because of the deplorable fact that virtually none of the botanical discoveries from the expedition were then published, Solander's competence has been far from fully recognized. As witnesses there exist fair copies of the drafts mentioned, based on the collections from a number of the places visited – Madeira, Brazil, Terra del Fuego, Tahiti, Polynesia, New Zealand – but no fair copy now seems to exist for Australia. It adds to their quality that the drafts mentioned above were made on board ship from living material. One invaluable product of the expedition was the corpus of drawings of the collected plants, the majority of which (in total 955) were completed by the artist Sydney Parkinson, who died on board on the return voyage between Java and Cape Town. In total, including many only in outline, they number more than 1,500. These drawings were intended to form the basis of one of the most spectacular and prestigious botanical publications ever seen, a florilegium of the *Endeavour* plants, which, it was anticipated, would occupy fourteen volumes. Banks and

Solander worked closely together on the project and – not without difficulties – engravers were found, leading to the production of some hundreds of plates (fig. 36). Solander's sudden death in May 1782 was a heavy personal blow to Banks, but none the less, only six months after his friend's passing away, he informed Solander's compatriot Johan Alströmer that the work was drawing near to completion: all that remained could be completed in just a few months, he wrote, if only the engravers could find time to put the finishing touches to it.

The importance of both Banks and Solander for the development of the Royal Botanic Garden at Kew needs to be recalled. Plants from his own and from other expeditions were, with exclusive rights, delivered by Banks to Kew, while Solander was the man behind most of the descriptions and notations in William Aiton's catalogue of Kew Gardens, *Hortus Kewensis*, published in 1789. Curiously enough, this situation was nearly repeated when about twenty years later Solander's successor as Banks's librarian – another Linnaean disciple, Jonas Dryander – as well as Robert Brown, who was to be his last librarian (see below), played similar roles for the second edition of *Hortus Kewensis*, published by Aiton between 1810 and 1813.[13]

It remains a mystery why the grand florilegium project, into which Banks had put an enormous amount of money, was not completed. Banks seems not to have lost interest in it, and in Dryander he now had a very competent botanist as his librarian – a man who could well have pushed the project closer to conclusion. Factors such as Banks's commitments to the material from Cook's third voyage on which the Captain was killed in 1780, financial difficulties, and the potential sales of the publication (coinciding with the American War of Independence) have all been blamed. But perhaps in the long run the loss of Solander himself was the ultimate cause. It was only in the early twentieth century that a number of the Australian plates were finally published[14] and then published again in full in a coloured de luxe edition of one hundred copies at the end of that century.[15] Fortunately, the *Endeavour* collections themselves were put at the disposal of science: they remained with Banks in his house until after his death in 1820, and in 1827 were incorporated into the British Museum collections.

Most, but not all, botanists visiting London were welcome at Soho Square, among them many Swedes: Carl Peter Thunberg, Linnaeus *filius* and Olof Swartz. The *Endeavour* collections proved of great importance to Johann Gaertner, the German botanist who published a fundamental thesis on fruits and seeds,[16] allowing him to include and discuss features discovered in plants collected on the voyage. However, their accessibility to Robert Brown (fig.37) – in particular the Australian specimens – is an aspect of special interest here.

Robert Brown and a revised system for plants

Brown, a Scotsman, was a twenty-seven-year-old army surgeon stationed in Ireland when, in December 1800, he received a letter from Banks requesting his services as the naturalist on Flinders's expedition to Australia. He accepted by return mail, arriving in London on Christmas Day to prepare himself among the *Endeavour* collections at Soho Square. Brown already had a reputation as a competent and careful botanist who had contributed many observations to Scottish botany in particular, and had worked with Banks for a period some years earlier.[17]

The expectations placed on him by Banks and others were to be richly fulfilled. It is beyond the scope of this paper to record the voyage in any detail, but it is appropriate to note its results. As mentioned, the *Endeavour* collections from Australia comprised somewhat less than 1,000 species, all from the east coast – Botany Bay and some places further north. Brown's collections resulted from sailing first around Australia with Flinders's *Investigator*, and then on his own to the east coast and Tasmania. That brought in about 3,900 new species.[18] His own 'Botany Bay' was to become King George's Sound in the far south-west, near present-day Albany – an extremely fortunate first landing on the continent, for in terms of its flora it is one of the richest spots on earth, abounding in novel forms. Brown's comprehensive but crabbed diary from the journey has recently been interpreted and published.[19] Whereas Solander had been able to fit his collections into the Linnaean system, it is clear that Brown saw quite other affinities and possible groupings in his material. In this he benefited from the significant progress in taxonomy that had occurred – especially in Paris – during the thirty years which had passed since the return of the *Endeavour*.

While on board, the diligent Brown had already prepared many of his descriptions, and like Solander he enjoyed the advantage of a skilful artist – in fact one of the most accomplished botanical artists ever, Ferdinand Bauer. About a year into the expedition, however, in August 1803, Brown admitted in a letter to Banks that 'In arranging the collections, I at first followed Jussieu's Genera plantatum sec. ordines naturales, but soon found the number of plants of doubtful affinity so numerous that I judged it better to follow the Linnaean method.' Antoine de Jussieu at the Jardin des Plantes in Paris had published a pioneering work with a coherent natural plant system, breaking almost totally with that of Linnaeus. The book has a supporting preface from three of the foremost French botanists of the time and publication was formally approved by the Marquis de Condorcet in May of the fateful year of 1789. So it was indeed a product of the French Enlightenment.[20]

As William Stearn has remarked, it was Brown's first-hand experience of the inadequacies of both systems that led him by his own observations to so much improve on that of Jussieu. This he accomplished in his fundamental *Prodromus Florae Novae Hollandiae and Insulae Van Diemen* (Australia and Tasmania), the first and only volume of which appeared in 1810 (fig.38).[21] After his return to London in 1805 he obtained a position at the Linnean Society and was allowed time to arrange his collections and to elaborate the *Prodromus*. In 1810 he estimated the number of species to be 3,400 of which 2,200 were described, no fewer than 1,700 of them new to science, as were 140 of the genera. Material from Banks's and Solander's collections from 1770 were included in this work, as were other smaller Australian collections that were by now available in London. It was at this time, during the work for the *Prodromus*, that Brown definitively broke with the Linnaean system and adopted a natural one. This system was entirely of his own invention, following critical assessments of other natural systems previously developed, and in particular that of de Jussieu. Throughout the *Prodromus*, taxonomical features are referred to and compared with those published by de Jussieu, with deviations noted and commented upon. Families are redefined, often by new characteristics which were to endure in the future, while the discussions extend well beyond the plants of Australia. It is characteristic of Brown that he disliked restricting himself geographically in his writing, preferring instead to discuss plants in a broad context unrestricted by geographical boundaries. His writings were rooted in his profound and extensive knowledge of botany. So the *Prodromus*, seemingly devoted to Australia, includes much general botany and forms an important foundation for the natural system as it came to be adopted. Together with Lamarck and De Candolle's *Flore française*,[22] the *Prodromus* is the first work in which such a system was employed at species level.

The *Prodromus* is no de luxe edition – on the contrary, it lacks illustrations, gives only short descriptions, and offers only a modest impression. Moreover, it was unfinished – the only volume published includes less than half of the material intended: pages 1–144 of volume I were never printed, while no part of volume II ever appeared. The print-run of this stunted volume was only 250 copies, most of which were never sold. Its scientific reputation is inversely proportional to all of that, and it can justly be regarded as the birthplace of global taxonomy in botany. There is a chain – Linnaeus/Solander/Brown – which would later continue into Hooker's *Flora Antarctica*, the same author's *Flora of Tasmania*, and Bentham's *Flora of Australia*,[23] to mention only a few. All of these, however, were geographically circumscribed in a way that Brown would have found unappealing.

Brown has to be left at this point, omitting all his coming fundamental observations and discoveries in botany – a pioneer as microscopist, discoverer of the cell nucleus and of cytoplasmic streaming, an embryologist and pollination biologist, and much more – but acknowledging that he was to become Banks's last librarian. He was instrumental in bringing the Banksian collections to British Museum, where he served the rest of his long life. He died as late as 1858, at the age of eighty-six. He was of course highly esteemed in Britain, although he was also to find himself at the centre of many controversies there. He was unequivocally praised on the Continent, where he regularly appeared at scientific meetings, not least in Germany. Alexander von Humboldt designated him '*Botanicorum facile princeps*', and Martius, his friend and renowned explorer of Brazil dubbed him '*Jupiter botanicus*'. By that point the nineteenth century was half-way through, but in the context of the present volume this can be allowed, since the greatest botanist the British Museum ever had deserves his share of acknowledgement in the anniversary year.

Notes and references

1 C. Linnaeus, *Species plantarum*, vols 1–2 (Holmiae, 1753).
2 C. Linnaeus, *Systema naturae, sive regna tria naturae systematice proposita per classes, ordines, genera & species* (Lugduni Batavorum, 1735).
3 On the reception of Linnaeus's system among European scientists see in particular F. Stafleu, *Linnaeus and the Linnaeans: The spreading of their ideas in systematic botany, 1735–1789* (Utrecht, 1971).
4 C. Linnaeus, *Classes plantarum* (Lugduni Batavorum, 1738).
5 See G. Eriksson, 'The botanical success of Linnaeus. The aspect of organization and publicity', in G. Broberg (ed.), *Linnaeus: Progress and prospects in Linnaean research* (Pittsburgh and Stockholm, 1980).
6 For a brief survey of their voyages with a map see R. E. Fries, 'De linneanska "apostlarnas" resor', *Svenska Linné-Sällskapets Årsskrift*

33–4 (1950–1), pp.31–40; also, R.E. Fries, *A Short History of Botany in Sweden* (Stockholm, 1950).

7   M.L. Pratt, *Imperial Eyes. Travel writing and transculturation,* (London and New York, 1992), pp.24–37.

8   In particular by S. Lindroth, 'Linnaeus in his European context', in G. Broberg (ed.), *Linnaeus: Progress and prospects in Linnaean research* (Pittsburgh and Stockholm, 1980).

9   L. Koerner, *Linnaeus. Nature and Nation* (Cambridge, Mass. and London, 2000).

10 B. Jonsell, 'Daniel Solander – the perfect Linnaean, his years in Sweden and relations with Linnaeus', *Archives of Natural History* 11 (1984), pp.443–50.

11 Concering this episode and the following see B. Jonsell, 'Linnaeus and his two circumnavigating apostles', *Proceedings of the Linnaean Society of New South Wales* 106 (1982), pp.6–19. The standard text (in Swedish) is A.H. Uggla, 'Daniel Solander och Linneé', *Svenska Linné-Sällskapets Årsskrift* 37–8 (1954–5), pp.23–64.

12 Concerning Solander in full see E. Duyker, *Nature's Argonaut. Daniel Solander 1733–1782. Naturalist and voyager with Cook and Banks* (Melbourne, 1998), together with E. Duyker and P. Tingbrand (ed. and trans.), *Daniel Solander: Collected correspondence 1753–1782* (Oslo etc., 1995).

13 See R. Desmond, 'The transformation of the Royal Gardens at Kew', in R.E.R. Banks *et al.* (eds), *Sir Joseph Banks: A global perspective* (Kew, 1994), pp. 105–15.

14 Published by J. Britten, *Illustrations of Australian Plants collected in 1770 during Captain Cook's Voyage* (London, 1901), p.5.

15 Sir Joseph Banks, *Banks' Florilegium: A publication in thirty-four parts of seven hundred and thirty-eight copperplate engravings of plants collected on Captain James Cook's first voyage round the world in HMS Endeavour 1768–1771. The specimens were gathered and classified by Sir Joseph Banks, Bart, and Daniel Solander and were accurately engraved between 1771 and 1784 after drawings taken from nature by Sydney Parkinson* (London, 1980–90).

16 J. Gaertner, *De fructibus et seminibus plantarum,* 2 vols (Stuttgart and Tübingen, 1788–91).

17 The standard biography is D.J. Mabberley, *Jupiter Botanicus: Robert Brown of the British Museum (*Braunschweig and London, 1985).

18 See W. Stearn, 'An introduction to Robert Brown's "Prodromus Florae Novae Hollandiae"', in *Three Prefaces on Linnaeus and Robert Brown* (Weinheim, 1962).

19 T. G. Vallance, D. T. Moore and E. W. Groves, *Nature's Investigator: The diary of Robert Brown in Australia, 1801–1805* (Canberra, 2001).

20 A. L. de Jussieu, *Genera plantarum* (Paris, 1789).

21 R. Brown, *Prodromus florae Novae Hollandiae and Insulae van-Diemen* (London, 1810).

22 J.B.A.P. Monnet de Lamarck and A.P. de Candolle, *Flore française,* 6 vols (Paris 1805–15); this forms the third edition of Lamarck's *Flore française* (Paris, 1778).

23 J.D. Hooker, *Flora Antarctica* (London, 1844–7) and *Flora Tasmaniae* (London, 1855–60); G. Bentham, *Flora australiensis* (London, 1863–78).

Figure 31
Carl Linnaeus (1707–78) at the age
of forty. From a pencil drawing by
J.E. Rehn, probably made in 1747.

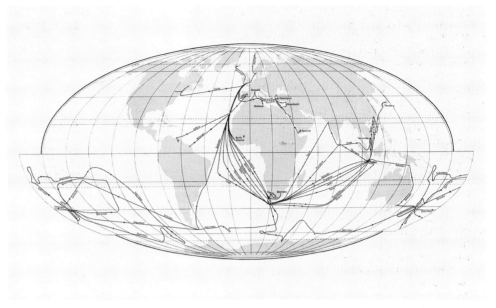

Figure 32
The voyages of the Linnaean apostles.
Map compiled by R.E. Fries (1951).

Figure 33
Daniel Solander (1733–82), c. 1776.
After the oil painting by J. Zoffany now
in the possession of the Linnean
Society of London.

Figure 34
Caricature of Daniel Solander, 1772,
published in London after the return
of HMS *Endeavour*.

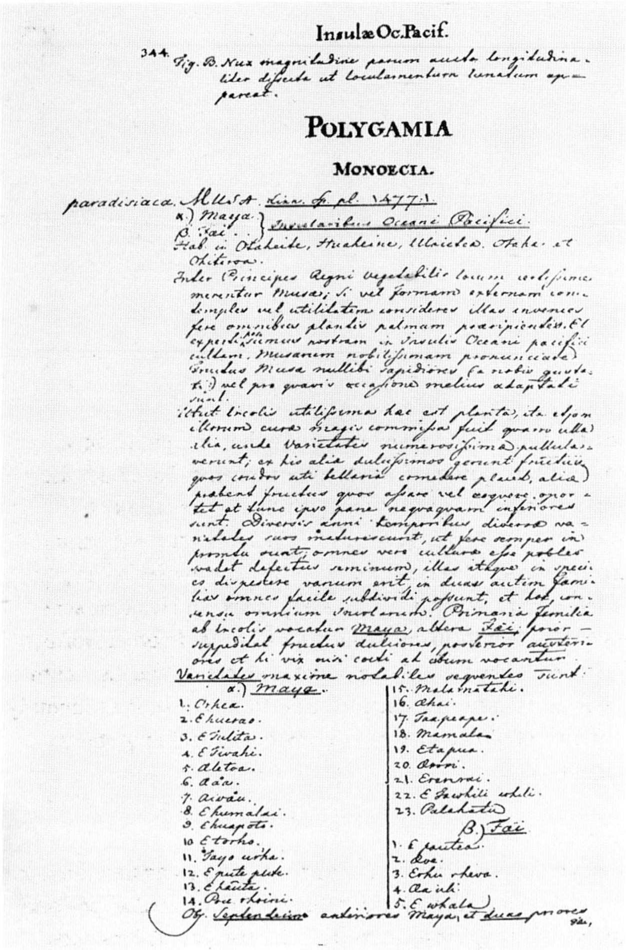

Figure 36
Banksia serrata collected
by Banks and Solander at Botany Bay.
Copperplate engraving by G. Smith,
from a pencil sketch by Sydney
Parkinson: pl.185 from Banks's
Florilegium. Reproduced from
E. Duyker, *Nature's Argonaut: Daniel
Solander 1733–1782, naturalist and
voyager with Cook and Banks*
(Melbourne, 1998).

Figure 35
Page of Solander's unpublished
manuscript 'Flora of Tahiti', with a
large number of banana varieties
listed. From F. Stafleu, *Linnaeus and the
Linnaeans. The spreading of their ideas
in systematic botany, 1735–1789*
(Utrecht, 1971).

Figure 37
Portrait of Robert Brown
by an unknown artist, probably
drawn shortly after his return to
England. From T.G. Vallance *et al.,
Nature's Investigator. The diary of
Robert Brown in Australia, 1801–1805*
(Canberra, 2001).

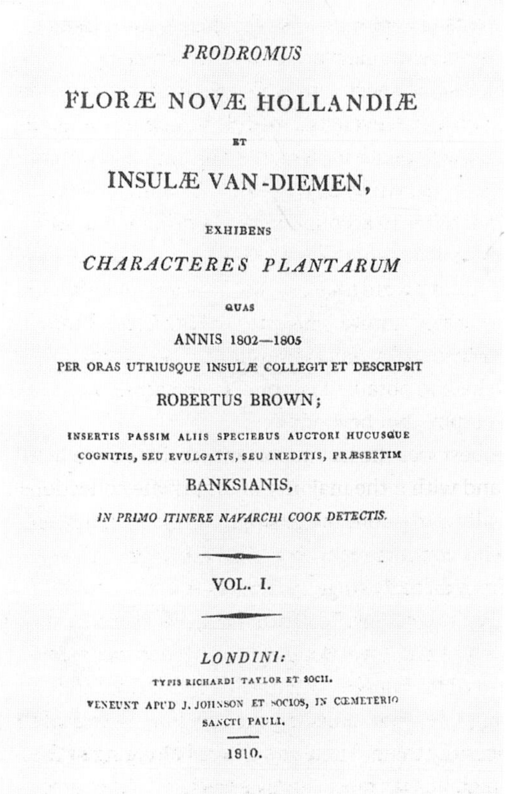

PRODROMUS
FLORÆ NOVÆ HOLLANDIÆ
ET
INSULÆ VAN-DIEMEN,

EXHIBENS

CHARACTERES PLANTARUM

QUAS

ANNIS 1802—1805

PER ORAS UTRIUSQUE INSULÆ COLLEGIT ET DESCRIPSIT

ROBERTUS BROWN;

INSERTIS PASSIM ALIIS SPECIEBUS AUCTORI HUCUSQUE
COGNITIS, SEU EVULGATIS, SEU INEDITIS, PRÆSERTIM

BANKSIANIS,

IN PRIMO ITINERE NAVARCHI COOK DETECTIS.

VOL. I.

LONDINI:

TYPIS RICHARDI TAYLOR ET SOCII.

VENEUNT APUD J. JOHNSON ET SOCIOS, IN CŒMETERIO
SANCTI PAULI.

1810.

Figure 38
Title page of Robert Brown's
*Prodromus florae Novae Hollandiae
et Insulae van-Diemen* (London, 1810).

Chapter 13

Joseph Banks, the British Museum and Collections in the Age of Empire
Neil Chambers

With the overseas activity that gathered pace from the 1760s onwards came rich new opportunities to collect.[1] Indeed, travel and collecting, particularly in natural history and ethnography, changed and grew on a global scale during the lifetime of Joseph Banks, a process he did much to encourage. In this period, the quantity and scope of material coming to Europe's museums from distant lands increased enormously, and this had important consequences for repositories, some of which struggled simply to keep pace. Many private individuals sought objects, and some mounted commercial exhibitions, creating realistic habitat groups and employing advanced preservation techniques. The two most eminent exponents of this type of museum in Banks's day were Sir Ashton Lever, and later William Bullock.[2] Commercial ventures like theirs differed from the collections kept by Banks, being more varied in content, whereas Banks's were used mainly in specialist research rather than in public displays for financial profit. All of these, however, drew on the results of exploration, as did the British Museum. The British Museum was one place to which increasing numbers of objects and specimens were sent from the growing empires of the world, yet even its capacity to cope was limited. By the time of Banks's death in 1820, the Museum in Montagu House had been outgrown by its collections and there were plans for new buildings to accommodate them. So it was to Smirke's redesigned Museum that Banks's great herbarium and natural history library were taken in 1827 in accordance with his will. There they joined natural and artificial products[3] brought or given to the Museum by Banks over more than fifty years, many of which he had obtained not only from within the boundaries of empire, but beyond them.

Banks's bequest was the last important service he rendered the Museum, and with it the majority of his private collections had passed finally into public ownership. The move had been anticipated by his conduct regarding collections throughout London, and from an early stage by the way in which he managed his own specimens. For, from 1778, the year he was elected President of the Royal Society, thereby becoming an *ex officio* trustee of the Museum, Banks started to divide his collections along lines that indicate generally how he regarded and ordered not only them, but many others belonging to the bodies with which he was most closely associated. Of course, not all these collections were concerned with natural history. For example, Banks assisted the British Museum in the acquisition of books and papers, a review of David Garrick's collection of Elizabethan and Jacobean plays being among the first tasks he undertook as a trustee in 1779. He even conveyed a number of classical antiquities to the Museum, mainly from the

Society of Dilettanti,[4] while ensuring that antiquities on a French ship captured in the Mediterranean by Horatio Nelson in 1803 came to the attention of the British government.[5] Nevertheless, Banks primarily handled natural history and ethnographic collections, and it is the pattern of what he gave to the British Museum, what he held back, and what he sent elsewhere that form the themes of this essay. In other words, emphasis is placed on Banks's role in assessing and distributing the imperial influx, a function he performed no less assiduously than that of dispatching collectors or marshalling contacts abroad.

Early exploration

It was Banks's exploits as a wealthy young civilian naturalist on the voyage of HMS *Endeavour* that first gave him Europe-wide fame, and brought him to royal notice (fig.39). This famous mission, under Lieutenant James Cook, was planned to observe the Transit of Venus across face of the Sun, from which the Sun's parallax might be determined, thereby enabling more accurate navigation at sea – itself a precondition of empire.[6] The voyage yielded, too, accurate charts, such as those of the islands of New Zealand and the East Coast of Australia, which Cook claimed for the Crown on Possession Island on 22 August 1770.[7] Along with detailed written accounts of the lands and cultures encountered, the voyage showed that the theoretical land mass called *Terra Australis* might not exist. Additionally, valuable experience had been gained, not least by Banks, who later became an authority on such voyages. On returning in July 1771 from the three-year voyage, Banks disembarked his collections, which were sent to his London home at 14 New Burlington Street. Thereafter his house became, in effect, an early 'museum of the South Seas', anticipating the opening of similar displays at the British Museum.

Reactions were marked. The Keeper of the Ashmolean Museum, the Revd William Sheffield,[8] felt 'utmost astonishment' at what he saw on a visit in 1772, and could 'scarce credit my senses'. In the first of three rooms in which the Banks collections were arranged, Sheffield encountered the 'Armoury', which contained all 'the warlike instruments, mechanical instruments and utensils of every kind, made use of by the Indians in the South Seas from Terra del Fuego to the Indian Ocean'.[9] The second held 'the different habits and ornaments of the several Indian nations', with a collection of insects, and 'the bread and other fruits preserved in spirits'. Here, too, was the great herbarium. The third and final room contained a very large collection of mammals, birds, fish and reptiles in spirit. This was also where the paintings and drawings of plants and some animals were located, these having been mostly completed by Sydney Parkinson, the gifted artist who accompanied the voyage as a member of Banks's team.

Apart from the ethnographic collection, which represented indeed a considerable achievement, the samples of flora at New Burlington Street were not surpassed by any other brought to Europe until the next century.[10] Recent estimates suggest that the voyage yielded over 30,000 plant specimens, comprising more than 3,600 species, of which some 1,400 were new to science. From the animal kingdom as a whole more than 1,000 species may have been collected, of which some of the insects and molluscs have survived. Few other actual specimens remain.[11] Moreover, Daniel Solander, an eminent pupil of Carl Linnaeus, was given leave from employment as an assistant at the British Museum to accompany Banks on *Endeavour*. He described the plants and animals they collected together, and Sheffield thought these descriptions 'fit to be put to the press'.[12] Although this was not done at the time, the engraved illustrations commissioned by Banks eventually appeared in the twentieth century.[13]

Nonetheless, Sheffield's admiring wonder is understandable, and was evidently shared by King George III who, by 1773, was being advised by Banks on the development of the Royal Gardens at Kew, themselves incorporated into Banks's schemes to increase and exploit plant discoveries from overseas. Some of the plants singled out by Sheffield for special comment might therefore have been discussed with the King already. New Zealand flax (*Phormium tenax*) had practical benefits for a maritime power seeking supplies of cordage and cloth, and Sheffield enthused: 'this will perhaps be the most useful discovery they made in the whole voyage'. He might have caught this idea from Banks and exaggerated it, for in his own assessment of the collections Banks concluded: 'Out of these, some considerable oeconomical purposes may be answerd, particularly with the fine Dyes of the Otaheitians, & the Plant of which the new Zelanders make their Cloth'.[14] Alongside scientific aims, the potential 'oeconomical purposes' of any natural or artificial product were of concern to naval commanders and entrepreneurs entering the Pacific during and following the 1760s. Sheffield's mention of the famous breadfruit (*Artocarpus altilis*, fig.40) reminds us why this was, and of how Banks fostered an inter-tropical network of botanic gardens with Kew as a 'clearing house', one to which the ill-starred William Bligh returned years later, after his second, successful breadfruit voyage.[15]

Such were the interrelated scientific and imperial issues beginning to emerge at New Burlington Street, which by 1777 had become too small to contain Banks's steadily growing library along with the other collections. Not everything in the 'immense magazine of curiosities' described by Sheffield (sometimes a little inaccurately) fell within Banks's core interests of botany and bibliography. As Banks moved into 32 Soho Square, which he retained for the remainder of his life, and as he obtained the over-arching positions he also held to the end – at the Royal Society, the British Museum, and Kew – the time had come to decide where many of his collections belonged. Apart from the small gifts he invariably made to friends, Banks appears to have reasoned that anything not strictly to do with the herbarium and library might be offered to one of the institutions with which he was connected. This

meant giving up the ethnographic collections *en masse* to the British Museum. The Museum was rapidly becoming more of a centre for such material than Soho Square, and Banks was certainly following a precedent set by the Admiralty with regard to Samuel Wallis's and George Carteret's collections, which were sent to the Museum in February 1770. Admiralty Secretary Philip Stephens, a supporter of Banks's efforts to gain Solander a place on *Endeavour* together with all the equipment Banks required, informed the trustees of the 'offer of several Curiosities from the late discovered Islands' in the Pacific.[16] These presumably formed an early nucleus for the South Sea Room, which the Museum trustees in 1775 directed should be established to receive gifts from Cook's voyages.[17]

Ethnography: status and dispersal

As a guide, but not necessarily an invariable rule, Admiralty procedure seems to have been that materials acquired on voyages of discovery, and placed under Admiralty control, belonged to the nation, and so might end up in its national museum. Accordingly, as a private individual, Banks suffered the indignation of foreign savants in 1782 rather than deprive the British Museum of the opportunity of first refusal of his entire collection of artefacts. Writing to Jan Ingenhousz, the Dutch plant physiologist, he defended his decision, saying: 'I am sorry that Mr. Jacquin is so angrey that I have not yet fulfilld my Promise of sending him arms & curiosities from the South Sea the reason I have not yet done it is that in order to give preference to the British Museum who engagd to fit up a room for the sole purpose of receiving such things I long ago sent all mine down there consisting of several Cart Loads.'[18]

Banks was culpable here for not cataloguing the objects beforehand, but neither, it seems, were they dealt with rapidly on receipt. Banks in any case expected that 'the major part of my things will be Sent me back again'. The donations were probably made – as a timely gesture – by himself in October 1778, shortly before his election as President of the Royal Society. Later, in November 1780, he led a series of gifts offered by officers and men from Cook's final voyage, consisting of a 'very large Collection of Artificial Curiosities Utencils, dresses &c from the South-Sea Islands, the West Coast of North America and Kamschatka lately visited by His Majesty's Ships the Resolution & the Discovery'.[19] On this occasion, Banks was given 'particular Acknowledgements . . . for his considerable and repeated liberalities to the Museum', while Solander, with assistance from two circumnavigators, gunner William Peckover and carpenter James Cleveley, was to arrange and label everything.[20] The South Sea Room was suitably modified by August 1781.[21]

It can be seen that Banks was directing the 'artificial products' of the voyages of discovery generally towards the British Museum, while he distributed the 'natural' collections of living plants and seeds to Kew, making a basic distinction between the two types similar to that applied at Soho Square. There, too, natural history and especially botany prevailed, while ethnographic material was sent to the British Museum. Banks was able to operate this trans-institutional regime because of his position as a senior figure in each of the bodies concerned. Indeed in 1781, when the Royal Society finally conceded that it was in no position to maintain a museum of its own, its President, who was also a Museum trustee, oversaw the transfer to the British Museum of the valuable collections,[22] parts of which may well survive today in institutions like the Natural History Museum, London. One of many options for historic collections like those of the Royal Society was therefore to pass into public possession, while individuals could specialize, as did Banks.[23] And if the Royal Society had relinquished its collections, strong in natural history, at least they had not passed beyond the control of the President. His personal influence over the routes by which collections reached London, and how they circulated once there, was fast becoming an important factor in shaping the development of these repositories.

Indeed, some sea captains saw Banks as the obvious person to decide on the allocation of their collections. One, George Dixon, a veteran of Cook's last voyage, approached Banks in this capacity in 1789. He had been dispatched by a syndicate of London merchants, who formed the King George's Sound Company, to open up a trade in otter furs between the north-west coast of America and the markets of China and Japan. Dixon, however, returned with more by way of cartographic and ethnographic results than profits from otter pelts. He commemorated Banks by naming an island on the north-west coast in his honour, and with Nathaniel Portlock he published in a two-volume edition an account of the voyage, dedicating his volume to Banks.[24] It was a compliment returned, for Banks had given advice on the mission and named Dixon's ship the *Queen Charlotte*. What is more, Dixon gave Banks 'Various Articles from the N:W: Coast of America', which are listed in the trustees' minutes since it was Banks who presented them to the Museum. They included mineral substances, in which Banks took an increasing interest, eating implements, beads and other ornaments, tobacco leaves used for chewing, and a native game.[25] This shows the extent to which Banks was regarded by some navigators as an authority to consult on private as well as public enterprises, not only as to how they might be mounted, but also as to the ultimate disposal of their physical collections. In 1780 James King had declared: '. . . I look up to you as the common Center of we discoverers'.[26] It was an epithet that might have served just as well for Banks at the British Museum.

For his part, Banks saw that he could match his position as adviser to business and government on exploration with that of being a trustee at the British Museum and unofficial director of Kew, one role supporting another. An example of how this worked, though still very much one embroiled in the same commercial and political rivalries that Dixon had encountered in the mid-1780s and early 1790s,[27] is provided by Archibald Menzies, the Scottish surgeon-botanist. Banks first gained Menzies a position under James Colnett on the *Prince of Wales*,[28] a ship accompanied by the *Princess Royal*, under Charles Duncan, in another vain attempt to seek a trade in furs. Menzies was away from 1786 to July 1789, when the *Prince of Wales* anchored in the Thames, and Banks received from the diligent Scot a box of the dried plants he had collected.[29] Menzies kept a set for himself, and sent material to the botanic gardens at Edinburgh and at Kew. He was allowed free access to Banks's library and herbarium to sort his specimens,[30] Soho being a powerful auxiliary to both Bloomsbury and Kew.

An altogether more significant international event provided the occasion for Menzies's next mission, on HMS *Discovery*,

from 1791 to 1795, under George Vancouver (fig.41). This was to seal the Convention of 28 October 1789 with Spain, and thereby to conclude the Nootka Sound crisis. This confrontation, resulting from British commercial and strategic activity in the preceding years, effectively ended wide-scale priority claims by the Spanish in the Pacific – although French ambitions remained. Banks obtained Menzies's appointment on *Discovery*;[31] he drafted the instructions,[32] themselves perhaps the most comprehensive statement of the scientific methods employed on such missions from 1768 to 1820, and Banks was to defend Menzies's conduct following serious disagreements with Vancouver on the return voyage.[33]

A familiar set of priorities can be seen in Banks's organization of the materials brought back by Menzies. Banks had already dispatched the plants and seeds to Kew[34] before the Home Secretary, William Henry Cavendish Bentinck, Duke of Portland, had even consulted the King as to where everything should go. Many of the living plants had been lost due to disagreements with Vancouver, and Banks was concerned that what remained should survive. Portland wrote merely to confirm that Banks's decision was approved, leaving it to decide what additional seeds might go to the Royal Gardens.[35] The herbarium specimens were taken to Soho Square, where they could be arranged. Menzies undertook this work, with the help of Banks, and more so that of his librarian, Jonas Dryander, and an assistant there, Samuel Toerner. Together they prepared sets of duplicates to be given to patrons and friends, one of which Banks was to receive. The artificial curiosities, meanwhile, were destined, as we should now expect, for the British Museum, to which Banks presented them a week after hearing from Portland of the King's wishes.[36]

Banks also had a contemporary copy made by his amanuensis, William Cartlich, of the checklist of 112 ethnographic items brought home from Otaheiti (Tahiti), the Sandwich Islands (Hawaii), Nootka, Cross Island, New Georgia, Port Trinidad, Cook's Inlet, and the north-west coast of America. These items had been held at Soho Square, but Banks seems to have learned from earlier experiences of sending such collections to be sifted at the Museum, and made a list before releasing them. However, the publication of Menzies's experiences was never completed, somewhat to Banks's annoyance, for he blamed Vancouver for the loss of many of the live plants between St Helena and England on the return journey.[37] This was somewhat ironic, for Banks, like Menzies, published little of his own collections, much to the frustration of subsequent generations of taxonomists.

By June 1808, the South Sea Room was being reorganized to reflect the growing numbers of coastlines and continents from which Museum objects were collected. Charles Konig (Karl Dietrich Eberhard König), Assistant Keeper in the Natural History Department, helped in the task and reported gifts from Banks at this time of cloth and matting from Madagascar. Konig moved in a quantity of 'artificial curiosities', including many from the north-west coast of America that had been offered by Banks, and which had been languishing in the basement.[38] Everything was set out in a geographical arrangement.[39] This was intended to 'illustrate particular Customs of different Nations; their Religion, their Government, their Commerce, Manufactures or Trades'.[40] As such, the displays were intended to provide a 'window' on the world for visitors, but with stated

Neil Chambers

purposes like these: many who climbed to Room 1 on the upper floor might have glimpsed reflections of the links and preoccupations of competing empires – and of Banks himself. The display covered Europe, Asia, Africa, South America, the east and west coasts of North America, Otaheite, the Sandwich Islands and Marquesas, the Friendly Islands (Tonga) and New Zealand, with various small articles being placed on a separate table.

In passing, it is also worth noting, in both the records and the published *Synopsis* (1808), a certain indifference of tone to the so-called 'Modern Artificial Curiosities'. The material comprises mostly unlisted 'donations', many of these, according to the *Synopsis*, not being 'strictly of a scientific nature'. Hence, while some might 'be set aside, to make room for others of more intrinsic value', the majority were stored 'in a less conspicuous part of the house' – a euphemism for anything consigned to the basement. In fact, some of the Museum's officers had little time for such material, and much disappeared in sales, was given away, or was left quietly in the 'lower apartments'. Banks was apt to give away objects, and what was not taken by the British Museum from his own collection might have been divided instead among members of his coterie, such as Lord Sandwich, Sir William Hamilton, Charles Francis Greville, Johan Alströmer, and the anthropologist Johann Friedrich Blumenbach. It is also probable that great collectors of exotica like Sir Ashton Lever, and later William Bullock, obtained material.[41] Even the angry Nicolaus Joseph Jacquin might eventually have been spared something. Nonetheless, the displays at the Museum remained popular, and, in their own way, foreshadowed much greater exhibitions to come.

Natural history: further donations and exchanges

The history of the dispersal of Banks's zoological specimens from the Cook voyages is as complex as that of the ethnographic items, and for similar reasons. Since Banks did not amass major private collections in branches of natural history other than botany, when the time came he looked to donate large portions of Pacific material elsewhere. In 1792 he made significant donations of zoological specimens to the British Museum, and also to the surgeon-anatomist John Hunter. These included material from the *Endeavour* mission, and from Cook's 'subsequent Voyages'. Banks, like the Museum, benefited from a series of gifts made by the naturalists and crews on Cook's second voyage, 1772–5. Indeed, immediately the ships arrived back late in July there was something of a sale of 'curiosities', with, for example, the London dealer George Humphrey obtaining many shells that he sold to the Duchess of Portland and to the Literary and Philosophical Society of Danzig amongst others. Demand in London and Europe generally was high for objects from these voyages, and as more returned in the years after Cook they were dispersed among a mix of naturalists, curio hunters and brokers, who sold and exchanged shells, skins, plants and artefacts with particular eagerness.

For Banks, material was forthcoming from Johann Reinhold Forster and Johann Georg Adam Forster, the father-and-son team that took Banks's place on the second mission, from Cook himself, and from other officers and sailors. Cook's collections went directly to Solander's apartments at the British Museum. Four casks of them were for Banks, containing birds and fish, with a box of plants from the Cape of Good Hope.[42] In

September the elder Forster offered duplicate specimens of insects to Banks and to the British Museum,[43] and in August he delivered a listed collection of birds, fish and other animals to Bloomsbury.[44] From what Solander understood,[45] the Forster collections were to be divided between the British Museum, the Royal Society, Banks, Marmaduke Tunstall and Sir Ashton Lever. This was a likely group of institutions and individuals variously interested in South Seas articles. The last-named, Lever, was something of a virtuoso, justly famed for his heterogeneous exhibitions.[46] From 1775 his museum was located at a former royal residence in Leicester Square, no less.

Banks could add to the proceeds of the second voyage all the plants, seeds and insects gathered on the third, 1776–80, by David Nelson, his personal collector who was paid at the rate of £35 a year.[47] In addition, the dying Charles Clerke, who commanded HMS *Discovery*, bequeathed his collections to Banks in a warm final letter.[48] In this he passed on 'the best collection of all kinds of matter ... that have fallen in our way in the course of the voyage'. It seems, too, that Banks received most of the birds from this mission, and portions of what the late William Anderson, naval surgeon, had found.[49] Seamen, like gunner's mate John Marra of the *Resolution*, also volunteered shells and other objects to Banks.[50] Lever, John Latham, the ornithologist, and the voracious naturalist and travel writer, Thomas Pennant, were all attracted to treasures of this kind.

Banks would have kept the plant collections, but many of the animals were given away. Indeed, in January 1792 Museum officers were invited to Soho Square to take every specimen that was not already was at the British Museum, thanks being given to 'Sir Joseph Banks, for his very valuable Donation.'[51] This was one of the larger accessions of such material to that date, and included many specimens preserved in spirit. It is evidence, too, of Banks's tendency to favour the British Museum in such major matters, and from 1792 onwards not to retain sizeable collections that lay outside botany and bibliography. Thus the Museum was also given first refusal of his ethnographic collections and, besides plants, it was also given the choice of his natural history collections. This latter gesture followed the remodelling in 1791 of the library at the rear of his Soho premises. Something as simple as architectural alterations, here supplied by George Dance Jnr, could explain the decision to relinquish large collections, although the choice of to whom would not have been taken lightly. Similarly, the transfer of the Royal Society's Repository to Bloomsbury coincided with the Society's move into new apartments at Somerset House, designed by Sir William Chambers. These lacked sufficient room for such collections.

In due course, other significant Banks collections made their circuitous ways to the British Museum. Even some of the material Banks gave to Hunter reached Bloomsbury through a donation from the Royal College of Surgeons in 1845, Hunter's collections having formed the basis of the College's museum in 1800.[52] Banks's original 1792 specimens were kept separate in the College's museum under the title of the 'New Holland Division'. When the College gave 348 specimens to the British Museum, some came from the 'New Holland Division', and a small number were registered as having belonged to Banks.[53] Moreover, when, like the Royal Society before it, the Linnean Society could no longer keep a museum, important collections of shells, insects and crustaceans that Banks had given in 1815

102 | Enlightening the British: Knowledge, discovery and the museum in the eighteenth century

went in turn to the British Museum.[54] These now provide a valuable source of type specimens, the insects having been worked on in the early 1770s by Johann Christian Fabricius, the Danish entomologist.

Yet Banks's earliest gifts to the Museum of birds and animals date from the period 1779–84. These indicate the widening range of his contacts abroad, rather than being material he acquired directly through exploration. This is another and important characteristic of the pattern of Banks's donations. For example, from Senegal came stuffed birds, and then a tiger cat; from South Carolina came a collection of fish; and by 1784 a collection of forty-nine dried bird skins from Brazil, Bombay and China had arrived, these last coming from William Pigou and John Duncan, both of whom were attached to the East India Company at Canton.[55] Banks might well have been prompted to give the bird skins by Edward Whitaker Gray, who went on to become a rather lax Keeper of the Department of Natural and Artificial Curiosities. Gray had recently been working on the Bird Room,[56] where Banks's birds were mounted for display at a cost of 3s.6d. each.[57] Banks was clearly not restricted to his own collecting activities, nor to voyages of discovery, but was able to increase his global reach by relying on his reputation in other countries, on his correspondence, and on the collectors he dispatched or with whom he was acquainted. Thus, in volume I of the 'Book of Presents', 1756–1823, we find that Banks is the most prolific individual donor. His gifts, however, include little by way of botany. Instead, zoology, mineralogy, books and manuscripts are most common, while the plants he received were retained, exchanged, or shared with Kew. Moreover, Banks could increasingly draw on colonial possessions.[58] In April 1790 he gave 'three Birds, the Skin of an Animal, and the Tail of a Sting Ray, from New South Wales', probably sent by Arthur Phillip, the first governor, from 1788 to 1792.[59] Banks's range of contacts was growing with his status,[60] and as the range of empire itself increased so too did the diversity of 'natural and artificial' products arriving at the British Museum through his agency.

This was of benefit, for voyages of discovery to the Pacific had effectively ceased since the declaration of war by revolutionary France in February 1793. Phillip's successors struggled on, relying on Banks as a dependable voice in London, until the situation changed at the turn of the century with the rising menace of Napoleon. French and British exploration was once again directed to the southern oceans, where it remained unclear whether or not Australia was a single landmass. Determining this would affect any claim to the continent as a whole, and what entry might be gained to its interior by land or boat. Since the *Endeavour* voyage, concern with such boundaries and their control had been an issue. Banks had been agitating for an equipped mission to open up the country from at least 1798.[61]

When, in keeping with polite appearances,[62] he obtained passports for a French voyage to these areas, Banks warned the First Lord of a 'Political manoeuvre'.[63] So it was that the *Investigator* was hastily dispatched under Matthew Flinders, partly in response to the launch from Le Havre on 19 October 1800 of the *Géograph* and the *Naturaliste*, under Nicolas Thomas Baudin.[64] The names of the French and indeed the British ships disguised with a fine Enlightenment veneer some of the real motives for their departure. Nevertheless, the *Investigator* was following in its scientific essentials an established programme defined by the example set on *Endeavour* and maintained by Banks. It deserves special mention here, for from the beginning the collections were to be passed on to the British Museum and Kew after being assessed at Soho Square. Indeed, the small scientific party that Banks assembled signed in his home an explicit agreement concerning the public ownership of these materials. They were the naturalist Robert Brown, Ferdinand Bauer and William Westall, two outstanding artists, Peter Good, an able gardener, and John Allen, a miner from Derbyshire. The Admiralty delegated their management to Banks. By this time, Banks's grasp of such arrangements qualified him to take complete charge in the eyes of Admiralty officials like Evan Nepean, who wrote confirming that 'Any proposal you make will be approved. The whole is left entirely to your decision'.[65]

It was not until November 1805 that most of the members of the scientific party were back in London with their collections, following a voyage disrupted primarily by the rotten state of some of the timber in *Investigator*, the shipwreck of the vessel chosen for the journey back to Britain, HMS *Porpoise*, and the detention of Matthew Flinders on Mauritius. Flinders had found, on sailing into Port Louis in the *Cumberland*, that the Peace of Amiens had collapsed, and from December 1803 to June 1810 he was confined on the island by its governor, a suspicious man who placed no trust in Flinders's passports, nor in the largely theoretical claims of science to be neutral in this period. At Soho Square, Banks supervised the disposal of the collections according to the contract which had earlier been drawn up. Despite what had been lost on Wreck Reef in August 1803, he could report to the Admiralty that the packages of seeds sent back periodically by Brown were already growing at Kew, where they provided 'the newest ornaments of that extensive and possibly unparalleled collection'.[66] Banks concluded that the Admiralty would order the remaining collections to be deposited 'in the national repository of the British Museum', and he advised sending there a number of bird skins, about 150 in all, some animals that were damaged on the voyage, a case of insects, and three boxes of minerals. The remainder was to stay at Soho Square where, on Banks's advice, Brown and Bauer were paid by the government to work on the collections. This extended employment followed the precedent set by the draughtsmen for Cook's second and third voyages, and did not in essence depart significantly from the pattern of work emerging since Cook's first voyage, or from known Admiralty procedures. The botanical material amounted to 3,600 plant species, and there were also some 2,000 drawings by Bauer to be assessed. Banks estimated that three years would be required to arrange the plants systematically, and to complete the most 'interesting part only of the immense collection of scetches'.

A new aspect was that Banks had found a miner for the voyage.[67] The surviving collections that he, Brown and Flinders made on the second leg of the voyage around Australia between July 1802 and June 1803 represent the earliest extant samples from Australia at the Natural History Museum, and are 'reasonably representative' of the rocks encountered. Little more could have been achieved given the disasters that took place.[68] Besides, Banks knew all too well that boring for deeper samples could be done more easily by settlers *in situ*, rather than by assigning such heavy work to voyagers.[69]

Neil Chambers

Thus in 1799 he appointed Mr Wapshot to make boring rods in London. These were loaded on a whaler sailing out with the new Governor, Philip Gidley King, since their weight was 'so considerable'.[70] The aim was to look for coal.[71] By 1801 proposals had even been put forward for the establishment of iron works in New South Wales.[72] This was one practical way of uncovering and utilizing the geology that had perforce been ignored by the *Investigator* expedition. Back in Britain, however, it was Banks who told the Admiralty in 1811 that the surviving *Investigator* earth collections should go the British Museum, the Lords of the Admiralty asking him to undertake 'the trouble of giving the necessary directions for depositing the specimens'.[73]

The Admiralty's trust in Banks was matched by that bestowed on him by his fellow trustees at the British Museum. In 1802 he proposed a direct system of exchange between himself and the Museum, which would allow only a disposal of duplicates.[74] This was unusual, but the trustees agreed, perhaps seeing in Banks an exceptional opportunity to increase the Museum's collections, their conditions being that once given any specimen would immediately become Museum property, and that they reserved the right to reject any application from Banks if it seemed unreasonable.[75] Banks accelerated the rate of his donations. At the very meeting where his request had been approved, on 9 April 1802, he deposited geese from Botany Bay, and a collection of Japanese minerals and fossils, sent by Isaac Titsingh.[76] These were followed in May by forty-nine skins of birds from Botany Bay, and in June by specimens of minerals from New South Wales, a pair of paddles from Western Port, with the head of an 'Argus Pheasant from Sumatra'.[77] The pheasant came from John Macdonald, a military engineer formerly stationed at Fort Marlborough, Bengkulu, while the increase of material from Australia at the turn of the century coincided with the arrival of Philip Gidley King in New South Wales, and the preceding governor, John Hunter, back in Britain. Other sources included, of course, Robert Brown, who sent seeds back for Kew, and men like Lieutenant James Grant, who had been exploring in *Lady Nelson* through Bass Strait to Western Port in the autumn of 1801 with George Caley, Banks's paid collector in the colony from 1800 to 1810.[78]

As if such an array were not enough, in March 1803 Banks presented specimens of a meteorite fall at Siena,[79] obtained from his correspondent Giovanni Fabbroni.[80] The event at Siena in June 1794 has recently been called 'perhaps the most consequential of historic falls',[81] and since the meteorite collection of the entire Museum comprised only seven pieces, this was an important contribution, one added to by Banks with others like the Benares and Wold Cottage stones. These joined fragments of Otumpa, a large iron meteorite found in Argentina, presented by the Royal Society in 1788,[82] and another from the L'Aigle fall received in 1803 from Jean Baptiste Biot.[83] In November 1803 came a number of fossilized and recent bones from the Emperor of Russia, a donation organized by Banks and sent by the President of the St Petersburg Academy, Nicolas Novossiltzoff.[84] It was, perhaps, the type of influx the trustees had been looking for. No other single donor matches Banks in these years for diversity of gifts presented. He, more than anyone else, seems to have been able to tap the manifold routes through which natural history flowed into, out of, and around Britain. As a whole, the Museum benefited far more from its dealings with Banks than he did in return, and it is certain that

he never intended to exploit the agreement obtained from the other trustees.[85] It should be added that Banks used his 'exchange account' only rarely, and then for the benefit of those wishing to conduct research or increase their museums.

Later administration and consolidation

Unfortunately these well-meaning exertions were not paralleled by the Museum's curation of its natural history collections. Gray died late in 1806, and his successor, George Shaw, was made Keeper of the Department of Natural History and Modern Curiosities, with Taylor Combe being placed in charge of a new Department of Antiquities. Shaw, though he published prolifically, did little more than Gray had to care for the specimens. The arrival of Konig, meanwhile, as an assistant, represented an important staff change. Banks had been asked to look at home and abroad for another naturalist[86] and settled on Konig, with whom he had a close working relationship. Their closeness was no surprise, since the German naturalist had been employed from 1801 to 1807 in Banks's own library and herbarium. Interested in botany to begin with, Konig later turned to mineralogy and palaeontology. He was made Keeper in 1813.[87] His assistant for the next year was the talented William Elford Leach, who was also a particularly generous benefactor to the Museum.[88] Leach worked enthusiastically during his seven years at the Museum to improve the collections, especially those in entomology. Something can be seen in this steady progression, and in Banks's dealings with these officers, of the relationship he maintained with their maritime and Admiralty counterparts. Some were picked for their posts by Banks, and in one or two cases strong attachments were formed leading to sustained mutual assistance and even dependence. Banks's first and formative contact of this kind at the Museum was with Daniel Solander. Solander introduced the ideas of his master, Linnaeus, to the arrangement of Museum collections, and, of course, he managed those of Banks.[89] These ideas were not superseded in the Museum until the days of Leach's generation, who preferred the more natural systems that were later developed in France.

This need for system, which Linnaeus had supplied admirably in the field, and which his students had used in their travels around the world, was one with which Banks was in sympathy.[90] Banks's activities as a trustee at the Museum show that, as with his own collections, an organized approach was paramount. A number of instances can be found of both Leach and Konig working with Banks to enlarge and consolidate the natural history collections. Both officers were willing to co-ordinate agreed opinions with Banks on the value of possible purchases, and on the organization of natural history in the Museum, which the other trustees then found hard to refuse. Their work together shows, too, an awareness that the preoccupation with foreign flora and fauna had distorted collecting, and consequently British natural history had been somewhat neglected. Banks's intention was never to deluge the Museum with random exotic specimens from which coherent collections could not be assembled. He was no pedlar of rarities merely for the sake of it, and appreciated the value of indigenous species and their place in an institution like the British Museum. Thus while Banks maintained a characteristically broad range of donations, concerted efforts were made to sharpen the focus of the collections at

Bloomsbury. These included attempts to create a more comprehensive British zoological collection, and to form a British mineralogy and a geological collection as well. Under the Principal Librarian, Joseph Planta, arrangements were initiated in 1811–12 'to compleat the Collection of Printed Books in the Library respecting the British Islands, & the several Possessions of the British Empire'.[91] By concentrating on such areas, it was hoped that achievable improvements could be made, and that those referring to the Museum would find adequate collections for the country of which it was the main repository.

In 1814, Leach had been concentrating on crustaceans, and preparing for the removal of the birds from their room.[92] British zoology was intended for the old Bird Room,[93] and the growth of this collection was to be a theme in the relationship between Leach and Banks. Consequently, when in February 1816 an important collection became available, Leach was eager to obtain it. This had been brought together by George Montagu, a former Army captain from the American colonies and a capable naturalist, who made good progress in the scientific study of British fauna, especially in Devon. His work and collections were wide-ranging, including ornithology, molluscs, crustaceans, fish, sponges and sea anemones.[94] On 10 February it was recommended to the trustees that 'the Collection of British Zoology made by the late Colonel Montagu of Knowle in Devonshire, valued at £1200, will be an useful addition to the Museum'.[95] To this Leach was willing to add '. . . a Collection of British Crustacea, Shells, and Insects, tending to render the first-mentioned Collection still more complete than it is at present, valued at £600, which he would be ready to give to the Museum in the event of the former Collection being purchased'. Leach was trying to encourage the Museum to acquire the Montagu collection by making it an offer that could not be refused. The purchase was referred at this meeting to Banks and to the Treasury.[96]

Banks thought Montagu's collection the 'most extensive of British Zoology offered to Sale'. He also stated that 'the British Museum should possess as complete a Collection as possible of the Zoology of the British Isles, tho' he [Banks] does not admit the expediency of forming a complete or even an Extensive Collection of Exotic Zoology'.[97] The latter view seems strange given the many foreign presents given by Banks, but perhaps was explained years before, in 1788, to Robert Ferryman, a clergyman living near Bath.[98] Banks commented that 'as far as my knowledge of the world will enable me to judge the Science of Zoology is not at present sufficiently in vogue to allow any professor of it whose scene of action is no larger than the British Islands to deserve for his Labors such support'.[99] The situation had evidently not changed much, and Banks was now taking the opportunity to lay greater emphasis on British zoology. Indeed, early in March, Leach had been to see Banks at Soho Square, writing subsequently to the Speaker that Banks advised the purchase of Montagu's collection.[100] In his June report, offering specimens from his own cabinet, Leach hoped to create 'the most complete assemblage of the animals of Great Britain that has hitherto been made'.[101] The combined efforts of Leach and Banks proved effective, and the purchase was authorized by the trustees, 'Sir Joseph Banks having signified his opinion that the price is reasonable and the acquisition valuable to the Museum.'[102] The sum, paid in instalments over three years, was £1,100.

It was Leach who suggested exhibiting British zoology in the old Bird Room.[103] A further twist in negotiations was the offer by J.F. Stephens, a victualling officer at the Admiralty. Following the incorporation of Montagu's collections, Stephens wanted to give specimens from his own extensive cabinet which were not represented in the Museum collections.[104] The trustees decided to write to the Admiralty to obtain leave for Stephens in August so that he could go through his material, and this was granted.[105] In this way, British zoology at the Museum was strengthened in 1816.[106] By November, Leach wanted to tour Britain looking for 'peculiar Species of Zoology', paying special attention to the coasts. This was 'for the purpose of collecting them for the Museum . . . Since the Trustees have resolved to confine their attention to British Zoology'.[107] Leach's request was granted, but he exceeded the duration allowed him by three months, which did not endear him to Planta. At the same meeting, Leach was given permission to make exchanges for insects 'at present wanting in the Museum Collection'. By 1817, Leach was back at the Museum sorting through the zoological collections, while the old Bird Room was being readied for the British zoology to which, as an officer, he had already contributed so much.[108]

His working relationship with Banks was still functioning too. In April 1817, the late John Francillon's collections of insects, and his drawings of insects and birds of Georgia, were offered for sale. Leach reported seeing '22242 specimens, 10832 species of insects and 5037 figures exhibiting the changes of the insects of Georgia together with figures of 266 species of American birds and above 1000 figures of insects and birds on single sheets of paper', all offered for £1,400. Leach predicted that if the Museum were to buy the collections its own holdings would then be the finest in Britain, and by exchanging duplicates they could become the finest in the world.[109] The Francillon collections were auctioned in three parts, in May and July 1817, and then June 1818, the latter two sales being predominantly of insects. In the first week of July 1817 Leach presented 600 species of insects gathered in France, and in addition to that 800 species of Brazilian insects collected by the naturalist William Swainson. At the same time he wanted the trustees to acquire the Francillon drawings, and any insects that might be sold at a moderate price.[110]

Late in July, however, Leach's hopes were disappointed. The Treasury responded that in the 'present Circumstances of the Country' Francillon's collections could not be afforded.[111] So, as work on the Museum's collections progressed during the year, Leach identified a number of duplicates as a potential source of funding by which to purchase some of the Francillon insects. He thought that £100 might be raised by auctioning this Museum material, of which he wanted to use no more than £70.[112] At the final auction, in June 1818, purchases were made on Banks's advice and authority, especially of the three orders of Hymenoptera, Neuroptera, and Diptera. These, Leach said, rendered 'that part of the collection of the Museum the most perfect in the world'.[113] The outlay of a mere £44 was covered by the Museum.[114] Once again, Leach had found in Banks a useful trustee for furthering his plans, but the formidable financial constraints that often prevented the Museum from buying even the most highly recommended collections should be noted here. For example, the purchase of Baron von Moll's collections in Munich in 1815 meant that those of the Marquis de Drée simply could not be afforded, as Banks lamented to his close friend, Sir Charles Blagden.[115] A tactic increasingly used was to decline a collection, and then take from auction the parts most necessary to the Museum. This happened more than once with natural history collections that had been valued at £1,000 or over. Failure to enter the market for collections at this time can be explained mostly by national economic conditions quite beyond the control of any single trustee. That the refusal of some purchases caused bitterness cannot be denied, but such acrimony, like most personal rivalries and differences, counted far less than the real restrictions by which trustees were circumscribed.

Donations continued to arrive, however, and as if to prove that items from abroad were still readily accepted by the Museum, Banks presented in 1817, 'two Varieties of the British ringed Snake; two Nests of the Edible Swallow of Java . . . a Lemur from Madagascar . . . and a horned Chameleon'.[116] He was sending animals to the Museum in much the way he had always done, and towards the end of his life he seems to have been passing on more and more.[117] By May 1819 Leach could report that the last twelve months had been good, because 'the Museum has been very considerably enriched, by specimens of Birds and Quadrupeds presented by the Admiralty, by Sir J. Banks, by the Hudson's Bay Company, Mr Bowdich and by the contribution of various individuals', himself included.[118] Two months later he reported presenting corallines collected in different parts of the world, including some found by Banks with Cook.[119] In May 1820, the year Banks died, Leach requested bottles and spirit to better curate 'a vast number of very rare animals in Spirit, which have been presented by Sir J. Banks; Major Smith and Dr Meryon; as well as those lately received from Mr Redman'.[120] Banks's final lifetime donation had not yet been received, for in June Leach recorded fifty rare kinds of birds from Ceylon, probably sent to Banks by Alexander Moon, superintendent of the Royal Botanic Garden at Colombo.[121]

As with zoology, Banks was clear that he did not collect minerals, but this did not mean that he was not concerned with their accumulation and use at the British Museum. Indeed, his refusal to accommodate minerals and other substances at his home was a positive gain for the Museum. Drawing on the international connections mentioned previously, and on his estates at Overton in Derbyshire, where mining offered profits to a landowner interested in structural geology, Banks maintained a steady supply of specimens to Bloomsbury.[122] When one Danish correspondent offered 'a small Set of Norwegian and Swedish Minerals', hoping they would find a place in 'Your Mineral Cabinet', Banks responded that 'I have Sir no collections of minerals myself', and forwarded this gift to the Museum, where 'the Public Treasuries of Science [are] preserved . . . for the honor of the Countrey & the use of Students'.[123] Likewise, when Sir William Hamilton sent Banks samples from Etna, Banks declined saying, 'I should thank you more for Collections of dried Plants made by Graefer than for Collections of the Produce of Etna which you Know is not exactly in my way it will do however for the British Museum where I will place it'.[124]

In these ways Banks maintained the scope of his gifts from abroad, as he did with Leach. Indeed, one of the most frequently repeated phrases in Konig's reports up to 1820 was 'through the medium of Sir Jos. Banks', so that the 'Book of

Presents' shows at least as much given to mineralogy as zoology, some of it coming from New World territories then being explored. In December 1809 Konig could report sight of minerals from New Holland (Australia), 'a continent as yet very little known with regard to its mineral productions', to be followed in February of the next year with 'crystallized White Topaz from New South Wales & another Article belonging to the secondary Fossils', all through Banks.[125] The number and variety of what Banks gave from 1810 to 1815 is remarkable.[126] Banks was the chief individual donor of such material in this period, through a series of separate gifts supplying specimens from the Pacific, the West Indies, North and South America, Russia and Ireland, as well as internally from Britain. It is as much in the British Museum as at his Derbyshire estates that we find Banks most active in the early earth sciences.

It was Banks who suggested and then oversaw the purchase in 1799 of Charles Hatchett's collection, which included a fine set of Russian minerals.[127] His report on the Hatchett collection, written with Charles Greville and Philip Rashleigh, stipulated that the Museum needed a good set of British minerals from places like 'Derbyshire, Cornwall or the Lead hills', and that a 'systematic Collection of Minerals is much wanted' for research. One collection from abroad which received particular comment was that made in accordance with Banks's instructions by Archibald Menzies on the northwest coast of America. This was to be kept separately, since it 'supplies a kind of mineralogical history of an extensive Coast very little known'.[128] Furthermore, numbers of arranged duplicates were to be exhibited for the public. In time, the Hatchett collection was united in the Mineral Room with two other major collections, those of Sir Hans Sloane and Clayton Mordaunt Cracherode. From these emerged the principal mineral collection of the Museum.

Working with Konig from May 1807, Banks saw some of the aims in his report achieved, and rooms provided to hold the resulting collections. These grew enormously, and by 1811 the ageing floors of the Museum were being strengthened to support them. With the death of Charles Greville, and the purchase of his collection in May 1810 for £13,727, Planta and Konig envisaged 'forming a systematic, and economical collection, and a collection for indigenous Minerals'.[129] This plan was discussed with Banks and the Speaker of the House of Commons before being presented to the Board of Trustees as a whole. Like Leach, Konig prepared the way for such changes by enlisting Banks's support. He could rely on this since these ideas were traceable, in part, to those proposed in 1799. Moreover, Konig now wished to see the principal mineral collection placed in the Saloon, a move he started in 1812. As the collections grew and were organized, Konig wanted them displayed in a series of connected rooms at the top of the main staircase. Needless to say, Banks was on the standing committee that approved the change to the Saloon, and further that the old Mineralogy Room be used for geology.

So closely did Banks become involved in these aspects that when the library and minerals of Baron von Moll were offered for sale in Munich,[130] the committee that convened to arrange a visit for Konig and Henry Hervey Baber met at Soho Square. This was on 14 February 1815, and it was from Soho Square that instructions for the two Museum representatives were issued.[131] Such a level of co-ordination was intended, within the limited Museum funds available, to extend the collections as fully as possible in their specialist fields. This was achieved by purchasing collections like those of the pioneering geologist William Smith, who (like Konig) Banks had done much to patronize. Smith's work had, of course, implications for landowners like Banks with mining interests on their estates, and laid an impressive foundation for the future of stratigraphy and palaeontology in the Museum.[132] With the acquisition of Von Moll's minerals, and in 1816 those of Count Beroldingen, Konig could claim that the main mineralogical collections were 'in such a state of order and systematic arrangement as to be supposed more extensively useful to the Student than any other Public assemblage of this kind'. He had also commenced arrangement of the 'Secondary fossils'.[133]

Seeking another room, this time for British mineralogy, Konig argued 'Nothing is more frequently enquired after, by native as well as by foreign visitors than a collection of British Minerals'.[134] Room 10 was chosen by the Museum surveyor as the only one capable of supporting such a collection.[135] Unsatisfied, Konig sought in 1819 to displace the exotic zoological specimens from Room 8 in preference for 'the whole of the splendid collection of Secondary Fossils' on which he had been working. Konig thought of relegating zoology to the basement so that 'the succession of the mineralogical collections (from the Saloon to the Room for British Minerals) would be no longer interrupted, and the landing place of the staircase would be cleared of the Quadrupeds which now disfigure it'.[136]

Judging from the *Synopsis* for 1820, this was one concession that could not be allowed: a balance was needed in the overall Museum treatment of natural history.[137] We see, though, that exotic zoology, like ethnographic collections, never held quite the same fascination for Konig as the earth sciences.

Conclusion

Banks could not fairly be accused of such partiality. He was willing to contribute to all fields of natural history and ethnography, but not necessarily to collect in them himself. Such eclecticism was more typical of Lever, and his approach should be contrasted with that of Banks.[138] Of Lever, Blagden commented: 'Mr. Lever wants anything that he happens not to have in his Museum, whether it tends to illustrate science or not: on the contrary, nothing can be an object to you, but what will conduce to the improvement of Natural History as a branch of Philosophy.'[139] In his early days, Lever's collections lacked system, a point to which Blagden certainly refers here, and the life-style of the showman brought him as much notice as his exhibits – not all of it good.[140] Lever would later try to remedy the former deficiency, but he continued to mount mixed exhibitions of natural and artificial products, with a particular strength in natural history, especially birds.[141] As such, his Museum has been regarded as something of a rival to the British Museum, although in practice the two collections probably tended to eclipse many lesser private museums, as Banks explained to Charles Willson Peale in 1794.[142]

In any case, it seems unlikely that such competition alone could account for the refusal of the British Museum to buy the entire Leverian Museum when Sir Ashton at last wanted to recoup his expenses.[143] The more prosaic, and historically more significant considerations of space and, crucially, finance help explain many of the purchases and refusals of the British Museum in its early years.[144] These factors affected a number of

major decisions from 1800 to 1820 in which the trustees had to accept or refuse 'offers' of major collections at a price, and when one was taken, or another passed over, there was alike a controversy that smouldered afterwards. Lever disposed of his collections by means of a lottery, although he was to sell only 8,000 of the 36,000 tickets he had printed. The winner in 1786 was James Parkinson who removed the Leverian museum to the Rotunda, in a less fashionable part of London, near Blackfriars Bridge. It survived there until 1806, when, finally, it was broken up and sold, portions being obtained by individuals such as William Bullock, but not the British Museum – a conspicuous omission.[145]

The British Museum had remained free, although access was regulated. In many respects the principles by which it was governed were therefore unlike those of commercial museums like Lever's, where charges were made, and a need to advertise and offer a degree of novelty applied. Bullock, one of Lever's successors as a leading museum proprietor in the capital, and an ambitious showman, mounted innovative dramatic displays in his Egyptian Hall, which was opened in Piccadilly in April 1812. One such display was entered through a mock basaltic cavern, like Fingal's Cave, which Banks had been the first to survey and record on Staffa in 1772. It was situated in the 'Pantherion', and showed animals grouped in a tropical forest, although they came from more than one area and continent.[146] It seems that Bullock was on more friendly terms with Banks than those enjoyed by Lever, and he was undoubtedly a better businessman than Lever. Despite this, both men claimed to possess substantial collections from Cook and Banks, claims that would repay further investigation.[147] When, by 1819 Bullock, also a great salesman and auctioneer, had tired of his collections of natural history, ethnography and other objects ancient and modern,[148] the British Museum simply could not afford to buy and house everything.[149] Bullock offered his collections to more than one institution, the University of Edinburgh being his first choice, suggesting that he had decided to relinquish them partly because the public were drawn increasingly to the British Museum, where admission policies had been liberalized. With no takers, Bullock was forced to auction everything, conducting the sale himself. Specimens called 'compounds' were noticed in some of the lots. These were assembled from more than one animal, a factor that might have adversely affected prices.[150] Whatever he claimed to have spent on the collections, Bullock took about £9,974 13s. – not much more than the sum for which he had offered everything to the British Museum. Leach, who rather harshly thought Bullock an indifferent naturalist, bid on behalf of the Museum, and also assisted the University of Edinburgh.

Banks thought such large private enterprises would ultimately be impermanent, however lavish the expenditure on them. He explained this in his short, cordial correspondence with Robert Ferryman,[151] and it was a view from which Ferryman did not dissent.[152] Yet if we see in the fate of Lever's and Bullock's collections a transition away from the assorted private cabinets of the past, however extensive and spectacular,[153] we see, too, with Banks's death the passing of a time when the landed gentry exerted such a pervasive influence over the course of collecting and of empire. During the preceding twenty years in particular, the Museum had been greatly enriched by the generation from which Banks came, but

Banks's bequest was different in kind from some other collections of his day. His was a specialist collection that could be consulted by scholars, along with the lively array of collections and shows then available in London. Indeed, Banks's herbarium provided the basis for a new specialist department in the Museum, under his former Soho Square curator, Robert Brown.[154] It was the finest plant collection to arrive since that of the founder, Sir Hans Sloane,[155] and led directly to the formal establishment of another discipline at the Museum. The library, its working partner, amounting to about 7,900 books, and 6,100 unbound tracts, in total about 14,000 items, went to the Department of Printed Books under Baber. The library covered much published material in the field of natural history, dating back almost to the beginning of printing. It had, too, a catalogue, the last part of which appeared in 1800; an updated version, interleaved and with manuscript additions, was also kept.[156] This was all made possible because, if nothing else, Banks had concentrated his collecting activities. In so doing, he held back the most prized of his collections until last. Up to 1827[157] it is to his role in mediating between the Museum and the expanding world of exploration and empire that consideration must be given, and to his sturdy committee work year after year, work touching on almost every aspect of the Museum, right down to its basement.

It is possible to detect, too, that in an institution that tended to favour antiquities in the first part of the nineteenth century, natural history was being nurtured, and perhaps even that there was greater overall activity and progress throughout the Museum than historians have sometimes been prepared to admit.

Acknowledgements

I am grateful to the Trustees of the British Museum, and to Christopher Date and Gary Thorn, for allowing me to make wide use of the papers in the British Museum Archives.

Notes and references

Note: references to manuscripts at the British Museum are made as follows: CE 1/- General Meetings; CE 3/- Standing Committee Minutes; CE 4/- Original Papers; CE 5/- Officers' Reports; CE 30/- Book of Presents. All citations use the relevant folio number.

The following further abbreviations are used: BL, British Library; BM, British Museum; NHM, Natural History Museum; RBG, Royal Botanic Gardens, Kew; *HRNSW, Historical Records of New South Wales* (Sydney, 1892–1901), 18 vols; ML, Mitchell Library, New South Wales.

1 For the 'second great age of European exploration', c.1760–1805, and its political and scientific impulses see R. MacLeod and P.F. Rehbock (eds), *Nature in its Greatest Extent* (Hawaii, 1988), especially the chapter by A. Frost, 'Science for political purposes: European explorations of the Pacific Ocean, 1764–1806'. For exploration and discovery in the seventeenth and eighteenth centuries see D. Howse (ed.), *Background to Discovery: Pacific exploration from Dampier to Cook* (Los Angeles, 1990). For Banks see J. Gascoigne, *Science in the Service of Empire: Joseph Banks, the British state and the uses of science in the age of revolution* (Cambridge, 1998).

2 W.S. Shepperson, 'William Bullock – an American failure', *Bulletin of the Historical and Philosophical Society of Ohio* 19 (1961), pp.144–52; W.H. Mullens, 'Some museums of Old London – I: The Leverian Museum', *Museums Journal* 15 (1915), pp.123–9, 162–72, followed by 'Some museums of Old London – II: William Bullock's

London Museum', *Museums Journal* 17 (1917–18), pp.51–7, 132–7, 180–7; T. Iredale, 'Bullock's Museum', *Australian Zoologist* 2 (1948), pp.233–7; R.W. and M. Force, *Art and Artifacts of the 18th Century: Objects in the Leverian Museum as painted by Sarah Stone* (Honolulu, 1968).

3 The terms 'natural and artificial curiosities' are mostly used to refer to collections that would today come under disciplines in natural history or anthropology.

4 BM CE 3/7 1892 (7 January 1785), CE 3/10 2662 (10 May 1817). Purkis to Banks CE 4/4 1334 (21 July 1816). See also L. Cust and S. Colvin, *History of the Society of Dilettanti* (London, 1914), pp.105–6.

5 Banks to Nelson, 8 August 1803, NMM CRK/2. See further, chapter 12.

6 For a number of articles on the scientific aspects of this voyage see *Notes and Records of the Royal Society* 24, no.1 (1969); *Pacific Studies* 1, no.2 (1978), and 2, no.1 (1978). See also H.B. Carter, 'The Royal Society and the voyage of HMS *Endeavour* 1768–71', *Notes and Records of the Royal Society* 49 (1995), pp.245–60.

7 J.C. Beaglehole (ed.), *The Endeavour Journal of Joseph Banks 1768–1771*, 2 vols, Sydney and London, vol.II, p.110. Banks does not dwell on this event. Cook had more to say about it: J.C. Beaglehole (ed.), *The Journals of Captain Cook . . . 1771–80*, 4 vols (reprinted Woodbridge, Hakluyt Society, 1999), vol.I, pp.386–9.

8 Sheffield, a shadowy figure, had an interest in early ethnographic collections from the Pacific, not least those given to the Ashmolean in 1776 by the Forsters: see R.F. Ovenell, *The Ashmolean Museum 1683–1894* (Oxford, 1986), chap.10.

9 R. Holt-White (ed.), *The Life and Letters of Gilbert White of Selborne*, 2 vols (London, 1901), vol.I, pp.210–12.

10 W.T. Stearn, 'The botanical results of the *Endeavour* voyage', *Endeavour* 32, no.100 (1968), p.9.

11 H.B. Carter, J.A. Diment, C.J. Humphries and A. Wheeler, 'The Banksian natural history collections of the *Endeavour* voyage and their relevance to modern taxonomy', *History in the Service of Systematics: Papers from the conference to celebrate the centenary of the British Museum (Natural History) 13–16 April, 1981*, Society for the Bibliography of Natural History: Special Publication 1 (London, 1981), pp.62–8.

12 This was probably a reference to the 'Solander Slips' used by Solander to catalogue at the British Museum and for Banks's collections. These are now bound in twenty-seven volumes in the Zoology Library, and a further twenty-four volumes in the Botany Library, all at the Natural History Museum. See: W.T. Stearn, 'Daniel Carlsson Solander (1733–1782), pioneer Swedish investigator of Pacific natural history', *Archives of Natural History* 11 (1984), pp.499–503; A. Wheeler, 'Daniel Solander and the zoology of Cook's voyage', *Archives of Natural History* 11 (1984), pp.505–15; E.W. Groves, 'Notes on the botanical specimens collected by Banks and Solander on Cook's first voyage, together with an itinerary of landing localities', *Journal of the Society for the Bibliography of Natural History* 4 (1962), pp.57–62; and on the Museum system of exchanging plant duplicates that persisted until the 1930s, J. Ramsbottom, 'Note: Banks's and Solander's duplicates', *Journal of the Society for the Bibliography of Natural History* 4 (1962), p.197.

13 The engraved plates Banks had prepared have been published by Alecto Historical Editions. There is a catalogue of the specimens, drawings, copper plates, related manuscripts and publications: J.A. Diment, C.J. Humphries, L. Newington, E. Shaughnessy, 'Catalogue of the natural history drawings commissioned by Joseph Banks on the Endeavour voyage 1768–1771', *Bulletin of the British Museum (Natural History): Historical Series* 11–13 (1984–7).

14 Banks to Lauraguais, 6 December 1771, ML 05.01.

15 The breadfruit voyages of William Bligh were mounted under Banks's direction to ship breadfruit and other plants of the Pacific to the West Indies to be used on the plantations. The first attempt ended in a mutiny on board HMS *Bounty*, 1787–9. The second was successful, HM Ships *Providence*, Bligh, *Assistant*, Nathaniel Portlock, 1791–3. For details of the plants delivered, including those to Kew, see D. Powell, 'The voyage of the plant nursery, HMS *Providence*, 1791–93', *Economic Botany* 31 (1977), pp.387–431. For an account of Banks's use of plant collectors, often from Kew, see D. Mackay, 'Agents of empire: the Banksian collectors and evaluation of new lands', in D.P. Miller and P.H. Reill (eds), *Visions of Empire: Voyages, botany, and representations of nature* (Cambridge, 1996), chap.3.

16 BM CE 1/3 667–78 (2 June 1770).
17 BM CE 1/3 740–2 (28 September 1775).
18 Banks to Ingenhousz, 31 May 1782, ML 74.03. Banks goes on in this letter to say that he had expected anything the Museum did not want to be returned to him, but that there had been a delay because, he suspected, the sorting of the material had been neglected.
19 BM CE 3/6 1632 (23 October 1770); CE 3/6 1743 (23 October 1778). See also more artificial curiosities from the South Seas from Williamson, Webber, Cleveley, the Collets – William and Joseph – and Hogg: BM CE 3/7 1745 (24 November 1780).
20 In August 1781 Cleveley was paid 15 guineas for assisting in the preparation of the South Seas Room: CE 3/7 1771 (10 August 1781).
21 Report by Solander, BM CE 4/1 599 (10 August 1781).
22 BM CE 1/4 828 (24 February 1781), CE 30/2 (15 June 1781).
23 For a discussion of the Royal Society's museum see M. Hunter, 'The cabinet institutionalized: the Royal Society's repository and its background', in O. Impey and A. MacGregor (eds), The Origins of Museums: The cabinet of curiosities in sixteenth- and seventeenth-century Europe (Oxford, 1985), chap.19. See also M. Hunter, Establishing the New Science: The experience of the early Royal Society (Woodbridge, 1989), especially chap.4.
24 N. Portlock and G. Dixon, A Voyage round the World, but more particularly to the North-West Coast of the America: performed in 1785, 1786, 1787, and 1788, in the King George and Queen Charlotte, Captains Portlock and Dixon, 2 vols (London, 1789).
25 BM CE 3/8 2005–6 (22 May 1789).
26 King to Banks, (October 1780), NHM B.L.D.T.C.I 304.
27 For a study of Banks's role as 'custodian' of the Cook 'model' of exploration, and generally of science and exploration in the growth of empire, 1780–1801, see D. Mackay, In the Wake of Cook: Exploration, science and empire, 1780–1801 (London, 1985), especially chaps 3 and 4.
28 Menzies to Banks, 7 September 1786, RBG Kew B.C. I 243; Etches to Banks, 29 September 1786, RBG Kew B.C. I 246.
29 Menzies to Banks, 21 July 1789, RBG Kew B.C. I 357.
30 Menzies to Rutherford, 19 October 1789, RBG Edinburgh.
31 Menzies to Banks, 8 October 1789, RBG Kew B.C. I 362.
32 Banks to Grenville, 20 January 1792, PRO H.O. 42/18 166–7 [with enclosures]; Banks to Menzies, 22 February 1791, BL Additional MS 33,979, fols 75–8.
33 Menzies to Banks, 14 September 1795, RBG Kew B.C. II 127.
34 Banks to Portland, 3 February 1796, NHM B.L. D.T.C. X(1) 15–16: '. . . tho' he [Menzies] lost no opportunities of making & writing down the necessary observations respecting the produce of the soil, the manners of the Natives, & such other matters as he was instructed to remark upon'.
35 Portland to Banks, 12 February 1796, S.L. Banks MS P N 1:18, and 'A Catalogue of Curiosities & natural productions brought home in his Majesty's Sloop Discovery from the North West Coast of America & the South Sea Islands by Mr. Archibald Menzies'.
36 BM CE 1/4 922 (13 February 1796).
37 Statement by Banks on the behaviour of George Vancouver [c. 1796], NHM B.L. D.T.C. X (1) 83–6. For Banks's warning about the importance of keeping a journal on the voyage as proof of conduct, as well as a record of the natural history and cultures encountered, see Banks to Menzies, 10 August 1791, HPNSW, vol.I, pt ii, pp.521–2. For accounts of the work of Menzies on these voyages, and for an assessment of the botanical results: E.W. Groves, and D.J. Galloway, 'Archibald Menzies MD, FLS (1754–1842), aspects of his life, travels and collections', Archives of Natural History 14 (1987), pp.3–34; E.W. Groves, 'Archibald Menzies (1754–1842) an early botanist on the northwestern seaboard of North America, 1792–1794, with further notes of his life and work', Archives of Natural History 28 (2001), pp.71–122.
38 Report by König, BM CE 5/1 57–8 (13 November 1807).
39 Reports by König, BM CE 5/1 106 (8 April 1808), 133 (9 July 1808).
40 BM CE 3/9 2391–2 (29 June 1808); Synopsis of the Contents of the British Museum (London, 1808), pp.4–5.
41 H.B. Carter, Sir Joseph Banks (1743–1820): A guide to biographical and bibliographical sources (Winchester, 1987), E: 'The Collections'. Also, on ethnographic objects, and their distribution and history: A.L. Kaeppler, 'Artificial Curiosities': Being an exposition of native manufactures collected on the three Pacific voyages of Captain James Cook, RN, at the Bernice Pauahi Bishop Museum January 18, 1978–August 31, 1978 . . . (Honolulu, 1978); A.L. Kaeppler (ed.),

Cook Voyage Artifacts in Leningrad, Berne, and Florence Museums (Honolulu, 1978); B. Hauser-Schäublin and G. Krüger (eds), James Cook, Gifts and Treasures from the South Seas: The Cook/Forster Collection, Göttingen (Munich and New York, 1998); B. Smith, European Vision and the South Pacific (New Haven and London, 2nd edn 1985).
42 Solander to Banks, 22 August 1775, RBG Kew B.C. I 51.
43 Solander to Banks, 5 September 1775, NHM B.L. D.T.C. I 98–9.
44 BM CE 4/1 289–92 (25 August 1775) being Johann Reinhold Forster's gift of birds, fish and animals from his voyage with Cook, which he calls a 'compleat Set of Specimens', with an accompanying list.
45 Solander to Banks, 5 September 1775, NHM B.L. D.T.C. I 98–9.
46 J. Gascoigne, Joseph Banks and the English Enlightenment: Useful knowledge and polite culture (Cambridge 1994), pp.68–9. Among others, Mullens , op. cit. (note 2) [Leverian Museum], pp.126–8 comments on this aspect. Susan Burney described the museum in July 1778: A.R. Ellis, (ed.), The Early Diary of Frances Burney 1768–1778, 2 vols (London, 1889), vol.II, p.249.
47 H. St. John, 'New species of Hawaiian plants collected by David Nelson in 1779', Pacific Science 30 (1976), pp.7–44.
48 Clerke to Banks, 18 August 1779, NHM B.L. D.T.C. I 266–7.
49 D. Medway, 'Some ornithological results of Cook's third voyage', Journal of the Society for the Bibliography of Natural History 9 (1979), pp.315–51; J.J. Keevil, 'William Anderson, 1748–1778: Master Surgeon, Royal Navy', Annals of Medical History 5 (1933), pp.511–24.
50 P.J.P. Whitehead, 'A guide to the dispersal of zoological material from Captain Cook's voyages, II', Pacific Studies (1978), p.78. Whitehead (p.64) points out the competitive element in all this, and the fact that the claim to Clerke's collections lodged by Daines Barrington on behalf of Lever was not valid.
51 BM CE 3/8 2049 (3 January 1792), CE 30/2 (13 January 1792).
52 P.J.P. Whitehead, 'Zoological specimens from Captain Cook's voyages', Journal of the Society for the Bibliography of Natural History 5 (1969), pp.165–7. Banks gave his opinion in 1796 on the relevance to medical science and anatomy of the Hunterian collection: Banks to Eden, [26 January 1796], NHM B.L. D.T.C. 10(1) 13–14.
53 Whitehead, op. cit. (note 52), pp.165–7. Collections purchased by the College from the British Museum in 1809 might also have contained Banks material that subsequently returned to Bloomsbury.
54 For the insects see M. Fitton, and S. Shute, 'Sir Joseph Banks's collection of insects', in R.E.R. Banks et al. (eds), Sir Joseph Banks: A global perspective(Kew, 1994), pp.209–11. For the shells see G.L. Wilkins, 'A catalogue and historical account of the Banks shell collection', Bulletin of the British Museum (Natural History): Historical Series 1 (1955), pp.71–119.
55 BM CE 30/2 (14 March 1779, 7 January 1780, 15 September 1780, 5 October 1781); (17 April 1783 – two birds from Lady Banks); (20 August 1784). For Pigou and Duncan [also signed by Duncan] to Banks, 31 May 1782, BL Additional MS 33,977, fol.148; Pigou [also signed by Duncan] to Banks, 31 December 1783, RBG Kew B.C. 1155; Duncan to Banks, 18 January 1784, BL Additional MS 33,977, fol.258.
56 BM CE 3/7 1825 (21 February 1783), 1829 (21 March 1783), 1859 (21 January 1784).
57 BM CE 3/7 1880–1 (3 September 1784).
58 For Banks's relationship with the colony on the east coast of Australia see J.M. Matra, 'A proposal for establishing a settlement in New South Wales' PRO C.O.201/1 57–61, printed in HRNSW, vol.I, pt ii, pp.1–8. Also H.B. Carter, Sir Joseph Banks (London, 1988), pp.212–16, and an account of the development of the colony and its strategic importance by A. Frost, 'The antipodean exchange: European horticulture and imperial designs', in Miller and Reill, op. cit. (note 15), chap.4.
59 BM CE 3/8 2021 (16 April 1790). The vast majority of animals, plants and minerals immediately dispatched from the colony at Sydney to Banks came at Arthur Phillip's orders, with a consignment of animals (live and dead), ethnographic material, insects, plants and seeds being sent by David Considen, an assistant surgeon. All the Phillip correspondence relating to this is in ML Banks MSS, while the Considen letter, from Port Jackson, was dated 18 November 1788, HRNSW, vol.I, pt ii, pp.220–1.
60 For comment on the types of colonial contact available to a man like Banks, and their importance, see J. Browne, 'Biogeography and empire', especially the sections 'Colonial officials' and 'Science of

empire', in N. Jardine, J.A. Secord, E.C. Spary (eds), *Cultures of Natural History* (Cambridge, 1996), pp.308–14.

61 Banks to King, 15 May 1798, *HRNSW*, vol.III, pp.382–3.

62 Gavin de Beer, *The Sciences were never at War* (London, 1960), especially 'The wars of Napoleon 1803–1815', Section IV.

63 Banks to Spencer [December 1800], PRO Adm. 1/4377.

64 E. Scott, *The Life of Captain Matthew Flinders, RN* (Sydney, 1914).

65 Nepean to Banks, 28 April 1801, ML 63.51.

66 Banks to Marsden, January 1806, *HRNSW*, vol.VI, pp.16–19. For more on the results of the voyage, especially the work of Bauer, see: D.J. Mabberley, *Ferdinand Bauer: The nature of discovery* (London, 1999), and D.J. Mabberley and D.T. Moore, 'Catalogue of the holdings in the Natural History Museum (London) of the Australian botanical drawings of Ferdinand Bauer (1760–1826) and cognate materials relating to the *Investigator* voyage of 1801–1805', *Bulletin of the Natural History Museum: Botany Series* 29, no. 2 (1999), pp.81–226.

67 Banks to Milnes, 20 January 1801, *HRNSW*, vol.IV, pp.290–1.

68 T.G. Vallance and D.T. Moore, 'Geological aspects of HMS *Investigator* in Australian waters, 1801–5', *Bulletin of the British Museum (Natural History): Historical Series* 10, no.1 (1982), especially p.29 and p.6. See also D.T. Moore, 'An account of those described rock collections in the British Museum (Natural History) made before 1918; with a provisional catalogue arranged by continent', *Bulletin of the British Museum (Natural History): Historical Series* 10, no.5 (1982), pp.141–77. For a wider assessment of the natural history: D.T. Moore and E.W. Groves, 'A catalogue of plants written by Robert Brown (1773–1858) in New South Wales: first impressions of the flora of the Sydney region', *Archives of Natural History* 22 (1997), pp.281–93; P.I. Edwards, 'Robert Brown (1773–1858) and the natural history of Matthew Flinders' voyage in HMS *Investigator*, 1801–1805', *Journal of the Society for the Bibliography of Natural History* 7 (1976), pp.385–407.

69 All the governors from Phillip onwards corresponded with Banks about iron, coal, copper and many other ores and minerals.

70 Banks to Navy Board, 25 March 1799, *HRNSW*, vol.III, pp.650–1.

71 Navy Board to Banks, 27 March 1799, *HRNSW*, vol.III, p.651; King to Banks, 3 April 1799, *HRNSW*, vol.III, p.658.

72 Kent to Banks, 1 November 1801, *HRNSW*, vol.IV, p.608.

73 Barrow to Banks, 21 March 1811, BM CE 4/3 997; CE 5/2 342 (5 April 1811).

74 BM CE 3/8 2133 (7 April 1797), and 2220 (April 1802). See also: CE 3/8 2271 (28 March 1806), and CE 1/4 994–6 (12 July 1806).

75 BM CE 3/8 2221 (9 April 1802).

76 Titsingh to Banks, 26 August 1797, BL Additional MS 33,980, fol.110; Titsingh to Banks, 10 December 1797, BL Additional MS 33,980, fols 124–5. Titsingh had recently been elected a Fellow of the Royal Society, on 22 June 1797.

77 BM CE 3/8 2222 (8 May 1802), and 2223 (11 June 1802). For the Argus Pheasant: Macdonald to Banks, 18 February 1797, BL Additional MS 33,980, fol.93.

78 The correspondence with these governors, navigators, botanists and collectors, c.1798–1805, shows the flow of material from New South Wales that reached Banks as the colony there developed. For more on Caley: J.B. Webb, *George Caley: Nineteenth-century naturalist* (New South Wales, 1995).

79 BM CE 3/8 2231 (11 March 1803).

80 Fabbroni to Banks [June 1794], BL Additional MS 33,982, fols 323–4; Fabbroni to Banks, 3 May 1796, BL Additional MS 8098, fols 349–50; Banks to Fabbroni, 1 July 1796, A.P.S. See also: W.C. Smith, 'A history of the first hundred years of the mineral collection in the British Museum', *Bulletin of the British Museum (Natural History): Historical Series* 3, no.8 (1969), p.259; M.M. Grady, *Catalogue of meteorites* (Cambridge, Mass., 2000), p.461.

81 R. Cowen, 'After the Fall', *Science News* 148, no. 16 (1995), pp.248–9.

82 BM CE 3/7 1978 (18 January 1788).

83 BM CE 3/8 2241 (13 January 1804), CE 30/2 (10 October 1803).

84 BM CE 30/2 (1 November 1803); CE 3/8 2238 (11 November 1803). See also: Banks to Novossiltzoff, 7 March 1803, RGB Kew B.C. II 275; Novossiltzoff to Banks, 7 July 1803, BL Additional MS 8099, fols 360–1, fol.362 being a list of the bones and horns sent.

85 See Report by Konig, CE 5/3 764 (10 June 1815) for an exchange by Banks in June 1815 using his 'account'. This concerned duplicate antlers of an Irish Moose deer. Konig supported their release, referring to the fossil bones from Siberia, sent to Banks by the Emperor of Russia, and donated by him in 1803. Konig was also able

to list other donations made by Banks in 1815 of fossilized hazelnuts. Moreover, some of the early experiments performed on minerals, and especially on meteorites, were made possible by use of Banks's 'account'. Among the scientific tests carried out on meteorites were those of Charles Hatchett, who obtained samples through Banks: BM CE 1/4 954 (13 February 1802); 959 (11 December 1802). Other tests performed on specimens taken from the collections included those of William Hyde Wollaston, in 1809 inventor of the reflecting goniometer. His were conducted in March 1809, BM CE 3/9 2412 (11 March 1809), and again in November 1815, Report by Konig CE 5/3 792 (10 November 1815). The analysis, too, of the chemist Edward Howard was encouraged by Banks, who felt that a new scientific field might be opening up with the study of various falls.

86 BM CE 1/4 996 (12 July 1806).

87 BM CE 1/5 1112–13 (1 September 1813).

88 A.E. Gunther, *The Founders of Science at the British Museum 1753–1900* (Halesworth, 1981), especially chaps 3–9.

89 BM CE 1/3 682 (26 September 1771) when Solander was granted leave in September 1771 to complete the arrangement and description of articles collected by Banks and himself with Cook. On Solander see further chapter 12.

90 F.A. Stafleu, *Linnaeus and the Linnaeans: The spreading of their ideas in systematic botany, 1735–1789* (Utrecht, 1971).

91 BM CE 3/9 2510–11 (11 January 1812).

92 Reports by Leach BM CE 5/3 706 (7 December 1814); 717 (13 January 1815); 738 (10 March 1815).

93 BM CE 4/4 1403 (26 July 1817).

94 R.J. Cleevely, 'Some background to the life and publications of Colonel George Montagu (1753–1815)', *Journal of the Society for the Bibliography of Natural History* 8, pt 4 (1978), pp.445–80.

95 BM CE 1/5 1141 (10 February 1816). See also: CE 4/3 1215 (5 July 1815).

96 See also: BM CE 3/9 2627 (9 March 1816), CE 4/3 1272 (1 March 1816).

97 BM CE 4/3 1176 (12 February 1816).

98 R.C. Murphy, 'Robert Ferryman, forgotten naturalist', *Proceedings of the American Philosophical Society* 103, no.6 (1959), pp.774–7. The correspondence between Banks and Ferryman is very small but friendly.

99 Banks to Ferryman, 5 February 1788, RBG Kew B.C. I 295 (2).

100 BM CE 4/3 1271 (1816).

101 Report by Leach BM CE 5/4 874 (14 June 1816).

102 BM CE 3/9 2634 (15 June 1816).

103 Report by Leach BM CE 5/4 874 (14 June 1816).

104 Report by Leach BM CE 5/4 842 (n.d. 1816). Montagu's collections were at the Museum by October 1816, along with Stephens's donation, and another from Charles Prideaux: Report by Leach CE 5/4 900 (1 October 1816). By July 1817 Room 11 was all but ready for Montagu's collection: Report by Planta BM CE 5/4 1005–6 (12 July 1817).

105 BM CE 3/10 2636 (13 July 1816).

106 Other purchases recommended by Leach in 1816: that of Latham, of Compton Street, for £25, being 1,300 Indian insects, Report by Leach BM CE 5/4 821 (n.d. 1816); that of Sims, of Norwich, for £15, being 3,187 insects, Reports by Leach CE 5/4 863 (10 May 1816) and CE 3/9 2632 (11 May 1816).

107 BM CE 3/10 2637 (13 July 1816).

108 Report by Leach BM CE 5/4 883–4 (2 July 1816), Leach worked hard to organize the animals to go into the room for British Zoology, which was almost ready by December 1817: Report by Leach CE 5/4 1044 (11 December 1817). See also: CE 4/4 1403 (26 July 1817).

109 Report by Leach BM CE 5/4 970–1 (10 April 1817). See also: C.F. Cowan, 'John Francillon, F.L.S., a few facts', *Entomologist's Record and Journal of Variation*, nos 7 and 8 (1986), pp.139–43; C. MacKechnie Jarris, 'A history of the British Coleoptera', *Proceedings and Transactions of The British Entomological and Natural History Society* 8, pt 4 (1976), pp.99–100.

110 Report by Leach BM CE 5/4 1014–15 (11 July 1817). For Swainson: Report by Leach CE 5/4 970–1 (10 April 1817).

111 BM CE 4/4 1409 (31 July 1817). See also: CE 3/10 2679 (8 November 1817).

112 BM CE 4/4 1404 (27 July 1817).

113 Report by Leach BM CE 5/5 1121–2 (c. June 1818).

114 For further gifts from Leach: BM CE 3/10 2742 (11 December 1819); Leach to Banks CE 4/3 1174 (11 February 1815); Reports by Leach

CE 5/3 692–3 (11 November 1814); CE 5/5 1218 (*c.* May 1819). For more payments by Leach, as authorized by Banks: £51 1s. 6d. for forty species of birds and fishes, and a rare turtle, purchased at the sale of Edward Donovan's collections, May 1818, Report by Leach CE 5/5 1106 (9 May 1818). Donovan worked and published on Lever's collections.

115 Banks to Blagden, 20 February 1815, R.S. B. 59.

116 BM CE 3/10 2665 (10 May 1817). Possible contact: Leschenhault de la Tour to Banks, 20 March 1817, BL Additional MS 8968, fol.25.

117 And would continue to do so. For a small collection of minerals from Greenland, 3 species of tortoise from the Cape of Good Hope, and thirty–five species of insect in 'Gum Amonia': BM CE 3/10 2711 (14 November 1818).

118 Report by Leach BM CE 5/5 1218 (n.d. May 1817).

119 Report by Leach BM CE 5/5 1240–1 (9 July 1819).

120 Report by Leach BM CE 5/6 1326 (12 May 1820).

121 Report by Leach BM CE 5/6 1339 (8 June 1820). Moon to Banks, 8 May 1819, NHM B.C. 183–4.

122 As one Derbyshire example, bones from a mine at Matlock: Report by Konig BM CE 5/1 114 (12 May 1808).

123 Aall to Banks, 1 April 1812, U.W.ML.; Banks to [Aall], [*c.* April/May 1812], U.W.ML. These British Museum references are to fossilized wood presented by Banks, which he collected in 1772: BM CE 30/2 (9 May 1812); Report by Konig CE 5/2 452 (10 May 1812); CE 3/9 2525 (2 June 1812). In February 1812 he also gave more Icelandic Manuscripts: CE 30/2 (8 February 1812). A major gift of Icelandic rocks came in 1814: Report by Konig CE 5/3 611 (7 January 1814), comprising 938 geological specimens from Iceland, found by Dr Berger during travels in that country, and presented through Banks.

124 Banks to Hamilton, 27 November 1878, BL Egerton MS 2641, fols 141–2.

125 Report by Konig BM CE 5/1 241 (8 December 1809); CE 3/9 2438 (10 February 1810).

126 For a number of donations from Banks to do with the earth sciences, 1810–15: BM CE 3/9 2476 (8 December 1810) [Twenty-six volcanic specimens mostly from Guadalupe]; 2492 (6 April 1811) [ores from India]; 2499 (8 June 1811) [New Holland minerals]; 2512 (11 January 1812) [specimen of a named 'Alluvial Mass' from Brazil in which diamonds were reputedly found]; 2533 (14 November 1812) ['Native Magnesia, Green Tourmaline and Crystallized Mica', from Professor Bruce, a good North American contact: Report by Konig CE 5/2 481 (13 November 1812)]; CE 3/9 2538 (9 January 1813) [Banks conveyed a 'Slab of Tourmaline' from New South Wales from William Bligh, whom Banks selected and approached to be Colonial Governor in 1805]; 2540 (13 February 1813) [grains of 'gold' from Wicklow in Ireland]; 2549 (12 June 1813) [volcanic substance erupted on the Pacific island of Bourbon in September of 1812]; 2557 (13 November 1813) [volcanic substances erupted in the West Indies]; 2559 (11 December 1813) [more volcanic substance erupted in the West Indies, on Barbados and St Vincent]; 2563 (8 January 1814) [in Banks's name, from the Geological Society, some minerals from Ireland]; 2566 (12 February 1814) ['Gold' and rocks from Wicklow in Ireland, through Banks, and donated by the Royal Society]; 2575 (1 June 1814) [new mineral from Siberia, Russian]; 2582 (12 November 1814) [meteorite stone from Moravia, conveyed by Banks on behalf of the Imperial Museum of Vienna, and an iron meteorite sent by Professor Bruce of New York]; 2589 (14 January 1815) [collection of volcanic specimens from Guadalupe]. Banks's international contacts in this field remained strong and useful. For more gifts in January 1811 of silver ore from Buenos Aires and specimens found in Fuller's Earth: Report by Konig CE 5/2 348–50 (11 January 1811). Or there was the collection of South American minerals on which Konig had been working, sent to Banks by Humboldt and donated by Banks to the Museum: CE 5/2 372 (8 March 1811). Indeed, Konig's grateful Officers' Reports for the period make frequent and detailed mention of the material listed above and more. For example, one not reported to the Standing Committee was native silver from Peru: Report by Konig CE 5/3 649 (13 May 1814).

127 BM CE 3/8 2155 (2 November 1798).

128 BM CE 4/2 723–5 (11 May 1799), and NHM B.L. D.T.C. XII 225–31.

129 Report by Konig BM CE 5/2 314–15 (13 July 1810).

130 BM CE 4/3 1167 (17 January 1815, etc.) [with enclosures]. See also: CE 4/3 1180 (21 March 1815) [with enclosures]; 1192 (2 April 1815); 1196 (2 April 1815).

131 BM CE 1/5 1134–5 (11 February 1815); CE 3/9 2592 (11 March 1815).

132 Report by Konig BM CE 5/4 880 (11 July 1816), 1040 (12 December 1817); CE 3/10 2639 (16 November 1816); 2679 (8 November 1817); 2683 (13 December 1817); CE 4/4 1328–9 (n.d. received 13 July 1816); 1413 (26 September 1817); 1423 (10 February 1818).

133 Report by Konig BM CE 5/4 858–9 (10 May 1816).

134 Report by Konig BM CE 5/4 897–8 (8 November 1816); CE 3/10 2640 (16 November 1816).

135 Report by Konig BM CE 5/4 950 (7 March 1817), and the present contents of Room 10 to go to 8, with the nearly empty Room 1 to take any overflow.

136 Report by Konig BM CE 5/5 1215 (7 May 1819).

137 *Synopsis of the Contents of the British Museum* (London, 1820), pp.57–61.

138 W.J. Smith, 'The life and activities of Sir Ashton Lever of Alkrington, 1729–1788', *Transactions of the Lancashire and Cheshire Antiquarian Society* 72 (1962), p.91 on the contrast between specialist research collections and those of Lever. There are also useful quotations touching on the behaviour of Lever as a young man, pp.64–7, on reactions to him, pp.72–4 and p.80, and on the reasons why he decided to sell his collections, pp.80–4. On the specialization of Banks and the more generalist approach of the showmen, see also T. Iredale, 'Museums of the past', *The Australian Museum Magazine* 2, no. 3 (1924), p.89. Fanny Burney made some cutting remarks in 1782 about Lever's showiness and eccentricity: C. Barrett, *Diary and Letters of Madame D'Arblay* (London, 1904), vol. II, pp.167–8.

139 Blagden to Banks, 28 October 1777, NHM B.L. D.T.C. I 148–51.

140 R.D. Altick, *The Shows of London* (Cambridge, Mass.), pp.28–33, including some interesting reactions to Lever's collections, not least from a correspondent in the *Gentleman's Magazine* 43 (1773), pp.219–21, on their mixed character: quoted pp.28–9. Significantly, Altick also questions the simplistic view that both men disliked and soon shunned one another, p.32. The exchanges between Banks and the many collectors of his period indicate a far more complex set of relationships than that. A bitter remark reported by Joseph Farington is the one frequently adduced here: J. Greig (ed.), *The Farington Diary* (London, 1924), vol. III, p.273. Altick agrees with the general opinion that Lever disposed of his collection by lottery because he had overreached himself, p.29, and points out too that Lever raised his prices in order to exclude troublesome 'common People'.

141 In the end a number of Lever's birds went to Vienna: A. Pelzeln, 'II – On the birds in the Imperial collection at Vienna obtained from the Leverian Museum', *The Ibis, A Quarterly Journal of Ornithology*, no.9 (1873), pp.14–54; 'XIII – On the birds in the Imperial collection at Vienna obtained from the Leverian Museum' loc. cit. 3, no. 10 (1873), pp.106–24. Others stayed in Britain, being purchased by Lord Stanley, with some passing to the Liverpool Museum: M.J. Largen, 'Bird specimens purchased by Lord Stanley at the sale of the Leverian Museum in 1806, including those still extant in the collections of the Liverpool Museum', *Archives of Natural History* 14, pt 3 (1987), pp.265–88.

142 Banks to Peale, 1 December 1794, A.P.S.

143 For one view of the reasons why Lever disposed of his Museum, and Banks's role in that event: W.J. Smith, 'A museum for a guinea', *Country Life* 127, no.3288 (1960), pp.494–5.

144 Smith, op. cit. (note 138), p.84. As we have seen, these factors became especially prominent from 1815 onwards, but had always been evident to varying degrees.

145 H.M. Platnauer and E. Howarth (eds), A. Newton, 'Notes on some old museums', *Museums Association: Report of Proceedings with the paper read at the Annual General Meeting held at Cambridge, July 7th, 8th & 9th, 1891* (London, 1891), pp.39–40. It may be that the poor condition of the Leverian collections by 1806, and the large amounts being spent at this time by the British Museum on the Townley Marbles, which also needed new accommodation, in part explain the omission. On the state of the Leverian collections: Altick, op. cit. (note 140), p.32.

146 E.P. Alexander, 'William Bullock: A little-remembered museologist and showman', *Curator* 28, no.2 (1985), pp.117–47. Bullock produced catalogues to educate the public about his collections, and, importantly, to promote them. A number are held at the Natural History Museum, London, and Mullens, op. cit. (note 2), p.132, gives a full list. Bullock's later career was one of eventual decline. He indulged in speculative silver mining in Mexico, and retirement communities in Cincinnati, pp.136–9, but made

significant contributions to the pre-Columbian collection of the British Museum from his visits to the Americas. See also: J. Edmondson, 'The Regency Exhibitionists: a fresh look at the Bullocks', *The Linnean: Newsletter and Proceedings of the Linnean Society of London* 5, no.1 (1989), pp.17–26; E.G. Hancock, 'One of those dreadful combats – a surviving display from William Bullock's London Museum, 1807–1818', *Museums Journal* 79, no.4 (1980), pp.172–5; R.D. Altick, 'Snake was fake but Egyptian Hall wowed London', *Smithsonian* 9, no.1 (1978), pp.68–77.

147 Whitehead, op. cit. (note 52), pp.167–71; Medway, op. cit. (note 49), pp.339–40; A.L. Kaeppler, 'Cook voyage provenance of the "Artificial Curiosities" of Bullocks Museum', *Man: The Journal of the Royal Anthropological Institute* 9, no.1 (1974), pp.68–92; J.C. King, 'New evidence for the contents of the Leverian Museum', *Journal of the History of Collections* 8, no.2 (1996), pp.167–86. The claims made in various catalogues to items from Banks are sometimes open to dispute.

148 Bullock to Banks, 31 March 1819, Brabourne 149–50. Altick, op. cit. (note 140), p.235, opens his chapter on Bullock by referring to the Egyptian Hall as a 'miscellaneous-exhibition branch of the trade for almost a century'.

149 Alexander, op. cit. (note 146), pp.126–7; J.M. Sweet, 'William Bullock's collection and the University of Edinburgh, 1819', *Annals of Science* 26, no.1 (1970), especially pp.24–5; Altick, op. cit. (note 140), p.241.

150 *The History of the Collections contained in the Natural History Departments of the British Museum* (London, 1904–12), 2 vols, and Appendix, especially vol.II, pp.208–45. See also Sweet, op. cit. (note 149), pp.27–31; Altick, op. cit. (note 146), p.72.

151 Banks to Ferryman, 2 February 1788, RBG Kew b.c. I 294 (2).

152 Banks to Ferryman, 4 February 1788, RBG Kew b.c. I 295.

153 Altick, op. cit. (note 140), p.288: 'With the dispersal of the Leverian Museum in 1806 and of Bullock's collection a decade later, the era of museums modelled after the miscellaneous cabinets of old-time virtuosi ended'.

154 W.T. Stearn, *The Natural History Museum at South Kensington: A history of the Museum 1753–1980* (London, 1998), pp.22–3 and 279–87; *History of the Collections,* op. cit. (note 150), pp.79–84. Also: D.J. Mabberley, *Jupiter Botanicus: Robert Brown of the British Museum* (London, 1985), pp.261–8.

155 For an assessment of Sloane's great herbarium see J.F.M. Cannon, 'Botanical collections', chap.8 in A. MacGregor (ed.), *Sir Hans Sloane: Collector, scientist, antiquary: founding father of the British Museum* (London, 1994).

156 J. Dryander (ed.), *Catalogus Bibliothecae Historico-Naturalis Josephi Banks Baroneti* (London, 1796–1800). In five volumes, compiled by Banks's librarian, Jonas Dryander, and supervised by Banks himself, the publication's structure reflected the intellectual scope of Banks's interests, and the organization of his library. The first was vol.II: *Zoologi*, in 1796, which was followed by vol.III: *Botanici*, 1797, vol.I: *Scriptores Generales*, 1798, vol.IV: *Mineralogi*, 1799, and finally vol.v *Supplementum et Index Auctores*, 1800.

157 This was when, after protracted negotiations, Banks's main collections were transferred, with Brown being placed in charge of what was called the Banksian Department: BM CE 4/5 1946–7 (17 July 1823) [description of Banks's library in Soho Square]; *History of the Collections*, op. cit. (note 150), pp.79–81 [description of Banks's herbarium in Bloomsbury].

Figure 39
Portrait of Sir Joseph Banks FRS, FSA
painted shortly after the return of
HMS *Endeavour*, 1771, by Benjamin
West. It shows Banks as a South Sea
explorer, surrounded by ethnographic
and botanical materials, many of
which eventually came to the British
Museum. Lincolnshire County Council.

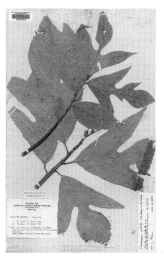

Figure 40
Specimen of *Artocarpus altilis*,
collected on Tahiti, Society
Islands, June–July 1769,
by Joseph Banks and Daniel
Solander during James Cook's
first voyage. London, Trustees
of the Natural History Museum.

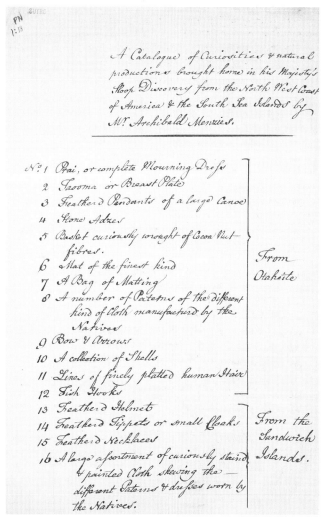

Figure 41
'A Catalogue of Curiosities &
natural productions brought
home in his Majesty's Sloop
Discovery from the North West
Coast of America & the South
Sea Islands by Mr. Archibald
Menzies.' Sutro Library,
California.

Chapter 14

'Ethnography' in the Enlightenment
John Mack

Much modern writing about historical ethnography has focused on the nature of the encounter between agents of Western culture and non-Western peoples, and how these came to be represented. The protagonists on the Western side were of mixed backgrounds. At one end, there were heroic voyagers lionized in their times by their peers. These might include natural historians, inspired by a search for new specimens with which to extend their taxonomic understanding of the natural world. They might also be mariners, often in search of supplies or local information about safe passage through waters to come. There were missionaries (in the eighteenth century usually members of one of the Catholic orders). And, of course, traders – most often attached to one of the larger trading companies – were also on the high seas. These travellers were supported by a motley crew of soldiery, mariners and administrators. On the other side, those with whom they met were equally of mixed backgrounds, not just ethnically, but of varying status amongst themselves – and these distinctions would often be unintelligible on initial contact. The negotiations – about goods and supplies, about cartographic or botanical knowledge – are the stuff of the ethnographic encounters. And the objects which were often acquired as part of such negotiation represent the origins of ethnographic collecting.

In this chapter the word 'ethnography' has been placed firmly in inverted commas. This is partly for the very obvious reason that the word itself was yet to be invented; but it is also to indicate that, for present purposes, the focus is much more on what was made of the reports of these encounters, on what would later become an intellectual discipline, than on the actual encounters themselves.

In a significant passage in his *Discourse on Inequality* of 1755, Rousseau reflects on the lack of direct experience of other human conditions amongst the leading minds of the French Enlightenment:

> Suppose a Montesquieu, a Buffon, a Diderot, a Duclos, a D'Alembert, a Condillac and other men of that stamp were to travel to instruct their compatriots, observing and describing as only they know how, Turkey, Egypt, Barbary, the Empire of Morocco, Guinea, the land of the Kaffirs, the interior and the East coast of Africa, the Malabars, Mogul, the banks of the Ganges, the kingdoms of Siam, Pegu and Ava, China, Tartary and above all Japan, and then in the other hemisphere, Mexico, Peru, Chile, and Magellan lands, not forgetting the Patagonians, true and false; Tucamen, Paraguay if possible, Brazil; finally the Caribbean islands, Florida and all the savage countries – the most important voyage of all, and the one that would have to be undertaken with the greatest possible care. Suppose that these new Hercules, on their return from these memorable journeys, then wrote at leisure the natural, moral and political history of what they had seen, we ourselves would see a new world spring from under their pens, and we should learn thereby to know our own world.[1]

Rousseau was writing nearly half a century before Joseph-Marie Degarando, the young philosopher from Lyon, wrote his *Considérations sur les méthodes à suivre dans l'observation des Peuples Sauvages* (translated as *The Observation of Savage Peoples*) which was conceived to inform the proposed expedition led by Nicolas-Thomas Baudin to the recently-discovered Australia. The great minds of the French Enlightenment had to make do with what they were served up in the traveller's accounts and the reports of missionaries, and others, without either direct experience themselves or the opportunity to develop their own questions to inform the enquiry of potential interlocutors. Montesquieu might have described the everyday life of a Persian seraglio in his *Lettres Persanes* of 1721; however, this was an imaginary, fictitious account in the mode of Mandeville's *Fable of the Bees*, designed to take a side-swipe at French society rather than as a substantial gesture towards ethnographic study.

What applies to France also applies to Scotland and indeed elsewhere in Britain and Europe. Hume, Ferguson, Smith, the Lords Kames and Monboddo – all reflected on the moral and human condition from the comfort of the armchair. There is an irony here, since amongst the Scots in particular there was a strong swing away from the Cartesian reliance on the primacy of reason to arrive at an understanding of human nature. Instead, what emerged was an assertion of the primacy of feeling, sensation and experience as the fundamentals of a definition of the basis of human action. Hume went further and included belief.[2] Yet none of these moral philosophers had the experience of travel, of cultural dislocation, as the spur to reflection that Rousseau had recommended. Introspection, rather than the mind-expanding effects of distant lands and exposure to unfamiliar cultures, was the leading stimulus of the Enlightenment imagination, a self-reflective approach, tempered only by the reading of such first-hand accounts of non-European cultural experience as others had thought to record. Unlike the natural sciences, where the leading figures of the eighteenth century – notably Sir Joseph Banks in the Pacific – served their apprenticeships as natural historians on voyages of discovery, the leading minds in the human sciences mostly stayed home.

Yet, if the moral philosophers of the Enlightenment (Scottish or French) did not themselves voyage to distant destinations in the manner of the natural historians, the questions they posed were no less fundamental. They sought to define human nature through its social and individual expressions. But on the basis of what evidence? The issue remains as to what they could actually know of non-Western cultures as the ground for their speculations on the human condition, and what they made of the evidence before them. The evidence was in two forms: the written accounts of the host of mariners, missionaries, traders, natural scientists, and administrators who had occasion to visit foreign lands; and objects brought back as a by-product of their various encounters. Each form of evidence will here be discussed in turn.

'Histories' and 'manners'

One of the most influential works of the Scottish Enlightenment was Adam Ferguson's classic *An Essay on the History of Civil Society* (1767). This is a general reflection drawing on a wealth of identifiable sources in selecting material for comment as examples of different stages in the development of the civil state. For his reflections on the character of so-called 'rude' societies, Ferguson relied on a limited number of usually identifiable works, the most prominent of these being Joseph-Marie Lafitau, *Moeurs des sauvages amériquains, comparées aux moeurs des premiers temps* of 1724, Pierre-François-Xavier de Charlevoix, *Histoire et description générale de la Nouvelle France* (Canada) of 1744, Abulgaze Bahadur Chan, *Genealogical History of the Tartars*, *A Collection of Dutch Voyages*, *A History of the Caribbees* (no author cited), Kolbe's *Description of the Cape of Good Hope*, and D'Arvieux's *History of the Wild Arabs*.

It was one indication of the relative paucity of sources available to be consulted that the two most prominent used by Ferguson, both by Jesuit missionaries writing about Native Americans, were by no means recent publications even in the late 1760s. Charlevoix's study was based on his work in the opening decade of the eighteenth century and a more formal royal expedition from 1720–2; Lafitau had lived among the Catholic Mohawk of Saint Louis du Sault (now known as the Kahnawake) from 1712 to 1717. And both works, which were in very limited supply in Britain, remained untranslated from French – in one case until the latter half of the nineteenth century[3], and in the other until less than thirty years ago.[4]

It is also interesting that, with the exception of Lafitau, all are presented by their titles as 'histories' of one sort or another. This has been seen as significant. Lafitau's *Manners* already heralds a more ethnographic style of description and he has, indeed, been regarded as more than just an early source on Iroquoian ethnography; he is also credited with anticipating a more anthropological style of analysis and being the first (well before Lewis Henry Morgan)[5] to describe matrilineal descent and classificatory kinship terminologies. But this is deceptive. As Christian Feest has recently pointed out,[6] Lafitau did not set out to write an ethnographic monograph but to characterize, through imagining native life before contact, a generic Native American culture: '. . . the trade with European nations has made the Indians lose many of their ancient folkways and altered their ways of living. I examine this culture and these customs as they were before their alteration, as they had been received from their ancestors.'[7] Lafitau proceeds to compare this imagined state to classical antiquity and European traditions of chivalry. He, like many of the period, was enthralled by the idea of the Great Chain of Being, engaged in that kind of time-shifting which emerged in a less benign form in nineteenth-century social evolutionary paradigms.

Yet things are not quite so unambiguous as this might make them appear. Lafitau's description is at once laudatory and critical. Whilst he expounds on the virtues of brave and chivalrous warriors, he is obliged to decry the torturing of captured enemies or the practice of geronticide – killing the elderly when they cease to contribute to society. Similar ambiguities are found in Charlevoix. It is worth examining a particular personification, the case of the famous Huron chief Kondiaronk. Charlevoix positively eulogizes Kondiaronk's abilities and charm; he was a man of exceptional ability and bravery, an eloquent speaker, an engaging guest at the table of the French Governor of Canada – 'the Indian of the highest merit that the French ever knew in Canada'. At his death Kondiaronk was given full French military honours and was buried in the cathedral at Montreal.[8] Charlevoix, however, recounts another side to the otherwise estimable character of the heroic Huron figure. We learn that he was instrumental in ambushing and killing a number of Iroquoian ambassadors and spreading the view that this was a piece of treachery enacted by unreliable and untrustworthy French colonialists.[9] From these and other sources, an older habit of mind which sought to construct a Golden Age of innocence and contentedness with nature was beginning to be compromised. The concept of nobility no longer went unchallenged in qualifying savagery. The philosophical construct was meeting the realities of tougher, more ignoble lives as Man's freedom was, to echo Rousseau, already starting to be characterized as enchained.

So what did Ferguson take from such sources? It is characteristic of Ferguson (and fellow Enlightenment philosophers) that what he chooses for comment are isolated details, usually of a strongly anecdotal character, and almost always unattributed to any particular society or culture.

> The writer [Charlevoix] has observed, that the nations among whom he travelled in North America, never mentioned acts of generosity or kindness under the notion of duty. They acted from affection, as they acted from appetite, without regard to its consequences. When they had done a kindness, they had gratified a desire; the business was finished, and passed from memory . . .[10]

Here, then, a somewhat casual, generalized impression of native motivation acts to illustrate a classic Scottish Enlightenment proposition. Implicit in the comment is the appeal to sense and feeling as the source of action. In this scheme of things 'reason' no longer holds sway in the definition of human nature – things simply do not lodge in the mind to become the basis of reasoning. They pass from memory. There is an assertion of common humanity, but at the same time the distancing assertion of an alternative moral condition: the presence in the European tradition of a sense of duty which is lacking in Native America.

Or again, drawing on Tacitus, Lafitau and Charlevoix as his acknowledged sources, Ferguson describes what he sees as the human predilection for games of chance:

> Games of hazard are not the invention of polished ages; men of curiosity have looked for their origin, in vain, among the monuments of an obscure antiquity; and it is probable that they belonged to times too remote and too rude even for the conjectures of antiquarians to reach. The very savage brings his furs, his utensils, and his beads to the hazard-table: he finds here the passions and agitations which the applications of tedious industry

John Mack

could not excite: and while the throw is depending, he tears his hair, and beats his breast, with a rage which the more accomplished gamester has learned to repress: he often quits the party naked, and stripped of all his possessions; or where slavery is in use, stakes his freedom to have one chance more to recover his former loss.[11]

What is served up in this highly coloured account of the ubiquity of the gaming table is an unspecific composite image. Particularity, detail, is not the issue: Ferguson is in search of general principles. Once seized of these, the construction of the character of civil society follows unimpeded by awkward facts. Dr Johnson, a few years later, remarked: 'I could write a better book of cookery than has ever yet been written; it should be a book upon philosophical principles'.[12] It was not a matter of deriving the general from the analysis of the particular, but of submerging the detail in the exposition of immutable principles. In the process the specificity of ethnographical reference – to the extent that it could be found in the source material – was forfeited.

Like most of his sources, Ferguson was writing a self-declared 'history'. Yet none of these texts recites the detail of chronological sequences of events, traces cause-and-effect, or indeed provides the reader with an expected diet of dates. The superstructure of a conventional history is not present. What we see is the emergent model that was to evolve through the later eighteenth and nineteenth centuries to Edward Burnet Tylor's *Early History of Mankind* (1865) and beyond – in Ferguson's case, a conjectured three-stage development from an original state of 'rudeness', through various applications of moral 'polish', to the maturity of 'civil society' (a term which later slipped into 'civilization'). Native Americans illustrate, in Ferguson's incipient model, the state of human infancy. For the armchair philosopher, such taxonomic games were an uncomplicated form of pseudo-judicial finding, underwritten by predetermined general laws and taken on the basis of written submissions without the need to confront actual witnesses.

Yet the Noble Savage, that entity close to nature and lurking within the psyche of everyman, was also loose in Europe itself. Not all 'savage' conditions could be classified in isolation from the reality. By Rousseau's time there were already some 'great minds' which had confronted other cultures, albeit in pursuit of other than anthropological aims. Ferguson took as the leading exemplars of his various stages of humanity Native Americans, Greeks, Romans, Dark Age English and Swedes. Others, however, ventured northwards deeper into the Baltic states. The Lapps (now referred to as the Saami) were the subject of some speculation in eighteenth-century Europe and they received some notable visitors – most notable of all perhaps Carl von Linné (otherwise Linnaeus), who visited Lapland in 1732. It is interesting that it should have been a serious student of the natural sciences who has provided us with the most impressive record of eighteenth-century Saami life, just as later in the century it should have been a meticulous navigator, the ill-fated Captain Bligh, who left us an admirably detailed account of Tahitian culture. The best 'ethnography' emerged in the service of other disciplines where detailed accounting was an essential and approved methodology.

Linnaeus's approach was that of scrupulous note-taking in the form of a comprehensive diary. The contrast with the impressions of a later observer, or rather, intruder into Lapland, the aristocratic Italian philosopher Giuseppi Acerbi, could

hardly be starker. Acerbi's approach is voyeuristic: he spies on saunas, he recoils at dirt and smell. Linnaeus certainly reports what anthropologists in later centuries would recognize as culture shock. But it was a culture shock with a resolution which was to lead to his admirable account of Saami life, customs and technology. 'O thou poor man! What hard destiny can have brought thee hither, to a place never visited by anyone before?' – not, as it happens, Linnaeus in a soliloquy of deep despond, but the reported words of a Saami woman offering hospitality and sympathy. This was an encounter which, together with the constant guidance of an excellent translator, brought Linnaeus to positive conclusions. He marvels at the Saami ability to tell one reindeer from another in a vast herd – like telling 'ants apart on an anthill'– at the balance of exploitation of resources, focusing on fishing in the summer months and reindeer milk and meat for the rest of the year. He sees Saami life as an expression of Ovid's silver age when ploughs and agriculture are yet to develop, when wars are unnecessary and when people move from place to place 'just like the patriarchs of old'. 'I witnessed with pleasure', he concludes, 'the supreme tranquility enjoyed by the inhabitants of this sequestered country.'[13] His is the style of participant observation mixed with scientific method and endeavour – as appropriate an attitudinal basis for thinking about the origins of ethnography as the tomes of moral philosophy.

'Miscellanies' and 'curiosities'

To this point the textual evidence available to Enlightenment thinkers has largely been considered. But what of more immediate and direct evidence? Objects too were beginning to become available for inspection and discussion. The whole thrust of this volume concerns the development of learning and of the institution of the museum in the eighteenth century. So what objects were available, and what significance were they accorded?

Sloane's collection actually reflects quite well the interests which Ferguson was later to pick up on and which have been discussed above. There were objects from the shores of North America, and there were two Saami drums, costumes, a sled and other materials – products of Sloane's wide network of contacts from around the known world. The Saami objects cannot be associated directly with Linnaeus, and indeed one of the drums is dated by an accompanying manuscript to c.1706,[14] before Linnaeus's visit to Lapland. But Linnaeus did visit Sloane in August 1736, and a decade later, in 1748, Sloane was also visited by Per Kalm, a pupil of Linnaeus who, like his mentor, was interested largely in the display of the natural history specimens and the degree of scientific order the system of physical arrangement achieved. Kalm too noted the existence of the Saami drum, but without comment.

The ethnographic objects Sloane assembled have been well-researched and recorded elsewhere. Bushnell[15] limited his count to thirty-four North American pieces, Braunholz[16] thought there were about 350 ethnographic objects in the original collection and King[17] gives a yet more generous estimate of at least 1,200 and provides the most complete description. Many of the objects listed in the original catalogues no longer exist and those that remain are important to contemporary students of historical ethnography on account of their rarity. But it has to be said that the ethnographic collection was almost entirely composed of modest objects, the kinds of acquisition which casual or chance encounter might be expected to produce: bows, arrows, clubs, knives, fishing gear, baskets, textiles, gourds, pipes, and so forth. Furthermore, the collection was dominated, again as might be expected, by objects from riverine or coastal regions, rather than from deeper into any island or continental interior.

Nonetheless, when, subsequent to Sloane's death and the bequest which established the British Museum, the collections were moved to Montagu House, their arrangement had an underlying rationale which strongly recalls the main tenets of Enlightenment thinking – as with the natural sciences, the arrangement of the collections was a direct conscious reflection of classificatory thinking. The 1761 guide to the collections, for instance, echoes much of what we have encountered in Lafitau. Displayed beside antiquities,

> ... we here find many modern Articles brought from distant nations, particularly from the several Parts of the new World of *America*, which serve to discover the Industry, Genius, and Manners of the Inhabitants. Happy for them were they now content with the little that once satisfied them; but the polite *Europeans*, since the Discovery of those Parts, have, by encreasing Wants, deprived them of their Ease, convincing them that they have many Things to wish for ... [18]

Some gloss on this is offered in the second edition of 1762 where, in a manner loosely suggestive of the arguments of David Hume, material to do with religion and belief is described together on the basis of its display in the same room or run of cases. American idols were juxtaposed with Japanese figures from pagodas, Islamic charms and inscription with Christian antidotes to witchcraft and enchantment. Comparison with the Roman preoccupation with household gods is introduced. And thus the whole conforms to a general scheme of ontological linkage.

Clearly, this classification can have none of the rigour of Linnaean or other taxonomy in the natural sciences. Indeed rigour, when it arrived, was largely associated with the racial classifications of the nineteenth century. At the same time, however, we can detect little of the detailed and informed engagement with objects as a form of historical evidence that we get in the reports of the discussions of the learned societies a century later.

The Society of Antiquaries of Scotland in Edinburgh, for instance, appears to have had no presentations on non-Caledonian subjects, with the exception of the occasional discussion of the Classics. It was established to do specifically for Scotland what the Society of Antiquaries in London considered on a broader basis, and it stuck rigorously to its brief – thus the diet at the regular meetings was a predictable confection of accounts based on parish histories, the record of Highland clan rivalries, or the history of the Caledonian bards. The Earl of Buchan's address as President on 'An Authentic account of the admirable Crichton' (January 1781) must have seemed a diversion in the miscellany of events. However, a society with such serious and influential luminaries of the Enlightenment as Lords Monboddo and Kames, and Honorary members of the stature of Diderot and the Comte de Buffon, was hardly engaged in a desperate search for light relief. There appears to have been no discussion in a formal context of wider ethnographical, as we would now say, or cultural matters.

Even so, the collections of the Society did begin to accumulate significant ethnographical objects to add to its Scottish focus. The inauguration of the Society, in 1780, had been a significant year. In May, a Caribbean bow and five arrows from the Island of Saint Vincent were donated by one Patrick Cruicksbank of Strickatho, although that was only a taster for a gift of more enduring importance. In July, the annals of the Society record the acquisition from Sir John Pringle, himself a moral philosopher and (in succession to Sir Hans Sloane) a royal physician, of 'a collection of the productions of Otaheite, the Sandwich Islands, and the west coast of North America, on the South Sea, made by the late Captain Cooke [*sic*] in his last voyage round the world and given to Sir John by Captain Cooke's widow ... '. Exotic objects were available, the museological context for the comparison of ancient British antiquity and non-European materials was in place – but, it seems, did not long divert the *philosophes* of Edinburgh.

Three terms stand out in such discussion as there is of ethnographic objects in the period. In catalogues, 'miscellanies' and 'artificial curiosities', a more general term for humanly created artefacts, recur. There is some overlap here: whilst all artificial curiosities might reasonably be classified as miscellanies, not all miscellanies were necessarily artificial curiosities. Miscellanies in Sloane's catalogues included ethnography, medical and scientific instruments and raw materials, objects made from obscure materials or other exotic sources, unique historical or personal relics. Ethnography lived in this category beside artificial body parts, medical instruments and remedies for a variety of physical conditions from gout to snake bites, a beaded necklace made by a woman without hands, as well as Christian relics and liturgical clothing.[19] Artificial curiosities were compared to natural curiosities on the basis of whether the object was worked by human hand (or, in some special circumstances, not).

In the vocabulary of moral philosophy, the third word 'curiosity' is central. It is incarnate in both the 1749 codicil to Sloane's will and the founding Act of Parliament of the British Museum: the will talks of 'satisfying the desire of the curious'[20] and the Act of Parliament of maintaining the Museum and collection 'not only for the Inspection and Entertainment of the learned and curious, but for the general Use and Benefit of the Public'.[21] There is already an excellent exposition of the range of meaning of this key term, curiosity, in its Enlightenment incarnation by Nicholas Thomas.[22] This essay echoes aspects of his discussion in the context of the remarks which have already been made.

In later usage the term 'curio' has come to refer to an artefact with a somewhat exotic or incompletely known provenance. This is the nineteenth-century meaning, one which has survived to the present and implies something like objectified oddity, something not 'of us', distanced, subject to intellectual processes which occasioned no self-reflection in the Victorian mind – at once idolatrous, fetishistic and ambivalent. From the documents concerning the foundation of the British Museum it will be evident that for the eighteenth century curiosity is in the eye of the beholder, rather than being an intrinsic quality in the object itself. It was in that sense still 'of us', or capable of being drawn into our world of sensible experience. For the eighteenth century, it is important to emphasize the observer's own sensation and experience, and his confidence in its validity, rather than rationality with its strategies of intellectual disavowal, as the classic definition of the Enlightenment philosophical programme. Thomas quotes Lord Kames's observation that 'love of novelty . . . prevails in children, in idlers and in men of shallow understanding; while curiosity might legitimately be indulged in order to acquire knowledge'.[23] Curiosity is an indulgence, an appetite, something innate to be satisfied, and something to be cultivated beyond the mere instinct for the new.

This is an important underlay to any discussion of the origins of museology in the Enlightenment. Thomas dwells on the apparently puzzling disjunction between the grand sweeping illustrations of William Hodges showing Cook's landings and his engagements with indigenous Polynesians, and the decontextualization of the objects which illustrate the narratives in the same volumes. In a museum context encounters are made in the same spirit. The objects are not imbued with significance 'in themselves' but with *potential* significance depending on the capacity for curiosity in the observer. Curiosity is lodged in the eye and mind of the beholder, not in the thing beheld.

In truth, however, ethnography did little to excite general curiosity in its first incarnations. Where it did, it was largely as an aside – an addendum to the main business of the men of science. Arguably what made the difference was Captain Cook. A description of a visit to the Museum by the German traveller Sophie von La Roche in 1786 makes the point. In her diary she recalls the impact made on her by the display of the collections of 'that luckless, excellent man' Captain Cook: '. . . all the pots, weapons and clothes from the South Sea islands just recently discovered, are on view there, just as they are shown in the prints illustrating the description of his voyage'.[24] The objects have a fascination at least in part because they are personalized to the encounters, and ultimately the demise, of a heroic figure. But, beyond that Sophie von La Roche goes on to reflect in a way expected of the curious on what all this might mean, concluding:

> On the whole . . . Roman, Greek and Carthaginian remains, swathings of Egyptian mummies, South Sea islanders' apparel and portraits of English royal personages or of those we see around us still, all prove that vanity and imperiousness led people at all times and in all places to ornament and [to] instruments of destruction, just as sounds of joy produced song, tripping merriment led to dance, passionate gesture to a groping after language.[25]

She was not alone. The Otaheite or South Sea Room, first proposed in 1775, was to be a major public draw. It is perhaps strange that the last part of the globe to become known to the Western world should have been the first in the British Museum to be set up with a specific geographic and cultural reference. That in large part reflects the influence of Sir Joseph Banks,

who, though a natural scientist at heart, garbed himself in a cloak of ethnographic interest. As a long-lived and influential trustee of the British Museum, his support for the display of Pacific collections was to prove crucial. Ironically, it was also the popularity of the South Sea Room which, well into the nineteenth century, saved ethnography from expulsion from Bloomsbury when it was in question as to which of the more popular public attractions could sustain attendance at a new venue and what in its absence could sustain the Bloomsbury site. In the outcome of that debate lie the origins of the Natural History Museum.

Notes and references
1 Jean-Jacques Rousseau, *A Discourse in Inequality* (1755), trans. Maurice Cranston (London, 1984), p.161.
2 See the discussion, for instance, in Gladys Bryson, *Man and Society: The Scottish enquiry of the eighteenth century* (Princeton, 1954), chap.1.
3 Pierre-François-Xavier de Charlevoix, *History and General description of New France*, trans. and ed. J.G. Shea (New York, 1868).
4 Joseph François Lafitau, *Customs of the American Indians compared with the Customs of primitive Times*, ed. and trans. W.N. Fenton and E.L. Moore (Toronto, 1974–7).
5 Lewis Henry Morgan, *Ancient Society of Researches in the Lines of Human Progress from Savagery through Barbarism to Civilisation* (New York, 1877). See also Meyer Fortes, *Kinship and the Social order: The Legacy of Lewis Henry Morgan* (London, 1969).
6 Christian F. Feest, 'Father Lafitau as ethnographer of the Iroquois', *European Review of Native American Studies* 15:2 (2001), pp.19–25.
7 Ibid., p.23.
8 Ter Ellingson, *The Myth of the Noble Savage* (Berkley and Los Angeles, 2001), pp.73–4.
9 Ibid., p.75.
10 Adam Ferguson, *An Essay on the History of Civil Society* (1767), ed. Duncan Forbes (Edinburgh, 1966), p.87.
11 Ibid., pp.93–4.
12 As quoted in Bryson, op. cit. (note 2), p.15.
13 As quoted in Ellingson, op. cit. (note 8), p.134.
14 J.C.H. King, 'Ethnographic collections: collecting in the context of Sloane's catalogue of "Miscellanies", in Arthur MacGregor (ed.), *Sir Hans Sloane: Collector, scientist, antiquary; founding father of the British Museum* (London, 1994), p.244, n.112.
15 David Bushnell Jnr, 'The Sloane collection in the British Museum', *American Anthropologist*, new ser. 8 (1906), pp.611–85.
16 H. J. Braunholz, *Sir Hans Sloane and Ethnography* (London, 1970).
17 King, op. cit. (note 14), pp.228–44.
18 [Edmund Powlett], *The General Contents of the British Museum with Remarks. Serving as a Directory in viewing that Noble Cabinet* (London, 1761), printed by R. and J. Dodsley, p.20.
19 Braunholz, op. cit. (note 16); King, op. cit. (note 14).
20 Marjorie Caygill, 'Sloane's will and the establishment of the British Museum', in MacGregor, op. cit. (note 14), p. 47.
21 Ibid, p. 50.
22 Nicholas Thomas, 'Licensed curiosity: Cook's Pacific voyages', in John Elsner and Roger Cardinal (eds), *The Cultures of Collecting* (Cambridge, Mass., 1994), pp.116–36.
23 Ibid., p.123.
24 Maria Sophie von la Roche, *Sophie in London, 1786: Being the Diary of Sophie v. la Roche*, trans. Clare Williams (London, 1933), p.109.
25 Ibid., p.110.

Chapter 15

European Responses to the Sacred Art of India
Partha Mitter

In the eighteenth century, closely following on the heels of the British seizure of India, European scholars began documenting Indian monuments methodically and comprehensively. They thus provided essential sources for the writing of an art history for India by the end of the nineteenth century. But while colonial documentation of ancient Buddhist and Hindu art and architecture was impressive, aesthetic appreciation of ancient Indian art remained inadequate and was informed by classical and neo-classical strictures on artistic taste. A typical comment was made by the art historian Vincent Smith who was convinced that, although Hindu sculpture enjoyed a respectable second rank within the world's art, it could hardly compare with the perfection of a classical Apollo or Aphrodite. Even today, judged by Western classical standards, the many-armed Hindu gods and goddesses are viewed as monsters: in other words, irrational or contra naturam.[1]

In order to understand eighteenth-century Western reactions to Indian art in the Enlightenment, it is essential to return to the beginnings of European explorations of the non-Western world at the close of the Middle Ages. The roots of Western ideas about Indian art are to be found in the medieval period, above all in the Graeco-Roman tradition it had inherited. In the Middle Ages, India had been reduced to a mythical land, where the earthly paradise was located and where monsters, lovingly described by the ancient Greeks, lived. Stories of monopods, cynocaephali, martikhora and many-armed creatures formed the collective fantasy of the educated. Significantly, Herman Schedel's 1493 Nuremberg Chronicle, compiled at the end of the Middle Ages, included among its compendium of monsters an anomalous multiple-armed creature, a creature that was, in fact, a garbled version of a Hindu god. The representation of Hindu gods as monsters was amazingly persistent. When the first travellers published descriptions of Hindu gods encountered during their visit to India, they preferred to quote what they had read in Pliny the Elder's Natural History rather than trust their own sight.[2]

The clash of classical and Indian taste in these encounters is, of course, important in this context. But perhaps even more crucial is the religious dimension to early Western responses to Indian art. First, the art which the travellers saw, namely, Hindu temple sculpture and architecture, was profoundly religious. Secondly, early European interest in Hindu sacred art is not at all surprising, given the fact that this was the age of faith in the West.

The reactions to Hindu gods demonstrate the clash of two major faiths, Christianity and Hinduism: the one a religion of the book that believed in unity, uniformity and the suppression of dissent, while the other was a form of pluralism that embraced a bewildering variety of views and beliefs accumulated over millennia. From the moment early explorers set foot on Indian soil, after long and hazardous land or sea journeys, they were faced with the problem of making sense of that vast theatre of idolatry that was India. For if, as the early Church Fathers had admonished (and the Bible confirmed), monotheism was God's precious gift to Adam, how was it that he had left such a teeming population of pagans in this dire abyss of idolatry? Idolatry fascinated, as well as perplexed, the first visitors to India.

Early reports, which contributed to the growing image of the Hindus, their religion and their religious art, were at once fragmented, discrete and disparate, and yet so sensational that they were extensively published in a number of European languages, obsessively read and endlessly discussed by the erudite. The full extent of idolatry, perpetrated by pagans the world over, dawned only slowly among the literati of the West. Initially, travellers felt confident (and with some justification) that Indians had been converted to Christianity by St Thomas the Apostle, and believed that they would prove to be valuable allies against the Turks, who were threatening Western Christendom. There is, for example, the story of the Portuguese explorer Vasco da Gama's arrival in South India in 1498:

> [In Calicut] they took us to a large church . . . built of hewn stone. Within this sanctuary stood a small image which they said represented Our Lady . . . Within this church the captain-major [da Gama] said his prayers, and we with him. [The priests] threw holy water over us [and] some white earth, which the Christians of this country are in the habit of putting on [their bodies].[3]

Only later did the Portuguese discover to their chagrin that the Brahmin priests were celebrating the worship of the local goddess, Mari Ammai.

One of the unquestionable gains of the early European travellers was their first-hand experience of India and its people. Yet they could not help constantly recalling the medieval legends they knew by heart. Brahmins, for instance, called gymnosophists or naked philosophers by the ancients, displayed in their simple lives all the traits of the Christian saint and philosopher. The legend was confirmed by a medieval text, the Alexander Romance, which described how the Brahmins had taught the brash young emperor the folly of hubris and worldly riches in a typical Indian fashion that has continued to hold westerners in its grip.[4]

In travel accounts from the fifteenth century, the more theological elements, such as the origins and nature of polytheism and tales about Brahmins mingled happily with sensational items like suttee (sati or self-immolation of widows) or the antics of Indian yogis. In an age when there were no package tours to exotic locations or the voyeuristic pleasures of television, these descriptions formed the stuff of collective fantasy. For the early travellers, the country was a virtual *terra incognita*. One can therefore appreciate the enormous problems they faced. From the outset, there were persistent attempts to fit the new material on Indian idolatry into the familiar mould of Biblical and Patristic literature – the accommodation of the unfamiliar into a familiar mind-set. Naturally, the travellers took as their guide the memorable passages in Pliny or the *Alexander Romance*. That redoubtable compiler of voyages, the Revd Samuel Purchas, for instance, devotes long chapters, in a weighty volume, to travellers to the East, from ancient times to his own period.[5]

One thing becomes quite clear: whether accounts were written by Catholics or Protestants, religious matters were paramount to all of them. Despite holding Hindus to be idolaters, Europeans could not help being moved by the fortitude of the widow to be burned at the funeral pyre, or shaken by the strong fervour with which Jains and Brahmins held their vegetarian principles. It was the particular form of idolatry practised by the Hindus that aroused the greatest curiosity among Europeans. Accordingly, different strategies were devised to answer the problems raised by Hinduism.

Western perceptions of alien religions, more than any other aspect of culture, take us to the very heart of the problem of translating concepts and values of one system into another, very different one. When scholars engage in the act of translating, they in fact search for equivalents that may make sense. But the problem was that Christianity and Hinduism represented two very different world views – what Husserl has called 'two different ways of bracketing respective experiences'.[6] From their perspective, European travellers faced a central problem of faith: were the Hindus monotheistic or polytheistic? It must be said that this is not the sort of question that engages Hindus. The binary opposition between monotheism and polytheism – if god is not one then he must be many – makes sense only in the West. In a monotheistic religion, God's divinity is absolute. He is the unique other – in sum precisely what humans are not. Thus monotheism must have polytheism as its binary opposite. The Indian religious universe is very different in its relativism. It is peopled with living beings, hierarchically ordered, and joined in a unifying chain of reincarnation. From this perspective, the supreme deity in Hinduism is transcendental, but at the same time God can relate to the devotee on a human level. Divinity in Hinduism can be on a number of levels, ultimately reaching the godhead.

The problem of accommodating idolatry arose initially in connection with the gods of ancient Greece and Rome. In an interesting paper, Francis Schmidt speaks of the shift in Western definition of non-Christians from idolaters to polytheists around 1580.[7] The question posed was this: how did the error of idolatry arise in view of God's gift of monotheism to mankind? Catholics appealed to the apocryphal text *The Wisdom of Solomon*, which fixed the transgression in the antediluvian era, while Protestants preferred to trust Maimonides, who viewed it as arising after the Flood. Europeans were also influenced by the prevailing notions of pagans: firstly, that Christianity, the most ancient religion, taught monotheism to pagans; secondly, that pagans let this knowledge lapse; lastly, that the higher forms of paganism prefigured the arrival of the Evangelists.

Given this framework, European visitors set about recovering the 'monotheism' concealed behind the garbled forms of Hindu polytheism. In so doing, they became aware of the syncretistic tendency of Hinduism to reconcile and unify different belief systems. The best-known visitor to Calicut after Vasco da Gama was the Italian, Ludovico di Varthema, in the sixteenth century. He concluded from his visit that even though the Hindus had received the revelation, they nonetheless persisted in worshipping many false gods. According to him, the Indians acknowledged one god, who created heaven and earth. But they also held that, as God did not wish to take on the task of judging, he sent his spirit, that is, the devil, to dispense justice. Having established the ultimate terms of Hindu monotheism to his satisfaction, Varthema proceeded to devote most of his attention to the demon worship of Calicut, based, as he claimed, on observation:

> In the midst of the chapel of the king of Calicut sits a devil made of metal on the seat in the flame of fire; he has four horns, four teeth and wears a triple crown like that worn by the Pope, and most terrible eyes. The said devil holds a soul in his mouth with the right hand, and with the other seizes a soul by the waist . . .[8]

It has been demonstrated elsewhere, however, that this is no Hindu god, but a conflation of different images of the Antichrist of the Middle Ages.[9] It should therefore be asked why Varthema, if, as he claims, he had visited the chapel of the king of Calicut, used medieval stereotypes to describe a Hindu god? It is clear that he wished to translate a strange and unfamiliar image into a language readily understood by his contemporaries. Yet at this time knowledge about Hindu religion and Hindu iconography was rudimentary. Thus Varthema was forced to fall back upon his inherited values. His values, in turn, were determined by his Christian background which considered all non-Christian religions as devil-inspired.

The fact that Varthema was describing something familiar was immediately grasped by his German illustrator, Georg Breu, who used several different traditions for his accompanying engraving (fig.42). The towering figure of Satan devouring sinners, while his attendant creatures torture the damned, is reminiscent of a celebrated fresco attributed to Francesco Traini at the Campo Santo in Pisa. The triple crown alludes to the image of those popes consigned to Hell; and most notably to that described by Dante. The reference to three crowns, four teeth and four horns plays on numbers, suggesting a reference to the dragon of the Apocalypse. The dragon, of course, represented the pagan empires of the East.[10]

In this way, Varthema established the traditional Western view of demon worship in India, a tradition that was to haunt Western imagination until the seventeenth century. The Dutchman Jan Huygen van Linschoten, who visited India briefly in the late sixteenth century, was associated with the Inquisition in Goa. Linschoten conceded that the Hindus acknowledged one god, but that this knowledge was perverted by devil worship, a perversion engineered by Satan himself. Predictably, for his description of Hindu gods, he turned to Varthema's celebrated devil of Calicut. Varthema's description was also used by Linschoten's engraver, Baptista à Doetechum, who placed this monster in the actual setting of the temple at Elephanta (fig.43). Finally, Linschoten offered the prayer that God should grant the Hindus enlightenment, because 'they are like us in all other respects, made after God's image and He will release them from Satan's bondage'.[11]

The seventeenth century marks a turning-point that paved the way towards a more objective study of Hinduism and to the discipline of comparative religion. This was anticipated in a very different tradition that used a classical framework to explain Hinduism. The circle of humanists that included the painter Peter Paul Rubens, the antiquary Girolamo Aleandro, the mythographer Lorenzo Pignoria and the French collector Nicholas Claude Fabri de Peiresc, was made up primarily of intellectuals and collectors of exotica. It was a group which expressed a genuine interest in other religions. In 1615, Pignoria republished Vincenzo Cartari's standard work, *Images of the Gods*, in which he included a Hindu god, this time not a monster but an image based on authentic sources. Pignoria traced the origins of the Hindu god Ganesha in Egyptian idolatry (fig.44).[12] In fact, his circle was ambitiously trying to formulate a universal theory of religion by the comparative study of paganism, a theory which traced all religions back to ancient Egypt. His Ganesha was a composite image, based on two sources. One source described the elephant-headed Hindu god; the other mentioned the four-headed Śiva Maheśa in the rock-cut temple at Elephanta, possibly the most famous Indian image in the West since the sixteenth century. Information on both was sent by the Jesuits in Goa between 1553 and 1560. Frances Yates has moreover demonstrated the abiding Renaissance and post-Renaissance interest in the concept of *ex oriente lux* (light from the east) – an interest in Egyptian hieroglyphs, Chaldean astrology and Indian gymnosophists, all examples of pagan wisdom prefiguring Christ's revelation.[13] Humanist attitudes therefore suggest a deep ambivalence towards idolatry condemned by the Church.

This changing cultural climate, one that also affected men of the cloth, eventually brought an end to monster stereotypes. The famous tract of 1630, *A Display of Two Foreign Sects in the Indies* by the English chaplain Henry Lord, was written to refute the pernicious vanity of the Hindus and Zoroastrians of India. Significantly, Lord's systematic refutation of paganism was also a stick with which to beat the Catholic religion. He described Hinduism as a 'counterfeit religion' that dared to break the law of the dread majesty of Heaven. How could a religion that denied God's revelation hold such high moral principles? He felt that he had demonstrated to everyone's satisfaction that Hindu vegetarianism and abstinence from alcohol were neither necessary nor logical. Moreover, these ideas were derived from the Greek philosopher Pythagoras, and therefore were not as ancient as the Old Testament. Indeed, he claimed, they were parodies of the Mosaic law, a view that continued the theological debate around Maimonides.[14]

Leaving this rhetoric aside, one notices in the work of Henry Lord some of the changes that were beginning to take place in the reporting of other religions. Dismissing Purchas's massive work as based merely on hearsay, Lord proceeded to give a description of Hinduism based on first-hand experience and Sanskrit texts, the *śāstras*, although the data itself was still viewed through a scriptural lens, many Hindu myths written about in such a way as to confirm the sanctity of the Old Testament. Thus God created the world, but to combat evil he created three gods, Brahmā, Vishnu and Śiva, who were charged respectively with creating, preserving and destroying evil; this was an interpretation that sought to reconcile these gods with the Christian Trinity.

In 1651 Abraham Rogerius's posthumous work, *The Open Door to the Mysteries of Hinduism*, was published; this was an event that was to have a profound effect on the Western world view and its representation of the Other. It was greeted with enthusiasm by scholars. Although the Dutch pastor did not live to see his work's triumphant reception, he would have had every reason to feel satisfied. Nothing perhaps expresses better the elation of having at last cracked the 'secret code' of pagan mysteries than Rogerius's title, *The Open Door*. A spirit of scientific enquiry informs the text, which is a painstaking investigation of Hindu doctrines and practices, and includes the translation by a Brahmin convert Padmanābha of a major Sanskrit text. The title page itself finally sheds the monster stereotype of Varthema, offering a general view of Hinduism (fig.45), although its draughtsmanship is not of the highest order.[15]

This publishing trend continued with the appearance in 1672 of Philip Baldaeus's *A True and Exact Description of the Most Celebrated Coasts of Malabar and Coromandel*, containing a full and sober account of Hinduism. Baldaeus claimed his work to be superior to that of previous authors in its reliability, and there is no doubt about the quality of the text. What is in question, however, is his authorship. There is evidence that the author of the text was the Jesuit priest Jacopo Fenicio, who had meticulously interviewed Brahmins for his sources. This text came into the possession of the Dutch artist Philip Angel, who then illustrated it with actual Indian paintings. Angel had presented it to the governor of Batavia in order to ingratiate himself with him. As tutor to the governor's son, Baldaeus had access to it, and he subsequently published it in his own name. Fig.46 illustrates an example from *A True and Exact Description of . . . Malabar* – the famous battle in the epic, *Rāmāyana*, reworked by Baldaeus's Dutch illustrator from the Indian miniature in Philip Angel's work.[16]

Any discussion of this early period is usefully concluded by going back five years to 1667, and to the most ambitious work on idolatry, *China Illustrata*, written by Athanasius Kircher. The papal librarian and possibly the greatest polymath in history, Kircher belonged to Pignoria's circle of comparative mythologists who traced the origin of all religions back to Egypt. Kircher's brand of cultural diffusionism, with its mixture of encyclopaedic learning and superhuman industry, albeit with a slight lack of common sense, has often been ridiculed. But his importance lies in his being one of the first to try to make sense of non-Christian religions, instead of dismissing them as forces of darkness. India fascinated Kircher and he dedicated a long section to it, including an early (though garbled) account of the importance of Buddhism in Asia. His German compatriot and emissary in northern India, Father Heinrich Roth, supplied him with texts and images from India. Kircher provided among others a curious illustration to the cosmological myth from Book 10 of the oldest Hindu religious text, the *Rg Veda*. The myth describes how the four great castes emerged from the different parts of the body of the creator god, Purusha or Brahmā.[17]

With Rogerius, Baldaeus and Kircher, the end of this long period – from the late Middle Ages to the threshold of the change that took place in the eighteenth century – is reached. Then, at last, the monster stereotype was discarded, and Hindu gods began to retrieve their true forms. Incidental details also became more convincing. But it was still another eighty years before the archaeological researches of the British Raj would disseminate faithful images of Hindu gods and accurate studies of Indian antiquities. This earlier transformation of European ideas about Hindus and Hinduism took place around 1757 with the founding of British rule in the aftermath of the Battle of Plassey. The East India Company suddenly found itself in possession of a vast territory in a virtually unknown subcontinent, with its own cultures and institutions. Thus began the long process of what Peter Marshall has termed 'the British discovery of Hinduism'; systematic acquisition of knowledge about India was a prerequisite for effective control over the territory and its population.[18]

One of the leading figures in this endeavour was Sir William Jones (1748–94), who is widely acknowledged to be the father of modern oriental studies in general and comparative philology in particular. A by-product of Jones's studies of the Hindu legal system was his discovery of a wealth of Sanskrit literature and its subsequent dissemination in continental Europe. His translation of the great fifth-century dramatist Kalidāsa's *Abhijñān Śakuntalam*, and the translation of a number of key Sanskrit texts by other English scholars, laid the intellectual foundations of the 'Oriental Renaissance' in the West that itself inspired the burgeoning Romantic movement in the nineteenth century.[19] Although Jones's tragic death at an early age removed his towering presence from the Asiatic Society of Bengal, his example was followed by a series of leading orientalists, who helped create an exalted image of ancient Indian philosophy and literature. Such a flattering evaluation of Indian Brahminical thought, based almost entirely on the interpretation of ancient texts, came into conflict with the actual practice of Hinduism by its adherents, including their worship of many-armed and erotic 'monstrous' gods. This seeming contradiction was conveniently explained away by means of a 'two-culture' theory. The highest achievements of Hindu philosophy and literature were the product of the enlightened Brahmin elite, while the superstitious masses wallowed in idolatry and superstition. This was a view that totally ignored the fact that both the philosophy of the *Upanishads* and the multi-limbed Hindu gods were products of the same culture.

The legacy of this 'two-culture' theory had an unfortunate impact on the development of art history and archaeology in India, and on the appreciation of ancient Indian art. It is important to stress that a sound knowledge of Indian sculpture and architecture did not necessarily lead to a greater understanding, a factor that has continued to pose problems of appreciation for the Western art historian. But here is the particular moment in the intellectual history of the Enlightenment which had a direct bearing on the collections at the British Museum. This eighteenth-century episode represents a remarkable interlude in Western representations of Hindu religion between the earlier 'monster' gods and the Revd Samuel Wilberforce's indignant outburst in 1837 that 'the hindoo gods were absolute monsters of lust, injustice, wickedness and cruelty'. The nineteenth century, and especially the Victorian period, witnessed the rise of evangelism, conversions and a contempt for other religions.[20]

One of the key issues facing the late eighteenth century was the problem of interpreting an erotic art form that was not for the private delectation of wealthy individuals (as were, for example, Japanese pillow books), but was an integral aspect of a major flourishing religion. This problem is still present today. Modern scholars, who are deeply imbued with Christian values, even if they are not practising Christians, have offered a variety of explanations – allegorical, sociological and ritualistic – for the 'uninhibited' sexuality of sacred sculptures in Hindu (and Jain) temples. Their main difficulty has been in the acceptance of erotic images in public places of worship. Western attempts to come to terms with Hindu sacred eroticism go back in fact to the early European travellers to India who often felt puzzled by or uncomfortable with the frank depictions of sexual acts on temple walls. A typical example is a seventeenth-century Dutch tract which noted with disapproval 'much immodest, heathen-style fornication and other abominations carved in various pagodes'.[21]

Set against this perspective, the late eighteenth-century interlude marked a refreshing openness towards ancient Hindu sculpture and Hinduism. In Britain, the main figures involved were the two famous collectors Charles Townley and his friend Sir Richard Payne Knight, who were in close contact with the *savants* of the French Enlightenment. Townley was the first known European to have acquired a group of erotic figures from a medieval Hindu temple (from central India or Gujarat?) now in the British Museum (fig.47), a group that was rediscovered in the 1960s.[22] Townley may have purchased it at a public auction of objects brought from India by East India Company officials. He also had in his possession a miniature model of a Hindu shrine with figures of deities.

These two very active members of the Society of Dilettanti made the first serious attempts at explaining the meaning of these images. With the benefit of late eighteenth-century discoveries in the fields of both classical and Hindu religion, they had the confidence for the first time to compare the cult of the Śiva *liṅga*, and scenes of lovemaking on the walls of the Hindu temples, with similar practices in ancient Greece and Rome. The Society of Dilettanti was closely involved with the dissemination in Britain of knowledge of classical civilization, following its initial impact on British consciousness through the regular arrival of art objects from Rome and through the direct intervention of the *Milordi* returning from their Grand Tour.[23]

One consequence of this was a new and intense awareness of the classical world and its visual culture in the eighteenth century. There was, in particular, a profound change in the perception of Graeco-Roman religion, partly as a consequence of the discovery of a great quantity of explicit sexual imagery and evidence of phallic cults in Herculaneum. Excavations on the site were begun around 1738; the discovery of the phallic objects there was reported to Sir Joseph Banks, Secretary to the Society of Dilettanti, by Sir William Hamilton, British envoy to the Court of Naples.[24] One can imagine the shock of disbelief with which the first excavators greeted the plethora of phallic objects buried in the town under the Vesuvian lava. Fearing a scandal, the authorities placed these objects in a 'secret' museum at Portici in Naples. By 1757, however, news of such finds reached the scholarly world which began studying in earnest the explicit sexual imagery and related cults of ancient Greece and Rome. The sheer quantity of phallic objects clearly stunned not only the antiquaries but the erudite world in general, in which the rude images began to be matched with the risqué stories already known from Homer and Hesiod.

Between 1780 and 1803, the renowned French anti-clerical scholar Pierre-Sylvain Maréchal brought out his monumental twelve-volume *Antiquitiés d'Herculanum*, a lavishly illustrated study of objects found at the site.[25]

Their initial excitement somewhat abated, these eighteenth-century students of ancient religion faced the problem of interpreting such sacred objects. One immediate casualty of this reassessment was the reputation of the 'chaste' Greeks, a product of Christian moralizing. They were now perceived to be the denizens of a primitive world expressing a primitive mentality. What helped this 'anthropological' radicalism was the fact that many of the Enlightenment philosophers were the same anticlerical freethinkers who were to inspire the French Revolution of 1789. This may be taken as a case where political revolution joined hands with sexual revolution.[26]

A small circle of English antiquaries who were out of sympathy with the Church joined forces with the French *savants*. The most colourful among them was, as already mentioned, the collector and critic Payne Knight, one of the first writers on universal phallic cults. He thereby anticipated later anthropologists in his *Discourse on the Worship of Priapus and its Connection with the Mystic Theology of the Ancients* (1786). A leading theoretician, who had contributed to the aesthetics of the Picturesque, Payne Knight was an interesting mixture of impressive erudition and the Hell-Fire Club tradition. His *Discourse* was owed partly to the visiting Frenchman, Pierre-François Hughes, called d'Hancarville, who joined the circle of Dilettanti for a brief period. D'Hancarville's *Veneres et priapi* (1784) and *Recherches sur l'origine, l'esprit et les progrès des arts de la Grèce* (1785) had appeared just before Payne Knight's controversial work.[27]

In this circle no one was more ambitious or respected than *citoyen* Charles Dupuis, a highly regarded intellectual of the Revolution, whose seven-volume *Origine de tous les cultes ou la religion universelle* (1794–6) proposed a grand universal religious system that combined sexuality, agricultural fertility and cosmic symbolism.[28] As with Sylvain Maréchal, Dupuis celebrated pagan religions at the expense of the Catholic Church. The Papal librarian and antiquary Winckelmann and the encyclopaedist Diderot had already underlined the intimate connection between love and religion in classical antiquity. Moreover, in his influential account of Herculaneum, Maréchal had presented paganism as a natural and noble religion, at once dignified and appealing to the senses.

These ideas had a two-fold effect on European representations of Indian religion and culture. The Enlightenment, it can be argued, had a profound impact on the reception of Hindu erotic art, while, conversely, a more secure knowledge of the *liṇga* cult and Hindu temple imagery provided the eighteenth century with the intellectual tools with which to come to terms with classical phallic practices. Payne Knight, for instance, made his friend Townley's Hindu erotic group the centrepiece of his argument on ancient paganism in his *Priapus* (fig 48).

How then did the Enlightenment philosophers interpret phallic cults? Certainly, they were indebted to the corpus of late seventeenth- and early eighteenth-century travel writings and ethnographic accounts which had deployed a syncretic method to make sense of Hinduism and other non-Christian religions,

previously condemned out of hand by Christian apologists. Syncretism was an explanatory device used since the time of Herodotus, one which equated the functions of known gods with those of alien deities in an attempt to come to terms with unfamiliar religions. Thus the *liṇga* cult prevailing in India, reported by a traveller such as La Créquinière, could be illuminated by an obscure phallic cult mentioned in the Old Testament.[29] In the process, Payne Knight, Dupuis and other eighteenth-century figures rediscovered a phenomenon whose importance remains undiminished today: the intimate connection made in ancient non-Christian religions between the sexual act and fertility. Later James Frazer was to construct his own grand theory with supporting evidence from anthropology.[30]

Payne Knight and d'Hancarville continued the tradition of comparative religion based on etymological diffusionism proposed about a century before by the humanist circle of Kircher, Peiresc, Rubens and Pignoria. As we have seen, in their theory on the origin of religion, the seventeenth-century humanists made Egypt the ultimate source and the centre of diffusion. In his *Recherches*, d'Hancarville suggested the ultimate source of all religions in an ancient and universal theology whose symbolism could be deciphered through the study of its artistic remains. Both d'Hancarville and Payne Knight found sexuality to be the common thread that bound all ancient religions together. The Enlightenment *savants* did more: they interpreted these sexual cults on different levels, not only in terms of fertility and life cycle with analogies drawn from solar and stellar symbolism, but also on a more complex mystical level. In the process they threw light on the fact that sexual organs displayed at Eleusis in Greece or in the Dionysiac cults of late antiquity were carriers of profound ideas about life, death and the renewal of life, as well as the intimate connection between sacred and profane love. Thereby they stumbled upon the essential nature of sacred sexuality. This early anthropological insight was a remarkable achievement of the period. And yet, even as scholars showered contempt on Christian allegorical rationalizations, the eighteenth-century perception of these cults was essentially allegorical – sexual imagery standing for a higher, abstract idea. These notions are not obsolete: modern interpretations of Hindu cults have continued to be allegorical. But Payne Knight's achievement was doubly remarkable. Unlike d'Hancarville's diffusionism, Payne Knight was convinced that the common artistic expressions found among mankind were a reflection of certain shared cultural forces and needs. Moreover, in a sense that anticipates Creuzer and Hegel, he placed greater emphasis on the symbolic content of art than on its formal aspects. Indeed, his pantheism expressed a remarkable openness and an eagerness to understand non-Christian religions, including his refusal to dismiss the sacred eroticism of Indian cults as obscene – an attitude which now especially seems refreshingly open and plural.[31]

Notes and references

1   See P. Mitter, *Much Maligned Monsters: History of European reactions to Indian art* (Oxford, 1977). On Smith, see P. Mitter, *Art and Nationalism in Colonial India 1850–1922* (Cambridge, 1994), p.311.
2   H. Schedel, *Liber Chronicarum* (Nuremberg, 1493).
3   A. Velho, *A Journal of the First Voyage of Vasco da Gama 1497–1499*, trans. and ed. by E.G. Ravenstein (Madras, 1995), pp.52–4. This is a

reprint of the 1898 Hakluyt Society edition. The editor prefers João de Sá as the author.

4   See D.J.A. Ross, *Alexander Historiatus* (London, 1963). J. Drew, *India and the Romantic Imagination* (Delhi, 1987); pt II contains a more recent discussion of the topic.

5   S. Purchas, *Purchas his pilgrimage, or relations of the world and the religions observed in all ages and places discovered . . .* (London, 1613).

6   Husserl quoted in E.D. Hirsch, *Aims of Interpretation* (Chicago, 1976).

7   F. Schmidt, 'Introduction: les polythéisms: dégénérescence ou progrès?', in F. Schmidt (ed.), *L'Impensable polythéisme* (Paris, 1988), pp.13–91.

8   See J.W. Jones, *The Travels of Ludovico di Varthema* (London, 1843), pp.136 ff.

9   Mitter, op. cit. *Much Maligned Monsters* (note 1), pp.17–19.

10   Ibid, chap.I, pt I.

11   Ibid, pp.21–2.

12   V. Cartari, *Le vere e nove imagini degli dei degli antichi,* pt II (Padua, 1615).

13   F. Yates, *Giordano Bruno and the Hermetic Tradition* (London, 1964).

14   H. Lord, *A Display of Two Forraigne Sects in the East Indies* (London, 1630).

15   A. Rogerius, *De Open Deure tot het verborgen Heydendom* (Leiden, 1651).

16   See Mitter, op. cit. *Much Maligned Monsters* (note 1), pp.57–64.

17   A. Kircher, *China Monumentis qua Sacris qua Profanis . . . illustrata* (Amsterdam, 1667).

18   P.J. Marshall, *British Discovery of Hinduism in the Eighteenth Century* (Cambridge, 1970).

19   R. Schwab, *La Renaisssance orientale* (Paris, 1950).

20   K.K. Dyson, *A Various Universe* (Oxford, 1978), p.162.

21   Mitter, op. cit. *Much Maligned Monsters* (note 1), p.74.

22   Ibid., chap.II. In the 1960s I rediscovered the piece which had been lying in the British Museum basement for a number of years through the kind help of the late Wladimir Zwalf. This then enabled me to match the image with Knight's text. David Gaimster's article, 'Sex and sensibility at the British Museum', *History Today*, 50 (9) (September, 2000), pp.10–15 makes no mention of the discovery of this fragment and its implications for Townley, Knight and the Society of Dilettanti.

23   F. Haskell and N. Penny, *Taste and the Antique* (New Haven and London, 1981).

24   See the catalogue of the exhibition, *The Arrogant Connoisseur: Richard Payne Knight 1751–1824,* ed. M. Clarke and N. Penny (Manchester, 1982), p.50.

25   P.-S. Maréchal, *Antiquites d'Herculanum*, 12 vols (Paris, 1780–1803).

26   F.E. Manuel, *The Eighteenth Century confronts the Gods* (Cambridge, Mass., 1959).

27   Mitter, op. cit. *Much Maligned Monsters* (note 1), chap.II. See also Clarke and Penny, op. cit. (note 24).

28   C. Dupuis, *Origine de tous les cultes ou la religion universelle*, 7 vols (Paris, 1794–6).

29   La Créquinière, *Conformité des coutumes des indiens orientaux avec celles des Juifs* (Brussels, 1904).

30   J. Frazer, *The Golden Bough*, 12 vols (London, 1890–1915).

31   See Mitter, op. cit. *Much Maligned Monsters* (note 1), chap.II for a further discussion of these ideas.

Figure 42
The *Deumo of Calicut*, engraving by
Georg Breu in Lodovico di Barthema
(Varthema), *Die Ritterlich vn Lobwirdig
Rayss...* (Augsburg, 1515). London,
British Library.

Figure 44
Hindu deities in Vincenzo Cartari,
*Le Vere e nove Imagini degli Dei delli
Antichi...*, part II (Padua, 1615).
London, British Library.

Figure 43
Idolum Indorum Pagodes, with
Elephanta on the left and a
'mosque' on the right. Engraving
by Baptista a Doetechum in Jan
Huygen Van Linschoten, *Itinerario*
(Amsterdam, 1596). London,
British Library.

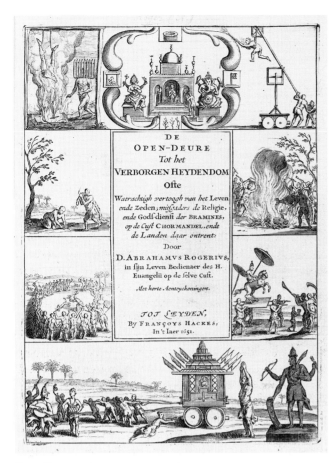

Figure 45
Title page from Abraham Rogerius,
*De Open-Deure tot het verborgen
Heydendom...* (Leiden, 1672).
London, British Library.

Figure 46
Battle of Rama and Ravana from Philip
Baldaeus, *Naauwkeurige Beschryvinge
van Malabar en Choromandel...*
(Amsterdam, 1672). London,
British Library.

Figure 47
Erotic fragment from India
(eleventh century AD), 75.5 x 45.5cm
(29³/₄ x 17⁷/₈ in). London, British
Museum, Department of Asia
(OA 1805,7-3,264).

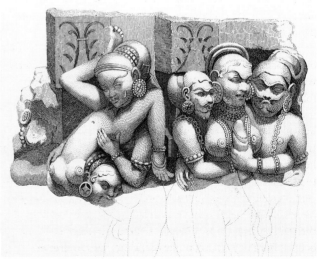

Figure 48
Townley's erotic fragment in Richard
Payne Knight, *An Account of the
Remains of the Worship of Priapus ...
to which is added, a discourse on the
Worship of Priapus ... and its connexion
with the Mystic Theology of the
Ancients* (London, 1786). London,
British Library.

Chapter 16
Dr Richard Mead (1673–1754) and his Circle
Ian Jenkins

The relative obscurity of Richard Mead now contrasts with his fame while alive.[1] According to Dr Samuel Johnson, he 'lived more in the broad sunshine of life than almost any other man'.[2] *Per Illustri, Celeberrimoque, Excellentissimoque Viro Doctori Mead*, reads the dedication on a drawing (fig.49) dedicated to Mead by the Venetian antiquary Antonio Maria Zanetti the elder (1680–1767).[3] An ancient Roman relief, then in the Palazzo Colonna in Rome and showing a Hermaphrodite, was no doubt an attractive subject for a man of Mead's liberal – not to say medical – tastes.[4]

This drawing must have been brought to England when Zanetti was himself in London in 1721.[5] He was one of many foreign visitors who were directed to Mead's house and table. On returning to Venice, Zanetti would honour his friend once more. While in England he had acquired a number of drawings by Parmigianino that were sold from the estate of Lord Stratford of Tart Hall, whose father was the great seventeenth-century collector Thomas Howard, 2nd Earl of Arundel (1585–1646).[6] Returning to Venice, Zanetti reproduced his drawings in a series of chiaroscuro woodcuts. One is signed and dated 1724 and titled *The Worship of Jupiter*; another is signed and dated 1741 and called *The Circumcision or Presentation of Christ* (fig.50). Both carry flattering dedications, the second being the most flamboyant – 'Per illustri, Eruditissimo, ac Munificentissimo Viro Domino Riccardo Mead, Artium Liberalium Splendidissimo Mecaenati'; it then goes on to name the original artist and the picture's provenance in the Arundel collection.[7]

Mead set up his first medical practice in Stepney, to the east of London, and in 1702 he published his treatise on poisons for which he was elected a Fellow of the Royal Society in the following year.[8] The treatise included the result of his investigations into venom and is obliquely referred to in the image on the reverse of a medal of Mead by Lewis Pingo (fig.51).[9] The infant Hercules is precociously demonstrating his heroic status by strangling a pair of snakes. The subject is a rendering in miniature of the bronze group by the seventeenth-century sculptor Alessandro Algardi, a version of which was in Mead's own collection and was illustrated in some editions of the treatise on poisons.[10] Mead's sculpture has since his death been at Burghley House, home of the Marquess of Exeter. The subject made eloquent reference to Mead's own youthful handling of vipers.

In spite of his interest in poisons, Mead's medical practice flourished. He was admitted to the College of Physicians in 1708 and elected a Fellow in 1716. His posthumous bust by Roubiliac, of which the British Museum has a cast, is still in their possession, presented by his friend Dr Anthony Askew (1722–74) in

1756.[11] Upon the death of another friend and fellow physician John Radcliffe (1650–1714), Mead took over Radcliffe's home in Bloomsbury Square, his substantial practice and his physician's gold-topped cane, now in the Royal College of Physicians.[12] He rose to become the principal physician of his day, and is said to have earned the colossal sum of between £5,000 and £6,000 a year. He served both George I and George II. This royal patronage is reflected in a portrait (fig.52) by Jacopo Amigoni of George II's Queen, Caroline of Ansbach (1683–1737), painted in 1735 and now in the National Portrait Gallery.[13] She is depicted as Fortuna with a cornucopia at her side. In place of the usual fruits of the field are miniature portraits of seven children.[14] Caroline was still Princess of Wales when, having nearly lost a daughter through smallpox, she approached Mead about the prospect of inoculating her other children. George I was sceptical of the benefits and wary of the dangers at a time when there was fierce resistance to the practice. In 1721 seven condemned felons were pardoned on condition that they undergo experimental inoculation.[15] They suffered no lasting ill-effects. Mead's standing rose and his reputation as a pioneer of medical inoculation was sealed when in 1748 he published his treatise on the subject.[16] As the inscription beneath her feet informs us, in 1736 the grateful Queen presented Amigoni's portrait to Mead.

For a final word on medical Mead, it should be noted that one of his principal contributions to the history of medicine was his publication on precautions against the spread of contagious disease.[17] In 1720 there was fear of the transmission to Britain of bubonic plague raging in the French port of Marseilles and much of Provence. Mead is credited with laying the foundations of a public health system in his outline proposals for quarantine and other preventative measures.[18]

Mead's professional interests need such definition since they are connected in a number of ways to his role as a collector of art and antiquity. The very first painting he purchased was *The Flaying of St Bartholomew* by 'Spagnoletto' (Jusepe de Ribera).[19] His physician's acumen found much to admire in the accurate rendering of the exposed muscles. While Roubiliac's bust of Mead is deposited in the Royal College of Physicians, the finest of all his painted portraits is owned by another medical institution, the Foundling Hospital. This was set up by two childless and kindly enemies of cant and cruelty, Thomas Coram (1668–1751) and William Hogarth (1697–1764).[20] Mead owned a portrait of Coram by Allan Ramsay (1713–1784) which has not been traced.[21] The same artist painted a portrait of Mead (fig.53), which he presented to the Hospital in 1747.[22] Ramsay enjoyed Mead's patronage and later his friendship. Mead was

Ian Jenkins

intimately connected with the Hospital. He campaigned for its Royal Charter, granted in 1739, and was a Governor there and Honorary Physician. Mead's portrait is a pair with, and has the same dimensions as, the painting of Coram by Hogarth, dated 1740, and also owned by the Hospital.[23]

Both portraits are exquisite characterizations of their respective sitters and share a rare luminosity. In contrast with the sea-raddled and diminutive Captain Coram in his coat of scarlet, the urbane and portly Mead is dressed in the fine but sober attire of a professional man. He is accompanied by a statue of the mythical and archetypal healing goddess Hygeia, set in a niche. This is probably the sculpture of her which Mead himself owned.[24]

Another (inferior) portrait of him, from the studio of Ramsay, is now in the National Portrait Gallery.[25] This time the mythical healer is Asclepius. The same god appears in a comparable portrait of Sloane, attributed to John Vanderbank, in the British Museum. The model for Sloane's Asclepius was a statuette he owned, now also in the British Museum.[26] The figure in Mead's portrait, however, is probably taken from Peter Paul Rubens's depiction of Sir Theodore Turquet de Mayerne (1573–1655), a version of which Mead himself owned.[27] James I brought Mayerne to England from France and made him Royal Physician, which office he also held under Charles I and Charles II. When he was not curing kings of their melancholy, Turquet dabbled in science and is said to have invented the first washable scribbling book. Mead's portrait of him is thought to be that in the North Carolina Museum of Art, Raleigh, and is taken as Rubens's original. The version in the National Portrait Gallery is seen as a copy of the late seventeenth or early eighteenth century. The chalk drawing of Mayerne by Rubens in the British Museum is likely to be an original study for the portrait, taken from life.[28]

The other object in Mead's lesser portrait is no less significant. It is the Hellenistic bronze head of a poet, then thought to be Homer and now Sophocles, which had been in Lord Arundel's collection and was at Tart Hall before Mead acquired it in 1720.[29] It was presented to the British Museum by the Earl of Exeter in 1760. It is such treasures as this that set Mead's antiquities apart from those of Sloane, who largely bought his collection in bulk, out of convention rather than from any especial discernment.[30] One contemporary records the following comparison: 'I was extremely entertained the other day with seeing Dr Mead's curiosities. They are much finer than Sir Hans Sloane's.'[31]

The Mead collection is documented through the catalogues and their manuscript annotations. These cover his library of over 10,000 volumes, his prints and drawings, his paintings and antiquities and natural history.[32] All this added up to what Matthew Maty, the compiler of a memoir of his life, so evocatively referred to as a 'Temple of Nature and Repository of Time'.[33] Mead's successful career had enabled him to settle at 49 Great Ormond Street, in a fine house which was demolished in the 1880s to make way for the Great Ormond Street Children's Hospital. A drawing (fig.54) shows it in 1882, already bearing a sign 'Hospital for Sick Children'. The roof, however, appears to have been stripped off both this property and the former French embassy next door, for these two buildings were being prepared for demolition.[34]

As an extension to this house, Mead built a gallery in 1732 to display his increasing art collection and liberally opened it to artists for study of his old master paintings and sculpture. He kept open house for his friends in the form of a dining club that met every Wednesday afternoon. The club is well described by Alastair Smart, making good use of the diary of Revd Dr Thomas Birch (1705–66) who, with his fellow historian and classicist Dr John Ward (c.1679–1758), was a founder member.[35] Birch makes frequent reference to the club and its members. They included the painters Allan Ramsay, William Hogarth and Jonathan Richardson and the sculptor John Michael Rysbrack. There was the poet Alexander Pope, the historian and antiquary George Vertue, the astronomer Edmund Halley, the antiquary and numismatist Martin Folkes. There was Browne Willis and Richard Bentley, both pioneers in the revival of interest in Gothic cathedrals, and the travellers Revd Thomas Shaw and Revd Richard Pococke, and of course the philanthropist Thomas Coram.

Around 1734, Mead employed James Gibbs to design a library for his books and manuscripts. It was for his books that in his day Mead was most renowned. Hence Alexander Pope's often quoted: 'Rare monkish manuscripts for Hearne alone, And books for Mead and butterflies for Sloane'.[36] The books themselves were in high-quality bindings and covered every category of learning.[37] At least thirty-five were dedicated to Mead himself and are an indication of his extensive patronage. Among many notable volumes was an edition of Shakespeare, which had been owned and read by Charles I on the eve of his execution.[38] The King gave it to the master of his bedchamber, Sir Thomas Herbert, and Mead bought it from the Herbert family. It is now in the Royal Library at Windsor, having been purchased in 1775 at the book-sale of the founder of British bibliomania, Anthony Askew, physician and classical scholar, and another of Mead's circle.[39] He travelled in Greece and Asia Minor and besides his books and manuscripts had a number of antiquities. These included the Athenian fifth-century marble gravestone of Xanthippos, afterwards acquired by Charles Townley and now in the British Museum.[40] Allan Ramsay's portrait of Askew hangs in Emmanuel College, Cambridge.[41]

An engraving bearing Mead's motto, *Non sibi sed toti*, is included in *Bibliotheca Meadiana*. It shows a long room with book presses down one side, and facing it more bookcases alternating with windows. Above the books are displayed paintings and portrait busts, which included a white marble portrait of Pope by Scheemakers, along with those of Shakespeare, Milton and assorted ancient worthies. The library also contained the cabinet of prints and drawings and cabinets of coins and medals. These were kept in an iron safe said to have belonged to Elizabeth I.[42]

It was said of Mead after his death that of all the physicians who had ever lived he gained the most and spent the most.[43] There are signs that already around 1750, he began to run into financial difficulties.[44] Horace Walpole writing to Horace Mann declared that Mead was 'undone': 'The world thinks he is immensely rich, but he is in fact deeply in debt . . . For his table alone', Walpole remarked, 'he is said to have allowed seventy pounds a week . . .'.[45] It is probably a consequence of his profligacy that even before the posthumous sales, Mead began to sell off his collection. The idea should also be entertained, however, that in his last years he was eager to find good homes for parts of the collection about which he especially cared.[46] Among those to purchase aspects of the collection in Mead's lifetime was Frederick, Prince of Wales (1707–51). Among the miniatures he bought, now in the Royal Collection, is 'one of the most famous images in British art' (fig.55), a remarkable work by Isaac Oliver (?1556–1617) which George Vertue had thought a portrait of Sir Philip Sydney, but is now catalogued as a melancholy young man and a personification of the Elizabethan malady of melancholy.[47] Prince Frederick also bought from Mead a volume of sixty-six drawings by Poussin, which had once been Cardinal Massimi's.[48] A further royal purchase at the drawings sale itself was two volumes of natural history subjects on vellum by Maria Sibylla Merian (1647–1717).[49] Sloane too had acquired some of her remarkable works, which formed part of the founding collection of the British Museum.[50] Among other natural history drawings at Mead's sale were over 200 in two volumes by Georg Dionysius Ehret.[51]

Not a few of the antiquities listed in Mead's catalogues have found their way into the British Museum. They include a fine bronze, which until recently belonged to the Methuen family of Corsham Court in Wiltshire.[52] It takes the form of a mask of Dionysus, originally the support for a fancy bucket-handle. Another interesting bronze has not previously been noted as coming from Mead's collection. It is one of a group of so-called 'magical hands' or 'hands of Sebazius', which came to the Museum in 1895 without a provenance.[53] A close reading of the Latin text of an entry in the catalogue of Mead's antiquities, however, shows it to be the one bought by Thomas Hollis.[54] This object has a very long history. It was found at Tournai on the Belgian-French border in the late sixteenth or early seventeenth century and was first published by Laurentius Pignorius in 1623.[55] At some point, a replica of it appears to have been made and this was later deposited in the Cabinet des Médailles in Paris.[56] This replica has been mistaken for the original and more recently it has been condemned as a forgery, while the British Museum's version is seen as a replica of this forgery.[57] The British Museum's bronze, however, has all the signs of antiquity, and the Paris version appears to be a reproduction of it.

Mead's interest in paintings was catholic. He had what we would now call 'old masters' as well as both contemporary and ancient works. He treated Watteau for consumption and put him up in his house: the painter gave his benefactor *The Italian Comedians*, now in the National Gallery of Art in Washington, and another painting entitled *A Pastoral Conversation*, which is lost but identified in a print.[58] By contrast with such modern works, Mead also had fragments of ancient Roman painting. He had, among others which are now in the British Museum, a head of a woman with a tall *modius*, formerly in the Palazzo Massimi.[59] It was featured in a volume of drawings by Pietro Santi Bartoli of paintings discovered in Rome. This had been commissioned by Camillo Massimi and was acquired in Rome through Mead's protégé, Allan Ramsay.[60] It was held back from the sale of the library and passed through the family. It used to be identified with a volume in the Royal Collection, but is now thought to be the one in Glasgow University Library, bearing the Massimi arms.[61] Mead's ancient paintings were praised by George Turnbull in his treatise on the subject, and some of Bartoli's drawings were engraved in the same volume.[62]

Another recent discovery concerns an entry in the sale catalogue of drawings: 'A large and curious collection of drawings from the antique, in 5 port folios, all pasted on blue paper.' These should be identified with three volumes now in the library of the Greek and Roman Department of the British Museum.[63] Executed in red or black chalk, there are around 400 drawings, mounted on blue paper. They are mostly by two separate hands, the more pleasing artist preferring red chalk and the other black. The drawings are all of sculpture in Rome in the early eighteenth century and are arranged in series, inscribed with the name of the collection: Spada, Chigi, Borghese, and so on. The three volumes seem to comprise a fragmentary record of a once apparently comprehensive survey of the ancient sculptures of Rome by palace or villa. Although fewer in number and less finished, they are comparable with the many similar drawings assembled by Richard Topham (1671–1730) and now in the College Library at Eton.[64] In short, many of the drawings in the British Museum can be identified as studies for the drawings at Eton. Indeed, there are some cases where the British Museum's volumes contain offsets from drawings in Eton. The making of an impression from a freshly worked chalk drawing was a simple way of gaining a *quasi* printed version of the original image in reverse.

Mead was Topham's kinsman and executor of his will. It was he who ensured that Topham's collection stayed together and he oversaw its installation in the central room of the new Eton College Library. Observing that some volumes appeared to contain duplicates, Mead, it may be surmised, retained them for his own library where they stayed until the sale after his death. They then passed through the hands of the sculpture-collectors Lyde Browne of Wimbledon and afterwards Charles Townley, and so to the British Museum.[65]

Topham's collection was assembled by mail-order through the painter and dealer Francesco Imperiali and contains in excess of 2,000 commissioned drawings of ancient subjects by named Italian artists. The hands involved in the British Museum's drawings are Bernardo Cifferi, who did those in red chalk, and Carlo Calderi, author of the black chalk images. There are some exceptions and these include five anonymous Italian drawings of two bronzes which, again exceptionally, are not ancient, but were thought in the eighteenth century to be by the sixteenth-century master Giambologna.[66] One drawing portraying Hercules with the Hydra, but omitting his club (fig.56), was inscribed, after Mead's death 'first Consul Smith's, now Mr Knight's of Whitehall, 1786'. The first is a reference to that well known art-Merchant of Venice, Consul Joseph Smith (1682–1770), who both knew Mead and praised him in a letter to A.F. Gori in Florence.[67] Knight is assumed to be the celebrated connoisseur of ancient bronzes, Richard Payne Knight (1751–1824). An engraving of Consul Smith's bronze was published by Desplaces after a drawing by A.M. Zanetti, with some slight variation.[68] The other bronze is after Giambologna's fountain figure of Neptune in Bologna. This too was probably owned by Consul Smith and is shown in a chiaroscuro woodcut engraving by J.B. Jackson (1701–c.1780).[69]

The Mead provenance added a premium to the value of objects at his sales. Many were the distinguished names who competed for the numerous treasures, and the annotated catalogues themselves provide an inventory of the great and the good of English collecting in the mid-eighteenth century.[70] In some cases the sale and purchase added new links in a chain of famous previous owners. From Cardinal Camillo Massimi, for example, Mead had acquired his copy of the Vatican Virgil.[71] It was bought at Mead's sale by Anthony Askew and Lord Lansdowne subsequently purchased it at Askew's posthumous sale of manuscripts in 1785, when Mead's Greek manuscripts formerly acquired by Askew were also sold.[72] It is now in the British Library. Mead's generation looked back on the Earl of Arundel as 'Father of Vertu in England' and the bronze, so-called Homer, came from him. Mead owned a portrait of the Earl by Rubens, now in the National Gallery. It was bought at Mead's sale by Lord Carlisle and presented to the Gallery in 1914 by Rosalind, Countess of Carlisle.[73] Mead also owned a Van Dyck drawing of him.[74]

Arundel's picture hung with the other portraits in Mead's house and together they comprised a gallery of the illustrious. It had long been the custom for cognoscenti to demonstrate their erudition by exhibiting the portraits of other learned men. The practice was begun at least as early as the second century BC in the library of the Attalid kings of Pergamum in Asia Minor.[75] Also ancient was the gathering of images into books. Varro, the man whom Antiquity itself named the 'most learned of the Romans' and Cicero, dubbed *homo polygraphotatos*[76] or 'much published man', compiled an album of 700 famous people.[77] It began with Homer and included a biography and an epigram attached to each portrait. Several of the portraits in Mead's collection were engraved and published in Thomas Birch's *Heads of Illustrious Persons of Great Britain*.[78] In Mead's gallery itself, under some images were suspended Latin couplets of Mead's own composition, praising the subject or his deeds. The portraits included many of general interest such as historical persons, artists, poets and philosophers. In particular, there were scholars and scientific men, including one image then identified as John Ray the naturalist (1627–1705) by Mrs Beale.[79] Some of Mead's scientific men were purchased by Dr William Hunter and are now at the Hunterian Museum in Glasgow. They include Dr William Harvey the physician (1578–1657) by van Bemmel and Isaac Newton by Kneller.[80] Hunter also bought the first item in the catalogue of Mead's antiquities, an Egyptian mummy and its case.[81]

As well as such modern figures, Mead collected heads of the ancients. They included a marble portrait of the Stoic philosopher Chrysippus, mounted on a modern term which is wrongly inscribed Xenokrates.[82] This formed a pair with a terminal bust of Theophrastus, the pupil of Aristotle. It came to Mead with a history and was said by the sixteenth-century Neapolitan antiquary Pirro Ligorio to have been found in the Villa of Cassius near Tivoli.[83] His contemporary Fulvio Orsini, curator of the Farnese collections in Rome, featured it in the *Imagines et Elogia Virorum Illustrium*, a self-conscious attempt at reconstructing Varro's album of *Imagines*. Mead acquired his head of Chrysippos from the Massimi collection. Such pedigrees rooted Mead's collection in a grand tradition, and this tradition was to reclaim its own when, after the Mead sale, both busts went back to Rome and the collection of Cardinal Alessandro Albani.[84]

That tradition is also illustrated by the first three items in the sale catalogue of pictures, which were portraits of the sixteenth-century humanists Erasmus and Petrus Aegidius, also known as Pieter Gillis (Giles), scholar and town clerk of Antwerp (figs 57–8). These pictures, together with a hitherto unidentified portrait of Paracelsus, were the cornerstones of Mead's gallery of famous men. Together they must have comprised an epitome of the active humanist. Mead believed that the first two were both by Hans Holbein and were the very pair given to More by Erasmus as a token of friendship. Holbein's portrait of Erasmus, Mead noted, has a date of 1523 and was said to have been in Arundel's collection.

There is great confusion here. Mead seems to have hold of a garbled version of two separate stories. The first concerns Holbein. One of Mead's portraits *is* by Holbein and was one of two paintings that Erasmus sent to England.[85] One of these – probably Mead's – was intended for William Warham, Archbishop of Canterbury. It is the model for many secondary portraits of Erasmus, and is probably again the picture seen by John Evelyn at Albury in 1655, when it was owned by Lord Arundel's grandson, later the 6th Duke of Norfolk.[86]

The other story derives from an episode in 1517, when on a diplomatic mission to the Low Countries, Thomas More was presented by Erasmus and Gillis with a diptych of themselves by the leading Antwerp painter of the day, Quentin Matsys.[87] He, and not Holbein, is the author of Mead's portrait of Gillis and, indeed, this picture appears to be one half of the Friendship Diptych. There are signs that this painting was originally smaller, and has been extended to make it conform to the size of the Holbein of Erasmus. Its original companion – Matsys's Erasmus – is thought to be the one in the Royal Collection. Both the Matsys of Gillis and the Matsys of Erasmus bear on the reverse the crowned CR brand of Charles I. Like the Holbein of Erasmus, the Matsys of Gillis was bought at Mead's sale by Viscount Folkestone. It remains in the Earl of Radnor's home, Longford Castle. The Friendship Diptych was presumably separated under Cromwell's Republic. The Erasmus remained or found its way back into the Royal Collection, while the Gillis eventually ended up with Mead.

More was delighted with his gift with its subtle reference in the inscriptions on the books to the mutual interests of the three friends. He wrote verses in its praise and sent them to Gillis with an injunction to burn them if they were not fit for Erasmus's own scholarly eyes. Alternatively, More asked for their return so that he could display them with the pictures themselves.[88] The verses were available to Mead in printed editions of Erasmus's letters and they were perhaps the inspiration for his own two-line compositions suspended under his pictures of Erasmus and Gillis. Mead's Latin is not easy but may be translated:

> Erasmus was the first to be able in abundance to bring forth the clear light of knowledge from the shadows.
> Erasmus esteemed Aegidius, who was illustrious to the Muses; painted by Holbein, each inspires the other.

To sum up, Mead's circle was a complex community of the living and the dead. There is the royal court at which he officiated as physician; there were the professional men of his own time, whose pictures he displayed and whose memory he preserved after they died; there is the immediate circle of friends who enjoyed his – by all accounts – lavish hospitality; there were the great collectors of the seventeenth century from whose collections some of his own treasures had come. There were the humanists of the sixteenth century, whose ambition he shared to 'bring forth knowledge from the shadows'. There were the ancients whose lives had been spent in the same quest and who were revered by all. Mead was himself called an 'Aesculapius both of the court and of the city'.[89] This medical god's 'temple of nature and repository of time' was demolished in the nineteenth century. It has left no physical trace and its collections were scattered in the previous century. Mead had lived in the 'broad sunshine of life' but fame, like the weather, is subject to change. He is buried in Temple Church and his monument in Westminster Abbey, dated 1754, is by Peter Scheemakers.[90]

Notes and references

1 For the life of Mead see M. Maty, *Authentic Memoirs of the Life of R. Mead* (London, 1755); A. Zuckermann, 'Dr Richard Mead (1673–1754): A biographical study' (PhD Dissertation, University of Illinois, Ann Arbor Michigan University Microfilms 1980) (1965); R.H. Meade, *In the Sunshine of Life – a Biography of Dr Richard Mead 1673–1754* (Philadelphia, 1974); C. Fell-Smith, 'Richard Mead MD', *Dictionary of National Biography*, vol.XIII (Oxford, 1998), pp.181–6; S. West, 'Dr Richard Mead', *The Dictionary of Art*, vol.XX (London, 1966), pp.910–11. On Mead as physician see *The Medical works of Richard Mead M.D.* (collected and published London, 1762, copy in the Wellcome Library); W. Macmichael, *The Gold-headed Cane* (London, 1827; facsimile edn 1953), pp.37–105. On Mead as collector see M. Webster, 'Taste of an Augustan collector I', *Country Life*, 29 January 1970, pp.249–51, and 24 September 1970, pp.765–7; D. Sutton, 'The Age of Walpole', *Apollo* 114 (1981), pp.328–39; I. Jenkins, 'Dr Mead (1673–1754) and Richard Topham's drawings of Roman sculpture', in M. Kunze and H. Wrede (eds), *300 Jahre Thesaurus Brandenburgicus*, Proceedings of an international colloquium (Stendal and Berlin, forthcoming).

For the sale catalogues of Mead's collection, the following abbreviations are used below:

Museum Meadianum: *Museum Meadianum sive Catalogus Nummorum Veteris Aevi cum aliis quibusdam Artis recentioris et naturae Operibus quae vir clarissimus Richardus Mead M.D.* (London, 1755).

Gems etc.: *Catalogue of the Genuine and Entire Collection of Valuable Gems, Bronzes, marble and other Busts and Antiquities of the Late Doctor Mead,* Langford, Tuesday 11 March 1755 and four following days.

Pictures: *A Catalogue of Pictures consisting of Portraits, Landscapes, Sea-Pieces, Architecture, Flowers, Fruits, Animals, Histories of the late Richard Mead, M.D.* Sold by auction 20, 21 and 22 March 1754 (printed 1755).

Prints and Drawings: *A Catalogue of the Genuine, Entire and Curious Collection of Prints and Drawings of the late Doctor Mead.* Langford, 13 January 1755 and thirteen following evenings.

Bibliotheca Meadiana: *Bibliotheca Meadiana sive Catalogus Librorum Richardi Mead*. Sale 18 November 1754 and 7 April 1755 (London).

2 J. Boswell, *The Life of Samuel Johnson L.L.D*, Modern Library (New York, n.d.), p.847.

3 British Museum, Mead vols of drawings in the library of the Department of Greek and Roman Antiquities, see below (note 63). Jenkins forthcoming, op. cit. (note 1).

4 A. Ajootian, 'Hermaphroditos', in *Lexicon Iconographicum Mythologiae Classicae* 5.1 (Zurich and Munich, 1990), p.281, 74 not illustrated; H. Wrede, 'Zu Antinous, Hermaphrodit und Odysseus', *Boreas* 9 (1986), p.131, pl.17.3.

5 For Zanetti see G. Lorenzetti, *Un Dilettante Incisore Veneziano del XVIII Secolo, Antonio Maria Zanetti di Girolomo* (Venice, 1917); A. Bettagno, *Caricatures di Anton Maria Zanetti* (Milan, 1970).

6 Lorenzetti, op. cit. (note 5), p. 18; A.E. Popham, *Catalogue of the Drawings of Parmigianino in 3 volumes*, vol.I (New Haven, 1971), p.32.

7 Lorenzetti, op. cit. (note 5), pp.52–7, 106.40 and 111.64.

8 R. Mead, *A Mechanical Account of Poisons in Several Essays* (London, 1702 and several other edns); V. Ferguson, 'A Bibliography of the Works of Richard Mead MD FRS (1673–1754)', unpublished typescript, 63 leaves (London, Wellcome Library).

9 C. Avery, in A. Weston-Lewis (ed.), *Effigies and Ecstasies: Roman baroque sculpture and design in the age of Bernini*, exh. cat., National Gallery of Scotland (Edinburgh, 1998), pp.94–5.

10 Mead Catalogues (note 1): Museum Meadianum, p.219; ibid.: Gems etc. 5th day, lot 71; J. Montagu, *Alessandro Algardi* (New Haven and London, 1985), p.406; Avery, op. cit. (note 9), pp.94–5.

11 Zuckerman, op. cit. (note 1), pp.234–5; A. Dawson, *Portrait Sculpture: A catalogue of the British Museum collection c.1675–1973* (London, 1999), pp.140–2, cat.53; J. Kerslake, *Early Georgian Portraits*, 2 vols, National Portrait Gallery (London, 1977), p.537; id. p.185, cat.528–38, lists eleven images of Mead.

12 Macmichael, op. cit. (note 1); Zuckermann, op. cit. (note 1), pp.76–7; Meade, op. cit. (note 1), p.99.

13 Kerslake, op. cit. (note 11), p.34, National Portrait Gallery (hereafter NPG) 4332.

14 For children in cornucopias see E. McGrath, 'Rubens's infant cornucopia', *Journal of the Warburg and Courtauld Institutes* 40 (1977), pp.315–18.

15 Meade, op. cit. (note 1), p.6; Zuckermann, op. cit. (note 1), pp.100–3.

16 R. Mead, *A Discourse on the Small Pox and Measles* (London, 1748).

17 R. Mead, *Short Discourse Concerning Pestilential Contagion, and the Measures to be used to Prevent it* (London, 1720).

18 Meade, op. cit. (note 1), pp.7–9; Zuckermann, op. cit. (note 1), pp.107–27.

19 Mead Catalogues (note 1): Pictures, xii. Purchased by 'Mr Qualm'. Not traced.

20 R. Nichols and S. Ray, *The History of the Foundling Hospital* (Oxford, 1935); R. McClure, *Coram's Children* (London and New Haven, 1981); B.Nicholson, *Treasures of the Foundling Hospital* (Oxford, 1972).

21 Mead Catalogues (note 1): Pictures vi, purchased by 'Dr Rawlinson'.

22 A. Smart, *Allan Ramsay, Painter, Essayist and Man of the Enlightenment* (New Haven and London, 1992), pp.80–1, fig.61; A. Smart and J. Ingamells (eds), *Allan Ramsay: A Complete Catalogue of his Paintings* (New Haven and London, 1999), p.157, cat.361, pl.13.

23 In 2002 both pictures could be seen hanging in their matching frames to good advantage in Tate Britain on either side of a doorway, with the subjects facing each other.

24 The type is that of the Kassel Hygeia from Ostia. This piece was, however, excavated in the later eighteenth century and cannot be the white marble one owned by Mead, which was in any case a statuette, 3 ft (91.4 cm) high: Mead Catalogue (note 1), Museum Meadianum p.218, bought by 'Dr Askew for the Earl of Litchfield'; ibid.: Gems etc. 4th day, lot 72. The Litchfield/Anson collection at Shugborough was dispersed in the nineteenth century: Adolph Michaelis, *Ancient Marbles in Great Britain* (Cambridge, 1882), p.41, n.174.

25 Kerslake, op. cit. (note 11), p.184, NPG 15.

26 A. Smith, *A Catalogue of Sculpture in the Department of Greek and Roman Antiquities, British Museum*, 3 vols (London, 1982), cat. 1695; I. Jenkins, 'Classical antiquities: Sloane's Repository of Time', in A. MacGregor (ed.), *Sir Hans Sloane: Collector, scientist, antiquary; founding father of the British Museum* (London, 1994), p.168.

27 D. Piper, *Catalogue of Seventeenth-Century Portraits in the National Portrait Gallery 1625–1714* (Cambridge, 1963), pp.228–9; Sutton, op. cit. (note 1), p.330.

28 A. Hind, *Catalogue of Drawings by Dutch and Flemish Artists in the British Museum,* vol.II: *Drawings by Rubens, Van Dyck and other artists of the Flemish School of the 17th Century* (London, 1923), p.29; Rubens cat.94.

29 Mead Catalogues (note 1): Museum Meadianum, pp.219–20; ibid. (note 1): Gems etc. 5th day, lot 75; H.B. Walters, *Catalogue of the Bronzes, Greek, Roman and Etruscan in the Department of Greek and Roman Antiquities, British Museum* (London, 1899–1904), 847.

30 Jenkins, op. cit. (note 26), p.170.

31 Duchess of Portland to Mrs Elizabeth Montagu, 1742, quoted by Zuckermann, op. cit. (note 1), p.236.

32 See Mead Catalogues (note 1).

33 Maty, op. cit. (note 1).

34 The drawing in the Wellcome Library is signed 'J.P. Emslie' and dated 1882.

35 The club is well-described by Smart, op. cit. (note 22), pp.66–7. He makes good use of British Library, Birch MS 4478c, 'Diary of Thomas Birch'.

36 Alexander Pope, *Moral Essays*: *Epistle IV to Richard Boyle, Earl of Burlington*, (n.p., n.d.), p.10.

37 Mead Catalogues (note 1): Books; A. Dobson, 'The Bibliotheca Meadiana', *Bibliographica* (London, 1895), *passim*; Meade, op. cit. (note 1), p.88.

38 Meade, op. cit. (note 1), p.88.

39 Baker & Leigh (auctioneers), *Bibliotheca Askeviana sive Catalogus Librorum Rarissimorum* (London, 1775); H. Barnes, 'On Anthony Askew, MD FRS and his library', *Proceedings of the Royal Society of Medicine Section of the History of Medicine* 9 (1915–16), pp.23–7; P. Potter, 'Taste sets the price: Mead, Askew, and the birth of bibliomania in eighteenth-century England', *Canadian Bulletin of Medical History* 12:2 (1995), pp.241–57. The Shakespeare was sold on the 2nd day, lot 347. It was purchased by a Mr George Stevens for £5 10s. The catalogue entry reads: 'In this Book is the writing of King Charles the First in these Words; Dum spiro spero C.R. Also in Mr Herbert's Hand, ex Dono Serenissimi Regis Car. Servo suo Humiliss. T. Herbert.'

40 Smith, op. cit. (note 26), BM Sculpture 628.

41 Smart and Ingamells, op. cit. (note 22), p.74, cat.18, fig.343.

42 Webster, op. cit. (note 1), vol.II, p.765.

43 Macmichael, op. cit. (note 1), p.105.

44 Zuckermann, op. cit. (note 1), pp.202–3.

45 P. Toynbee (ed.), *The Letters of Horace Walpole, Fourth Earl of Orford*, 16 vols (Oxford, 1903–5), vol.III, p.3.

46 A parallel is to be drawn here with the last efforts of Sir William Hamilton (1730–1803) to place well his second collection of vases, bronzes and gems: I. Jenkins, 'Seeking the bubble reputation', in L. Burn (ed.), *Sir William Hamilton, Collector and Connoisseur* (Journal of the History of Collections 9, no.2) (1997), p.201.

47 C. Lloyd and V. Remington, *Masterpieces in Little Portrait miniatures from the collection of Her Majesty Queen Elizabeth II* (London, 1996), p.20; the 'melancholy young man' is p.86, cat.20.

48 M. Clayton, *Poussin, Works on Paper: Drawings from the collection of Her Majesty Queen Elizabeth II* (Houston and London, 1995), p.10.

49 E. Ruecker and W. Stearn, *Marià Sibilla in Surunam: Commentary to the facsimili edition of 'Metamorphuis Infectorum Surinamensium'* (Amsterdam, 1705) based on original watercolours in the Royal Library, Windsor Castle (London, 1982).

50 J. Rowlands, *Holbein: The paintings of Hans Holbein the Younger, complete edition* (Oxford, 1994), p.258.

51 Mead Catalogues (note 1): Prints and Drawings, 14th night, lot 65; E. Slatter, 'Dr Richard Mead's Commission and Ehret's Drawings at the Wellcome Institute'. Unpublished MS in various libraries, including those of the Wellcome Institute, Royal Society and Department of Prints and Drawings at the British Museum (1995), 40 pp.

52 Mead Catalogues (note 1): Museum Meadianum, p. 232; ibid.: Gems etc., 5th day, lot 35; I. Jenkins, 'The masks of Dionysos/Pan-Osiris-Apis', *Jahrbuch des Deutschen Archäologischen Instituts* 109 (1994), pp.273–99 *passim*.

53 Walters, op. cit. (note 29), p.876.

54 Mead Catalogues (note 1): Museum Meadianum, p.216; ibid.: Gems etc. 1st day, lot 35.

55 L. Pignorius, *Magnae deum matris ideae et Attidis initia ex vetustis monumentis nuper Tornaci erutis* (Paris, 1623), with engraving; Bernard de Montfaucon, *L'antiquitée expliquée et représentée en figures*, 15 vols (Paris, 1722–4), vol.II, pt 2, pl.137.

56 Paris, Bibliothèque Nationale, Cabinet des Médailles, inv. no. 4522/173/17B.

57 G. Faider-Feytmans, *Les bronzes romains de Belgique* (Mainz, 1979), p.212; B28, pls 197–8; M. Vermaseren, *Corpus Cultus Iovis Sabazii*, I: *The Hands* (Leiden, 1983), p.19 cat.44.

58 Mead Catalogues (note 1): Pictures xiv; M. Grasselli and P. Rosenberg, *Watteau 1684–1721*, exh. cat. National Gallery of Art (Washington, 1984), pp.439–43, cat.71.

59 Mead Catalogues (note 1): Museum Meadianum, p.242; ibid.: Gems etc. 5th day, lot 63; R. Hinks, *Catalogue of the Greek, Etruscan and Roman Paintings and Mosaics in the British Museum* (London, 1933), no.56, pl.18.

60 Smart, op. cit. (note 22), p.40.

61 C. Pace, 'Pietro Santi Bartoli: drawings in Glasgow University Library after Roman paintings and mosaics', *Papers of the British School at Rome* 47 (1979), pp.126–31.

62 G. Turnbull, *Treatise on Ancient Painting* (London, 1741).

63 Mead Catalogues (note 1): Prints and Drawings, 8th night, lot 70; Jenkins forthcoming, op. cit. (note 1).

64 L. Connor, 'The Topham collection of drawings in Eton College Library', *Eutopia* 2:1 (1993), pp.25–39.

65 Townley acquired other things from Mead, now in the British Museum, including an inscription, GR 1805. 7–3.4650; other inscriptions, GR 1805. 7–3. 190 and 203, came to Townley via Matthew Duane; an east-Greek Hellenistic marble relief, Smith, op. cit. (note 26) 704 came to Townley via Anthony Askew. Information supplied by B.F. Cook.

66 Mead Catalogue of Drawings (note 3), vol.3, fols 2–6.

67 Ibid., fol. 2; F. Haskell, *Painters and Patrons. A study in the relation between Italian art and society in the Age of the Baroque* (London, 1963), p.301; A.F. Gori, *Dactyliotheca Smithiana* (Venice, 1767), vol.II, p.292. The image was engraved by G.B. Brustolon after P.A. Novelli.

68 P. Laverack, *Daniel Katz Ltd 1968–1993* (London, 1993), p.82.

69 C. Avery and A. Radcliffe, *Giambologna 1532–1608, Sculptor to the Medici*, exh. cat., Victoria and Albert Museum (London and Vienna, 1978–9), pp.82–3; C. Avery, A. Radcliffe and M. Leithe-Jasper (eds), *Giambologna 1529–1608. Ein Wendepunkt der Europäischen Plastik* exh. cat. (Vienna, 1978), cat. no.20c.

70 Michaelis, op. cit. (note 24), pp.50–1.

71 D.H. Wright, 'The study of ancient Virgil illustrations from Raphael to Cardinal Massimi', in I. Jenkins (ed.), *Cassiano dal Pozzo's Paper Museum* 1 (Quaderni Puteani 2) (Turin, 1992), pp.137–53.

72 Barnes, op. cit. (note 39), pp.23–7; Potter, op. cit. (note 39), pp.241–57.

73 National Gallery, London, no.2968.

74 Mead Catalogues (note 1): Prints and Drawings, 14th night, lot 59.

75 Pliny, *Natural History*, book 35. 2. 9–11.

76 Cicero, *Letters to Atticus*, book 134. 18.

77 W. Smith, *A Dictionary of Greek and Roman Biography and Mythology in three Volumes* (London, 1876), *s.v.* Varro.

78 T. Birch, *The Heads and Characters of Illustrious Persons of Great Britain, with their Portraits engraven by Mr Houbraken and Mr Vertue. With their Lives and Characters by T. Birch*, 2 vols (London, 1743, 1751).

79 Mead Catalogues (note 1): Pictures, p.v. Bequeathed to the British Museum by Sir William Watson, friend of Ray, 1788, now in the Natural History Museum, South Kensington; this is not now thought to be Ray and is not like his true portraits. Piper, op. cit. (note 27), p.295. See further Lisa Jardine, p.49 (above).

80 The British Library's annotated copy of the Mead Pictures sale is inscribed 'Mr Oram/Dr Hunter' or simply 'Oram' against a number of items: p.v, William Harvey, John Locke, Walter Charlton; p.vi, John Radliffe, Isaac Newton.

81 Mead Catalogues (note 1): Museum Meadianum, p.213; Gems etc. 1st day, lot 68.

82 Mead Catalogues (note 1): Museum Meadianum, p.221; Gems etc. 1st day, lot 65; G. Richter, *Portraits of the Greeks*, 3 vols (London, 1965), p.192, figs 1127–9. Mead's bas relief of Demosthenes at the Altar is now in Trinity College, Dublin, but thought a fake: Mead Catalogues (note 1): Museum Meadianum, p.226; ibid.: Gems etc. 5th day, lot 70.

83 Mead Catalogues (note 1): Museum Meadianum, p.221; ibid.: Gems etc. 1st day, lot 66; Richter, op. cit. (note 82), p.177.1, figs 1022–3; L. Giuliani, in H. Beck and P. Bol (eds), *Forschungen zur Villa Albani: Katalog der Antiken Bildwerke*, vol.1 (Berlin, 1989), cat.152, pls 268–9.

84 The Chrysippus is now in Munich.

85 Rowlands, op. cit. (note 50), pp.58 and 128, cat.13, pl.26.

86 It was bought at the Mead sale by Viscount Folkestone and entered the collection of the Earl of Radnor. It is now on loan to the National Gallery.

87 L. Campbell, M. Mann Phillips, H. Herbrüggen and J. Trapp, 'Quentin Matsys, Desiderius Erasmus, Pieter Gillis and Thomas More', *Burlington Magazine* 120 (1972), pp.716–24; L. Silver, *The Paintings of Quinten Massys with Catalogue Raisonné* (Oxford, 1984), pp.105 ff., 235–7, cat.58.

88 Campbell *et. al.*, op. cit. (note 87), p.717.

89 Printed notice in the Mead file of the National Portrait Gallery, London: 'Harrison May 1, 1795'.

90 Meade, op. cit. (note 1), pp.109–11.

Figure 51
Lewis Pingo, bronze medal of Richard
Mead (1754). London, British Museum,
Department of Coins and Medals.

Figure 49
A.M. Zanetti the Elder, relief showing
a Hermaphrodite once in
the Palazzo Colonna, Rome (c. 1720),
black chalk on paper. London,
British Museum, Department of Greek
and Roman Antiquities.

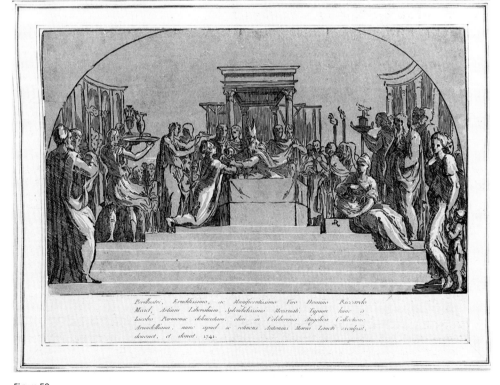

Figure 50
A.M. Zanetti, *The Circumcision and
Presentation of Christ* (1741),
chiaroscuro woodcut after
Parmigianino. London, British Museum,
Department of Prints and Drawings.

Figure 52
Jacopo Amigoni, *Queen Caroline
of Ansbach* (1735), oil on canvas.
By courtesy of the National Portrait
Gallery, London.

Figure 53
Allan Ramsay, *Portrait of
Dr Richard Mead* (1747), oil on canvas.
Coram Foundation, Foundling
Museum, London, UK/Bridgeman
Art Library.

Figure 54
J.P. Emslie, *49 Great Ormond
Street* (1882), watercolour on paper.
London, The Wellcome Library.

Figure 55
Isaac Oliver, *Portrait of a melancholy young man* (*c*. 1590), watercolour on vellum. London, The Royal Collection.

Figure 56
Anon, Italian drawing, *Bronze of Hercules with the Hydra* (*c*. 1720), black chalk on paper. London, British Museum, Department of Greek and Roman Antiquities.

Figure 57
Hans Holbein, *Portrait of Erasmus* (1523), panel, 75.7 x 51.4cm (29 x 20¼in). London, National Gallery.

Figure 58
Quentin Matsys, *Portrait of Pieter Gillis*, one half of the Friendship Diptych (1517), panel. Longford Castle.

Chapter 17

The Rise and Decline of English Neoclassicism

Joseph M. Levine

It is no accident that the rise and growth of the British Museum should coincide with the rise and decline of British neoclassicism. This is not to say that the success of the British Museum was the cause of the failure of neoclassical culture, but rather that it was inadvertently complicit in it. No doubt this must seem paradoxical since the first years of the Museum were marked by a series of magnificent classical acquisitions: beginning with Sir William Hamilton's astonishing collection of ancient vases (1772), and proceeding to the Townley Marbles (1804); the Elgin and Phigaleian Marbles (1814–16); and finally Payne Knight's extensive collection of Greek and Roman objects (1824). By 1807 a new department of antiquities had been created to rival the library and the natural history collections, and it soon became necessary for the Museum to find more space. It was only natural to commission a great Greek temple to house all these things, which of course resulted in today's imposing neoclassical building. And for a time it must have seemed that the development of the Museum and the prosperity of neoclassicism must forever coincide. But there were some early signs of trouble.

The term 'neoclassicism' is itself problematical. It was coined first by art historians, who were not altogether approving, later in the nineteenth century, to describe the high artistic culture of the period beginning about 1750 and continuing into the first decades of the new century. Like most such terms it has been stretched out of shape and much contested. It has been used sometimes to describe a particular period style in the fine arts, architecture, decoration, even music, although others have argued that the classical form is timeless and ever-recurring.[1] The term is used here rather to describe an attitude, an episode in intellectual history, when a long-standing admiration for the cultural forms of classical antiquity drew to a climax and inspired much direct imitation and appropriation. I shall concentrate on neoclassicism as a specific frame of mind, as the intellectual or cultural context which furnished the inspiration and justification for most of the ambitious art of the period – and its style. And I shall address a question that has been, generally and surprisingly, overlooked: why did this attitude develop in England in the manner and at the time that it did, and why did it gradually fade away?

Of course, what needs to be determined first is just what the appeal of antiquity was to early modern England, waxing and waning with changing circumstances over so many generations. From this perspective neoclassicism should probably best be seen as the climactic instance in a very long history; in particular as the interaction of two long-term conditions that eventually brought about its triumph.[2] In the first place, there

was the political situation, in Italy first, in England afterwards, which seemed to create for the governing classes an increasing practical utility for the classics. This, more than anything else, won them patronage and installed them in the schools, and explains their long and continuous life. In the second place, there was the developing knowledge of Greek and Roman antiquity, which brought about a deeper and more direct acquaintance with the classical sources and thereby facilitated a more accurate imitation and a more active emulation of the ancient culture. If this is right, eighteenth-century neoclassicism may be seen as a result of a long-standing desire to adapt the ancient models to modern life, enhanced by an especially congenial political situation, and reinforced by an increasing access to antiquity. And if this is so, it is to the governing classes in England that we may assign the principal credit for creating and fostering the new art that was eventually to triumph throughout much of Europe and America.[3] This may help to explain not only why and how neoclassicism came to flourish, but also why and how it began to fade away.

To demonstrate the truth of this contention would require, among other things, a history of English education from the days of Thomas More and Erasmus until recent times. It would show how Englishmen, beginning with the Crown itself, gradually subscribed to the notion that a sound political education required an intimate knowledge of the classics, and that an exclusive diet of Latin and Greek was the necessary preparation for practical life. From Thomas Elyot's *Boke of the Governor* (1531) to its numerous eighteenth-century progeny, the lessons which had once been set out in Cicero and Quintilian, and the Greeks before them, were reiterated incessantly.[4] If one hoped to participate in public life, it was necessary above all to learn to speak and write persuasively, and that could be done only by imitating the best of the ancient authors. The first and highest art of neoclassicism was therefore rhetoric (about which much was accordingly written), and its most splendid achievements were the orations of its politicians. Eloquence was undoubtedly the loftiest of the arts,[5] 'the most beautiful of all the daughters of wisdom', according to Mrs Montagu, and 'with the best dowry'.[6] When Joshua Reynolds decided to deliver his celebrated *Discourses on Art* to the Royal Academy, he drew naturally on classical rhetoric, in particular on Cicero and Quintilian, to help frame his own theory and to elevate his art.[7]

Of course, true eloquence required free political institutions. England's 'mixed constitution' was thought to embody the same principles of liberty and moral integrity, and to require the same kinds of deliberation and eloquence, that had once been associated with ancient Athens and Rome. Whigs, Tories, and Radicals all agreed upon the importance of free public debate,[8] and nearly everyone believed that 'free states are the best nursery-bed of the arts'.[9] As a result, the best hope for eloquence seemed to lie in a recapitulation of the style, form, and message – indeed the whole culture – of Cicero and Demosthenes. It was this attitude, which was endlessly reiterated throughout the period, that explains the close association between politics, education, and rhetoric, that characterized the age.[10]

But changing political circumstances necessarily affected the force of this message. From the first it was assumed that there was a real affinity between the actual circumstances of the Greek and Roman world and their modern counterparts. 'No nation under heaven', writes the critic and painter Jonathan Richardson, 'so nearly resembles the ancient Greeks and Romans as ours. There is a haughty courage, an elevation of thought, a greatness of taste, a love of liberty, a simplicity and honesty among us, which we inherit from our ancestors'.[11] By the eighteenth century it was parliament that provided the great public stage that seemed akin to the free public assemblies of Athens and Rome. And it was parliament that was the chief ambition of 'the nation-forming class'.[12] The more that modern England seemed to resemble the political and social institutions of the ancient world, the easier and more appropriate did comparison and imitation appear. A host of works were written to draw out the parallels between ancient and modern history.[13] When the elder Pitt spoke everyone remembered Demosthenes, and no one had to be reminded of Roman example when Edmund Burke took up the cudgels against Warren Hastings in the guise of Cicero against Verres.[14] A canon of British orators emerged to rival the ancients, until a proud Englishman could boast that: 'The annals of the world do not afford more brilliant proofs of the powers of the human genius, and of the extent of the human understanding, than are to be found in the debates of the British senate.'[15] Under these circumstances, it is not surprising that politicians wished to have themselves represented in portrait sculpture in classical costume and pose. What a galaxy of neoclassical heroes could be assembled from the tombs in Westminster Abbey alone!

To give a public speech was thus to invite criticism, not merely of politics, but of style and form and delivery. Keen observers like Horace Walpole or Nathaniel Wraxall never failed to analyse the orations they heard for their rhetorical merit. Classical allusions were commonplace. As Walpole put it, even when 'a Minister was much abused, he at least had the satisfaction of hearing himself abused very classically.'[16] Parliament was a stage, and the quality of the performance was everything. It was William Pitt the Elder who had shown the way, and with his immediate successors created the golden age of English oratory. It was Chatham who had personally supervised his son's education in the classics with the deliberate and successful intention of making him his successor; and it was his old rival, Henry Fox, who may even have outdone him by turning *his* son, Charles James Fox, into one of the best Greek scholars of the age.[17] Their rivalry as orators was notorious. Wraxall found it hard to judge who was best in the knowledge of Greek and Latin sources. 'Fox's oratory was more impassioned; Pitt's could boast greater correctness of diction. The former

exhibited, while speaking, all the Tribunitarian rage; the latter displayed the consular dignity.'[18] When at last the younger Pitt died in 1806, he was given a splendid neoclassical monument in Westminster Abbey; when Fox died shortly afterwards, he too was given a monument in the Abbey, as well as a bronze statue in Bloomsbury Square. Both were honoured with busts by Nollekens that were distributed throughout the British Isles. Fox was also commemorated by the Duke of Bedford in a Temple of Liberty modelled by Henry Holland after an ancient Greek original.[19] Classical oratory had become both the stimulus and the occasion for much of the neoclassical art of the period.

It followed naturally that the governing classes should take an interest in the whole range of activities of their classical prototypes and try to emulate them there too. The letters of such as Cicero and Pliny the Younger offered a window on the world of upper-class Rome that seemed to provide models and mirrors for the private as well as the public lives of the English country gentleman. From the beginning of the Renaissance, antiquaries had been accumulating a detailed knowledge of the culture of antiquity, using the material remains as well as literature to determine how the Greeks and Romans lived, fought and worshipped. Vast compilations had accumulated to inform the learned, while neat digests and handbooks were created for the rest, complete with copious engraved illustrations.[20]

It was natural in these circumstances that many great men should think of emulating the ancients by building or rebuilding their stately homes and decorating them in what they imagined to be classical style. What better for that purpose than to go abroad and see directly the remains of the ancient world, and bring back whatever they could to fill up their libraries and adorn their estates? It was the great lords and wealthy gentlemen who first began to flood into Rome and Naples to complete their Grand Tours, accompanied by classical tutors or travel guides, followed by artists and architects, eager to copy and purchase antiquities for their cabinets and thus lay the foundations for the museums that were to follow. By 1754 a great many of the peers and at least ninety-six members of the House of Commons had gone on the Grand Tour.[21] It was a thrill, expressed again and again in public and private (as George Grenville put it in 1774), to look upon 'those spots and buildings where perhaps a Brutus raised his dagger, or a Tully saved his country.' Boswell was so moved by the sight of Rome, he resolved to speak only Latin while he was there; and Johnson, who never did get there, remarked plaintively that 'A man who has not been to Italy, is always conscious of his inferiority from his not having seen what it is expected a man should see'.[22] Among other things, Grenville was astonished by 'the profusion of marbles' that he found there. With this in mind, he wrote to his cousin, 'you will easily imagine . . . I have not been insensible to the opportunities of enriching myself and my country with the spoils of Roman grandeur'.[23] Winckelmann was only afraid that some mad Englishman might take it into his head to carry off the whole of Trajan's Column.[24]

The artists followed their patrons, eager to oblige them by painting or carving their portraits, often posed in classical costume or before the ancient monuments, or holding them in hand; by furnishing them with antiques, restoring or copying them for their collections; and eventually, by building and decorating their houses. By 1749 there were already at least sixteen British artists in Rome, enough to form a short-lived academy, not to mention a busy group of sculptors and architects.[25] In a few years there were many more, including the leading founders of the Royal Academy: the architect William Chambers, the sculptor Joseph Wilton, the painter Joshua Reynolds. The point, James Barry was told, was that in Rome above all, 'you will find among the works of the ancients, the most perfect forms in the most graceful attitudes, and with the justest expressions'.[26] For the artists, it was not least among their objectives that they hoped to meet and acquire their future patrons on the spot. 'I am now in such a situation in Rome,' George Dance wrote to his father in 1762, 'that I cannot fail of making acquaintance with some of the greatest people of England, and I assure you the acquaintance one makes with English noblemen in Rome are of great consequence when one meets them in England. Their having known you abroad makes them interest themselves for you more than otherwise they wou'd think of.'[27]

Meanwhile, news of the discoveries of Pompeii and Herculaneum began to circulate in England and Roman travellers soon added those sites to their itineraries, while the Greek remains at Paestum and Sicily brought further excitement. Sir William Hamilton set up his ambassador's shop in Naples and opened his doors to scores of English travellers whom he guided expertly to the classical sites in search of Virgil's tomb and Horace's villa, all the while building the amazing collections that were to find their way (at least in part) to the British Museum.[28] The voracious appetites of Northern visitors led to fresh excavations in search of treasure, and the traffic in antiquities from Hadrian's villa and other places near Rome, orchestrated by the artist Gavin Hamilton and the banker Thomas Jenkins, became notorious. One principal beneficiary was Lord Shelburne, whose Lansdowne House was carefully prepared to display them.[29] Another was Townley, who filled his house in Westminster with marbles, bronzes, coins, gems, and drawings, arranged in a manner so 'classically correct . . . that the interior of a Roman villa might be inspected in our metropolis.' It looked to one visitor like a scene out of Cicero or Pliny.[30] His friend Thomas Hope may have done even better with his Duchess Street mansion. 'Every man of taste will congratulate himself', wrote a satisfied observer in 1800, 'that England is the seat of the arts; and that so many genuine remains of ancient sculpture are preserved in our cabinets.'[31]

Inevitably the Grand Tour was extended eastward and a host of English visitors, led by a few noble lords and under-written by the Society of the Dilettanti, began to discover and describe the remains of ancient Greece. Already in Rome in 1756, young Robert Adam had expressed a wish, that was often reiterated and soon to be fulfilled by his successors, to view the Temples of Athens, Thebes, and Sparta, and the fields of Marathon and Thermopylae, 'to be where harangued Demosthenes, where fought Epaminondas, and where Pericles counselled'.[32] To visit Greece was less comfortable than Italy, to be sure, but as the Turks eased their restrictions, and politics and commerce encouraged traffic, explorers flooded into Athens and the Troad, rejoicing again to be at the sites of their literary and historical heroes, and eager to take back what they could to England. We are at the beginning of the Greek revival.

This is a familiar story, which probably needs no further elaboration, except to emphasize that this was the immediate background for some of the collectors who did so much to create the British Museum. Among the many tourists who turned up in Athens to describe the excitement around 1800 was Robert Smirke, the young architect who was eventually to design the Museum's neoclassical building. Exactly as his predecessors had done a generation before in Rome – George Dance and Robert Adam and many another – he wrote letters and recorded his discoveries and his enthusiasm. He particularly admired the architecture, and carefully sketched the Acropolis, where one could still see with astonishment 'the perfection to which art had been carried in those ages and conceive with that the refinements of the mind which necessarily must have kept pace with those perfections.' It was just then that Lord Elgin's company began to dismantle the frieze on the Parthenon. Despite a twinge of regret, Smirke had no doubt that it was all for the best. 'It is rather fortunate for the English', he wrote, 'that such a man is commandant, for by this, works of art will be introduced into the country and in all probability become public property, which will not only be ornamental, but I should think extremely useful to the Painter, Sculptor, or Architect.'[33] Nothing was too small to escape his attention; he admired the forms of everything he saw. He tried to take casts, but settled for carrying off what fragments he could, including one large piece of marble from the Erechtheion too bulky to smuggle past the guards. With a single helper, he picked it up and tossed it over the walls, where it rolled along for some distance. 'Fortunately, no one was passing at the time, we wrapt our handkerchiefs over it and brought it safely home, from where I afterward got the useful part cut off.' Eventually he ran out of money and time, but he had learned, so he thought, 'the merits of a style of architecture which, though it has always been a favorite with me, I have I am sure, never felt its just force, nor do I think it would have been ever possible, if I had not seen it so strikingly in Athens'.[34] He returned to England, eager to put his knowledge to practical use.

Nevertheless, and despite the affinity that was felt between ancient and modern times, hardly anyone really expected that neoclassicism should be an exact reproduction of antiquity. The act of imitation was always an act of adaptation, and even the strictest pedants allowed for some flexibility. But this is just where increasing knowledge began to widen the gap. Imitation became more self-conscious and difficult with the growing recognition that there were insurmountable differences as well as similarities between past and present. It was Horace Walpole (among others) who pointed out the growing significance of modern finance to politics. How awkward would the ancient historians have been had they had to encumber their narratives with 'three per cents, discounts, premiums, South Sea annuities and East India Bonds!'[35] Was it possible that the models and lessons of the past might not be so directly useful in the present? Did the times and personalities in fact resemble each other closely enough?[36] With the coming of the Industrial Revolution in the new century and the expansion of the franchise, neoclassical politics, or what some have called 'civic humanism', seemed to become increasingly irrelevant to modern life. For the first time serious questions began to be asked about the exclusive place of the classics in education.[37]

But if times were changing, so too was knowledge of the past. The neoclassical sensibility had been naturally dependent on an increasing knowledge of, and access to, antiquity.

Imitation required understanding, and for a long time after the Renaissance, understanding of the ancient world deepened as classical philology and archaeology grew steadily more competent. The literary sources were gradually discovered, edited, interpreted and translated; the material remains were collected, unearthed, classified and criticized. A rhetorical climate had whetted the appetite for knowledge, and for a while every fragment of antiquity seemed to throw new light on the ancient culture that was so much admired and imitated. But then, unexpectedly, it turned out that too much knowledge could be a dangerous thing. Instead of helping, it seemed that history could get in the way and even undermine the whole enterprise.

All along, it is true, some doubts had been expressed, and neoclassicism had always been distinguished from earlier classicisms by a certain self-consciousness and an ironic detachment, which has sometimes given it a bad name. The neoclassical monuments that bestrewed the grounds of Stowe (including one of the first Greek revival buildings in Europe) had an overt political programme, but they soon became famous as a tourist site, rather for their historical associations than for their practical value. 'A classical park or garden', Thomas Lyttleton complained as early as 1779, 'is as ridiculous an expression as a classical plum pudding or a classical sirloin of beef. It is an unworthy action to strip the classics of their heroes, gods and goddesses, to grow green amid the fogs of our unclassical climate.'[38] Nostalgia for the ancients as a lost civilization was quite different from the desire to replicate it immediately for use in the present. It did not help that the original works had usually to be restored to neoclassical perfection before export – freshly polished and given new arms and heads – and that they were often seen and studied in plaster copies. More disturbing was the gradual realization by their admirers that the originals were themselves merely late Roman or Greek copies.[39] When ruins began to be admired – and actually *created* – for their own intrinsic value, the neoclassical moment was clearly in jeopardy. As Rose Macaulay once put it, 'We do not find Cicero or Verres writing to order ruined temples for their villas, nor Pliny describing the prospects in his Tuscan garden as terminating in broken triumphal arches, nor Horace rejoicing in ruins on his Sabine farm.'[40] A growing sense of history was beginning to intrude.

This can be seen, among other things, in a deepening disagreement about the appropriate dress for modern heroic representation. Should James Wolfe be portrayed dying on the plains of Quebec in classical or modern costume? West opted for modernity over the objections of Joshua Reynolds, who urged him 'to adopt the classic costume of antiquity, as much more becoming the inherent greatness of a subject than the modern garb of war'.[41] Even in sculpture, which had led the way, direct imitation of antiquity began to seem problematical. Thus the statue of Admiral Holmes by Joseph Wilton (1766), which had once been acclaimed as a model of neoclassical style, eventually fell into disgrace. At first, 'the worshippers of antique costume were gratified with beholding a British Admiral drest like a Roman, standing with his right hand resting on a mounted cannon, over which was displayed the English flag.' But as time passed, according to the nineteenth-century author, 'many lovers of historical truth and nature exclaimed against a clumsy fiction by which the first century shook hands with the

eighteenth'.[42] When Samuel Johnson died, it was Reynolds who led the fight to have his old friend sculpted in classical dress for his monument in St Paul's. For the time being he won, but the cause was already failing. In a few years, the sculptor Francis Chantrey wondered, 'why a plain English gentleman . . . should consent to be habituated in any other way in marble than that which he appeared in real life?' He found it hard to accept what he called 'the vague spell of classicality'.[43]

Paradoxically, the more exact and historical the knowledge of the ancients, the less satisfactory did the early examples of neoclassicism seem. When the Greek revival began it was at the expense of the Romanists, who did not give up without a fight. Sir William Chambers, James Paine, even Robert Adam, resisted.[44] Sir John Soane admired Adam's successful attempt at Keddleston to unite 'the magnificence of a Roman villa with all the comforts of an English nobleman's residence'. Nevertheless, he believed with many in his generation that Adam had not quite reached 'the sublimity of the great restorers of architecture'. And it was not long afterwards that it became hard to accept that 'the depraved compositions of Adam were not only tolerated but had their admirers'.[45] But this was the age of Wilkins and Smirke, the National Gallery and the British Museum, a neoclassical Greek architecture more pedantic and correct, and more appropriate certainly to a museum, but less obviously appealing for ordinary life.[46]

The history of how the Elgin Marbles were acquired makes a fitting climax to our story: their collection by a noble lord who hoped to reinvigorate British art with their example; their purchase by a parliament that basically accepted that argument; and their installation in the British Museum. The public debate that accompanied their purchase is especially revealing. A comparison with the Townley Marbles now suggested to some (Flaxman, for example) that they were only copies and inferior works; whereas to others (like Payne Knight) it was the Elgin Marbles which seemed the less authentic because of their imperfect state, too realistic for their neoclassical sensibilities.[47] Perhaps it was William Hazlitt who best expressed the modern view, preferring the marbles 'for their mouldering imperfect state', because they were able to transport the onlookers directly to the ancient Greece of the Parthenon; whereas he thought that a Hellenistic masterpiece like the Apollo Belvedere was overrated just because it looked like an eighteenth-century gentleman (perhaps he was thinking of Reynolds's famous portrait of Admiral Keppel).[48] In any case, the undeniable fact was that the Elgin marbles failed to rejuvenate a declining British neoclassical art. Their greatest advocate, Benjamin Robert Haydon, was unable to find any patronage for his grand classicizing ambitions.[49]

Of course, the Marbles continued to be admired anyway, as they are today, but to less effect, surrounded and obscured by the spoils of a dozen other early civilizations. Slowly and almost imperceptibly, the neoclassical aspiration was turning from an ethical ideal and practical guide to life to an historical curiosity, from an integral part of the culture of the governing classes to something to be safely admired in a museum, a special subject only in the schools and universities where it had once ruled without competition. Like the classics in general, for better or for worse, the art of antiquity has been turned into history and returned to its own time, still appealing, no doubt, but very distant and very different from our own.

Joseph M. Levine

Notes and references

1   A dictionary definition is provided by the article in the *Encyclopedia of World Art*, vol.x (1958), cols 514–15. 'The term "neoclassic" designates a clearly defined movement in European style and taste from about the mid-eighteenth century to the first decades of the nineteenth ... it particularly sought to reflect the forms of the apogee of Greco-Roman civilization.' The author adds: 'Pure and simple form was the ideal, simplicity was emphasized, whatever was accidental or realistic was eliminated.' For anticipations of this neoclassical aesthetic in artists from Mantegna to Poussin see Mario Praz, *On Neoclassicism*, trans. Agnes Davidson (London, 1969). And for the history of the term – which was of course used as much for literary history as the history of the arts, but even more elastically – see James William Johnson, *The Formation of English Neo-Classical Thought* (Princeton, 1967), pp.3–30; Renée Wellek, 'The term and concept of Classicism in literary history', *Discriminations: Further concepts of criticism* (New Haven, 1970), pp.55–89; B.H. Bronson, 'When was Neo-Classicism?', *Studies in Criticism and Aesthetics 1660–1800. Essays in Honour of S.H. Monk* (Minneapolis, 1967), pp.13–35. 'Neoclassicism', according to the *Pelican History of Art*, 'is a movement of some complexity still awaiting its historian', Margaret Whinney, *Sculpture in Britain 1580–1830*, rev. John Physick (London, 1988), p.277.

2   The same case has been argued in Joseph M. Levine, 'Why Neoclassicism? Politics and culture in eighteenth-century England', *British Journal for Eighteenth-Century Studies* 25 (2002), pp.75–101.

3   For English precedence, an admittedly controversial notion, see J. Locquin, 'La rétour à l'antique dans l'école anglaise et dans l'école française avant David', *La Renaissance de l'art française* 8 (1922), pp.472–81; S.F. Kimball, 'Les influences anglaises dans la formation du style Louis XVI', *Gazette des Beaux-Arts* 5 (1931), pp.29–44, 231–55; and E.K. Waterhouse, 'The British contribution to the Neo-Classical style in painting', *Proceedings of the British Academy* 40 (1954), pp.57–74.

4   See the essay on Thomas Elyot in Joseph M. Levine, *The Autonomy of History: Truth and method from Erasmus to Gibbon* (Chicago, 1999), pp.53–71.

5   'For it unites the beauties of them all. It joins the harmony of sound, the beauty of action, comeliness of composition, to good breeding.' Thomas Reid, *Lectures in the Fine Arts*, ed. Peter Levy (The Hague, 1973), p.51, quoted in Stephen Copley, 'The fine arts in eighteenth-century polite culture', in John Barrell (ed.), *Painting and the Politics of Culture: New essays on British art 1700–1850* (Oxford, 1992), p.29. In general, see Wilbur S. Howell, *Eighteenth-Century British Logic and Rhetoric* (Princeton, 1971).

6   Elizabeth Montagu to Thomas Lyttleton (1761), Emily Climenson (ed.), *Elizabeth Montagu, The Queen of the Blue-Stockings* (London, 1906), vol.II, pp.253–6.

7   Reynolds's debt is frequently expressed, as in a key passage at the beginning of the third discourse (1770), where he writes: 'The poets, orators, and rhetoricians of antiquity, are continually enforcing this position; that all the arts receive their perfection from an ideal beauty.' Robert R. Wark (ed.), *Discourses on Art* (New Haven, 1975), p.42. For some explicit references to Cicero see pp.42–3, 100, 133, 163; to Quintilian, pp.48, 104.

8   For a good example of Tory neoclassicism see William King, whose Latin orations at Oxford caused a sensation. David Greenwood, *William King: Tory and Jacobite* (Oxford, 1969), pp.141–2, 193–233. For the radicals see the republican Thomas Hollis, who joined to his politics a vigorous patronage of the neoclassical arts; see *Memoirs of Thomas Hollis* (London, 1780).

9   William Young, *The History of Athens Politically and Philosophically Considered* (London, 1786), p.139. 'All politeness', declared the Earl of Shaftesbury, 'is owing to Liberty'; see Lawrence Klein, 'Liberty, manners, and politeness in early eighteenth-century England', *Historical Journal* 32 (1989), pp.583–605.

10 The advice to the gentleman was endlessly reiterated: study the classics 'to make them useful and subservient to you in supporting the dignity and station you are to fill in life'. *Letters concerning Education addressed to a Gentleman entering the University* (London, 1785). For some characteristic examples see John Hill, *Observations on the Greek and Roman Classics* (London, 1753); Sir William Jones to Lord Althorp, Garland Cannon (ed.), *The Letters of Sir William Jones* (Oxford, 1970), vol.I, pp.125–6, 146–9, etc.; Vicessimus Knox, *Personal Nobility, or Letters to a Young Nobleman in the Conduct of his Studies* (London, 1793).

11 Jonathan Richardson, 'Essay on the theory of painting' (1715), reprinted in *The Works ...* (London, 1773), p.122.

12 See Lewis Namier, *The Structure of Politics at the Accession of George III*, 2nd edn (London, 1968), p.1.

13 See, for example, *A Parallel between the Roman and British Constitution* (London, 1747); or the work by Edward Wortley Montagu, *Reflections on the Rise and Fall of the Antient Republicks adapted to the Present State of Britain* (1759) and *The Parallel: Or the Conduct and Fate of Great Britain in regard to our present Contest with France; exemplified from the Histories of Macedon and Athens* (London, 1756). For some other parallel histories see Frank Turner, 'British politics and the demise of the Roman Republic', *Historical Journal* 29 (1986), pp.577–99.

14 Geoffrey Carnall, 'Burke as the modern Cicero', in G. Carnall and C. Nicolson (eds), *The Impeachment of Warren Hastings* (Edinburgh, 1989), pp.76–90; H.V. Canter, 'The impeachments of Verres and Hastings: Cicero and Burke', *Classical Journal* 9 (1913–14), pp.199–211. See Nathaniel Wraxall, *Posthumous Memoirs*, 2nd edn (London, 1836), vol.III; and for the speech, Burke, *Works* (Boston 1839), vol.VIII, p.534.

15 Thomas Browne, *The British Senate: Or a Selection of the most Admired Speeches of the English Language* (London, 1808), vol.I, p.237; C. William Hazlitt, *The Eloquence of the British Senate* (London, 1808). And for the British canon in America, Chauncey Goodrich, *Select British Eloquence* (New York, 1853).

16 'Whenever a leader of the opposition was to be popular, he was presently likened to the greatest names of antiquity, and to be canonized by the appellation of some Brutus or Camillus ... If any young patriot was to be recommended as the idol of the party, Horatius Coccles, young Scipio, or Marcellus, fitted them to a hair.' Horace Walpole in *Old England*, 14 February, 1747, quoted by Romney Sedgwick, 'Horace Walpole's political articles', in Warren H. Smith (ed.), *Horace Walpole: Writer, politician, connoisseur* (New Haven, 1967), pp.46–7.

17 When Fox was asked how he got his fluency in public speaking, he replied, 'I believe it may be attributed to this circumstance: when I was a lad, my father used every morning to make me translate, before him and the rest of the family, those portions of Livy, Virgil, etc, which I had read in the morning with my tutor.' Samuel Rogers, *Table-Talk* (London, 1856), p.113; Edward Creasy, *Memoirs of Eminent Etonians* (London, 1850), p.212.

18 Nathaniel Wraxall, *Historical Memorials of my own Time*, ed. Richard Asckam (1815, reprinted London, 1904), p.632.

19 John Kenworthy-Brown, 'The Temple of Liberty at Woburn', *Apollo* 130 (1989), pp.27–33; N.B. Penny, 'The Whig cult of Fox in early nineteenth-century culture', *Past and Present* 70 (February 1976), pp.94–105. An earlier bust of Fox by Nollekens was commissioned by Catherine the Great in 1792 to be placed between Cicero and Demosthenes.

20 See my essay, 'The antiquarian enterprise, 1500–1800', in J.M. Levine, *Humanism and History* (Ithaca, 1987), pp.73–106.

21 Romney Sedgwick, *History of Parliament: House of Commons 1715–54* (London 1970), vol.I, p.139. Indispensable now is the new *Dictionary of British and Irish Travellers in Italy 1701–1800*, compiled from the archives of Brinsley Ford, by John Ingamells (New Haven and London, 1997).

22 Frank Brady and Frederick Pottle (eds), *Boswell on the Grand Tour 1765–66* (London, 1955), vol.II, pp.63–5, 84–6; George Birkbeck Hill (ed.), *Boswell's Life of Johnson*, rev. L.F. Powell (Oxford, 1934), vol.III, p.36.

23 George Grenville to Morton Pitt, 14 May 1774, in Georgiana Lady Chatterton (ed.), *Admiral Lord Gambier Memorials*, 2 vols (London, 1861), vol.I, pp.96–9. This is an exact echo of Joseph Spence writing to his mother, 2 August 1732, in Slava Klima (ed.), *Letters from the Grand Tour* (Montreal, 1975), pp.114–16.

24 Winckelmann to Stosch, 26 February 1768, reproduced in Adolf Michaelis, *Ancient Marbles in Great Britain*, trans. C.A.M. Fennell (Cambridge, 1882), p.88.

25 James Russel, *Letters from a Young Painter Abroad* (London, 1750), vol.II, p.361. For a list of more than a hundred British visitors to Rome, chiefly artists, see Lindsay Stainton, 'Hayward's List: British visitors to Rome 1753–75', *Walpole Society* 49 (1983); *British Artists in Rome,* exh. cat. Kenwood House (London, 1974).

26 Dr Joseph Sleigh to Barry, 31 December 1763, in Dr Fryer (ed.), *The Works of James Barry* (London, 1809), vol.I, pp.11–12. See in general Frances Haskell and Nicholas Penny (eds),

The Most Beautiful Statues: The taste for antique sculpture (Oxford, 1981).

27 5 February 1762, Dance Letters, Royal Institute of British Architects (hereafter RIBA), pp.19–20. In the same vein, see William Chambers, quoted in Derek Hudson, *Sir Joshua Reynolds: A personal study* (London, 1958), p.46.

28 See the articles in I. Jenkins and K. Sloan (eds), *Vases and Volcanoes: Sir William Hamilton and his collections* (London, 1996), and 'Sir William Hamilton: Collector and connoisseur', *Journal of the History of Collections* 9 (1997), pp.187–303.

29 According to Wraxall (op. cit. [note 18], p.273), it formed 'an asylum of taste and science'. See Lord Edward Fitzmaurice (ed.), *The Letters of Gavin Hamilton at Lansdowne House* (Devizes, 1879); and David Irwin, 'Gavin Hamilton: archaeologist, painter, and dealer', *Art Bulletin* 44 (1962), pp.87–102. See also Thomas Ashby, 'Thomas Jenkins in Rome', *Papers of the British School at Rome* 6 (1913), pp.487–511; Brinsley Ford, 'Thomas Jenkins: banker, dealer and unofficial agent', *Apollo* (1974), pp.416–25; Carlo Pietrangeli, 'Archaeological excavations in Italy 1750–1850', *The Age of Neo-Classicism* (London, 1972), pp.xlvi–lii; and 'The discovery of classical art in eighteenth-century Rome', *Apollo* 107 (1983), pp.380–91. Pietrangeli enumerates thirteen major English collections that were served by Hamilton and Jenkins.

30 James Dalloway in John Nichols, *Illustrations of the Literary History of the Eighteenth Century*, vol.III (London, 1818), pp.721–46; see Brian Cook, 'The Townley Marbles in Westminster and Bloomsbury', *British Museum Yearbook* 2 (1977), pp.34–78.

31 James Dalloway, *Anecdotes of the Arts in England* (London, 1800), p.viii; David Watkin, *Thomas Hope and the Neo-Classical Idea* (London, 1968).

32 John Fleming, *Robert Adam and his Circle* (London, 1962), p.214.

33 Robert Smirke, Travel Journals, Athens, 20 July 1803, RIBA, box 5, vol.II, pp.19v., 33.

34 Ibid., 8 August 1803, p.73. For Smirke see J. Mordaunt Crook, *The British Museum: A case-study in architectural politics* (London, 1972), pp.73–150.

35 Horace Walpole, *Memoirs of George II*, ed. John Brooke, (New Haven, 1985),vol.III, p.39.

36 Walpole to Mann, 28 December 1761, in W.S. Lewis (ed.), *Correspondence*, vol.XXI (New Haven, 1960), pp.557–60.

37 See for example John Barrell, *The Political Theory of Painting from Reynolds to Hazlitt* (New Haven, 1986), pp.338–9. Barrell draws on the works of J.G.A. Pocock.

38 T. Frost, *The Life of Thomas Lord Lyttleton* (London, 1876), pp.313–14. The complaint was anticipated in the satirical poem, *Of Taste* (1756) and grew more insistent over time, viz. John Claudius Loudon, *A Treatise on Forming Country Residences* (London, 1806), vol.II, pp.360–61.

39 See A.D. Potts, 'Greek sculpture and Roman copies: Anton Mengs and the eighteenth century', *Journal of the Warburg and Courtauld Institutes* 43 (1980), pp.150–75. Not untypical is the example of Gavin Hamilton who found a torso of Venus in the Barberini Palace and sold it to Thomas Jenkins, who had it reworked and given a head, probably by the notorious Roman sculptor and restorer, Bartolomeo Cavaceppi, who then sold it in 1765 as an uninjured antique to the English collector William Weddell, for a great sum. See Magaret Whinney, *Sculpture in Britain 1530–1830* (Harmondsworth, 1964), p.135. Nollekens made his first reputation

40 stitching together the parts of different statues and supplying the missing parts; see J.T. Smith, *Nollekens and his Times* (London, 1828), vol.I, p.251.

41 Rose Macaulay, *Pleasure of Ruins* (London, 1953), pp.7–8.

42 Reynolds had published his views in the seventh discourse of 1776: *Discourses*, op. cit. (note 7), pp.134–41. He expressly compares sculpture and oratory there. On the general problem, see Edgar Wind, 'The revolution of history painting', in Jayne Anderson (ed.), *Hume and the Heroic Portrait* (Oxford, 1986), pp.88–99.

43 Allan Cunningham, *Lives of the British Painters, Sculptors and Architects* (London, 1830), vol.III, pp.73–4.

44 John Holland, *Memorials of Francis Chantrey* (London, 1851), pp.199–201. 'Commercial enterprise, which created the money and paid for the work, had little taste for classical dress or allegory, and preferred their great men to be recognizable, and in the attitudes they might have adopted in life', Whinney, op.cit. (note 39), p.203.

45 When Chambers got his copy of the *Antiquities of Ionia* he protested to his patron, Lord Charlemont, that it 'showed some of the worst architecture I ever saw', 4 February 1770, *Manuscripts and Correspondence of Lord Charlemont,* Historical Manuscripts Commission (London, 1891–4), vol.I, p.298. See Dora Wiebenson, *Sources of Greek Revival Architecture* (University Park, 1969), app.III, pp.126–31. In 1823 James Elmes remembered how odd the new-fangled Doric had first seemed, without its base, like 'a shirt without ruffles'. See J. Mordaunt Crook, *The Greek Revival* (London, 1968), pp.15–17; and Michael McCarthy, 'Documents on the Greek Revival in architecture', *Burlington Magazine* 114 (1972), pp.760–69.

46 Joseph Gwilt, *Encyclopedia of Architecture* (1842): I quote from the 2nd edn (London, 1851); Soane's lectures on Adam were delivered in 1815. See Arthur T. Bolton, *The Architecture of Robert and James Adam* (London, 1922), vol.I, pp.110–12.

47 Some of the criticisms are assembled by Crook, op. cit. (note 34). For the growing classicism of such as George Dance, Thomas Harrison and Soane, and the 'Greek purists' Wilkins, Smirke and Inwood, see John Summerson, *Architecture in Britain* (Baltimore, 1954), pp.254, 270ff.

48 'You have lost your labour, my Lord Elgin; your marbles are overrated – they are not Greek, they are Roman of the time of Hadrian . . .' When the marbles turned up in England, the distinguished connoisseur Sir George Beaumont recommended that they be restored immediately, 'as at present, they excite rather disgust than pleasure in the minds of the people in general, to see parts of limbs, and bodys, stumps of arms, etc.' Kathryn Cave (ed.), *The Diary of Joseph Farington*, vol.IX (New Haven, 1982), 3 June 1808, p.3290. Canova was approached to restore them but refused on the ground that 'it would be sacrilege in him or any man to presume to touch them with a chisel'. *Memorandum on the Subject of the Earl of Elgin's Pursuits in Greece* (London, 1815), pp.39–40; J.H. Smith, 'Lord Elgin and his collection', *Journal of Hellenic Studies* 36 (1916), p.255.

48 See Stephen A. Larrabee, 'Hazlitt's criticism of Greek sculptures', *Journal of the History of Ideas* 2 (1941), p.84.

49 'The Elgin Marbles will produce a revolution in the art of this country', Haydon wrote optimistically to his father in 1806, 'but I fear the low taste of the patrons . . . they have no conception of its public function', F.W. Haydon (ed.), *Correspondence and Table-Talk* (Boston, 1877), vol.I, pp.255–6.

Chapter 18

Bodies of Enlightenment
Sculpture and the eighteenth-century museum

Malcolm Baker

Today's notion of 'the museum' has been shaped, to a very great extent, both by the way in which that type of institution was conceived in the Enlightenment and by the role it played in articulating and advancing Enlightenment ideals and values. The most obvious manifestation of this debt has, of course, been the frequent adoption of classical architectural models for museum buildings, but equally visible, if far less remarked upon, has been the prominent presence of sculpture within these institutions. Now seen as an appropriate decorative addition, this sculptural peopling of the rationally arranged spaces of the museum draws on a pattern established in the Enlightenment. Just as Enlightenment notions of citizenship drew on Graeco-Roman textual tradition and authority, so it was fitting that one of the public institutions that grew out of these notions should give prominence to those antique marbles, pieces that offered a visual equivalent to classical texts. Equally, it was considered appropriate to represent and to commemorate sculpturally those modern thinkers responsible for shaping Enlightenment beliefs, above all in the form of portrait busts. In these two ways sculpture – especially sculpture in marble – may be viewed as a register of Enlightenment concerns and aspirations so that its prominence in a range of institutions of that age, including museums, is not surprising.

But the relationship established between sculpture and the other parts of a collection (whether paintings or archaeological artefacts), as well as that between sculpture and the architecture of the institution, has connections with older traditions of using sculpture within princely collections, albeit with certain very significant differences. This chapter will argue that the key role played by sculpture in the Enlightenment museum was established through a reworking of earlier modes of sculptural display, in the light of new concerns and ideals, and with an awareness of a different and wider audience. As well as registering the shift from private to public (at least in broad terms), this re-configuration of the sculptural component of the museum or art collection involved both the formulation of new aesthetic attitudes and ways of viewing, together with a changing notion of history. In its use of sculpture, as in so many other of its aspects, the Enlightenment museum was shaping and privileging the material culture of the past to meet needs that were modern, and by so doing was attempting, in some way, to define modernity.

While sculpture might be seen as a central element in the museums of the late eighteenth and early nineteenth centuries, its nature and position were far from agreed and straight-forward. As Ian Jenkins has shown, the use made of sculpture at the British Museum, especially after the arrival of the Parthenon sculptures, was vigorously debated and contested.[1] Similarly,

Alex Potts and others have demonstrated that the disposition and interpretation of antique sculpture in Ludwig I's Glyptothek in Munich was agreed only after much debate, with different positions being taken by Ludwig's architect, Leo von Klenze, and his adviser on sculpture, Johann Martin von Wagner.[2] What may now seem so familiar was established as a norm only after the consideration, and indeed testing, of various options.

When the British Museum was founded in 1753 through the acquisition of Sir Hans Sloane's collection, along with the Cotton and Harley manuscripts, sculpture was neither a prominent nor a substantial part of its holdings. Sloane's antiquities included a few marbles and inscriptions, but the most significant sculpture consisted of small-scale sculptures. These were classified as man-made objects which complemented the natural rarities and belonged in a collection that had many of the characteristics of a *Wunderkammer*. But, unlike many of those 'cabinets of curiosities' elsewhere, such objects were not complemented or amplified by any substantial collection of antique monumental sculpture. This, in part, reflected the way in which collecting patterns in Britain differed from those in Italy or Germany where princely or noble initiatives prompted the formation of both types of collection. So, while in Europe the Electors of Saxony had assembled in Dresden both elaborate enamelled fantasies by Johann Melchior Dinglinger and highly finished bronzes by Giambologna, and the Medici had organized the Tuscan Grand-Ducal collections to incorporate both turned ivory cups and the Venus de' Medici, in England the noble collections of antiquities, such as that formed by the Earls of Pembroke at Wilton, were separate from those cabinets of curiosity formed by Richard Mead, Sloane and others. Although the mid-eighteenth-century donation of the Arundel Marbles to the University of Oxford by the Pomfret family brought monumental sculpture and curiosities into the same institution, they remained largely distinct collections, with the marble sculpture consigned to the Radcliffe Camera rather than the Ashmolean Museum.

However, it is worth stressing that collections such as that at Wilton were seen by more than members of the family and their peers; indeed, the publication of various guide-books, one of them produced in a number of editions, suggests that this collection was seen by a wide range of visitors. Conversely, while the British Museum was set up as an institution for the public, the viewing public that was actually admitted to the British Museum was still relatively restricted, making the distinction between public and private collections less marked than it might at first seem. (Only with the foundation of the National Gallery in 1824 and later Henry Cole's South

Kensington Museum was the museum-visiting public really widened.) Thus, during the eighteenth century, sculpture was to be seen solely in private collections such as those at Wilton and Holkham – the marbles and casts assembled by Matthew Brettingham for Lord Leicester – and it was in these contexts that the innovations in display were made. At the British Museum it was only with the acquisition of the Townley Marbles in 1805 that sculpture as it is usually recognized (and certainly was at this period) became prominent, indeed dominant, in determining the character of the Museum.

What has been described here is how the earliest public museums in Britain were formed essentially from cabinets of curiosities, and how collections of monumental sculpture – predominantly antique – were incorporated only at a later stage. As argued below, sculpture was to play a significant role in these Enlightenment bodies, but insofar as the sculptural bodies – the figures, busts and groups – consisted of antique sculpture in marble, this characteristic of the Enlightenment museum appeared in Britain some time after it had been established elsewhere in Europe. To understand what happened belatedly in England, it is therefore necessary to establish the ways in which various prominent European museums, those which have been described as 'enlightened' in their arrangement and openness, used sculpture. How, for instance, did their presentation and interpretation of sculpture relate to earlier patterns and protocols of display? But before looking at the different ways in which monumental sculpture played a prominent role at the Upper Belvedere in Vienna, the Museo Pio-Clementino in Rome, the Royal Museum in Stockholm, the Glyptothek in Munich and the Louvre in Paris, it is worth analysing briefly those collections and displays of sculpture, mostly in private collections, that preceded them.

In one sense, large-scale sculpture in marble or bronze has almost always had public functions, much of it having been designed with a wide audience in mind. This consideration seems to have been taken into account in the planning of the Belvedere Statue Court at the Vatican where the Apollo Belvedere was placed in 1503 and where, three years later, the Laocoön was set up; here, the various statues were treated as an ensemble, with the most celebrated works placed within corner niches.[3] Even in the sixteenth century, the Belvedere Court was already available to a far wider range of viewers than were admitted to the papal apartments. In this way, it was a cross between a public space in which sculpture was to be seen – a public square with a figure of the ruler, for example – and the arrangement of sculpture from a private collection found in a courtyard or garden.

Rather more typical of modes of display being adopted in the principal Roman princely collections was the later sixteenth-century arrangement in the Villa Medici.[4] Although various proposed arrangements might have made this connection still more strongly, the disposition of the sculpture at the Villa Medici and in its gardens both suggested an illustrious mythological genealogy for the family and, through references to Mount Parnassus, left the viewer in no doubt as to Cardinal Ferdinando de' Medici's renowned patronage of the arts. While, as Carole Paul has pointed out, this arrangement is unusual in the preponderance of sculpture over painting – in the Farnese gallery, for example, the relationship of the roles is reversed – the Villa Medici is but one instance of a princely use

of sculpture collections in which the iconographical significance of figures was considered to be of most importance. In this instance the subjects were used to articulate and support a family's genealogical and other status-enhancing claims.[5] Often as significant, however, was the potential that sculpture provided for decoration, a factor at all the sites discussed so far. Nonetheless, when some of these same pieces were moved from the Villa Medici in Rome to be incorporated in the Uffizi displays in Florence, as these were being reworked by Raimondo Cocchi after 1773, we get a hint of rather different concerns and preoccupations. Newly arranged in Florence, antique sculptures were juxtaposed with painting, not simply to form a decoratively harmonious and balanced mixed display but to suggest, in more self-conscious way, the idea of a dialogue between painting and sculpture – the *paragone* – enacted before the spectator through the arrangement of celebrated antique marbles in conjunction with paintings.

This precedent notwithstanding, the first decisive reworking of a princely (or in this case imperial) collection of sculpture and painting is usually identified with the reorganization by Christian von Mechel of the Hapsburg collection in the Upper Belvedere in Vienna from 1778 onwards. Certainly, Mechel's overwhelming interest was in the paintings and it was in their redisplay that the most influential innovations were made and into which, as Debora Meijers has demonstrated, Enlightenment notions of classification and system were introduced.[6] But even if the arrangement of the paintings in this new way on the first floor has received more attention, it should not be forgotten that the ground floor housed a sculpture display. In his catalogue Mechel gives little away about its arrangement, stating simply that: 'Before leaving the Upper Belvedere, the curious visitor will be stopped again in the vaulted rooms of the ground floor ... where many pieces of interest may be seen among the great quantity of antique and modern sculptures.'[7] Rather frustratingly, he gives no more details. However, even if it did not follow the scheme of national schools and periods pioneered in the paintings display above, it must have differed considerably from the *Wunderkammer*-like displays set up earlier in the Stallburg.
A similar shift may be seen in the reconfiguration of other princely collections, most notably that at Dresden. Here the antique works were supplemented by two further rooms, one with modern copies after the antique and the other with modern sculptures. The impression given here is of an increasing tendency to group marble sculpture together, already anticipated in the placing together of busts in the *Antiquarium* in Munich, in spaces that were designed for that sole purpose. Such arrangements were also pre-dated by the pioneering sculpture galleries which were being established in eighteenth-century England to house marbles acquired on the Grand Tour.[8] Through the arrangement of marbles in these (sometimes purpose-built) interiors, as in the generally later institutional (or semi-institutional) European galleries, the conditions were being created in which sculpture could be given close and sustained attention.

The display in which these new preoccupations were most apparent was the arrangement in the Museo Pio-Clementino, initiated by Pope Clement XIV in 1771 and continued by Pius VII (fig.59). Yet although it was intended solely as a public display space for sculpture, effectively developing the potential of the

Malcolm Baker

Belvedere Sculpture Court around which it was constructed, its arrangement still had much in common with earlier princely galleries. While there were some groupings that took account of works coming from the same sites, the disposition of the marbles was determined by iconographical and, above all, decorative considerations. In Feoli's engravings of the different galleries, Roman portrait busts can be seen, for example, below busts of Greek gods and heroes. Also apparent in these prints – the production and distribution of which are in themselves quite complex – is an alternating pattern of large figures and smaller pieces articulating the walls. While it may not have been innovative in its principles of arrangement, the Museo Pio-Clementino was, not surprisingly, a much imitated model. Gustavus III of Sweden visited Rome in 1783 and was shown the new galleries by the Pope. Then, having acquired his marbles of the Muses and Endymion, he started to plan a combination of museum and palace, taking account also of German precedents in his ideas for the display of paintings. In the event, his assassination meant that this palace-museum was never built, but a museum open to the public was nonetheless set up. This not only gave still more prominence to the antique sculpture, but did so by consciously imitating some of the modes of display adopted in the Vatican.[9]

In France, new displays at the Louvre were already being planned by Comte d'Angiviller in the pre-revolutionary period, making it more of a public museum. Then, following Bonaparte's Italian campaign, the appropriation of the most celebrated works from the Vatican collections, including the Apollo Belvedere and the Laocoön, meant that, as one popular song put it:

> Rome is no more in Rome
> Every hero, every great man
> Has changed country
> Rome is no more in Rome
> It is all in Paris

When the collections were reorganized, as Andrew McClellan has shown, the paintings were arranged so as to articulate a history of art, albeit one that rejected the notion of rise and decline as it had been developed by Johann Joachim Winckelmann and, more relevantly here, Quatremère de Quincy.[10] A different approach, however, was taken with the antique sculpture in an arrangement eventually developed by Ennio Quirino Visconti, the son and brother of successive directors of the Museo Pio-Clementino. Here a chronological display was considered incompatible with the proper veneration of the great masterpieces of antique sculpture. Instead, the various rooms were centred around celebrated individual figures, linked together in a chain and so punctuating the vistas – an arrangement that owed much to the recent configuration of the sculpture at the Vatican. The Enlightenment notion of a public museum was of course of central importance here, but the arrangement of the Louvre's sculpture still harked back to an earlier tradition.[11] Indeed, the adoption of chronology and a fully historical approach as the basis for displaying sculpture was only clearly apparent with the establishment in 1830 of the Glyptothek in Munich, where rooms were still arranged around individual masterpieces but the sequence of rooms was laid out to follow an historical progression.

Through this museological Grand Tour, an attempt has been made to outline the main developments in the display of sculpture that were taking place in the eighteenth century. This, then, was the context in which the displays of the British Museum's collection of sculpture were being formulated, first in its presentation of the newly acquired Townley collection in the first decade of the nineteenth century and then, by the middle of the century, in its display of this and the Parthenon Marbles in Robert Smirke's new building. How might these developments, and the ways in which they were adopted by the British Museum, be read? To what degree, for example, may such displays be considered as registers of Enlightenment thinking?

One issue here is how the relationship between sculpture and other parts of a collection might be configured. The various cases described above show that a range of options was being explored. Common to all these museum and private displays, however, was the new prominence being given to sculpture. Above all, sculpture was being displayed in conditions that allowed it increasingly to be the object of sustained attention. This might be achieved through the creation of rooms dedicated solely to the display and viewing of sculpture, as we have seen in the examples of the Museo Pio-Clementino, the Louvre and the Munich Glyptothek. Perhaps the most striking examples, however, were those galleries designed for private patrons, such as the sculpture gallery at Woburn, designed with the sole purpose of displaying the Duke of Bedford's sculptures. This was a collection that consisted not only of antique marbles but also modern works, some of them newly commissioned. While some eighteenth-century Roman collections included a few modern figures and groups – the most striking example being Bernini's marbles in the Villa Borghese, where great care was taken with their display – the emphasis was still very much on the antique.[12] At Woburn, by contrast, not only were antique and modern combined on almost equal terms, but the culmination of the display was an early nineteenth-century work – Canova's *Three Graces* – by an artist considered one of the few moderns whose work could equal that of the ancients. More importantly in this context, it exemplified a new type of modern sculpture created for just these viewing conditions that the displays discussed above encouraged and made possible.

One striking feature of this period was the formulation of this new type of sculpture, partly in response to the development of more avowedly public galleries and display spaces. But a more important issue, in the context of this volume, consists of the ways in which certain characteristics of Enlightenment thought were inscribed in the displays and interpretation of sculpture in the various museums described above. A key factor here was a new and different awareness of history. As Anthony Grafton has argued, a significant historiographical shift took place in the eighteenth century with the marrying together of the antiquarian study of artefacts and narrative history.[13] One outcome of this marriage was a new kind of museum display as analysed by Stephen Bann in *The Clothing of Clio*, beginning with Alexandre Lenoir's Musée des Monuments Français.[14] And, of course, any serious display of antique sculpture at the end of the eighteenth century had to take account of the work of Winckelmann. The ways in which such histories of art were being constructed were grounded, in part, in those systems of taxonomy and categorization central to the Enlightenment project. But, while displays of paintings with their careful articulation of filiations of master, pupil and school, as well as their increasingly chronological structure, paralleled the systematization of the natural sciences, displays of sculpture were slow to follow suit, despite the fact that Winckelmann's novel formulation of the progress and decline of art was concerned above all with sculpture.[15]

It is perhaps worth noting in parenthesis that the application of such systems to the natural world did, however, have a consequence for at least one category of sculpture. For, as those parts of the *Wunderkammer* concerned with *naturalia* became separate, more scientifically ordered collections in their own right, other frameworks of meaning and display had to be found for the small-scale sculptures in ivory and boxwood. One option was to create a distinct category for these small, richly decorated *objets d'art*, as was done in the Grünes Gewölbe in Dresden. But an alternative was to ally the smaller figurative sculpture with the monumental works in marble, constituting sculpture of various sorts as a category of 'art'. This was done, for instance, with the ivories by Francis van Bossuit in the sale of Anthony Grill's collection in Amsterdam in 1728; here, figures and reliefs that, twenty-one years earlier, had been included within the *Wunderkammer* of the previous owner were now associated with marbles and paintings, presented unequivocally on the catalogue's title page as art.[16] The way in which this united category of art was being formulated was one aspect of the emerging notion of the aesthetic, with its concept of the autonomous work of art – yet another facet of Enlightenment thinking that had important implications for galleries for the display of sculpture.

If these were all, to varying degrees, Enlightenment concepts that were of concern to those setting up new museums and to those determining how sculpture was to be displayed and interpreted, no single factor was more important than the growing recognition of public audiences beyond that of a prince, his family and peers. Limited though its range of visitors may have been, the British Museum and the other institutions discussed here were all considered public museums. This had, it might be suggested, a special significance in the case of sculpture, much of which through its monumental nature and setting had been viewed by a wider public than other categories of artistic production. Indeed, it must be significant that, during the mid-eighteenth century, one particular genre of sculpture – the equestrian monument of the ruler – had itself been tellingly reworked to take account of a different audience. Jean-Baptiste Pigalle's monument to Louis XV, for example, included a figure of the citizen, signalling as it were the shift (in Jürgen Habermas's terms) to the bourgeois public sphere.[17] The same, indeed, might be said of the galleries already discussed. To place in these galleries a class of sculpture – antique marbles – that had formerly been the private property of a ruler and viewed largely by him and his court was to make them, like the picture collections, no longer exclusive in their address. But, with sculpture, the connotations were especially significant, not only in that sculpture had had often performed public functions, but also because the medium was seen as having the potential to carry a greater weight of political meaning. Earlier in the century, sculpture's association with authority made it well suited to articulate civic, humanist notions about the

public role of the noble and landed classes. According to theorists such as the 3rd Earl of Shaftesbury, the possession of freehold land and title gave the landed gentleman the autonomy and freedom from interest which allowed him to take on a public role requiring civic virtue.[18] Since such ideas were closely associated with notions of the classical citizen, it was not surprising that the representations of those who upheld civic virtue through their disinterested action for the public good in the 'Senate' – by which was meant the House of Lords – were so frequently shown in the guise of Romans. When figures of Lord Foley and his family, for example, were placed on the monument in the chapel attached to the house at Great Witley, Worcestershire, all the males were shown in classicizing dress, so indicating their fitness for public office.[19] By the late eighteenth century, sculpture was seen as equally appropriate for use in institutions that increasingly laid stress on their public rather than private benefit. Indeed, no medium was more fitted to Enlightenment needs.

These, then, are some of the ideas that underpinned the use of sculpture in galleries throughout Europe, including the British Museum in London. Sculpture collections were slowly beginning to be reorganized on new principles. And, while many of the features of the displays in these museums recalled earlier sculpture displays within princely palaces, their underlying structure was increasingly driven as much by ideas about history as a concern with decorative effects or subject-matter. But, as other papers in this volume make us well aware, the people who were shaping these new institutions placed as much importance on the text as the artefact, the two ideally being seen as complementary – the encyclopaedia and the museum. It is no coincidence (as Klaus Herding has pointed out) that several German periodicals from this period use the word *Museum* in their title.[20] Demonstration of new truths was attempted or achieved through both word and image, and this meant that the library was at the heart of institutions such as the British Museum, where the manuscript and book collections of Harley, Cotton and Sloane were as significant as the artefacts and specimens assembled by the last of these great collectors.

Acknowledgement of the centrality of the library means that any consideration of sculpture in the eighteenth-century museum must also take account of a category of sculpture that was flourishing at this period: the portrait bust and, more specifically, those series of busts of authors and other worthies that formed such a conspicuous part of the Enlightenment library. The tradition of portraits of great men had, of course, been established long before; the interest of collectors in ancient Roman busts had much to do with their supposed identities and the way such images could be displayed as exemplary figures. In introducing the collection of antique sculpture assembled by the Earl of Pembroke, the 1786 Wilton House guide-book, for example, comments:

> Bustoes he was particularly fond of, as they expressed with more strength and exactness, the lineaments of the face. Besides, the viewing of these brought to the spectator's mind the history and glorious exploits of ancient Kings and Heroes.[21]

When these heroes were thinkers and authors, there was no more appropriate context for their display than the library (fig.60). The *locus classicus* for the use of busts in this way is the

Malcolm Baker

book by Gabriel Naudé, translated by John Evelyn, on the
formation and decoration of a library. According to Naudé and
Evelyn, the use of 'likely statues of all the gallant men' would
allow the viewer to 'make judgement of their of the wit of
authors by their Books, and by their bodies'.[22] Such images
were intended to serve as 'a puissant spurre to excite a generous
and well-born Soul to follow their track and to continue firm
and stable in the wayes and beaten paths of some noble
enterprise and resolution'. Outside France, Naudé's advice was
heeded by many prestigious academic bodies. These included
All Souls in Oxford (with John Cheere's busts of former
Fellows); Trinity College, Dublin (with Claudius Gilbert's
bequest 'for the purchase of busts of men eminent for
learning'); and not least Trinity College, Cambridge, where the
Wren Library was adorned with plaster busts of ancient and
modern authors and then by marble busts of those eminent in
the new science – Bacon, Newton, Ray and Willoughby.[23]

To create one of these images – that of the seventeenth-
century naturalist John Ray – the sculptor Louis-François
Roubiliac obtained permission from the newly appointed
Trustees of the British Museum to see the painted portrait that
had belonged to Sloane; he was thus one of the Museum's
earliest users. More significantly in this context, the terracotta
model for the Trinity College marble was one of a large group of
terracotta and plaster busts purchased at the sculptor's
posthumous sale in 1762 by the future Principal Librarian of the
British Museum, Dr Matthew Maty – the figure in the Museum's
early history who best exemplifies Enlightenment thinking.
Maty gave all these busts to the Museum, and it is these images,
rather than any antique marbles, that form the most substantial
group of monumental sculpture that the Museum acquired in
the eighteenth century. Despite Aileen Dawson's rigorous
enquiries, we do not know exactly how and where these busts
were displayed until they were later moved into the Print
Room.[24] But we may assume that they were acquired not
because of their authorship or aesthetic qualities, aware as
Maty would have been of these, but because a high proportion
of the portrait sculptures included in this group were of subjects
involved in the new science. The acquisition and display of
these busts would therefore seem to represent an attempt to use
portrait sculpture to promote British Enlightenment figures as
models for emulation. Here again, we see an earlier tradition
being adapted to suit Enlightenment needs.

There is, however, a distinction here between the use of
busts in an Enlightenment institution and the use of sculpture –
especially antique statuary – as described above. In the latter
case, the antiquities constituted the collection itself and must be
seen as the focus of attention, the subject worthy of study,
ordering and classification. By contrast, in the former
case – that of the portrait busts of intellectual worthies –
sculpture functioned not as the collection *per se*, but as a means
of interpreting, commenting on and directing attention to the
relationship between the constituent parts of the collection
proper, whether this was made up of books, artefacts or
specimens or all three. And, as well as serving as a heuristic
device for the use of the reader, the busts, through those
thinkers represented, set a standard for the study of the subjects
covered by the Museum's collections, so fulfilling the role of
'puissant spurre' for scholars using them.

It may be that this distinction was not quite as hard and
fast as has been suggested here, and that the Enlightenment
museum even offered a possibility of drawing together
'sculpture as commentary' and 'sculpture as collection and
subject'. Although this opportunity was not seized at the British
Museum, it had almost happened earlier at the Louvre when
D'Angiviller's proposed scheme for the *Grande Gallerie*
envisaged the integration into the display of antiquities those
statues of Enlightenment figures known as the *Grands
Hommes* – the busts of worthies writ large, as it were.[25] This
linkage was to remain an Enlightenment aspiration rather than
a feature of the Enlightenment museum as it was realized. The
marriage of 'sculpture as collection' with 'sculpture as
commentary' had to wait for those nineteenth-century
museums – the heirs to Enlightenment institutions – with their
familiar pantheons of artists' busts and figures. And, at that
point, sculpture often merged into the architecture of the
institution and no longer had that central position that it had
enjoyed at the end of the eighteenth century, a period in which
marble figures carried so much of the meaning of a new type of
museum, each in its way constituting bodies of Enlightenment.

Notes and references
1   I. Jenkins, *Archaeologists and Aesthetes in the Sculpture Galleries of
    the British Museum 1800–1939* (London, 1992).
2   A. Potts, 'Die Skulpturenaufstellung in der Glyptothek', in K.
    Vierneisel and G. Leinz (eds), *Glyptothek München 1830–1980*
    (Munich, 1980), pp.258–83. Here and throughout this paper I draw
    on the work of a range of scholars working over the past twenty
    years on sculpture collections and display.
3   F. Haskell and N. Penny, *Taste and the Antique* (New Haven and
    London, 1981), pp.7–15, 23–30. For the Belvedere courtyard and the
    later disposition of sculpture at the Vatican see Potts, op. cit.
    (note 2); J. Collins, 'The Gods' Abode: Pius VI and the invention of
    the Vatican Museum', in C. Hornsby (ed.), *The Impact of Italy: The
    Grand Tour and beyond* (London, 2000), pp.173–94; A. Potts, 'The
    Classical ideal on display', in *Viewing Antiquity: The Grand Tour,
    antiquarianism and collecting* (Ricerche di storia dell'Arte 72) (Rome,
    2000), pp.29–36.
4   For these various Roman collections see M. Künze, *Römische
    Antikensammlungen in 18. Jahrhunderts* (Mainz, 1998) and H. Beck
    and P. Bol, *Forschungen zur Villa Albani: Antike Kunst und die Epoche
    der Aufklärung* (Berlin, 1982).
5   C. Paul, *Making a Prince's Museum: Drawings for the
    late-eighteenth-century redecoration of the Villa Borghese* (Los
    Angeles, 2000).
6   D. Meijers, *Kunst als Natur. Die Habsburger Gemälde Gallerie in Wien
    um 1780* (Vienna, 1995).
7   C. von Mechel, *Verzeichniss der Gemälde der Kaiserlich Königlichen
    Bilder Gallerie in Wien* (Vienna, 1783).
8   The development of the sculpture gallery in England is best
    documented by J. Kenworthy-Browne, 'Private Skulpturengalerien
    in England 1730–1830', in Vierneisel and Leinz, op. cit. (note 2),
    pp.334–53. For a discussion of the shift in viewing practices
    involved here see M. Baker, *Figured in Marble: The making and
    viewing of eighteenth-century sculpture* (London and Los Angeles,
    2000), pp.159–68; A. Yarrington, 'The *Three Graces* and the Temple
    of Feminine Virtue', *Sculpture Journal* 7 (2002), pp.30–42; and the
    chapter on 'Classical figures' in A. Potts, *The Sculptural Imagination:
    Figurative, modernist, minimalist* (New Haven and London, 2000),
    pp.24–59. This needs to be seen in the context outlined in the
    chapter on 'The exhibition as a medium for the presentation of art',
    in O. Bätschmann, *The Artist in the Modern World* (New Haven and
    Cologne, 1997).
9   P. Bjurström, 'Physiocratic ideals and national galleries', in P.
    Bjurström (ed.), *The Genesis of the Art Museum in the Eighteenth
    Century* (Stockholm, 1993), pp.28–60.
10 A. McClellan, *Inventing the Louvre: Art, politics and the origins of the
    modern museum in eighteenth-century Paris* (Cambridge, 1995).

11 Despite this concern with public understanding and the provision of labels identifying the works and their subjects, some visitors still, as McClellan describes, managed to mistake busts of Plato and Alexander for the Duc de Brissac and the Prince de Condé.

12 The relationship seems sometimes to echo the make-up of Rossi's celebrated book of engravings of sculpture in which works by Bernini and other moderns are mixed in with far more numerous antique marbles.

13 A. Grafton, *The Footnote: A curious history* (London, 1997).

14 S. Bann, *The Clothing of Clio* (Cambridge, 1984). For a reworking of these ideas and an argument for the emergence of a new sense of history in the early nineteenth century see also S. Bann, *Romanticism and the Rise of History* (New York, 1995).

15 For Winckelmann see A. Potts, *Flesh and the Ideal: Winckelmann and the origins of art history* (New Haven and London, 1994). For different views of the antiquarian context see F. Haskell, *History and its Images: Art and the interpretation of the past* (New Haven and London, 1993), and T. DaCosta Kaufmann, 'Antiquarian connoisseurship and art history before Winckelmann', in C. Schneider *et al.* (eds), *Shop Talk: Studies in honour of Seymour Slive* (Cambridge, Mass., 1995), pp.130–2; and of the connoisseurial context see G. Warwick, *The Arts of Collecting: Padre Sebastiano Resta and the market for drawings in early modern Europe* (Cambridge, 2000) and C. Gibson-Wood, *Jonathan Richardson: Art theorist of the English Enlightenment* (New Haven and London, 2000).

16 For Bossuit see M. Baker, 'Francis van Bossuit, Böttger stoneware and the "Judith" reliefs', in R. Kahsnitz and P. Volk, *Skulptur in Süddeutschland 1400–1700. Festschrift für Alfred Schädler* (Munich, 1998), pp.281–94. Grill's sale took place in Amsterdam on 14 April 1728 and included a number of ivories by Bossuit that may be identified with pieces in the sale of Petronella della Court on 20–21 October 1707, also in Amsterdam. For more on these see the entries (based on information from the present writer) in *De Wereld binnen Handbereik*, exh. cat., Amsterdams Historisch Museum (Amsterdam, 1992).

17 This issue was addressed in the Henry Moore Institute's conference 'Public Monuments and Urban Spaces in Eighteenth-Century Europe', held at Leeds in March 2002. A book based on this subject is currently being edited by Charlotte Rousseau.

18 For the classic exposition of this doctrine see J.G.A Pococke, 'Civic Humanism in Anglo-American thought', in his *Politics, Language and Time* (Chicago, 1989), pp.80–103, and, in a much fuller form, J.G.A. Pococke, *The Machiavellian Moment: Florentine political thought and the Atlantic republican tradition* (Princeton, 1975).

19 The ideological connotations involved in Michael Rysbrack's use (and, more to the point, the Foley heir's choice) of a classicising mode are discussed in M. Baker, *Figured in Marble* (London 2000), pp.108–27.

20 K. Herding, 'Conception et philosophie bourgeoises du musée en Allemagne à la fin du xviiie et au début du xixe siècle', in E. Pommier (ed.), *Les Musées en Europe à la veille de l'ouverture du Louvre* (Paris, 1995), pp.439–60; see also H. Bock, 'Collections privées et publiques. Les prémices du musée public en Allemagne', loc. cit., pp.59–78.

21 J. Kennedy, *A Description of the Antiquities and Curiosities in Wilton House*, 2nd edn (Sarum, 1786).

22 G. Naudé, trans. J. Evelyn, *Instructions concerning erecting of a Library* (London, 1661), p.85.

23 For accounts of the busts of the libraries at Trinity College, Cambridge, and Trinity College, Dublin, and a wider discussion of the tradition of using sculpture within the library, see M. Baker, 'The portrait sculpture', in D. McKitterick (ed.), *The Making of the Wren Library* (Cambridge, 1995), pp.110–37; id., 'The making of portrait busts in mid-eighteenth England: Roubiliac, Scheemakers and Trinity College, Dublin', *Burlington Magazine* 137 (1995), pp.821–31.

24 A. Dawson, *Portrait Sculpture: A catalogue of the British Museum collection c.1675–1975* (London, 1999).

25 McClellan, op. cit. (note 10), pp.82–4.

Figure 59
Vincenzo Feoli, *View of the Galleria dei Busti* of the Museo Pio-Clementino, Rome (*c.* 1810), engraving. London, British Museum, Department of Prints and Drawings.

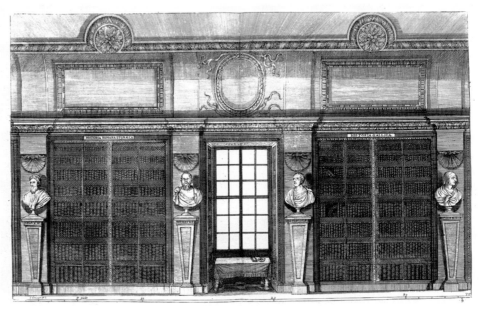

Figure 60
Franz Ertinger, *View of the Bibliothèque de Ste Geneviève*, engraving from Claude du Molinet, *Le Cabinet de la bibliothèque Ste Geneviève* (Paris, 1692). London, Victoria and Albert Museum.

Chapter 19

Napoleon and Egyptology
Britain's debt to French enterprise
T.G.H. James

In 1803 a book in two volumes was published in London which contained an account of some of the activities of the French army in Egypt from the invasion in the summer of 1798 up to the time when its author boarded the ship *La Muiron* carrying Napoleon Bonaparte back to France on 22 August 1799, not much more than a year after French forces had landed in Egypt.[1] The great conqueror was beating a clandestine retreat, partly, it might be thought, to escape the ignominy of failure and the shame of surrender to a British counter-force, and partly – perhaps for him more importantly – to scramble back to France to ensure his own future after the imminent collapse of the administration known as the Directory.[2]

The book was *Travels in Upper and Lower Egypt, in company with several divisions of the French Army, during the campaigns of General Bonaparte in that country; and published under his immediate patronage.* Its author was Dominique Vivant Denon (1747–1825), a member of a minor noble family who had in his youth practised the arts, and developed a connoisseurship in engraved gems and medals. He subsequently served as a diplomat in Russia, Sweden and Italy, and was in Venice at the time of the French Revolution. In spite of having had his properties in France confiscated, and with a considerable expectation of arrest and execution, he returned to Paris, succeeded in securing his rehabilitation, met Napoleon in the *salon* of Josephine de Beauharnais, and sufficiently gained the great man's favour as to be included informally among the members of the Commission des Sciences et des Arts which was being assembled in early 1798 to accompany the French army overseas on its next enterprise, the destination of which had not yet been revealed. It seems that Denon was something of a supernumerary member of the Commission, a position which allowed him to act with considerable freedom of movement once he was in the field. He may not have known where they were going until the expedition was launched, but he must have received more than a hint that he should pack pencils and paint brushes, and furnish himself with an adequate supply of good drawing paper.[3] His destination was to be Egypt, and a return will be made later to his activities there, to consider his harvest of drawings used to illustrate the published diary of his exploits on the expedition, *Voyage dans la Basse et la Haute Égypte,* and to contemplate its immense success both as a lively account of parts of the Egyptian campaign and as a prime influence in the development of interest in Egypt. The bulk of his Egyptian drawings have been housed in the Department of Prints and Drawings at the British Museum since the 1830s.

By the fortunate occasion of the brief and uneasy truce between France and Britain after the signing of the Treaty of Amiens in 1802, Denon was able to arrange for the English translation of his work to be published in London the year after its publication in Paris. It was not as splendidly produced as the French original and lacked many of the plates, but it had, nevertheless, a great success, being the first publication to bring to the attention of the English-speaking public the land and monuments of Egypt in the post-Napoleonic period. For, after the resounding triumph of British arms in Egypt, the British people were, perhaps for the first time, alerted to the exotic grandeur of eternal Egypt. One may wonder, however, what the readers of Denon's volumes made of the dedication to Bonaparte, carefully translated into English:

> To combine the lustre of your Name with the Splendour of the Monuments of Egypt, is to associate the glorious annals of our own time with the history of the heroic age; and to reanimate the dust of Sesostris and Mendes, like you Conquerors, like you Benefactors. Europe, by learning that I accompanied you in one of your most Memorable Expeditions, will receive my Work with eager interest. I have neglected nothing in my power to render it worthy of the Hero to whom it is inscribed.

The flattery worked. In 1802 Denon was appointed Director of the Musée Central des Arts in Paris. In 1804 he became Director-General of Museums, serving as such until 1815, and being chiefly responsible for the building up of the collections of the Louvre, accompanying the French armies on their various excursions through Europe to select what artistic treasures should be brought back to Paris. Denon was in effect Napoleon's chief agent in matters of art, and very largely responsible for the stimulation of interest in Egypt that followed the French expedition to that country, in spite of its ignominious ending with the treaty of capitulation of Alexandria in the Autumn of 1801.

Before examining more fully the question of why the proper study of ancient Egypt should be attributed, in part at least, to Napoleon and his grandiose plans for the conquest of that country, some consideration should first be given to the state of interest in Egypt among the educated classes in Europe during the eighteenth century. A fascination with the land of the Pharaohs had survived the decline of Egypt after the Roman annexation which followed the collapse of the Ptolemaic Dynasty in 33 BC. Substantial traces of Egyptian religious practices survived, in garbled form, in the mystery cults which were so popular in Imperial Rome and the Empire. In Egypt itself, the use of the hieroglyphic script and its related cursive forms of hieratic and demotic was superseded by the much more practical Coptic script, essentially a derivative of the Greek alphabet. A treatise on the ancient pictorial script, called *Hieroglyphica*, written possibly in the fifth century by

Horapollo,[4] provided, seemingly, the best introduction to the strange writing, remaining a key text throughout the period from late antiquity to the eighteenth century. Horapollo, however, was scarcely a reliable authority. His credentials were distinctly shaky: he may have been Greek, or Egyptian, or Graeco-Egyptian; his treatise may have been written in Greek, or originally in Egyptian translated into Greek by an equally shadowy Philippos. Unfortunately, *Hieroglyphica* in later times possessed the respectability of being written in a classical language, apparently not long after the demise of the Egyptian script as a functional medium. It could therefore be trusted just as much as the writings of Plutarch on Egyptian religion, and of Herodotus on Egyptian history. Such classical writings were thought to be just as trustworthy as the Bible: they were the only ancient sources available to pre-Napoleonic students of ancient Egypt – they cannot yet be called Egyptologists – apart from the visual evidence of the surviving monuments of Egyptian antiquity, including sculptures retrieved from sites in Italy, notably in Rome and at Hadrian's villa at Tivoli.

The impenetrable nature of the hieroglyphic script, together with the exotic character of Egyptian monuments, were powerfully attractive to scholars and to the literate public. The elements of this attraction remain much the same today: pyramids, temples, obelisks, mummies and tombs, with their incomprehensible but very suggestive scenes of arcane ceremonies. The Age of Enlightenment brought a more focused approach to interest in ancient Egypt. Antiquities trickled back to Europe along the trade routes. An Egyptian Society was founded in London in 1741, holding its first meeting in Lebeck's Head Tavern in Chandos Street, Charing Cross, on 11 December, considered to be the day of the Feast of Isis. The Society's purpose was 'the promoting and preserving Egyptian and other ancient learning'. It met once a fortnight during the winter to inspect Egyptian antiquities owned by members, and to hear papers on these objects and on ancient Egypt generally. The Egyptian Society had a distinguished membership, including the Dukes of Montagu and Richmond, the Earl of Sandwich, well-known travellers who had published accounts of their travels in Egypt and the Levant, such as Richard Pococke, Frederik Norden and Charles Perry, and others who had commercial interests in the Near East, like members of the Lethieullier family. The Society's energetic programme, unfortunately, soon exhausted the antiquities available for discussion, and it was disbanded after its twenty-second meeting on 16 April 1743.[5]

A notable absentee from the membership of the Egyptian Society was Sir Hans Sloane. By 1741, when the Society was founded, he was already aged eighty-one and may reasonably have felt unenthusiastic about turning out once a fortnight to engage in mock Egyptian ceremonies in Charing Cross, many miles from his home in Chelsea. There is moreover no evidence that he ever showed a particular interest in ancient Egypt, although his collection did contain about 150 Egyptian antiquities – mostly small objects, amulets, scarabs, divine bronzes, *ushabti* figures, and one inscribed stone stela of a man named Nekau.

The volumes on Egyptian travels published during the mid-eighteenth century by Pococke, Norden and Perry, did much to stimulate public interest in Egypt.[6] The volumes produced by F.L. Norden (1700–42) in particular were very well received, and frequently reprinted. Norden was a Danish naval captain who in 1738 had been sent by King Christian VI to survey Egypt. Subsequently he settled in London and was readily welcomed in scientific and literary circles, being elected a Fellow of the Royal Society in 1740. Sadly, he died in 1742 and was denied the chance to prepare his narrative and plates for publication. His *Travels in Egypt and Nubia* were to appear in English in 1757, having been first published in French in 1755. The illustrations cover a wide range of ancient Egyptian monuments, engraved not very competently from Norden's very accomplished drawings (fig. 61). In many cases, for example, the hieroglyphic signs in the texts are poorly reproduced, although the original drawings provided fairly accurate copies. The printed results might not have been so disappointing had Norden himself been able to supervise the making of the plates. Artists trained in the classical tradition found it difficult to draw Egyptian subjects, especially sculptures, two-dimensional reliefs and paintings, without introducing an un-Egyptian muscularity. Translation from drawing to engraved plate provided a further opportunity to render Egyptian figuration in a distorted and bizarre manner.[7]

As far as the British Museum was concerned, ancient Egypt rated low in the scale of significant areas of collecting during its first half-century. Apart from the small number of items in Sloane's bequest, the Lethieullier family presented and bequeathed the few Egyptian antiquities in the Museum's possession, including two mummies which then, as ever, attracted much public attention.[8] In 1766, the first monumental pieces arrived as a gift from King George III. They had been excavated – if that is the right word to use – by the disreputable Edward Wortley Montagu in the region of Alexandria. He sent them back to his brother-in-law, the 3rd Earl of Bute, who wasted little time in presenting them to the King.

Although interest in ancient Egypt formed part of the general fascination with antiquity of the serious-minded throughout the eighteenth century, there was in Britain little active debate among scholars and amateurs on the nature of the hieroglyphic script and its decipherment. The futility of wild speculation was characterized by the marginal writings of John Turberville Needham (1713–81), a priest, a respected scientist (Fellow of the Royal Society in 1746), who was also a member of the Egyptian Society and a Fellow of the Society of Antiquaries. His principal thesis was that there was identity between Egyptian hieroglyphs and the Chinese script. John Needham's views on hieroglyphs were vigorously opposed by William Stukeley (1687–1765), the distinguished antiquary, also a Fellow of the Royal Society, Secretary of the Egyptian Society, and a founder-member of the Society of Antiquaries. He had written a paper, delivered to the Antiquaries in 1743, 'On hieroglyphics and Chinese letters', in which he maintained that both these forms of writing had been invented by Adam, hieroglyphics being for sacred writings, and Chinese for civil texts. His later attack on Needham's views in 1762 was based on particular details of the scripts, but also cast a doubt on the sources used by Needham for his Egyptian evidence.[9]

Such debates did nothing to advance the proper explication of Egyptian writings, but, in the words of Warren R. Dawson, an early twentieth-century antiquary, historian of science, authority on mummies, and amateur Egyptologist in general, himself somewhat in the mould of an eighteenth-century gentleman scholar, they were:

> . . . interesting as showing the delusions, the prejudices, and the scepticism of scholars, and they form the background against which the luminous figure of Champollion stands out in bold relief when he brought his critical acumen and genius to bear upon unlocking the door that revealed a new and wonderful chapter in the world's history . . .

Jean-François Champollion (1790–1832) (fig. 62) will indeed be the ultimate hero of this chapter, for it was he who finally reaped the harvest of what had been cultivated by Napoleon through the agency of the scholars of his Commission in Egypt, and the fortuitous, but fortunate, discovery of the Rosetta Stone.

Needham and Stukeley were not cranks, seeking esoteric or quasi-scientific explanations for the many unusual elements in the ancient culture of that antique land. They were respected scientists, out of their depth, attempting to unravel the secrets of a script for which there were at that time no truly ascertainable facts. Their own deliberations and disputes were characteristic of the time, the Age of Enlightenment, and they were fired by the desire to shed light on an immensely difficult, apparently impenetrable subject. Their approach to the problems of the hieroglyphs was not only flawed, but wholly misdirected. To penetrate the script was almost the easiest part of the matter; there remained the question of cracking the language expressed by the script. There were a few scholars who understood the need to consider language, such as the Abbé Jean Jacques Barthélemy (1716–95), who was the first to claim that the ovals which we now call cartouches probably contained royal names, an observation that would be proved to be valid and important when serious attempts at decipherment were undertaken in the early decades of the nineteenth century.[10]

Georg Zoëga (1755–1809), a Danish antiquary who spent many years in Rome studying obelisks, understood the linguistic problem and made a serious study of Coptic, the language used in the Egyptian Christian church and written in an augmented Greek script. It was thought by some scholars – rightly – to be the last stage of the ancient language of Egypt. Zoëga published an important work on obelisks and a catalogue of Coptic manuscripts in the Museo Borgiano, both of which works were later to prove useful to Champollion.[11] But decipherment remained totally elusive, and the burgeoning of the study of ancient Egypt was wholly frustrated until the Napoleonic expedition to Egypt resulted in publication of a large number of inscriptions copied from the monuments, including those on the Rosetta Stone.

Everything changed, or at least began to change, after 1798 when French forces landed on Egyptian soil. The idea of the invasion was not a simple whim of Napoleon to divert attention from difficulties he faced with the Directory in Paris. The possible annexation of Egypt as a French colony was at this stage seriously proposed – if not initiated – by Baron François de Tott, as a result of a secret mission undertaken in 1777 for the French authorities. De Tott, of Hungarian origin, knew the Levant well, and was entrusted with the commission to inspect French establishments there. Secretly he was charged with exploring the possibility of making Egypt a French colony. His report was positive, but no action followed. The idea of annexing Egypt, however, did not die.[12] It remained a matter

for consideration by French politicians, and became a topic of debate between Talleyrand and Napoleon with no encouragement from the Directory. As a colony Egypt was potentially of considerable value to France in view of its agricultural potential. Politically, as far as France's struggle with Britain was concerned, the annexation of Egypt would help to secure French power in the eastern Mediterranean, and prove a threat to British power in India. The possibility of a canal at Suez was also seriously considered. In September 1797 Napoleon wrote to Talleyrand from Italy:

> If it happens that when we make peace with England we have to give up the Cape of Good Hope, we must occupy Egypt. That country has never belonged to a European nation. The Venetians alone had a certain but very precarious preponderance there several centuries ago. We could leave here with 25,000 men, escorted by eight or ten ships of the line or Venetian frigates, and take it. Egypt does not really belong to the Sultan. I shall be glad, Citizen Minister, if you will enquire in Paris and let me know what reaction our expedition to Egypt would produce on the Porte. With armies such as ours, for which all religions are alike, Mohammedans, Copts, Arabs, pagans, etc., all that is unimportant; we would respect one as much as the other.[13]

Egypt became for Napoleon a bone to be worried to death. In 1798 when the intended invasion of Britain ceased to be an immediate concern, Egypt became the priority, and plans were rapidly developed and enthusiastically put into effect. Not least among Napoleon's intentions was to discover and record all that could be found out about Egypt, ancient and modern, scientific and cultural. To this end he convinced the Directory to authorize the setting up of the Commission des Sciences et des Arts, on 16 March 1798. It was made up of scholars of all disciplines (usually called 'savants' even in English writings on their activities), about 150 in all, including engineers and artists. This extraordinarily enlightened initiative would in due course result in the great *Description de l'Égypte*, which appeared between 1809 and 1828 (fig. 63) – the first scientific publication which (in part) provided the stimulus for the careful recording of ancient Egyptian monuments and the development of the specialist field of study to be known as Egyptology.

Dominique Vivant Denon, who had persuaded Napoleon to allow him to accompany the expedition to Egypt (though probably not as a member of the Commission), came into his own after the invasion. He had considerable freedom of action, and in the early months engaged in the search for, and the selective acquisition of, ancient monuments for a national museum in Paris. He was already assuming for himself the kind of role he would later pursue in the annexation of works of art in the train of Napoleonic conquests in Europe. For example, in a mosque in Alexandria, on the site of the earlier church of St Athanasius, he inspected a huge breccia libation tank. 'This monument', he commented, 'which is without doubt a sarcophagus of ancient Egypt, will perhaps be hereafter illustrated by volumes of dissertations. It may be considered a very valuable antique, and as one of our most precious spoils in Egypt, with which it is to be wished that our national museum may be enriched'.[14] Its fate was rather different. It was included amongst those antiquities ceded by the French to the British after the Capitulation of Alexandria in 1801 and is now in the British Museum (fig. 64). It was always thought, quite correctly, to be royal, though it was initially identified as being the sarcophagus of Alexander the Great. When the texts carved on it, inside and out, could be read, it was found to be the last resting place of King Nectanebo II (360–343 BC) of the Thirtieth Dynasty, the last native-born Egyptian Pharaoh. Denon also cast his eye over the two obelisks, one prone, one upright, on the sea-front of Alexandria. They were already called Cleopatra's Needles, and he thought they might well be brought back to France to embellish Paris.

Wherever he went, Denon drew, and many of his informal sketches were made, as he claimed, on horseback, as he followed the French forces led by General Desaix in their pursuit of the Mamelukes into Upper Egypt (fig.65). This brilliant campaign, executed with great panache and daring by Napoleon's best commander in Egypt, began in August 1798, and continued throughout the autumn and winter, well into the spring of 1799. Denon spent most of this time following the army, often being closely involved in combat, and rarely having the opportunity to make his drawings in comfortable conditions. His diary, which forms the basis of the text of *Voyage dans la Basse et la Haute Égypte*, records the progress of Desaix's forces in a very lively manner, including some moments when the splendour of Egyptian monuments overcame the desire to pursue the enemy. It happened, for example, at Dendera in Middle Egypt, site of a very well-preserved temple of the Graeco-Roman Period.[15] It was the first largely intact ancient structure south of Cairo and the pyramids available for close inspection, and the army came to a halt:

> Without any orders having either been given or received, every officer, every soldier left the road and rushed to Tentyra [Dendera]; spontaneously the whole army remained there for the rest of the day ... What a day! What bliss to have braved all to find such a feast!

Egyptologists today would not wax so extravagantly over the temple of Dendera – architecturally Egypt has much better things to show – but for Denon, and indeed for other travellers in Egypt, this late temple with its striking façade, in a romantic, isolated setting, was something special, and became in a sense an icon of Egyptian architecture to be reproduced time and again in drawing, painting, porcelain, bronze, and other materials. It offered a false pattern, yet one which promoted the particularity of Egyptian art.

A further demonstration of the impact of Egyptian monuments on unsuspecting visitors came on 27 January 1799, when the army, rounding a bend in the Nile, perceived in the distance the panorama of ancient Thebes. Denon reported that the whole force came spontaneously to a halt and clapped their hands at the sight. 'Without an order being given', wrote Lieutenant Desvernois, 'the men formed their ranks and presented arms to the accompaniment of the drums and bands.' Denon was there with pencil at the ready; soldiers offered him their knees on which to rest his drawing pad; others stood close to shield him from the strong sun. He was overcome by the sight of so many majestic monuments, and by 'the electrifying emotion of an army of soldiers whose refined sensibility made me rejoice in being their companion, and proud of being a Frenchman'.[16]

In the meanwhile, other members of the Commission, artists and draughtsmen, were separately concerned with making drawings of the monuments, and especially of the scenes and inscriptions in tombs and temples. This work would continue throughout the stay of the French in Egypt, and the results would eventually form the bulk of the ancient records included in the *Description de l'Égypte*.

In Cairo, Napoleon, among other concerns, did not forget the scientific purposes of the French invasion of Egypt, and in order to regularize the activities of the members of the Commission he established an Institut d'Égypte, inspired by the prestigious Institut de France of which he had been elected a member in December 1797.[17] The Institut d'Égypte was organized into four sections, each with a maximum membership of twelve: Mathematics, Physics, Political Economy, and Literature and Arts. Its guiding architect was Gaspard Monge, a very distinguished scientist and probably the outstanding scholar of the Commission. He had come to know Napoleon in 1796 in Italy when he headed the Commission pour la Recherche des Objets Artistiques et Scientifiques en des Pays Conquis. Among the paintings removed to Paris under his supervision was the *Mona Lisa*.

In its deliberations, the Institut d'Égypte was charged with discussing the state of the sciences in Egypt, the collection and study of natural, industrial and historical information about Egypt, and any other matter on which it might be consulted by the government. It was installed in a fine house in the Turkish style which had belonged to Hassan Kashef, with space for accommodation, a library, collections of natural history, geological specimens and antiquities, and also a laboratory. It was an ambitious project and was met with enthusiastic approval by those members of the Commission who were made members of the Institut, less so by those who were not so chosen.

The first meeting of the Institut took place on 25 August 1798.[18] Monge was elected its President, Napoleon modestly accepting the position of Vice-President. The subjects discussed scarcely matched up, in most cases, to the grandiose aspirations of the Institute, and were often practical, ranging from the quality of the army's baking ovens and the question of whether beer could be brewed in Egypt without hops, to a debate on the situation in Egypt concerning criminal and civil law and the teaching of law.

The proceedings of the Institut were published in *La Décade égyptienne* from 1 October 1798 until 21 March 1801. Matters more germane to the purpose of the Institut were regularly discussed once the members of the Commission had begun their work of surveying the country, collecting information, and bringing back to Cairo their specimens, including antiquities. Denon, however, was not much interested in the deliberations of the Institut, although his name was included in the list of members of the Section of Literature and Art; he was, after all, away from Cairo following General Desaix into Upper Egypt for much of his time in the country. He was not, apparently, at the meeting of the Institut on 27 July 1799 when a letter was read in which Michel-Ange Lancret, an engineer and member of the Mathematical Section, announced the discovery of a stone 'which may prove very interesting to examine'.[19] This was the first report on a matter which soon was to transform the possibilities of discovering the language and culture of ancient Egypt, to initiate what was to become the science of Egyptology. It was without a doubt, from the Egyptological point of view, the supreme result of the Napoleonic expedition to Egypt. It is not known whether Napoleon himself knew about the discovery before he left the country in October 1799, but it would not be unreasonable to credit him with the find which would have such far-reaching results.

Rosetta, or Rashid as it is called by the Egyptians, lies about thirty miles to the north-east of Alexandria and is a pleasant, well-settled small port on the banks of the western branch of the Nile, lying just a mile or two from the river's mouth. In July 1799 frantic efforts were being made to reinforce the defences of the town in the expectation of an attack by Turkish troops about to come ashore at Aboukir to the west of Alexandria. A small fort, originally built by the Sultan Qait Bey in the fifteenth century, renamed Fort St Julien by the French, was in the process of being strengthened (fig.66). The work was supervised by Lieutenant Pierre François Xavier Bouchard, who by a happy chance was one of the savants included in the original Commission des Sciences et des Arts. He had, therefore, an understanding of the secondary, scientific, purpose of the expedition to Egypt, and possessed a better education (at the recently established École Polytechnique) than many of his fellow engineer officers.

During the clearance of rubble in the fort, a group of workmen – probably local labourers – turned up a slab of dark-coloured stone about 1m (3ft 4in) in height, bearing on one side inscriptions carved in small characters set out in three bands, the top recognizably hieroglyphics, the bottom Greek, and the centre a script with very strange cursive signs (fig.67). When the stone had been cleaned and could be closely examined it was, not unexpectedly, the Greek text which first commanded attention. Surprisingly there were in Rosetta at that time officers in the French garrison who understood enough Greek to make out at least the gist of the text. It is probable that the first reading of the Greek text was something of a corporate effort, with Bouchard and Michel-Ange Lancret (another member of the Commission) principally worrying away at the inscription. It was seen to be a text concerning one of the Ptolemaic rulers of Egypt. It also emerged from the last sentence on the stela that the text should be inscribed in hieroglyphs, the documentary script, and Greek, on hard stone, and placed in all the principal temples of Egypt. At a very early stage, therefore, it was appreciated that the stone might provide the key for the decipherment of hieroglyphs, and of the cursive script to be called enchorial, and now known as demotic.

Lancret reported the discovery to the Institut on 27 July, and in mid-August, the Rosetta Stone itself was brought to Cairo by Lieutenant Bouchard. Everybody, so it was said, came to look at it after the discovery was made public in the *Courrier d'Égypte* on 15 September. Arrangements were made to have the inscriptions copied, and in January 1800 the results, obtained by three different methods, were sent to Paris. More careful translation of the Greek section revealed that the stela bore the text of a decree issued on 27 March 196 BC, recording the granting of a royal cult to the king, Ptolemy V Epiphanes, by the priests of Egypt in conclave in Memphis, in return for his many favours to them.[20]

The subsequent history of the Rosetta Stone may be sketched quite briefly.[21] In the early months of 1800 the members of the Commission des Sciences et des Arts attempted to leave Egypt with their papers and collections of specimens, including antiquities and the Stone. Their departure, however, was frustrated, and the Stone was lodged in Alexandria until the French finally capitulated to British arms in August 1801.

On the advice of William Richard Hamilton, secretary to Lord Elgin, British Ambassador in Constantinople, the French were obliged to hand over most of the collections made in the course of the Napoleonic expedition. After much argument it was agreed that the natural history and similar collections could be retained by the scientists, but that the antiquities, including the Rosetta Stone, should be ceded to the British. Among the antiquities which were in due course to be presented by King George III to the British Museum were the great sarcophagus of Nectanebo II already mentioned, a number of granite statues of the lion-goddess Sakhmet, and a colossal fist of a statue of Ramesses II from Memphis.

The Rosetta Stone arrived in Portsmouth in February 1802 and was at first placed in the rooms of the Society of Antiquaries. There copies of the texts were made and distributed to many learned societies in Britain and abroad; plaster casts were presented to the Universities of Oxford, Cambridge and Edinburgh, and to Trinity College, Dublin. At the end of the year it finally entered the British Museum.

The race to decipher the two Egyptian scripts represented on the Rosetta Stone began as soon as copies of the texts got into the hands of interested scholars.[22] The first seriously to address decipherment on the basis of the new evidence was Antoine Isaac Silvestre de Sacy, a learned orientalist who had refused to be part of Napoleon's Commission des Sciences et des Arts. In his efforts he was joined, and later opposed, by one of his students, Johan David Åkerblad, a Swedish diplomat, also very learned in oriental languages. De Sacy did not long pursue his quest for decipherment when he realized that his lines of enquiry were leading nowhere. But he retained his general interest and followed the progress of others. First among these was Jean François Champollion, who since childhood had been fascinated by the Egyptian scripts. In his late teens he became a pupil of de Sacy in the Collège de France and the École Speciale des Langues Orientales Vivantes. Champollion's obsessive pursuit of decipherment, and his disregard for the opinions of others, rendered him a somewhat unattractive scholar, and Silvestre de Sacy from about 1814 showed less interest in the results achieved by his pupil and more in those of Thomas Young. The latter was already a distinguished physician and natural philosopher and a Fellow of the Royal Society before the discovery of the Rosetta Stone. He was also a considerable linguist, and became interested in decipherment when he was given some fragments of Egyptian papyri in 1814 by Sir William Boughton.

Young made considerable progress in clarifying the nature of the hieroglyphic script, and made many discoveries which were accepted by Champollion, who did not always assign proper credit to his rival. But the single-minded devotion and linguistic brilliance of the French scholar ensured his success. In 1822 his *Lettre à M. Dacier*, addressed to the Secretary of the Académie des Inscriptions et Belles-Lettres, he set out his principal findings on decipherment. This communication marked the final stage in the decipherment race, and earned for Champollion the title 'Father of Egyptology'.[23]

So the new discipline was launched. Within fifteen years Egyptian texts were being read and translated with increasing confidence. Amateurs and scholars quartered Egypt in search of new texts, learning how important it was to copy carefully. Denon's *Voyage dans la Basse et la Haute Égypte* remained in print, continuing to stimulate the interest of readers. Meanwhile, the great *Description de l'Égypte* completed its publication in 1828, making available a mass of material from Egyptian monuments (fig. 68).[24] This great work might well be considered the most important result of the Napoleonic invasion of Egypt. But its value as a source of reference for hieroglyphic texts was flawed, much of its content being superseded within thirty years by other mammoth publications. The same cannot be said of Champollion's work, which was fundamental to the understanding of Egyptian scripts, and thereby the history, religion and culture of the ancient Egyptians. And it all could be traced back to the discovery of the Rosetta Stone, to the activity of the French troops in the Delta, to the invasion of Egypt, and ultimately to the vision of Napoleon Bonaparte.

Notes and references

1 Dominique Vivant Denon, *Voyage dans la Basse et la Haute Égypte* (Paris, 1802); English translation, *Travels in Upper and Lower Egypt*, 2 vols (London, 1803).

2 For general information on the French expedition J. Christopher Herold, *Bonaparte in Egypt* (London, 1963), has principally been used.

3 For Denon in general see the catalogue of the Louvre exhibition, *Dominique Vivant Denon. L'Oeil de Napoléon* (Paris, 1999). His Egyptian exploits are dealt with in chap.IV by Chantal Orgogozo.

4 On Horapollo and the post-classical interest in Egyptian hieroglyphics see E. Iversen, *The Myth of Egypt and its Hieroglyphs in European Tradition* (Copenhagen, 1961).

5 British Egyptological activities in the eighteenth century are addressed generally in T.G.H. James, *The British Museum and Ancient Egypt* (London, 1982), pp.4–6; also id., *Egypt Revealed* (London, 1997), pp.39–54.

6 The publications in question are: R. Pococke, *A Description of the East, and some other Countries*, 2 vols (London, 1743, 1745); C. Perry, *View of the Levant* (London, 1743); F.L. Norden, *Travels in Egypt and Nubia*, 2 vols (London, 1757). On the authors see M.L. Bierbrier, *Who was Who in Egyptology*, 3rd edn (London, 1995).

7 Norden's original drawings reveal the care he devoted to copying texts; see M.L. Buhl, *Les Dessins archéologiques et topographiques de l'Égypte ancienne, faits par F.L. Norden 1737–1738* (Copenhagen, 1993).

8 See M.L. Bierbrier, 'The Lethieullier family and the British Museum', *Pyramid Studies and other essays presented to I.E.S. Edwards* (London, 1988), pp.220–8.

9 W.R. Dawson, 'An eighteenth-century discourse on hieroglyphs', *Studies presented to F. Ll. Griffith* (London, 1932), pp.465–73.

10 See R. Solé and D. Valbelle, *The Rosetta Stone: The story of the decoding of hieroglyphics* (London, 2001), p.22.

11 G. Zoëga's two important works are *De origine usu obeliscorum* (Rome, 1797) and *Catalogus codicum Copticorum manuscriptorum qui in Museo Borgiano Velitris adservantur* (Rome, 1819).

12 For the early considerations on the annexation of Egypt see Herold, op. cit. (note 2), pp.5–16.

13 English translation in John Eldred Howard, *Letters and documents of Napoleon*, vol.I: *The rise to power* (London, 1961), pp.208–9 (no.258).

14 Denon, op. cit. (note 1), vol.I, p.72. The tank is now British Museum, no. EA10.

15 Ibid., vol.I, pp.286–8.

16 Ibid., vol.II, p.226. For Desvernois, see Herold, op. cit. (note 2), p.251.

17 Denon, op. cit. (note 1), in general chap.VI; for the organization of the Institut, p.169.

18 Herold, op. cit. (note 2), pp.151ff.

19 For Lancret's announcement see Solé and Valbelle, op. cit. (note 10), p.6; for the discovery of the Stone, pp.1–5.

20 On the content of the inscription on the Rosetta Stone see Solé and Valbelle, op. cit. (note 10), pp.128–34; also R. Parkinson, *Cracking Codes: The Rosetta Stone and decipherment* (London, 1999), pp.25ff., 198–200.

21 For fuller accounts see Solé and Valbelle, op. cit. (note 10), pp.29ff.; Parkinson, op. cit. (note 20), pp.21–5.

22 The decipherment race is well described in Solé and Valbelle, op. cit. (note 10), pp.46–100, with the special contributions of Thomas Young, pp.63–74, 139–48; also Parkinson, op. cit. (note 20), pp.31–41.

23 On the *Lettre à M. Dacier* see particularly Solé and Valbelle, op. cit. (note 10), pp.78–86.

24 Of the ten volumes of plates, five are devoted to antiquities, two to modern Egypt, two to natural history, and one is an atlas. Of the nine text volumes, four were for antiquities, three for modern Egypt, and two for natural history. Publication began in 1809 under the patronage of Napoleon and ended in 1828 in the reign of Charles X.

Figure 61
Engraving in Norden's *Travels* (1757)
of a peripteral temple of King
Amenophis III (*c*.1390–1352 BC), on
the Island of Elephantine: a valuable
record of a monument dismantled for
building materials in the 1820s.

Figure 62
Jean-François Champollion
(1790–1832), decipherer of
hieroglyphs and the 'Father of
Egyptology'. After a posthumous
portrait by Léon Cogniet (1831).

Figure 63
The mortuary temple of King
Ramesses II (*c*.1279–1213 BC), now
called the Ramesseum, but known in
the early nineteenth century as the
Memnonium. An engraving in the
Description de l'Égypte (1827).

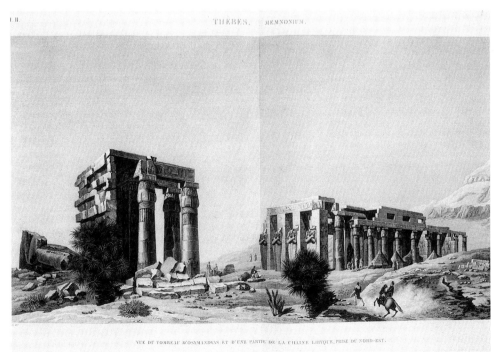

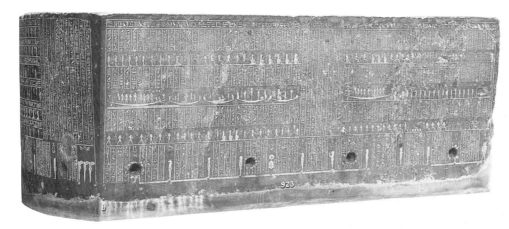

Figure 64
The breccia sarcophagus of King
Nectanebo II of the Thirtieth Dynasty
(360–343 BC), l.313.5cm (122¹/₂ in).
Found in a mosque in Alexandria,
where it was used as an ablutions tank;
first thought to be the sarcophagus of
Alexander the Great. British Museum,
Department of Ancient Egypt and
Sudan (EA 10).

Figure 65
Vivant Denon's illustration
of French surveyors measuring the
Great Sphinx at Giza (1802). The artist
has enhanced his representation with
details of the head which were not
to be seen in 1798.

Figure 66
The fort of Qait Bey in Rosetta,
renamed Fort St Julien by the French,
in which Lieutenant Bouchard found
the Rosetta Stone in 1799.

Figure 67
The Rosetta Stone (196 BC),
a granite stela carrying three bands
of text: the top in hieroglyphs, the
middle in cursive demotic, the bottom
in Greek, ht (max) 1.14m (3ft 9in).
London, British Museum, Department
of Ancient Egypt and Sudan (EA 24).

Figure 68
A frontispiece plate from the
Description de l'Égypte (1827)
consisting of a capriccio of Egyptian
monuments, some fanciful, some
based on genuine originals, and
peopled with troops of the Napoleonic
army in Egypt.

Chapter 20

Martin Folkes and the Study of the English Coinage in the Eighteenth Century

Hugh Pagan

Two hundred and fifty years ago, at the time of the foundation of the British Museum, there was as yet no national coin collection. Of the two major collections containing English coins that had existed in the middle of the seventeenth century, the more important, that formed by Sir Robert Cotton, long preserved in Cotton House adjacent to the Palace of Westminster, had followed the migrations of Cotton's books and manuscripts to new premises in the early years of the eighteenth century. Access to the coins had, however, always been difficult, and in 1747, when the coin collection was rediscovered by Martin Folkes, it was noted that the coins had been presumed lost in the fire that had destroyed part of the manuscript collection in 1731.[1] The other significant collection that had then existed, the old Royal Collection, can be glimpsed in outline from the inventory of Charles I's art collections made by Abraham van der Doort before the outbreak of the Civil War, but it was of a somewhat incoherent nature and does not seem to have contained more than a handful of English coins predating the reign of James I. There is no evidence as to what, if anything, survived of it at the Restoration and, although by 1771 George III was in possession of a large collection of English and European coins and medals, most of it had probably been assembled within his own reign.[2] In any case, this was not a collection to which the public had any access at all, and it was not until the mid-1820s that it was handed over to the British Museum as part of a general financial settlement between George IV and the government.

Against this background, it is easy to understand that the historical study of the English coinage had not got very far by the beginning of the eighteenth century. Some of the documentary evidence for the coinage had been used by William Lowndes for a publication of 1695, and some preliminary attempts to attribute English medieval coins to their correct rulers had been made by coin collectors, most notably by John Sharp, Archbishop of York (1645–1714).[3] Even Sharp's attributions, however, had often been wrong, and almost everything remained to be done. The first serious attempt to take the study forward was made by the Society of Antiquaries of London in January 1722, when a group of its members agreed to undertake 'a complete description and history of all the coins relating to Great Britain from the earliest times to our own', but nothing positive followed. The Society's President, Peter Le Neve, volunteered, or was proposed by others, to take on by himself the whole of the medieval and later English coinage,

but evidently found the task was too much for him. Another group of Society members was named for the same purpose in 1724, among whom specialists in the coinage after 1066 were more numerous, but they too achieved nothing.[4]

The honour of having written the first book on the English coinage was thus to fall on Stephen Martin Leake, a future Garter King of Arms, whose book *Nummi Britannici Historia, or An Historical Account of English Money from the Conquest*, appeared in 1726. His book was, however, not much more than a compilation from existing published material, and there is no evidence that Martin Leake had any specialist knowledge of the coins that he mentions, or that he was aware of the gradual progress with datings and attributions that was beginning to be made in discussion and correspondence between collectors. Meanwhile, the Society of Antiquaries retained an interest in the history of the coinage of Great Britain, but its only publishing vehicle at this date was its *Vetusta Monumenta* series of engraved plates, sporadically issued and in an inconveniently large format.[5] It is no surprise therefore that in 1731 the Society was persuaded to give its approval to one of its members, Martin Folkes, who wanted to compile a scholarly illustrated book of his own on the English coinage.[6]

There is no better introduction to Martin Folkes (figs 69–70) than to quote the opening part of a celebrated description of him written about 1752 by his sometime friend, the antiquary William Stukeley:[7]

> Martin Folkes has an estate of near £3000 got by his father in the law. He is a man of no aeconomy. Before of age he married Mrs Bracegirdle off the stage. His mother griev'd at it so much she threw herself out of a window & broke her arm. His only son broke his neck off a horse back at Paris. His eldest daughter ran away with a book keeper & who used her very ill. Quarrelling with Sir Hans Sloan about the Presidentship of the Royal Society, & being baffled, he went to Rome with his wife, & daughters, dog, cat, parrot, and monkey. There his wife grew religiously mad. He went to Venice and got a dangerous hurt upon his leg. Returning he was successor to Sir Hans, President of the R[oyal] S[ociety]. Losing his teeth, he speaks so as not to be understood. He constantly refuses all papers that treat of longitude. He chuses the Councel & Officers out of his junto of sycophants that meet him every night at Rawthmills coffee house or that dine with him on thursdays at the Miter, Fleet Street. He has a great deal of learning, philosophy, astronomy: but knows nothing of natural history. In matters of religion an errant infidel & loud scoffer. Professes himself a godfather to all monkeys, beleives nothing of a future state, of the Scriptures, of revelation. He perverted Duke of Montagu, Richmond, Ld Pembroke, & very many more of the nobility, who had an opinion of his understanding; &

this has done infinite prejudice to religion in general, made the nobility throw off the mask, & openly deride & discountenance even the appearance of religion, which has brought us into that deplorable situation we are now in, with thieves, & murderers, perjury, forgery, &.

This description requires some amplification and explanation and the salient facts of Folkes's life are these. Born in 1690, he had inherited from his parents both money and a small landed estate at Hillington, near King's Lynn in Norfolk. As a result, after a university education at Cambridge, he was not forced to embark on a career, and was able instead to pursue his intellectual interests, initially in mathematics generally, but afterwards more particularly in astronomy and metrology. This obtained him election to the Royal Society as early as 1714 and, from the 1720s onwards, he became deeply involved in the activities and internal politics both of the Royal Society and of the Society of Antiquaries; he was in fact eventually to become the only individual ever to be elected president of both organizations. He presided over the Royal Society from 1741 to 1752, and over the Antiquaries from 1751 to his death in June 1754, although his tenure of office in both societies was largely nominal after the severe stroke which he suffered in the autumn of 1751. What is worth stressing is that, as Stukeley more or less has to admit, he was on terms of genuine friendship with the scientists and antiquaries with whom he socialized, and that these included such great noblemen as the 2nd Duke of Montagu, the 2nd Duke of Richmond, and the 9th Earl of Pembroke.[8] In a recent article by David Haycock,[9] the extent of Folkes's circle of friends is somewhat underplayed – even Stukeley had been a close friend of his until 1750 – and it was certainly personal friendships between Folkes and fellow numismatists that got his book on coins under way.

No evidence survives as to the reason why he suddenly took an interest in coins in the early 1730s, but it may reasonably be supposed that it might have stemmed from his underlying interest in metrology. Of the two numismatic publications by him that appeared in his lifetime, the first, his *Table of English Gold Coins*, first published in 1736, is concerned with the weights and values of the coins rather than with their physical appearance. His second, the *Table of English Silver Coins*, a more substantial book, published in 1745, makes much use of data of a metrological character; it shows, for example, that Folkes had weighed, with surprisingly varied results, no fewer than eight examples of the rare surviving groats of Edward I.[10]

However, it was not with metrology that he began his self-imposed task. The first we hear of its progress is in more or less simultaneous letters of July 1732 from Folkes to the antiquary Browne Willis, and from the engraver Vertue to another antiquary, Maurice Johnson. They reveal that George Vertue was at that time preparing a series of engraved plates of English gold coins for Folkes's intended book.[11] These letters, and four others written by Folkes to Willis in the same year, show that by July, Vertue had provided Folkes with a proof of a plate illustrating gold coins attributed to Edward III, Henry IV and Richard II, and that he was at work on another plate illustrating coins of James I. By September, Vertue had also executed a proof of a plate illustrating gold coins of Mary I and Elizabeth I, and the correspondence indicates that a further plate of gold coins of Elizabeth I, as well as a plate or plates of Charles I's gold coins, were also envisaged.

What is apparent from this exchange of letters is that Folkes's first objective was not the writing of a text, but the preparation of a set of engraved plates. This may seem surprising, but it reflected the needs of the time. A corpus of reliable illustrations of English regal coins was the most important requirement, one which would enable numismatic scholars to see, as the starting point for future research, what varieties of coins were known for which rulers. Since there was no public or private collection that, by itself, contained a good enough selection of such coins, Folkes, to achieve this end, clearly had to borrow widely from the collections of his friends. These surviving letters show that at this time English gold coins had already been made available to Folkes by the Earl of Pembroke, by the Countess of Pomfret, by the painter and coin collector Hugh Howard, and by Willis himself.[12]

After a letter of 14 November 1732, the correspondence between Folkes and Willis breaks off, and does not resume until 1736. Folkes had in fact left England on 25 March 1733 (with his wife, daughters, dog, and so on) and did not return to this country until 1 September 1735.[13] When he returned, he had changed his mind about the need to give priority to the preparation of plates, and all that he did at first was to send the manuscript text of his *Table of English Gold Coins* to the printer William Bowyer. As published, this is no more than a unillustrated list of the denominations, weights and values of the gold coins struck by English monarchs from Edward III to George II.

This had been published by the late summer of 1736, and it is apparent from a letter of Folkes to Willis, dated 8 September 1736, that, on receiving his copy of the Table, Willis had written quite a detailed letter to Folkes drawing his attention to some of its inadequacies. In his own letter, Folkes does his best to deflect Willis's criticisms, and in the course of it he remarks that: 'I am much oblig'd for your kind wishes … that I would go on with the gravings: which I hope to do soon, if I live. But I am ashamed to own my being abroad so many years from my papers, have so addled my hand from them, that I am frequently at a loss to make out things I had formerly done.'[14] It appears that no further engraved plates were prepared for some years, and the idea of an illustrated publication on the English coinage may temporarily have been dropped altogether. What is clear however is that Folkes took on board the criticisms of the *Table of English Gold Coins* expressed by Willis, and doubtless by others as well. Its companion volume, the *Table of English Silver Coins*, which, as we have seen, finally appeared in 1745, is no mere list but a proper book on the history of the English coinage between the Norman Conquest and the early years of the reign of George II. Its coverage of the coins of the Norman and Plantagenet dynasties is sketchy, but becomes fuller with the accession of Henry VII; Folkes manages to provide a continuous narrative of the history of the coinage from the reign of Edward VI onwards, considerably helped for the later reigns by information and documents provided by friendly officials at the Tower mint. However, because Folkes had decided not to proceed with the preparation of plates, it appeared without any illustrations at all, therefore making it very difficult for its readers to relate Folkes's text to actual coins. Indeed, as it was going through the press, Folkes's recognition of this failing effectively brought him back to the point at which he had stopped before he left England in 1733. On 13 February 1745, it

Hugh Pagan

was agreed between him and the Society of Antiquaries that he would prepare, and the Society would pay for and publish, a plate volume with accompanying descriptive text that would act as a companion to his two unillustrated volumes of Tables.[15]

For this purpose Folkes already possessed some six plates of gold coins that had been engraved for him by Vertue in 1732, to which additional plates of gold coins could now be added. However, it remained necessary to prepare a complete new series of plates illustrating the silver coins, and a start was evidently made on these shortly afterwards, since the first plate of silver coins, those of William I and William II, was completed by 15 July 1745.[16] By the time of Folkes's death in 1754, forty-two plates were in existence, twelve illustrating gold coins and the rest silver coins.[17] A good number of these plates must have been prepared without access to the Cotton collection, which was not rediscovered by Folkes until May 1747, well after the engraving of the plates of silver coins had begun. The collection would not, in any case, have been of much help. A manuscript list compiled by Folkes shows that by then it contained only sixty-six silver coins struck between 1066 and the death of Queen Elizabeth I, among which as few as half a dozen were obvious rarities.[18] This makes the fact that Folkes was able to provide something over 450 high-quality coins from his own collection and from the collections of his friends, for illustration on these forty-two plates, all the more remarkable an achievement.

Such detail about the plates produced in Folkes's lifetime is material because when the illustrated version of his book was finally published by the Society of Antiquaries in 1763, nine years after his death, it was to contain twenty-six further plates which had nothing to do with Folkes. Even the plates which had been prepared for Folkes were extensively reworked, with additional coins crammed into any available space which Folkes's engraver had left blank (figs 71–2). These amplifications can be simply explained by the fact that a watershed had been crossed in the intervening years. When Folkes took up his task, the compilation of volumes of this kind was a matter for private scholars, relying on a network of like-minded friends for information and for the loan of relevant material for illustration. Once the Cotton and Sloane collections had been brought together in the newly created British Museum in Montagu House, there was however both the nucleus of a proper national coin collection and a knowledgeable numismatist on the Museum's staff to work on it: Dr Andrew Gifford, Assistant Librarian in the Department of Manuscripts.[19]

The Society of Antiquaries had at first been uncertain as to how to complete the unfinished volume after Folkes's death,[20] but, by February 1757, Gifford was already involved with the project.[21] In the end it was Gifford who was to decide which additional coins to illustrate and who provided short written descriptions, both of those coins and of others already engraved for Folkes. Gifford's attitude to Folkes's book seems at the start to have been conservative. He left Folkes's combined text (of 1736 and 1745) unaltered, and many of his descriptions of the coins included in the earlier plates are brief and uninformative. However, as his work on the volume progressed, he gradually began to increase the level of annotation and to record which of the coins illustrated were in the British Museum and which were in private collections known to him. In the portions of his text that describe the plates of gold coins and six

supplementary plates at the end, this information is given more or less as a matter of course. By the end of this process, Gifford had added illustrations and descriptions of at least 700 further coins to the volume as Folkes had left it, making the book considerably more helpful for any one who wanted to use it to identify coins in their own possession. In its final form it is as much Gifford's monument as Folkes's.[22]

But, in any revamping of another author's intended publication, there is loss as well as gain. As a result of Gifford's anxiety to illustrate as many coins as possible, a few deceptive modern forgeries crept in, and insufficient care was taken to check the accuracy of some of the added illustrations, which had been largely provided by Francis Perry, the engraver. Perry is recorded as having been 'painstaking and industrious',[23] but he only had one eye and he was in no way the equal of George Vertue either as draughtsman or as engraver. Additionally, the reworking of the copper plates prepared for Folkes meant in some cases that coins, very accurately drawn and engraved in 1732 or in the years after 1745, were represented on the revised plates by rather less accurate illustrations done in the later 1750s. Here one can instance the unique surviving sovereign groat of Henry VII, beautifully engraved on a plate done for Folkes, but re-engraved less well in a different place for Gifford, with the consequence that numismatists have not clearly recognized that the coin, which seems to have been known at least since 1732, is genuine and not a mid-eighteenth century forgery.[24] One might also regret the insertion of additional coins in the blank spaces left on Folkes's plates which almost invariably spoils the aesthetic appearance of the plates. This is certainly contrary to what Folkes himself would have wanted, for in one of his letters to Willis he records that 'the beauty of the plates' was one of the factors dictating his arrangement of the coins.[25]

Finally, lest it be thought that all this is mere antiquarianism, it should be stressed that the plates prepared for Folkes and Gifford have had a utility to numismatists, and a life expectancy which can scarcely have been anticipated. When half a century later Rogers Ruding needed illustrations for the first edition of his famous book, *The Annals of the Coinage of Britain*, the Society of Antiquaries gave him permission to reuse the surviving copper plates of all Folkes's and Gifford's plates, and they were used again to illustrate the two subsequent editions of Ruding's work, the last of which appeared in 1840. More tellingly, it was still the case well into the second half of the twentieth century that the engraved plates in the 1840 edition of Ruding provided an illustrated record of the English coinage not yet superseded by any subsequent photographically illustrated publication, and in many respects that still remains true today.

Notes and references
1   Letter from Maurice Johnson Jnr to William Stukeley, 20 June 1747, printed in W.C. Lukis (ed.), *The Family Memoirs of the Rev. William Stukeley, M.D., and the Antiquarian and other Correspondence of William Stukeley* (London, 1887), vol.III (Surtees Society 80), p.354.
2   The composition of this portion of the royal coin collection in 1771 is recorded in a manuscript, 'Catalogue of the several series of modern medals & coins in His Majesty's collection 1771', reused and updated in 1814 as the second volume of a two-volume manuscript catalogue of the royal coin collection as a whole (now bound together in the Department of Coins and Medals, British Museum).

The collection as it existed in 1771 was notably weak in coins of George III's two immediate predecessors, from which it may be inferred that they, at least, had taken no particular interest in it, and there is a variety of evidence for the expansion of the collection in the early years of George III's reign.

3   Archbishop Sharp's contribution to the study of the English coinage was discussed by the present writer in H. Pagan, 'Presidential Address to the British Numismatic Society for the year 1987', *British Numismatic Journal* 57 (1987), pp.173–80.

4   Revd Rogers Ruding, *Annals of the Coinage of Britain and its Dependencies* (London, 1817), vol.IV, pp.xiii–xiv. Ruding correctly states that William Stukeley, who was a member of both groups and who on each occasion took on responsibility for the Ancient British series, did get as far as issuing a series of engraved plates of ancient British coins, but this should be interpreted as a personal undertaking by Stukeley, rather than as his contribution to a collective project.

5   The first volume of the Society of Antiquaries' *Vetusta Monumenta* series, published in 1747, contains six broadly relevant plates (pls 20, 37, 38, 43, 55, 56). These had originally been issued as separate engravings and carry dates between 1725 and 1739. The two plates of English coins dated 1739 which conclude this sequence were produced during the period in which, as it would seem, Folkes had temporarily abandoned the idea of an illustrated volume on the coinage (see further below).

6   Ruding, op. cit. (note 4), vol.I, p.xiv, quoting 'Vertue's MS in the Society [of Antiquaries]'.

7   Lukis, op. cit. (note 1), vol.I (London, 1882) (*Surtees Society* 72), pp.98–100 (extract from Stukeley's commonplace book). It should be noted that in this passage Stukeley confuses Folkes's actress wife, Lucy Bradshaw, with the older and more celebrated actress Mrs Bracegirdle (for whom see *DNB*), and that Folkes was certainly of age at the time of his marriage on 18 October 1714.

8   It is appropriate to record here that Folkes's personal prestige in north-west Norfolk was sufficient to secure him a reasonable vote when he stood as a candidate for the borough of King's Lynn at the general election of 1747, against sitting MPs who had the support of the locally all-powerful Walpole family (Romney Sedgwick wrongly attributed this candidacy to a fictitious 'Morton Folkes', see R. Sedgwick, *History of Parliament, House of Commons, 1715–1754* (London, 1970), vol.I, p.290).

9   D. Haycock, '"The cabal of a few designing members": The presidency of Martin Folkes PRS, and the Society's first charter', *Antiquaries Journal* 80 (2000), pp.273–84.

10 M. Folkes, *Table of English Silver Coins* (London, 1745), p.8.

11 Folkes to Browne Willis, late July 1732 (letter survives in a transcript by William Cole, British Library, Additional MS 5833, fol.149 (refoliated 152), in which Cole renders Browne Willis's endorsement as 'Recd. July 38 [*sic*] 1732'); Vertue to Maurice Johnson, 29 July 1732, printed in J. Nichols, *Literary Anecdotes* (London, 1812–15), vol.III, p.249.

12 Folkes's next four letters to Browne Willis are dated 17 September, 31 October, 4 November and 14 November, 1732, and likewise survive in transcripts by William Cole, British Library, Additional MS 5833, fols 150–4 (refoliated 153–7).

13 J. Ingamells, *A Dictionary of British and Irish Travellers in Italy 1701–1800* (Newhaven and London, 1997), pp.365–6.

14 Folkes to Browne Willis, 8 September 1736 (transcript by William Cole, British Library, Additional MS 5833, fol.154 (refoliated 157).

15 In his annotated copy of the 1763 edition of Folkes's book (in the possession of the present writer), Richard Gough, Director of the Society of Antiquaries 1771–97, added a marginal ink note offering his own rather broad-brush summary of the Society of Antiquaries' role in the volume's publishing history. It reads as follows: 'The Soc[iet]y after having engraved a few tables of our gold & silver coins by a[rch]b[isho]p Sharpe & others were prevail'd on to resign the undertaking to Mr. Folkes. After he had presented his book to em 1745 they resolved to complete it at their own expense. Mr. F. furnishd the plan of the plates, & letterpress for 50 plates & offerd his assistance & to make up his own plates then & give em to the Society. After they had purchasd his plates & on his decease

Mr. Wm Folkes offered em some MS papers of the author & they bo[ugh]t at Dr. Mead's sale a small book of Eng. coins from Eliz. to the Commonwealth with his MSS notes for £3.10.'

16 Letter from George North to Andrew Coltee Ducarel, printed in Nichols, op. cit. (note 11), vol.v, p.430.

17 A complete set of proofs of these plates, as they existed at the date of Folkes's death, is bound up with one of the Society of Antiquaries' sets of the original unillustrated editions of Folkes's volumes of 1736 and 1745. Another partial set of proof plates accompanies Society of Antiquaries MS 657, Josiah Colebrooke's manuscript cited in note 20 below.

18 Folkes's list, compiled on 16 May 1747 and preserved in the Department of Coins and Medals, British Museum, records silver coins only. It is uncertain whether this is because the collection by that date contained no gold coins of British rulers of the medieval and early modern period or because Folkes omitted to list any such coins, but Cotton's collection is known to have suffered significant losses during the century after his death, and it may well be that all the medieval and early modern gold in the collection had vanished by the 1740s.

19 It should be explained that before the establishment of a Department of Antiquities at the British Museum in the early years of the nineteenth century, the Museum's coin collection fell within the curatorial responsibility of the staff of the Department of Manuscripts. Rather strangely to modern eyes, Gifford (1700–84) combined his duties at the British Museum with the position he had held since 1730 as minister of the Baptist chapel in Eagle Street, Holborn.

20 Having purchased the existing copper plates and the copyright of Folkes's text from Folkes's heirs, the Society's Council distributed sets of proof plates to each Council member in December 1755, inviting their comments. Only one full set of written comments survives in the Society's archives, that by Andrew Coltee Ducarel (Society of Antiquaries MS 274), but significant written comments seem also to have been made at this juncture by John Ward (the Society's Director) and by Andrew Gifford, and also by Josiah Colebrooke (not at the time a member of the Society's Council but active in the Society's affairs and a personal friend of Folkes). In consequence, primary responsibility for the editing of the volume initially devolved on Ward, with Gifford helping with the completion of the plates and Colebrooke supplying written descriptions of the coins featured on them. Colebrooke's manuscript of his descriptions is MS 657, compiled by him at intervals in 1756 and 1757, but it seems subsequently to have been decided that these descriptions were too lengthy to be used in the published volume. After Ward's death in October 1758, Gifford took over complete responsibility both for the plates and for the accompanying letterpress.

21 In a letter to Ducarel, dated 16 February 1757, printed in Nichols, op. cit. (note 11), vol.IX, p.417, the Suffolk antiquary Thomas Martin enquires how publication of Folkes's book is progressing, and expresses the hope that 'perhaps Dr. Gifford can let me have some spare plates'.

22 Gifford's own annotated copy of Folkes's book in its 1763 version, bequeathed by him to the library of the Baptist College, Bristol, was acquired some years ago for the library of the Department of Coins and Medals, British Museum. The annotations are not, however, of any particular consequence.

23 Perry's career and surviving output are adequately summarized by F.M. O'Donoghue in *DNB*.

24 The fullest discussion of this coin is that by E.J. Winstanley, 'The sovereign groat of Henry VII', in R.A.G. Carson (ed.), *Mints, Dies and Currency: Essays dedicated to the memory of Albert Baldwin* (London, 1971), pp.161–4. Although Winstanley quotes a passage from Thomas Snelling, *Miscellaneous Views of the Coins (etc.)* (London, 1769), p.43, recording that the coin had first come to light in the collection of 'Mr. Thomas Granger', Winstanley was not aware that Granger, Clerk to the East India Company's Committee of Private Trade, had died as far back as 22 March 1732, and that the coin must presumably have been known before that date.

25 Folkes to Browne Willis, 14 November 1732 (see note 12).

Figure 69
Martin Folkes, engraving by John Faber
(1737) after John Vanderbank (1736).

Figure 70
Martin Folkes, engraving by James
McArdell after Thomas Hudson
(undated).

Figure 71
Martin Folkes, *A Table of English Gold
Coins*, pl.ɪ: (a) version of 1732; (b)
version in published volume of 1763.

(a)

(b)

Figure 72
Martin Folkes, *A Table of English Silver
Coins*, pl.xvɪɪ: (a) version of c.1750; (b)
version in published volume of 1763.

(a)

(b)

Chapter 21

The Antiquary *en plein air*

Eighteenth-century progress from topographical survey to the threshold of field archaeology

Arthur MacGregor

In common with other proto-scientific pursuits, the practice of antiquarian research in the eighteenth century showed an increasing tendency to look for its primary material in an outdoor arena. If the archetype of the solitary scholar in his study embraced the figure of the antiquary from the early years of the Renaissance to the generation that gave birth to Dr Richard Mead, Sir Hans Sloane and their contemporaries,[1] by the end of the 'long Enlightenment' he had undoubtedly been displaced in importance by his cousin in the field, characteristically winning new discoveries by engaging with the landscape. Certainly, the ever closer scrutiny of ancient artefacts – usually pre-selected for their primary appeal as collectors' pieces – offered only limited prospects for the advancement of knowledge at this time, as did the repeated combing of classical texts in search of understanding of miscellaneous objects from a past whose topography remained as yet largely undifferentiated, beyond the constraints imposed on it by Old Testament chronology. All this decontextualized material simply lacked the potential to communicate very innovatively. For this reason, and although natural history entered a period when taxonomies began to make strides at the microscope bench, the potential for the armchair antiquary to expand the frontiers of his subject diminished in inverse proportion to the expanding horizons of those investigators for whom artefacts formed only incidental links in a chain of evidence that was anchored in monuments in the field.

It would be over-optimistic to suggest that this transition had been fully effected during the eighteenth century: convention ascribes that turning-point to the latter half of the nineteenth century. Nonetheless, a number of conceptual and methodological advances can be claimed for our era, around which the present-day concerns of field archaeology were ultimately to crystallize.

The English topographical tradition

The roots of this nascent movement indeed reach back to the very origins of the antiquarian tradition in England, to the world of John Leland (c.1503–52), whose *Itinerary* of the English landscape, compiled before 1543, was punctuated by images of principally medieval monuments, many of them freshly scarred by encounters with the forces of Reformation secularization,[2] and of William Camden (1551–1623), whose *Britannia*, published initially in 1586, forms the first milestone in this new discipline (characterized by its author as 'the backward looking curiosity'), against which all other advances have to be measured. Published in six Latin editions, the

Britannia's influence was felt with new vigour when it was translated into English by Philemon Holland in 1610 (2nd edn, 1637), enlarged and extended in scope in a new edition edited by Edmund Gibson in 1695 (2nd edn, 1722), and revived again by Richard Gough in 1789 (2nd edn, 1806).[3]

Few indications of antiquarian interest in the landscape can be detected in the first half of the seventeenth century, save for the surprising intervention of James I (prompted, it seems, by purely venal considerations) when he commanded Inigo Jones (1573–1652) to discover whatever he could about the monument at Stonehenge. As an architect steeped in the traditions of classical and Renaissance Italy, Jones responded by producing a schematized plan of the site in which its various features were regularized into a design of circles and equilateral triangles in fulfilment of his preconception as to its origins – specifically, that it was of Roman construction and hence comprehensible within the rules of Vitruvian proportion (fig.73). His plan encapsulates one of the fundamental problems facing the early antiquary in the field – that of identifying exactly which were the significant features that needed to be recorded. That the physiognomy of the casually surviving (often damaged and incomplete) remains of the monument might itself have an evidential significance was by no means immediately clear, and the fortuitous appearance bequeathed to it by history compared to its original, pristine form – which, it was perceived, could readily be re-created – had at best an ambivalent value. We can easily comprehend Jones's decision to attempt to recover the essence of the monument whose original regularity, he surmised, 'time had eroded'.[4]

The decades following the Restoration of Charles II (in 1660), and the subsequent founding of the Royal Society, saw the appearance of a series of studies which were to impinge more directly on the best antiquarian practice of the eighteenth century, stamping it with the character and the modes of operation of the Royal Society itself. Of these, Sir William Dugdale's *Antiquities of Warwickshire* (1656) is acknowledged as setting new standards in the treatment of local history that make it stand out from the run of antiquarian writing that had preceded it, enjoying the advantage of being 'adorned with many cuts'.[5] Robert Plot, with his *Natural History* of Oxfordshire (1677) and of Staffordshire (1686), in expressing a determination to concentrate on '*things*' to the exclusion of '*persons* and *actions*', and to treat of these 'only of such, as are very remote from the present *Age*, whether found under ground, or whereof there yet remain any footsteps above it', formalizes the new agenda for the treatment of material culture.[6] His observation that such items, 'being all made and fashioned out of natural things', were therefore appropriate for consideration under the rubric of natural history, looks back in one sense to the Plinian concept in which all man-made objects were classified according to the raw materials from which they were produced; more immediately, it reflects the comprehensive terms of the credo of the Royal Society. Martin Lister adopted a comparable viewpoint in relation to the antiquities he published, claiming that his interest in them lay 'only in the relation they may have to the advancement of Natural Philosophy and Arts'.[7] Perhaps the most fully integrated programme of this kind was that elucidated by Edward Lhwyd (1660–1709) for his projected *Archaeologia Britannica*, which aimed to situate the study of archaeological remains within a scheme that took as its starting point the geology and botany of the Celtic realms and which culminated in an analysis of their respective languages. The plan was never brought to a conclusion, although examples survive of the preparatory surveys carried out by Lhwyd.[8] It is demonstrable therefore that the eighteenth-century development of archaeological interest in the field is intimately linked to the highly integrated approach of natural historians and philosophers; its practitioners saw their researches not in the light of an emerging new discipline, but essentially as one line of advance in a process of inquiry that proceeded on a broad front.[9]

Aubrey and Stukeley: antiquarian innovators

Despite this proper emphasis on the unified nature of early antiquarian research, it was only by focusing to some degree on the materials of archaeological fieldwork, and on the particular problems they posed, that any potential they might have for the advancement of knowledge could be exploited. That opportunity was first fully grasped by John Aubrey (1626–97), who sought to apply to the antiquities of the countryside the disciplines of recording, comparison and analysis that were by then more familiar in the natural sciences.

If Aubrey's fieldwork had entirely lived up to his rhetoric it might be expected that in his treatment of field monuments those methodologies would have been carried through with full scientific rigour: 'These Antiquities are so exceeding old that no Bookes doe reach them', he wrote on one occasion, 'so that there is no way to retrive them but by comparative antiquitie, which I have writt upon the spott from the Monuments themselves'.[10] In the same vein, in his *Monumenta Britannica, or a Miscellanie of British Antiquities*, he claimed further to have 'arranged these Monuments together, for the neer resemblance they have to one another', interpreting megalithic sites 'by comparative Arguments' and attempting 'to work-out and restore after a kind of Algebraical method, by comparing them that I have seen, one with another; and reducing them to a kind of Æquation'.[11] The very concept of allowing the monuments to speak for themselves – whether observing a mathematical paradigm or not – rather than turning optimistically to historical or scriptural sources, was itself a conceptual novelty ('As the Divines doe interpret Scripture by Scripture', Aubrey says elsewhere, 'so shall I explaine these obsolete Antiquities one by another'),[12] but comparison of his actual output with his declared ambitions shows considerable discrepancies in this respect.[13] Dogged by the extremely abbreviated view of pre-Roman chronology that was to prevail well into the

nineteenth century, Aubrey was bound to see all of prehistory not only as virtually contemporaneous but as located on the very eve of the Roman invasion. Another black hole opened up between the collapse of the Empire and the Norman Conquest, into which he was reluctant to cast any remains of the least sophistication.[14] Perhaps inevitably, it is hard to find evidence of success on Aubrey's part in conjuring much order from the prodigious confusion that characterized British prehistory in his day.

Between the poles of his proclaimed ambitions and his methodological impediments, however, there remains no shortage of valuable material that secures Aubrey's place as one of the innovators of his age. Michael Hunter has drawn parallels between the way in which the camps, barrows and roads are treated successively in the *Monumenta* and the comparable classificatory system that marks Aubrey's *Naturall Historie of Wiltshire* – evidence of a systematic approach applied in a novel context.[15] If prehistoric chronology defeated him (as well it might), his 'Discourses Chronological' on handwriting, on costume history and particularly on architecture show him succeeding brilliantly in his application of the comparative principles he had earlier elucidated and in drawing valid conclusions from them.[16]

When these methods were turned on the landscape, the limits of knowledge within which Aubrey and his contemporaries operated led to a great many disparate elements being run together in a dramatic but, from a twenty-first-century perspective, disastrously foreshortened narrative: in his own grand scheme, for example, we find him planning to 'trace-out the way the victorious Roman Eagle tooke her Course' by plotting the distribution of what are now recognized as Bronze Age barrows – interpreted by him as the mass graves of British heroes hewn down by the legions.[17] But even in this mistaken instance, Aubrey left a valuable legacy in the form of measured plans of individual monuments (fig.74) – some compiled by himself and some by others – whose accuracy he was keen to stress. He particularly distanced himself from Inigo Jones's approach to recording, criticizing Jones's plan of Stonehenge on the grounds that 'he framed the monument to his own Hypothesis, which is much differing from the Thing itself'.[18] He also constructed a map of ancient Wessex in which many of his own observations were combined to reconstitute an entire ancient landscape (fig.75). In his *Memoir* of Aubrey, John Britton characterized him in the following terms:

> He may be regarded as essentially an *Archæologist*, and the first person in this country who fairly deserved the name. Historians, chroniclers, and topographers there had been before his time; but he was the first who devoted his studies and abilities to archæology, in its various ramifications . . . No one before him investigated or understood anything of the vast Celtic temple at Avebury, and other monuments of the same class.[19]

Further expression was to be given to Aubrey's approach to the archaeological landscape by William Stukeley (1687–1765), whose preoccupations with matters druidical have long obscured the valuable work he carried out in the field in his earlier years. Stukeley is known to have copied out large parts of the unpublished manuscript of the *Monumenta Britannica* for his own use, and unquestionably the fundamental framework of Aubrey's methodology had a direct bearing on the way Stukeley framed his own researches.

Even Richard Mead can claim oblique credit in Stukeley's enterprise, for it seems that too many evenings spent quaffing the doctor's French wine left the still youthful Stukeley with a predisposition to gout, so that in his own words, '. . . in the spring, I was oblig'd to ride for my health, and that brought me to the humour and love of travelling; whereby I indulg'd myself in the study of the antiquities of my country'.[20] Over a period of fifteen years, between 1710 and 1725, he traversed the country on a dozen expeditions, some account of which he published in his *Itinerarium Curiosum* of 1724. The range of phenomena that caught his attention harmonized with the broad run of scholarly interest of the period, making him almost a predictable candidate for election to the Royal Society in 1718, and he was further to be found among the founding Fellows of the Society of Antiquaries, formally inaugurated in the winter of 1717–18 with Stukeley acting as Secretary.

An early visit to Stonehenge and an encounter with one of Loggan's engraved views of the monument resolved Stukeley 'to make an exact Model of that most noble and stupendous piece of Antiquity, which', he says, 'I have accomplish'd and from thence drawn the groundplot of its present ruins, and the view of it in its pristine State, and propose from thence to find out the original Architectonic Scheme by which it was erected, together with its design, use, Founders, etc.'[21] By 1719 he had visited the site in person and had also conceived plans to make a similarly detailed record of the remains of Avebury, then suffering unprecedented destruction, in order 'to preserve the memory of this most illustrious Work of the highest Antiquity'.[22] Like Aubrey's fieldwork before him, the written records that Stukeley compiled, along with his conjectural reconstructions of monuments, have proved of less permanent value than his plans and drawings: indeed, Stuart Piggott characterized their combined output of drawings as more valuable than almost the entire output of the next hundred years.[23]

Stukeley's primary concerns at Stonehenge and Avebury were to establish the layout of the constituent elements of the monuments and their place within the landscape. The detail and care that went into his plans is impressive (at Stonehenge, his surveys were made with the aid of a theodolite and, elsewhere, there is evidence for the use of the compass and the chain), while on occasion he would incorporate three-dimensional details for clarity of expression. His prospects of the surrounding landscape, though pleasingly idiosyncratic in style, remain vivid and persuasive documents (fig.76), while his handling of individual monuments bears comparison with most contemporary topographical drawing (fig.77). The manner in which he naturally communicates in terms of maps and plans has been said to have established the basis of a convention in British field archaeology that survives to this day.[24] (Surveying had indeed been considered an appropriate accomplishment for young gentlemen since the seventeenth century; it may be that the enclosure movement played a part in advancing it still further in the course of the 1700s.) When these monuments interacted directly with one another Stukeley was capable of making intelligent deductions, allowing him to work out some degree of relative chronology. He also speculated on the means by which the megaliths could have been transported and erected by the use of sledges and

rollers, cradles and levers,[25] and his investigation and recording of several Bronze Age burial mounds set new standards of recording and observation.[26]

Stukeley's descent into ever more speculative obsession with the Druids, and with their role in the erection of the monuments he had so signally brought to attention, are usually seen as compromising the text of the two volumes that might otherwise have proved definitive for their age, his *Stonehenge,* published in 1740, and *Abury* of 1743.[27] A further, less eccentric misconception, concerning a spurious medieval source for the history of Roman Britain, was to cast a blight over the work of another antiquary who was otherwise to represent the best of mid-eighteenth-century achievement in field survey.

William Roy and the *Military Antiquities of the Romans*

William Roy (1726–90) was another child of his time, though he emerged in a very different milieu from the rather pastoral background of the predecessors already mentioned – in the aftermath of Scotland's last disastrous flirtation with Jacobitism as part of the Duke of Cumberland's final solution to the festering problem of Stuart-led dissent. Having successfully suppressed the rebellion of 1745 and faced with the task of pacifying the Highlands on a permanent basis, Cumberland and his generals had 'found themselves greatly embarrassed for want of a proper Survey of the Country' and accordingly, Lieutenant-Colonel David Watson (c.1713–61), Quartermaster-General for Scotland, conceived the idea of compiling a definitive map of the Highland area. As his assistant in charge of the project, Watson appointed the twenty-one-year-old Roy who, between 1748 and 1752, led a small team of military and civilian personnel to complete this unprecedented task.[28] So successful were they, indeed, that they had no sooner finished it than the survey was extended to cover also the south of the country, the work of a further three years.

It was during the latter part of this exercise, it seems, that Roy developed a fascination for the Roman monuments that proliferated in the broad frontier area of the Lowlands. In later life he looked back on it as a very natural interest, musing on how 'military men . . . are naturally led to compare present things with the past; and being thus insensibly carried back to former ages, they place themselves among the ancients, and do, as it were, converse with the people of those remote times' – a desirable frame of mind for any antiquary.[29] The opportunities for comparing solutions adopted by the Roman generals in controlling a hostile native population on their northern flank with contemporary military strategies intrigued the still youthful (though by now highly experienced) surveyor. There is no doubt that his ideas were further stimulated, and formalized, by a growing acquaintance with Captain (later Lieutenant-General) Robert Melville (1723–1809), whose researches into the geography of Tacitus' *Agricola* explored the literary dimensions of the evidence which Roy was then charting on the ground – for once, history and archaeology working hand-in-hand.[30] Two of Roy's mapping achievements have earned lasting admiration from the antiquarian community: firstly, a map of Roman Scotland which, remarkably, is held not to have been superseded in some aspects until the issuing of the Ordnance Survey's *Map of Roman Britain* in 1924;[31] and secondly, a 1:36,000 survey of the entire length of the Antonine Wall, together with plans and sections of several of its associated forts (fig.78). The quality and scale of these surveys, carried out to the best military standards by the best of the Army's (civilian) surveyors, makes Stukeley's ground-plots, of only a generation earlier, look decidedly amateur.

Almost immediately the mapping work was completed, a great exodus of the officer corps from Scotland (prompted by the build-up to the Seven Years War) drew Roy in its wake to southern England, where he was himself commissioned into the Corps of Engineers and had his attention diverted elsewhere for the better part of a decade. In 1764, however, there was a renewed burst of effort on Roy's part to collect and compile further maps, plans and sketches that were to form the basis of an impressive folio volume, the *Military Antiquities of the Romans in North Britain*. The project was largely completed by 1773 but his findings were not published until twenty years later by the Society of Antiquaries, three years after the author's death.[32]

While Roy's original maps and plans have achieved the status of national treasures (and they compare favourably with anything produced in Europe at that date), his interpretative text has not fared nearly so well. Profiting from the insights gained from Melville's close knowledge of the classical sources, Roy was disastrously misled into relying most heavily on a text now known to be entirely spurious – the so-called *De Situ Britanniae*, attributed to a fictitious monk of Westminster named Richard of Cirencester. This was a hoax perpetrated by an Englishman, Charles Bertram, then living in Copenhagen, transmitted to the learned world via the Society of Antiquaries in 1756 by the unwitting Stukeley and published *in extenso* by Bertram himself in the following year. So extensive was Roy's reliance on this text that much of his own analysis has simply been jettisoned from scholarly use.[33] Nonetheless, Roy deserves to be remembered as much more than a misguided antiquary; there can be no doubt that he set new standards in archaeological surveying. His volume has rightly been characterized as 'one of our archaeological classics . . . a storehouse of trustworthy topographical information regarding Roman sites [that] can never be entirely superseded'.[34] It is also worth seeing the initial reluctance that Roy evidently felt in supplying a textual accompaniment to his survey of the Antonine Wall in the context of the motto of the Royal Society itself – *Nullius in Verba*. For Roy, the evidence of his plans and sections was self-sufficient and did not stand in need of verbal exposition. It was indeed necessary for knowledge to be summarized and collated, as Richard Yeo has stated (p.30), but Roy and the other archaeological topographers showed the learned world that there was more than one means by which this could be achieved.[35]

It is also clear that Roy's antiquarian interest was born out of a wider involvement with the military Survey of Scotland and, in 1763, he was to propose for the first time 'a general survey of the whole Island at public cost'. Although rejected on that occasion, the proposal was ultimately to lead, in 1791, to the foundation of the Ordnance Survey, from whose work the progress of archaeology was to benefit ever after. Although the scientific world had moved on from the early days when the study of antiquity sat comfortably within the broad agenda of the Royal Society, it is noteworthy how closely Roy remained part of that world; his experiments with the use of barometers as a means of establishing altitude – an essential element of

relief map-making – were aided by Sir Joseph Banks himself and were reported through the pages of the Society's *Philosophical Transactions*.[36] Furthermore, his commissioning of ultra-accurate equipment from steel surveying chains to glass measuring rods and culminating in Jesse Ramsden's famous three-foot diameter theodolite, made him a deserving recipient of the Society's Copley Medal.[37] He also made genuine contributions to the archaeological understanding of the military geography of Roman Britain, especially through the knowledge he was to develop of the distribution and character of marching camps and other temporary fortifications.[38] While inclined to dismiss his own work 'rather as the lucubrations of his leisure hours, than as tending to any great utility', Roy recognized too that his familiarity with contemporary military practice gave him valuable insights denied to many of the authors who had preceded him, and indeed he permitted himself to observe that it was 'a misfortune, that few of the commentators who have treated on this subject, however well qualified in other respects, have been military men'.[39]

James Douglas and the Chatham Lines

In 1781 William Roy, by now Deputy Quartermaster-General and about to be promoted to Major-General, produced, in the course of his military duties, a 'Report concerning the positions for an army in front of Chatham Lines'. The officer commanding the Lines at this point was Colonel (later General) Hugh Debbieg, one of Roy's youthful companions on the Survey of Scotland; a recent recruit to Debbieg's staff of engineers was a Captain of an antiquarian turn of mind, James Douglas (1753–1819). This momentary coincidence of talent might reasonably have been expected to set off Douglas, still in his late twenties, on a course of research that would mirror that of the venerable Roy. However, the task that Douglas was to set himself, and the manner of his achieving it, are noteworthy for their originality of conception; Douglas owed little in this respect to his older contemporaries.

The disturbance of ancient graves at Chatham Lines had first been brought about by the building of new soldiers' kitchens in 1756, but it was the repair of the Lines and the construction of a new redoubt in 1779–82 that opened up possibilities for Douglas's involvement. He ensured that, as each of the grave-groups was uncovered, it was preserved independently, including such bones as could be recovered; he was also careful to exclude from these assemblages such material as he perceived to be extraneous.[40] Elected to the Society of Antiquaries in 1780, he read a paper to the Fellowship on certain Roman remains found at Chatham. His parallel interest in fossils led to an invitation to address the Royal Society, on which occasion he expanded the conclusions drawn from his specimens in order to draw 'some inferences on the antiquity of the earth' and to speculate on the possibility of 'an antediluvian world inhabited by animals and, *perhaps*, by human beings'. This was dangerous territory for a man who was shortly to give up the Army for the Church; indeed, it may have been that Douglas's liberal views on these matters prejudiced his chances for preferment in his new profession.[41]

It was as a man of the cloth, however, that Douglas had the opportunity to extend his investigations to other cemeteries in Kent, including several unpublished sites excavated earlier by the Revd Bryan Faussett (1720–76). He drew together these discoveries into a handsome folio volume titled *Nenia Britannica, or a sepulchral history of Great Britain from the earliest period to its general conversion to Christianity* (1793), from which work his contribution can be assessed.[42] The first thing to note is that in chronological terms his interests had shifted later than those of his predecessors: British and Roman remains are given consideration, but only by way of background to the Saxon rites and ceremonies, evidence for which was drawn from 'several hundred burial places, opened under a careful inspection by the author'. In the course of a great deal of polemic, Douglas sets out his credo for the empirical study of antiquity in the cause of history. The opportunities offered by comparison of 'relics' discovered in one context with those from another are signalled, and the necessity of paying attention to the most accurately datable finds such as coins and inscriptions is highlighted. There is a recognition that research of this kind must be collaborative, involving 'the work of other antiquaries, whose labours will doubtless produce a succession of discoveries which, by degrees, will convey a great accession of light to the dark pages of history'. 'No position in the work has been assumed on mere conjecture', he claims, 'and when deductions have been made they have been founded on scrupulous comparison of the facts.'[43]

Douglas's comparisons are indeed drawn from wide-ranging sources and are argued in detail in lengthy footnotes, on occasion ranging over five pages at a time. The individual tumuli he investigated (and on occasion recorded structurally in some detail – if schematically: see fig.79) are described in this exhaustive way. The individual grave-goods associated with each burial are similarly treated and individually illustrated, providing a visible underpinning for Douglas's contention that he would advance no claims that he could not adequately justify from the evidence before him. He buttresses his arguments with references ranging from Pliny and Virgil to John Dee, Winckelmann and Sir William Hamilton. On occasion, to corroborate the testimony of his own eyes, he mentions the presence of exemplary witnesses such as Sir Joseph Banks and his friend Sir Charles Blagden, who attended the opening of certain graves in Greenwich Park where exceptional environmental conditions had led to the survival of Anglo-Saxon textiles and even human hair.[44]

No one before that time had made such a close study of field monuments in association with their contents;[45] Douglas's *Nenia* has with justification been called the first modern excavation report, in its integrated treatment of the artefacts – all drawn to a commendable standard by his own hand[46] – and the graves which produced them. The conclusions he drew from this evidence were equally original and noteworthy. The following quotation comes from the summing-up of his entire thesis, where he considers the totality of the evidence he has recovered himself or noted from discoveries by others in Kent and Sussex, and places it in a national context:

> The discovery of coins, the workmanship of relics, arms and nature of the burial places, either considered externally or internally, shew them to belong to a similar people, to a people in a state of peace, and in general possession of the country. Their situation near villages of Saxon names, their numbers proportioned to a small clan of people existing at a peculiar æra afford the critical evidence of their owners. They are scattered all over Britain in places which the Saxons occupied, and are not discovered in the parts of Wales which they had not subdued ... From their being scattered in such situations near places of Saxon names, at a convenient distance for sepulture, and no remains of British sepulchres near them, inferences may be deduced that the Saxons had totally extirpated the Britons from the parts they then occupied.[47]

Quite apart from his methodological advances, therefore, Douglas is noteworthy for having been the first excavator to recognize the Anglo-Saxons when he saw them. Hitherto, they had proved every bit as elusive as the inhabitants of remote prehistory. Douglas's assiduous interrogation of the monuments and their contents had, however, established the general characteristics of at least one group of these peoples in a thesis which could only have been conceived in the field; it was not to be surpassed until the work of E.T. Leeds in the twentieth century.

Colt Hoare, Cunnington and *Ancient Wiltshire*

A final illustration of progress dependent on the development of early field archaeology – a process that might be said to have been stimulated as much by Romantic as by Enlightenment values[48] – carries the subject forward to the opening years of the nineteenth century in terms of the personalities involved and the published work they compiled, and back to the still-fraught world of prehistory in the matter of the material with which they struggled. If a single model is sought for the elegant volumes of *Ancient Wiltshire* which form the joint monument of William Cunnington (1754–1810) and Sir Richard Colt Hoare (1758–1838),[49] it can be suggested – on their own authority – that their principal source of inspiration was provided by Douglas's *Nenia Britannica*;[50] but, in their preoccupation with providing an interpretation of the entire archaeological landscape of their county, they also looked beyond him, back across the century and more in which antiquarian attention had been drawn to the more spectacular monuments of the Wiltshire landscape, to the works of Aubrey and Stukeley. To the degree that the work of Cunnington and Colt Hoare represented an attempt to investigate and to explain the topography of a whole region, it may also be said to prefigure, albeit in a limited way, the landscape archaeology of our own time.[51]

The very nature of this new collaborative effort reflected, or even adumbrated, some of the wider social changes that had already begun to take place in the eighteenth century and that were to gather momentum in the century to come. Cunnington, a sagacious wool merchant and mercer of Heytesbury, was drawn to contemplation of earthworks and megaliths while riding on the Downs for the sake of his health.[52] He was undoubtedly the archaeological hero of the piece. It was Cunnington who saw the potential of monuments to yield new insights into the past inhabitants of the landscape, who had the ability to formulate the questions to be asked of the monuments and to undertake their interrogation in the field, and it was he who compiled a typology of the 'Camps and other earthen works' he encountered in an attempt to impose some degree of system on the past (fig.80).[53] The wealthy Colt Hoare's contributions in this respect were slighter, but his input was crucial to the success their project was to enjoy; he was not merely the paymaster of the project, but also an effective planner and organizer of field campaigns. He came fully into his own as compiler of the text that was to enshrine their joint findings, a coherent and expansive narrative distilled from the detail of Cunnington's notebooks. Nor did they work alone, and the roles played by their various collaborators are also worthy of mention.

The weightiest figure among them was the Revd Thomas Leman (1751–1826), whose familiarity with the classical sources recommended him to Colt Hoare as a suitable mentor for the project. It could be argued, however, that the principal benefit of his involvement, from a modern point of view, is to highlight the solidly independent value of Cunnington's own fieldwork. This succeeded very much on its own terms and signalled the irrefutable conclusion that the discipline had ultimately arrived at a point where it could free itself from the tyranny of the brand of literary scholarship enshrined in the person of the stultifying Revd Leman.[54] Their three-cornered relationship is a fascinating one, with Leman constantly seeking to undermine Cunnington's hypotheses by vain reference to classical authors, Cunnington's growing confidence in rebutting these suggestions on the basis of the evidence of his own eyes and of his trowel,[55] and Colt Hoare anxiously holding the ring, committed to his patronage of the field project, yet reluctant to abandon totally the received wisdom of the traditional learning that had shaped his own education, an epistemology that had been reinforced on the Grand Tour and hitherto had enjoyed a monopoly of access to the past.[56]

There were others with a hand in the project too. There was Philip Crocker, a young surveyor and draughtsman on periodic loan to Colt Hoare from the Ordnance Survey (recently established on the lines envisaged by William Roy), to whose talents the maps, plans, topographical views and illustrations of artefacts in *Ancient Wiltshire* owe so much (fig.81).[57] There were two excavators, Stephen and John Parker, father and son, on whom Cunnington relied, not only for the back-breaking work on the barrows, but also for prospecting for unrecorded sites beyond the limited territory he himself could cover on horseback. And finally there were Cunnington's three daughters, who maintained the 'Moss House Museum', a wonderfully Romantic installation in the garden of the Cunnington house, where they pasted labels on the urns and other artefacts in order to preserve details of their original relationships,[58] arranging them tumulus by tumulus and making them available to visitors during the periodic absences of their father.[59] The whole ensemble has a rather endearing early nineteenth-century air to it – more redolent of the novels of Jane Austen than of the desiccated academic world of Anthony Wood and Thomas Hearne, on whom we rely for a window on the antiquarian world at the beginning of our period.[60]

But a more significant change had overtaken the practice followed by these searchers into antiquity. *Ancient Wiltshire* opens with a dramatic motto: 'We speak from facts, not theory'.[61] It was a declaration that had been heard in the mouths of earlier researchers in the field and it was an ideal that was to prove beyond the capacities of many who followed in the course of the nineteenth century. But no one could now continue to subscribe to Samuel Johnson's contention that 'All that is known of the ancient state of Britain is contained in a few pages. We can know no more than what the old writers have told us.'[62] Cunnington had been prepared to assign some of his Wiltshire remains to as much as one thousand years before Julius Caesar, and in 1797, John Frere was to venture so far (in a letter to the Secretary of the Society of Antiquaries) as to

place the flint implements he had recovered at Hoxne, Suffolk, in 'a very remote period indeed; even beyond that of the present world'.[63] By stepping out of doors, the antiquary had extended his horizons more than anyone could have dreamed possible.

Acknowledgements

I am grateful to my colleagues Professor Andrew Sherratt and Dr Stephen Briggs, who read the text in manuscript and made many useful comments upon it.

Notes and references

1   See, for example, the image of the 'museum or study' reproduced from Comenius by Richard Yeo elsewhere in this volume (fig.16), 'where a student, apart from men, sitteth alone' with his books.

2   By 1550 Leland had become insane. For his life see T.D. Kendrick, *British Antiquity* (London, 1950), pp.45–64.

3   Even within the successive early Latin editions, increasing numbers of illustrations of archaeological finds appear, earning Camden the epithet 'the pioneer in antiquarian book illustration in this country' (Kendrick, op. cit. [note 2], p.151). For Camden's work as a whole see ibid., pp.143–56, and for a discussion of the various editions see Stuart Piggott, 'Introduction: William Camden and the *Britannia*', in *The Times* facsimile reprint of the 1695 edition (London, 1971), pp.5–13.

4   This potent phrase comes from P. Ucko, M. Hunter, A.J. Clark and A. David, *Avebury Reconsidered: From the 1660s to the 1990s* (London, 1991), p.64; see also Christopher Chippindale, *Stonehenge Complete* (London, 1983), p.57. The plan originally appeared in Inigo Jones's *The most notable Antiquity of Great Britain, vulgarly called Stone-Heng on Salisbury Plain* (London, 1655), plan no.2. Jones (p.8) expressed himself of the opinion that the monument was 'erected by a people, grand masters in the Art of building, and liberall sciences, whereof the ancient *Britans* [were]utterly ignorant'.

5   The appreciative characterization is by Anthony Wood, who declared his 'tender affections and insatiable desire for knowledg were ravish'd and melted downe by the reading of that book', which he accounted 'the best book of its kind that hitherto was made extant' (*The Life and Times of Anthony Wood, Antiquary, of Oxford, 1632–1695, described by Himself*, vol.1, ed. A. Clark [Oxford, 1891], p.209).

6   Robert Plot, *The Natural History of Stafford-shire* (Oxford, 1686), p.392.

7   'A letter from Dr. Lister of York, containing an account of several curious observations made by him about antiquities', *Philosophical Collections* 4 (1681), p.87.

8   Only vol.1, *Glossography* (Oxford, 1707) of the *Archaeologia Britannica* was to be completed before Lhwyd's premature death at the age of forty-nine.

9   An example of the adoption for antiquarian purposes of the methodology as well as the spirit of the Royal Society's programme is formed by the questionnaires devised by Plot, Lhwyd and others as a means of information-gathering (see Stuart Piggott, *William Stukeley, an Eighteenth-Century Antiquary*, 2nd edn [London, 1985], pp.21–3). The large degree of overlap in the personnel involved in both antiquarianism and natural history makes this identity of purpose unsurprising. From the following century comes similar testimony from the Cornish antiquary and naturalist William Borlase (1696–1772): of his twin interests, he wrote, 'so far are they from being incompatible studies, that they travel sociably together, lodge in the same space or room in one bed and breast, and for one and the same hire appear so readily upon all calls, that whatever remarkable escapes the one, is no sooner seen than it is noted, observed and registered by the other' (P.A.S. Poole, *William Borlase* [Truro, 1986], p.86). Having delivered the manuscript of his *Antiquities of Cornwall* to the printer in 1753, Borlase returned to his native county and 'sedulously set about the other half of my task, the *Natural history*, for which I had been gathering collections on every side for many years' (ibid., p.104).

10 Quoted in Chippindale, op. cit. (note 4), p.68.

11 Bodleian Library, Oxford: John Aubrey, 'Monumenta Britannica' (MS Top. Gen. c.24), fols 25v, 30.

12 Ibid., fol.39 [erased].

13 See the discussion in Michael Hunter, *John Aubrey and the Realm of Learning* (London, 1975), pp.178–91.

14 In matters of ability, Aubrey had a very low opinion of the Anglo-Saxons; on one occasion he declared certain masonry remains to be most probably British in origin, 'for the Saxons were dunces' (Bodleian Library, MS Hearne's Diaries 158, fol.162).

15 Hunter, op. cit. (note 13), pp.192–3. Taking up this theme elsewhere, Aubrey avowed that 'being but an ill Orator myselfe', he intended 'to make the Stones give evidence for themselves' (Aubrey, op. cit. [note 11], fol. 30), while his use of the term 'the reall Designe' has been persuasively linked to the 'Real Character' from which his contemporaries – notably John Wilkins – hoped to distill a rational style of scientific discourse (Ucko *et al.*, op. cit. [note 4], pp.69–70).

16 See Hunter, op. cit. (note 13), pp.162–6.

17 Aubrey, op. cit. (note 11), fol.139; see also Hunter, op. cit. (note 13), p.173. Favouring at first a contention that 'the greatnesse, and numerousness of the Barrowes (the Beds of Honour where now so many Heroes lie buried in Oblivion) doe speak plainly to us, that Death & Slaughter once rag'd and that here were the Scenes where terrible Battles were fought; wherein fell so many thousands, mentioned by the Historians', Aubrey evidently came in time to the opposite conclusion, surmising that warriors could never have afforded the 'great deale of time and leisure to collect so many thousands of loads of earth' and concluding that they were instead the 'Burying-places for the great persons of those times' (ibid., fol. 62v). Later Stukeley was to declare unequivocally that they were not 'tumultuary burials of the slain' but 'single sepulchres of kings, and great personages, buried during a considerable space of time, and that in peace' (William Stukeley, *Stonehenge, a Temple restor'd to the British Druids* [London, 1740], p.43).

18 The unprecedented pains that Aubrey took to invest his plans with a high degree of accuracy are noteworthy: following a visit to the site in 1663 in the company of King Charles II and the Duke of York, he records that 'I surveyd that old Monument of *Aubury* with a plain-table'. The result was the first realistic (if less than wholly accurate) representation of the site ever made (Aubrey, op. cit. [note 11], fols 25, 40; see also Ucko *et al.*, op. cit. [note 4], p.30, pl.7, and pp.66–7, 108–10 for discussion of his draughting techniques).

19 John Britton, *Memoir of John Aubrey, F.R.S.* (London, 1845), p.3.

20 Quoted from the definitive biography by Stuart Piggott, op. cit. (note 9), pp.33–4. For the range of recently published material available to Stukeley, much of it seemingly inspired by the appearance of Gibson's edition of Camden's *Britannia*, see ibid., pp.18–21.

21 Stukeley to Maurice Johnson, 6 June 1716, quoted in Piggott, op. cit. (note 9), p.40.

22 Bodleian Library, MS Eng. misc. c.323, fol.173. Stukeley explains his motive in embarking on the survey of the beleaguered monuments as hoping that it 'may rescue some part from impending ruin when the Country finds an advantage in preserving its poor reliques', and that 'future times may hence be able to ascertain its purport, when this sort of learning will be more cultivated'. Elsewhere he professes an aim 'to perpetuate the vestiges of this celebrated wonder & of the barrows avenues cursus &c for I forsee that it will in few years be universally plowd over & consequently defac'd' (ibid.; Piggott, op. cit. [note 9], pp.50, 89). The destruction wrought on field monuments had similarly acted as a spur to Aubrey's work: he lamented earthworks 'yearly eaten-out by the Plough', megalithic monuments quarried for their building stone, and damage inflicted by rampaging soldiers during the Civil War (see Hunter, op. cit. [note 13], p.166.

23 Piggott, op. cit. (note 9), p.92.

24 Ibid., p.61. As an illustration of Stukeley's meticulous approach to topographical drawing, Piggott mentions the (often precisely dated) amendments he made not only to the original drawings but also to the proof copies of the engraved plates produced from them; on one occasion he revisited Avebury with the proofs in hand in order to check them against the landscape (ibid., pp.36–7). Ucko *et al.* (op. cit. [note 4], p.66) mention that Stukeley compiled several plans of Stonehenge in which he strove for accuracy, although in his *Stonehenge* he published only a 'Geometrical Ground-plot' with certain profiles. In terms of exactitude, his work falls short of the best work of the day, as exemplified by a series of plans of Stonehenge compiled in the early eighteenth century by the architect John Wood and published in 1747, characterized as representing 'as accurate a Plan of the whole Work as the Nature of it can admit' (John Wood, *Choir Gaure, Vulgarly called Stonehenge, on Salisbury Plain, Described, Restored, and Explained* [Oxford, 1747], p. 48); even this series, however, included one geometrically 'correct' plan attempting to represent the stones 'In the perfect State they seem to have been Intended by the Architect of the work'. Stukeley was indeed unimpressed by Wood's display of skill and criticized him for 'mesuring of the stones, designed to be rude, as if they were the most nice and curious Grecian pillars in any of their capital temples' (Ucko *et al.*, op. cit [note 4], pp.68–9, pl.17).

25 Another illustration of the characteristic preoccupations of the Royal Society being applied to Stonehenge comes in 1720, when Edmond Halley (1656–1742) exhibited to the Fellowship a fragment of sarsen from the site, estimating 'from the general wear of the weather upon the stones . . . that the work must be of an extraordinary antiquity, and for ought he knew, 2 or 3,000 years old' (Stukeley, op. cit. [note 17], p.5). However ingeniously, Stukeley and Halley began to go further off course when they noted that the stones were aligned with 'a certain exactness, with consistent variation from the cardinal points', from which systematic error they deduced that the monument had been laid out with the aid of a magnetic compass; plotting the periodic variations in the earth's magnetic field as best they could they seemed to detect a regular cyclical variation, from which they further calculated that Stonehenge was most probably laid out c.460 BC (ibid., pp.56–66).

26 Stukeley's barrow-digging was supported with labour and funds supplied by Lord Pembroke. Credited with the first sectional drawing of such a monument, Stukeley accorded unprecedented attention to the fabric of the tumuli themselves, as in the following: 'The manner of composition of the barrow was good earth, quite thro', except a coat of chalk of about two foot thickness . . . under the turf. Hence it appears that the method of making these barrows was to dig up the turf for a great space round, till the barrow was brought to its intended bulk. Then with the chalk, dug out of the environing ditch, they powder'd it all over' (Stukeley, op. cit. [note 17], p. 44). Piggott, op. cit. (note 9), p.93, estimates his excavating technique 'far superior to anything normally undertaken before the middle of the [nineteenth] century'.

27 These two volumes were originally conceived as parts of a four-volume series in folio on 'the history of the antient *Celts*, particularly the first inhabitants of *Great Brittan*', to be illustrated with over 300 engraved plates (William Stukeley, *Itinerarium Curiosum, Centuria I* [London, 1724], preface). Ucko *et al.*, op. cit. (note 4), pp.53, 55, point out that the strong attraction manifested by Stukeley for the Druids (or more specifically, his ambition of 'reconciling Plato & Moses, & the Druid & Christian Religion') can be traced to his earliest writings, and that the widely-held view that it was a foible of his old age is erroneous.

28 The extraordinarily talented team included three assistant engineers who later – like Roy – were to rise to the rank of general officers: David Dundas (1735–1820), Hugh Debbieg (1732–1810) and George Morrison ([?]1704–99) – and as chief draughtsmen the topographical artist Paul Sandby (1725–1809). The ambitious nature of this project stands in striking contrast to the poor state of official mapping in Britain up to that time, characterized by the Society of Arts as 'wholly destitute of any public encouragement'; the Society tried without success to promote a competition in which £100 would be paid by the Government for the first accurate survey of any county at 1 inch to the mile: see Tim Owen and Elaine Pilbeam, *Ordnance Survey: Map makers to Britain since 1791* (Southampton, 1992), p.3.

29 William Roy, *The Military Antiquities of the Romans in North Britain* (London, 1793), p.i.

30 See Robert Melville, *A Critical Inquiry into the Constitution of the Roman Legion* (Edinburgh, 1773).

31 Yolande O'Donoghue, *William Roy 1726–1790: Pioneer of the Ordnance Survey*, exh. cat., British Library (London, 1977), p.28.

32 The publishing history of the *Military Antiquities* is carefully reconstructed by George MacDonald, 'General William Roy and his *Military Antiquities of the Romans in North Britain*', Archaeologia 68 (1916–17), pp.190–220. Roy's text, as received by the Antiquaries in 1790, formed the basis of communications read at the Society's meetings on no fewer than eight occasions during the following year (ibid., p.210); he had been elected FSA on 21 March 1776.

33 The extent of Roy's reliance on this source is evident from the subtitle to his *Military Antiquities* (op. cit. [note 29], title page): 'A

treatise, wherein the ancient geography of that part of the island is rectified, chiefly from the lights furnished by Richard of Cirencester'. The vitiating effect of Bertram's 'egregious hoax' on Roy's work is made plain in MacDonald, op. cit. (note 32), pp.161–228.

34 MacDonald, op. cit. (note 32), p.161.

35 Roy's own comment in relation to his plate showing the Antonine Wall was that 'a short description may suffice, since from a general plan of this kind, topographically expressed, a much truer notion may be obtained . . . than what, without such assistance, could possibly be conveyed in many words' (op. cit. [note 29], pp.155–6).

36 William Roy, 'Experiments and observations made in Britain, in order to obtain a rule for measuring heights with the barometer', *Philosophical Transactions* 67 (1777), pp.653–788.

37 The Copley Medal was awarded in recognition of his achievement in laying out on Hounslow Heath with unprecedented accuracy a base-line from which the triangulation of the whole of England was to proceed: see William Roy, 'An account of the measurement of a base on Hounslow-Heath', *Philosophical Transactions* 75 (1785), pp.385–480.

38 Roy contended (op. cit. [note 29], pp.iv–v) that these temporary structures had not then been recognized in any other part of the Roman Empire. His success in identifying their locations had grown from his recognition that their relationships to one another could be predicted from the daily marching distances of the Roman military units.

39 Roy, op. cit. (note 29), p.v. Roy's own observations were framed on the perception – representing a newly elucidated historical principle noteworthy on its own account – that 'The nature of a country will always, in a great degree, determine the general principles upon which every war must be conducted' (p.i), and that these principles were themselves 'fixed and general, varying only with local circumstances and situation of the country' (p.v).

40 James Douglas, *Nenia Britannica: or, a sepulchral history of Great Britain from the earliest period to its general conversion to Christianity* (London, 1793), pp.3, 10, and *passim*. 'It is only by the local deposit of the relics, when accurately surveyed', he writes here, while taking a side-swipe at Stukeley's untrustworthiness in this respect, 'that a perfect knowledge can be acquired of their respective owners'. Elsewhere (p.53), he pronounces that 'want of attention to this caution has frequently led antiquaries into the greatest of errors', citing in a 2½-page footnote Chifflet's 'incorrect' account of the opening of the tomb of Childeric and declaring himself convinced that 'several graves were opened at Tournay in a very careless and desultory manner', their contents being 'promiscuously' combined. His criticism of Chifflet's retrospective account of this accidental discovery is a little unjust, and the disparate material found in that interment is now viewed as representing multiple elements of a single monument (see Arthur MacGregor, 'The afterlife of Childeric's ring', in M. Henig and D. Plantzos (eds), *Classicism to Neo-classicism* (BAR International Series 793) (Oxford, 1999), p.154.

41 Ronald Jessup, *Man of many Talents: An informal biography of James Douglas 1753–1819* (London, 1975), pp.58–9.

42 The sub-title (Douglas, op. cit. [note 40]) continues to the effect that the volume includes 'a complete series of the British, Roman, and Saxon sepulchral rites and ceremonies, with the contents of several hundred burial places, opened under a careful inspection of the author . . . tending to illustrate the early part of and to fix on a more unquestionable criterion for the study of antiquity'.

43 Ibid., pp.v–vi. In the same vein he declares that 'the great plan I have in view will be to draw a line between all speculative fancies in antiquities and hypotheses founded on reason and practical observation' (quoted in Jessup, op. cit. [note 41], p.92). Elsewhere Douglas comments contemptuously on the indoor antiquaries who assembled collections without submitting them to any sort of analysis, castigating those who 'hoard up antique relics as children collect gegaws'; in his view, 'they often expose the more reflecting antiquary whose only view in collecting them is to throw light upon history or place some doubtful custom of an antient people in a more accurate light, to the pleasantry of his friends, and the ridicule of the unlettered part of the world' (ibid., p.70).

44 Ibid., p. 56.

45 Mention has been made, however, of the work of the Revd Bryan Faussett, who opened large numbers of Saxon graves in Kent in the decades immediately preceding Douglas's arrival there. (Douglas benefited from being able to examine the material from Faussett's excavations, preserved together by his heir.) Faussett was misled into suggesting that the populations he uncovered were 'chiefly, of Romans Britonized, and Britons Romanized', with representatives of both groups who, 'having mixed and intermarried with each other, had naturally learned, and in some measure adopted, each other's customs'. He did go on to conjecture, however, that in chronological terms, at least one of the cemeteries he excavated 'served . . . long after the Romans . . . had entirely evacuated and quitted this isle', that it 'might have continued to be a burying-ground after the arrival of the Saxons' even up to the time of Cuthbert, although he erred in surmising that 'nothing which I have discovered here seems to have belonged to that people': see Charles Roach Smith, *Inventorium Sepulchrale: an account of some antiquities dug up by . . . the Rev. Bryan Faussett* (London, 1856), pp.37–8.

46 Douglas even etched the aquatint plates from which the illustrations in the *Nenia Britannica* were printed.

47 Douglas, op. cit. (note 40), p.177. In a scientific metaphor typical of the age, the author claims (p. 183) to have argued his case 'from a chain of facts'.

48 If we may identify as typically 'Romantic' a preoccupation with ethnicity rather than material culture, it is clear that manifestations of this movement extend to the earliest decades of the eighteenth century; thereafter, they form a continuous – if muted – counterpoint to the main themes embodied in the primary antiquarian agenda focused on the physical world, as presented here. See Andrew Sherratt, *Economy and Society in Prehistoric Europe: Changing perspectives* (Edinburgh, 1997), pp.44–54.

49 Sir Richard Colt Hoare, *The Ancient History of Wiltshire*, 2 vols (London, 1812–21). Vol.I carries a dedication to Cunnington, 'a tribute that is due to justice and friendship'; vol.II is dedicated to Banks, 'who, in every class of enlightened science, so well knows how to estimate, appreciate, and instruct.' Colt Hoare himself was evidently in no doubt about the status of *Ancient Wiltshire* itself as a work of 'enlightened science'.

50 Douglas first visited Colt Hoare at Stourhead in 1809; his direct contributions to *Ancient Wiltshire* must have been of exceedingly limited value, to judge from his theories about Stonehenge, which he pronounced 'a temple of the Sun of the Mithraic order' (Kenneth Woodbridge, *Landscape and Antiquity. Aspects of English culture at Stourhead 1718 to 1838* [Oxford, 1970], p.227). Cunnington seems to have been characteristically more sceptical of Douglas and, in response to certain criticisms of Stukeley made by Douglas in his *Nenia*, Cunnington was to write that 'Mr Douglas has erred as widely as Stukeley in more parts of his work than I shall take the trouble to notice': see R.H. Cunnington, *From Antiquary to Archaeologist. A biography of William Cunnington 1754–1810* (Princes Risborough, 1975), pp. 30–1.

51 See Cunnington, op. cit. (note 50), pp.xiv–xv. In the introduction to *Ancient Wiltshire*, Colt Hoare announces his intention 'to divide the different parts of the county into so many *stations*, from which I shall diverge and give an account of all the antiquities that are within reach of it in a morning's ride.'

52 With a turn of phrase reminiscent of Stukeley, Cunnington records that his physician had advised him that he must 'ride out or die' (Cunnington, op. cit. [note 50], p.5).

53 Despite Cunnington's progress in erecting a typological classification of the barrows, he was at a loss in trying to make sense of their respective relationships and interpreting the significance of their contents: 'After all the experience we have had', he was to write, 'I am almost of the opinion that the Britons had no regular system in regard to the tumulus nor many other things practised at the interment of their dead, but appear to have been more influenced by caprice than by established rules' (Woodbridge, op. cit. [note 50], p.211).

54 One such closely-argued rebuttal from Cunnington to Leman, dated 1809, is reproduced as appendix III in Woodbridge, op. cit. (note 50): 'I contend', writes Cunnington in his opening salvo, 'that the information to be gathered from the Roman & Greek Historians will afford little information as data for illustrating Abury, Stonehenge Marden etc. etc., the Works of an ancient people like the Celtic Britons. The information to be gathered from Caesar and Tacitus relate to the Britons in their times – therefore all theories drawn from such sources in regard to our Celtic Britons are ever at war with the facts.'

55 With commendable attention to detail, Colt Hoare had specially made knives forged with blades in the form of a pointed oval, 7in long and 2in wide (17.8 × 5.1cm), to replace the masons' trowels with which the excavators began their investigations (Cunnington, op. cit. [note 50], p.72).

56 Something of the awkward balance he maintained comes through in his opening remarks: 'traces of British population are every where apparent upon our extensive downs; and numerous Roman roads, towns, villas, &c. mark the power and residence of that conquering and civilizing nation' (Colt Hoare, op. cit. [note 49], vol.I, p.I).

57 While conceding that Crocker's plans of the Wiltshire earthworks were 'something new', Stuart Piggott (*Ancient Britons and the Antiquarian Imagination* [London, 1989], p.156) observes that he had little understanding of what he was recording and that in terms of technique *Ancient Wiltshire* shows no real advance over the eighteenth century. The absence of plans and sections of the monuments excavated is perhaps unsurprising, since Cunnington's digging strategy seems to have been focused on recovering the contents rather than recording the structure of the monument. Elsewhere, however, he shows himself perfectly capable of intelligently observing and recording the stratigraphy encountered: see 'Further account of tumuli opened in Wiltshire, in a letter from Mr. William Cunnington, F.A.S. to Aylmer Bourke Lambert, Esq. F.R.S. F.A.S. and F.L.S. communicated by Mr. Lambert', *Archaeologia* 15 (1806), pp.338–46.

58 In 1801 Leman had counselled Cunnington on the importance of labelling all the finds, 'describing with accuracy the very spot in which you found them. The people who succeed us may possibly know more about these things than we do ... but we ought to mark the steps *we* have advanced and afford *them* all the information we can with clearness ...' For once Leman was offering good advice which Cunnington evidently did not take entirely to heart, for in 1806 we find Colt Hoare – clearly conscious of his collaborator's poor health – writing to him in the following terms: 'I beg your daughters will affix paper labels to as many of the articles as they can ... Only conceive in case of accident, what confusion would arise and how our labour would be lost, if I did not know the history of our articles ...' (reproduced in Cunnington, op. cit. [note 50], pp.21, 91).

59 Colt Hoare's friend Richard Fenton left the following description of the Moss House museum: 'Nothing could be more curious and systematic than the arrangement of the museum: the contents of every tumulus were separate, and the articles so disposed as in the case of ornaments, such as beads, in such elegant knots and festoons, as to please the eye which looks to nothing farther ... In one drawer were displayed all the utensils employed to fabricate arrow-heads, other weapons and implements that required sharp points ... together with bone in its wrought and unwrought state, evidently proving it to have been the sepulchre of an artist, whose employ this was ...' (Richard Fenton, *A Tour in quest of Genealogy through several parts of Wales, Somersetshire and Wiltshire* [London, 1811], pp.251–2). After Cunnington's death the contents of the museum were to become the cause of some dissension between Colt Hoare (who had funded most of the excavations from which the exhibits were recovered) and the daughters, who regarded the collection as their inheritance and who believed that 'a considerable sum of money would be paid by the government & which to us who are just beginning life would be *particularly advantageous*'. The Trustees of the British Museum declined to pay their asking price, however, and eventually the collection passed to Colt Hoare for a consideration of £200; later, in 1883, it was purchased (along with other material acquired by Colt Hoare *c*.1800 and originating in northern Germany) by the Wiltshire Archaeological Society for £280 and deposited in the Society's museum at Devizes (Cunnington, op. cit. [note 50], pp.91–2; Woodbridge, op. cit. (note 50), p.232).

60 As a further sign of the times, it is noteworthy that Cold Hoare arranged for a number of the urns recovered in Cunnington's excavations to be modelled by Josiah Wedgwood (Cunnington, op. cit. [note 50], p.28).

61 Colt Hoare, op. cit. (note 49), p.7. His introduction continues: '... I shall describe to you what we have found; what we have seen; in short, I shall tell you a plain unvarnished tale, and draw from it such conclusions as shall appear not only reasonable, but even uncontradictable.'

62 Curiously, though, with a characteristic excess of deference to traditional scholarship and in contradiction to the entire archaeological thesis that was to follow, Colt Hoare inscribes this very statement in his introduction (op. cit. [note 49], pp.9–10).

63 'Account of flint weapons discovered at Hoxne in Suffolk. By John Frere, Esq. F.R.S. and F.A.S. In a letter to the Rev. John Brand, Secretary', *Archaeologia* 13, 2nd edn (1807), pp.204–5. Frere presents his dramatic finds, backed up by close stratigraphic observations, in the most modest, self-effacing terms. He reports also the discovery in a sandy layer above the flints of 'some extraordinary bones, particularly a jaw-bone of enormous size, of some unknown animal, with the teeth remaining in it'; by the time its existence was brought to his notice, however, it had been presented to Sir Ashton Lever and was now, he conjectured, 'probably in Parkinson's Museum' (see this volume, p.83), and its subsequent fate is unknown.

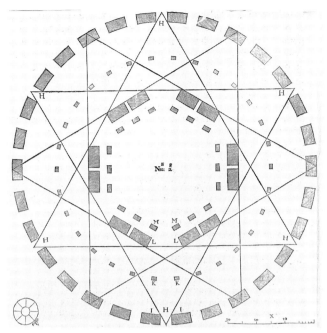

Figure 73
Inigo Jones, 'Stoneheng restored',
from *The most notable Antiquity of ...
Stonheng* (1655): 'The Groundplot
of the work, as when first built,
in a greater form, with the foure
equilaterall triangles making the
Scheme, by which the whole work was
composed'. Taylorian Institute, Oxford.

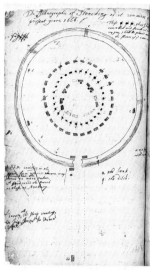

Figure 74
Aubrey's 'Ichnographie of Stoneheng
as it remaines to the present yeare
1666', from his *Monumenta Britannica*.
Aubrey attempts to show here more
accurately than Inigo Jones the degree
to which the monument remained
standing, although unlike his earlier
plane-table survey of Avebury it
remains schematized. Bodleian Library,
Oxford (MS Top. Gen. c.24, fol.64v).

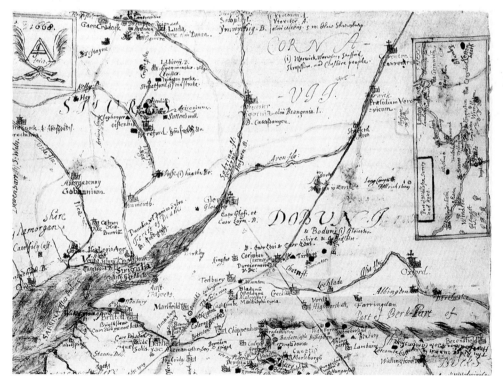

Figure 75
Aubrey's map of ancient Wessex, from
his *Monumenta Britannica* (before
1689). Aubrey wrote (fol.149v): 'I
deemed it worth the little labour to
prick downe in a Mappe these
Remaines of Antiquity, which I beheld
with so much delight; and peradventure
by this meanes some that have more
learning and leisure then my selfe, may
retrieve the places of many of those
memorable Battailes mentioned by
Tacitus and other Historians.' Bodleian
Library, Oxford (MS Top. Gen. c.24,
fol.251).

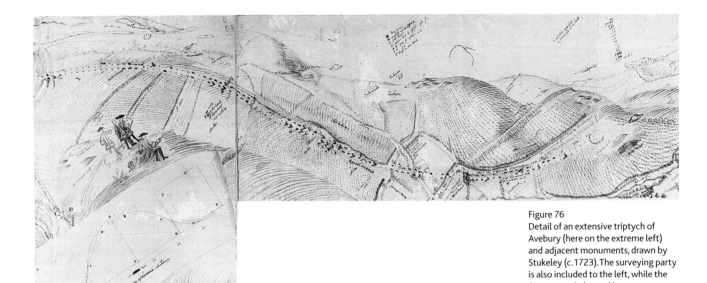

Figure 76
Detail of an extensive triptych of
Avebury (here on the extreme left)
and adjacent monuments, drawn by
Stukeley (c.1723). The surveying party
is also included to the left, while the
Sanctuary circles and barrows on
Overton Hill are shown to the right.
Bodleian Library, Oxford (MS Eng.
misc. b.65, fol.43r).

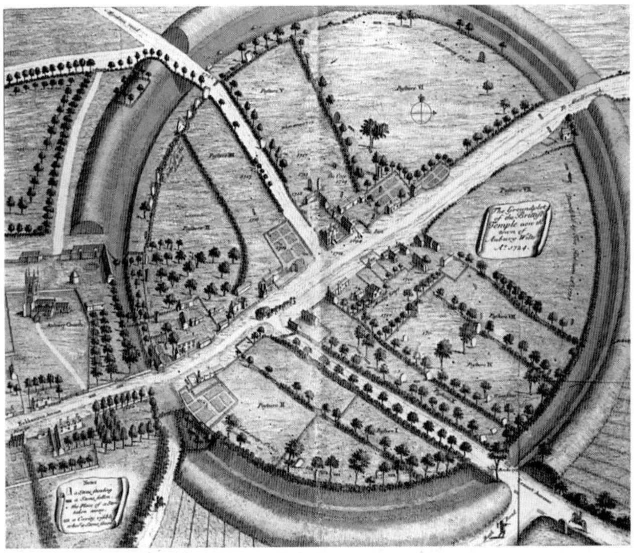

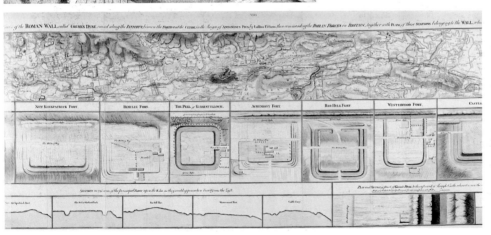

Figure 77
The 'great frontispiece plate' from
Stukeley's *Abury* (1740), described
(pp.19, 22) as a 'ground-plot
representing the true state of the
town and temple, when I frequented
it' and as 'done from innumerable
measurements'. Many draft versions
of this plate, all with minor variations,
are discussed by Ucko *et al.* As a
record of the site it was not to be
superseded until the lengthy
campaign of excavation and survey
led by Alexander Keiller on the eve of
the Second World War. Ashmolean
Museum, Oxford.

Figure 78
Detail of William Roy's plan showing
the course of the Antonine Wall,
together with associated forts;
surveyed in 1755, drawn up in 1773,
and published in his *Military
Antiquities of the Romans in North
Britain* (1793). British Library, London,
Department of Manuscripts (King's
MS 248, fol. 43).

Figure 79
James Douglas, plan of Tumulus I on Chatham Lines, uncovered in September 1779, together with its contents. From _Nenia Britannica_ (1793), pl.II. Ashmolean Museum, Oxford.

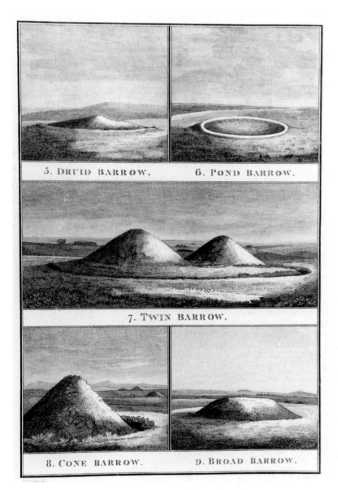

Figure 80
Ancient Wiltshire: part of Cunnington's typology of barrows (1812). Drawn by Philip Crocker, engraved by James Basire. Society of Antiquaries, London.

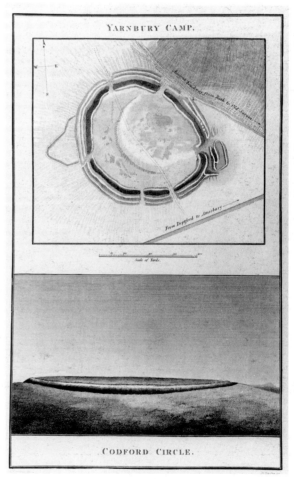

Figure 81
Ancient Wiltshire: Yarnbury Camp and Codford Circle (1812). Drawn by Philip Crocker, engraved by James Basire. Society of Antiquaries, London.

Chapter 22

Record and Reverie

Representing British antiquity in the eighteenth century

Sam Smiles

This chapter is intended as an examination of the ways in which the visual arts contributed to an understanding of British antiquity in the eighteenth century, both in terms of making accurate visual records of the remnants of the past and in producing imaginative constructions of national history. Both enterprises were novel, and the interplay between them is itself revealing of wider debates concerning the limits of knowledge. Coinciding as they do with the foundation and early development of the British Museum, there is at the very least an indirect link between such endeavours and the growth of the Museum's collections, even if those collections at first paid scant regard to British antiquity. It is well known that it took fifty years from the establishment of the British Museum until, in 1807, antiquities were separated from the natural history collections in their own department. Moreover, despite moves to establish a special room for British antiquities in the 1820s, it was not until 1866 that British and Medieval Antiquities (with ethnography) achieved full departmental status. Indeed, as late as the 1850s, the entire collection of British antiquities comprised less than twenty cases of artefacts, with no dedicated curator until the appointment of Augustus Wollaston Franks in 1851.[1]

If the eighteenth-century recuperation of British antiquity is therefore chiefly associated with the Society of Antiquaries rather than the British Museum, it is worth remembering the connections between the two institutions. There is evidence that plans were afoot, in the winter of 1753–4, to house the Society of Antiquaries in a complex that would have contained both the British Museum and the Royal Society. Although nothing came of it (the Society of Antiquaries had already moved to its own premises in Chancery Lane), the relationship between the Society and the Museum remained cordial. William Stukeley was nominated by the Society as a Trustee of the British Museum in 1753 and a number of curators at the British Museum were also Fellows of the Society of Antiquaries, Francis Douce, Henry Ellis and Taylor Combe among them. As Keeper of the new Department of Antiquities and, from 1813, Director of the Society of Antiquaries as well, Combe was surely instrumental in the Museum's acquisition in 1814 of six cases and three fragments of ancient paintings from St Stephen's Chapel, Westminster. The product of the Society of Antiquaries' first major investigative survey of a medieval structure, these material remains had been exhibited in the Society's meeting-room, and it is a measure of their confidence in the British Museum that they were able to make such a donation.[2]

These links demonstrate that the Museum might have moved more resolutely towards British antiquity than it in fact did. Certainly, if we turn our attention to the wider context of the period, it is evident that the retrieval of the past was of increasing concern as the eighteenth century wore on. It is also clear that the business of recording that past was a live issue for artists and antiquaries alike. In outlining some of the prominent issues involved in these endeavours, the variety of graphic approaches to British antiquity that were on offer, and the extent to which any decision about which to use was a matter of careful consideration, are both issues of particular interest. Indeed, the contrast between record and reverie may best be understood as a division between different modes of cognition.[3] The power of the graphic arts to produce a credible and often a more compelling view of the past than text-based studies could achieve should be emphasized above all. Moreover, this essay will suggest that the arts' ability to restage British antiquity helped prepare the ground both for its public estimation and for its formal recognition by the British Museum.

The fundamental question for those involved with imaging British antiquity can be simply expressed: how should the past be known? In answer, two broadly differentiated positions might be sketched out. For some, the past was accessible through scrupulous recording of extant material remains. The seemingly incontestable evidence of physical relics would offer a check to the ambiguities of text-based study. William Borlase, the Cornish antiquary, wrote as much in a letter of 1749: 'The materials, style, measurement and appurtenances of monuments are things not to be new moulded by, or made to comply with every fanciful conjecture, but remaining always the same, will be impartial authorities to appeal to . . .' It was essential, therefore, to make an accurate record of them by graphic means for, as Borlase concluded, it was 'next to an impossibility to convey an adequate idea of the simplest monument by words and numerical figures, or indeed to find out the justness and extravagance of a conjecture without seeing what the monument really is'.[4] Here, then, can be observed the articulation of an empirical methodology whose reliance on physical data is seen as a surer route to knowledge than any submission to written texts alone. Indeed, the recipient of these remarks, Charles Lyttleton, Dean of Exeter, was preoccupied precisely with the need to use empirical knowledge to challenge the received history of his cathedral. His account of the history of its fabric, completed in 1754, relied on first-hand scrutiny of the architecture to establish a credible dating for the building sequence, especially where no medieval records survived. Borlase's other requirement, that accurate drawings be made, was also part of Lyttleton's scholarly approach. He compiled a portfolio of drawings of Romanesque churches, made by professional artists. The possession of such a compendium allowed Lyttleton to analyse visually, and therefore comprehend, the characteristics of Romanesque architecture by virtue of comparative examples.[5] As will be seen, the Society of Antiquaries would prosecute such dissemination of graphic information in their own publications later in the century. Since neither of these two methods – accurate scrutiny of physical evidence and the recording of it through visual means – would be unusual today, it is important to remember that in the early eighteenth century these were pioneering endeavours. The past, it would seem, could be known not only through the pursuit of exacting scholarship but also by scrupulous attention to physical data.

The key figure arguing for visual representation of antiquity was Richard Gough. Director of the Society of Antiquaries from 1771, he actively promoted the use of artists to record what remained of the medieval legacy. Gough believed that the production of an exact record would perform a service to posterity, no matter whether the structure itself was subsequently mutilated, restored or demolished. Because of their visual accuracy, such delineations would save these buildings for scholarship, functioning analogously to modern-day campaigns of rescue archaeology. Beyond this, however, lay a more significant project. Gough understood that a proper history of British medieval architecture could be supplied only when a full survey of its major monuments had been attempted. It was essential that a systematic analysis be conducted, if the course of architectural evolution was to be understood.[6] Typologies of style could then be used to place buildings in their correct sequence, even when written records had vanished. This made an exact visual record absolutely essential; only by collecting, analysing and ordering the data visible in the material fabric could scholars hope to retrieve a proper understanding of what remained, and even what had been destroyed. As Gough wrote in 1768:

> One cannot enough regret the little regard hitherto paid to Gothic architecture, of which so many beautiful models are daily crumbling to pieces before our eyes. England can boast specimens of all its stages from the simplest to the most improved. Had the remains of antient buildings been more attended to, we should before now have seen a system of Gothic architecture in its various areas: we should have all its parts reduced to rules; their variations and their dates fixed together.[7]

Gough was something of a victim of his own pioneering efforts, however, for the standards of accuracy he required, and the artistic competence he therefore sought, were in relatively short supply in the mid-eighteenth century. Although the production of topographical prints and drawings was quickening, and an interest in British antiquity as part of the historical fabric of the nation was developing, it was not until the 1780s and afterwards that a combination of topographical publications and picturesque tourism became a truly popular phenomenon. A generation earlier, however, Gough found it difficult to attract good artists to his project, and even in the early 1780s this problem persisted. This is not to say that capable artists, able to undertake Gough's requirements, did not exist. It is more the case that the disciplined record he required was not necessarily conformable with academic honours and the development of an artistic reputation. As he complained, with some feeling, 'The walk of fame for modern artists is not sufficiently enlarged. Emulous of excelling in History, Portrait or Landscape, they

overlook the unprofitable, though not the less tasteful, walk of Antiquity, or, in Grecian and Roman forget Gothic and more domestic monuments.'[8]

Within the Society of Antiquaries, of course, Gough had a more lasting success. It is fair to see his influence combining with that of antiquaries already well versed in drawing, like Stukeley and Borlase, and keen to champion its utility. In 1784, John Carter was the first artist appointed to the Society to record objects shown at its meetings, as well as producing his own illustrated publications on British antiquity (fig.82). In 1792, the Society elected Thomas Underwood as its Draughts-man in Ordinary, while simultaneously embarking on an ambitious programme to record the architecture of British cathedrals and other religious houses. Carter, elected to a fellowship of the Society in 1795, made the drawings for St Stephen's Chapel, Westminster, published in 1795, and Exeter Cathedral, published in 1797, among others. Carter was something of a zealot for the re-evaluation of Britain's Middle Ages. His numerous writings are marked by a passionate advocacy for the glorious medieval past and, in particular, the reign of Edward III, which he viewed as one of the great cultural achievements of Europe. He was prompted in large part by the disfigurement of medieval architecture at the hands of modern restoration and improvement campaigns, notoriously those associated with the architect James Wyatt. Carter deprecated the destruction of material evidence. For him, the urgency of the antiquarian project was underlined by the reckless destruction of what was left of the medieval record.[9] As he put it in a book devoted to the evolution of medieval architecture,

> The absolute necessity of a publication of this nature being set about at this hour, will be evident to many, when the unrestrained rage given way to on all occasions, either for a partial alteration of the features of our ancient edifices, or for their entire demolition, is considered.[10]

In publishing visually accurate engravings of selected religious buildings, the Society of Antiquaries was attempting to do for the medieval legacy what the Society of Dilettanti had achieved for classical architecture, with their sponsorship of illustrated accounts of Athens and Ionia in the 1750s and 1760s. But if the project was to succeed, it required that drawing become a form of notation purged of stylistic mannerisms or other detrimental 'artistic' qualities. Carter himself was emphatic that his drawings were produced 'not alone to please the eye . . . but to give information and instruction to the rising generation of Antiquaries and Architectural Professors'.[11] He was, moreover, implacably hostile to those delineators of architecture who sacrificed detail in a bid to capture the picturesque appeal of a building. He attacked head-on those

> picturesque appearances produced by the skill of the Artist, in a certain disposal of light and shade toward what is called 'effect' in drawing; an effect of that kind we perceive when gazing on an object with the eyes half open, in a sort of dim fascination on the senses, whereby we catch a momentary gleam of the sublime; such sort of pencilled performances tending more to accredit the modern Delineator than the antient Architect.[12]

Although caution should be observed in believing that any drawing can be entirely freed from a stylistic language, Carter's exemplary accuracy has proved useful to modern-day scholars, seeking to establish the appearance of medieval architecture before major campaigns of restoration in the eighteenth and nineteenth centuries.[13]

This concentration on drawing as pure notation and the eschewing of artistic effect when representing British antiquity is, however, but part of the picture. The second half of the eighteenth century is notable for a revival of interest in the British 'archaic' and medieval eras, and some significant paintings and sculptures set out to represent aspects of early British history. This, too, was a pioneering development. As the title of this essay indicates, however, in contrast to the prosecution of an empirical understanding of the past in antiquarian scholarship, the representation of antiquity in the creative arts had at best a tangential relationship to antiquarian research. Indeed, their attempts to produce a credible image of the past were circumscribed by aesthetic considerations that deliberately eschewed accuracy. This phenomenon might be usefully characterized as reverie, to indicate its connotations of dreaming or musing on the past in an abstracted way, when compared to the exact record promoted by some antiquaries. Reverie, on this analysis, legitimately applies to ambitious works of art with British antiquity as their subject-matter, for British antiquity in eighteenth-century painting and sculpture is a poetic creation, rather than a literal representation, and thus follows the characteristic recommendation of academic training. Joshua Reynolds, in his fourth Discourse to the students of the Royal Academy, delivered in 1771, outlined the need for the history painter to elevate invention over 'minuteness and particularity' and deliberately to 'deviate from vulgar and strict historical truth, in pursuing the grandeur of his design'. Painters working in the grand or great style, as Reynolds calls it, must strike the imagination and, if necessary, play fast and loose with the historical record. For Reynolds, 'All this is not falsifying any fact; it is taking an allowed poetical licence'.[14] While such an approach may have suited the dictates of contemporary aesthetics, it ran completely counter to the antiquaries' use of the arts to record empirical data.

Some idea of the incompatibility of antiquarian and artistic attitudes to the past can be obtained when reviewing two treatments of Edward III at the close of the century. In the 1780s, George III commissioned Benjamin West to produce a cycle of pictures for the Audience Chamber at Windsor Castle on the theme of Edward III and his achievements, especially the creation of the Order of the Garter. West went to considerable trouble to research the fourteenth century. He read historical accounts of the creation of the Order of the Garter, he examined manuscripts, arms and accoutrements in the royal collections and he made use of illustrated costume books to provide a credible mise-en-scène for his paintings.[15] This quest for accuracy was certainly more particular than Reynolds had recommended in his Discourses, and it is a hallmark of West's more general attitude to history painting, vividly announced in his refusal to classicize the protagonists depicted in The Death of General Wolfe (1770). Yet West was enough of a grand style painter to recognize the need to balance historical accuracy and the ideal, and paintings in the Windsor cycle, such as The Institution of the Order of the Garter (1787) speak the language of high art as well as presenting a picture of the past (fig.83). In 1805 West's cycle was reviewed in the Gentleman's Magazine by John Carter, whose own standards of truth and accuracy we considered earlier. Carter subjected West's achievement to a withering

critique, castigating the artist for his historical inaccuracy and complaining of his disregard for easily available documentary and material evidence. The crux of Carter's assault is that West had made an approximation to the court of Edward III when he could have shown a minutely accurate, reliable and verifiable image. West's picture, in the view of an exacting antiquary, is no more than a piece of theatre whose fancy dress signifies 'Middle Ages' to the ignorant, but, to the knowledgeable, is a riot of anachronisms and inventions. In Carter's own words, 'How can we account for our historic delineator touching so lightly on national documents, and marking, with a zealous hand all the extravagance and whim found in the warehouses of masquerade tinsel and gewgaw finery?' The bleak answer to such a question is supplied by Carter, dismayed by the squandered opportunity at Windsor. The real world of Edward III had become 'a sacrifice to that contempt which is so generally evinced for the study of our antiquities'.[16]

As this incident reveals, the prosecution of antiquarian research through the provision of highly faithful images put that enterprise at loggerheads with the more poetic interpretations offered by history painters. But at this remove, it might be argued that the separation between both of these approaches was not unbridgeable. Carter himself, it should be noted, was prepared to produce historicist images of the Middle Ages, albeit he considered his own productions to be based on sound evidence, in place of the theatrical deceit practised by artists like West. He exhibited pen-and-wash drawings at the Royal Academy in the 1780s and 1790s, including recreations of episodes taken from Walpole's Castle of Otranto, and, in 1786, he exhibited his own picture of Edward III at the Royal Academy. He reproduced it in a publication of the same year, accompanied with a lengthy text which indicates the archaeological exactitude of his details: Lord Berkeley, seen on the left conversing with a nobleman, is taken from his own monument in Berkeley Church, Gloucestershire; the Bishop's robes are copied from a brass plate in the Abbey Church in St Albans; the musicians in the gallery owe their instruments to the crosier of William of Waltham, in New College, Oxford (fig.84).[17] Here, then, is the kind of performance that West should have given in his Institution of the Order of the Garter, completed in the following year. Yet, notwithstanding its archaeological accuracy, Carter's picture is a confection that simulates the world of Edward III. What propelled Carter to do this, as also in his highly evocative verbal descriptions of the Middle Ages, was surely a recognition that the past would not revive until its disjointed members had been reunited. Beyond the systematic description, analysis and comparison of visible remains lay the larger project of a comprehensive view of medieval culture. For all the fervour of his denunciation of artists like West, in attempting to make a coherent whole out of the relics of antiquity, Carter differed from West in degree, rather than kind. Furthermore, if the project of historical revivification requires that an artist selects and organizes from a fragmented and uncertain past, when Carter offered recreations of the Middle Ages, no matter how accurate they were, he was closer to the hated Wyatt than he would have cared to admit. For the restoration of cathedrals and the production of history paintings both invoke the historical imagination and to similar ends, to produce an image of the past suitable for modern usage.

One category of history painting, images of Celtic Britain before or during the Roman occupation, can be seen as important for precisely that reason. For here the power of reverie to create a credible past allowed poetic suggestion of what might have been to fabricate an image of British antiquity that stood in the place of textual and archaeological evidence. With insufficient material evidence available to counter its graphic representation, the earliest British history became the creature of imaginative projection and worked its beguiling effect on the public unchecked. Indeed, it was precisely because that history lacked an authoritative narrative and was at the mercy of a medley of rival antiquarian suppositions, based on contradictory accounts from the classical era, that its image could lead an independent life. Fortunately for artists, British historiography, especially as it became a self-consciously rigorous mode of enquiry, tended to disdain the pre-Roman period. David Hume's *History of England* (1754–62) is unrepentant in its refusal to offer any searching account of Britain's remotest antiquity. For Hume,

> The adventures of barbarous nations, even if they were recorded, could afford little or no entertainment to men born in a more cultivated age. The convulsions of a civilized state usually comprise the most instructive and most interesting part of its history; but the sudden, violent, and unprepared revolutions incident to barbarians, are so much guided by caprice, and terminate so often in cruelty, that they disgust us by the uniformity of their appearance; and it is rather fortunate for letters that they are buried in silence and oblivion.[18]

In like manner, when introducing his *History of Scotland* in 1759, William Robertson emphatically dismissed any attempt at writing about barbarian Europe, finding it 'impossible to give any authentic account of the different kingdoms established there. Everything beyond that short period to which well attested annals reach, is obscure, an immense space is left to imagination to occupy . . .'[19] Once beyond the reach of reliable textual sources, in other words, the Augustan historian should abandon the chase.

But if Robertson was right, the imagination would not merely occupy that immense space, as it had in the production of fabulous medieval chronicles and pseudo-histories, but would continue to occupy it in his own times. Alongside the imagination's possession of that space would also emerge new methods of enquiry, fostered largely in antiquarian scholarship, promoting philology and archaeology as worthy contributions to the study of the past. As is well known, the middle of the eighteenth century witnessed the flourishing of the Celtic revival, whose scholarship regarding cultural longevity, as expressed in language and customs, blazed a trail into antiquity that historians like Hume and Robertson were not able to follow.[20] The Honourable Society of Cymmrodorion was established in 1751 to promote these researches, also manifested in such publications as John Parry and Evan Williams's *Antient British Music* (1742) and Evan Evans's *Some Specimens of the Poetry of the Antient Welsh Bards* (1764). Thomas Gray's poem *The Bard* (1757) helped to naturalize this burgeoning interest in antiquity and cultural continuity and was followed, in its turn, by William Mason's influential verse drama *Caractacus* of 1759 and James Macpherson's *Ossian* cycle of the 1760s. Those ambitious artists, whom Gough was unable to recruit for his campaign of recording physical monuments, were available to

give form to these new imaginative developments. As early as 1761 Paul Sandby exhibited a lost painting of *The Bard* at the Society of Artists, and a few years later, probably in the early 1760s, Macpherson tried unsuccessfully to recruit John Hamilton Mortimer to provide illustrations for *Ossian*.[21]

Certainly, the possibility of the arts drawing on British history was very much in the air at the mid-century. In 1750, John and Paul Knapton and Robert Dodsley proposed to publish fifty prints after designs by Nicholas Blakey and Francis Hayman, representing episodes in national history, from the landing of Julius Caesar to the Glorious Revolution.[22] The earliest scenes represented concerned Celtic Britain, with Blakey's *Landing of Julius Caesar* (1751), and Hayman's *Caractacus* (1751; fig.85) and *The Druids* (1752; fig.86). With these images discussion concerning the limits of empirical data and artistic protocols can be extended. For the pre-Roman era, there was little material evidence equivalent to that readily available for the Middle Ages, notwithstanding the burgeoning tradition within antiquarian scholarship concerning the Druids and the culture of Ancient Britain. Here, then, the strictures expressed by antiquaries such as John Carter were less damaging; indeed, we might say that only the imagination of the artist could have made a whole from the fragmentary knowledge available to scholars. Ancient Britain was not easily imagined. Passages preserved in classical texts had to be reconciled with some limited excavation and surveying and a variety of speculations concerning megalithic structures. The evidence that survived was confused and contradictory, and contemporary interpretations of it were discordant. In the murky world of British antiquity the artist alone could make concrete and definite what otherwise would remain hypothetical and ambiguous. The artist could do this, furthermore, precisely because his graphic abilities anchored imaginative projections in the world of the real. If at bottom this was essentially a rhetorical performance, it nevertheless produced a tangible impression of the past that no discursive text could equal. The Britons who opposed Roman arms now became valorous defenders of liberty, zealous to defend their way of life against foreign oppression. Caractacus, in particular, was valorized as the ultimate noble barbarian; fired with patriotism to resist Roman might until he was betrayed, his nobility of spirit secured his freedom from Claudius in Rome. Hayman's print, *The Noble Behaviour of Caractacus, before the Emperor Claudius* is effectively a species of mythography, condensing Caractacus's heroism and barbarian nobility of spirit into one potent image.

In November 1758 the Society for the Encouragement of Arts, Manufactures and Commerce proposed to award a prize or 'Premium for the Improvement of History Painting in this Country'. The original list of six suggested subjects for competition, English and classical, included *Boadicea telling her Distress to Cassibelan and Paulinus in the presence of her two Daughters*. In early 1759 the Committee of Premiums decided that candidates should choose their subjects from English history alone, consciously promoting national subjects over those of classical origin. As John Sunderland has observed, this decision ran counter to the kind of Grand Style history painting Reynolds would shortly enunciate at the Royal Academy, for paintings of national history, in their presumed fidelity to a recent past, were prone to historicist temptation, lacking the universal qualities of classical and biblical narratives.[23] The

Committee of Premiums' decision is thus a significant reinforcement of that mid-century tendency to find a positive place for British antiquity in contemporary culture. The winner of the Society of Arts' top 100-guinea premium in 1764 was John Hamilton Mortimer, for his painting of *St Paul Preaching to the Ancient Britons* (fig.87), exhibited at the Free Society. Just over a decade later, in 1777, Mortimer exhibited a finished drawing of the same subject at the Society of Artists, which was later engraved (fig.88). The difference between the two images is a testament to Mortimer's awareness of antiquarian research into pagan Britain, moving from the generalized image of 1764, with its obvious debt to Bolognese seventeenth-century painting, to a much more historicist production in 1777. As with Hayman's conversion scene of 1752, showing Bishop Aristobulus's mission (fig.86), the world of Celtic Britain conjured into existence here offers a radical challenge to Hume and Robertson's account of unrewarding barbarism, fortunately buried in silence and oblivion. In contrast, Hayman and Mortimer ground their subjects in that contemporary understanding of Celtic Britain which asserted its cultural achievements, especially the arcane knowledge of those patriot-philosophers the Druids. No matter that Christianity in both pictures is presented as the superior belief, the Druids and their Celtic followers are depicted as intelligent and cultivated, their paganism is no more reprehensible than that of a Greek or Roman.

The nobility of archaic British culture was articulated in eighteenth-century texts, most notably William Stukeley's *Stonehenge, a Temple Restor'd to the British Druids* (1740) and Robert Henry's *History of Great Britain* (1771).[24] During a period when British identity was being considered as never before, especially in the context of patriotic exhortation in the struggle against France, there was comfort indeed in constructing a history of Britain that asserted the cultural dignity of the dawn of the nation. For many, this process implied a celebration of Anglo-Saxon achievements; for others, especially but not uniquely in the Celtic fringes, the Ancient Britons demonstrated that liberty and martial valour stretched even further back in the historical record. Hayman and Mortimer reinforce that perception of nobility by dignifying their Ancient Britons with poses that utilize the decorum of the high art tradition. In like manner, Alexander Runciman's Ossianic ceiling decorations for Penicuik House, Midlothian, also date from the 1770s. Significantly, Runciman had first proposed the life of Achilles to his patron, Sir James Clerk, whose new Palladian mansion had recently been completed. In celebrating instead not the world of the *Iliad*, but episodes from Ossian, the Homer of the north, Runciman, too, was able to assert the nobility and longevity of British culture. As with Hayman and Mortimer, Runciman's quotation from artistic tradition helps to dignify his subject. In his design for *The Death of Oscar*, the hero's pose fuses Michelangelo's *Adam* from the Sistine ceiling with the classical statue of the *Dying Gladiator* (fig.89). As spectators, therefore, we are made witnesses of a culture redeemed from the condescension of classical history and those, like Hume and Robertson, who accepted its prejudices. What had been merely the antipodes of civilization is now made visible as a civilization in its own right. Historical recreations such as these, for all their fanciful imagining, are thus tokens of a desire to explore the roots of national history in remote antiquity and to find there, at the nation's originating moment, patriotism, the defence of

liberty, the growth of knowledge and enlightenment. As with Carter's enthusiasm for the reign of Edward III, so here in Celtic Britain, the modern nation might find comfort and inspiration.

It is therefore demonstrable that the contribution of the graphic arts to understanding British antiquity was far from peripheral. To think of images as merely illustrating the past, whether as records of material remains or as historical reconstructions, is to misunderstand the importance of the arts in making the past visible. The production of scrupulous records of empirical data, from which systematic and comparative analyses could be derived for the first time, put the graphic media in an extraordinarily influential position for the furtherance of architectural scholarship. Equally, however, the production of history paintings with British antiquity as their subject-matter helped to create and dignify the image of the past in the public mind. Although these endeavours might confront one another on occasion, it would be wrong to see accurate record as the acceptable face of enlightenment research and the poetics of history painting as mere whimsy, vulnerable to cruel exposure of its shortcomings by the development of historical and archaeological knowledge. Both ways of understanding the past helped to give British antiquity a cognitive shape and a place in the imagination of the nation.

Notes and references

1 See in particular, Marjorie Caygill, *The Story of the British Museum* (London, rev. edn 1992), pp.31–42; Ian Jenkins, *Archaeologists and Aesthetes in the Sculpture Galleries of the British Museum, 1800–1939* (London, 1992), pp.16–18; Arthur MacGregor, 'Antiquity inventoried: Museums and "national antiquities" in the mid nineteenth century', in V. Brand (ed.), *The Study of the Past in the Victorian Age* (Oxford, 1998), pp.129–36.

2 See Joan Evans, *A History of the Society of Antiquaries* (Oxford, 1956), pp.111, 151, 202.

3 For an extended treatment of this topic see Sam Smiles, *Eye Witness: Artists and visual documentation in Britain, 1770–1830* (Brookfield and Aldershot, 2000), *passim*.

4 Letter from William Borlase to Charles Lyttleton, 6 November 1749, British Library, Stowe MS 752 118 LB 50, quoted in P.A.S. Poole, *William Borlase* (Truro, 1986), pp.128–9.

5 Lyttleton's book of drawings is now in the collection of the Society of Antiquaries. His account of Exeter Cathedral was published as 'Some remarks on the original foundation and construction of the present fabric of Exeter Cathedral', in Society of Antiquaries, *Some Account of the Cathedral Church of Exeter* (London, 1797), pp.1–12. For Lyttleton's work at Exeter see Sam Smiles, 'Data, documentation and display in eighteenth-century investigations of Exeter Cathedral', *Art History* 25 (2002), pp.500–19.

6 See John Frew, 'An aspect of the early Gothic revival: the transformation of medievalist research', *Journal of the Warburg and Courtauld Institutes* 43 (1980), pp.174–85; Rosemary Sweet, 'Antiquaries and antiquities in eighteenth-century England', *Eighteenth-Century Studies* 34 (2001), pp.181–206.

7 Richard Gough, *Anecdotes of British Topography. Or, an historical account of what has been done for illustrating the Topographical Antiquities of Great Britain and Ireland* (London, 1768), p.xx.

8 Richard Gough, *Sepulchral Monuments in Great Britain* (London, 1786), p.9.

9 See J. Mordaunt Crook, *John Carter and the Mind of the Gothic Revival* (London, 1995), *passim*.

10 John Carter, *The Ancient Architecture of England, including the Orders during the British, Roman, Saxon, and Norman Eras; and under the reigns of Henry III and Edward III,* first published 1795 (London, 1837), n.p.

11 'J.C.', 'Publication of antiquities by the Antiquarian Society', *Gentleman's Magazine* 73 (1803), 1, pp.106–7.

12 Ibid.

13 See, for example, the essays on the west front of Exeter Cathedral by J.P. Allan and S.R. Blaylock, 'The West Front 1 – The structural

history of the west front', and Eddie Sinclair, 'The West Front II – The west front polychromy', in Francis Kelly (ed.), *Medieval Art and Architecture at Exeter Cathedral*, British Archaeological Association: Conference Transactions for the Year 1985 (London, 1991), pp.94–133.

14 Discourse IV, delivered 10 December 1771, in Robert R. Wark (ed.), *Sir Joshua Reynolds: Discourses on art* (New Haven and London, 1975), pp.58–60.

15 See Wendy Greenhouse, 'Benjamin West and Edward III: a neoclassical painter and medieval history', *Art History* 8 (1985), pp.178–91.

16 'An Architect' [John Carter], 'The pursuits of architectural innovation no. LXXXVIII. Windsor Castle, continued', *Gentleman's Magazine* 75, II (1805), pp.818–19.

17 John Carter, op. cit. (note 10).

18 David Hume, *The History of England,* ed. Hewson Clarke (London, rev. edn 1813), p.3.

19 William Robertson, *The History of Scotland* (London, 1759), pp.1–2.

20 See Edward D. Snyder, *The Celtic Revival in English Literature, 1760–1800* (Cambridge, Mass. 1923), *passim*.

21 For information on this commission see Sam Smiles, 'J.H. Mortimer and Ancient Britain: An unrecorded project and a new identification', *Apollo* 142 (1995), pp.42–6.

22 It should be noted, however, that this enterprise was a commercial failure and publication ceased after the production of the first six prints.

23 See John Sunderland, 'Samuel Johnson and history painting', in D.G.C. Allan and John L. Abbott (eds), *The Virtuoso Tribe of Arts and Sciences: Studies in the eighteenth-century work and membership of the London Society of Arts* (Athens and London, 1992), pp.183–94.

24 For a further discussion of the enthusiasm for Celtic Britain in this period see Sam Smiles, *The Image of Antiquity: Ancient Britain and the Romantic imagination* (New Haven and London, 1994), *passim*.

Figure 83
Benjamin West, *The Institution of
the Order of the Garter* (1787), oil
on canvas, 287 x 448.3cm (113 x
176½ in). London, The Royal Collection
© 2002. Her Majesty Queen Elizabeth II.

Figure 82
James Basire after John Carter,
*Specimens of English Ecclesiastical
Costume* (1817), engraving.
By permission of the Syndics of
Cambridge University Library.

Figure 84
John Carter *Specimens of the Ancient
Sculpture and Painting now remaining
in this kingdom* (1786), etching.
By permission of the Syndics of
Cambridge University Library.

Figure 85
Charles Grignion after Francis
Hayman, *The Noble Behaviour of
Caractacus before the Emperor
Claudius* (1751), engraving. New
Haven, Yale Center for British Art,
Paul Mellon Collection.

Figure 86
Simon François Ravenet after Francis
Hayman, *The Druids; or, the Conversion
of the Britons to Christianity* (1752),
engraving. New Haven, Yale Center for
British Art, Paul Mellon Collection.

Figure 87
John Hamilton Mortimer, *St Paul preaching to the Ancient Britons* (1764), oil on canvas, 350 x 366cm (138 x 144in), Guildhall, High Wycombe. Photograph: Photo Archive, Paul Mellon Centre, London.

Figure 88
Joseph Haynes after John Hamilton Mortimer, *St Paul preaching to the Britons* (1780), etching. New Haven, Yale Center for British Art, Paul Mellon Collection.

Figure 89
Alexander Runciman, *The Death of Oscar* (c.1770–2), pencil, pen and wash, 35.4 x 49.5cm (14 x 19¹/₂ in). Edinburgh, National Gallery of Scotland.

Afterword
Keith Thomas

The chapters which make up this book tell us much about the intellectual background to the foundation of the British Museum, the cultural climate in which it developed and the purposes which it was meant to serve. Its obvious forerunners are examined – cabinets of curiosities, collections of art and antiquities, private libraries and learned or semi-learned societies. The book's contributors also deal with the antiquarian investigations of the eighteenth century, with the study of coins and medals and with the accumulation of *materia medica*. They describe the contemporary interest in the classical world, the scientific voyages which explored the natural history of the globe and the establishment of parallel collections and museums, both in provincial Britain and on the continent of Europe. From St Petersburg to Vienna, from Rome to Stockholm, the eighteenth century was a great age of museum foundation and collection development. Outside Europe, too, museums sprang up: in Charleston, in Calcutta and in Jakarta.

All this provides a context for the early history of the British Museum. But history is a dangerous trade. Individuals do not always welcome inquiries into their origins, lest the results should prove to be embarrassing. The same is true of institutions; and it is certainly the case with the British Museum. For its foundation two hundred and fifty years ago was based upon a number of assumptions which are no longer held.

First, and most important, was the polymathic ideal: the notion that any one individual could and should attempt to grasp the whole of human knowledge. The British Museum Act stated that 'all arts and sciences have a connexion with each other'; and the Museum was intended to be a visual and tangible encyclopædia of human knowledge. Yet nowadays scholars and scientists have become specialists: even within the same academic discipline, they are sometimes barely capable of understanding what their colleagues are up to. In parallel with this growth of academic specialization, the British Museum has greatly reduced its original scope. It never really developed its collection of oil paintings and, with the beginning of the National Gallery in 1824 and the foundation of the Victoria and Albert Museum in 1852, the primary responsibility for collecting and displaying fine art went elsewhere. The transfer of the Museum's portraits to the National Portrait Gallery in 1879 completed this process. The Museum also withdrew from most areas of natural science. The medical and anatomical specimens went to the Royal College of Surgeons in 1809 and much of the mineralogical collection was sold off in the same decade. The physical sciences were taken up by the Science Museum from 1857; and the British Museum's natural history collections moved from Bloomsbury to South Kensington in the 1880s, becoming legally independent in 1963. Finally, in 1972, the British Library Act removed the national collection of books and manuscripts. The British Museum has thus lost its universal and encyclopædic coverage, even if the breadth and depth of its

remaining collections, and the huge range of cultures it covers, reflect some of its original aspirations.

Secondly, the founders of the British Museum believed in the intrinsic superiority of British, or at least European, civilization. It was in Western Europe that the arts and sciences appeared to be the most advanced. The social theorists of the British Enlightenment held that civilization progressed in stages and that the highest stage – that of commercial society – was to be found only in the West. Of course, the other cultures were not all seen as equally barbarous. There was still much to be learned from the classical past of Greece and Rome; China and Egypt provided aesthetic models to be imitated in art and decoration; and the Noble Savage was invoked by romantic commentators as a device for criticising the moral faults of the contemporary West. But Hinduism was widely condemned as a system of idolatry; and it was not until the beginning of the twentieth century that the artefacts of Africa or Polynesia became a source of artistic inspiration. The norm of civilization was always a Western one and the collections of the British Museum were seen as proof of the point. Today, however, there is doubt about the unique value of Western civilization, much more reluctance to proclaim its superiority, and more readiness to concede the validity of other ways of living and thinking.

Thirdly, many of the contents of the early British Museum were trophies, symbols of superior military power and conquest. Joseph Banks in Australia and Napoleon Bonaparte in Egypt brought back objects which were fascinating because they were exotic, and reassuring because their possession was proof of European hegemony. The British Museum, as it is today, would have been inconceivable without the reality of British naval and military might. Of course, the spirit of the times was not always narrowly nationalistic; Sloane himself had contemplated the possibility of his collections going to St Petersburg or to some alternative Continental centres. But collections of works of art, rare animals and similar treasures had always been regarded by rulers as symbols of prestige. In the eighteenth century the holdings of the British Museum were visible testimony to the power, the learning, and the taste of the nation which had acquired them. Today, the Trustees of the Museum do not regard the greatness of its collections as evidence of Britain's supremacy. They prefer to stress the Museum's role as the custodian of humanity's treasures. It is there to serve the people of every nation.

Fourthly, the British Museum, as originally conceived, was meant to be useful in a practical way. In his first will of 1739, Sloane explained that his collections were intended for 'the use and improvement of physic, and other arts and sciences, and the benefit of mankind'. The Founding Act said that the Museum was there for 'the advancement and improvement' of all the arts and sciences; it expressed the hope that the collections would 'give help and success to the most useful experiments'. Plant-hunting had a strongly utilitarian dimension and *materia medica* were meant to have a therapeutic utility. Classical antiquities had an exemplary value: moral, literary and aesthetic. They were an inspiration to architects and to industrial designers, like Josiah Wedgwood, for the link between art and commerce was very close. Today, by contrast, when the benefits of the Museum are discussed, the talk is of pleasure, interest or instruction, but seldom of utility.

Fifthly, little has been said in the preceding chapters about the notion that, in its early days, the British Museum might have been intended to serve any kind of religious purpose. Yet Sloane's first will stressed that his collection tended to 'the manifestation of the glory of God' and 'the confutation of atheism and its consequences'; and, right up until the 1960s, the Board of Trustees was usually chaired by the Archbishop of Canterbury. It is hard to tell how important religious motivation was to the founders of the Museum, but it is certain that religious objectives no longer play any explicit part in the Museum's affairs.

Sixthly, the British Museum was meant to raise the tone. It was intended to disseminate learning and to improve taste. It had a civilizing function. Today, its educational role is still stressed, but there is a good deal of inhibition about claiming to raise taste or elevate cultural standards. Just as the BBC appears to have abandoned the improving objectives set it by Sir John Reith, so the British Museum, along with other contemporary cultural institutions, is much less likely to admit a civilizing intention than it once would have been.

Yet, despite all these changes, the Museum's basic ideals have survived. One of them is free access. In 1753 Sloane's

Trustees ruled that the collection should be preserved 'for the use and benefit of the publick, who may have free access to view and peruse the same'; and the British Museum Act of 1753 prescribed free access 'to all studious and curious persons'. There is room for disagreement about how these provisions were interpreted in the early years of the Museum. Yet despite financial and political pressures, the principle of free access remains intact today; and the 'studious and curious persons' envisaged in 1753 now come, not just from Britain or Europe, but from all over the world.

Another enduring feature is the British Museum's legal independence. The distinctively English common-law device of the trust was adopted in Sloane's will and in the British Museum Act. Sloane listed some sixty-three Trustees. Fortunately, there are not quite so many today. But the continuing existence of the Board of Trustees has ensured the survival of the collection and its independence from the whims of the government of the day: now, as then, an essential precaution.

The Museum also continues to advance knowledge, as well as to conserve it. It makes an essential contribution to research in archaeology and cultural history, and it conducts specialized investigations into a huge range of subjects, from numismatics and art history to the scientific conservation of material objects.

Finally, the Museum remains global in its scope. In its concern to represent the diversity of human cultures, it is a force for understanding and for tolerance. It remains faithful to the Enlightenment ideal of dissipating ignorance, superstition and prejudice. As it reaches its 250th anniversary, everyone can take pleasure in its enduring success and in the central place it continues to occupy in the world of learning.

Index

Page numbers in *italics* refer to illustrations.

Index